Introduction to Electronic Commerce

Introduction to Electronic Commerce 2/e

Efraim Turban
University of Hawaii

David King
JDA Software Group, Inc.

Judy Lang
Lang Associates

with contributions from

Linda Lai
Macau Polytechnic University, China

Judy McKay
Swinburne University of Technology, Australia

Peter Marshall
University of Tasmania, Australia

Carol Pollard
Appalachian State University

Deborrah Seballos
Cagayan de Oro College, Philippines

Dennis Viehland
Massey University, New Zealand

Linda Volonino
Canisius College

Prentice Hall
Upper Saddle River, NJ 07458

Library of Congress Cataloging-in-Publication Data

Turban, Efraim.
  [Introduction to e-commerce]
  Introduction to electronic commerce/Efraim Turban, David King, Judy Lang;
with contribution by Linda Lai . . . [et al.]. — 2e.
    p. cm.
  Prev. ed. published under title: Introduction to e-commerce.
  Includes bibliographical references and index.
  ISBN 978-0-13-603324-0
  1. Electronic commerce. I. King, David R. II. Lang, Judy, 1950- III. Title.
HF5548.32T87 2009
658.8'72—dc22

                                                  2008025903

Executive Editor: Bob Horan
Editorial Director: Sally Yagan
Editor in Chief: Eric Svendsen
Assistant Editor: Kelly Loftus
Marketing Manager: Anne Fahlgren
Marketing Assistant: Susan Osterlitz
Permissions Project Manager: Charles Morris
Senior Managing Editor: Judy Leale
Associate Managing Editor: Suzanne DeWorken
Senior Operations Specialist: Arnold Vila
Operations Specialist: Carol O'Rourke
Art Director: Steve Frim

Creative Director: Christy Mahon
Cover design: Jodi Notowitz
Cover Art: John Bleck
Interior Design: Jill Little
Manager, Rights and Permissions: Zina Arabia
Manager, Visual Research: Beth Brenzel
Composition: Integra
Full-Service Project Management: BookMasters, Inc./Sharon Anderson
Printer/Binder: Edwards Brothers, Inc.
Typeface: 10/12 ACaslon Regular

Pearson Education Ltd., London
Pearson Education Singapore, Pte. Ltd
Pearson Education, Canada, Inc.
Pearson Education–Japan
Pearson Education Australia PTY, Limited

Pearson Education North Asia, Ltd., Hong Kong
Pearson Educación de Mexico, S.A. de C.V.
Pearson Education Malaysia, Pte. Ltd
Pearson Education Upper Saddle River, New Jersey

Prentice Hall
is an imprint of

www.pearsonhighered.com

10 9 8 7 6 5 4 3 2 1
ISBN-13: 978-0-13-603324-0
ISBN-10:   0-13-603324-5

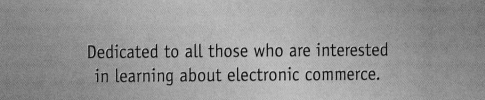
Dedicated to all those who are interested
in learning about electronic commerce.

Contents in Brief

www.prenhall.com/turban

Contents

Part 3 Business-to-Business E-Commerce   172

Part 6 EC Strategy and Implementation   474

www.prenhall.com/turban

Online Chapters

Part 7 Applications and Site Development

INTERNET EXERCISES

TEAM ASSIGNMENTS AND ROLE PLAYING

REAL-WORLD CASE: MOLDING A NEW VISION FOR
 E-COMMERCE AT D-M-E

Online Chapter Files

Preface

As we enter the third millennium, we are experiencing one of the most important changes to our daily lives—the move to an Internet-based society. Internet World Stats (internetworldstats.com) reported in December 2007 that almost 71 percent of the U.S. population (over 238 million) surf the Internet. More interesting is the fact that more than 90 percent of people between the ages of 5 and 17 surf the Internet on a regular basis. It is clear that these percentages will continue to increase, and similar trends exist in most other countries. As a result, much has changed at home, school, work, and in the government—and even in our leisure activities. Some of these changes are spreading around the globe. Others are just beginning in some countries.

One of the most significant changes is in how we conduct business, especially in how we manage marketplaces and trading. For example, the senior author of this book pays all of his bills online; trades stock online; buys airline and event tickets online; buys books online; chats with friends all over the world; searches for services, information, and knowledge; and purchased his computer, printer, and memory sticks online, to cite just a few examples.

Electronic commerce (EC) describes the manner in which transactions take place over networks, mostly the Internet. It is the process of electronically buying and selling goods, services, and information. Certain EC applications—such as buying and selling stocks and airline tickets on the Internet—are growing very rapidly, exceeding non-Internet trades. But EC is not just about buying and selling; it is also about electronically communicating, collaborating, and discovering information (sometimes referred to as *e-business*). It is about e-learning, e-government, social networks, and much more. Electronic commerce will have an impact on a significant portion of the world, affecting businesses, professions, and, of course, people.

The impact of EC is not just in the creation of Web-based businesses. It is the building of a new industrial order. Such a revolution brings a myriad of opportunities as well as risks. Bill Gates is aware of this, and the company he founded, Microsoft, is continually developing new Internet and EC products and services. Yet Gates has stated that Microsoft is always 2 years away from failure—that somewhere out there is an unknown competitor who could render its business model obsolete (Heller 2005). Gates knows that today's competition is not among products or services, but among business models. What is true for Microsoft is true for just about every other company. The hottest and most dangerous new business models out there are on the Web.

The years between 2005 and 2008 have been characterized by the emergence of Web 2.0, which expanded the boundaries of e-commerce from trading, information search, and collaboration with a business orientation to personal life support and then back to business. Companies are now adopting social computing technologies that were designed for individual use (such as blogs, wikis, file sharing, and social networks) to increase the effectiveness and efficiency of their operations.

Forrester Research reports that the easy connections that social computing has given us have made a major impact not only on the social structure that exists outside of the business world, but also on the global economy. Because of the pervasiveness of social computing, Forrester suggests that individuals take information from each other more often rather than from institutional sources like mainstream media outlets and corporations. For a company to survive, Forrester suggests that their marketing initiatives must fundamentally change from a top-down information flow to one where communities and social computing initiatives are made a part of their products and services (reported by Blacharski 2006).

In revising *Introduction to Electronic Commerce*, we paid great attention to the above developments. The reason is that so-called "social computing" is changing not only our lives and the way we do business, but also the field of e-commerce itself.

The purpose of this book is to describe what EC is—how it is being conducted and managed—as well as to assess its major opportunities, limitations, issues, and risks—all in the social-computing business environment. It is written from a managerial perspective. And because EC is an interdisciplinary topic, it should be of interest to managers and professional people in any functional area of business in all industries. People in government, education, health services, and other areas also will benefit from learning about EC.

Today, EC and e-business are going through a period of consolidation in which enthusiasm for new technologies and ideas is accompanied by careful attention to strategy, implementation, and profitability. Most of all, people recognize that e-business has three parts; it is not just about technology, it is also about commerce and people.

This book is written by experienced authors who share academic as well as real-world practices. It is a concise text that can be used in one-semester or one-quarter courses. It also can be used to supplement a text on Internet fundamentals, management information systems (MIS), or marketing.

FEATURES OF THIS BOOK

Several features are unique to this book.

Managerial Orientation

Electronic commerce can be approached from two major aspects: technological and managerial. This text uses the second approach. Most of the presentations are about EC applications and implementation. However, we do recognize the importance of the technology; therefore, we present the essentials of security in Chapter 10 and the essentials of infrastructure and system development in Online Chapter 14, which is located on the book's Web site (prenhall.com/turban). We also provide some detailed technology material in the files, appendices, and tutorials on the book's Web site. Managerial issues are provided at the end of each chapter.

Real-World Orientation

Extensive, vivid examples from large corporations, small businesses, and government and not-for-profit agencies from all over the world make concepts come alive. These examples show students the capabilities of EC, its cost and justification, and the innovative ways real corporations are using EC in their operations. Examples cover both large and small (SME) companies.

Solid Theoretical Background and Research Suggestions

Throughout the book, we present the theoretical foundations necessary for understanding EC, ranging from consumer behavior to the economic theory of competition. Furthermore, we provide Web site resources, many exercises, and extensive references to supplement the theoretical presentations.

Most Current Cutting-Edge Topics

The book presents the most current topics relating to EC, as evidenced by the many 2005 to 2008 citations. Topics such as social networking, e-learning, e-government, e-strategy, Web-based supply chain systems, collaborative commerce, mobile commerce, and EC economics are presented from the theoretical point of view as well as from the application side.

Integrated Systems

In contrast to other books that highlight isolated Internet-based systems, we emphasize those systems that support the enterprise and supply chain management. Intra- and interorganizational systems are highlighted as are the latest innovations in global EC and in Web-based applications.

Global Perspective

The importance of global competition, partnerships, and trade is increasing rapidly. EC facilitates export and import, the management of multinational companies, and electronic trading around the globe. International examples are provided throughout the book.

Online Support

More than 100 files are available online to supplement text material. These include files on generic topics such as data mining and intranets, cases, technically oriented text, and much more.

User-Friendliness

While covering all major EC topics, this book is clear, simple, and well organized. It provides all the basic definitions of terms as well as logical conceptual support. Furthermore, the book is easy to understand and is full of interesting real-world examples and "war stories" that keep readers' interest at a high level. Relevant review questions are provided at the end of each section so the reader can pause to review and digest the new material.

WHAT'S NEW IN THIS EDITION?

The following are the major changes in this edition:

- **New Co-author.** We welcome Judy Lang (Lang Associates) who brings expertise in several e-business areas.
- **New Chapter.** A new chapter on social networks and industry disruptors (Chapter 8) covers the most cutting-edge technologies and includes case studies of some of the industry players and leaders.

▶ **Chapters with Major Changes.**
- ▶ Chapter 1 now includes social networks, new business models, and other leading-edge topics.
- ▶ Chapter 4 includes new coverage of advertising models and strategies.
- ▶ Chapter 6 includes the addition of major innovations in e-supply chains and e-supply chain strategies as well as several other challenging innovations demonstrated in new cases.
- ▶ Chapter 10 has been completely rewritten, moving from a generic view of security to an e-commerce orientation.
- ▶ Chapter 12 has significantly upgraded the concepts of business planning, e-strategy, and business models.

▶ **Chapters with Less Significant Changes.** All data in the chapters were updated. More than 30 percent of all cases have been replaced. About 50 percent of all end-of-chapter material has been updated and/or expanded. Managerial issues were updated as were figures and tables. Duplications were eliminated and explanations of exhibits have been made more understandable. New topics were added in many of the sections to reflect the Web 2.0 revolution.

▶ **Online Files.** The online files were updated and reorganized. Many new files have been added.

ORGANIZATION OF THE BOOK

The book is divided into 12 chapters grouped into 6 parts. Two additional chapters (13 and 14), two appendices, and one tutorial are available as online supplements.

PART 1—INTRODUCTION TO E-COMMERCE AND E-MARKETPLACES

In Part 1, we provide an overview of today's business environment as well as the fundamentals of EC and some of its terminology (Chapter 1) and a discussion of electronic markets and their mechanisms (Chapter 2).

PART 2—INTERNET CONSUMER RETAILING

In Part 2, we describe EC B2C applications in two chapters. Chapter 3 addresses e-tailing and electronic service industries (e.g., travel, e-banking). Chapter 4 deals with online consumer behavior, market research, and online advertising.

PART 3—BUSINESS-TO-BUSINESS E-COMMERCE

In Part 3, we examine the one-to-many B2B models (Chapter 5), including auctions and the many-to-many models, including exchanges. Chapter 6 describes the e-supply chain, intrabusiness EC, and collaborative commerce.

PART 4—OTHER EC MODELS AND APPLICATIONS

Part 4 begins with several interesting applications such as e-government, e-learning, and consumer-to-consumer EC as presented in Chapter 7. Chapter 8 covers the topics of Web 2.0 and social networks. Chapter 9 explores the developing applications in the world of wireless EC (m-commerce and l-commerce).

PART 5—EC SUPPORT SERVICES

Chapter 10, the first chapter of Part 5, begins with a discussion of the need to protect privacy and intellectual property. It also describes various types of computer fraud and crime, and discusses how to minimize these risks through appropriate security programs. Chapter 11 describes two major EC support services—electronic payments and order fulfillment.

PART 6—EC STRATEGY AND IMPLEMENTATION

Chapter 12 discusses strategic issues in implementing and deploying EC. The chapter also presents global EC and EC for small businesses, the economics of EC, and cost/benefit justification. Online Chapter 13 is unique; it describes how to build an *Internet company* from scratch, as well as how to build a storefront. It takes the reader through all the necessary steps and provides guidelines for success. It also deals with legal, ethical, and societal issues. Finally, Online Chapter 14 deals with EC applications development, including the upcoming wave of Web services.

HOW THIS BOOK DIFFERS FROM *ELECTRONIC COMMERCE 2008*

This book was derived in part from *Electronic Commerce 2008* by Efraim Turban et al., Prentice Hall 2008. The major differences are:

▶ This book is about half the size of EC 2008 (624 pages versus 910 pages; 12 chapters versus 18 chapters).

▶ *EC 2008* is designed for one or two semesters; this book is designed for one quarter or semester.

▶ *EC 2008* is designed for upper division and graduate levels.

▶ *EC 2008* has a strong research orientation with twice as many references and research topics for each chapter.

▶ In many places, more technical details are available in *EC 2008*.

▶ Several chapters were eliminated in this book (e.g., auctions) or combined (e.g., B2B is one chapter instead of two).

▶ This book includes some simplified cases and examples.

▶ This book is more up-to-date (2009 versus 2008).

LEARNING AIDS

The text offers a number of learning aids to the student:

▶ **Chapter Outlines.** A listing of the main headings ("Content") at the beginning of each chapter provides a quick overview of the major topics covered.

▶ **Learning Objectives.** Learning objectives at the beginning of each chapter help students focus their efforts and alert them to the important concepts to be discussed.

▶ **Opening Vignettes.** Each chapter opens with a real-world example that illustrates the importance of EC to modern corporations. These cases were carefully chosen to call attention to the major topics covered in the chapters. Following each vignette, a short section titled "What We Can Learn . . . " links the important issues in the vignette to the subject matter of the chapter.

- **EC Application Cases.** In-chapter cases highlight real-world problems encountered by organizations as they develop and implement EC. Questions follow each case to help direct student attention to the implications of the case material.

- **Insights and Additions.** Topics sometimes require additional elaboration or demonstration. Insights and Additions boxes provide an eye-catching repository for such content.

- **Exhibits.** Numerous attractive exhibits (both illustrations and tables) extend and supplement the text discussion. Many are available online.

- **Review Questions.** Each section ends with a series of review questions about that section. These questions are intended to help students summarize the concepts introduced and to digest the essentials of each section before moving on to another topic.

- **Marginal Glossary and Key Terms.** Each Key Term is defined in the margin when it first appears. In addition, an alphabetical list of Key Terms appears at the end of each chapter with a page reference to the location in the chapter where the term is discussed.

- **Managerial Issues.** At the end of every chapter, we explore some of the special concerns managers face as they adapt to doing business in cyberspace. These issues are framed as questions to maximize readers' active engagement with them.

- **Chapter Summary.** The chapter summary is linked one-to-one with the learning objectives introduced at the beginning of each chapter.

- **End-of-Chapter Exercises.** Different types of questions measure students' comprehension and their ability to apply knowledge. Questions for Discussion are intended to promote class discussion and develop critical-thinking skills. Internet Exercises are challenging assignments that require students to surf the Internet and apply what they have learned. More than 250 hands-on exercises send students to interesting Web sites to conduct research, investigate an application, download demos, or learn about state-of-the-art technology. The Team Assignment and Role Playing exercises are challenging group projects designed to foster teamwork.

- **Real-World Cases.** Each chapter ends with a real-world case, which is presented in somewhat more depth than the in-chapter EC Application Cases. Questions follow each case relating the case to the topics covered in the chapter.

SUPPLEMENTARY MATERIALS

The following support materials are also available.

Online Instructor's Resource Center: prenhall.com/turban

This convenient online *Instructor's Resource Center* includes all of the supplements: Instructor's Manual, Test Item File, TestGen, PowerPoint Lecture Notes, and Image Library (text art).

The **Instructor's Manual**, written by Jon Outland, includes answers to all review and discussion questions, exercises, and case questions. The **Test Item File**, written by Linda Volonino, is an extensive set of multiple-choice, true/false, and essay questions for each chapter. New to this edition, the Test Item File also contains questions tagged to the AACSB Assurance of Learning Standards. It is available in Microsoft Word, **TestGen**, and WebCT- and BlackBoard-ready test banks. The **PowerPoint Lecture Notes** by Judy Lang are oriented toward text-learning objectives.

Companion Web Site: prenhall.com/turban

The book is supported by a Companion Web site that includes:

- ▶ Two online chapters (Chapters 13 and 14).
- ▶ An appendix on the impacts of EC.
- ▶ An appendix on e-CRM.
- ▶ Online Files for Chapters 4 and 5 that cover business intelligence, EDI, and extranets.
- ▶ An interactive tutorial on preparing an e-business plan.
- ▶ Self-Study Quizzes, by Jon Outland, include multiple-choice, true/false, and essay questions for each chapter. Each question includes a hint and coaching tip for students' reference. Students receive automatic feedback after submitting each quiz.
- ▶ All of the Internet Exercises from the end of each chapter in the text are provided on the Web site for convenient student use.

Materials for Your Online Course

Prentice Hall supports adopters using online courses by providing files ready for upload into both WebCT and BlackBoard course management systems for our testing, quizzing, and other supplements. Please contact your local PH representative for further information on your particular course.

ACKNOWLEDGMENTS

Many individuals helped us create this text. Faculty feedback was solicited via reviews and through individual interviews. We are grateful to the following faculty for their contributions.

CONTENT CONTRIBUTORS

The following individuals contributed material for this edition.

- ▶ Linda Volonino of Canisius College updated Chapters 10 and 12.
- ▶ Linda Lai of the Macau Polytechnic University of China updated Chapter 7.
- ▶ Carol Pollard of Appalachian State University updated Online Chapter 14, available on the book's Web site. Judy McKay (Swinburne University of Technology, Australia) and Peter Marshall (University of Tasmania, Australia) contributed materials to Chapters 3 and 6.
- ▶ Deborrah Seballos (Cagayan de Oro College, Philippines) contributed material to several chapters via her Internet search efforts.

REVIEWERS

We wish to thank the faculty who participated in reviews of this text and our other EC titles.

David Ambrosini, Cabrillo College

Timothy Ay, Villanova University

Deborah Ballou, University of Notre Dame

Christine Barnes, Lakeland Community College

Martin Barriff, Illinois Institute of Technology

Sandy Bobzien, Presentation College

Stefan Brandle, Taylor University

Joseph Brooks, University of Hawaii

Bruce Brorson, University of Minnesota

Clifford Brozo, Monroe College-New Rochelle

Stanley Buchin, Boston University

John Bugado, National University

Ernest Capozzolli, Troy State University

Mark Cecchini, University of Florida

Sandy Claws, Northern University

Jack Cook, State University of New York at Geneseo

Larry Corman, Fort Lewis College

Mary Culnan, Georgetown University

Chet Cunningham, Madisonville Community College

Roland Eicheleberger, Baylor University

Ted Ferretti, Northeastern University

Colin Fukai, Gonzaga University

Vickie Fullmer, Webster University

Dennis Galletta, University of Pittsburgh

Ken Griggs, California Polytechnic University

Varun Grover, University of South Carolina

Tom Gruen, University of Colorado at Colorado Springs

Norman Hahn, Thomas Nelson Community College

Harry Harmon, University of Central Missouri

James Henson, Barry University

Sadie Herbert, Mississippi Gulf Coast Community College

James Hogue, Wayland Baptist University

Brian Howland, Boston University

Chang Hsieh, University of Southern Mississippi

Paul Hu, University of Utah

Jin H. Im, Sacred Heart University

Jeffrey Johnson, Utah State University

Kenneth H. Johnson, Illinois Institute of Technology

Robert Johnson, University of Connecticut

Morgan Jones, University of North Carolina

Charles Kelley, California Baptist University

Douglas Kline, Sam Houston State University

Mary Beth Klinger, College of Southern Maryland

Tanvi Kothari, Temple University

Joanne Kuzma, St. Petersburg College

Charles Lange, DeVry University

Byungtae Lee, University of Illinois at Chicago

Chunlei Liu, Troy State University

Lakshmi Lyer, University of North Carolina

Joseph Maggi, Technical College of the Lowcountry

Ross Malaga, Montclair State University

Steve Mann, Humphreys College

Michael McLeod, East Carolina University

Susan McNamara, Northeastern University

Mohon Menon, University of South Alabama

Stephanie Miller, University of Georgia

Ajay Mishra, State University of New York at Binghamton

Bud Mishra, New York University

Robert Moore, Mississippi State University

Lawerence Muller, LaGuardia Community College, CUNY

Suzy Murray, Piedmont Technical College

William Nance, San Jose State University

Lewis Neisner, University of Maryland

Katherine A. Olson, Northern Virginia Community College

Robert Oullette, University of Maryland University College

Somendra Pant, Clarkson University

Wayne Pauli, Dakota State University

Craig Peterson, Utah State University

Sarah Pettitt, Champlain College

Dien D. Phan, University of Vermont

H.R. Rao, State University of New York at Buffalo

Catherine M. Roche, Rockland Community College

Jorge Romero, Towson University

Greg Rose, California State University at Chico

Linda Salchenberger, Loyola University of Chicago

George Schell, University of North Carolina at Wilmington

Sri Sharma, Oakland University

Seungjae Shin, Mississippi State University-Meridian

Sumit Sircar, University of Texas at Arlington

Hongjun Song, University of Memphis

Kan Sugandh, DeVry Institute of Technology

John Thacher, Gwinnett Technical College

Goran Trajkovski, Towson University

Dothang Truong, Fayetteville State University

Linda Volonino, Canisius College

Andrea Wachter, Point Park University

Ken Williamson, James Madison University

John Windsor, University of North Texas

Gregory Wood, Canisius College

Walter Wymer, Christopher Newport University

James Zemanek, East Carolina University

Several individuals helped us with the administrative work. Special mention goes to Christy Cheung of Hong Kong Baptist University who helped with editing, drawing figures, URL verification, and more. We also thank the many students of San Yet—Sun University in Taiwan for their help in searches and diagramming. We thank Daphne Turban, Sarah Miller, and all these people for their dedication and superb performance shown throughout the project.

We also recognize the various organizations and corporations that provided us with permissions to reproduce material. Special thanks go to Dion Hinchcliffe for allowing us to use his figures.

Thanks also to the Prentice Hall team that helped us from the inception of the project to its completion under the leadership of Executive Editor Bob Horan. The dedicated staff includes Assistant Editor Kelly Loftus, Editorial Assistant Mauricio Escoto, Senior Managing Editor Judy Leale, and Media Project Manager Denise Vaughn.

REFERENCES

Blacharski, D. "How Social Computing Is Changing the World." *ITWorld.com*, February 27, 2006. itworld.com/Tech/2987/nls_itinsights_social_060301/pfindex.html (accessed February 2008).

Computer Industry Almanac. "Worldwide Internet Users Top 1 Billion in 2005." January 4, 2006. c-i-a.com/pr0106.htm (accessed February 2008).

Heller, R. "Strengths and Weaknesses: Assess the Strengths and Weaknesses of Your Business, as Well as the Opportunities and Threats, with SWOT Analysis." *Thinking Managers*, 2005.

Internet World Stats. "Internet Usage Statistics: The Big Picture." December 31, 2007. internetworldstats.com/stats.htm (accessed February 2008).

CHAPTER 1

OVERVIEW OF ELECTRONIC COMMERCE

Content

Learning Objectives

Upon completion of this chapter, you will be able to:

1. Define electronic commerce (EC) and describe its various categories.

2. Describe and discuss the content and framework of EC.

3. Describe the major types of EC transactions.

4. Describe the digital revolution as a driver of EC.

5. Describe the business environment as a driver of EC.

6. Describe some EC business models.

7. Describe the benefits of EC to organizations, consumers, and society.

8. Describe the limitations of EC.

9. Describe the contribution of EC to organizations responding to environmental pressures.

10. Describe online social and business networks.

DELL—USING E-COMMERCE FOR SUCCESS

The Problem/Opportunity

Founded in 1985 by Michael Dell, Dell was the first company to offer personal computers (PCs) via mail order. Dell designed its own PC system (with an Intel 8088 processor running at 8 MHz) and allowed customers to configure their own customized systems using the build-to-order concept (see Chapter 2, Appendix 2A). This concept was, and is still, Dell's cornerstone business model. By 1993, Dell had become one of the top five computer makers worldwide, threatening Compaq, which started a price war. At that time, Dell was taking orders by fax and snail mail and losing money. Losses reached over $100 million by 1994. The company was in trouble.

The Solution
DIRECT MARKETING ONLINE

The commercialization of the Internet in the early 1990s and the introduction of the World Wide Web in 1993 provided Dell with an *opportunity* to expand rapidly. Dell implemented aggressive online order-taking and opened subsidiaries in Europe and Asia. Dell also started to offer additional products on its Web site. This enabled Dell to better Compaq, and in 2000 Dell became number one in worldwide PC shipments. At that time, Internet sales topped $50 million per day (about $18 billion per year). Today, Dell (*dell.com*) sells about $60 billion a year in computer-related products online, from network switches to printers, employing over 40,400 people.

Direct online marketing is Dell's major electronic commerce (EC) activity. Dell sells to the following groups:

- Individuals for their homes and home offices, B2C
- Small businesses (up to 200 employees), B2B
- Medium and large businesses (over 200 employees), B2B
- Government, education, and health-care organizations, B2B

Consumers shop at Dell.com using an electronic catalog. The sales are completed using mechanisms described in Chapters 2 and 3.

In addition, Dell sells refurbished Dell computers and other products in electronic auctions at *dellauction.com*. As will be discussed in Chapter 2, online auctions are an important sales channel. In 2006, Dell opened physical stores, mainly in reaction to customer demands.

Business-to-Business EC. Most of Dell's sales are to businesses. Whereas B2C sales are facilitated by standard shopping aids (e.g., catalogs, shopping carts, credit card payments; see Chapters 2 and 3), B2B customers obtain additional help from Dell. Dell provides each of its nearly 100,000 business customers with Premier Dell service.

For example, British Airways (BA) considers Dell to be a strategic supplier. Dell provides notebooks and desktops to 25,000 BA users. Dell offers two e-procurement services to BA purchasing agents. The more basic service, Premier Dell, allows BA (and other businesses) to browse, buy, and track orders on a Dell Web site customized for the user's requirements. The site enables authorized users to select preconfigured PCs for their business unit or department. A more advanced version, Premier B2B, supports e-procurement systems. This provides automatic requisition and order fulfillment once an authorized user has chosen to buy a PC from Dell. BA has placed the e-procurement tools on its E-Working intranet. This allows authorized staff to purchase PCs through a portal that connects directly into Dell's systems.

In addition to supporting its business customers with e-procurement tools, Dell also is using EC in its own procurement. Dell developed an e-procurement model that it shares with its suppliers and other business partners. One aspect of this model is the use of electronic tendering to conduct bids (see Chapter 5). Dell uses electronic tendering when it buys the components for its products.

In 2000, Dell created a B2B exchange at *dell.b2b.com*. This venture was a failure, like most other exchanges (see Chapter 5).

E-Collaboration. Dell has many business partners with whom it needs to communicate and collaborate. For example, Dell uses shippers, such as UPS and FedEx, to deliver its computers to individuals. It also uses third-party logistics companies to collect, maintain, and deliver components from its suppliers, and it has many other partners.

Dell has a superb communication system with its over 15,000 service providers around the globe.

E-Customer Service. Dell uses a number of different tools to provide superb customer service around the clock. To leverage customer relationship management (CRM)—a customer service approach that is customer centered for lasting relationships—Dell provides a virtual help desk for self-diagnosis and service as well as direct access to technical support data. In addition, a phone-based help desk is open 24/7. Customers can also arrange for a live chat with a customer care agent. Product support includes troubleshooting, user guides, upgrades, downloads, news and press releases, FAQs, order status information, a "my account" page, a community forum (to exchange ideas, information, and experiences), bulletin boards and other customer-to-customer interaction features, training books (at a discount), and much more.

Dell keeps a large customer database. Using data mining tools, it learns a great deal about its customers and attempts to make them happy. The database is used to improve marketing as well.

Intrabusiness EC. To support its build-to-order capabilities, significantly improve its demand-planning and factory execution accuracy, reduce order-to-delivery time, and enhance customer service, Dell partnered with Accenture to create a new, high-performance supply chain planning solution. Now in place in Dell's plants around the world, the program, which paid for itself five times over during the first

12 months of operation, enables Dell to adapt more quickly to rapidly changing technologies and the business environment, maintaining its position as a high-performance business. Dell also has automated its factory scheduling, demand-planning capabilities, and inventory management using information technology and e-supply chain models.

Affiliate Program. Dell provides affiliate partners the opportunity to link from their Web sites to Dell.com. Dell pays 2 to 4 percent on any qualified sale made from clicking on Dell's link at the partners' sites (referring buyers).

The Results

Dell has been one of *Fortune's* top five "Most Admired" companies since 1999, and it continuously advances in the rankings of the *Fortune* 500 and the *Fortune Global* 500. Dell has over 100 country-oriented Web sites, and profits are nearing $4 billion a year. If you had invested $10,000 in Dell's initial public offering (IPO) in 1987, you would be a millionaire just from that investment.

Dell actively supports EC research at the University of Texas in Austin (Dell's headquarters also are in Austin). It also contributes heavily to charity. Dell has partnered with the National Cristina Foundation (NCF) to provide computer technology to people with disabilities, students at risk, and economically disadvantaged persons. Paired with the company's recycling program, used computers are refurbished and then distributed through NCF. Through Dell's TechKnow Program, the company donates computers to urban middle schools. The students learn about computers by taking them apart and reassembling them, loading software, setting up and running printers, upgrading hardware, diagnosing and correcting basic hardware problems, and

using the Internet. Upon completion of the program, students take home the computers they build and receive a year of free Internet access. Dell also awards grants each year to governmental and educational institutions to organize, promote, stage, and recycle computer equipment in a free "No Computer Should Go to Waste" collection event in their communities.

Dell's major competitor is HP. In 2006, HP regained its "top PC maker" position, leaving Dell in second place (Ames 2007). In 2006, Dell opened physical stores to match its competitors and customer demands. Still, over 90 percent of its business is online and through mail orders. It also launched a blog called Direct2Dell (*direct2dell.com*). Dell also is expanding its business not only in the computer industry but also in consumer electronics. It is clearly an example of EC success. However, rapidly changing business conditions (Section 1.4) and preferences for notebook computers, forced Dell to restructure its operations in 2007.

Sources: Compiled from Ames (2007), Kraemer and Dedrick (2001), Ferguson and Davis (2007), National Cristina Foundation (2006), and *dell.com* and *dellauction.com* (accessed January 2008).

WHAT WE CAN LEARN . . .

Dell exemplifies the major EC business models. First, it pioneered the direct-marketing model for PCs, and then it moved online. Second, Dell supplemented its direct marketing with the build-to-order model on a large scale (mass customization). In doing so, Dell benefited from the elimination of intermediation with the first model and from extremely low inventories and superb cash flow from the second model. To meet the large demand for its quality products, Dell introduced other EC models, notably e-procurement for improving the purchasing of components, collaborative commerce with its partners, and intrabusiness EC for improving its internal operations. Finally, Dell uses e-CRM (CRM supported electronically; see Online Appendix B for details) with its customers. By successfully using e-commerce models, Dell became a world-class company, triumphing over all of its competitors. Dell's EC business models have become classics and best practices and are followed today by many other manufacturers, notably automakers.

This chapter defines EC and lists the types of transactions that are executed in it. Various EC models and the benefits and limitations of EC are also examined. Finally, a visual preview of the book's chapters is provided.

1.1 ELECTRONIC COMMERCE: DEFINITIONS AND CONCEPTS

Let's begin by looking at what the management guru Peter Drucker had to say about EC:

> The truly revolutionary impact of the Internet Revolution is just beginning to be felt. But it is not "information" that fuels this impact. It is not "artificial intelligence." It is not the effect of computers and data processing on decision making, policymaking, or strategy. It is something that practically no one foresaw or, indeed even talked about 10 or 15 years ago; e-commerce—that is, the explosive emergence of the Internet as a major, perhaps eventually the major, worldwide distribution channel for goods, for services, and, surprisingly, for managerial and professional jobs. This is profoundly changing economics, markets and industry structure, products and services and their flow; consumer segmentation, consumer values and consumer behavior; jobs and labor markets. But the impact may be even greater on societies and politics, and above all, on the way we see the world and ourselves in it. (Drucker 2002, pp. 3–4)

DEFINING ELECTRONIC COMMERCE

electronic commerce (EC)
The process of buying, selling, transferring, or exchanging products, services, or information via computer networks.

Electronic commerce (EC) is the process of buying, selling, transferring, or exchanging products, services, and/or information via computer networks, including the Internet. EC can also be defined from the following perspectives:

▶ **Business process.** From a business-process perspective, EC is doing business electronically by implementing business processes over electronic networks, thereby substituting information for physical business processes.

▶ **Service.** From a service perspective, EC is a tool that addresses the desire of governments, firms, consumers, and management to cut service costs while improving the quality of customer service and increasing the speed of service delivery.

▶ **Learning.** From a learning perspective, EC is an enabler of online training and education in schools, universities, and other organizations, including businesses.

▶ **Collaborative.** From a collaborative perspective, EC is the framework for inter- and intraorganizational collaboration.

▶ **Community.** From a community perspective, EC provides a gathering place for community members to learn, transact, and collaborate. The most popular type of community is *social networks*, such as MySpace.

EC often is confused with e-business.

DEFINING E-BUSINESS

e-business
A broader definition of EC that includes not just the buying and selling of goods and services, but also servicing customers, collaborating with business partners, and conducting electronic transactions within an organization.

Some people view the term *commerce* only as describing transactions conducted between business partners. If this definition of commerce is used, the term *electronic commerce* would be fairly narrow. Thus, many use the term *e-business* instead. **E-business** refers to a broader definition of EC, not just the buying and selling of goods and services, but also servicing customers, collaborating with business partners, engaging in e-learning, and conducting electronic transactions within an organization. According to McKay and Marshall (2004), e-business is the use of the Internet and other information technologies to support commerce and improve business performance. However, some view e-business as comprising those activities that do not involve buying or selling over the Internet, such as collaboration and intrabusiness activities (online activities between and within businesses); that is, it is a narrowly defined complement of e-commerce. In this book, we use the broadest meaning of electronic commerce, which is basically equivalent to e-business. The two terms will be used interchangeably throughout the text.

PURE VERSUS PARTIAL EC

EC can take several forms depending on the *degree of digitization* (the transformation from physical to digital) of (1) the *product* (service) sold, (2) the *process* (e.g., ordering, payment, fulfillment), and (3) the *delivery method*. Exhibit 1.1 explains the possible configurations of these three dimensions. A product may be physical or digital, the process may be physical or digital, and the delivery method may be physical or digital. These alternatives create eight cubes, each of which has three dimensions. In traditional commerce, all three dimensions of the cube are physical (lower-left cube); in pure EC, all dimensions are digital (upper-right cube). All other cubes include a mix of digital and physical dimensions.

If there is at least one digital dimension, we consider the situation EC, but only *partial EC.* For example, purchasing a computer from Dell's Web site or a book from Amazon.com is partial EC because the merchandise is physically delivered. However, buying an e-book from Amazon.com or a software product from Buy.com is *pure EC,* because the product, payment, and delivery to the buyer are all digital.

EC Organizations. Purely physical organizations (companies) are referred to as **brick-and-mortar (old-economy) organizations**, whereas companies that are engaged only in EC are considered **virtual** or **pure-play organizations**. **Click-and-mortar** (or **click-and-brick organizations**) are those that conduct some EC activities, usually as

brick-and-mortar (old-economy) organizations
Old-economy organizations (corporations) that perform their primary business off-line, selling physical products by means of physical agents.

virtual (pure-play) organizations
Organizations that conduct their business activities solely online.

click-and-mortar (click-and-brick) organizations
Organizations that conduct some e-commerce activities, usually as an additional marketing channel.

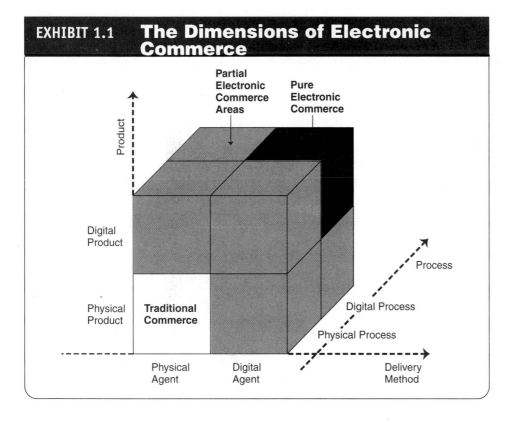

EXHIBIT 1.1 The Dimensions of Electronic Commerce

an additional marketing channel. Gradually, many brick-and-mortar companies are changing to click-and-mortar ones (e.g., Wal-Mart online and Marks & Spencer, see Online File W1.1).

INTERNET VERSUS NON-INTERNET EC

Although some people still use a stand-alone computer exclusively, the vast majority of people use computers connected to a global networked environment known as the Internet, or to its counterpart within organizations, an intranet. An **intranet** is a corporate or government network that uses Internet tools, such as Web browsers, and Internet protocols. Another computer environment is an **extranet**, a network that uses the Internet to link multiple intranets.

Most EC is done over the Internet, but EC also can be conducted on private networks, such as *value-added networks* (VANs; networks that add communications services [e.g., security, volume] to existing common carriers), on local area networks (LANs) using intranets, or even on a single computerized machine. For example, buying food from a vending machine and paying with a smart card or a cell phone can be viewed as an EC activity.

An example of non-Internet EC would be field employees (such as sales reps) who are equipped with mobile handwriting-recognition computers so they can write their notes in the field immediately after a sales call. (For a more in-depth example, see the Maybelline Case at Online File W1.2.)

ELECTRONIC MARKETS AND INTERORGANIZATIONAL AND INTRAORGANIZATIONAL INFORMATION SYSTEMS

EC can be conducted in an **electronic market (e-marketplace)** where buyers and sellers meet online to exchange goods, services, money, or information. Electronic markets may be supplemented by connecting interorganizational or intraorganizational information systems. **Interorganizational information systems (IOSs)** are those where only routine transaction processing and information flow take place between two or more organizations using a standard protocol, such as *electronic data interchange* (EDI; see Chapter 5). EC activities that take place within individual organizations are facilitated by **intraorganizational information systems**.

These systems also are known as *intrabusiness EC*.

Section 1.1 ▶ REVIEW QUESTIONS

1. Define EC and e-business.

2. Distinguish between pure and partial EC.

3. Define click-and-mortar and pure-play organizations.

4. Define electronic markets, IOSs, and intraorganizational information systems.

5. Describe non-Internet EC.

1.2 THE EC FRAMEWORK, CLASSIFICATION, AND CONTENT

The opening case illustrates a new way of conducting business—electronically, using the Internet, intranet, and private networks. The case demonstrates several ways that businesses can use EC to improve the bottom line. Dell is not the only company that has moved its business online. Thousands of other companies, from retailers (e.g., see Online File W1.1, Marks & Spencer) to hospitals, are moving in this direction.

intranet
An internal corporate or government network that uses Internet tools, such as Web browsers, and Internet protocols.

extranet
A network that uses the Internet to link multiple intranets.

electronic market (e-marketplace)
An online marketplace where buyers and sellers meet to exchange goods, services, money, or information.

interorganizational information systems (IOSs)
Communications systems that allow routine transaction processing and information flow between two or more organizations.

intraorganizational information systems
Communication systems that enable e-commerce activities to go on within individual organizations.

EC is not yet a significant global economic force (less than 5 percent of all transactions in most industries). However, some predict that it could become globally significant within 10 to 20 years (Drucker 2002). Networked computing is the infrastructure for EC, and it is rapidly emerging as the standard computing environment for business, home, and government applications. *Networked computing* connects multiple computers and other electronic devices that are located in several different locations by telecommunications networks, including wireless ones. This connection allows users to access information stored in several different physical locations and to communicate and collaborate with people separated by great geographic distances and/or by time.

AN EC FRAMEWORK

The EC field is a diverse one, involving many activities, organizational units, and technologies (e.g., see Khosrow-Pour 2006). Therefore, a framework that describes its content is useful. Exhibit 1.2 introduces one such framework.

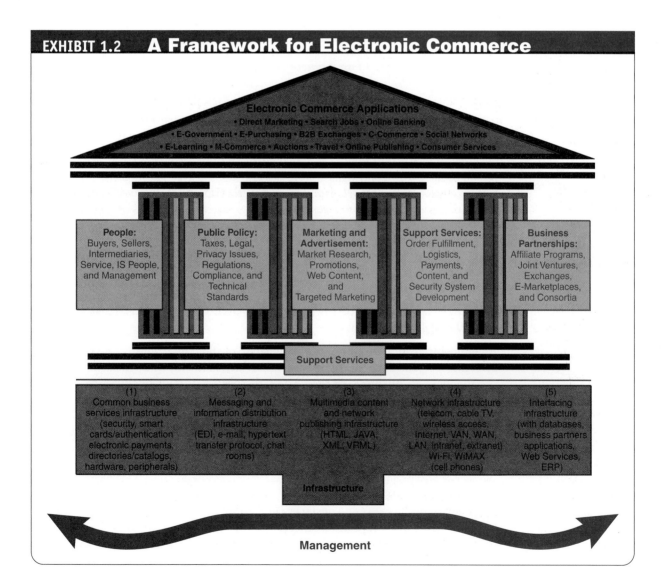

EXHIBIT 1.2   A Framework for Electronic Commerce

Electronic Commerce Applications
• Direct Marketing • Search Jobs • Online Banking
• E-Government • E-Purchasing • B2B Exchanges • C-Commerce • Social Networks
• E-Learning • M-Commerce • Auctions • Travel • Online Publishing • Consumer Services

People:
Buyers, Sellers, Intermediaries, Service, IS People, and Management

Public Policy:
Taxes, Legal, Privacy Issues, Regulations, Compliance, and Technical Standards

Marketing and Advertisement:
Market Research, Promotions, Web Content, and Targeted Marketing

Support Services:
Order Fulfillment, Logistics, Payments, Content, and Security System Development

Business Partnerships:
Affiliate Programs, Joint Ventures, Exchanges, E-Marketplaces, and Consortia

Support Services

| (1) Common business services infrastructure (security, smart cards/authentication electronic payments, directories/catalogs, hardware, peripherals) | (2) Messaging and information distribution infrastructure (EDI, e-mail, hypertext transfer protocol, chat rooms) | (3) Multimedia content and network publishing infrastructure (HTML, JAVA, XML, VRML) | (4) Network infrastructure (telecom, cable TV, wireless access, Internet, VAN, WAN, LAN, intranet, extranet) Wi-Fi, WiMAX (cell phones) | (5) Interfacing infrastructure (with databases, business partners applications, Web Services, ERP) |

Infrastructure

Management

As can be seen in the exhibit, there are many EC applications (top of exhibit), some of which were illustrated in the opening case about Dell; others will be shown throughout the book (see also Papazoglou and Ribbers 2006; Lee et al. 2006; and Jelassi and Enders 2005). To execute these applications, companies need the right information, infrastructure, and support services. Exhibit 1.2 shows that EC applications are supported by infrastructure and by the following five support areas (see pillars in the exhibit):

▶ **People.** Sellers, buyers, intermediaries, information systems specialists, other employees, and any other participants comprise an important support area.

▶ **Public policy.** This includes legal and policy and regulatory issues, such as privacy protection and taxation, that are determined by governments. Included as part of public policy is the issue of technical standards, which are established by government and/or industry-mandated policy-making groups. Compliance with the regulations is an important issue.

▶ **Marketing and advertisement.** Like any other business, EC usually requires the support of marketing and advertising. This is especially important in business-to-consumer (B2C) online transactions, in which the buyers and sellers usually do not know each other.

▶ **Support services.** Many services are needed to support EC. These range from content creation to payments to order delivery.

▶ **Business partnerships.** Joint ventures, exchanges, and business partnerships of various types are common in EC. These occur frequently throughout the *supply chain* (i.e., the interactions between a company and its suppliers, customers, and other partners).

The infrastructure for EC is shown at the bottom of Exhibit 1.2. *Infrastructure* describes the hardware, software, and networks used in EC. All of these components require good *management practices*. This means that companies need to plan, organize, motivate, devise strategy, and restructure processes, as needed, to optimize the business use of EC models and strategies. Management also deals with strategic and operational decisions (see Chapter 12 and examples throughout the book).

This text provides details on the major components of the framework. The infrastructure of EC is described in Online Chapter 14.

CLASSIFICATION OF EC BY THE NATURE OF THE TRANSACTIONS OR INTERACTIONS

A common classification of EC is by the nature of the transactions or the relationship among participants. The following types of EC are commonly distinguished.

Business-to-Business (B2B). All of the participants in **business-to-business (B2B)** e-commerce are either businesses or other organizations (see Chapters 5 and 6). For example, several of Dell's and Marks & Spencer's applications involve B2B with their suppliers. Today, over 85 percent of EC volume is B2B (Mockler et al. 2006).

Business-to-Consumer (B2C). **Business-to-consumer (B2C)** EC includes retail transactions of products or services from businesses to individual shoppers. The typical shopper at Dell online or at Amazon.com is a *consumer* or *customer*. This EC type is also called **e-tailing** (see Chapter 3).

Business-to-Business-to-Consumer (B2B2C). In **business-to-business-to-consumer (B2B2C)** EC, a business provides some product or service to a client business. The client business maintains its own customers, who may be its own employees, to whom the product or service is provided without adding any value to it. One example of B2B2C is a company

business-to-business (B2B)
E-commerce model in which all of the participants are businesses or other organizations.

business-to-consumer (B2C)
E-commerce model in which businesses sell to individual shoppers.

e-tailing
Online retailing, usually B2C.

business-to-business-to-consumer (B2B2C)
E-commerce model in which a business provides some product or service to a client business that maintains its own customers.

that pays AOL to provide its employees with Internet access rather than having each employee pay an access fee directly to AOL. Another example is wholesaler-to-retailer-to-consumer merchandising, such as airlines and travel units that provide travel services, such as airline tickets and hotel rooms, to business partners, such as travel agencies, who then sell the services to customers. As a final example, Godiva (see Case 1.1) sells chocolates directly to business customers. Those businesses may then give the chocolates as gifts to employees or to other businesses. Godiva may mail the chocolate directly to the recipients (with complements of . . .). An interesting example of B2B2C can be found in wishlist.com.au. The term B2B frequently includes B2B2C as well.

Consumer-to-Business (C2B). The **consumer-to-business (C2B)** category includes individuals who use the Internet to sell products or services to organizations and individuals who seek sellers to bid on products or services (see Chapter 2). Priceline.com is a well-known organizer of C2B transactions.

Mobile Commerce. EC transactions and activities conducted in full or in part in a *wireless environment* are referred to as **mobile commerce**, or **m-commerce** (see Chapter 9). For example, people can use Internet-enabled cell phones to do their banking or order a book from Amazon.com. Many m-commerce applications involve mobile devices. Some people define m-commerce as those transactions conducted when people are away from their home or office (i.e., they are mobile); such transactions can be done both on wireless or wireline systems. (See the Maybelline case at Online File W1.2.) If such transactions are targeted to individuals in specific locations, at specific times, they are referred to as **location-based commerce**, or **l-commerce**.

Intrabusiness EC. The **intrabusiness EC** category includes all internal organizational activities that involve the exchange of goods, services, or information among various units and individuals in that organization. Activities can range from selling corporate products to one's employees to online training and collaborative design efforts (see Chapter 6). Intrabusiness EC is usually performed over intranets and/or *corporate portals* (gateways to the Web).

Business-to-Employees (B2E). The **business-to-employees (B2E)** category is a subset of the intrabusiness category in which the organization delivers services, information, or products to individual employees, as Maybelline is doing (see Online File W1.2). A major category of employees is *mobile employees*, such as field representatives. EC support to such employees is also called B2ME (*business-to-mobile employees*).

Collaborative Commerce. When individuals or groups communicate or collaborate online, they may be engaged in **collaborative commerce**, or **c-commerce** (see Chapter 6). For example, business partners in different locations might design a product together (see Boeing, Case 1.2), using screen-sharing; manage inventory online, as in the Dell case; or jointly forecast product demand, as Marks & Spencer does with its suppliers (Online File W1.1).

Consumer-to-Consumer (C2C). In the **consumer-to-consumer (C2C)** category (see Chapter 7), consumers transact directly with other consumers. Examples of C2C include individuals selling residential property, cars, and so on in online classified ads (e.g., see Case 2.2 on Craigslist in Chapter 2). The advertisement of personal services over the Internet and the selling of knowledge and expertise online are other examples of C2C. In addition, many auction sites allow individuals to place items up for auction.

Peer-to-Peer Applications. **Peer-to-peer (P2P)** technology can be used in C2C, B2B, and B2C (see Chapter 7). This technology enables networked peer computers to share data files and processing with each other directly. For example, in a C2C peer application, people can exchange (swap) music, videos, software, and other digitizable goods electronically.

consumer-to-business (C2B)
E-commerce model in which individuals use the Internet to sell products or services to organizations or individuals who seek sellers to bid on products or services they need.

mobile commerce (m-commerce)
E-commerce transactions and activities conducted in a wireless environment.

location-based commerce (l-commerce)
M-commerce transactions targeted to individuals in specific locations, at specific times.

intrabusiness EC
E-commerce category that includes all internal organizational activities that involve the exchange of goods, services, or information among various units and individuals in an organization.

business-to-employees (B2E)
E-commerce model in which an organization delivers services, information, or products to its individual employees.

collaborative commerce (c-commerce)
E-commerce model in which individuals or groups communicate or collaborate online.

CASE 1.1
EC Application

BUY CHOCOLATE ONLINE? TRY GODIVA.COM

The Business Opportunity

The demand for high-quality chocolate has been increasing rapidly since the early 1990s. Several local and global companies are competing in this market. Godiva Chocolatier is a well-known international company based in New York whose stores can be found in hundreds of malls worldwide. The company was looking for ways to increase its sales, and after rejecting the use of a CD-ROM catalog, it had the courage to try online sales as early as 1994. The company was a pioneering click-and-mortar e-business that exploited an opportunity years before its competitors.

The Project

Teaming with Fry Multimedia (an e-commerce pioneer), Godiva.com (*godiva.com*) was created as a division of Godiva Chocolatier. The objective was to sell online both to individuals (B2C) and to businesses (B2B). Because its online activities began in 1994, the Godiva.com story parallels the dynamic growth of e-commerce. Godiva.com went through difficult times—testing e-commerce technologies as they appeared; failing at times, but maintaining its commitment to online selling; and, finally, becoming the fastest-growing division of Godiva, outpacing projections. Godiva.com embodies a true success story. Here we present some of the milestones encountered.

The major driving factors in 1994 were Internet user groups of chocolate lovers, who were talking about Godiva and to whom the company hoped to sell its product online. Like other pioneers, Godiva had to build its Web site from scratch without EC-building tools. A partnership was made with *Chocolatier* Magazine, allowing Godiva.com to showcase articles and recipes from the magazine on its site in exchange for providing an online magazine subscription form for e-shoppers. The recognition of the importance of relevant content was correct, as was the need for fresh content. The delivery of games and puzzles, which was considered necessary to attract people to EC sites, was found to be a failure. People were coming to learn about chocolate and Godiva and to buy—not to play games. Another concept that failed was the attempt to make the Web site look like the physical store. It was found that different marketing channels should look different from one another.

Godiva.com is a user-friendly place to shop. Its major features include electronic catalogs, some of which are constructed for special occasions (e.g., Mother's Day and Father's Day); a store locator (how to find the nearest physical store and events at nearby stores); a shopping cart to make it easy to collect items to buy; a gift selector and a gift finder; custom photographs of the products; a search engine by product, price, and other criteria; instructions on how to shop online (take the tour); a chocolate guide that shows exactly what is inside each box; a place to click for live assistance or for a paper catalog; and the ability to create an address list for shipping gifts to friends or employees. The site also features "My Account," a personalized place where customers can access their order history, account, order status, and so on; general content about chocolate (and recipes); and tools for making shipping and payment arrangements.

Godiva.com sells both to individuals and to corporations. For corporations, incentive programs are offered, including address lists of employees or customers to whom the chocolate is to be sent—an example of the B2B2C EC model.

Godiva.com continues to add features to stay ahead of the competition. The site is now accessible using wireless technologies. For example, the store locator is available to wireless phone users, and Palm Pilot users can download mailing lists.

The Results

Godiva.com's online sales have been growing at a double-digit rate every year, outpacing the company's "old economy" divisions as well as the online stores of competitors.

Sources: Compiled from Reda (2004) and from *godiva.com* (accessed January 2008).

Questions

1. Identify the B2B and B2C transactions in this case.
2. Why did Godiva decide to sell online?
3. List the EC drivers in this case.
4. Visit *godiva.com*. How user-friendly is the site?
5. Describe B2B2C at Godiva.

E-Learning. In **e-learning**, training or formal education is provided online (see Chapter 7). E-learning is used heavily by organizations for training and retraining employees (called e-training). It also is practiced at virtual universities.

E-Government. In **e-government** EC, a government entity buys or provides goods, services, or information from or to businesses (G2B) or from or to individual citizens (G2C) (see Chapter 7).

Exchange-to-Exchange (E2E). An **exchange** describes *a public electronic market* with many buyers and sellers (see Chapter 5). As B2B exchanges proliferate, it is logical for exchanges to connect to one another. **Exchange-to-exchange (E2E)** EC is a formal system that connects two or more exchanges.

Nonbusiness EC. An increased number of nonbusiness institutions, such as academic institutions, nonprofit organizations, religious organizations, social organizations, and government agencies, are using EC to reduce their expenses or to improve their general operations and customer service. (Note that in the previous categories one can usually replace the word *business* with *organization.*)

Many examples of the various types of EC transactions will be presented throughout this book.

A BRIEF HISTORY OF EC

EC applications were first developed in the early 1970s with innovations such as *electronic funds transfer* (EFT) (see Chapter 11), whereby funds could be routed electronically from one organization to another. However, the use of these applications was limited to large corporations, financial institutions, and a few other daring businesses. Then came *electronic data interchange* (EDI), a technology used to electronically transfer routine documents, which expanded electronic transfers from financial transactions to other types of transaction processing (see Chapter 5 and wikipedia.org for more on EDI). EDI enlarged the pool of participating companies from financial institutions to manufacturers, retailers, services, and many other types of businesses. Such systems were called *interorganizational system* (IOS) applications, and their strategic value to businesses has been widely recognized. More new EC applications followed, ranging from travel reservation systems to stock trading.

The Internet began as an experiment by the U.S. government in 1969, and its initial users were a largely technical audience of government agencies and academic researchers and scientists. When the Internet became commercialized and users began flocking to participate in the World Wide Web in the early 1990s, the term *electronic commerce* was coined. EC applications rapidly proliferated. A large number of so-called *dot-coms*, or *Internet start-ups*, also appeared (see Cassidy 2002). One reason for this rapid expansion was the development of new networks, protocols, and EC software. The other reason was the increase in competition and other business pressures (see discussion in Section 1.4).

Since 1995, Internet users have witnessed the development of many innovative applications, ranging from online direct sales to e-learning experiences. Almost every medium- and large-sized organization in the world now has a Web site, and most large U.S. corporations have comprehensive portals through which employees, business partners, and the public can access corporate information. Many of these sites contain tens of thousand of pages and links. In 1999, the emphasis of EC shifted from B2C to B2B, and in 2001 from B2B to B2E, c-commerce, e-government, e-learning, and m-commerce (see Ariguzo et al. 2006). In 2005, *social networks* (Chapter 8) started to receive quite a bit of attention, as did l-commerce and wireless applications. Given the nature of technology and the Internet, EC will undoubtedly continue to shift and change. More and more EC successes are emerging (see Mullaney 2004). For a comprehensive ready-reference guide to EC including statistics, trends, and in-depth profiles of over 400 companies, see Plunkett (2006) and en.wikipedia.org/wiki/E-commerce.

consumer-to-consumer (C2C)
E-commerce model in which consumers sell directly to other consumers.

peer-to-peer (P2P)
Technology that enables networked peer computers to share data and processing with each other directly; can be used in C2C, B2B, and B2C e-commerce.

e-learning
The online delivery of information for purposes of training or education.

e-government
E-commerce model in which a government entity buys or provides goods, services, or information from or to businesses or individual citizens.

exchange
A public electronic market with many buyers and sellers.

exchange-to-exchange (E2E)
E-commerce model in which electronic exchanges formally connect to one another for the purpose of exchanging information.

CASE 1.2
EC Application

BOEING CHANGES THE NATURE OF ITS BUSINESS WITH GLOBAL COLLABORATION

Boeing, the $61.5 billion Chicago-based aerospace company, has been a major player in the global economy for almost a century. But now the company is undertaking a far-reaching transformation as it uses cutting-edge materials and electronics and high-level technology for the design and assembly process of its new passenger plane—the Boeing 787. The new plane, nicknamed the "Dreamliner," is Boeing's bid for market leadership in competition with Airbus. The new midsize passenger jet will have an outer shell and about half of its parts made of carbon-fiber-reinforced plastic, which makes it lighter and gives it better fuel economy. In July 2007, the company had about 700 firm orders from 34 airlines for the new 787, which seats from 250 to 330 passengers in varying configurations. The list price is about $150 million per plane.

The previous state of the art in aviation manufacturing was to have global partners work from a common blueprint to produce parts—actually, whole sections of the airplane—that were then physically shipped to a Boeing assembly plant near Seattle to see if they fit together. Prior to the 787, wood mock-ups of planes would be constructed to see if parts built by partners around the world would really fit together. When the process failed, the cost in time and production was extreme.

The new business model takes Boeing from manufacturer to a high-end technology systems integrator. In 2004, Boeing's IT systems people were consolidated into the Boeing Technology Group. Now parts are designed from concept to production concurrently by partners (including companies in Japan, Russia, and Italy) and "assembled" in a computer model maintained by Boeing outside its corporate firewall. Boeing's role is integrator and interface to the airlines, while the partners take responsibility for the major pieces, including their design. Boeing still takes the hit if the planes fail and deliveries are late, but the actual cost of development and manufacturing is spread across its network of *collaborators*. At the same time, building such global relationships might help the company sell its planes overseas. The biggest savings are in the time saved through the online collaboration process (from 33 to 50 percent), creating a huge competitive advantage.

Collaboration is a necessity for Boeing for several reasons. Airplanes are huge and enormously complex.

Politically, sales of a "global product" are enhanced when people in other countries are building parts of the airplane. Companies in these countries may then buy from Boeing. Basic collaboration is done through information-flow tools such as Microsoft Office and SharePoint. Boeing and partners are using Dassault Systemes 3D and Product Lifecycle Management solutions.

Other IT tools used are a product suite from Exostar LLC, with which Boeing can share two-dimensional drawings, conduct forward and reverse auctions (Chapter 2), and respond to RFPs (Chapter 5). The plane is designed at Global Collaboration Environment, a special online site maintained by Boeing.

Three levels of collaboration are facilitated between teams and companies. In the first level—*design collaboration*—all parties involved log in and make their changes electronically in the blueprints, and the team works together. Quality is improved because the computer finds the mistakes. The next level involves *suppliers working with their supply chains*. The third level is real-time collaboration that involves a considerable amount of product life cycle management across multiple countries enabled by technology that differentiates Boeing's new model from the previous kinds of global relationships. Boeing also uses the new partnership to solicit ideas on how to improve designs, integration, and so on. This results in cost-cutting.

Boeing maintains 10 multimedia rooms at its complex in Everett, Washington, for use by collaboration teams. These are open 365 days a year, 24 hours a day. A visualization application developed by Boeing allows the teams to do real-time design reviews of complex geometry without any lag time as the models load. Meetings are conducted in English, with sidebar conversations, as needed, in a team member's native language. Collaborative design also speeds the design process, helping Boeing to avoid expensive penalties from its customers if the plane is not delivered on time, and it gives the company more flexibility in simultaneously designing multiple versions of the 787 that are part of its wide-ranging appeal in the marketplace.

Finished designs are stored in another Dassault product, Enovia, which also is maintained by Boeing. This has become an enormous data-management task. The issue of security has also been a concern; however, security technology has developed to the point that the security of the information is assured.

(continued)

CASE 1.2   (continued)

All of this has helped Boeing accelerate the design process. The company introduced a completed plane on July 7, 2007. However, the company experienced some delays in delivery to the first customers due to non–IT-related problems.

Sources: Compiled from Cone (2006), *Workforce-Performance* (2006), Berstein (2006), and *boeing.com* (accessed January 2008).

Questions

1. Describe online collaboration and its benefits to Boeing.
2. List the levels of collaboration and the parties involved.
3. How does technology facilitate collaboration?

THE INTERDISCIPLINARY NATURE OF EC

The Google Revolution

During its early years, EC was impacted by companies such as Amazon.com (Chapter 3), eBay, and Yahoo! However, since 2001 no other company has had more of an impact on EC than Google. As will be seen in Chapter 4, Google related Web searches to targeted advertisements much better than companies such as DoubleClick did. Today, Google is much more than just a search engine; it employs several innovative EC models, is involved in many EC joint ventures, and impacts both organizational activities and individual lives, as described in the Real-World Application Case at the end of this chapter and in Chapter 4.

EC Failures

Starting in 1999, a large number of EC companies, especially e-tailing and B2B ones, began to fail (see disobey.com/ghostsites; Cassidy 2002; and Kaplan 2002). Well-known B2C failures include eToys, Xpeditor, MarchFirst, Drkoop.com, Webvan.com, and Boo.com. Well-known B2B failures include Chemdex.com, Ventro.com, and Verticalnet.com. (Incidentally, the history of these pioneering companies is documented in The Business Plan Archive [businessplanarchive.org] by David Kirch.) A survey by Strategic Direction (2005) found that 62 percent of dot-coms lacked financial skills and 50 percent had little experience with marketing. Similarly, many companies failed to ensure they had the inventory and distribution setup to meet initial demand. The reasons for these and other EC failures are discussed in detail in Hwang and Stewart (2006) and in Chapters 3 and 5.

Does the large number of failures mean that EC's days are numbered? Absolutely not! First, the dot-com failure rate is declining sharply. Second, the EC field is basically experiencing consolidation as companies test different business models and organizational structures. Third, most pure EC companies, including giants such as Amazon.com, are expanding operations and generating increasing sales and profit.

EC Successes

The last few years have seen the rise of extremely successful virtual EC companies such as eBay, Google, Yahoo!, VeriSign, AOL, and E-Trade. Click-and-mortar companies such as Cisco, Wal-Mart online, General Electric, IBM, Intel, and Schwab also have seen great success (see Papazoglou and Ribbers 2006; and Jelassi and Enders 2005). Additional success stories include start-ups such as Alloy.com (a young-adults-oriented portal), Bluenile.com, FTD.com, Expedia.com, and Campusfood.com (see Online File W1.3). For more on the history of e-commerce, see Tian and Stewart (2006).

From just a brief overview of the EC framework and classification, you can probably see that EC is related to several different disciplines. The major EC disciplines include the following: *computer science, marketing, consumer behavior, finance, economics, management information systems, accounting, management, human resource management, business law, robotics, public administration,* and *engineering.*

THE FUTURE OF EC

In 1998, B2C sales in the United States were about $43 billion, or 1 percent of total retail sales (Greenberg 2004). Today's predictions about the future size of EC, provided by respected analysts such as AMR Research, Jupiter Media, Emarketer.com, and Forrester, vary. For example, 2006 global online shopping and B2B transactions are estimated to be about $7 trillion (Tian and Stewart 2006). According to Jupiter Media (2006), online retail spending will increase from $81 billion in 2005 to $95 billion in 2006, growing to $144 billion in 2010. By 2010, 78.5 percent of online users will use the Internet to shop, compared to 65 percent in 2005 (Marketingcharts.com 2007). Forrester estimates that almost $400 billion of store sales—or 16 percent of total retail sales—are directly influenced by the Web as consumers research products online and purchase them offline. This will grow at a 17 percent compound annual growth rate (CAGR), resulting in more than $1 trillion of store sales by 2012 (Mendelsohn et al. 2007). According to Forrester Research (2006), online sales reached $176 billion in 2005 and were expected to grow to $211 billion in 2006. Excluding travel, online sales account for nearly 5 percent of the U.S. retail market (vs. less than 2 percent in 2000). The number of Internet users worldwide was estimated at 700 million in mid-2006 (Mann 2006). EC growth will come not only from B2C, but also from B2B and from newer applications such as e-government, e-learning, B2E, and c-commerce. Overall, the growth of the field will continue to be strong into the foreseeable future. Despite the failures of individual companies and initiatives, the total volume of EC has been growing by 15 to 25 percent every year; as Lashinsky (2006) said: "The boom is back."

WEB 2.0 AND WEB 3.0

Web 2.0

The second-generation of Internet-based services that let people generate content, collaborate, and share information online in perceived new ways—such as social networking sites, wikis, communication tools, and folksonomies.

The term **Web 2.0** was coined by O'Reilly Media in 2004 to refer to a supposed second generation of Internet-based services that let people generate and control content, collaborate, and share information online in perceived new ways—such as social networking sites, wikis, communication tools, blogs, and folksonomies. O'Reilly Media, in collaboration with MediaLive International, used the phrase as a title for a series of conferences. Since then, it has become a popular, if ill-defined and often criticized, buzzword in the technical and marketing communities.

O'Reilly (2005) provides the following examples to illustrate the differences between Web 2.0 and the previous generation, referred to as Web 1.0.

He also provided a road map (see O'Reilly 2005), which later was expanded by Angermeier (2005) (see Exhibit 1.3). The tools of Web 2.0 are described in Chapters 2, 8, and 14. The applications are described throughout the book, especially in Chapter 8.

Schonfeld (2006a) believes a major characteristic of Web 2.0 is the global spread of innovative Web sites. As soon as a successful idea is deployed as a Web site in one country, similar sites appear around the globe. He presents 23 Web 2.0 type sites in 10 countries. Web 2.0 will be followed by Web 3.0, which will probably emerge by 2010 (see Chapter 8).

Web 1.0		Web 2.0
DoubleClick	→	Google AdSense
Ofoto	→	Flickr
Akamai	→	BitTorrent
mp3.com	→	Napster
Britannica Online	→	Wikipedia
personal Web sites	→	blogging
Evite	→	upcoming.org and EVDB
domain name speculation	→	search engine optimization
page views	→	cost per click
screen scraping	→	Web services
publishing	→	participation
content management systems	→	wikis
directories (taxonomy)	→	tagging ("folksonomy")
stickiness	→	syndication

EXHIBIT 1.3   Mind Map of Web 2.0

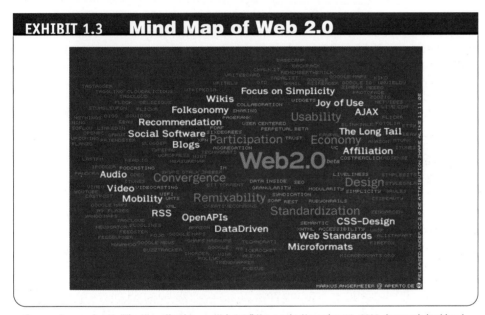

Source: Angermeier, M. "The Huge Cloud Lense Web 2.0." Kosmar.de, November 11, 2005. *kosmar.de/archives/2005/11/11/the-huge-cloud-lens-bubble-map-web20* (accessed January 2008). Reprinted by permission of Markus Angermeier.

Now that you are familiar with the concepts of EC, let's see what drives it (Sections 1.3 and 1.4).

Section 1.2 ▶ REVIEW QUESTIONS

1. List the major components of the EC framework.
2. List the major transactional types of EC.
3. Describe the major landmarks in EC history.
4. List some EC successes and failures.
5. Define Web 2.0.

1.3 THE DIGITAL REVOLUTION DRIVES EC

The major driver of EC is the digital revolution.

THE DIGITAL REVOLUTION AND ECONOMY

The digital revolution is upon us. We see it every day at home and work, in businesses, schools, and hospitals, on roads, and even in wars. One of its major aspects is the digital economy.

The Digital Economy

digital economy

An economy that is based on digital technologies, including digital communication networks, computers, software, and other related information technologies; also called the Internet economy, the new economy, or the Web economy.

The **digital economy** refers to an economy that is based on digital technologies, including digital communication networks (the Internet, intranets, extranets, and VANs), computers, software, and other related information technologies. The digital economy is sometimes called the *Internet economy,* the *new economy,* or the *Web economy.* According to Sharma (2006) and Choi and Whinston (2000), this platform displays the following characteristics:

- A vast array of digitizable products—databases, news and information, books, magazines, TV and radio programming, movies, electronic games, musical CDs, and software—are delivered over a digital infrastructure anytime, anywhere in the world.
- Consumers and firms conduct financial transactions digitally through digital currencies or financial tokens that are carried via networked computers and mobile devices.
- Microprocessors and networking capabilities are embedded in physical goods such as home appliances and automobiles.
- Information is transformed into a commodity.
- Knowledge is codified.
- Work and production are organized in new and innovative ways.

The term *digital economy* also refers to the convergence of computing and communications technologies on the Internet and other networks and the resulting flow of information and technology that is stimulating EC and vast organizational changes. This convergence enables all types of information (data, audio, video, etc.) to be stored, processed, and transmitted over networks to many destinations worldwide (see also Sharma 2006 and Turban et al. 2007).

The digital economy is creating an economic revolution, which, according to the *Emerging Digital Economy II* (U.S. Department of Commerce 1999), was evidenced by unprecedented economic performance and the longest period of uninterrupted economic expansion in U.S. history (1991–2000), combined with low inflation. Because of the growth of the Internet and its usage, hardware advances (e.g., PCs, cell phones), progress in communications capabilities (e.g., VoIP, worldwide broadband adoption), advanced usage of digital media (e.g., Internet video, blogs, and wikis), and IT spending for better productivity, the future of the digital economy is looking good. Exhibit 1.4 describes the major characteristics of the digital economy.

The digital revolution accelerates EC mainly by providing competitive advantage to organizations. The digital revolution enables many innovations, some of which are listed in Insights and Additions 1.1. Many, many other innovations characterize the digital revolution, and new ones appear daily.

The digital revolution drives EC by providing the necessary technologies, as well as by creating major changes in the business environment, as described in the next section.

EXHIBIT 1.4   Major Characteristics of the Digital Revolution

Area	Description
Globalization	Global communication and collaboration; global electronic marketplaces.
Digital system	From TV to telephones and instrumentation, analog systems are being converted to digital ones.
Speed	A move to real-time transactions, thanks to digitized documents, products, and services. Many business processes are expedited by 90 percent or more.
Information overload	Although the amount of information generated is accelerating, intelligent search tools can help users find what they need.
Markets	Markets are moving online. Physical marketplaces are being replaced by electronic markets; new markets are being created, increasing competition.
Digitization	Music, books, pictures, and more (see Chapter 2) are digitized for fast and inexpensive distribution.
Business models and processes	New and improved business models and processes provide opportunities to new companies and industries. Cyberintermediation and no intermediation are on the rise.
Innovation	Digital and Internet-based innovations continue at a rapid pace. More patents are being granted than ever before.
Obsolescence	The fast pace of innovation creates a high rate of obsolescence.
Opportunities	Opportunities abound in almost all aspects of life and operations.
Fraud	Criminals employ a slew of innovative schemes on the Internet. Cybercons are everywhere.
Wars	Conventional wars are changing to cyberwars.
Organizations	Moving to digital enterprises.

Section 1.3 ▶ REVIEW QUESTIONS

1. Define the digital economy.
2. List the characteristics of the digital revolution.

Insights and Additions 1.1 Interesting and Unique Applications of EC

▶ According to Farivar (2004), VIP patrons of the Baja Beach Club in Barcelona, Spain, can have radio frequency identification (RFID) chips, which are the size of a grain of rice, implanted into their upper arms, allowing them to charge drinks to a bar tab when they raise their arm toward the RFID reader. An RFID is a tiny tag that contains a processor and antenna; it can communicate wirelessly with a detecting unit in a reader over a short distance (see Lebbecke 2006 and Chapter 6). "You don't call someone crazy for getting a tattoo," says Conrad Chase, director of Baja Beach Clubs international. "Why would they be crazy for getting this?"

▶ Pearson Education, Inc., the publisher of this book, in collaboration with O'Reilly & Associates, offers professors reasonably priced, customized textbooks for their classes by compiling material from thousands of Pearson's publications and the instructors' own materials. The customized books are either electronic or more expensive hard copies.

▶ In Japan, a person can wave a Casio watch over a scanner to purchase products from a vending machine, pay for food in a cafeteria, or pay for gasoline.

▶ Dryers and washers in college dorms are hooked to the Web. Students can punch a code into their cell phones or sign in at *esuds.net* and check the availability of laundry machines. Furthermore, they can pay with their student ID or with a credit card and receive e-mail alerts when their wash and dry cycles are complete. Once in the laundry room, a student activates the system by swiping a student ID card or keying in a PIN number. The system

(continued)

Insights and Additions 1.1 *(continued)*

automatically injects premeasured amounts of detergent and fabric softener, at the right cycle time.

▶ More than 60 percent of all airline tickets sold in the United States are electronic tickets. It costs more to purchase a ticket from a local travel agent or by phone directly from the airline. In some airports, travelers can get their boarding passes from a machine. Most airlines allow travelers to print their boarding passes from home.

▶ In January 2004, NASA's Web site received more than 6.5 billion hits in a few days—the biggest Internet government event to date—because people were interested in viewing the Mars Exploration Rover's landing on Mars.

▶ Several banks in Japan issue smart cards that can be used only by their owners. When using the cards, the vein on the palm of the owner's hand is compared with a stored template of the vein stored on the smart card. When the owner inserts the card into ATM or vendors' card readers that are equipped with the system, it will dispense the card owner's money. The police are alerted if anyone other than the card's owner tries to use it.

▶ Jacobi Medical Center in New York tracks the whereabouts of patients in the hospital. Each patient has an RFID in a plastic band strapped to the wrist. Each time a patient passes an RFID reader, the patient's location is transmitted in real time to the responsible staff member. The RFID is linked to the hospital's computer network, connecting the patient's records to labs, billing, and the pharmacy.

▶ To find adoptive parents for himself and a baby sister after both parents died of cancer, a Chinese boy in Zhengzhou, China, created a special Web site that described the children and showed photos. Within a short time, dozens of people from many countries expressed an interest (Zhengzhou Evening News [in Chinese], September 27, 2004).

▶ According to *People's Daily Online* from China (2006), distressed parents have created a blog to track down their missing 24-year-old son (*blog.sina.com.cn/m/xunzi*). The blog is linked to some celebrity blogs to get more attention.

▶ Using his blog site (*oneredpaperclip.blogspot.com*), Kyle MacDonald of Canada was able to trade a red paper clip into a three-bedroom house. He started by advertising in the barter section of Craigslist.com that he wanted something bigger or better for one red paper clip. In the first iteration, he received a fish-shaped pen, and he posted on Craigslist again and again. Following many iterations and publicity on TV, he finally, after one year, received a house (see Chapter 2 for details).

▶ Camera-equipped cell phones are used in Finland as health and fitness advisors. A supermarket shopper using the technology can snap an image of the bar code on a packet of food. The phone forwards the code number to a central computer, which sends back information on the item's ingredients and nutritional value. The computer also calculates how much exercise the shopper will have to do to burn off the calories based on the shopper's height, weight, age, and other factors.

1.4 THE BUSINESS ENVIRONMENT DRIVES EC

Economic, legal, societal, and technological factors have created a highly competitive *business environment* in which customers are becoming more powerful. These environmental factors can change quickly, vigorously, and sometimes in an unpredictable manner. Companies need to react quickly to both the problems and the opportunities resulting from this new business environment. Because the pace of change and the level of uncertainty are expected to accelerate, organizations are operating under increasing pressures to produce more products, faster, and with fewer resources.

THE BUSINESS ENVIRONMENT

Most people, sports teams, and organizations are trying to improve their *performance*. For some, it is a challenge; for others, it is a requirement for survival. Yet, for some it is the key to improved life, profitability, or reputation.

Most organizations measure their performance periodically, comparing it to some metrics and to the organization's mission, objectives, and plans. Unfortunately, in business,

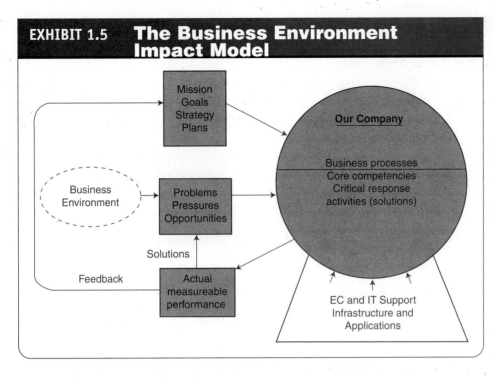

EXHIBIT 1.5   The Business Environment Impact Model

performance often depends not only on what you do, but also on what others are doing, as well as on forces of nature. In the business world, such events are referred to, in totality, as the *business environment*. Such an environment can create significant pressures and impact performance in uncontrollable, or sometimes even in unpredictable, ways.

The Business Environment Impact Model

The model shown in Exhibit 1.5 illustrates how the business environment (left) creates problems and opportunities that drive what organizations are doing in their business processes (the "our company" box). Other drivers are the organization's mission, goals, strategy, and plans. Business processes include competencies, activities, and responses (what we term *critical response activities* or *solutions*) to the problems, constraints, and opportunities. Organizational activities in business processes result in measurable performance, which provides solutions to problems/opportunities, as well as feedback on the mission, strategy, and plans.

Notice that in the figure EC and IT provide support to organizations' activities and to actual performance, countering business pressures. We will demonstrate this throughout the book.

Business Pressures and Opportunities

In this text, business pressures are divided into the following categories: market (economic), societal, and technological. The main types of business pressures in each category are listed in Exhibit 1.6. Some of these create problems, others create opportunities.

Organizational Response Strategies

How can organizations operate in such an environment? How can they deal with the threats and the opportunities? To begin with, many traditional strategies are still useful in today's environment. However, because some traditional response activities might *not*

EXHIBIT 1.6   Major Business Pressures

Market and Economic Pressures	Societal Pressures	Technological Pressures
Strong competition Global economy Regional trade agreements (e.g., NAFTA) Extremely low labor cost in some countries Frequent and significant changes in markets Increased power of consumers	Changing nature of workforce Government deregulation, leading to more competition Compliance (e.g., Sarbanes-Oxley Act) Shrinking government subsidies Increased importance of ethical and legal issues Increased social responsibility of organizations Rapid political changes	Increasing innovations and new technologies Rapid technological obsolescence Increases in information overload Rapid decline in technology cost versus manual labor cost (technology becomes more attractive)

work in today's turbulent and competitive business environment, many of the old solutions need to be modified, supplemented, or discarded. Alternatively, new responses can be devised. Critical response activities can take place in some or all organizational processes, from the daily processing of payroll and order entry to strategic activities such as the acquisition of a company. Responses can also occur in the supply chain, as demonstrated by the cases of Boeing (Case 1.2), Dell (opening case), and in Marks & Spencer (Online File W1.1). A response activity can be a reaction to a specific pressure already in existence, or it can be an initiative that will defend an organization against future pressures. It can also be an activity that exploits an opportunity created by changing conditions.

Many response activities can be greatly facilitated by EC. In some cases, EC is the only solution to these business pressures. Representative major EC-supported response activities are provided in Exhibit 1.7 and in Online File W1.4.

Section 1.4 ▶ REVIEW QUESTIONS

1. List the components of the business environment impact model and explain the model.
2. List the major factors in today's business environment.
3. List some of the major response activities taken by organizations.

1.5 EC BUSINESS MODELS

business model
A method of doing business by which a company can generate revenue to sustain itself.

One of the major characteristics of EC is that it enables the creation of new business models (see Rappa 2006). A **business model** is a method of doing business by which a company can generate revenue to sustain itself. The model also spells out where the company is positioned in the value chain—that is, by what activities the company adds value to the product or service it supplies. (The *value chain* is the series of value-adding activities that an organization performs to achieve its goals, such as making profit, at various stages of the production process.) Some models are very simple. For example, Wal-Mart buys merchandise, sells it, and generates a profit. In contrast, a TV station provides free broadcasting to its viewers. The station's survival depends on a complex model involving advertisers and content providers. Public Internet portals, such as Yahoo!, also use a complex business model. One company might have several business models.

EXHIBIT 1.7   Innovative Organizational Responses

Response Strategy	Descriptions
Strategic systems	Improve strategic advantage in industry.
Agile systems	Increase ability to adapt to changes and flexibility.
Continuous improvements and business process management	Use enterprise systems to improve business processes. Introduce e-procurement.
Customer relationship management	Introduce programs to improve customers' relationships using the Internet and EC models.
Business alliances and Partner Relationship Management (PRM)	Create joint ventures, partnerships, e-collaboration, virtual corporations and others for win–win situations (even with competitors). (See Case 1.3.)
Electronic markets	Use both private and public electronic market to increase efficiency and effectiveness.
Cycle time reduction	Increase speed of operation and reduce time-to-market (see Online File W1.5).
Empowering employees, especially at the frontline (interacting with customers, partners)	Provide employees with computerized decision aids so they can make quick decisions on their own (see Davenport 2006).
Supply chain improvements	Reduce problems along the supply chain, expedite flows, and reduce inventories.
Mass customization in a build-to-order system	Produce customized products (services), rapidly at reasonable cost to many, many customers (mass), as Dell does. See Appendix 2A.
Intrabusiness use of automation	Many intrabusiness activities, from sales force automation to inventory management, can be improved with e-commerce and m-commerce.
Knowledge management	Appropriate creation, storage, and dissemination of knowledge using electronic systems increases productivity, agility, and competitiveness.
Customer selection, loyalty, and service	Identify customers with the greatest profit potential; increase likelihood that they will want the product or service offering; retain their loyalty.
Human capital	Select the best employees for particular tasks or jobs, at particular compensation levels.
Product and service quality	Detect quality problems early and minimize them.
Financial performance	Better understand the drivers of financial performance and the effects of nonfinancial factors.
Research and development	Improve quality, efficacy, and, where applicable, safety of products and services.

Business models are a subset of a business plan or a business case. These concepts frequently are confused. (In other words, some equate a *business model* with a *business plan*.) However, as Online Chapter 13 and Online Tutorial 1 show, business plans and cases differ from business models (also see Lee et al. 2006 and Currie 2004).

THE STRUCTURE AND PROPERTIES OF BUSINESS MODELS

Several different EC business models are possible, depending on the company, the industry, and so on. Weill and Vitale (2001) developed a framework for evaluating the viability of e-business initiatives. According to this methodology, eight elementary, or "atomic," e-business models can be combined in different ways to create operational e-business initiatives. The eight atomic business models are *direct marketing, intermediary, content provider, full-service provider, shared infrastructure, value net integrator, virtual community,* and *consolidator of services* for large organizations. For example, the Amazon.com business model combines direct marketing, the intermediary role, virtual community, and content provider. Each atomic model can be described by four characteristics: strategic objectives, sources of revenue, critical success factors, and core competencies required. However, all business models share common elements.

According to McKay and Marshall (2004), a comprehensive business model is composed of the following six elements:

▶ A description of the *customers* to be served and the company's relationships with these customers, including what constitutes value from the customers' perspective (*customers' value proposition*)

▶ A description of all *products* and *services* the business will offer

▶ A description of the *business process* required to make and deliver the products and services

▶ A list of the *resources* required and the identification of which ones are available, which will be developed in-house, and which will need to be acquired

▶ A description of the organization's *supply chain*, including *suppliers* and other *business partners*

▶ A description of the revenues expected (*revenue model*), anticipated costs, sources of financing, and estimated profitability (*financial viability*)

Models also include a *value proposition*, which is an analysis of the benefits of using the specific model (tangible and intangible), including the customers' value proposition cited earlier.

A detailed discussion of and examples of business models and their relationship to business plans is presented in Online Chapter 13. For a list of components and key issues of EC business models, see Lee et al. (2006).

This chapter now presents two of the elements that are needed to understand the material in Chapters 2 through 12: revenue models and value propositions.

revenue model
Description of how the company or an EC project will earn revenue.

Revenue Models

A **revenue model** outlines how the organization or the EC project will generate revenue. For example, the revenue model for Godiva's online EC initiative shows revenue from online sales. The major revenue models are:

▶ **Sales.** Companies generate revenue from selling merchandise or services over their Web sites. An example is when Wal-Mart, Amazon.com, or Godiva sells a product online.

▶ **Transaction fees.** A company receives a commission based on the volume of transactions made. For example, when a homeowner sells a house, he typically pays a transaction fee to the broker. The higher the value of the sale, the higher the total transaction fee. Alternatively, transaction fees can be levied per *transaction*. With online stock trades, for example, there is usually a fixed fee per trade, regardless of the volume.

▶ **Subscription fees.** Customers pay a fixed amount, usually monthly, to get some type of service. An example would be the access fee for AOL. Thus, AOL's primary revenue model is subscription (fixed monthly payments).

> ▶ **Advertising fees.** Companies charge others for allowing them to place a banner on their sites. This is how Google has made its fortune. (See Chapter 4 and the Real-World Application Case at the end of this chapter.)
>
> ▶ **Affiliate fees.** Companies receive commissions for referring customers to others' Web sites.
>
> ▶ **Other revenue sources.** Some companies allow people to play games for a fee or to watch a sports competition in real time for a fee (e.g., see *espn.go.com*). Another revenue source is licensing fees (e.g., *datadirect-technologies.com*). Licensing fees can be assessed as an annual fee or a per usage fee. Microsoft takes fees from each workstation that uses Windows NT, for example.

A company uses its *revenue model* to describe how it will generate revenue and its *business model* to describe the process it will use to do so. Online File W1.6 summarizes five common revenue models. For example, Godiva's online revenue model shows that customers can order products online. The customers can pick up the merchandise at a Godiva store or, for an extra charge, have it shipped to their homes. The revenue comes from sales, which take place both off-line and online.

The revenue model can be part of the value proposition or it may complement it.

Value Proposition

Business models also include a value-proposition statement. A **value proposition** refers to the benefits, including the intangible, nonquantitative ones, that a company can derive from using the model. In B2C EC, for example, a value proposition defines how a company's product or service fulfills the needs of customers. The value proposition is an important part of the marketing plan of any product or service.

Specifically, how do e-marketplaces create value? Amit and Zott (2001) identify four sets of values that are created by e-business: search and transaction cost-efficiency, complementarities, lock-in, and novelty. *Search and transaction cost-efficiency* enables faster and more informed decision making, wider product and service selection, and greater economies of scale—cost savings per unit as greater quantities are produced and sold (e.g., through demand and supply aggregation for small buyers and sellers). *Complementarities* involve bundling some goods and services together to provide more value than from offering them separately. *Lock-in* is attributable to the high switching cost that ties customers to particular suppliers. *Novelty* creates value through innovative ways for structuring transactions, connecting partners, and fostering new markets.

value proposition
The benefits a company can derive from using EC.

Functions of a Business Model

According to Chesbrough and Rosenbloom (2002), business models have the following functions or objectives:

▶ Articulate a customer value proposition.

▶ Identify a market segment (*who* will use the technology for *what* purpose; specify the revenue-generation process).

▶ Define the venture's specific value chain structure.

▶ Estimate the cost structure and profit potential.

▶ Describe the venture's positioning within the value network linking suppliers and customers (includes identification of potential complementors and competitors).

▶ Formulate the venture's competitive strategy.

TYPICAL EC BUSINESS MODELS

There are many types of EC business models. Examples and details of EC business models can be found throughout this text (and also in Rappa 2007; Currie 2004; and Afuah and Tucci 2003). The following list describes some of the most common or visible models. Details are provided throughout the text.

1. **Online direct marketing.** The most obvious model is that of selling products or services online. Sales may be from a *manufacturer* to a customer, eliminating intermediaries or physical stores (e.g., Godiva), or from *retailers* to consumers, making distribution more efficient (e.g.,Wal-Mart). This model is especially efficient for digitizable products and services (those that can be delivered electronically). This model has several variations (see Chapters 3 and 5). It is practiced in B2C (where it is called *e-tailing*) and in some B2B types of EC.

2. **Electronic tendering systems for procurement.** Large organizational buyers, private or public, usually make large-volume or large-value purchases through a **tendering (bidding) system**, also known as a reverse auction. Such tendering can be done online, saving time and money. Pioneered by General Electric Corp., e-tendering systems are gaining popularity. Indeed, several government agencies mandate that most of their procurement must be done through e-tendering (see Chapter 5).

3. **Name your own price.** Pioneered by Priceline.com, the **name-your-own-price model** allows buyers to set the price they are willing to pay for a specific product or service. Priceline.com (Chapter 2) will try to match a customer's request with a supplier willing to sell the product or service at that price. This model is also known as a *demand-collection model*.

4. **Find the best price.** According to this model, also known as a *search engine model* (see Bandyopadhyay 2001), a customer specifies a need and then an intermediate company, such as Hotwire.com, matches the customer's need against a database, locates the lowest price, and submits it to the consumer. The potential buyer then has 30 to 60 minutes to accept or reject the offer. A variation of this model is available for purchasing insurance: A consumer can submit a request for insurance to Insweb.com and receive several quotes. Many companies employ similar models to find the lowest price. For example, consumers can go to **eloan.com** to show price comparisons of different vendors and find the best interest rate for auto or home loans. A well-known company in this area is Shopping.com, which is described with similar companies in Chapter 3. Companies such as Half.com offer products and services at deep discounts, as much as 50 percent off the retail price (see Chapter 3).

5. **Affiliate marketing. Affiliate marketing** is an arrangement whereby a marketing partner (a business, an organization, or even an individual) refers consumers to a selling company's Web site (see Chapter 4). The referral is done by placing a banner ad or the logo of the selling company on the affiliated company's Web site. Whenever a customer who was referred to the selling company's Web site makes a purchase there, the affiliated partner receives a commission (which may range from 3 to 15 percent) of the purchase price. In other words, by using affiliate marketing, a selling company creates a *virtual commissioned sales force*. Pioneered by CDNow (see Hoffman and Novak 2000), the concept is now employed by thousands of retailers and manufacturers. For example, Amazon.com has over 1,000,000 affiliates, and even tiny Cattoys.com offers

---

tendering (bidding) system
Model in which a buyer requests would-be sellers to submit bids; the lowest cost or highest value bidder wins.

name-your-own-price model
Model in which a buyer sets the price he or she is willing to pay and invites sellers to supply the good or service at that price.

affiliate marketing
An arrangement whereby a marketing partner (a business, an organization, or even an individual) refers consumers to the selling company's Web site.

individuals and organizations the opportunity to put its logo and link on their Web sites to generate commissions.

6. **Viral marketing.** According to the **viral marketing** model (see Chapter 4), an organization can increase brand awareness or even generate sales by inducing people to send messages to other people or to recruit friends to join certain programs. It is basically Web-based word-of-mouth marketing and is used extensively in social networks (Chapter 8).

7. **Group purchasing.** In the off-line world of commerce, discounts are usually available for purchasing large quantities. So, too, EC has spawned the concept of *demand aggregation*, wherein a third party finds individuals or **SMEs (small-to-medium enterprises)**, aggregates their small orders to attain a large quantity, and then negotiates (or conducts a tender) for the best deal. Thus, using the concept of **group purchasing**, a small business, or even an individual, can get a discount. This model, also known as the *volume-buying model*, is described in Chapter 5. One leading aggregator is Letsbuyit.com (see also Krishnan and Ravi 2003). Online purchasing groups also are called **e-co-ops**.

8. **Online auctions.** Almost everyone has heard of eBay, the world's largest online auction site. Several hundred other companies, including Amazon.com and Yahoo!, also conduct online auctions. In the most popular type of auction, online shoppers make consecutive bids for various goods and services, and the highest bidders get the items auctioned. E-auctions come in different shapes (Chapter 2) and use different models. For example, eBay is using about 40,000 "assistants" in a model where the assistants perform order fulfillment (see Chapter 2).

9. **Product customization and service personalization.** With **customization**, a product is created according to the buyer's specifications. Customization is not a new model, but what is new is the ability to quickly configure customized products online for consumers at costs not much higher than their noncustomized counterparts (see Chapters 3 and 5). Dell is a good example of a company that customizes PCs for its customers.

   Many other companies are following Dell's lead: The automobile industry is customizing its products and expects to save billions of dollars in inventory reduction alone every year by producing made-to-order cars (see Li and Du 2004). Mattel's My Design lets fashion-doll fans custom-build a friend for Barbie at Mattel's Web site; the doll's image is displayed on the screen before the person places an order. Nike allows customers to customize shoes, which can be delivered in a week. Lego.com allows customers to configure several of their toys. Finally, De Beers allows customers to design their own engagement rings.

   Configuring the details of the customized products, including the final design, ordering, and paying for the products, is done online. Also known as *build-to-order*, customization can be done on a large scale, in which case it is called *mass customization*. For a historical discussion of the development of the idea of mass customization, see Appendix 2A at the end of Chapter 2.

   Similarly, when a service or information is created to meet the customer specification, it is called **personalization**. This is frequently done through portals ("My . . ."). Personalization usually is provided for free.

10. **Electronic marketplaces and exchanges.** Electronic marketplaces existed in isolated applications for decades (e.g., stock and commodities exchanges). But as of 1996, hundreds of e-marketplaces have introduced new efficiencies to the trading process. If they are well organized and managed, e-marketplaces can provide significant

---

viral marketing
Word-of-mouth marketing in which customers promote a product or service to friends or others.

SMEs
Small-to-medium enterprises.

group purchasing
Quantity (aggregated) purchasing that enables groups of purchasers to obtain a discount price on the products purchased.

e-co-ops
Another name for online group purchasing organizations.

customization
Creation of a product or service according to the buyer's specifications.

personalization
The creation of a service or information according to specific customer specifications.

benefits to both buyers and sellers. Of special interest are *vertical* marketplaces, which concentrate on one industry (e.g., GNX.com for the retail industry and Chemconnect.com for the chemical industry, see Chapter 5).

11. **Information brokers (infomediaries).** Information brokers (see Chapters 3 through 7) provide privacy, trust, matching, search, content, and other services (e.g., Bizrate.com, Froogle.com).

12. **Bartering.** Companies use bartering (see Chapter 2) to exchange surpluses they do not need for things that they do need. A market maker (e.g., Web-barter.com or Tradeaway.com) arranges such exchanges.

13. **Value-chain integrators.** This model offers services that aggregate information-rich products into a more complete package for customers, thus adding value. For example, Carpoint.com provides several car-buying–related services, such as financing and insurance.

14. **Value-chain service providers.** These providers specialize in a supply chain function such as logistics (UPS.com) or payments (PayPal.com, now part of eBay) (see Chapters 6 and 11).

15. **Supply chain improvers.** One of the major contributions of EC is in the creation of new models that change or improve supply chain management, as shown in the opening case about Dell. Most interesting is the conversion of a *linear* supply chain, which can be slow, expensive, and error prone, into a *hub*.

16. **Social networks, communities, and blogging.** Many companies are developing commercial benefits from social networks (see Section 1.7 and Chapter 8), communities, and blogging (e.g., for paid advertising or as a sales channel).

17. **Negotiation.** The Internet offers negotiation capabilities between individuals (e.g., Ioffer.com) or between companies (e.g., in exchanges, Chapter 5). Negotiation can also be facilitated by intelligent agents.

SPECIAL EC BUSINESS MODEL: SECOND LIFE

virtual world

A user-defined world in which people can interact, play, and do business. The most publicized virtual world is Second Life.

One of the most interesting EC models is the *virtual world*. A **virtual world** is a user-defined world in which people can interact, play, and do business. The most publicized virtual world is Second Life (secondlife.com). More information about Second Life is provided in Case 1.3 and at en.wikipedia.org/wiki/Second_Life.

Any of the business models presented in this section and others can be used alone or in combination with each other or with traditional business models. One company might use several different business models. The models can be used for B2C, B2B, and other forms of EC. Although some of the models are limited to B2C or B2B, others can be used in several types of transactions, as will be illustrated throughout the text.

Section 1.5 ▶ REVIEW QUESTIONS

1. Define business model.
2. Describe a revenue model and a value proposition.
3. Describe the following business models: name your own price, affiliate marketing, viral marketing, and product customization.
4. Identify business models related to buying and those related to selling.
5. Compare customization with personalization.
6. Describe Second Life.

CASE 1.3
EC Application

SECOND LIFE

In 2003, a 3D virtual world called Second Life was opened to the public. The world is entirely built and owned by its residents. In 2003, the virtual world consisted of 64 acres, and by 2007 it had grown to 65,000 acres and was inhabited by 8,610,000 residents from around the planet (SecondLife.com 2007). The virtual world consists of a huge, digital continent; people; entertainment; experiences; and opportunities.

Thousands of new residents join Second Life each day and create their own avatar through which they travel around the Second Life world meeting people, communicating, having fun, and buying virtual land and other virtual properties where they can open a business or build a personal space. They are limited only by their imaginations and their ability to use the virtual 3D applications. Avatars have unique names and move around in imaginative vehicles including helicopters, submarines, and hot-air balloons.

Second Life is dedicated to creativity, and everything in Second Life is resident-created. Residents retain the rights to their digital creations and can buy, sell, and trade with other residents and are able to sell them at Second Life marketplaces. Residents can also socialize and participate in group activities. Businesses succeed by the ingenuity, artistic ability, entrepreneurial acumen, and the owners' reputation.

Residents get some free virtual land (and they can buy more) where they build a house or business. They can then sell the virtual properties or the virtual products or services they create. Residents can also sell real-world products or services. For example, Copeland and Kelleher (2007) report that more than 25,000 aspiring entrepreneurs trade virtual products or services at Second Life. Stevan Lieberman is one of these. He uses his expertise in legal intellectual property and the site to solicit work mainly from programmers who are looking to patent their code.

Second Life is managed by Linden Labs, which provides Linden dollars (in 2007 they faced regulatory problems) that can be converted to U.S. dollars. Second Life uses several Web 2.0 tools such as blogs, wikis, RSS, and tags (from *del.icio.us*). These tools are described in Chapter 2.

Many organizations use Second Life for 3D presentations of their products. Even governments have opened virtual embassies on the site's "Diplomacy Island." Many universities offer educational courses and seminars in virtual classrooms (see "EduIslands" on the site). Some companies are conducting recruitment at the site.

Roush (2007) describes how to combine Second Life with Google Earth. Such combinations enable investigation of phenomena that would otherwise be difficult to visualize or understand.

Real-world businesses use the virtual world, too. For example, IBM uses it as a location for meetings, training, and recruitment (Reuters 2006). American Apparel is the first major retailer to set up shop in Second Life (Jana 2006). Starwood Hotels uses Second Life as a relatively low-cost market research experiment in which avatars visit Starwood's virtual Aloft hotel. The endeavor has created publicity for the company and has provided feedback on the design of the hotel. Feedback is solicited from visiting avatars and will be reflected in brick and mortar when the first real-world Aloft hotels open in 2008 (Carr 2007). The Mexican Tourism Board and Morocco Tourism are examples of 3D presentations of major tourist attractions. Many companies use Second life as a hot place to go to try new business ideas (see Rosedale 2007). For example, you can test drive a Toyota Scion, play with prototype toys, and become a virtual architect.

Sources: Carr (2007); Copeland and Kelleher (2007); Jana (2006); Reuters (2006); Rosedale (2007); Roush (2007); and secondlife.com (accessed October 2007).

Questions

1. Enter the Second Life site (*secondlife.com*) and identify EC activities there. (You need to register for free and create an avatar.)

2. Which of the types of transactions listed in Section 1.2 are observable at the site?

3. Which of the business models listed in Section 1.5 are observable at the site?

4. How can a university utilize the site?

5. If you were a travel agent, how would you utilize the site?

6. Have your avatar communicate with five others. Write a report on your experience.

7. You are planning to build a swimming pool in your "First Life" backyard. How can Second Life be of help?

1.6 BENEFITS AND LIMITATIONS OF EC

Few innovations in human history encompass as many benefits as EC does. The global nature of the technology, the opportunity to reach hundreds of millions of people, its interactive nature, the variety of possibilities for its use, and the resourcefulness and rapid growth of its supporting infrastructures, especially the Web, result in many potential benefits to organizations, individuals, and society. These benefits are just starting to materialize, and they will increase significantly as EC expands. It is not surprising that some maintain that the EC revolution is as profound as the change that accompanied the Industrial Revolution (Drucker 2002).

THE BENEFITS OF EC

EC provides benefits to organizations, individual customers, and society. These benefits are summarized in Exhibit 1.8. An example of how EC technologies assist the Department of Homeland Security can be found in Insights and Additions 1.2. More details are shown in Online File W1.7.

EXHIBIT 1.8   Benefits of E-Commerce

Benefit	Description
Benefits to Organizations	
Global reach	Locating customers and/or suppliers worldwide, at reasonable cost and fast.
Cost reduction	Lower cost of information processing, storage, distribution.
Supply chain improvements	Reduce delays, inventories, and cost.
Business always open	Open 24/7/365; no overtime or other cost.
Customization/personalization	Make it to consumers' wish, fast and at reasonable cost.
Sellers specialization (niche market)	Seller can specialize in a narrow field (e.g., dog toys); yet make money.
Ability to innovate, use new business models	Facilitate innovation and enable unique business models.
Rapid time-to-market and increased speed	Expedite processes; higher speed and productivity.
Lower communication cost	The Internet is cheaper then VAN private lines.
Efficient procurement	Enabler of e-procurement saves time and reduces cost.
Improved customer service and relationship	Direct interaction with customers, better CRM
Fewer permits and less tax	May need fewer permits and avoid sales tax.
Up-to-date company material	All distributed material is up-to-date.
Help SME to compete	EC may help small companies to compete against large ones through special business models.
Lower inventories	Using customization, inventories can be minimized.
Lower cost of distributing digitalizable product	Delivery online can be 90 percent cheaper.
Benefits to Consumers	
Ubiquity	Can shop any time from any place.
More products/services	Large selection to choose from (vendor, products, styles).
Customized products/services	Can customize many products and/or services.
Cheaper products/services	Can compare and shop for lowest prices.
Instant delivery	For digitized products.
Information availability	Easy finding what you need, with details, demos, etc.
Convenient auction participation	Do auctions any time and from any place.

(continued)

EXHIBIT 1.8   (continued)

No sales tax	Sometimes.
Enable telecommuting	Can work or study at home.
Electronic socialization	Can socialize online in communities, yet be at home.
Find unique items	Online auctions can be used to find collectibles.
Benefits to Society	
Enabler of telecommuting	Facilitate work at home; less traffic, pollution.
More public services	Make education, health, and so on, available to more people. Rural area can share benefits; more services for the poor.
Improved homeland security	Facilitate Department of Homeland Security (see Insights and Additions 1.2).
Increased standard of living	Can buy cheaper and more.
Close the digital divide	Allow people in developing countries and rural areas to accept more services and purchase what they really like.

Insights and Additions 1.2 Enhancing Homeland Security Electronically

The U.S. Department of Homeland Security (DHS) must determine which preexisting applications and data can help the organization meet its goals; migrate data to a secure, usable, state-of-the-art framework; and integrate the disparate networks and data standards of 22 federal agencies, with 170,000 employees, that merged to form the DHS. The real problem is that federal agencies have historically operated autonomously, and their IT systems were not designed to interoperate with one another. Essentially, the DHS needs to link large and complex silos of data together.

Major problems have occurred because each agency has its own set of business rules that dictate how data are described, collected, and accessed. Some of the data are unstructured and not organized in relational databases, and they cannot be easily manipulated and analyzed.

Commercial applications, mostly data warehouse and data mart technologies, are being used for the major integration activities. Informatica, one of several software vendors working with the DHS, has developed data integration solutions that will enable the DHS to combine disparate systems to make information more widely accessible throughout the organization (see *informatica.com*).

The new DHS system will have information-analysis and infrastructure-protection components. The DHS not only has to make sense of a huge mountain of intelligence gathered from disparate sources, but then it must get that information to the people who can most effectively act on it. Many of these people are outside the federal government.

Sources: Compiled from Foley (2003) and Peters (2003).

Facilitating Problem Solving

One of the major benefits of EC is its ability to solve complex problems that have remained unsolved for generations. Such problems might require several EC and IT tools. Problems exist in small organizations and large ones, as well as in cities and even countries.

THE LIMITATIONS AND BARRIERS OF EC

Barriers to EC can be classified as either technological or nontechnological. The major barriers are summarized in Exhibit 1.9.

According to a 2006 study (Harmonyhollow.net 2006), the major barriers to EC are (1) resistance to new technology, (2) implementation difficulties, (3) security concerns,

EXHIBIT 1.9   Limitations of Electronic Commerce

Technological Limitations	Nontechnological Limitations
Lack of universal standards for quality, security, and reliability.	Security and privacy concerns deter customers from buying.
The telecommunications bandwidth is insufficient, especially for m-commerce.	Lack of trust in EC and in unknown sellers hinders buying.
Software development tools are still evolving.	People do not yet sufficiently trust paperless, faceless transactions.
It is difficult to integrate Internet and EC software with some existing (especially legacy) applications and databases.	Many legal and public policy issues, including taxation, have not yet been resolved or are not clear.
Special Web servers are needed in addition to the network servers, which add to the cost of EC.	National and international government regulations sometimes get in the way.
Internet accessibility is still expensive and/or inconvenient.	It is difficult to measure some of the benefits of EC, such as online advertising. Mature measurement methodologies are not yet available.
Order fulfillment of large-scale B2C requires special automated warehouses.	Some customers like to feel and touch products. Also, customers are resistant to the change from shopping at a brick-and-mortar store to a virtual store.
	In many cases, the number of sellers and buyers that are needed for profitable EC operations is insufficient.
	Online fraud is increasing.
	It is difficult to obtain venture capital due to the failure of many dot-coms.

(4) lack of technology skills, (5) lack of potential customers, and (6) cost. Van Toorn et al. (2006) believe that the barriers are sectoral barriers (e.g., government, private sector, international organizations), internal barriers (e.g., security, lack of technical knowledge, and lack of time and resources), and external barriers (e.g., lack of government support). Van Toorn et al. (2006) also list the top barriers with regards to global EC: cultural differences, organizational differences, incompatible B2B interfaces, international trade barriers, and lack of standards.

Despite these barriers, EC is expanding rapidly. For example, the number of people in the United States who buy and sell stocks electronically increased from 300,000 at the beginning of 1996 to over 40 million by the spring of 2007 (FastPitch 2007). In Korea, about 60 percent of all stock market transactions took place over the Internet in the summer of 2004, versus 2 percent in 1998 (*Seoul Digital City* 2004).

The benefits presented here may not be convincing enough reasons for a business to implement EC. Much more compelling, perhaps, are the omnipresence of the digital revolution and the influence of EC on the business environment, as described in Sections 1.3 and 1.4.

Section 1.6 ▶ REVIEW QUESTIONS

1. Describe some EC benefits to organizations, individuals, and society.

2. List the major technological and nontechnological barriers and limitations to EC.

3. Describe some contributions of EC to Homeland Security.

1.7 SOCIAL AND BUSINESS NETWORKS

The most interesting e-commerce application in recent years has been the emergence of social and business networks. Originating from online communities (Chapter 8), these networks are growing rapidly and providing many new EC initiatives.

SOCIAL NETWORKS

Social networks are Web sites that connect people with specified interests by providing free services, such as photo presentation, e-mail, blogging, and so on. The transactions in social networks are mostly people-to-people. But as we will see in Chapter 8, corporations are starting to have an interest in this EC feature (e.g., see linkedin.com, a network that connects businesses by industry, functions, geography, and areas of interest).

According to Lashinsky (2006) and Schonfeld (2006b), the action today is with the following social networks:

▶ Facebook.com—facilitates socialization by students
▶ YouTube.com and Metcafe.com—users can upload and view video clips
▶ Flickr.com—users share photos
▶ MySpace.com—provides a platform to find friends and make contacts, upload and share videos and more (see Case 1.4)
▶ Myheritage.com—face recognition in genealogy; recognizes faces in different stages of peoples' lives
▶ Cyworld.rate.com—Asia's largest social network
▶ Habbohotel.com—Entertaining country-specific sites (18 countries in 2008) for kids and adults
▶ YUB.com—A social network for discount shoppers

social networks
Web sites that connect people with specified interests by providing free services such as photo presentation, e-mail, blogging, and so on.

CASE 1.4
EC Application
MYSPACE: THE WORLD'S MOST POPULAR SOCIAL NETWORKING WEB SITE

MySpace is an interactive social network of user-submitted blogs, profiles, groups, photos, MP3s, and videos and an internal e-mail system. It has become an increasingly influential part of contemporary pop culture. The site claims to have over 200 million members (the world's fourth most popular English-language Web site) and draws 230,000 new members each week.

MySpace also is used by some independent musicians and filmmakers, who upload songs and short films on their profiles. These songs and films can also be embedded in other profiles, an interconnectedness that adds to MySpace's appeal.

Contents of a MySpace Profile
Each member's profile contains two "blurbs": "About Me" and "Who I'd Like to Meet." Profiles also can contain

optional sections about personal features such as marital status, physical appearance, and income. Profiles also contain a blog with standard fields for content, emotion, and media. MySpace also supports uploading images and videos.

Users can choose a certain number of friends to be displayed on their profile in the "Top Friends" area. In 2006, MySpace allowed up to 24 friends to be displayed. The "Comments" area allows the user's friends to leave comments. MySpace users can delete comments or require all comments to be approved before posting. The site gives users some flexibility to modify their user pages, or "MySpace editors" are available to help.

(continued)

CASE 1.4   (continued)

MySpace Celebrities

MySpace has led to the emergence of MySpace celebrities, popular individuals who have attracted hundreds of thousands of "friends," leading to coverage in other media. Some of these individuals have remained only Internet celebrities, others have been able to jump to television, magazines, and radio.

Major Issues Surrounding MySpace

The following are several major issues surrounding MySpace use.

Accessibility

Sometimes user profiles have accessibility problems, because the site is set up so that anyone can customize the layout and colors of their profile page with virtually no restrictions. Poorly constructed MySpace profiles can freeze up Web browsers. Also, new features, such as song and video sharing through streaming media, and the huge number of MySpace users joining daily means that more users are online for longer periods; this increase in usage slows down the MySpace servers at peak times.

Restricting Access

Many schools and public libraries in the United States and the United Kingdom have begun to restrict access to MySpace because it has become "such a haven for student gossip and malicious comments" and because MySpace was consuming up to 40 percent of the daily Internet bandwidth, impeding delivery of Web-based courses. Regular administrative functions can also be slowed down, making the normal running of universities difficult.

Potential Damage to Students

The *Chicago Tribune's* RedEye printed an article concerning MySpace and an individual's search for employment. The author argued that young college graduates compromise their chances of starting careers because of the content they post on their accounts. An employer might not hire a highly qualified candidate because the candidate maintains an account that suggests overly exuberant behavior.

Security and Safety

MySpace allows registering users to be as young as 14. Profiles of users with ages set to 14 to 15 years are automatically private. Users whose ages are set at 16 or over do have the option to restrict their profiles, as well as the option of merely allowing certain personal data to be restricted to people other than those on their "friends list." The full profiles of users under age 18 are restricted to direct MySpace friends only.

Globalization and Competition

In 2006, News Corporation took MySpace to China, where it is spreading rapidly (in Chinese, of course). In Korea, a competitor, Cyworld, launched a U.S. version in 2006 (see Schonfeld 2006b and Chapter 8).

Other Issues

Other issues affecting MySpace are musicians' rights, the user agreement, social and cultural issues, and legal issues. These and other issues are discussed in Chapter 8.

Revenue Model and Competition

When News Corporation purchased MySpace in July 2005 for $580 million, many questioned the wisdom of paying so much for a site with no income and questionable advertisement revenue sources. However, in August 2006 Google paid MySpace almost the entire purchase sum for allowing Google to place its search engine and advertising on MySpace pages. This is helpful to MySpace, too, because now its users do not have to leave the site to conduct a Google search.

As of 2006, MySpace's major competitors included Facebook, Xanga, Wayn, Reunion, Friendster, and Xuqa See Chapter 8 for details.

Sources: Compiled from Cashmore (2006); Miller (2005); Sellers (2006); and *en.wikipedia.org/wiki/MySpace* (accessed October 2007).

Questions

1. Why does MySpace attract so many visitors?
2. List the major issues faced by the company.
3. What are the benefits to MySpace and Google from their collaboration?

Business-Oriented Networks

Business-oriented networks are social networks whose primary objective is to facilitate business. For example, YUB.com is a network of shoppers looking for discounts and bargains. Another example is Craigslist.com, the classified ad super site that offers many social-oriented features (see Case 2.2 in Chapter 2). Yet, its major objective is to help people find accommodations, barter items, or conduct other business-oriented activities. Many B2B portals offer community services for thousands of members.

For example, Carnival Cruise Lines is sponsoring a social networking site (carnivalconnections.com) to attract cruise fans. Visitors can use the site to exchange opinions, organize groups for trips, and much more. It cost the company $300,000 to set up the site, but Carnival anticipates that the cost will be covered by increased business. For details, see Fass (2006). Similarly, in 2007 Coca-Cola created a social network for young lovers of the drink.

One of the most interesting emerging business-social networks is Xing.com (xing.com).

Example: Xing.com. Originating in Germany, Xing.com is a business network that attracts millions of executives, sales representatives, and job seekers from many countries, mostly in Europe. The site offers secure services in 16 languages. Users can use the site to:

- Establish new business contacts.
- Systematically expand their networks.
- Easily manage their contacts.
- Market themselves in a professional business context.
- Identify experts and receive advice on any topic.
- Organize meetings and events.
- Manage contacts from anywhere.
- Control the level of privacy and ensure that their personal data are protected.

For additional details, take the site's "Guided Tour." Services also are available for mobile device users. For further discussion, see Chapter 8.

Revenue Models of Social and Business Networks

Most of the social-networking sites expect to earn revenue from advertising (as MySpace does with Google). In contrast, business-oriented networks may collect registration fees or even transaction fees. Due to the huge number of members, fees can be minimal. Recruiters, for example, already use the social networks to find people whom other people know. This enables a warm call by the recruiter ("Hi, your friend Mr. Z suggested we contact you.). For details on how recruiters use social networks, see Totty (2006). How many of these networks will survive is not known, but some already have been sold for hundreds of millions of dollars (e.g., Google paid $1.65 billion for YouTube in 2006).

Section 1.7 ▶ REVIEW QUESTIONS

1. What is a social network? Identify major features offered by social networks.

2. Describe MySpace. Why is it so popular?

3. What are some major issues faced by social network sites?

4. What is a business-oriented network?

5. Describe Xing.com and list five of its major benefits.

6. List some revenue sources in social networks.

1.8 THE DIGITAL ENTERPRISE

The task facing each organization is how to put together the components that will enable it to transform itself within the digital economy and gain competitive advantage by using EC. The first step is to put in the right infrastructure—connective networks, related databases, and hardware and software needs—upon which applications can be structured. The second step is to create (or transform) to the *digital enterprise*.

digital enterprise
A new business model that uses IT in a fundamental way to accomplish one or more of three basic objectives: reach and engage customers more effectively, boost employee productivity, and improve operating efficiency. It uses converged communication and computing technology in a way that improves business processes.

corporate portal
A major gateway through which employees, business partners, and the public can enter a corporate Web site.

THE DIGITAL ENTERPRISE

The term *digital enterprise* has a number of definitions. It usually refers to an enterprise such as Dell, which uses computers and information systems to automate most of its business processes. Davis (2005) believes that the **digital enterprise** is a new business model that uses IT in a fundamental way to accomplish one or more of three basic objectives: reach and engage customers more effectively, boost employee productivity, and improve operating efficiency. It uses converged communication and computing technology in a way that improves business processes. The major characteristics of the digital enterprise are illustrated in Exhibit 1.10, where they are compared with those of a traditional enterprise.

The digital enterprise shifts the focus from managing individual information resources—devices, applications, and datasets—to *orchestrating the services and workflows* that define the business and ultimately deliver value to customers and end users.

A digital enterprise uses networks of computers to electronically connect:

▶ All its internal parts via an *intranet*, which is the counterpart of the Internet.
▶ All its business partners via the *Internet*, or via a secured Internet, called an extranet, or via value-added private communication lines.

The vast majority of EC is done on computers connected to these networks. Many companies employ a **corporate portal**, which is a gateway for customers, employees, and partners to reach corporate information and to communicate with the company. For additional details, see Tatnall (2006) and Chapters 2 and 6.

The major concern of many companies today is how to transform themselves to take part in the digital economy, where e-business is the norm. For example, Harrington (2006) describes why and how, as a CEO, he transformed the Thomson Corp. (now

EXHIBIT 1.10 The Digital Versus Brick-and-Mortar Company

Brick-and-Mortar Organizations (Enterprises)	Digital Organizations (Enterprises)
Selling in physical stores	Selling online
Selling tangible goods	Selling digital goods as well
Internal inventory/production planning	Online collaborative inventory forecasting
Paper catalogs	Smart electronic catalogs
Physical marketplace	Marketspace (electronic)
Use of telephone, fax, VANs and traditional EDI	Use of the Internet and extranets
Physical and limited auctions	Online auctions, everywhere, any time
Broker-based services, transactions	Electronic infomediaries, value-added services
Paper-based billing	Electronic billing
Paper-based tendering	Electronic tendering (reverse auctions)
Push production, starting with demand forecast	Pull production, starting with an order
Mass production (standard products)	Mass customization, build-to-order
Physical-based commission marketing	Affiliated, virtual marketing
Word-of-mouth, slow and limited advertisement	Explosive viral marketing
Linear supply chains	Hub-based supply chains
Large amount of capital needed for mass production	Less capital needed for build-to-order; payments can flow in before production starts
Large fixed cost required for plant operation	Small fixed cost required for plant operation
Customers' value proposition is frequently a mismatch (cost > value)	Perfect match of customers' value proposition (cost = value)

Cengage Learning) from a traditional $8 billion publishing business into an electronic information services provider and publisher for professionals in targeted markets. In 5 years, revenue increased over 20 percent and profit increased by more than 65 percent. If the transformation is successful, many companies will reach the status of our hypothetical toy company shown in Online File W1.8, which uses the Internet, intranets, and extranets in an integrated manner to conduct various EC activities.

It may take 5 to 10 years for companies to become fully digitized like the hypothetical Toys, Inc. Major companies, such as Schwab, IBM, Intel, and General Electric, are moving rapidly toward such a state.

Section 1.8 ▶ REVIEW QUESTIONS

1. Define a digital enterprise.
2. Compare traditional and digital enterprises.
3. What is a corporate portal?
4. Identify EC transaction models (e.g., B2B) in Online File W1.8.

1.9 OVERVIEW OF THIS BOOK

This book is composed of 12 chapters grouped into 6 parts, as shown in Exhibit 1.11. Additional content is available online at the book's Web site. The Web site provides a seventh part, with two additional chapters, a tutorial, two appendices and online supplemental material for each chapter.

The specific parts and chapters of this textbook are as follows.

PART 1: INTRODUCTION TO E-COMMERCE AND E-MARKETPLACES

This section of the book includes an overview of EC and its content, benefits, limitations, and drivers, which are presented in Chapter 1. Chapter 2 presents electronic markets and their mechanisms, such as electronic catalogs and auctions. Chapter 2 also includes a presentation of some Web 2.0 tools and mechanisms.

PART 2: INTERNET CONSUMER RETAILING

This part includes two chapters. Chapter 3 describes e-tailing (B2C), including some of its most innovative applications for selling products online. It also describes the delivery of services, such as online banking, travel, and insurance. Chapter 4 explains consumer behavior in cyberspace, online market research, and Internet advertising.

PART 3: BUSINESS-TO-BUSINESS E-COMMERCE

Part 3 is composed of two chapters. In Chapter 5, we introduce B2B EC and describe primarily company-centric models (one buyer—many sellers, one seller—many buyers). Electronic exchanges (many buyers and many sellers) also are described in Chapter 5. Chapter 6 deals with e-supply chain topics, c-commerce, and corporate portals.

PART 4: OTHER EC MODELS AND APPLICATIONS

Several other EC models and applications are presented in Part 4. E-government, e-learning, and C2C are the major subjects of Chapter 7. Chapter 8 is devoted to Web 2.0 applications and social networks. In Chapter 9, we introduce the topics of m-commerce.

EXHIBIT 1.11   Plan of the Book

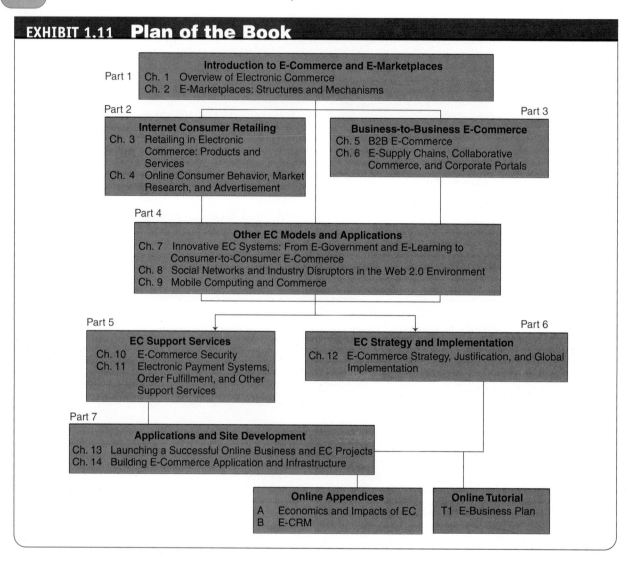

PART 5: EC SUPPORT SERVICES

Part 5 examines issues involving the support services needed for EC applications. Chapter 10 delves into EC security. Of the many diverse Web support activities, we concentrate on two: payments and order fulfillment (Chapter 11).

PART 6: EC STRATEGY AND IMPLEMENTATION

Part 6 includes one chapter, Chapter 12, on EC strategy and implementation, including going global and the impact of EC on small businesses. Chapter 12 also deals with the economics of EC.

ONLINE PART 7: APPLICATIONS AND SITE DEVELOPMENT

Two additional complete chapters are available online at the book's Web site (prenhall. com/turban). Chapter 13 is dedicated to the construction of small-scale e-stores. Chapter 14 addresses EC application development processes and methods, including the emerging topics of software as a service, Web Services, and service-oriented architecture (SOA).

ONLINE TUTORIAL

One tutorial is available at the book's Web site (prenhall.com/turban):

▶ Tutorial T1: E-Business Plan

ONLINE APPENDICES

Two appendices are available on the book's Web site (prenhall.com/turban).

Appendix A: Economics and Impacts of EC
Appendix B: E-CRM

ONLINE SUPPLEMENTS

A large number of online files organized by chapter number support the content of each chapter.

MANAGERIAL ISSUES

Many managerial issues are related to EC. These issues are discussed throughout the book and also are summarized in a separate section (like this one) near the end of each chapter. Some managerial issues related to this introductory chapter are as follows.

1. **Is it real?** For those not involved in EC, the first question that comes to mind is, "Is it real?" We believe that the answer is an emphatic "yes." Just ask anyone who has banked from home, purchased company stocks online, or bought a book from Amazon.com. Randy Mott, Wal-Mart's Chief Information Officer (CIO), gives an interesting tip for organizations and managers: "Start EC as soon as possible; it is too dangerous to wait." Jack Welch, former Chief Executive Officer (CEO) of General Electric, has commented, "Any company, old or new, that doesn't see this technology literally as important as breathing could be on its last breath" (McGee 2000).

2. **Why is B2B e-commerce so attractive?** B2B EC is attractive for several reasons. First, some B2B models are easier to implement than traditional off-line models. In contrast, B2C has several major problems, ranging from channel conflict with existing distributors to lack of a critical mass of buyers. Also, the value of transactions is larger in B2B, and the potential savings are larger and easier to justify. Rather than waiting for B2C problems to be worked out, many companies can start B2B by simply buying from existing online stores or selling electronically by joining existing marketplaces or

an auction house. The problem is determining where to buy or sell.

3. **There are so many EC failures—how can one avoid them?** Beginning in early 2000, the news was awash with stories about the failure of many EC projects within companies as well as the failure of many dot-coms. Industry consolidation often occurs after a "gold rush." About 100 years ago, hundreds of companies tried to manufacture cars, following Ford's success in the United States; only three survived. The important thing is to learn from the successes and failures of others. For lessons that can be learned from EC successes and failures, see Chapters 3, 6, and Online Chapter 13.

4. **How can we exploit social/business networking?** There are major possibilities here. Some companies even open their own social networks. Advertising is probably the first thing to consider. Recruiting can be a promising avenue as well. Offering discounted products and services should also be considered. Finally, sponsoring a site may be rewarding as well.

5. **What should be my company's strategy toward EC?** A company can choose one of three basic strategies: lead, wait, or experiment. This issue is

revisited in Chapter 12, together with related issues such as the cost-benefit trade-offs of EC, integrating EC into the business, outsourcing, going global, and how SMEs can use EC. Another strategic issue is the prioritization of the many initiatives and applications available to a company.

6. **What are the top challenges of EC?** The top 10 *technical issues* for EC (in order of their importance) are security, adequate infrastructure, data access,

back-end systems integration, sufficient bandwidth, network connectivity, up time, data warehousing and mining, scalability, and content distribution. The top 10 *managerial issues* for EC are budgets, project deadlines, keeping up with technology, privacy issues, the high cost of capital expenditures, unrealistic management expectations, training, reaching new customers, improving customer ordering services, and finding qualified EC employees. Most of these issues are discussed throughout this book.

SUMMARY

In this chapter, you learned about the following EC issues as they relate to the learning objectives.

1. **Definition of EC and description of its various categories.** EC involves conducting transactions electronically. Its major categories are pure versus partial EC, Internet-based versus non-Internet-based, and electronic markets versus interorganizational systems.

2. **The content and framework of EC.** The applications of EC, and there are many, are based on infrastructures and are supported by people; public policy and technical standards; marketing and advertising; support services, such as logistics, security, and payment services; and business partners—all tied together by management.

3. **The major types of EC transactions.** The major types of EC transactions are B2B, B2C, C2C, m-commerce, intrabusiness commerce, B2E, c-commerce, e-government, and e-learning.

4. **The role of the digital revolution.** EC is a major product of the digital and technological revolution, which enables companies to simultaneously increase both growth and profits. This revolution enables digitization of products, services, and information.

5. **The role of the business environment as an EC driver.** The business environment is changing rapidly due to technological breakthroughs, globalization, societal changes, deregulations, and more. The changing business environment forces organizations to respond. Traditional responses may not be sufficient because of the magnitude of the pressures and the pace of the changes involved. Therefore, organizations must frequently innovate and reengineer their operations. In many cases, EC

is the major facilitator of such organizational responses.

6. **The major EC business models.** The major EC business models include online direct marketing, electronic tendering systems, name-your-own-price, affiliate marketing, viral marketing, group purchasing, online auctions, mass customization (make-to-order), electronic exchanges, supply chain improvers, finding the best price, value-chain integration, value-chain providers, information brokers, bartering, deep discounting, and membership.

7. **Benefits of EC to organizations, consumers, and society.** EC offers numerous benefits. Because these benefits are substantial, it looks as though EC is here to stay and cannot be ignored.

8. **Barriers to EC.** The barriers to EC can be categorized as technological and nontechnological. As time passes and network capacity, security, and accessibility continue to improve through technological innovations, the barriers posed by technological limitations will continue to diminish. Nontechnological barriers also will diminish over time, but some, especially the behavioral ones, may persist for many years in some organizations, cultures, or countries.

9. **Social and business online networks.** Social and business networks attract huge numbers of visitors. Many of the visitors are young future EC customers. Therefore, advertisers are willing to spend money on advertising, either to an entire group or to individuals (e.g., using Google's technology). Already among the most visited sites, they offer many innovative applications as well.

KEY TERMS

Affiliate marketing	24	Digital economy	16	Intraorganizational information systems	6
Brick-and-mortar (old-economy) organizations	5	Digital enterprise	34	Location-based commerce	
		E-business	4	(l-commerce)	9
Business model	20	E-co-ops	25	Mobile commerce (m-commerce)	9
Business-to-business (B2B)	8	E-government	11	Name-your-own-price model	24
Business-to-business-to-consumer (B2B2C)	8	E-learning	11	Peer-to-peer (P2P)	9
		E-tailing	8	Personalization	25
Business-to-consumer (B2C)	8	Electronic commerce (EC)	4	Revenue model	22
Business-to-employees (B2E)	9	Electronic market (e-marketplace)	6	SMEs	25
Click-and-mortar (click-and-brick) organizations	5	Exchange	11	Social networks	31
		Exchange-to-exchange (E2E)	11	Tendering (bidding) system	24
Collaborative commerce (c-commerce)	9	Extranet	6	Value proposition	23
		Group purchasing	25	Viral marketing	25
Consumer-to-business (C2B)	9	Interorganizational information systems (IOSs)	6	Virtual (pure-play) organizations	5
Consumer-to-consumer (C2C)	9			Virtual world	26
Corporate portal	34	Intrabusiness EC	9	Web 2.0	14
Customization	25	Intranet	6		

QUESTIONS FOR DISCUSSION

1. Compare brick-and-mortar and click-and-mortar organizations.

2. Why is buying with a smart card from a vending machine considered EC?

3. Why is it said that EC is a catalyst for fundamental changes in organizations?

4. How does EC facilitate customization of products and personalization of services?

5. Explain how EC can reduce cycle time, improve employees' empowerment, and facilitate customer support.

6. Which of the EC limitations do you think will be more easily overcome—the technological or the nontechnological limitations? Why?

7. Why are social networks, such as MySpace, considered EC?

8. Why is Second Life considered to be a Web 2.0 application?

INTERNET EXERCISES

1. Visit Amazon.com's site (**amazon.com**) and locate recent information in the following areas:

   a. Find the five top-selling books on EC.

   b. Find a review of one of these books.

   c. Review the customer services you can get from Amazon.com and describe the benefits you receive from shopping there.

   d. Review the products directory.

2. Go to **ups.com** and find information about recent EC projects that are related to logistics and supply chain management. How is UPS using wireless services?

3. Go to **nike.com** and design your own shoes. Next visit **office.microsoft.com/en-us/templates/ CT102530531033.aspx** and create your own electronic business card. Finally, enter **jaguar.com**

and configure the car of your dreams. What are the advantages of each activity? The disadvantages?

4. Visit **chemconnect.com**. What kind of EC does this site represent? What benefits can it provide to buyers? To sellers?

5. Enter **espn.go.com** and identify and list all of the revenue sources on the site.

6. Enter **ediets.com**. Find the personalized activities. Explain their benefits. Also, identify eDiets' revenue model.

7. Enter **lowes.com**. View the "design it" online feature and the animated "How Tos." Examine the Project Calculators and Gift Advisor features. Relate these to the business models and other EC features of this chapter.

8. Enter **secondlife.com**. Identify the various business models and revenue models used.

TEAM ASSIGNMENTS AND ROLE PLAYING

1. Each team will research two EC success stories. Members of the group should examine both companies that operate solely online as well as some that extensively employ a click-and-mortar strategy. Each team should identify the critical success factors for their companies and present a report to the class.

2. Each team member studies three social networks (see **wikipedia.org** for a list). Then the team makes a presentation on the features of the companies, the revenue models, any unique characteristics, and the IT support.

3. Each team member enters **secondlife.com**, registers, and goes to the "Orientation Island" to find out how to navigate, meet people, buy, and sell. Each member creates an avatar, gets virtual land, and builds something. Each member spends $10 to buy Linden dollars and spends the money on a product or service of choice and then sells the same item in order to make money. Visit five properties of other residents, meet them and write about your experience. Each team should prepare a report on the positive and negative aspects of the experience.

Real-World Case

GOOGLE IS CHANGING EVERYTHING

Introduction

Of all the companies associated with EC, probably no other company has impacted our work and life as much as Google has. More than that, according to Carr (2006), Google's unconventional IT and EC management strategy is both effective and efficient, and it offers a glimpse into how organizations might deploy technology in the future. Google runs on close to 500,000 servers. Google has grown more quickly than any other EC company, and it started to generate profit faster than most start-ups. By 2006, its revenue had reached $9.3 billion (estimates for 2007 are $11.8 billion), about the same as IBM and more than Ford and General Motors combined (Goldberg 2006).

Google is known primarily for its search engine and its related targeted-advertising tools. Google delivers its advertisers far more revenue per click in search results than its competitors (mainly Microsoft and Yahoo!) do. In Chapter 4, we will explain Google's ad-matching strategy. However, Google is doing many other things. Let's examine some of Google's many EC activities.

A Glimpse at Google's Activities

Google's goal is to deliver technologies to organize the world's information and make it universally accessible and useful. For example, Google is trying to reinvent the spreadsheet as a Web-based application that makes it simple for users to input and share data. Google Spreadsheet is a free Web-based application that can be shared with up to 10 users simultaneously, overcoming a key limitation of Microsoft's Excel.

How Does Google Compete?

Google is meeting the competitive challenges it faces head on. Google offers an expanding repertoire of tools in line with its core competency in search technology. The major tools are:

▶ Froogle (*froogle.google.com*) is a product-comparison search engine for online shopping. A similar search tool is Google Catalogs (*catalogs.google.com*), which searches a database of mail-order catalogs.

▶ Google News (*news.google.com*) searches news-oriented Web sites and displays articles according to a computer algorithm that rates them based on how many news sites are publishing the articles, how recently the articles were published, and, for searches, keyword occurrence.

▶ Google Earth (*earth.google.com*) is a collection of zoomable aerial and satellite 3D photos of the earth that enables you to find information linked to geographic location.

▶ Google Maps (*maps.google.com*), and Google Maps for Mobile (*google.com/gmm*) present countless maps of cities and streets around the globe. It enables you to get driving instructions from one location to another.

▶ Google Scholar (*scholar.google.com*) searches the scholarly literature, including peer-reviewed papers, theses, books, preprints, abstracts, and technical reports. Many hits are abstracts or citations, not full articles, and some are "cloaked" behind subscription-only journal subscriptions.

▶ Google also has introduced Google Wireless (*google.com/mobile*) where you get Search, Maps, GMail, SMS, GOOG411 (find local businesses), and YouTube and Google Groups (*groups.google.com*) where you can discuss online and via email, create custom pages with rich formats, and customize your page with your own graphics.

Strategically, Google is leveraging its widely recognized brand name and search technology expertise into areas beyond Web searching. Sometimes these projects bring Google into direct competition with the EC giants mentioned earlier.

▶ Google Print (*books.google.com*) is similar to Amazon.com's "search inside the book" feature. Users can search by keyword (e.g., "books about Nelson Mandela") and then search for keywords or phrases within the books.

▶ Gmail (*gmail.google.com*) is Google's offering in the huge Web-based e-mail market that is currently dominated by Microsoft's Hotmail and Yahoo! Mail. Gmail offers new services, such as grouping related messages together and keyword searching through e-mail messages.

▶ Google Mini (*google.com/mini*) is a cost-effective appliance that businesses can use to deploy corporate searches that mimic the main Google Web search engine.

▶ Google Desktop (*desktop.google.com*) searches the contents of computer files, e-mail messages, books, and even recently viewed Web pages. This is a dramatic improvement on the Windows "Find" feature, which only searches computer files, and then mostly by file name. Google Desktop preempts technology that Microsoft is intending to put into Longhorn.

▶ Orkut (*orkut.com*) is a social-networking service that competes in one of the fastest-growing Internet markets—Web sites that connect people through networks of friends or business contacts to find new friends or contacts. In order to sign in at Orkut, you must have a Google account.

In 2006, Google expanded into the software business, offering Google Office (initially free, to compete with Microsoft). Also, Google offers a set of Web programs (e.g., for e-mail, communications, and scheduling). For more on Google products, visit *google.com/intl/eN/options/*. The strategic moves Google is making are all in line with its mission statement: "to organize the world's information and make it universally useful and accessible."

Disruptors of Google, Will They Succeed?

Many companies want to displace or to become as successful Google. The following are just two examples.

Intelligent Search Engine—Will It Work?
The various search engine models are based on keywords, which may result in poor or incorrect answers. People can improve a search by adding one or two keywords (which many people do not like to do) for an advanced search. Powerset.com, a new start-up, wants to use natural-language queries (by typing your question in normal conversational syntax) instead of keywords. Powerset has cut a deal with Xerox's PARC labs, a top research company in natural-language understanding. Major unknowns are the quality of natural-language processing and whether searchers

will be willing to key in the long natural-language queries instead of simple, short keywords. However, if successful, this concept may disrupt the search engine industry and intensify the industry wars.

According to Sloan (2007), Web advertisers are moving beyond search by using powerful science to figure out what people want—sometimes before the searchers even know. This is an iterative process. Queries are made in natural language and improvements are made in several iterations. This slows the process, but you get better answers.

Wikia.com and Collaborative Innovation

Wikia.com is a for-profit Web site affiliated with the Wikipedia Foundation (which is a nonprofit organization). Wikia is growing very rapidly; 30,000 contributors created 500,000 Wikia articles in 45 languages in a 2-year period (see McNichol 2007). One of its projects is to use its community's brain to build a better search engine than Google. The idea is to tap into the users' enthusiasm (see McNichol 2007 for details).

Enterprise Search

An enterprise search identifies and enables specific content across the enterprise to be indexed, searched, and displayed to authorized users. Google has partnered with BearingPoint, an IT consulting firm, to supply enterprise search capabilities. BearingPoint has experience in extending Google to provide search services to specific industries. A crucial enterprise search issue is programming search engines to crawl through all the various data sources at a company and index their contents.

Enterprise searches can be integrated with other applications to improve performance. For example, Cognos Go! Search Service is a BI (business intelligence) search utility. It offers a familiar search interface for accessing strategic enterprise information, such as reports, metrics, analyses, and business events, that answer critical business questions with a simple keyword search. Oracle offers a search engine for enterprise systems, such as ERP and CRM.

Example

Kaiser Permanente (*kaiserpermanente.org*), America's largest nonprofit health maintenance organization (HMO), has almost 9 million members. The amount of available medical knowledge doubles about every 7 years, so keeping up with new knowledge is an important aspect of good caregiving by HMOs.

When Kaiser Permanente developed a clinical-knowledge corporate portal for its 50,000 doctors, nurses, and other caregivers, enterprise search was a part of the plan. The Permanente Knowledge Connection, available from anywhere in the Kaiser wide area network, gives medical staff access to diagnostic information, best practices, publications, educational material, and other clinical resources. The portal's resources are distributed across the entire United States. Putting the right information quickly and easily into caregivers' hands is essential to the clinical portal's success.

Kaiser turned to the Google Search Appliance, which enabled the HMO to index 150,000 documents across the Kaiser network. Clinicians now search the site in situations that range from leisurely research to urgent care, from the exam room to the emergency room. Doctors and nurses use the search engine to help them reach diagnoses and specify treatments, check the side effects of new medications, and consult clinical research studies and other medical publications. Google's spell-checking capability is especially useful in the medical profession: Doctors' handwriting can be problematic and pharmaceutical product names are difficult for small businesses.

Sources: Compiled from Carr (2006), Brown (2006), and Hicks (2004).

Questions

1. Use Google to conduct a search. What advertisements appear next to the search results?

2. What is Google trying to do with spreadsheets?

3. What is an enterprise search?

4. Identify potential revenue models in Google's activities described here and on its Web site.

5. How do Google's services benefit a company such as Kaiser?

6. Why is Google considered to be a Web 2.0 company?

CHAPTER 2

E-MARKETPLACES: STRUCTURES AND MECHANISMS

Content

How Blue Nile Inc. Is Changing the Jewelry Industry

Managerial Issues

Real-World Case: Stormhoek Vineyards Excels with Web 2.0 Tools

Appendix 2A: Build-to-Order Production

Learning Objectives

Upon completion of this chapter, you will be able to:

1. Define e-marketplaces and list their components.

2. List the major types of e-marketplaces and describe their features.

3. Describe the various types of EC intermediaries and their roles.

4. Describe electronic catalogs, shopping carts, search engines, and portals.

5. Describe the major types of auctions and list their characteristics.

6. Discuss the benefits, limitations, and impacts of auctions.

7. Describe bartering and negotiating online.

8. Describe the major mechanisms for delivering Web 2.0.

HOW BLUE NILE INC. IS CHANGING THE JEWELRY INDUSTRY

Blue Nile Inc. (*bluenile.com*), a pure-play online e-tailer that specializes in diamonds and jewelry, capitalized on online diamond sales as a dot-com start-up in 1999. The company provides a textbook case of how EC fundamentally undercuts the traditional way of doing business.

The Opportunity

Using the B2C EC model—knocking out expensive stores and intermediaries and then slashing prices (up to 35 percent less than rivals to gain market share), Blue Nile captured a high market share in a short time, inducing more and more people to buy online and making a sizable profit.

How did the start-up defy conventional wisdom that diamonds could not be sold online? Basically, Blue Nile offers a huge selection of diamonds and more information on diamonds than a jewelry expert offers in a physical store.

It features educational guides in plain English and provides independent (and trusted) quality ratings for every stone. A customer can look over a rating scale for cut, clarity, color, and so on and then conduct a price comparison with Diamond.com (*diamond.com*) and other online stores. Most important is the 30-day money-back guarantee (now an online industry standard). This provides customers a comfort level against fraud and gives Blue Nile a competitive edge against stores that take the stones back but charge a fee to do so.

The Results

Blue Nile sales were $319 million in 2007, and growing 24 percent annually. The company went public in 2004 (one of the most successful IPOs of 2004) and became the eighth-largest specialty jewelry company in the United States.

To sell $319 million in jewelry, a traditional retail chain needs 300 stores and close to 2,200 employees. Blue Nile does it with one 10,000-square-foot warehouse and 115 staffers. The company also bypasses the industry's tangled supply chain, in which a diamond can pass through five or more middlemen before reaching a retailer. Blue Nile deals directly with original suppliers, such as Thaigem.com (*thaigem.com*; see Online File W2.1).

This is one reason why in the United States some 465 small jewelry stores closed in 2003 alone. Many of the survivors specialize in custom-crafted pieces. Large rivals try to fight back, streamlining the supply chain, emphasizing customer service, and even trying to sell some products online.

The future seems to be clear, as summarized by Roger Thompson, a small jeweler in Lambertville, New Jersey, "Anyone with half a brain, who wants a diamond engagement ring will go to the Internet." So, he stopped selling diamonds. In the meantime, grooms with at least half a brain make proposals with Blue Nile rings, saving $3,000 to $5,000 each.

Sources: Adapted from Mullaney (2004), *BusinessWeek* Online (2006a), and *bluenile.com* (accessed January 2008).

WHAT CAN WE LEARN . . .

Blue Nile is a pure-play online store (a storefront) that uses electronic catalogs, virtual shopping carts, and superb customer service to sell diamonds and jewelry. Storefronts, carts, portals, and catalogs are the major mechanisms for selling online, and they are described here and in Online Chapter 13. This case also shows the impact of online sales on an industry. Because of low operating costs and global reach, Blue Nile and other online jewelers quickly conquered an impressive market share, driving hundreds of small traditional jewelry retailers out of business. For further discussion, see Online Appendix A.

2.1 E-MARKETPLACES

Markets (electronic or otherwise) have three main functions: (1) matching buyers and sellers; (2) facilitating the exchange of information, goods, services, and payments associated with market transactions; and (3) providing an institutional infrastructure, such as a legal and regulatory framework that enables the efficient functioning of the market (see Zwass 2003 for details).

ELECTRONIC MARKETS

The major place for conducting EC transactions is the electronic market (e-market). An **e-marketplace** (also called *e-marketspace*) is a virtual marketplace in which sellers and buyers meet and conduct different types of transactions. Customers exchange these goods and services for money (or other goods and services if bartering is used). The functions of an e-market are the same as that of a physical marketplace; however, computerized systems tend to make markets much more efficient by providing more updated information to buyers and sellers.

According to Bakos (1998), electronic markets play a central role in the economy, facilitating the exchange of information, goods, services, and payments. In the process, they create economic value for buyers, sellers, market intermediaries, and for society at large.

In recent years, markets have seen a dramatic increase in the use of IT and EC (Turban et al. 2007). EC has increased market efficiencies by expediting or improving the functions listed in Exhibit 2.1. Furthermore, EC has been able to significantly decrease the cost of executing these functions.

The emergence of *electronic marketplaces*, especially Internet-based ones, changed several of the processes used in trading and supply chains. These changes, driven by technology, resulted in:

▶ Greater information richness of the transactional and relational environment

▶ Lower information search costs for buyers

e-marketplace
An online market, usually B2B, in which buyers and sellers exchange goods or services; the three types of e-marketplaces are private, public, and consortia.

EXHIBIT 2.1 **Functions of a Market**		
Matching of Buyers and Sellers	**Facilitation of Transactions**	**Institutional Infrastructure**

• Determination of product offerings
   Product features offered by sellers
   Aggregation of different products
• Search (of buyers for sellers and
  of sellers for buyers)
   Price and product information
   Organizing bids and bartering
   Matching seller offerings with
     buyer preferences
• Price discovery
   Process and outcome in
     determination of prices
   Enabling price comparisons
• Others
   Providing sales leads
	• Logistics
	   Delivery of information, goods,
	     or services to buyers
	• Settlement
	   Transfer of payments to sellers
	• Trust
	   Credit system, reputations,
	     rating agencies like *Consumer*
	     Reports and BBB, special
	     escrow and online trust
	     agencies
	• Communication
	   Posting buyers' requests
		• Legal
		   Commercial code, contract law,
		     dispute resolution, intellectual
		     property protection
		   Export and import law
		• Regulatory
		   Rules and regulations,
		     monitoring, enforcement
		• Discovery
		   Provides market information
		     (e.g., about competition,
		     government regulations)

Sources: Compiled from Y. Bakos (1998) and E-Market Services (2006).

▶ Diminished information asymmetry between sellers and buyers

▶ Greater temporal separation between time of purchase and time of possession of physical products purchased in the e-marketplace

▶ Greater temporal proximity between time of purchase and time of possession of digital products purchased in the e-marketplace

▶ The ability of buyers and sellers to be in different locations

EC leverages IT with increased effectiveness and lower transaction and distribution costs, leading to more efficient, "friction-free" markets. An example of such efficiency is the Blue Nile case. For more on e-marketplaces, see Li and Du (2005).

E-MARKETPLACE COMPONENTS AND PARTICIPANTS

The major components and players in a marketspace are customers, sellers, goods and services (physical or digital), infrastructure, a front end, a back end, intermediaries and other business partners, and support services. A brief description of each follows:

▶ **Customers.** The 1.6 billion people worldwide who surf the Web are potential buyers of the goods and services offered or advertised on the Internet. These consumers are looking for bargains, customized items, collectors' items, entertainment, socialization, and more. They are in the driver's seat. They can search for detailed information, compare, bid, and sometimes negotiate. Organizations are the largest consumers, accounting for more than 85 percent of EC dollar activities.

▶ **Sellers.** Millions of storefronts are on the Web, advertising and offering a huge variety of items. These stores are owned by companies, government agencies, or individuals. Every day it is possible to find new offerings of products and services. Sellers can sell direct from their Web sites or from e-marketplaces.

▶ **Products and services.** One of the major differences between the marketplace and the marketspace is the possible digitization of products and services in a marketspace. Although both types of markets can sell physical products, the marketspace also can sell **digital products**, which are goods that can be transformed to digital format and instantly delivered over the Internet. In addition to digitization of software and music, it is possible to digitize dozens of other products and services, as shown in Online File W2.2. Digital products have different cost curves than those of regular products. In digitization, most of the costs are fixed, and variable costs are very low. Thus, profit will increase very rapidly as volume increases, once the fixed costs are paid for.

▶ **Infrastructure.** The marketspace infrastructure includes electronic networks, hardware, software, and more. (EC infrastructure is introduced in Chapter 1; also see Online Chapter 14.)

▶ **Front end.** Customers interact with a marketspace via a **front end**. The components of the front end can include the *seller's portal*, electronic catalogs, a shopping cart, a search engine, an auction engine, and a payment gateway. (For details, see Beynon-Davies 2004 and Chapter 11.)

▶ **Back end.** All the activities that are related to order aggregation and fulfillment, inventory management, purchasing from suppliers, accounting and finance, insurance, payment processing, packaging, and delivery are done in what is termed the **back end** of the business.

▶ **Intermediaries.** In marketing, an **intermediary** is typically a third party that operates between sellers and buyers. Intermediaries of all kinds offer their services on the Web. The role of these electronic intermediaries (as will be seen throughout the text and especially in Chapters 3 and 5) is frequently different from that of regular

---

digital products
Goods that can be transformed to digital format and delivered over the Internet.

front end
The portion of an e-seller's business processes through which customers interact, including the seller's portal, electronic catalogs, a shopping cart, a search engine, and a payment gateway.

back end
The activities that support online order fulfillment, inventory management, purchasing from suppliers, payment processing, packaging, and delivery.

intermediary
A third party that operates between sellers and buyers.

intermediaries (such as wholesalers). For example, online intermediaries create and manage the online markets. They help match buyers and sellers, provide some infrastructure services, and help customers and/or sellers to institute and complete transactions. They also support the vast number of transactions that exist in providing services, as demonstrated in the WebMD case (Case 2.1). Most of these online intermediaries operate as computerized systems.

▶ **Other business partners.** In addition to intermediaries, several types of partners, such as shippers, use the Internet to collaborate, mostly along the supply chain.

▶ **Support services.** Many different support services are available, ranging from certification and escrow services (to ensure security) to content providers.

CASE 2.1
EC Application
WEBMD

WebMD is the largest online medical services company in the United States. Although the company is known mainly for its consumer portal, *webmd.com*, the most visited medical-related Web site, its core business is being an e-intermediary.

The health-care industry is huge (close to $2 trillion per year, the largest in terms of GNP). Almost $600 billion is spent just on administrative expenses. The government (federal and state) provides large amounts of money to health-care providers (e.g., physicians, hospitals, drug companies), and it attempts to control costs. A major instrument for cost control is the Health Insurance Portability and Accountability Act of 1996 (HIPAA), which requires digital medical records and standardized documents for the health-care industry. WebMD is attempting to capitalize on this legislation by providing computer-related information and services to both the providers and purchasers (government, insurance companies, HMOs, and consumers) of services, mainly in terms of standardized electronic transactions.

WebMD's major objective is to reduce costs for the participants by facilitating electronic communication and collaboration because paper-based transactions are 20 to 30 times more expensive than electronic ones. It also seeks to speed cycle time.

WebMD operates via several separate, but electronically linked, divisions:

▶ **WebMD Envoy.** This division (now a subsidiary of Emdeon) is the leading clearinghouse for real-time transactions (over $2.5 billion a year) among over 300,000 medical and dental providers, 600 hospitals, 650 software vendors, 36,000 pharmacies and laboratories, and 1,200 government and commercial health

agencies. Transactions are secure; large customers use EDI (Chapter 5), and others use the Internet. The system handles all types of transactions, from clinical data to billing.

▶ **WebMD Practice Services.** This division provides software and programs that help physicians and other providers manage their businesses. Hundreds of different applications are available (this service is referred to as Intergy EHR). Some provide access to patient information, whereas others retrieve medical knowledge. Practice Services is a leading provider of payment and transaction services at the vanguard of bringing innovative practice management solutions to the rapidly changing health-care industry.

▶ **WebMD Health.** This information gateway has portals for both consumers and professionals. For consumers, information is provided about wellness, diseases, and treatments. For professionals (physicians, nurses, medical technicians, etc.), the Medscape portal provides medical news, medical education, research-related information, and more.

▶ **Porex.** The medical product unit manufactures and sells specialty medical products.

Many services are available on the WebMD Health portal, including the following:

▶ **News Center.** Visitors can find the latest in health news.
▶ **A-Z Guides.** Guides are available on topics ranging from medical tests to prescription drugs to common symptoms.
▶ **Health Search.** This enhanced search tool enables users to find the information they need, quickly and completely.

(*continued*)

CASE 2.1   (continued)

▶ **WebMD Video.** Videos are offered on a number of health-related topics.

▶ **Family and Pregnancy.** Parents, future parents, grandmothers, grandfathers, and caregivers can find useful information on family and pregnancy.

▶ **Blogs for Experts.** The portal features various blogs (see Section 2.7) devoted to specific topics within the health-care industry.

▶ **Blogs for Readers.** The site also features blogs for nonexperts on multiple topics.

According to O'Buyonge and Chen (2006), the success of WebMD is a result of the proper value proposition in its business model. Most important are the value-added services provided to health-care providers, insurers, and other B2B participants.

WebMD's future as an intermediary is not clear. On the one hand, disintermediation is possible due to the fact that the largest customers may develop their own B2B connections. On the other hand, the need

to comply with HIPAA may facilitate the role of WebMD, especially for small- and medium-sized health-care participants.

Sources: Compiled from O'Buyonge and Chen (2006), Southwick (2004), and *webmd.com* (accessed January 2008).

Questions

1. Visit *webmd.com* to learn more about the types of intermediation it provides. Write a report based on your findings.

2. What kinds of reintermediation do you foresee for the company?

3. WebMD Health does not bring in much revenue. Should the company close it? Why or why not?

4. What impact can WebMD have on the health-care industry? (Use the chapter's framework in your answer.)

Section 2.1 ▶ REVIEW QUESTIONS

1. What is the difference between a physical marketplace and an e-marketplace (marketspace)?

2. List the components of a marketspace.

3. Define a digital product and provide five examples.

2.2 TYPES OF E-MARKETPLACES AND MECHANISMS: FROM STOREFRONTS TO PORTALS

There are several types of e-marketplaces. The major B2C e-marketplaces are *storefronts* and *Internet malls*. B2B e-marketplaces include private *sell-side* e-marketplaces, *buy-side* e-marketplaces, and *exchanges*. The gateways to these e-marketplaces are the portals.

ELECTRONIC STOREFRONTS

storefront
A single company's Web site where products or services are sold.

An electronic or Web **storefront** refers to a single company's Web site where products and services are sold. It is an electronic store. The storefront may belong to a manufacturer (e.g., geappliances.com and dell.com), to a retailer (e.g., walmart.com and wishlist.com.au), to individuals selling from home, or to another type of business. Note that companies that sell services (such as insurance) might refer to their storefronts as *portals*. An example of a service-related portal is a hotel reservation system, as shown in Online File W2.3. In general, all storefronts have their own portals.

A storefront includes several mechanisms that are necessary for conducting the sale. The most common mechanisms are an *electronic catalog*; a *search engine* that helps the consumer find products in the catalog; an *electronic cart* for holding items until checkout; *e-auction facilities*; a *payment gateway* where payment arrangements can be made;

a *shipment court* where shipping arrangements are made; and customer services, including product and warranty information. The first three mechanisms are described in Section 2.4; e-auctions are described in Section 2.5; payment mechanisms are described in Chapter 11; and shipments are discussed in Chapter 11. Customer services, which can be fairly elaborate, are covered throughout the book.

ELECTRONIC MALLS

In addition to shopping at individual storefronts, consumers can shop in electronic malls (e-malls). Similar to malls in the physical world, an **e-mall (online mall)** is an online shopping location where many stores are located. For example, Hawaii.com (hawaii.com) is an e-mall that aggregates Hawaiian products and stores. It contains a directory of product categories and the stores in each category. When a consumer indicates the category he or she is interested in, the consumer is transferred to the appropriate independent *storefront*. This kind of a mall does not provide any shared services. It is merely a directory. Other malls do provide shared services (e.g., choicemall.com). Some malls are actually large click-and-mortar retailers; others are virtual retailers (e.g., buy.com).

e-mall (online mall)
An online shopping center where many online stores are located.

Visualization and Virtual Realty in Shopping Malls

To attract users to shopping malls, vendors use rich media, including virtual reality (VR). Lepouras and Vassilakis (2006) proposed an architecture for a VR Mall. The major task of VR is to relate the content via digital representation to the potential buyers. This was illustrated in the discussion of Second Life (secondlife.com) presented in Chapter 1.

TYPES OF STORES AND MALLS

Stores and malls are of several different types:

- **General stores/malls.** These are large marketspaces that sell all types of products. Examples are amazon.com, choicemall.com, shop4.vcomshop.com, spree.com, and the major public portals (store.yahoo.com, aol.com, and msn.com). All major department and discount stores also fall into this category.
- **Specialized stores/malls.** These sell only one or a few types of products, such as books, flowers, wine, cars, or pet toys. Amazon.com started as a specialized e-bookstore but today is a generalized store. 1-800-Flowers.com sells flowers and related gifts; fashionmall.com/beautyjungle specializes in beauty products, tips, and trends; and cattoys.com sells cat toys.
- **Regional versus global stores.** Some stores, such as e-grocers or sellers of heavy furniture, serve customers who live nearby. For example, parknshop.com serves the Hong Kong community; it will not deliver groceries to New York. However, some local stores will sell to customers in other countries if the customer will pay the shipping, insurance, and other costs (e.g., see hothothot.com).
- **Pure-play online organizations versus click-and-mortar stores.** Stores can be pure online (i.e., virtual or pure-play) organizations, such as Blue Nile, Amazon.com, Buy.com, or Cattoys.com. They do not have physical stores. Others are physical (i.e., *brick-and-mortar*) stores that also sell online (e.g., Wal-Mart with walmart.com, 1–800-Flowers.com with 1-800-Flowers.com, and Woolworths with woolworths.com.au). This second category is called *click-and-mortar*. Both categories will be described further in Chapter 3.

TYPES OF E-MARKETPLACES

In general conversation, the distinction between a mall and a marketplace is not always clear. In the physical world, malls often are viewed as collections of independent stores (i.e., shopping centers) where the stores are isolated from each other and prices are generally fixed. In contrast, marketplaces, some of which are located outdoors, often are viewed as places where many vendors compete and shoppers look for bargains and are expected to negotiate prices.

On the Web, the term *marketplace* has a different and distinct meaning. If individual customers want to negotiate prices, they may be able to do so in some storefronts or malls. However, the term *e-marketplace* usually implies B2B, (not B2C that is usually conducted in storefronts and malls). We distinguish two types of e-marketplaces: private and public.

Private E-Marketplaces

private e-marketplaces
Online markets owned by a single company; may be either sell-side and/or buy-side e-marketplaces.

sell-side e-marketplace
A private e-marketplace in which one company sells either standard and/or customized products to qualified companies.

buy-side e-marketplace
A private e-marketplace in which one company makes purchases from invited suppliers.

Private e-marketplaces are those owned and operated by a single company (see Chapter 5). As can be seen in the Raffles Hotel case (Online File W2.3), private markets are either sell-side or buy-side. In a **sell-side e-marketplace**, a company, for example, Cisco will sell either standard or customized products to qualified companies; this type of selling is considered to be *one-to-many*. It is similar to a B2C storefront. In a **buy-side e-marketplace**, a company purchases from many suppliers; this type of purchasing is considered to be many-to-one. For example, Raffles Hotel buys its supplies from approved vendors that come to its marketplace. Private marketplaces are frequently open only to selected members and are not publicly regulated. We will return to the topic of private e-marketplaces in Chapter 5.

Public E-Marketplaces

public e-marketplaces
B2B marketplaces, usually owned and/or managed by an independent third party, that include many sellers and many buyers; also known as *exchanges*.

Public e-marketplaces are B2B markets. They often are owned by a third party (not a seller or a buyer) or by a group of buying or selling companies (a consortium), and they serve many sellers and many buyers. These markets also are known as *exchanges* (e.g., a stock exchange). They are open to the public and are regulated by the government or the exchange's owners. An example of a public marketplace, NTE.net, is provided in Online File W2.4. Public e-marketplaces are presented in detail in Chapter 5.

INFORMATION PORTALS

information portal
A single point of access through a Web browser to business information inside and/or outside an organization.

A portal is a mechanism that is used in e-marketplaces, e-stores, and other types of EC (e.g., in intrabusiness, e-learning, etc.). With the growing use of intranets and the Internet, many organizations encounter information overload at a number of different levels. Information is scattered across numerous documents, e-mail messages, and databases at different locations and in disparate systems. Finding relevant and accurate information often is time-consuming and requires access to multiple systems.

As a consequence, organizations lose a lot of productive employee time. One solution to this problem is the use of *portals*. A portal is an information gateway. It attempts to address information overload by enabling people to search and access relevant information from disparate IT systems and the Internet, using advanced search and indexing techniques (such as Google's desktop), in an intranet-based environment. An **information portal** is a single point of access through a Web browser to critical business information located inside and outside of an organization. Many information portals can be personalized for the users.

Types of Portals

Portals appear under many descriptions and shapes. One way to distinguish among them is to look at their content, which can vary from narrow to broad, and their community or audience, which also can vary. The following are the major types of portals:

▶ **Commercial (public) portals.** These portals offer content for diverse communities and are the most popular portals on the Internet. Although they can be customized by the user, they are still intended for broad audiences and offer fairly routine content, some in real time (e.g., a stock ticker and news about a few preselected items). Examples of such sites are yahoo.com, aol.com, and msn.com.

▶ **Corporate portals.** Corporate portals provide organized access to rich content within relatively narrow corporate and partners' communities. They also are known as *enterprise portals* or *enterprise information portals*. Corporate portals appear in different forms and are described in detail in Chapter 6.

▶ **Publishing portals.** These portals are intended for communities with specific interests. These portals involve relatively little customization of content, but they provide extensive online search features and some interactive capabilities. Examples of such sites are techweb.com and zdnet.com.

▶ **Personal portals.** These target specific filtered information for individuals. They offer relatively narrow content and are typically very personalized, effectively having an audience of one.

▶ **Mobile portals.** Mobile portals are portals that are accessible from mobile devices (see Chapter 9 for details). Although most of the other portals mentioned here are PC based, increasing numbers of portals are accessible via mobile devices. One example of such a mobile portal is i-mode (my-imode.com), which is described in Chapter 9.

▶ **Voice portals.** Voice portals are Web sites, usually portals, with audio interfaces. This means that they can be accessed by a standard telephone or a cell phone. AOLbyPhone is an example of a service that allows users to retrieve e-mail, news, and other content from AOL via telephone. It uses both speech recognition and text-to-speech technologies. Companies such as Tellme.com (tellme.com) and BeVocal (bevocal.com) offer access to the Internet from telephones and tools to build voice portals. Voice portals are especially popular for 1–800 numbers (Enterprise 800 numbers) that provide self-service to customers with information available in Internet databases (e.g., find flight status at delta.com).

▶ **Knowledge portals.** Knowledge portals enable access to knowledge by knowledge workers and facilitate collaboration (see Chapter 6).

mobile portal
A portal accessible via a mobile device.

voice portal
A portal accessed by telephone or cell phone.

Agent-Based E-Marketplaces

E-marketplaces, especially for B2B and mega B2C (such as Amazon.com) can become plagued by information overload. To overcome the problem, Guan (2006) suggests using intelligent (or software) agents. As we will see in Chapter 3, software agents already provide comparisons (e.g., froogle.com, comparefare.com) and even personal recommendations (e.g., at amazon.com and netflix.com). Various search engines can help explore catalogs, and monitoring agents watch auctions. But today's state of the art is still limited.

1. Describe electronic storefronts and e-malls.
2. List the various types of stores and e-malls.
3. Differentiate between private and public e-marketplaces.
4. What are information portals? List the major types.
5. Describe agent-based e-marketplaces.

2.3   PARTICIPANTS, TRANSACTIONS, INTERMEDIATION, AND PROCESSES IN E-COMMERCE

Now that we are familiar with marketplaces, their types, components, and participants, let's look at what is going on in these markets. We begin by describing the participants.

SELLERS, BUYERS, AND TRANSACTIONS

A major EC activity is electronic trading. Typically, a seller (retailer, wholesaler, or manufacturer) sells to customers. The seller buys from suppliers: either raw material (as a manufacturer) or finished goods (as a retailer). This process is illustrated in Exhibit 2.2.

The selling company is shown in the center of the figure, marked as "our company." Internally, processes in the different functional areas are supported by enterprise software, (B2B), or government agencies (B2G). The customers place orders, and the seller fulfills them.

Our company buys materials, products, and so on from suppliers (B2B), distributors (B2B), or from the government (G2B) in a process called *e-procurement*. Sometimes intermediaries are involved in this process (see Chapter 5 for details).

THE ROLES AND VALUE OF INTERMEDIARIES IN E-MARKETPLACES

Intermediaries (brokers) play an important role in commerce by providing value-added activities and services to buyers and sellers. There are many types of intermediaries. The most well-known intermediaries in the physical world are wholesalers and retailers.

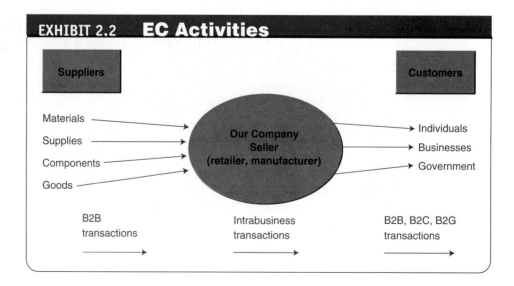

EXHIBIT 2.2   EC Activities

In cyberspace, there are, in addition, intermediaries that provide and/or control information flow. These electronic intermediaries are known as **infomediaries**. The information flows to and from buyers and sellers via infomediaries, as shown in Online File W2.5. Frequently, intermediaries aggregate information and sell it to others (see en.wikipedia.org/wiki/Wikipedia:Syndication).

Online intermediaries are companies that facilitate transactions between buyers and sellers and receive a percentage of the transaction's value (see en.wikipedia.org/wiki/Business-to-consumer_electronic_commerce). These firms make up the largest group of B2C companies today. The two types of online intermediaries are brokers and infomediaries.

infomediaries
Electronic intermediaries that provide and/or control information flow in cyberspace, often aggregating information and selling it to others.

Brokers

A *broker* is a company that facilitates transactions between buyers and sellers. The following are different types of brokers:

- **Buy/sell fulfillment.** A corporation that helps consumers place buy and sell orders (e.g., E*TRADE).
- **Virtual mall.** A company that helps consumers buy from a variety of stores (e.g., Yahoo! Stores).
- **Metamediary.** A firm that offers customers access to a variety of stores and provides them with transaction services, such as financial services (e.g., Amazon zShops).
- **Search agent.** A company that helps consumers compare different stores (e.g., Shopping.com).
- **Shopping facilitator.** A company that helps consumers use online shops by providing currency conversion, language translation, payment features, and delivery solutions, and potentially a user-customized interface, (e.g., MyOrbital.com).

Infomediaries

Web sites that gather and organize large amounts of data and act as intermediaries between those who want the information and those who supply the information are called *infomediaries* (Webopedia 2007). There are two types of infomediaries:

1. The first type offers consumers a place to gather information about specific products and companies before they make purchasing decisions. It is a third-party provider of unbiased information; it does not promote or try to sell specific products in preference over other products or act on behalf of any vendors (e.g., Autobytel.com and BizRate.com).

2. The second type is not necessarily Web-based. It provides vendors with consumer information that will help the vendor develop and market products. The infomediary collects the personal information from the buyers and markets that data to businesses. The advantage of this approach is that consumer privacy is protected and some infomediaries offer consumers a percentage of the brokerage deals.

Producers and consumers might interact directly in an e-marketplace: Producers provide information to customers, who then select from among the available products. In general, producers set prices; sometimes prices are negotiated. However, direct interactions are sometimes undesirable or unfeasible. In that case, intermediation is needed. Intermediaries, whether human or electronic, can address the following five important limitations of *direct interaction*, which are shown in Online File W2.6.

E-Distributors in B2B

e-distributor

An e-commerce intermediary that connects manufacturers with business buyers (customers) by aggregating the catalogs of many manufacturers in one place—the intermediary's Web site.

A special type of intermediary in e-commerce is the B2B **e-distributor**. These intermediaries connect manufacturers with business buyers (customers), such as retailers (or resellers in the computer industry). E-distributors basically aggregate the catalogs or the product information from many manufacturers, sometimes thousands of them, in one place—the intermediary's Web site. An example is W.W. Grainger (see Chapter 5 for details).

DISINTERMEDIATION AND REINTERMEDIATION

Intermediaries are agents that mediate between sellers and buyers. Usually, they provide two types of services: (1) They provide relevant information about demand, supply, prices, and requirements and, in doing so, help match sellers and buyers. (2) They offer value-added services such as transfer of products, escrow, payment arrangements, consulting, or assistance in finding a business partner.

disintermediation

Elimination of intermediaries between sellers and buyers.

Intermediaries that provide only (or mainly) the first type of service might be eliminated; a phenomena called **disintermediation**. An example is the airline industry and its push for buying electronic tickets directly from the airlines. This is resulting in the disintermediation of travel agents from the purchasing process. In another example, discount stockbrokers who only execute trades manually are disappearing; brokers who manage electronic intermediation are not only surviving, but might actually be prospering (e.g., E*TRADE). This phenomenon, in which disintermediated entities or newcomers take on new intermediary roles, is called **reintermediation** (see Chapters 3 and 5).

reintermediation

Establishment of new intermediary roles for traditional intermediaries that have been disintermediated.

Disintermediation is more likely to occur in supply chains involving several intermediaries, as illustrated in the opening case. Online File W2.7 Boise Cascade illustrates an intermediary that does both B2C and B2B.

THE PURCHASING PROCESS

Customers buy goods online in different modes. The most common mode is purchasing from catalogs at fixed prices. Sometimes prices are negotiated or discounted. Another mode is *dynamic pricing*, which refers to nonfixed prices, such as those in *auctions* or stock (commodity) markets. The buyer uses the process illustrated in Exhibit 2.3.

The process starts with logging into a seller's site, registering (if needed), and entering into an online catalog or the buyer's "my account." E-catalogs can be very large, so a search mechanism may be needed. Also, the buyer needs to compare prices. Some sellers will provide comparisons with competing vendors. Otherwise, the buyer may need to leave the site to do the comparison. If not satisfied, the buyer will abandon the site. If satisfied, the buyer will select the item and place it in a *shopping cart*. The buyer might then return to the catalog to choose more items. When shopping is completed, the buyer goes to a checkout page where a shipment option is selected from a menu. A payment option may be available (e.g., credit card, PayPal, after billing, in installments, and so on). After checking all details for accuracy, the buyer *submits* the order.

In the remainder of this chapter, we will describe the major mechanisms that support this process.

Section 2.3 ▶ REVIEW QUESTIONS

1. Describe the transaction process between a seller and its customers and suppliers.
2. List the roles of intermediaries in e-markets.
3. Describe e-distributors.
4. What are disintermediation and reintermediation?
5. Describe the purchasing process.

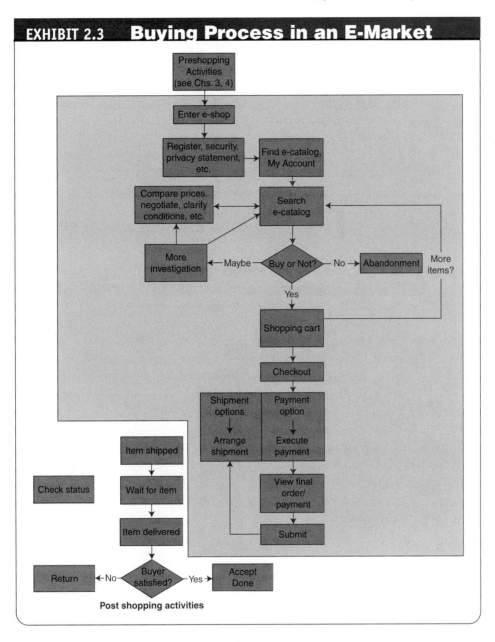

EXHIBIT 2.3   Buying Process in an E-Market

2.4 ELECTRONIC CATALOGS AND OTHER MARKET MECHANISMS

To enable selling online, a Web site usually needs EC *merchant server software* (see Online Chapter 13). The basic functionality offered by such software includes electronic catalogs, search engines, and shopping carts.

ELECTRONIC CATALOGS

Catalogs have been printed on paper for generations. Recently, electronic catalogs on CD-ROM and the Internet have gained popularity. **Electronic catalogs** consist of a product database, directory and search capabilities, and can be interactive (Cox and

electronic catalogs
The presentation of product information in an electronic form; the backbone of most e-selling sites.

Koelzer 2006). They are the backbone of most e-commerce sales sites. For merchants, the objective of electronic catalogs is to advertise and promote products and services. For the customer, the purpose of such catalogs is to locate information on products and services. Electronic catalogs can be very large; for example, the Library of Congress Web catalog (catalog.loc.gov) contains millions of records.

The majority of early online catalogs were replications of text and pictures from print catalogs. However, online catalogs have evolved to become more dynamic, customized, and integrated with selling and buying procedures. As online catalogs have become more integrated with shopping carts, order taking, and payment, the tools for building them are being integrated with merchant suites and Web hosting (e.g., see smallbusiness.yahoo.com/merchant).

Electronic catalogs can be classified on three dimensions:

1. **The dynamics of the information presentation.** In *dynamic catalogs*, information is presented in motion pictures or animation, possibly with supplemental sound. Dynamic catalogs can be in real time, changing frequently, such as with prices of stocks (and commodities) on stock exchange tickers.

2. **The degree of customization.** In *customized catalogs*, content, pricing, and display are tailored to the characteristics of specific customers.

3. **Integration with business processes.** Catalogs can be classified according to the degree of integration with the following business processes or features: order taking and fulfillment; electronic payment systems; intranet workflow software and systems; inventory and accounting systems; suppliers' or customers' extranets; and paper catalogs. Many sellers advise customers on item availability and possible delivery dates.

Although used occasionally in B2C commerce, *customized catalogs* are especially useful in B2B e-commerce. For example, e-catalogs can show only the items that the employees in a specific organization are allowed to purchase. E-catalogs can be customized to show the same item to different customers at different prices, reflecting discounts or purchase-contract agreements. Extranets, in particular, can deliver customized catalogs to different business customers.

For a comprehensive discussion of standards and multilingual strategies for online catalogs, see Beckman et al. (2004), jcmax.com/advantages.html, and purchasing.about.com.

Online Catalogs Versus Paper Catalogs

The advantages and disadvantages of online catalogs are contrasted with those of paper catalogs in Online File W2.7. Although online catalogs have significant advantages, such as ease of updating; the ability to be integrated with the purchasing process; coverage of a wide spectrum of products; interactivity; customization; and strong search capabilities, they do have a few disadvantages and limitations. For example, customers need computers and Internet access to view online catalogs. Nevertheless, paper catalogs will be supplemented by, if not actually replaced by, electronic ones.

A representative tool for building online catalogs is Microsoft's Commerce Server 2006—a .NET tool for creating Web sites that include search capabilities, the ability to feature large numbers of products, enhanced viewing capabilities, and ongoing support.

Customized Catalogs

A *customized catalog* is a catalog assembled specifically for a buying company or tailored to loyal individual shoppers or to a segment of shoppers (e.g., frequent buyers). There are two approaches to creating customized catalogs.

The first approach is to let the customers identify the products of interest to them from the total catalog, as is done by software products such as QuickSilver from Broadvision (broadvision.com). Such software allows the creation of catalogs with branded value-added capabilities that make it easy for customers to find the products they want to purchase, locate the information they need, and quickly configure their order.

The second approach is to let the system automatically identify customer characteristics based on the customer's transaction records. However, to generalize the relationship between the customer and items of interest, data-mining technology (Chapter 4) might be needed. This second approach can be combined with the first one.

As an example of the second approach, consider the following scenario, which uses Oracle's 9i server: Joe Smith logs on to the Acme Shopping site, where he has the option to register as an account customer and record his preferences in terms of address details, interest areas, and preferred method of payment. Acme Shopping offers a wide range of products, including electronics, clothing, books, and sporting goods. Joe is interested only in clothing and electronics—specifically related to photography.

After Joe has recorded his preferences, each time he returns to Acme's electronic store the first page will show him only the clothing and electronics departments. Furthermore, when Joe goes into the electronics department, he sees only cameras and accessories in his preferred price range. Such *customization* gives consumers a value-added experience and adds to their reasons for revisiting the site, thus building brand loyalty to that Internet store.

Against the backdrop of intense competition for Web time, customization and personalization provide a valuable way to match consumers with the products and information in which they are most interested as quickly and painlessly as possible. An example of how corporations customize their catalogs for corporate clients is provided in Online File W2.7.

Implementing E-Catalogs

Implementing e-catalogs on a small scale is fairly simple (see Online Chapter 13). However, transforming a large-scale catalog to an e-catalog necessitates the creation of a matching customer support system. See Schmitz et al. (2005) for a discussion of the topic, examples of successes and failures, and suggestions for implementation. Large online catalogs need a search engine. Advanced search engines use keywords for conducting searches.

SEARCH ENGINES AND INTELLIGENT AGENTS

A **search engine** is a computer program that can access databases of Internet resources, search for specific information or keywords, and report the results. For example, customers tend to ask for product information (e.g., requests for product information or pricing) in the same general manner. This type of request is repetitive, and answering such requests is costly when done by a human. Search engines deliver answers economically and efficiently by matching, for example, questions with FAQ (frequently asked question) templates, which respond with "canned" answers.

Google, AltaVista, and Lycos are popular search engines. Portals such as AOL, Yahoo!, and MSN have their own search engines. Special search engines organized to answer certain questions or search in specified areas, include Ask.com, Northern Light, Mama, and Looksmart. Thousands of different public search engines are available (see searchengineguide.com). In addition, hundreds of companies have search engines on their portals or storefronts. These are known as desktop search engines (e.g., see what Google is offering). A search engine for online catalogs is Endeca InFront (from endeca.com).

search engine
A computer program that can access databases of Internet resources, search for specific information or keywords, and report the results.

SHOPPING CARTS

electronic shopping cart

An order-processing technology that allows customers to accumulate items they wish to buy while they continue to shop.

An **electronic shopping cart** is an order-processing technology that allows customers to accumulate items they wish to buy while they continue to shop. In this respect, it is similar to a shopping cart in the physical world. The software program of an electronic shopping cart allows customers to select items, review what has been selected, make changes, and then finalize the list. Clicking on "buy" will trigger the actual purchase.

Shopping carts for B2C are fairly simple (visit amazon.com to see an example), but for B2B a shopping cart may be more complex. A B2B shopping cart could enable a business customer to shop at several sites while keeping the cart on the buyer's Web site to integrate it with the buyer's e-procurement system.

Shopping-cart software is sold or provided for free as an independent component (e.g., monstercommerce.com and easycart.com). It also is embedded in merchants' servers, such as smallbusiness.yahoo.com/merchant. Free online shopping carts (trials and demos) are available at volusion.com and gomerchant.com. For more on shopping carts, see Online Chapter 13.

Product Configuration

A key characteristic of EC is the self-customization of products and services, as done by Dell. Manufacturers need to produce the customized products in an economic way so that the price of the products will be competitive. *Product configuration* systems support the acquisition of the customer requirements while automating the order-taking process, and they allow customers to configure their products by specifying their technical requirements. It allows manufacturers to produce customized products efficiently in large quantities through a process called *mass customization* (see Appendix 2A at the end of this chapter).

Sophisticated product configuration systems use artificial intelligence (AI) tools because they need to support the interaction with the customers and understand their needs. For an overview, see Blecker (2006).

ONLINE CLASSIFIED ADS

Electronic catalogs are used mainly for presenting products. Another mechanism for presenting products and services is electronic classified ads, which are similar to classified ads in newspapers. Notice that e-classifieds are used mainly by individuals who provide a service or are looking for one, as well as offering items for sale. E-classifieds can be interactive and can include much more information than newspaper ads. Some classified providers charge a fee from the advertisers (e.g., Yahoo!), others are free or charge only for certain services in certain geographical areas (e.g., Craigslist.com). The competition in classified ads is fierce, because the trend is to charge for posting. Many newspapers and commercial Internet portals offer classified ads. Popular are listings for jobs and apartments or houses to rent or sell. Some sites provide visual views of apartments (e.g., apartments.com). A popular classifieds site is Craigslist.com, described in Case 2.2.

Section 2.4 ▶ REVIEW QUESTIONS

1. List the dimensions by which electronic catalogs can be classified.
2. List the benefits of electronic catalogs.
3. Explain how customized catalogs are created and used.
4. Describe an electronic shopping cart.
5. Describe e-classified ads and their advantages.

CASE 2.2
EC Application
CRAIGSLIST: THE ULTIMATE ONLINE CLASSIFIED SITE

If you want to find (or offer) a job, housing, goods and services, social activities, and much more in over 300 cities in more than 50 countries worldwide for free, go to *craigslist.org*. The site has much more information than you will find in all the newspapers in the individual cities. For example, more than 500,000 new jobs are listed from the more than 10 million new classified ads received by Craigslist every month. Craig Newmark, the founder of Craigslist, has said that everything is for sale on the site except the site itself. Although many other sites offer free classifieds, no other site even comes close to Craigslist.

In addition, Craigslist features 80 topical discussion forums with more than 40 million user postings. No wonder that Craigslist has over 4 billion page views per month, making it the seventh most visited site in the English language. Craigslist is considered by many as one of the few Web sites that could change the world, because it is simply a free notice board with more than 4 billion readers (Naughton 2006).

Users cite the following reasons for the popularity of Craigslist:

▶ It gives people a voice.
▶ It promotes a sense of trust, even intimacy.
▶ Its consistency and down-to-earth values.
▶ Its simplicity.
▶ Its social networking capabilities.

As an example of the site's effectiveness, we provide the personal experience of one of the authors who needed to rent his condo in Los Angeles. The usual process would take 2 to 4 weeks and $400 to $700 in newspaper ads plus the local online for-rent services to get the condo rented. With Craigslist, it took less than a week at no cost. As more people discover Craigslist, the traditional newspaper-based classified ad industry will probably be the loser; ad rates may become lower, and fewer ads will be printed.

eBay owns 25 percent of Craigslist. Craigslist charges for "help wanted" ads and apartment broker listings in some larger cities. In addition, Craigslist may charge ad placers, especially when an ad has rich media features. Classified advertising is Craigslist's real money-making feature. According to Copeland (2006a), offline classifieds generate $27 billion in annual profits, and online classifieds could quadruple that amount in 4 years. Both Google and Microsoft are attempting to control this market. So, it is likely that Craigslist.org will be purchased soon.

Sources: Compiled from Brandon (2006), Naughton (2006), Copeland (2006a), *craigslist.org* (accessed July 2008), and *Time* (2006).

Questions

1. Identify the business model used by Craigslist.
2. Visit *craigslist.org* and identify the social network and business network elements.
3. Why is Craigslist considered to be a site that can "change the world"?
4. What do you like about the site? What do you dislike about it?

2.5 AUCTIONS AS EC MARKET MECHANISMS

One of the most interesting market mechanisms in e-commerce is electronic auctions (Nissanoff 2006). They are used in B2C, B2B, C2C, G2B, G2C, and more.

DEFINITION AND CHARACTERISTICS

An **auction** is a market mechanism that uses a competitive process by which a seller solicits consecutive bids from buyers (forward auctions) or a buyer solicits bids from sellers (reverse auctions). Prices are determined dynamically by the bids. A wide variety of online markets qualify as auctions using this definition. Auctions, an established method of commerce for generations, deal with products and services for which conventional marketing channels are ineffective or inefficient, and they ensure prudent execution of sales. For example,

auction
A competitive process in which a seller solicits consecutive bids from buyers (forward auctions) or a buyer solicits bids from sellers (backward auctions). Prices are determined dynamically by the bids.

auctions can expedite the disposal of items that need to be liquidated or sold quickly. Rare coins and other collectibles are frequently sold in auctions.

There are several types of auctions, each with its own motives and procedures. Auctions can be done *online* or *offline*. They can be conducted in public auction sites, such as at eBay. They also can be done by invitation to private auctions.

This section presents the essential information about auctions that is necessary for understanding related material in Chapters 3 through 5. See also Saarinen et al. (2006) for e-auction information.

TRADITIONAL AUCTIONS VERSUS E-AUCTIONS

Traditional, physical auctions are still very popular. However, the volume traded on e-auctions is significantly larger and continues to increase.

Limitations of Traditional Offline Auctions

Traditional offline auctions, regardless of their type, have the following limitations: They generally last only a few minutes, or even seconds, for each item sold. This rapid process may give potential buyers little time to make a decision, so they might decide not to bid. Therefore, sellers might not get the highest possible price; bidders might not get what they really want, or they might pay too much for the item. Also, in many cases the bidders do not have much time to examine the goods. Bidders have difficulty learning about the locations and times of the auctions and cannot effectively compare what is offered at each location. Bidders must usually be physically present at auctions; thus, many potential bidders are excluded.

Similarly, it might be difficult for sellers to move goods to an auction site. Commissions are fairly high because a location must be rented, the auction needs to be advertised, and an auctioneer and other employees need to be paid. Electronic auctioning removes these deficiencies.

Electronic Auctions

The Internet provides an infrastructure for executing auctions electronically at lower cost, with a wide array of support services and with many more sellers and buyers. Individual consumers and corporations both can participate in this rapidly growing and very convenient form of e-commerce. Forrester Research projects that the Internet auction industry will reach $65.2 billion in sales by 2010 (123jump.com 2006).

electronic auction (e-auction)
Auctions conducted online.

Electronic auctions (e-auctions) are similar to offline auctions except that they are done online. E-auctions have been in existence since the 1980s over LANs (e.g., flowers; see Saarinen et al. 2006) and were started on the Internet in 1995. Host sites on the Internet serve as brokers, offering services for sellers to post their goods for sale and allowing buyers to bid on those items.

Major online auction sites, such as eBay, offer consumer products, electronic parts, artwork, vacation packages, airline tickets, and collectibles. Excess supplies and inventories are auctioned off by B2B marketers. Another type of B2B online auction is increasingly used to trade special types of commodities, such as electricity transmission capacities and gas and energy options. Furthermore, conventional business practices that traditionally have relied on contracts and fixed prices are increasingly being converted into auctions with bidding for online procurements (e.g., Raffles Hotel, Online File W2.3).

Of course, many consumer goods are not suitable for auctions, and for these items conventional selling—such as posted-price retailing—is more than adequate. Yet the flexibility offered by online auction trading offers innovative market processes for many other goods. For example, instead of searching for products and vendors by

CASE 2.3
EC Application
INNOVATIVE AUCTIONS

The following are some examples of innovative implementations of e-auctions:

1. Every year, Warren Buffett, the famous U.S. stock investor and investment guru, invites a group of seven people to lunch with him. The seven pay big money for the pleasure. The money is donated to the needy in San Francisco. In the past, Buffett charged $30,000 per group. As of July 2003, Buffett places the invitation on an online auction (eBay). In 2003, bidders pushed the bid from $30,000 to $250,100. The winning bid in 2007 was $650,200. One of the winners commented that he was willing to pay whatever was needed so that he could express to Buffett his appreciation for his investment guidance. Before the auction, he had no chance to be invited.

2. A Harley-Davidson motorcycle autographed by celebrities and offered by talk-show host Jay Leno fetched $800,100 on eBay to benefit tsunami victims.

3. Richard Dan operates an eBay store in Maui, Hawaii, called Web Auctions Hawaii (see trading assistants list on *ebay.com*). Initially he was selling unclaimed items from his pawnbroker business. Now he is also one of eBay's 40,000 "trading assistants." Web Auction Hawaii

and other trading assistants handle advertisements, auction listings, appraisals, descriptions, authentication, payments, shipments, insurance, and more. Dan also advises sellers as to which eBay category is the best for their particular item. Dan is helping non-profit organizations, estate administrators, and others to sell just about anything, including the four mules he helped sell in September 2004. Dan's basic charge is $25 per item plus a 25 percent commission. (Dan only handles items with an expected price of over $200.)

Sources: Compiled from Wagner (2007) and Woolard (2005).

Questions

1. Why is Warren Buffett so successful with his auctions?

2. You can place your item for sale on eBay without a trading assistant and save on the commission. Why do people use Dan's services?

3. What are the advantages of fund-raising via auctions? Are there any limitations?

visiting sellers' Web sites, a buyer can solicit offers from all potential sellers. Such a buying mechanism is so innovative that it has the potential to be used in almost all types of consumer goods auctions (as will be shown later when reverse auctions and "name-your-own-price" auctions are discussed). Some examples of innovative auctions are provided in Case 2.3.

DYNAMIC PRICING AND TYPES OF AUCTIONS

A major characteristic of auctions is that they are based on dynamic pricing. **Dynamic pricing** refers to prices that are not fixed but that are allowed to fluctuate as supply and demand in a market change. In contrast, catalog prices are fixed, as are prices in department stores, supermarkets, and many electronic storefronts.

Dynamic pricing appears in several forms. Perhaps the oldest forms are negotiation and bargaining, which have been practiced for many generations in open-air markets. It is customary to classify dynamic pricing into four major categories based on how many buyers and sellers are involved. These four categories are shown in Exhibit 2.4 and are briefly outlined in the following text.

dynamic pricing
Prices that change based on supply and demand relationships at any given time.

One Buyer, One Seller

In this configuration, one can use negotiation, bargaining, or bartering (pictured in the upper-left-hand box in Exhibit 2.4). The resulting price will be determined by each

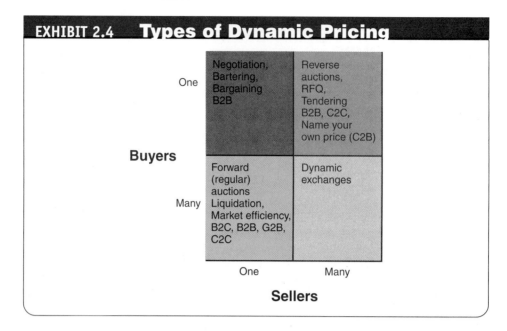

EXHIBIT 2.4   Types of Dynamic Pricing

		One	Negotiation, Bartering, Bargaining B2B	Reverse auctions, RFQ, Tendering B2B, C2C, Name your own price (C2B)
Buyers		Many	Forward (regular) auctions Liquidation, Market efficiency, B2C, B2B, G2B, C2C	Dynamic exchanges
			One	Many
			Sellers	

party's bargaining power, supply and demand in the item's market, and (possibly) business environment factors. This model is popular in B2B (see Chapter 5).

One Seller, Many Potential Buyers

forward auction

An auction in which a seller entertains bids from buyers. Bidders increase price sequentially.

In this configuration (in the bottom-left-hand box of Exhibit 2.4), the seller uses a **forward auction**, an auction in which a seller entertains bids from multiple buyers. The four major types of forward auctions are *English* and *Yankee* auctions, in which bidding prices increase as the auction progresses, and *Dutch* and *free-fall* auctions, in which bidding prices decline as the auction progresses. Each of these can be used for either liquidation or for market efficiency (see Gallaugher 2002). For additional details on forward auctions, see Cook (2006).

American Power Conversion Corp. (APC; apcc.com) needed a channel for end-of-life (old models) and refurbished power-protection products. These were difficult to sell in regular distribution channels. Before using auctions, the company used special liquidation sales that were not very successful. APC decided to use auctions to sell these items. APC turned to FreeMarkets to help it establish an online auction. (Note: FreeMarkets was integrated into Ariba.com.) It also helped the company determine the best auction strategies (such as starting bid price and auction running length). The site became an immediate success. APC also started to auction some of its regular products (only merchandise for which there would be no conflict with the company's regular distributors).

One Buyer, Many Potential Sellers

Two popular types of auctions in which there is one buyer and many potential sellers are reverse auctions (tendering) and "name-your-own-price" auctions. In auctions in this category (pictured in the upper-right-hand corner of Exhibit 2.4) one buyer solicits bids from many sellers or suppliers. An item the buyer needs is placed on an RFQ (request for quote), and potential sellers bid on the item, *reducing the price sequentially* (see Exhibit 2.5, page 63, for an illustration of this process.) These auctions are called *reverse auctions* because *suppliers* bid on goods or services the buyer needs. In reverse auctions, the price is reduced sequentially, and the lowest bid wins. These auctions are used mainly in B2B (both large and small businesses) or G2B; they also can be combined with negotiations.

Reverse Auctions. When there is one buyer and many potential sellers, a **reverse auction** (also called a **bidding** or **tendering system**) is in place. In a reverse auction, the buyer places an item he or she wants to buy for bid (or *tender*) on a *request for quote* (RFQ) system. Potential suppliers bid on the item, reducing the price sequentially (see Exhibit 2.5). In electronic bidding in a reverse auction, several rounds of bidding may take place until the bidders do not reduce the price further. The winner is the one with the lowest bid (assuming that only price is considered). Reverse auctions are primarily a B2B or G2B mechanism. (For further discussion and examples, see Chapter 5.)

B2B reverse auctions are gaining popularity as an online mechanism for buying goods and services. Hedgehog.com/onlinereverseauctions.htm presents the opportunities, advantages, and economic benefits of such B2B e-auctions. For more on reverse auctions, see Carbone (2005).

Although most C2C auctions are of a forward nature, increasingly, individuals are conducting reverse auctions. For example, a person who wants to buy a used car might create a *request-for-bid* (RFB, for individuals) for the car of their dreams and let those who have such cars contact them. C2C auctions are provided by eBay.

The Name-Your-Own-Price Model. Priceline.com pioneered the **"name-your-own-price" model**. In this model, a would-be buyer specifies the price (and other terms) that he or she is willing to pay to any willing and able seller. Priceline.com presents consumers' requests to sellers, who fill as much of the guaranteed demand as they wish at prices and terms requested by buyers. Alternately, Priceline.com searches its own database that contains vendors' lowest prices and tries to match supply against requests. Priceline.com asks customers to guarantee acceptance of the offer if it is at or below the requested price by giving a credit card number. This is basically a C2B model, although some businesses use it, too (see Online File W2.8 for details).

reverse auction (bidding or tendering system)
Auction in which the buyer places an item for bid (tender) on a request for quote (RFQ) system, potential suppliers bid on the job, with the price reducing sequentially, and the lowest bid wins; primarily a B2B or G2B mechanism.

"name-your-own-price" model
Auction model in which a would-be buyer specifies the price (and other terms) he or she is willing to pay to any willing and able seller. It is a C2B model that was pioneered by Priceline.com.

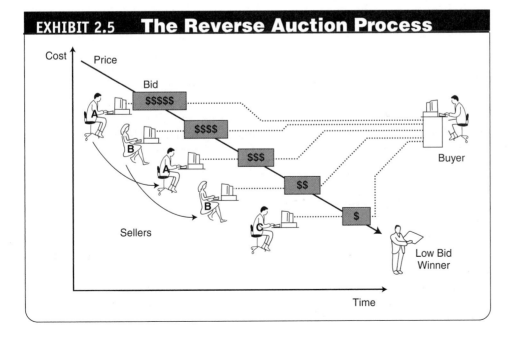

EXHIBIT 2.5   The Reverse Auction Process

double auction
Auctions in which multiple buyers and their bidding prices are matched with multiple sellers and their asking prices, considering the quantities on both sides.

vertical auction
Auction that takes place between sellers and buyers in one industry or for one commodity.

auction vortal
Another name for vertical auction portal.

Many Sellers, Many Buyers

When there are many sellers and many buyers, buyers and their bidding prices are matched with sellers and their asking prices based on the quantities on both sides. Stocks and commodities markets are typical examples of this configuration (as shown in the bottom-right-hand box of Exhibit 2.4). Buyers and sellers can be individuals or businesses. Such an auction is called a **double auction**.

A **vertical auction** is one that takes place between sellers and buyers in one industry or for one commodity (e.g., flowers, cars, or cattle). It is considered vertical because activity goes up and down the supply chain in a single industry, rather than horizontally between members of supply chains in different industries. Specialized sites for such auctions (in one industry) are sometimes referred to as **auction vortals**. Vertical auctions are particularly useful in B2B. At eBay "anything goes" (i.e., almost anything can be sold), but many auction sites specialize in one area. For example, policeauctions.com specializes in selling unclaimed or seized properties.

BENEFITS, LIMITATIONS, AND IMPACTS OF E-AUCTIONS

E-auctions are becoming important selling and buying channels for many companies and individuals. E-auctions enable buyers to access goods and services anywhere auctions are conducted. Moreover, almost perfect market information is available about prices, products, current supply and demand, and so on. These characteristics provide benefits to all.

Benefits of E-Auctions

According to Nissanoff (2006), the auction culture will revolutionize the way customers buy, sell, and obtain what they want. A listing of the benefits of e-auctions to sellers, buyers, and e-auctioneers is provided in Insights and Additions 2.1.

Limitations of E-Auctions

E-auctions have several limitations. The most significant limitations are minimal security, the possibility of fraud, and limited participation.

Minimal Security. Some of the C2C auctions conducted on the Internet are not secure because they are done in an unencrypted environment. This means that credit card numbers could be stolen during the payment process. Payment methods such as PayPal (paypal.com) can be used to solve the payment problem (see Chapter 12). In addition, some B2B auctions are conducted over highly secure private lines.

Possibility of Fraud. Auction items are in many cases unique, used, or antique. Because the buyer cannot see the items, the buyer may get defective products. Also, buyers can commit fraud by receiving goods or services without paying for them. Thus, the fraud rate on e-auctions is relatively high. For a discussion of e-auction fraud and fraud prevention, see Online File W2.9.

Limited Participation. Some auctions are by invitation only; others are open to dealers only. Limited participation may be a disadvantage to sellers, who usually benefit from as large a pool of buyers as possible.

Impacts of Auctions

Because the trade objects and contexts for auctions are very diverse, the rationale behind auctions and the motives of the different participants for setting up auctions are quite different. The following are some representative impacts of e-auctions.

Insights and Additions 2.1 Benefits of E-Auctions

Benefits to Sellers	Benefits to Buyers	Benefits to E-Auctioneers
• Increased revenues from broadening bidder base and shortening cycle time. • Opportunity to bargain instead of selling at a fixed price. • Optimal price setting determined by the market (more buyers, more information). • Sellers can gain more customer dollars by offering items directly (saves on the commission to intermediaries; also, physical auctions are very expensive compared with e-auctions). • Can liquidate large quantities quickly. • Improved customer relationship and loyalty (in the case of specialized B2B auction sites and electronic exchanges).	• Opportunities to find unique items and collectibles. • Participation in e-auctions can be entertaining and exciting. • Buyers can bid from anywhere, even with a cell phone; they do not have to travel to an auction place. • With the help of a third party, buyers can remain anonymous. • Possibility of finding bargains, for both individuals and organizations. • Price transparency allows buyers to be careful in making offers.	• Higher repeat purchases. Jupiter Research (*jupiterresearch.com*) found that auction sites, such as eBay, tend to garner higher repeat-purchase rates than the top B2C sites, such as Amazon.com. • High "stickiness" to the Web site (the tendency of customers to stay at sites longer and come back more often). Auction sites are frequently "stickier" than fixed-priced sites. Stickier sites generate more ad revenue for the e-auctioneer. • Easy expansion of the auction business.

Auctions as a Coordination Mechanism. Auctions are used increasingly as an efficient coordination mechanism for establishing a price equilibrium. An example is auctions for the allocation of telecommunications bandwidth.

Auctions as a Social Mechanism to Determine a Price. For objects that are not traded in traditional markets, such as unique or rare items, or for items that are offered randomly or at long intervals, an auction creates a marketplace that attracts potential buyers, and often experts. By offering many of these special items at a single place and time and by attracting considerable attention, auctions provide the requisite exposure of purchase and sale orders, and hence liquidity of the market in which an optimal price can be determined. Typical examples are auctions of fine arts or rare items. For example, wine collectors can find a global wine auction at winebid.com.

Auctions as a Highly Visible Distribution Mechanism. Some auctions deal with special offers. In this case, a supplier typically auctions off a limited number of items, using the auction primarily as a mechanism to gain attention and to attract those customers who are bargain hunters or who have a preference for the gambling dimension of the auction process. The airline seat auctions by Cathay Pacific, American Airlines, and Lufthansa fall into this category (see Saarinen et al. 2006).

Conducting Auctions

Auctions are conducted usually on specialized sites. The most well-known site is eBay (see Case 2.4).

EBAY—THE WORLD'S LARGEST AUCTION SITE

The Opportunity

eBay is one of the most profitable e-businesses. The successful online auction house has its roots in a 50-year-old novelty item—Pez candy dispensers. Pam Omidyar, an avid collector of Pez dispensers, came up with the idea of trading them over the Internet. When she expressed this idea to her boyfriend (now her husband), Pierre Omidyar, he was instantly struck with the soon-to-be-famous e-business auction concept.

The Solution

In 1995, the Omidyars created a company called AuctionWeb. The company was renamed eBay and has since become the premier online auction house in many countries, with millions of unique auctions in progress and over 500,000 new items added each day. Almost 194 million registered buyers and sellers use eBay. Today, eBay is much more than an auction house, but its initial success was in electronic auctions.

eBay's initial business model was to provide an electronic infrastructure for conducting mostly C2C auctions. eBay auctions do not require an auctioneer; technology manages the auction process.

On eBay, people can buy and sell just about anything. The company collects a submission fee upfront, plus a commission that is a percentage of the final sale amount. The submission fee is based on the amount of exposure the seller wants the item to receive, with a higher fee if the seller would like the item to be among the featured auctions in a specific product category, and an even higher fee if the seller wants the item to be listed on the eBay homepage under *Featured Items*. Another attention-grabbing option is to publish the product listing in a boldface font (for an additional charge).

The auction process begins when the seller fills in the appropriate registration information and posts a description of the item for sale. The seller must specify a minimum opening bid. If potential buyers feel this price is too high, the item may not receive any bids. Sellers can set the opening bid lower than the *reserve price*, a minimum acceptable bid price, to generate bidding activity.

If a successful bid is made, the seller and the buyer negotiate the payment method, shipping details, warranty, and other particulars. eBay serves as a liaison between the parties; it is the interface through which sellers and buyers can conduct business. eBay does not maintain a costly physical inventory or deal with shipping, handling, or other services that businesses such as Amazon.com and other retailers must provide. The eBay site basically serves individuals, but it also caters to small businesses.

In 2001, eBay started to auction fine art in collaboration with Icollector.com (*icollector.com*) of the United Kingdom and with the art auction house Sotheby's (*sothebys.com*), whose auction page is on eBay's main menu. Due to lack of profit, as of May 2003, eBay and Sotheby's discontinued separate online auctions and began placing emphasis on promoting Sotheby's live auctions through eBay's Live Auctions technology while continuing to build eBay's highly successful arts and antiques categories. Sotheby's Web site still exists, but now is focused on supporting Sotheby's live auction business.

In addition, eBay operates globally, permitting international auctions to take place. Country-specific sites are located in over 31 countries, including the United States, Canada, France, Sweden, Brazil, the United Kingdom, Australia, Singapore, and Japan. eBay also has equity in or owns several country-specific sites, such as those in China, India, Korea, and Japan, that generate 46 percent of eBay's business. Buyers from more than 150 other countries participate. eBay also operates a business exchange in which SMEs can buy and sell new and used merchandise in B2B or B2C modes.

eBay has over 60 local sites in the United States that enable users to easily find items located near them, to browse through items of local interest, and to meet face-to-face to conclude transactions. In addition, some eBay sites, such as eBay Motors, concentrate on specialty items. Trading can be done anywhere, anytime. Wireless trading also is possible.

In 2002, eBay Seller Payment Protection was implemented to make it safer to sell on eBay. Now sellers are protected against bad checks and fraudulent credit card purchases. The service offers credit card chargeback protection, guaranteed electronic checks, secure processing, and privacy protection. After a few years of successful operation and tens of million of loyal members, eBay decided to leverage its large customer base and started to do e-tailing, mostly at fixed prices. This may have been in response to Amazon.com's decision to start auctions or it might have been a logical idea for a diversification. By 2003, eBay operated several specialty sites. In addition to eBay Motors cited earlier, *half.com*, the famous discount e-tailer, is now part of eBay, as is PayPal, the P2P payment company.

(continued)

CASE 2.4 (continued)

A special feature is eBay Stores. These stores are rented to individuals and companies. The renting companies can use these stores to sell from catalogs or conduct auctions. In 2002, eBay introduced the Business Marketplace, located at *ebay.com/businessmarketplace*. This site brings together all business-related listings on eBay to one destination, making it easier for small businesses to find the equipment and supplies they need. eBay also offers software for building customized storefronts that eBay hosts (Prostores products), and provides templates for building standard storefronts.

Many individuals are using eBay Stores and Marketplace to make a living. Some of them are very successful. Holden (2006) describes how 10 different entrepreneurs have tapped into the power of eBay and are making millions.

In 2006, eBay launched "eBay Express," which enables instant-purchasing using a shopping cart to buy multiple items at the prices set by the sellers. eBay also allows Web site affiliates to run contextual ads for eBay auctions in exchange for a cut of resulting ad sales (the program is called eBay AdContext). eBay also features the eBay Community Wiki, where buyers and sellers can exchange best practices and tips. eBay owns Skype, a VoIP provider of Internet communication. Users can use Skype to streamline complex auctions (e.g., if you want to buy a car, on eBay you might want to ask the seller questions about the vehicle) and to facilitate communication between buyers and sellers with regards to product customization.

The Results

The impact of eBay on e-business has been profound. Its founders took a limited-access offline business model and, by using the Internet, were able to bring it to the desktops of consumers worldwide. This business model consistently generates a profit and promotes a sense of community—a near addiction that keeps traders coming back.

eBay is the world's largest auction site, with a community of close to 194 million registered users as of spring 2006, about half of them outside the United States. According to company financial statements, in 2004, eBay transacted over $40 billion in sales for a net revenue close to $6 billion and a net income of about $500 million.

As a matter of fact, the only place where people are doing more business online than offline (and considerably more, at that) is auctions. For comparison, e-tailing is less than 5 percent of total retail sales.

Sources: Compiled from eBay (2006a), Search Engine Roundtable (2006), Stroebel (2003), Coffin (2004), Prince (2004), Schonfeld (2005), Park (2006), and Holden (2006).

Questions

1. What were the drivers of eBay?
2. What are eBay's critical success factors?
3. Describe the eBay auction process.
4. Why does eBay sell in fixed prices, too?
5. Why does eBay provide a marketplace?
6. Why do some consider eBay to be a social network?

Auctions as an EC Component. Auctions can stand alone or they can be combined with other e-commerce activities. An example of the latter is the combination of *group purchasing* with reverse auctions, as described in Online File W2.10.

Section 2.5 ▶ REVIEW QUESTIONS

1. Define auctions and describe how they work.
2. Describe the benefits of electronic auctions over traditional (offline) ones.
3. List the four types of auctions.
4. Distinguish between forward and reverse auctions.
5. Describe the "name-your-own-price" auction model.
6. List the major benefits of auctions to buyers, sellers, and auctioneers.
7. What are the major limitations of auctions?
8. List the major impacts of auctions on markets.

2.6 BARTERING AND NEGOTIATING ONLINE

Two emerging mechanisms are gaining popularity (as can be seen in Chapter 10) in EC: e-bartering and e-negotiation.

ONLINE BARTERING

bartering
The exchange of goods or services.

Bartering, the exchange of goods and services, is the oldest method of trade. Today, it is done primarily between organizations. The problem with bartering is that it is difficult to find trading partners. Businesses and individuals might use classified ads to advertise what they need and what they offer, but they still might not be able to find what they want. Intermediaries can be helpful, but they are expensive (20 to 30 percent commission) and very slow.

e-bartering (electronic bartering)
Bartering conducted online, usually in a bartering exchange.

E-bartering (electronic bartering)—bartering conducted online—can improve the matching process by attracting more partners to the barter. In addition, matching can be done faster, and, as a result, better matches can be found. Items that are frequently bartered online include office space, storage, and factory space; idle facilities; and labor, products, and banner ads. (Note that e-bartering can have tax implications that need to be considered.)

bartering exchange
A marketplace in which an intermediary arranges barter transactions.

E-bartering is usually done in a **bartering exchange**, a marketplace in which an intermediary arranges the transactions. These exchanges can be very effective. Representative bartering Web sites include barteryourservices.com, barterwww.com, and barterdepot.com. The process works like this: First, the company tells the bartering exchange what it wants to offer. The exchange then assesses the value of the company's products or services and offers it certain "points" or "bartering dollars." The company can use the "points" to buy the things it needs from a participating member in the exchange.

Bartering sites must be financially secure. Otherwise users may not have a chance to use the points they accumulate. (For further details, see virtualbarter.net and barternews.com.)

Consumer-to-Consumer Barter Exchanges

More and more individuals use the bartering method. For additional sites, see Copeland (2006a). The following are some examples of bartering sites:

- **SwapVillage.** SwapVillage (swapvillage.com) offers a complete swapping service, from item listings to actual exchanges. Users can swap items, Village$ (SwapVillage's currency), or a combination of the two.
- **SwapThings.** This site (swapthings.com) is dedicated to bringing together large numbers of people on the Internet and facilitating the swap of durable goods such as music CDs, video games, movies, books, antiques, collectibles, and electronics.
- **Trade Away.** Trade Away (tradeaway.com) offers consumers and businesses the opportunity to get exchanges for their unused goods or services without the use of cash.
- **WebSwap.** WebSwap (webswap.com) matches swappers interested in exchanging goods, allowing use of money to equalize deals if necessary. In addition to swapping, users can buy and sell goods.
- **BarterBee.** BarterBee (barterbee.com) users swap CDs, DVDs, and games.
- **Lala.com.** Lala.com (lala.com) helps people swap CDs. Sign-up is free. Just list the discs you're trying to peddle and draft a wish list of the discs you want. When another user requests one of your discs, Lala mails you a prepaid envelope to

send it in. Once your disc is received, the first available disc on your wish list is sent to you. Lala charges $1 for every CD you receive and 49 cents for shipping; 20 percent of the trading revenue goes to the "Z" Foundation, a nonprofit founded by Lala.com to help working musicians obtain health care. Similar sites are Peerflix and Bookins.

▶ **Craigslist.org.** The barter option in craigslist.org enabled Kyle MacDonald to turn a paper clip into a house. See Case 2.5 for details.

Many other variations of bartering exist both in B2B and C2C. Although many barters are done on a one-to-one basis, several bartering exchanges facilitate three-way (or more) trades. For example, see swaptree.com and Copeland (2006b).

ONLINE NEGOTIATING

Dynamic prices also can be determined by *negotiation.* Negotiated pricing commonly is used for expensive or specialized products. Negotiated prices also are popular when large quantities are purchased. Much like auctions, negotiated prices result from interactions and bargaining among sellers and buyers. However, in contrast with auctions, negotiation also deals with nonpricing terms, such as the payment method and credit. Negotiation is a well-known process in the offline world (e.g., in real estate, automobile purchases, and contract work). In addition, in cases where there is no standard service or product to speak of, some digital products and services can be personalized and "bundled" at a standard price. Preferences for these bundled services differ among consumers, and thus they are frequently negotiated. More discussions on electronic negotiations can be found in

---

CASE 2.5
EC Application
TURNING A PAPER CLIP INTO A HOUSE

When Kyle MacDonald told people about his idea, people thought that he had lost his mind. MacDonald's idea was to trade a paper clip for something more valuable, and to do so many times until he traded for a house. His goal was to do it within 1 year. And indeed, he did it. Kyle was inspired by a childhood barter game called Bigger and Better, but this time he used e-commerce technology.

MacDonald's first step was to post a message "for barter" on *craigslist.org*. In 2 days, he bartered the paper clip for a fish-shaped pen, which he then swapped for a doorknob with a smiley face. The swapping continued, next to a Coleman camping stove.

To reach a larger audience, Kyle created a special Web site—*oneredpaperclip.com*—where he received more responses, as well as strange offers, ranging from body parts to souls. With some publicity in TV and newspapers, the offers kept coming. The camping stove was traded for a power generator, and with a few more trades he owned a snowmobile. By the time he had acquired a truck, he was getting closer to his goal. Soon, he received a half day with the rock legend Alice Cooper. Then his trades

concentrated in show-business ventures. Finally, after 14 trades, the town of Kipling, Saskatchewan, Canada, offered him a three-bedroom house for a speaking role in a new film.

Today, a swapping marketplace called SwapAce uses *oneredpaperclip.com.au* to advertise swapping, and Kyle MacDonald uses *oneredpaperclip.com* as a blogging space.

Sources: Compiled from Anonymous (2006), *oneredpaperclip.com*, and CBC News (2006).

Questions

1. Is such a barter possible offline? Why or why not?
2. Why did Kyle use Craigslist.org to begin with, and why did he shift to a special Web site?
3. Speculate on why people were willing to swap and get inferior items.
4. Do you think that many people can conduct such a deal? Why or why not?

Bichler et al. (2003). A Web 2.0–type peer-to-peer (P2P) negotiation can be seen in ioffer.com. For more on negotiation in P2P money lending, see the ZOPA and Prosper cases in Online File W8.2.

Section 2.6 ▶ REVIEW QUESTIONS

1. Define bartering and describe the advantages of e-bartering.

2. What is the function of bartering exchanges?

3. Explain the role of online negotiation in EC.

2.7 WEB 2.0 MECHANISMS AND TOOLS

E-marketplaces, shopping carts, e-catalogs, and auctions are the major Web 1.0 mechanisms. Other mechanisms and tools are used for user-generated content, collaboration, file sharing, and other Web 2.0 applications. Most notable are blogs, wikis, RSS, and podcasts. A brief description is provided in this section.

BLOGGING (WEBLOGGING) AND BLOGS

Weblogging (blogging)
Technology for personal publishing on the Internet.

blog
A personal Web site that is open to the public to read and to interact with; often dedicated to specific topics or issues.

The Internet offers the opportunity for individuals to publish on the Web using a technology known as **Weblogging**, or **blogging**. A **blog** is a personal Web site that is open to the public and on which the owner expresses his or her feelings or opinions. Blogs became very popular after the terrorist attacks of September 11, 2001. People were looking for as many sources of information as possible and for personal connections to the tragedy. Blogs comfort people in times of stress. They offer a place where people express their ideas, and they can result in two-way communication and collaboration, group discussion, and so on.

Many types of blogs are available. According to Yap (2006), the most common types of blogs are professional blogs, which focus on professions, job aspects, and career building; personal blogs, which often take the form of an online diary, containing thoughts, poems, experiences, and other personal matters; topical blogs, which focus on a certain topic or niche, discussing specific aspects of the chosen subject; and business blogs, which are discussions about business and/or the stock market. Other types of blogs include, but are not limited to, science blogs, culture blogs, educational blogs, political blogs, and photo blogs. Flynn (2006) estimates that one new blog is created every second. There were more than 1.6 million daily postings (or 66,600 hourly postings) on the blogsphere as of June 2006 (Sifry 2006). The January 1, 2007, issue of *Time* was dedicated to blog communities. It described the story of 15 citizens—including a French rapper, a relentless reviewer, and a lonely girl—who are members of the new *digital democracy* (Grossman 2006).

Creating Blogs

It is becoming easier and easier to create blogs. Programs from blogger.com, pitas.com, and others very user-friendly. Blog space is free; the goal is to make it easy for users to create Web journals or blogs. Bloggers (the people who create and maintain blogs) are handed a fresh space on their Web site to write in each day. They can easily edit and add entries, broadcasting whatever they want by simply clicking the send key. Blogging software such as WordPress or Movable Type helps bloggers update their blogs easily. Free blog generators, such as Blogger, lets users host their content (on Google servers) without having to install any software or obtain a domain.

The crucial features that distinguish a blog from a regular Web page, according to Rapoza (2006) are trackbacks, blogrolls, pings, Feedblitz (an e-mail list management solution), and RSS feeds. Bloggers also use a special terminology. See samizdata.net for a dictionary of blog terms.

Datta (2006) suggests seven principles for building effective blogs:

1. Focus on a narrow niche, ideally one whose audience has a predilection for high-margin products.
2. Set up the blog so that each post gets its own permanent URL.
3. Think of a blog as a database, not a newspaper-like collection of dispatches.
4. Blog frequently and create at least half a dozen posts every weekday.
5. Use striking images that liven up the pages and attract readers.
6. Enable comments and interact with readers.
7. Make friends with other bloggers, online and off.

Commercial Uses of Blogs

The blog concept has transferred quickly to the corporate world. According to the 2006 Workplace E-mail, Instant Messaging & Blog Survey from the American Management Association (AMA) and The ePolicy Institute, 8 percent of U.S.–based organizations operate business blogs. Of that number, 55 percent operate external, or "facing out," blogs to communicate with customers and other third parties. Another 48 percent have established internal blogs to enhance employees' communication with one another (many operate both). Even CEOs are diving into the blogosphere, with 16 percent using blogs to build trust-based relationships, polish corporate reputations, promote social causes, and accomplish other professional goals. Blogging provides the ability to supplement corporate public relations, press releases, and brochures with more personal, "from the heart" talk and offer convenient links to related sources. A skillfully written, content-rich business blog can help organizations position executives as industry thought leaders, build brand awareness, facilitate two-way communication, and accomplish other important business goals. Blogs have gone from self-indulgent hobbies to flourishing businesses with the Web 2.0 wave (see Chapter 8). See Sloan and Kaihla (2006) for a survey of commercial uses of blogs. Case 2.6 illustrates how one company uses blogs for building its corporate reputation and providing CRM. Another application is provided in the Real-World Case at the end of this chapter.

A 2007 Forrester Research survey asked medium and large U.S. companies about their use of blogs. Blogging at some level (or planning to do so) was reported by 54 percent of the companies; 46 percent reported no plan to invest in blogs, primarily because they see no business value in it (McGillicuddy 2007). For examples of applications, see Weber (2007).

Potential Risks of Blogs

Some people see risks in corporate blogging (e.g., Lewin 2004). Two obvious examples are the risk of revealing trade secrets (in corporate-related blogs) and of making statements that are or that could be construed as libel or defamation. Many companies have corporate policies on blogging. Groove Networks (a Microsoft company) is one such example (see Ozzie 2002); the company even has corporate lawyers review the contents of its blogs.

CASE 2.6
EC Application
STONYFIELD FARM ADOPTS BLOGS FOR PUBLIC RELATIONS

Stonyfield Farm is the third largest organic company in the world, producing more than 18 million cups of yogurt each month and generating more than $300 million in annual sales in 50 states. The company's core values are promoting healthy food and protecting the environment. It guarantees the use of only natural ingredients in its products and donates 10 percent of its profit each year to efforts that protect the earth.

The company employs "word-of-mouth" marketing approaches that are compatible with its grassroots "people-friendly" image. Since 2005, Stonyfield has turned to blogs to further personalize its relationship with its customers and connect with even more people. The blogs provide the company with what the management calls a "handshake" with customers. Stonyfield publishes four different blogs on its Web site: (1) "Healthy Kids" encourages healthy food consumption in public schools; (2) "Strong Women Daily" features fitness, health tips, and stress-coping strategies; (3) "Baby Babble" provides a forum for child development and balancing work with family; and (4) "The Bovine Bugle" provides reports from organic dairy farms.

Stonyfield hires a journalist and almanac writer to post new content to each of the blogs daily, 5 days a week. When readers subscribe to the blogs, they receive automatic updates and are able to interact with the blogs (e.g., responding to postings). The blogs have created a positive response for the Stonyfield brand by providing readers with topics that inspire them and pique their interests. They are also, of course, persuaded to try and buy Stonyfield products. The management believes that blogs are an excellent public relations method.

Sources: Compiled from Needleman (2005), *BusinessWeek* Online (2006b), and *stonyfield.com* (accessed January 2008).

Questions

1. How does Stonyfield Farms manage its business blogs?

2. How do the blogs help Stonyfield Farms build its corporate reputation?

According to Flynn (2006), blog-related risks can be minimized by establishing a strategic blog management program that incorporates the three Es of electronic risk management:

1. **Establish comprehensive, written rules and policies.** Make sure employees understand that all company policies apply to the blogosphere, regardless of whether employees are blogging at the office or from home.

2. **Educate employees about blog-related risks, rules, and regulations.** Be sure to address rights and privacy expectations, as well as the organization's blog-related risks and responsibilities.

3. **Enforce blog policy with disciplinary action and technology.** Take advantage of blog search engines to monitor the blogosphere and to keep track of what is being written about your company.

Bloggers and Politics

Bloggers become more and more active in politics. In France, politicians pursued millions of voters in the blogosphere during the 2007 presidential elections. In the United States, when Senator Tom Daschle (who lost the 2004 Senate election in South Dakota) went to court at the last minute to sue his opponent, several hundred bloggers in South Dakota and elsewhere attacked him, saying that the lawsuit was "pathetic" and showed desperation. One blogger even broadcasted the court hearing on the blog site.

Wikis

A wikilog, or wiki, is an extension of a blog. Whereas a blog usually is created by an individual (or maybe a small group) and might have an attached discussion board, a **wikilog**, or **wikiblog** or **wiki**, is essentially a blog that enables everyone to participate as a peer. Anyone can add, delete, or change content. It is like a loose-leaf notebook with a pencil and eraser left in a public place. Anyone can read it, scrawl notes, tear out a page, and so on. Creating a wikilog is a *collaborative* process. For description and details, see Tapscott and Wiliams (2006) and usemod.com/cgi-bin/mb.pl?WikiLog. For further discussion, see Chapter 8 and en.wikipedia.org/wiki/wiki. A commercial use of a wiki is presented in the Real-World Case at the end of this chapter.

wikilog (wikiblog or wiki)
A blog that allows everyone to participate as a peer; anyone can add, delete, or change content.

RSS

RSS (short for "Rich Site Summary," "RDF site summary," or "Really Simple Syndication") is an XML format for syndicating Web content (A Web site that wants to allow other sites to publish some of its content creates an RSS document and registers the document with an RSS publisher. It is most often used to publish frequently updated digital content, such as blogs, news stories, or podcasts. A user who can access RSS-distributed content can use the content on a different site. This enables the *sharing* of Web content. Users can view it as a distributable "What's New" on a site, and it is popular with bloggers. Major sites such as CNET, BBC, CNN, Disney, TechTarget, ZDNet, Red Herring, and Wired use RSS to share content among themselves. RSS offers a number of key benefits to users:

RSS
An XML format for syndicating and sharing Web content.

- **Timeliness.** Users can automatically receive updates from their favorite Web sites when new content becomes available.
- **Efficiency.** Users can quickly scan over headlines and summaries and only read the content of interests.
- **Coverage.** Users receive updates from multiple Web sites into one location—their RSS reader or aggregator.

RSS technology also solves problems such as long delays caused by increased site traffic and expedites the gathering and distribution of news. For an RSS tutorial, see mnot.net/rss/tutorial. According to eMarketer (2005), RSS is one of the "top 10 e-business trends for 2005." Several advertisers have begun to use RSS as a platform for targeted advertisements. For details see en.wikipedia.org/wiki/RSS_(file_format).

Podcasting A **podcast** is a media file that is distributed by subscription (paid or unpaid) over the Internet using syndication feeds (such as RSS news feeds) for playback on mobile devices and personal computers. Like "radio," it can mean both the content and the method of syndication. A podcast is a collection of audio files in MP3 format, represented by an RSS 2.0 news feed. The host or author of a podcast is often called a *podcaster*, who can offer direct download or streaming of its content. A podcast distinguishes itself from other digital audio formats by its ability to download automatically using software capable of reading feed formats such as RSS.

podcast
A media file that is distributed over the Internet using syndication feeds for playback on mobile devices and personal computers. As with the term *radio*, it can mean both the content and the method of syndication.

The term *podcast* is derived from Apple's portable music player, the iPod. A pod refers to a container of some sort; thus, the idea of broadcasting to a container, or *pod*, correctly describes the process of podcasting.

Although podcasters' Web sites might also offer direct download or streaming content, a podcast is distinguished from other digital audio formats by its ability to be downloaded automatically, using software capable of reading feed formats such as RSS.

Podcasting is emerging as an e-commerce tool (see Gibson 2007 and Weber 2007). For example, podcasts create a new channel for Web sites to communicate with customers. Because podcasts are audio files, it enables companies to deliver audio-specific content, including music, speeches, radio-style presentations, and more (see en.wikipedia.org/wiki/Podcasting).

MASHUPS

mashup
A Web site that combines content data from more than one source to create a new user experience.

Mashups are tools that help users combine data and other content from two (or more) Web sites to create new applications. An example is housingmaps.com. The site plots apartments for rent and homes for sale on Craigslist.org on Google Map. Users can preview a listing by simply clicking one of the pushpins. A similar service is available at bidnearby.com, where users can search and locate classifieds from Craigslist as well as local physical auctions.

For a list of thousands of mashups, their traffic, and ratings, see programmableweb.com. Also, see several articles and blogs by R. D. Hof at *BusinessWeek Online.* (e.g., July 25, 2005 and February 17, 2006).

The following are some additional applications of mashups:

▶ Pubwalk (pubwalk.com) combines bar listings with reviews from City Search with Google Map. Each pushpin has a pop-up window with bar (or restaurant) information, including rating and pictures. Finally, you can plot and print the driving directions to get to a desired one!

▶ Google Transit (google.com/transit) lets you plan public transportation trips in dozens of cities. After you provide the addresses from and to, the planner gives directions, combining walking, buses, and trains, and approximates travel times and fares. Finally, you can compare, and have an alternative to, the cost of driving.

Section 2.7 ▶ REVIEW QUESTIONS

1. Define blog and blogger.
2. Discuss the critical features that distinguish blogs from regular Web pages.
3. Describe the potential advantages and risks of blogs.
4. Define wikis and compare them to blogs.
5. Discuss the commercial uses of blogs.
6. Define RSS. What can it be used for?
7. Define podcasting.
8. Describe mashups.

MANAGERIAL ISSUES

1. **What about intermediaries?** Many EC applications will change the role of intermediaries. This might create conflict between a company and its distributors. It might also create opportunities. In many cases, distributors will need to change their roles. This is a sensitive issue that needs to be planned for during the transformation to the e-business plan.

2. **Should we auction?** A major strategic issue is whether to use auctions as a sales channel. Auctions do have some limitations, and forward auctions might create conflicts with other distribution channels. If a company decides to use auctions, it needs to select auction mechanisms and determine a pricing strategy. These decisions determine the success of the auction and the ability to attract and

retain visitors on the site. Auctions also require support services. Decisions about how to provide these services and to what extent to use business partners are critical to the success of high-volume auctions.

3. **Should we barter?** Bartering can be an interesting strategy, especially for companies that lack cash, need special material or machinery, and have surplus resources. However, the valuation of what is bought or sold may be hard to determine, and the tax implications in some countries are not clear.

4. **Should we sponsor blogs and wikis?** Although the cost of Web 2.0 tools is low, issues regarding security and content control need to be examined (see Chapter 8). Blogs and wikis can be very beneficial in some, but not all, cases. Consult a legal expert prior to a final decision.

5. **Can we blog for business?** With one new blog created every second, the hype surrounding the blogosphere is understandable. Everyone, it seems, is blogging. Is blogging just a hobby? Can we make real (big or small) money from our blogs? How can we turn our passion into an online business? Many companies are beginning to use blogging successfully.

SUMMARY

In this chapter, you learned about the following EC issues as they relate to the learning objectives.

1. **E-marketplaces and their components.** A marketspace, or e-marketplace, is a virtual market that does not suffer from limitations of space, time, or borders. As such, it can be very effective. Its major components include customers, sellers, products (some digital), infrastructure, front-end processes, back-end activities, electronic intermediaries, other business partners, and support services.

2. **The role of intermediaries.** The role of intermediaries will change as e-markets develop; some will be eliminated (disintermediation), others will change their roles and prosper (reintermediation). In the B2B area, for example, e-distributors connect manufacturers with buyers by aggregating electronic catalogs of many suppliers. New value-added services that range from content creation to syndication are mushrooming.

3. **The major types of e-marketplaces.** In the B2C area, there are storefronts and e-malls. In the B2B area, there are private and public e-marketplaces, which may be vertical (within one industry) or horizontal (across different industries). Different types of portals provide access to e-marketplaces.

4. **Electronic catalogs, search engines, and shopping carts.** The major mechanisms in e-markets are electronic catalogs, search engines, software (intelligent) agents, and electronic shopping carts. These mechanisms facilitate EC by providing a user-friendly shopping environment.

5. **Types of auctions and their characteristics.** In forward auctions, bids from buyers are placed sequentially, either in increasing (English and Yankee) mode or in decreasing (Dutch and free-fall) mode. In reverse auctions, buyers place an RFQ and suppliers submit offers in one or several rounds. In "name-your-own-price" auctions, buyers specify how much they are willing to pay for a product or service and an intermediary tries to find a supplier to fulfill the request.

6. **The benefits and limitations of auctions.** The major benefits for sellers are the ability to reach many buyers, to sell quickly, and to save on commissions to intermediaries. Buyers have a chance to obtain bargains and collectibles while shopping from their homes. The major limitation is the possibility of fraud.

7. **Bartering and negotiating.** Electronic bartering can greatly facilitate the swapping of goods and services among organizations, thanks to improved search and matching capabilities, which is done in bartering exchanges. Software agents can facilitate online negotiation.

8. **The major mechanisms of Web 2.0.** Many organizations are exploiting blogs and wikis to promote collaboration, advertise products and services, obtain feedback from customers, and more. Both blogs and wikis are authored by individuals, but wikis can be edited. Other mechanisms include RSS and podcating for content distribution, and mashups for content integration.

KEY TERMS

QUESTIONS FOR DISCUSSION

1. Compare marketplaces with marketspaces. What are the advantages and limitations of each?

2. Compare and contrast competition in traditional markets with that in digital markets.

3. Explain why sell-side and buy-side marketplaces in the same company are usually separated, whereas in an exchange they are combined.

4. Discuss the need for portals in EC.

5. Discuss the advantages of dynamic pricing over fixed pricing. What are the potential disadvantages of dynamic pricing?

6. The "name-your-own-price" model is considered a reverse auction. However, this model does not include RFQs or consecutive bidding. Why is it called a reverse auction?

7. You want to sell your old bicycle, and you are considering auctioning it at eBay or advertising it on Craigslist.org. Discuss the two options.

8. Compare wikis and blogs.

9. Relate blogs and wikis to collaboration.

INTERNET EXERCISES

1. Visit **bluenile.com, diamond.com,** and **jewelry exchange.com**. Compare the sites. Comment on the similarities and the differences.

2. Enter **blogger.com** and find out how to create your own blog. Create a blog based on your personal interests.

3. Visit **ticketmaster.com, ticketonline.com,** and other sites that sell event tickets online. Assess the competition in online ticket sales. What services do the different sites provide?

4. Examine how bartering is conducted online at **tradeaway. com, barteryourservices.com, u-exchange.com,** and **barter-www.com**. Compare the functionalities and ease of use of these sites.

5. Enter **pages.ebay.com/mobile** and investigate the use of eBay via cell phone.

6. Enter **mfgquote.com** and review the process by which buyers can send RFQs to merchants of

their choice. Evaluate all of the online services provided by the company. Write a report based on your findings.

7. Enter eBay's online partner (**elance.com**). Post a project and see how professionals bid on this work. Summarize your experience.

8. Enter **respond.com** and send a request for a product or a service. Once you receive replies, select the best deal. You have no obligation to buy. Write a short report based on your experience.

9. Enter **icollector.com** and review the process used to auction art. Find support services, such as currency conversion and shipping. Take the tour of the site. Prepare a report on buying collectibles online.

10. Enter **yahoo.com** and find what personalization methods it uses.

11. Enter Timberland Boot Studio (**timberland.com**) and design a pair of boots. Compare it to building your own sneakers at **nike.com**.

TEAM ASSIGNMENTS AND ROLE PLAYING

1. Reread the opening case and discuss the following:
   a. Discuss the key success factors for Blue Nile.
   b. Amazon.com makes only a 15 percent margin on the products it sells. This enables Amazon.com to sell diamond earrings for $1,000 (traditional jewelers charge $1,700 for the same). Do you think that Amazon.com will succeed in selling this type of jewelry as Blue Nile did in selling expensive engagement rings?
   c. Competition between Blue Nile and Amazon.com will continue to increase. In your opinion, which one will win (visit their Web sites and see how they sell jewelry).
   d. Why is "commoditization" so important in the diamond business?
   e. Compare the following three sites: **diamond.com**, **ice.com**, and **bluenile.com**.
   f. Follow the performance of Blue Nile's stock since 2003 (symbol: NILE).

2. Each team examines two or three of the following sites: **prosper.com**, **swapthing.com**, **swaptree.com**, **peerflix.com**, **lala.com**, **swapvillage.com**, **bigvine.com**, etc. Compare their business and revenue models.

3. Create an eBay group. Enter **ebay.com**, click the "Community" button, click "Groups," sign in to enter, click "Start Group," and follow the instructions to create a group of five members in your class and select a common interest (e.g., collecting stamps or toy trains). You will moderate the group, invite the group to discussions, and create polls. Write a report on your experience.

Real-World Case

STORMHOEK VINEYARDS EXCELS WITH WEB 2.0 TOOLS

Stormhoek Vineyards is a small winery in South Africa (*stormhoek.com*). Annual sales in 2005 were only $3 million, but with Web 2.0 technologies sales grew to $10 million in 2007 and are projected to reach $30 million in 2010. The company devised a marketing campaign called "100 Geek Dinners in 100 Days." Each dinner was to be hosted by one person and used for wine tasting by several dozen guests in the United Kingdom and the United States. How can you get 100 people to host a wine tasting and how do you find 40 to 60 guests for each event? The answer: Web 2.0 technologies. Here is what the company did:

▶ **Blogging.** The CEO of Orbital Wines, Stormhoek's parent company, in collaboration with a well-known blogger, Mr. Macleod, wrote dozens of blog entries about the events, soliciting volunteer hosts, including bloggers and wine enthusiasts.

▶ **Wiki.** Each volunteer was provided with contact and location information on a wiki. The wiki technology was mainly used for customer relations management (CRM). The wiki included wine-related cartoons and other entertainment and advertising.

▶ **Podcasts.** Web-content feed (enabled by an RSS) was used to push information to participants' inboxes. Information included wine news, wine analyses, and descriptions of the 100 parties.

▶ **Video Links.** The corporate blog supported video links. Bloggers could cut and paste embedded links to YouTube videos (Chapter 8) directly into an entry.

▶ **Shopping.** The blog site acted as a portal to Stormhoek and included support for order placement and shopping carts for promotional "swag," such as posters and T-shirts.

▶ **Mashups.** An interactive map was integrated into the wiki using mashup software. This allowed dinner hosts to display a map of the location of the event. Also, guests could click an event on the map to make a reservation, get a reservation confirmation, send a query to the host, and receive photos of the house and the hosts. The company's wiki also had a link to the host-blogger's home page.

The parties were attended by over 4,500 people, and the publicity enabled the vineyard to triple sales in 2 years (mainly in the UK). The only problem was a profusion of blog spam—random comments that were automatically posted by marketers for promotions. This required a daily purging and cleaning of the blog from unwanted postings.

The blogging resulted in word-of-mouth publicity (see Chapter 4). The blogging was done by a professional blogger (Hugh Macleod at *gapingvoid.com*). The blog offered a free bottle of wine. Macleod also organized the 100 dinners described earlier. RSS pioneer Dave Winer attended one of the dinners. A final word: Stormhoek wine is really good! Viral marketing cannot sell bad wine.

Sources: Compiled from Bennett (2007), McNichol (2007), and *stormhoek.com* (accessed January 2008).

Questions

1. What was the corporate blog used for?
2. What were the hosts' blogs used for?
3. What capabilities were introduced by the mashups?
4. How did the wiki help in communication and collaboration?
5. Why do you think the Web 2.0 technologies were successful in increasing sales?
6. What is blog spam and why is it a problem?

BUILD-TO-ORDER PRODUCTION

The concept of *build-to-order* means that a firm starts to make a product or service only after an order for it is placed. It also is known as *demand-driven manufacturing (DDM), customization, personalization,* and *pull technology.* This concept is as old as commerce itself and was the only method of production until the Industrial Revolution. According to this concept, if a person needs a pair of shoes, he or she goes to a shoemaker, who takes the person's measurements. The person negotiates quality, style, and price and pays a down payment. The shoemaker buys the materials and makes a customized product for the customer. Customized products are expensive, and it takes a long time to finish them. The Industrial Revolution introduced a new way of thinking about production.

The Industrial Revolution started with the concept of dividing work into small parts. Such division of labor makes the work simpler, requiring less training for employees. It also allows for specialization. Different employees become experts in executing certain tasks. Because the work segments are simpler, it is easier to automate them. As machines were invented to make products, the concept of build-to-market developed. To implement build-to-market, it was necessary to design standard products, produce them, store them, and then sell them.

The creation of standard products by automation drove prices down, and demand accelerated. The solution to the problem of increased demand was mass production. In mass production, a company produces large amounts of standard products at a very low cost and then "pushes" them to consumers. Thus began the need for sales and marketing organizations. Specialized sales forces resulted in increased competition and the desire to sell in wider, and more remote, markets. This model also required the creation of large factories and specialized departments, such as accounting and personnel, to manage the activities in the factories. With mass production, factory workers personally did not know the customers and frequently did not care about customers' needs or product quality. However, the products were inexpensive and good enough to fuel demand, and thus the concept became a dominant one. Mass production also required inventory systems at various places in the supply chain, which were based on forecasted demand. If the forecasted demand was wrong, the inventories were incorrect. Thus, companies were always trying to achieve the right balance between not having enough inventory to meet demand and having too much inventory on hand.

As society became more affluent, the demand for customized products increased. Manufacturers had to meet the demand for customized products to satisfy customers. As long as the demand for customized products was small, it could be met. Cars, for example, have long been produced using this model. Customers were asked to pay a premium for customization and wait a long time to receive the customized product, and they were willing to do so. Note that the process starts with product configuration (Blecker 2006); namely, the customer decides what the product is going to look like, what operations it will perform, and what capabilities it will have (e.g., the functionalities in Dell).

Slowly, the demand for customized products and services increased. Burger King introduced the concept of "having it your way," and manufacturers sought ways to provide customized products in large quantities, which is the essence of mass customization, as pioneered by Dell. Such solutions were usually enhanced by some kind of information technology. The introduction of customized personal computers (PCs) by Dell was so successful that many other industries wanted to try mass customization. EC can facilitate customization, even mass customization. In many cases, EC is doing it via personalization (Anke and Sundaram 2006). To understand how companies can use EC for customization, let's first compare mass production, also known as a push system, and mass customization, also known as a pull system, as shown in Exhibit 2A.1.

Notice that one important area in the supply chain is order taking. Using EC, a customer can self-configure the desired product online. The order is received in seconds. Once the order is verified and payment arranged, the order is sent electronically to the production floor. This saves time and money. For complex products, customers may collaborate in real time with the manufacturer's designers, as is done at Cisco Systems. Again, time and money are saved and errors are reduced due

EXHIBIT 2A.1   Push Versus Pull Production Systems

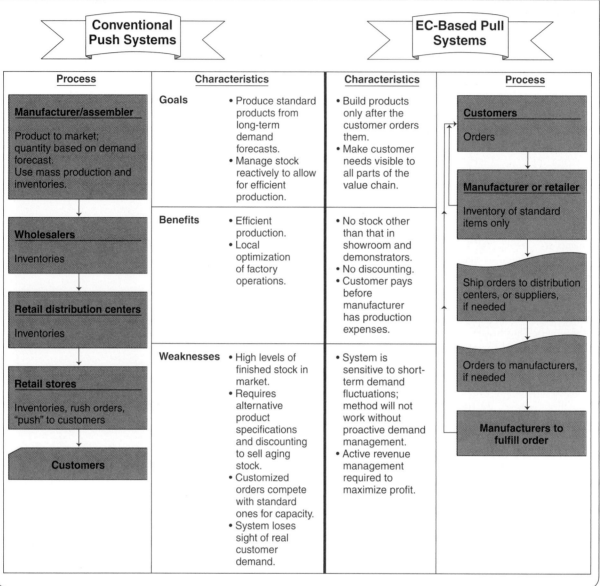

Conventional Push Systems		EC-Based Pull Systems	
Process	**Characteristics**	**Characteristics**	**Process**
Manufacturer/assembler Product to market; quantity based on demand forecast. Use mass production and inventories.	**Goals** • Produce standard products from long-term demand forecasts. • Manage stock reactively to allow for efficient production.	• Build products only after the customer orders them. • Make customer needs visible to all parts of the value chain.	**Customers** Orders
Wholesalers Inventories	**Benefits** • Efficient production. • Local optimization of factory operations.	• No stock other than that in showroom and demonstrators. • No discounting. • Customer pays before manufacturer has production expenses.	**Manufacturer or retailer** Inventory of standard items only Ship orders to distribution centers, or suppliers, if needed
Retail distribution centers Inventories			
Retail stores Inventories, rush orders, "push" to customers **Customers**	**Weaknesses** • High levels of finished stock in market. • Requires alternative product specifications and discounting to sell aging stock. • Customized orders compete with standard ones for capacity. • System loses sight of real customer demand.	• System is sensitive to short-term demand fluctuations; method will not work without proactive demand management. • Active revenue management required to maximize profit.	Orders to manufacturers, if needed **Manufacturers to fulfill order**

to better communication and collaboration. Other contributions of EC are that the customers' needs are visible to all partners in the order fulfillment chain (fewer delays, faster response time), inventories are reduced due to rapid communication, and digitizable products and services can be delivered electronically.

A key issue in mass customization is knowing what the customers want. In many cases, the seller can simply ask the customer to configure the product or service. In other cases, the seller tries to predict what the customer wants. EC is very helpful in this area due to the use of online market research methods such as collaborative filtering (see Chapter 4 and Chandra 2005). Using collaborative filtering, a company can discover what each customer wants without asking the customer directly. Such market research is accomplished more cheaply by a machine than by human researchers.

From the production point of view, EC also can enable mass customization. In the factory, for example, IT in general and e-commerce in particular can help in expediting the production changeover from one item to another. Also, because most mass production is based on the assembly of standard components, EC can help a company create the production process for a product in minutes and identify needed components and their location. Furthermore, a production schedule can be generated automatically, and needed resources can be deployed, including money. This is why many industries, and particularly the auto manufacturers, are planning to move to build-to-order using EC. By doing so, they are expecting huge cost reductions, shorter order-to-delivery times, and lower inventory costs.

Mass customization on a large scale is not easy to attain (Zipkin 2001; Warschat et al. 2005), but if performed properly, it may become the dominant model in many industries.

RETAILING IN ELECTRONIC COMMERCE: PRODUCTS AND SERVICES

Learning Objectives

Upon completion of this chapter, you will be able to:

1. Describe electronic retailing (e-tailing) and its characteristics.
2. Define and describe the primary e-tailing business models.
3. Describe how online travel and tourism services operate and their impact on the industry.
4. Discuss the online employment market, including its participants, benefits, and limitations.
5. Describe online real estate services.
6. Discuss online stock-trading services.
7. Discuss cyberbanking and online personal finance.
8. Describe on-demand delivery of groceries and similar products/services.
9. Describe the delivery of digital products and online entertainment.
10. Discuss various e-tail consumer aids, including comparison-shopping aids.
11. Describe disintermediation and other B2C strategic issues.

Content

AMAZON.COM: TAKING E-TAILING TO THE NEXT LEVEL

The Opportunity

It was not a business problem, but an opportunity that faced entrepreneur Jeff Bezos: He saw the huge potential for retail sales over the Internet and selected books as the most logical product for e-tailing. In July 1995, Bezos started Amazon.com, an e-tailing pioneer, offering books via an electronic catalog from its Web site (*amazon.com*).

Over the years, the company has recognized that it must continually enhance its business models and electronic store by expanding product selection, improving the customer's experience, and adding services and alliances. Also, early on the company recognized the importance of order fulfillment and warehousing. It invested hundreds of millions of dollars in building physical warehouses designed for shipping small packages to hundreds of thousands of customers. Amazon.com's challenge was, and remains, how to succeed where many have failed—namely, how to compete in selling consumer products online, showing profit and a reasonable rate of return on the huge investment it has made.

Reaching Out to Customers

In addition to its initial electronic bookstore, Amazon.com has expanded its offerings to a vast array of products and services segmented into three broad categories: media (books, music, DVDs, etc.); electronics and other merchandise (including its new wireless reading device, "Kindle"; office supplies; cameras; toys; etc.); and other (nonretail activities, such as Web services, Amazon Enterprise Solutions, etc.). Key features of the Amazon.com superstore are easy browsing, searching, and ordering; useful product information, reviews, recommendations, and personalization; broad selection; low prices; secure payment systems; and efficient order fulfillment.

The Amazon.com Web site has a number of features that make the online shopping experience more enjoyable. Its "Gift Ideas" section features seasonally appropriate gift ideas and services. AmazonConnect allows customers to select their favorite authors, read about them, and then receive e-mails from those authors.

Amazon.com also offers various marketplace services. Amazon Auctions hosts and operates auctions on behalf of individuals and small businesses throughout the world. The Shops service hosts electronic storefronts for a monthly fee, offering small businesses the opportunity to have customized storefronts supported by the richness of Amazon.com's order-fulfillment processing. Customers can use Web-enabled cell phones, PDAs, or Pocket PCs to access Amazon.com and shop anywhere, anytime. Amazon.com also can be accessed via AT&T's #121 voice service. Amazon.com is recognized as an online leader in creating sales through customer intimacy and customer relationship management (CRM), which are cultivated by informative marketing front ends and one-to-one advertisements. In addition, sales are supported by highly automated, efficient back-end systems. When a customer makes a return visit to Amazon.com, a cookie file (see Chapter 4) identifies the user and says, for example, "Welcome back, Sarah Shopper," and then proceeds to recommend new books from the same genre of the customer's previous purchases and a range of other items. It also provides detailed product descriptions and ratings to help consumers make informed purchase decisions. The site has an efficient search engine and other shopping aids. Amazon.com has a superb warehousing system that gives the company an advantage over the competition.

Customers can personalize their accounts and manage orders online with the patented "1-Click" order feature. 1-Click includes an electronic wallet (see Chapter 11), which enables shoppers to place an order in a secure manner without the need to enter their address, credit card number, and other information each time they shop and allows customers to view their order status, cancel or combine orders that have not yet entered the shipping process, edit the shipping options and addresses on unshipped orders, modify the payment method for unshipped orders, and more.

In 1997, Amazon.com started an extensive associates program. By 2006, the company had more than 2 million partners worldwide that refer customers to Amazon.com. Amazon.com pays a 4 to 10 percent commission on any resulting sale. Starting in 2000, Amazon.com has undertaken alliances with major "trusted partners" that provide knowledgeable entry into new markets. For example, clicking "Office Supplies" allows customers either to select from Amazon's office supplies or to browse those of Office Depot; clicking "Health and Personal Care" allows customers to benefit from great deals offered by Weight Watchers. In yet another extension of its services, in September 2001 Amazon signed an agreement with Borders Group Inc., providing Amazon.com's users with the option of picking up their merchandise at Borders' physical bookstores (In-Store pickup). Amazon.com also is becoming a Web fulfillment contractor for national chains such as Target. Amazon.com also has its own search engine, called A9.com (*a9.com*), and offers a range of Web services to developers (Amazon Web Services).

The Results

Amazon.com maintained its position as the number one e-tailer in 2006, generating revenues of $11 billion, with a net profit of $190 million. Annual sales for Amazon.com have trended upward, driven largely by product diversification and its international presence. This pioneer e-tailer now offers over 17 million book, music, and DVD/video titles to some 20 million customers. Amazon.com also offers several features for international customers, including over 1 million Japanese-language titles.

In January 2002, Amazon.com declared its first profit—for the 2001 fourth quarter. However, despite increasing sales and net profits, in percentage terms Amazon.com saw a drop in profitability in 2006, which it attributed to huge spending on further developing its technology infrastructure and its investment in the Amazon Prime discount shipping program. Like all businesses—and especially e-tailing ones—Amazon.com, the king of e-tailers, which has shown all others the potential of B2C EC, will continue to walk the fine line of profitability, at least in the short run.

Sources: Compiled from *BusinessWire* (2006), Parker (2006), and *Internetretailer.com* (2006a).

WHAT WE CAN LEARN . . .

The case of Amazon.com, the most recognized e-tailer in the world, demonstrates some of the features and managerial issues related to e-tailing. It demonstrates the evolution of e-tailing, some of the problems encountered by e-tailers, and the solutions employed by Amazon.com to expand its business. It also is indicative of a key trend in Internet retailing: that the biggest online retailers are still growing and becoming more dominant, with the top 500 e-retailers accounting for 61 percent ($83.6 billion) of all online sales in 2007 (Hanks 2007). However, some experts argue that online retailers will need to better understand customer behaviors and preferences if they are to achieve a better convergence between technological capability and customer desires (*Internetretailer.com* 2006b). In this chapter, we will look at the delivery of both products and services online to individual customers. We also will discuss e-tailing successes and failures.

3.1 INTERNET MARKETING AND ELECTRONIC RETAILING

The Amazon.com case illustrates how commerce can be conducted on the Internet. Indeed, the amount and percentage of goods and services sold on the Internet is increasing rapidly, despite the failure of many dot-com companies. According to *Internetretailer.com* (2007a), approximately 45 percent of adult U.S. Internet users shop online and/or research offline sales online. With estimates of 150 million Internet users in the United States, this suggests that in 2006 there were approximately 80 million online shoppers. However, as the number of Internet users reaches saturation, the rate of increase of online shoppers will slow. One of the challenges for electronic retailers, therefore, is to increase the amount spent online. As discussed in Chapters 1 and 2, companies have many reasons to market and sell their goods and services online. Innovative marketing strategies and a deep understanding of online consumer behavior and preferences will be required for sustained success in a competitive online environment.

This chapter presents an overview of Internet retailing, its diversity, prospects, and limitations. (For more-detailed analysis, see Soopramanien and Robertson 2007.) Retailing, especially when conducted in a new medium, must be supported by an understanding of consumer buying behavior, market research, and advertising, topics that will be presented in Chapter 4. Let's begin our discussion of EC products and services with an overview of electronic retailing.

OVERVIEW OF ELECTRONIC RETAILING

A retailer is a sales *intermediary,* a seller that operates between manufacturers and customers. Even though many manufacturers sell directly to consumers, they supplement their sales through wholesalers and retailers (a *multichannel approach*). In the physical world, retailing is done in stores (or factory outlets) that customers must visit in order to make a purchase. Companies that produce a large number of products, such as Procter & Gamble, must use retailers for efficient distribution. However, even if a company sells only a relatively few products (e.g., Kodak), it still might need retailers to reach a large number of customers.

Catalog sales offer companies and customers a relief from the constraints of space and time: Catalogs free a retailer from the need for a physical store from which to distribute products, and customers can browse catalogs on their own time. With the ubiquity of the Internet, the next logical step was for retailing to move online. Retailing conducted over the Internet is called **electronic retailing**, or **e-tailing**, and those who conduct retail business online are called **e-tailers**. E-tailing also can be conducted through auctions. E-tailing makes it easier for a manufacturer to sell directly to the customer, cutting out the intermediary (e.g., Dell and Godiva in Chapter 1). This chapter examines the various types of e-tailing and related issues.

The concept of retailing and e-tailing implies sales of goods and/or services to individual customers—that is, B2C EC. However, the distinction between B2C and B2B EC is not always clear. For example, Amazon.com sells books mostly to individuals (B2C), but it also sells to corporations (B2B). Amazon.com's chief rival in selling books online, Barnes & Noble (barnesandnoble.com), has a special division that caters only to business customers. Wal-Mart (walmart.com) sells to both individuals and businesses (via Sam's Club). Dell sells its computers to both consumers and businesses from dell.com, Staples sells to both markets at staples.com, and insurance sites sell to both individuals and corporations.

electronic retailing (e-tailing)
Retailing conducted online, over the Internet.

e-tailers
Retailers who sell over the Internet.

SIZE AND GROWTH OF THE B2C MARKET

The statistics for the volume of B2C EC sales, including forecasts for future sales, come from many sources. Reported amounts of online sales *deviate substantially* based on how the numbers are derived, and thus it is often difficult to obtain a consistent and coherent picture of the growth of EC. Some of the variation stems from the use of different definitions and classifications of EC. For example, when tallying financial data some analysts include the investment costs in Internet infrastructure, whereas others include only the value of the actual transactions conducted via the Internet. Another issue is how the items for sale are categorized. Some sources combine certain products and services; others do not. Some sources include online travel sales in the data for EC retail; others do not. Sometimes different time periods are used in the measurement. When reading data about B2C EC sales, therefore, it is very important that care is taken in interpreting the figures.

The sites listed in Exhibit 3.1 provide statistics on e-tailing as well as on other Internet and EC activities. Typical statistics used in describing e-tailing and consumer behavior include Internet usage by demographic (online sales by age, gender, country, etc.); online sales by item; online sales by vendor; and buying patterns online.

The following are some general statistics about online sales. Data from the U.S. Census Bureau (2007) suggest that B2C EC grew by some 25.2 percent in 2004, to $71 billion that increased to $88 billion in 2005, an increase of 23.9 percent. This 2005 figure, however, although large in dollar terms and representing extraordinary growth over the past decade, still sees B2C EC sales as representing only about 2.4 percent of total retail sales in the United States. Preliminary data for the third quarter of 2007 showed that EC retail had increased to approximately 3.4 percent of total retail. However, data from the U.S. Census Bureau do not include online travel. When travel is included in the data, B2C sales fall in the range of $165 billion, as estimated by Forrester (Mulpuru 2006), to $176.4 billion, as estimated by ClickZ.com (Burns 2006). Both figures suggest that B2C sales continue to grow in excess of 20 percent per annum, with expectations of total sales of $211.4 billion for 2006, with some suggesting that by the end of 2006 online sales could represent 4 percent of total retail sales (*Internetretailer.com* 2006b). This is compared against growth rates of approximately 8.1 percent in total retail sales in the United States (U.S. Census Bureau 2006). Forrester Research expects U.S. online sales to grow from $132 billion in 2006 to $271 billion in 2011, still comprising just 9 percent of overall retail sales (Linn 2007). Also, profitability is up, and marketing costs per order are declining.

According to comScore Networks, Internet sales exceeded the $100 billion mark for the period January 1 through December 23, 2006. The total was the first time online retail (excluding travel) surpassed $100 billion (*DiamondView. com* 2006).

EXHIBIT 3.1	**Representative Sources of EC Statistics**

AM Research (*amresearch.org*)
Business 2.0 (*business2.com*)
ClickZ Network (*clickz.com*)
Fulcrum Velocity Analytics (*cyberdialogue.com*)
DoubleClick (*doubleclick.com*)
Ecommerce Info Center (*ecominfocenter.com*)
Forrester Research (*forrester.com*)
Gartner (*gartner.com*)
Gomez (*gomez.com*)
JupiterResearch (*jupiterresearch.com*)
Lionbridge (*lionbridge.com*)
Nielsen/Netratings (*nielsen-netratings.com*)
Ominture SiteCatalyst (*omniture.com*)
Shop.org (*shop.org*)
U.S. Census Bureau (*census.gov/estats*)
Yankee Group (*yankeegroup.com*)

WHAT SELLS WELL ON THE INTERNET

With approximately 80 million shoppers online in the United States in 2007, e-tailers appreciate the need to provide excellent choice and service to an ever-increasing cohort of potential customers. Hundreds of thousands of items are available on the Web from numerous vendors. Exhibit 3.2 shows categories that are all selling well online. For some current trends in B2C see Online File W3.1.

CHARACTERISTICS OF SUCCESSFUL E-TAILING

Many of the same basic principles that apply to retail success also apply to e-tail success. Sound business thinking, visionary leadership, thorough competitive analysis and financial analysis, and the articulation of a well–thought-out EC strategy are essential. So, too, is ensuring appropriate infrastructure, particularly a stable and scalable technology infrastructure to support the online and physical aspects of EC business operations. Newly required capabilities (e.g., capabilities in logistics and distribution) might need to be obtained through external strategic alliances. Offering quality merchandise at good prices, coupled with excellent service, and cross-channel coordination and integration in which customers can almost seamlessly operate between the online and physical environments of a business are also important elements in successful e-tailing. In a sense, the online and traditional channels are not very different. However, e-tailers can offer expanded consumer services not offered by traditional retailers. For a comparison of e-tailing and retailing, see Exhibit 3.3.

With all else being equal in the online environment, goods with the following characteristics are expected to facilitate higher sales volumes:

- High brand recognition (e.g., Lands' End, Dell, Sony)
- A guarantee provided by highly reliable or well-known vendors (e.g., Dell, L.L.Bean)
- Digitized format (e.g., software, music, or videos)
- Relatively inexpensive items (e.g., office supplies, vitamins)
- Frequently purchased items (e.g., groceries, prescription drugs)
- Commodities with standard specifications (e.g., books, CDs, airline tickets), making physical inspection unimportant
- Well-known packaged items that cannot be opened even in a traditional store (e.g., foods, chocolates, vitamins)

The next section examines business models that have proved successful in e-tailing.

Section 3.1 ▶ REVIEW QUESTIONS

1. Describe the nature of B2C EC.
2. What sells well in B2C?
3. What are the characteristics of high-volume products and services?
4. Describe the major trends in B2C.

EXHIBIT 3.2   What Sells Well on the Internet?

Category	Description
Travel	Expedia and Travelocity are major players in this category. Online travel agents offer a range of services, including travel booking, hotel reservations, car rentals, and vacation packages.
Computer hardware and software	Dell and Gateway are the major online vendors of computer hardware and software. Computer hardware and software is the largest category of products sold online.
Consumer electronics	According to the U.S. Census Bureau (2006), 59 percent of consumer electronics are now sold online. These include digital cameras, printers, scanners, and wireless devices.
Office supplies	B2C and B2B sales of office supplies are increasing rapidly, all over the world, as companies increasingly use the Internet to place orders for stationery and the like.
Sport and fitness goods	Sporting goods sell very well on the Internet. However, it is difficult to measure the exact amount of sales because only a few e-tailers sell sporting goods exclusively online (e.g., *fogdog.com*).
Books and music	Amazon.com and Barnesandnoble.com are the major sellers of books. However, hundreds of other e-tailers sell books on the Internet, especially specialized books (e.g., technical books, children's books).
Toys	Total retail sales of toys (both traditional and online) dropped by about 4 percent in 2005. However, the proportion of sales of toys sold online increased to about 6 percent in 2006. (Direct Marketing Association 2006). In 2007, online sales of toys dropped again due to toy recalls, specifically those toys made in China (Biz Report 2007).
Health and beauty	A large variety of health and beauty products—from vitamins to cosmetics and fragrances—are sold online by most large retailers and by specialty stores.
Entertainment	This is another area where dozens of products, ranging from tickets to events (e.g., *ticketmaster.com*) to paid fantasy games (see Section 3.8), are embraced by millions of shoppers worldwide.
Apparel and clothing	With the possibility of buying customized shirts, pants, and even shoes, the online sale of apparel also is growing. Guaranteed returns policies and improving features on fitting clothing without first trying it on have increased the customers' comfort zone for buying apparel online.
Jewelry	Online sales of jewelry are booming. With claims of prices about 40 percent less than would be paid in traditional stores, the trend toward online jewelry sales is likely to continue.
Cars	The sale of cars over the Internet is just beginning (people still like to "kick the tires"), but could be one of the top sellers on the Internet in the near future. Customers like the build-to-order capabilities, but even selling used cars online has advantages and is increasing rapidly. Support services such as financing, warranties, and insurance also are selling well online.
Services	Sales in service industries, especially travel, stock trading, electronic banking, real estate, and insurance, are increasing—more than doubling every year in some cases.
Pet supplies	Pet supplies is a new category in the top-seller list. As family pets become more and more integrated as members of the family, online spending on toys, edible treats, food, pet accessories, and veterinary products and services is soaring.
Others	Many other products, ranging from prescription drugs to custom-made shoes are offered on the Internet. Many items are specialized or niche products.

Sources: Biz Report (2007), U.S. Census Bureau (2006), and Direct Marketing Association (2006).

EXHIBIT 3.3   Retailing Versus E-Tailing

	Retailers	E-Tailers
Physical expansion (when revenue increases as the number of visitors grows)	• Expansion of retailing platform to include more locations and space	• Expansion of e-commerce platform to include increased server capacity and distribution facilities
Physical expansion (when revenue does not increase as the number of visitors grows)	• May not need physical expansion • Expand marketing effort to turn "window shoppers" into effective shoppers	• May still need physical expansion to provide sustainable services • Expand marketing to turn "pane shoppers" into effective shoppers
Technology	• Sales automation technologies such as POS systems	• Front-end technologies benefit from browsing • Back-end technologies • "Information" technologies
Customer relations	• More stable due to nonanonymous contacts • More tolerable of disputes due to visibility • "Physical" relationships	• Less stable due to anonymous contacts • More intolerant of disputes due to invisibility • "Logical" relationships
Cognitive shopping overhead	• Lower cognitive shopping overhead due to easy-to-establish mutual trust	• Higher cognitive shopping overhead due to hard-to-establish mutual trust
Competition	• Local competition • Fewer competitors	• Global competition • More competitors
Customer base	• Local area customers • No anonymity • Fewer resources needed to increase customer loyalty • Customers remain loyal for future purchases	• Wide area customers • Anonymity • More resources needed to increase customer loyalty • Customers shift loyalty

Sources: Compiled from Lee and Brandyberry (2003) and *NPD.com* (2001).

3.2 E-TAILING BUSINESS MODELS

In order to better understand e-tailing, let's look at it from the point of view of a retailer or a manufacturer that sells to individual consumers. The seller has its own organization and must also buy goods and services from others, usually businesses (B2B in Exhibit 3.4). As also shown in Exhibit 3.4, e-tailing, which is basically B2C (right side of the exhibit), is done between the seller (a retailer or a manufacturer) and the buyer. The exhibit shows other EC transactions and related activities because they may impact e-tailing. In this section, we will look at the various B2C models and their classifications.

CLASSIFICATION BY DISTRIBUTION CHANNEL

A business model is a description of how an organization intends to generate revenue through its business operations. More specifically, it is an analysis of the organization's customers and, from that, a discussion of how that organization will achieve

EXHIBIT 3.4 E-Tailing as an Enterprise EC System

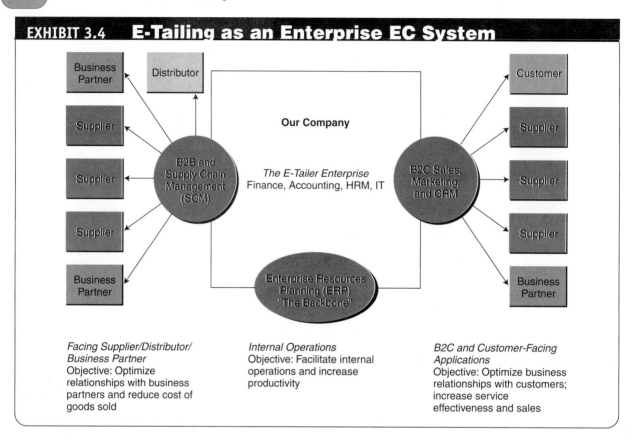

Facing Supplier/Distributor/
Business Partner
Objective: Optimize
relationships with business
partners and reduce cost of
goods sold

Internal Operations
Objective: Facilitate internal
operations and increase
productivity

B2C and Customer-Facing
Applications
Objective: Optimize business
relationships with customers;
increase service
effectiveness and sales

profitability and sustainability by delivering goods and services (value) to those customers (McKay and Marshall 2004). E-tailing business models can be classified in several ways. For example, some classify e-tailers by the scope of items handled (general purpose versus specialty e-tailing) or by the scope of the sales region covered (global versus regional), whereas others use classification by revenue models (see Chapter 1). Here we will classify the models by the distribution channel used, distinguishing five categories:

1. **Direct marketing by mail-order retailers that go online.** Most traditional mail-order retailers, such as QVC, Sharper Image, and Lands' End, simply added another distribution channel—the Internet. Several of these retailers also operate physical stores, but their main distribution channel is direct marketing.

2. **Direct marketing by manufacturers.** Manufacturers, such as Dell, Nike, LEGO, Godiva (Chapter 1), and Sony, market directly online from company sites to individual customers. Most of these manufacturers are click-and-mortar, also selling in their own physical stores or via retailers. However, the manufacturer may be a pure-play company (e.g., Dell).

3. **Pure-play e-tailers.** These e-tailers do not have physical stores, only an online sales presence. Amazon.com is an example of a pure-play e-tailer.

4. **Click-and-mortar retailers.** These are of two sorts, depending on how the businesses were originally founded. Originally, click-and-mortar referred to traditional businesses that developed Web sites to support their business activities in some way (e.g., walmart.com, homedepot.com, and sharperimage.com). For details, see en.wikipedia.org/wiki/Bricks_and_clicks. However, we are now seeing the reverse trend. A small number of successful e-tailers are now creating physical storefronts, leveraging the brand power of the online environment to support more traditional trading activities via stores. For example, Expedia.com, one of the largest online travel companies in the world, has opened physical stores. Dell, a pioneer of e-tailing and one of the largest sellers of computers online, has also opened physical stores.

5. **Internet (online) malls.** As described in Chapter 2, these malls include large numbers of independent storefronts.

We will examine each of these distribution channel categories in the pages that follow.

Direct Marketing by Mail-Order Companies

In a broad sense, **direct marketing** describes marketing that takes place without intermediaries. Direct marketers take orders directly from consumers, bypassing traditional wholesale or retail distribution.

    Firms with established, mature mail-order businesses have a distinct advantage in online sales, given their existing payment processing, inventory management, and order-fulfillment operations, as shown in Online File W3.2.

direct marketing
Broadly, marketing that takes place without intermediaries between manufacturers and buyers; in the context of this book, marketing done online between any seller and buyer.

Direct Sales by Manufacturers

The parties in direct marketing have a great opportunity to influence each other. Sellers can understand their markets better because of the direct connection to consumers, and consumers gain greater information about the products through their direct connection to the manufacturers. Dell is primarily using direct marketing combined with a build-to-order approach (see Appendix 2A for more on build-to-order), customizing its products. Insights and Additions 3.1 describes the process by which customers can configure and order cars online.

Pure-Play E-Tailers

Virtual (pure-play) e-tailers are firms that sell directly to consumers over the Internet without maintaining a physical sales channel. Amazon.com is a prime example of this type of e-tailer. Virtual e-tailers have the advantage of low overhead costs and streamlined processes. However, one drawback can be a lack of established infrastructure (or back office) to support the online front-office activities. Virtual e-tailers are *general purpose* or *specialized* e-tailers.

    General e-tailers, such as Amazon.com (see the opening case), selling a vast range of goods and services online, capitalize on the Internet to offer such variety to a diverse group of customers geographically without the need to maintain a large physical retail (storefront) network.

virtual (pure-play) e-tailers
Firms that sell directly to consumers over the Internet without maintaining a physical sales channel.

Insights and Additions 3.1 Selling Cars Online: Build to Order

The world's automobile manufacturers are complex enterprises with thousands of suppliers and millions of customers. Their traditional channel for distributing cars has been the automobile dealer, who orders cars and then sells them from the lot. When a customer wants a particular feature or color ("options"), the customer might have to wait weeks or months until the "pipeline" of vehicles has that particular car on the production line.

In the traditional system, the manufacturers conduct market research in order to estimate which features and options will sell well, and then they make the cars they wish to sell. In some cases, certain cars are ultimately sold from stock at a loss when the market exhibits insufficient demand for a particular vehicle. The automakers have long operated under this "build-to-stock" environment, building cars that are carried as inventory during the outbound logistics process (ships, trucks, trains, and dealers' lots). General Motors (GM) estimates that it holds as much as $40-billion worth of unsold vehicles in its distribution channels. Other automakers hold large amounts as well.

Ford, GM, and Toyota, along with other automakers around the world, have announced plans to implement a build-to-order program, much like the Dell approach to building computers. These auto giants intend to transform themselves from build-to-stock companies to build-to-order companies, thereby cutting inventory requirements in half, while at the same time giving customers the vehicle they want in a short period (e.g., 1 to 2 weeks). However, according to Weiner (2006) this transformation has so far been "doomed to failure by rigid production processes, inflexible product structures, the lack of integrated logistics processes, and inadequate networking of

manufacturers, suppliers and customers." Only when a network of suppliers producing standard modules for cars using standardized processes and IT systems will the dream of a truly agile and responsive supply chain delivering build-to-customer-order capability be realized.

As an example of this trend toward build-to-order mass customization in the new car market, Jaguar car buyers can build a dream car online. On Jaguar's Web site (*jaguar.com*), consumers are able to custom configure their car's features and components, see it online, price it, and have it delivered to a nearby dealer. Using a virtual car on the Web site, customers can view in real time more than 1,250 possible exterior combinations out of several million, rotate the image 360 degrees, and see the price updated automatically with each selection of trim or accessories. After storing the car in a virtual garage, the customer can decide on the purchase and select a dealer at which to pick up the completed car. (Thus, conflicts with the established dealer network channel are avoided.) The Web site helps primarily with the research process—it is not a fully transactional site. The configuration, however, can be transmitted to the production floor, thereby reducing delivery time and contributing to increased customer satisfaction. Similar configuration systems are available from all the major car manufacturers. Customers can electronically track the progress of the car, including visualization of the production process in the factory. Another similarly impressive Web site with similar functionality is *hummer.com*.

Sources: Compiled from *jaguar.com* (accessed January 2008), *hummer.com* (accessed January 2008), Weiner (2006), and Knowledge@Wharton (2005).

Specialty e-tailers can operate in a very narrow market, as does Cattoys.com (cattoys.com), described in Online File W3.3, or Rugman.com (rugman.com), which specializes in offering more than 12,000 Oriental and Persian rugs online. Such specialized businesses would find it difficult to survive in the physical world, because they would not have enough customers and could not hold the variety of stock in each physical location.

click-and-mortar retailers

Brick-and-mortar retailers that offer a transactional Web site from which to conduct business.

Click-and-Mortar Retailers

A **click-and-mortar retailer** is a combination of both the brick-and-mortar retailer and an online transactional Web site. Many click-and-mortar retailers started life as a traditional storefront with a physical retail presence only and over time adopted an online transactional capability as well (mortar only to click-and-mortar). Another type of click-and-mortar business is those that started their business online and then expanded to physical storefronts as well (click-only to click-and-brick).

Brick-and-mortar retailers conduct business in the physical world, in traditional brick-and-mortar stores. Traditional retailing frequently involves a single distribution channel, the physical store. In some cases, traditional sellers also might operate a mail-order business.

In today's digital economy, click-and-mortar retailers sell via stores, through voice phone calls to human operators, over the Internet through interactive Web sites, and by mobile devices. A firm that operates both physical stores and an online e-tail site is said to be a click-and-mortar business selling in a **multichannel business model** (see Reda 2002). Examples of brick-only to brick-and-click would be department stores, such as Macy's (macys.com), Sears (sears.com), and Nordstrom (nordstrom.com), as well as discount stores, such as Wal-Mart (walmart.com) and Target (target.com). It also includes supermarkets and all other types of retailing.

Expedia in the travel industry and Dell in the computer industry are examples of companies moving from click-only to click-and-brick. For many years, some catalog companies, such as Argos in the United Kingdom, have had storefronts, but these served to display catalogs, to offer advice, and to accept orders and payments for goods, which were then delivered via the usual catalog-delivery modes. This is precisely the approach Dell has adopted in opening its physical stores in Dallas and New York. Dell has for some time operated kiosks in shopping malls in the United States, but the physical stores add a new dimension to their move to click-and-mortar. Various models of computers are on display in the stores, and Dell staff is available to offer advice and support and to assist customers in personalizing their purchases. However, the stores hold no inventory, so interested customers must still place their orders online from within these stores, assisted by Dell staff. The difference from the Web site is that customers are able to touch and feel and compare different Dell models before buying. Dell has not really altered its direct-to-customer model, because the physical stores do not currently have the capability to transact directly (*Ebcenter.org* 2006).

Although there may be practical advantages to being a virtual seller, such as lower overhead costs, it has many drawbacks and barriers, which are described later. Therefore, many experts suggest that the ultimate winners in many market segments will be the companies that are able to leverage the best of both worlds using the click-and-mortar approach.

Retailing in Online Malls

Online malls, as described in Chapter 2, are of two types: referring directories and malls with shared services.

Referring Directories. This type of mall is basically a directory organized by product type. Catalog listings or banner ads at the mall site advertise the products or stores. When users click on the product and/or a specific store, they are transferred to the storefront of the seller, where they then complete the transaction. An example of a directory is hawaii.com/marketplace. The stores listed in a directory either own the site collectively or they pay a subscription fee or a commission to the third party (e.g., a portal) that advertises their logos. This type of e-tailing is basically a kind of affiliate marketing. Other examples of referring directories can be found at insurancefinder.com and bedandbreakfast.com.

Malls with Shared Services. In online malls with shared services, a consumer can find a product, order and pay for it, and arrange for shipment. The hosting mall provides these services, but they usually are executed by each store independently. (To see the variety of services provided, consult smallbusiness.yahoo.com.) The buyer must repeat the process in each store visited in the mall, but it is basically the same process. The storefront owners pay rent and/or transaction fees to the owner. Both

brick-and-mortar retailers
Retailers who do business in the non-Internet, physical world in traditional brick-and-mortar stores.

multichannel business model
A business model where a company sells in multiple marketing channels simultaneously (e.g., both physical and online stores).

EXHIBIT 3.5   Other B2C Business Models

Model Name	Description	Location in Book
Transaction brokers	Electronically mediate between buyers and sellers. Popular in services, the travel industry, the job market, stock trading, and insurance.	Chapter 3
Information portals	Besides information, most portals provide links to merchants, for which they are paid a commission (affiliate marketing). Some provide hosting and software (e.g., *store.yahoo.com*), some also sell.	Chapters 3 and 5
Community portal	Combines community services with selling or affiliate marketing (e.g., *virtualcommunities.start4all.com*).	Chapter 8
Content creators or disseminators	Provide content to the masses (news, stock data). Also participate in the syndication chain (e.g., *espn.com*, *reuters.com*, and *cnn.com*).	Online Chapter 13
Viral marketing	Use e-mail or SMS to advertise. Also can sell direct or via affiliates (e.g., *blueskyfrog.com*).	Chapters 4 and 9
Market makers	Create and manage many-to-many markets (e.g., *chemconnect.com*); also auction sites (e.g., *ebay.com* and *dellauction.com*). Aggregate buyers and/or sellers (e.g., *ingrammicro.com*).	Chapter 5
Make (build)-to-order	Manufacturers that customize their products and services via online orders (e.g., *dell.com*, *nike.com*, and *jaguar.com*).	Chapters 2, 3, and 4
B2B2C	Manufacturer sells to a business, but delivers to individual customers (*godiva.com*).	Chapters 2, 3
Service providers	Offer online payments, order fulfillment (delivery), and security (e.g., *paypal.com* and *escrow.com*).	Chapters 3 and 11

manufacturers and retailers sell in such malls. Yahoo! provides a rich example of this type of shared-services mall. When a user goes to Yahoo!, clicks on "shopping," then "all categories," "pets," "dogs," and then "dog toys," for example, a large range of dog toys, sourced from many different e-tailers, is displayed for shoppers. You can see the name of the company selling the item, the price and availability, and so on. In addition, when two e-tailers supply the same product, users are provided with a comparison of the price at each of those stores. Alternatively, users can go directly to one of the vendors' sites; in this case, users will not know that they are in the Yahoo! environment until the checkout process. Other malls with shared services are firststopshops.com and shopping.msn.com.

Ideally, the customer would like to go to different stores in the same mall, use one shopping cart, and pay only once. This arrangement is possible in Yahoo! stores (smallbusiness.yahoo.com/ecommerce).

OTHER B2C MODELS AND SPECIAL RETAILING

Several other business models are used in B2C. They are discussed in various places throughout the book. Some of these models also are used in B2B, B2B2C, G2B, and other types of EC. A summary of these other models is provided in Exhibit 3.5. Representative special B2C services are discussed in Online File W3.4.

Section 3.2 ▶ REVIEW QUESTIONS

1. List the B2C distribution channel models.
2. Describe how mail-order houses are going online.
3. Describe the direct marketing model used by manufacturers.

4. Describe virtual e-tailing.

5. Describe the click-and-mortar approach.

6. Describe e-malls.

7. Describe online wedding and gift services. (See Online File W3.4.)

3.3   TRAVEL AND TOURISM SERVICES ONLINE

Online travel bookings and associated travel services are one of the most successful e-commerce implementations, with estimates of sales of $73.4 billion in 2006 (Burns 2006), approaching 30 percent of the total travel spending (*Omniture.com* 2006). This is expected to increase to 34 percent of total travel spending by 2010, valued at about $104 billion (*Omniture.com* 2006). According to Jupiter Research, half of all leisure travelers book online and 43 percent of those use the Internet to research their trips (Leggatt 2007). The most popular types of Web sites are online travel agencies (such as Expedia, Travelocity, and Priceline), search engine Web sites (such as Google and Yahoo!), and company-owned Web sites for airlines, hotels, and the like (*Tia.org* 2005). This outstanding performance is underpinned by increased Web traffic of more than 10 percent to major travel sites, higher conversion of visitors to sales, and increased average value per sale, all suggesting that people are becoming more confident and trusting of booking travel-related services online (*Internetretailer.com* 2006c). By 2007, the growth in the number of new customers stopped, but the purchases per customer increased due to the fact that people are taking more short vacations and fewer longer ones (TravelBizMonitor 2008).

Some major travel-related Web sites are expedia.com, travelocity.com, zuji.com (now owned by Travelocity but operating separately), and priceline.com. Online travel services also are provided by all major airlines (e.g., britishairways.com), vacation services (e.g., blue-hawaii.com), large conventional travel agencies (e.g., expedia.com), trains (e.g., amtrak.com), car rental agencies (e.g., autoeurope.com), hotels (e.g., marriott.com), commercial portals (e.g., cnn.com/travel), and tour companies (e.g., atlastravelweb.com). Publishers of travel guides such as Fodors and Lonely Planet provide considerable amounts of travel-related information on their Web sites (fodors.com and lonelyplanet.com), as well as selling travel services there. The online ticket consolidator ebookers.com and the travel information broker tiscover.com are linking up to create a comprehensive online travel resource.

The revenue models of online travel services include direct revenues (commissions), revenue from advertising, lead-generation payments, consultancy fees, subscription or membership fees, revenue-sharing fees, and more. With such rapid growth and success, the travel industry seems to have matured beyond initial concerns such as trust, loyalty, and brand image. However, competition among online travel e-tailers is fierce, with low margins, little customer loyalty, and increasing commoditization of products and services. Thus, guaranteed best rates and various loyalty programs are likely to be popular ways of affecting customer behavior.

Three important trends will drive further changes in the online travel industry. First, online travel agents may try to differentiate themselves through customer-service messaging and other related services, presenting themselves as adding value to the customer. Second, the number of travel meta search facilities, or "travel bots"—online sites or services that search through a range of related sites to find the best price or compare the value of travel products for a consumer—is likely to increase (*Hedna.org* 2005). Third, online travel companies are likely to increasingly use the growing phenomenon of social networking sites (such as myspace.com) to provide content to would-be travelers and also use these sites to study the behavior of potential customers (see discussion later in this section).

SERVICES PROVIDED

Virtual travel agencies offer almost all of the services delivered by conventional travel agencies, from providing general information to reserving and purchasing tickets, accommodations, and entertainment. In addition, they often provide services that most conventional travel agencies do not offer, such as travel tips provided by people who have experienced certain situations (e.g., a visa problem), electronic travel magazines, fare comparisons, city guides, currency conversion calculators, fare tracking (free e-mail alerts on low fares to and from a city and favorite destinations), worldwide business and place locators, an outlet for travel accessories and books, experts' opinions, major international and travel news, detailed driving maps and directions within the United States and several other countries (see infohub.com), chat rooms and bulletin boards, and frequent-flier deals. In addition, some offer several other innovative services, such as online travel auctions.

SPECIAL SERVICES

Many online travel services offer travel bargains. Consumers can go to special sites, such as those offering stand-by tickets, to find bargain fares. Lastminute.com (lastminute.com) offers very low airfares and discounted accommodation prices to fill otherwise-empty seats and hotel rooms. Last-minute trips also can be booked on americanexpress.com, sometimes at a steep discount. Special vacation destinations can be found at priceline.com, tictactravel.com, stayfinder.com, and greatrentals.com. Flights.com (flights.com) offers cheap tickets and also Eurail passes. Travelers can access cybercaptive.com for a list of thousands of Internet cafés around the world. Similar information is available via many portals, such as Yahoo! and MSN.

Also of interest are sites that offer medical advice and services for travelers. This type of information is available from the World Health Organization (who.int), governments (e.g., cdc.gov/travel), and private organizations (e.g., tripprep.com, medicalert.org, and webmd.com).

Other special services include:

- **Wireless services.** Several airlines (e.g., Cathay Pacific, Delta, and Qantas) allow customers with cell phones with Internet access to check their flight status, update frequent-flyer miles, and book flights. British Air offers a broadband Internet connection for passengers onboard. Qantas (qantas.com.au) has announced that as of early 2007 customers will be able to send and receive in-flight e-mails, SMSs, and calls via their own mobile phones and personal electronic devices, such as Blackberries (*Qantas.com.au* 2006).

- **Direct marketing.** Airlines sell electronic tickets over the Internet. When customers purchase electronic tickets online (or by phone), all they have to do is print the boarding pass from their computer's printer or upon arrival at the airport enter their credit card at an *electronic kiosk* to get a boarding pass. Alternatively, travelers can get a boarding pass at the ticket counter. Using direct marketing techniques, airlines are able to build customer profiles and target specific customers with tailored offers.

- **Alliances and consortia.** Airlines and other travel companies are creating alliances to increase sales or reduce purchasing costs. For example, some consortia aggregate only fares purchased over the Internet. Several alliances exist in Europe, the United States, and Asia. For example, zuji.com is a travel portal dedicated to Asia-Pacific travelers. It is a consortium of regional airlines, Travelocity, some hotel chains, and car-rental providers that specializes in tour packages in the region. The company also has a booking engine for travel agents, enabling them to store their customers' e-mail addresses (a B2B2C service).

Travel-Oriented Social Networks

Since 2005, online leisure travelers' use of social computing technologies, such as blogs, RSS, wikis, and user reviews, for researching travel has skyrocketed. Travel e-businesses, marketing executives, and managers realized that social computing was increasingly playing a larger role in corporate online strategy, even if all a company did was monitor what travelers were saying about a certain company in third-party forums. Companies that implement social computing technologies on their own Web sites probably need to view it primarily as supporting business goals, such as improving customer communication or increasing engagement of customers, and less as a sales or customer service tool.

As travelers forge connections and share information with like-minded travelers online, their needs and expectations change. They want more relevance and more correct information. Social computing has shifted online travel from passive selling to active customer engagement, which affects how travel companies and agents distribute and market their products (Epps et al. 2007). Several social networks have travel channels that cater to travelers. One such network is Wikia.com. In a special report, Harteveldt (2006) provided guidelines for travel e-commerce and marketing executives and managers on how travelers embrace social computing technologies. Case 3.1 shows an example of a social network for travelers.

Travel Recommendation. One of the characteristics of Web 2.0 is personalization. For an example of how it is being done in the travel industry, see Online File W3.5.

BENEFITS AND LIMITATIONS OF ONLINE TRAVEL SERVICES

The benefits of online travel services to travelers are enormous. The amount of free information is tremendous, and it is accessible at any time from any place. Substantial discounts can be found, especially for those who have time and patience to search for them. Providers of travel services also benefit: Airlines, hotels, and cruise lines are selling otherwise-empty spaces. Also, direct selling saves the provider's commission and its processing.

Online travel services do have some limitations. First, many people do not use the Internet. Second, the amount of time and the difficulty of using virtual travel agencies can be significant, especially for complex trips and for inexperienced Internet surfers. Finally, complex trips or those that require stopovers might not be available online because they require specialized knowledge and arrangements, which may be better done by a knowledgeable, human travel agent. Therefore, the need for travel agents as intermediaries remains, at least for the immediate future.

CORPORATE TRAVEL

The corporate travel market is huge and has been growing rapidly in recent years. Corporations can use all of the travel services mentioned earlier. However, many large corporations receive additional services from large travel agencies. To reduce corporate travel costs, companies can make arrangements that enable employees to plan and book their own trips. Using online optimization tools provided by travel companies, such as those offered by American Express (americanexpress.com), companies can try to reduce travel costs even further. Travel authorization software that checks availability of funds and compliance with corporate guidelines is usually provided by travel companies such as American Express. Expedia Inc. (expedia.com), Travelocity (travelocity.com), and Orbitz (orbitz.com) also offer software tools for corporate planning and booking.

An example of how a major corporation uses online corporate travel services is described in Online File W3.6. For further discussion, see B2B travel in Chapter 5.

WAYN: A SOCIAL NETWORK FOR TRAVELERS

WAYN (which stands for "Where Are You Now?") is a social networking Web site (*wayn.com*) with a goal of uniting travelers from around the world. WAYN was launched in London in May 2003. It has grown from 45,000 to about 10 million members as of 2008. About 2 million members are in the United Kingdom. It also is strong in the United States, Canada, Australia, New Zealand, and other countries in Western Europe. It is growing by 20,000 members daily.

As with many other social networking services, WAYN enables its users to create a personal profile and upload and store photos. Users can then search for others with similar profiles and link them to their profiles as friends. It also is possible to send and receive messages using discussion forums. Because it is designed for travelers, members are able to search for contacts based on a particular location. Using a world map, users can visually locate where each of their contacts are situated around the world. The goal of the service is for members to keep friends informed of where they are while traveling and, in turn, to be able to locate their friends.

In addition, users can send SMSs to any of their contacts worldwide; chat online using WAYN's Instant Messenger; and plan trips and notify their friends about them. Using WAYN, users can create discussion groups, ask for recommendations, and send smiley icons to all. Finally, chat bots (avatars) are dynamic and fully active, representing one of the best ways of meeting people in the WAYN community.

WAYN is one of the very few sites that did not lose new subscriptions after introducing fees for its premier membership service, making it one of the few social networking communities that has managed to quickly become profitable.

WAYN is now popular in 220 countries, becoming a global brand. It is not aimed at any particular age group, but it seems to be most popular with the 18-to-25 age group. It also has a strong position among the 35-to-45-plus age group. Members can find out who will be traveling to their next intended destination, at the same time as they are.

Sources: PRWeb.com (2003), *wayn.com* (accessed January 2008), and *en.wikipedia.org/wiki/WYAN* (accessed January 2008).

Questions

1. Visit *wayn.com*. What options do you find most exciting on the site?
2. Why has WAYN been so successful even though the site requires subscription fees?

IMPACT OF EC ON THE TRAVEL INDUSTRY

It was not uncommon in the mid-late 1990s for people to forecast the demise of travel agents, arguing that all travel agency services would be replaced by the rise of travel superstores on the Internet (e.g., see Bloch and Segev 1997). Others suggested that only the value-added activities of travel agencies that could not be automated would be performed by travel organizations that would serve certain targeted markets and customers (also see Van der Heijden 1996). Travel superstores, providing many products, services, and entertainment, might enter the industry, as well as innovative individuals operating as travel agents and undertaking some aspects of service tasks from their homes.

The Internet has had a large impact on the role of travel agents. This has occurred through direct impacts, with customers increasingly using the Internet to make bookings. It has also occurred somewhat indirectly, with airlines and hotel chains, for example, encouraging customers to book direct or through online wholesalers, bypassing travel agents. However, others argue that travel agents will become the "leisure consultants" of the future, gaining an advantage through their overall knowledge of the industry and their independent advice. In these cases, both a physical and virtual presence are seen as essential, and investing in content (information, travel advice, and the like) is seen as an absolute requirement for success in this competitive market (Atkinson 2005).

Major companies, such as Expedia and Orbitz, provide excellent service via their Web sites and search through their own extensive databases and networks to offer attractive deals and packages to customers. Rapid growth of late, however, has occurred in the use of travel search engines, or travel bots. The use of intelligent agents in travel services are discussed on Online File W3.7.

Section 3.3 ▶ REVIEW QUESTIONS

1. What travel services are available online that are not available offline?
2. List the benefits of online travel services to travelers and to service providers.
3. What role do software (intelligent) agents have in online travel services? What future applications may be possible? (See Online File W3.7.)

3.4 EMPLOYMENT PLACEMENT AND THE JOB MARKET ONLINE

The job market is very volatile, and supply and demand are frequently unbalanced. Traditionally, job matching has been done in several ways, ranging from ads in classified sections of newspapers to the use of corporate recruiters, commercial employment agencies, and headhunting companies. The job market has now also moved online. The online job market connects individuals who are looking for a job with employers who are looking for employees with specific skills. It is a very popular approach, and, increasingly, both job seekers and prospective employers are turning away from traditional print-based advertising and recruitment methods in preference of online advertisements and recruitment activities. In addition to online job ads and placement services available through specialized Web sites (such as careerbuilder.com), larger companies are increasingly building career portals on their corporate Web sites as a way of trimming recruitment costs and reducing the time to fill vacancies (Cox 2006). Advantages of the online job market over the traditional one are listed in Exhibit 3.6.

EXHIBIT 3.6	**Traditional Versus Online Job Markets**	
Characteristic	**Traditional Job Market**	**Online Job Market**
Cost	Expensive, especially in prime space	Can be very inexpensive
Life cycle	Short	Long
Place	Usually local and limited if global	Global
Context updating	Can be complex, expensive	Fast, simple, inexpensive
Space for details	Limited	Large
Ease of search by applicant	Difficult, especially for out-of-town applicants	Quick and easy
Ability of employers to find applicants	May be very difficult, especially for out-of-town applicants	Easy
Matching of supply and demand	Difficult	Easy
Reliability	Material can be lost in mail	High
Communication speed between employees and employers	Can be slow	Fast
Ability of employees to compare jobs	Limited	Easy, fast

THE INTERNET JOB MARKET

The Internet offers a rich environment for job seekers and for companies searching for hard-to-find employees. Nearly all *Fortune* 500 companies now use the Internet for some of their recruitment requirements, and studies reveal that online resources are now the most popular way to find suitably qualified applicants for job vacancies (*Careerbuilder.com* 2006). Online job recruitment revenues and volume overtook print ad classifieds at the end of 2005 (Cox 2006), and in 2006 were estimated to reach $2.3 billion (*Careerbuilder.com* 2006). The U.S. market is dominated by three major players: Monster, Careerbuilder, and Yahoo! HotJobs, which together comprise about 55 percent of the market. In Australia, the leading site is seek.com.au. Employers spent more on online recruitment advertising than newspaper job ads—$5.9 billion to $5.4 billion—for the first time in 2006 (Walsh 2006).

The following parties use the Internet job market:

> ▶ **Job seekers.** Job seekers can reply to employment ads. Or, they can take the initiative and place their résumés on their own homepages or on others' Web sites, send messages to members of newsgroups asking for referrals, and use the sites of recruiting firms, such as careerbuilder.com, Yahoo! HotJobs (hotjobs.yahoo.com), and monster.com. For entry-level jobs and internships for newly minted graduates, job seekers can go to collegerecruiter.com. Job seekers can also assess their market value in different U.S. cities at wageweb.com and use the Web to compare salaries and conditions, obtain information about employers, and get career advice. Passive job seekers, those just keeping an eye on opportunities, are using this medium, as well as those actively seeking new employment.

> ▶ **Employers seeking employees.** Many organizations, including public institutions, advertise openings on their Web sites. Others advertise job openings on popular public portals, online newspapers, bulletin boards, and with recruiting firms. Employers can conduct interviews and administer interactive intelligence, skills, and psychological tests on the Web. Some employers, such as Home Depot, have kiosks in some of their stores on which they post job openings and allow applicants to complete an application electronically. Forty percent of large U.S. firms are using computerized assessments to screen new hires or to identify up-and-comers for training and development. The tests are designed to predict success by measuring behavioral or personality traits and comparing a candidate's profile with those of people who have succeeded in similar jobs (Rose 2008).

> ▶ **Classified ads.** Classified ads for job openings and job seekers are available at craigslist.org, kijiji.com, linked.com, and in the online classified sections of many newspapers. Also, several social networks allow posting of job openings.

> ▶ **Job agencies.** Hundreds of job agencies are active on the Web. They use their own Web pages to post available job descriptions and advertise their services in e-mails and at other Web sites. Job agencies and/or employers use newsgroups, online forums, bulletin boards, Internet commercial résumé services, and portals such as Yahoo! HotJobs and AOL. Most

portals are free; others, such as marketing.theladders.com, charge membership fees but offer many services.

▶ **Government agencies and institutions.** Many government agencies advertise openings for government positions on their Web sites and on other sites; some are required by law to do so. In addition, some government agencies use the Internet to help job seekers find jobs elsewhere, as is done in Hong Kong and the Philippines. An initiative by the Australian Government, Jobsearch (jobsearch.gov.au), the largest free job board in the country, offers free advertising to employers. It claims the largest candidate database in Australia and has over 1 million visitors per month, with an average of 75,000 jobs on offer at any one time. It links this online presence to an Australia-wide network of touch-screen kiosks. Employers are notified when a candidate's résumé matches an advertised job (*Jobsearch.gov.au* 2006).

A Consortium of Large Employers and College Careers Advisors

Most large employers, such as GE, IBM, and Xerox, spend hundreds of thousands of dollars annually on commissions to online job companies and on recruitment activities. For colleges, an important performance metric is the employability of their graduates; hence, providing career advice and services is an important part of campus life. To save money, a number of leading companies joined a nonprofit consortium that created a career portal called jobcentral.com. The National Association of Colleges and Employers created other sites, including the NACELink Network (nacelink.com). These nonprofit associations have now merged to form JobCentral, providing people at all education levels timely information about careers and employment opportunities nationwide (*JobCentral.com* 2006). The site is used primarily to catalog job postings from the sites of the member employers. It also provides a rich resource of information about occupations, career development, relocation information, and the like. Having the job postings of a number of large employers in one place makes it easy for job searchers to explore available openings.

Global Online Portals

The Internet is very helpful for anyone looking for a job in another country. An interesting global portal for Europe is described in Online File W3.8. An interesting global site for placing/finding jobs in different countries is xing.com (see Internet Exercise 9). A similar service is provided by linkedin.com.

BENEFITS AND LIMITATIONS OF THE ELECTRONIC JOB MARKET

As indicated earlier, the electronic job market offers a variety of benefits for both job seekers and employers. These major advantages are shown in Exhibit 3.7.

Probably the biggest limitation of the online job market is the fact that some people do not use and do not have access to the Internet, although this problem has declined substantially. Nonetheless, the potential for an ever-increasing gap between those with skills and access to the Internet and those without is of concern. To overcome this problem, companies might use both traditional advertising approaches and the Internet.

EXHIBIT 3.7   Advantages of the Electronic Job Market for Job Seekers and Employers

Advantages for Job Seekers	Advantages for Employers
• Can find information on a large number of jobs worldwide	• Can advertise to large numbers of job seekers
• Can communicate quickly with potential employers	• Can save on advertisement costs
• Can market themselves directly to potential employers (e.g., *quintcareers.com*)	• Can reduce application-processing costs by using electronic application forms
• Can write and post résumés for large-volume distribution (e.g., Personal Search Agent at *careerbuilder.com*, *brassring.com*)	• Can provide greater equal opportunity for job seekers
• Can search for jobs quickly from any location	• Increased chance of finding highly skilled employees
• Can obtain several support services at no cost (e.g., *hotjobs.yahoo.com* and *monster.com* provide free career-planning services)	• Can describe positions in great detail
	• Can conduct interviews online (using video teleconferencing)
• Can assess their market value (e.g., *wageweb.com* and *rileyguide.org*; look for salary surveys)	• Can arrange for testing online
• Can learn how to use their voice effectively in an interview (*greatvoice.com*)	• Can view salary surveys for recruiting strategies
• Can access newsgroups that are dedicated to finding jobs (and keeping them)	

However, the trend is clear: Over time, more and more of the job market will be on the Internet. One solution to the problem of limited access is the use of Internet kiosks, as used by companies such as Home Depot.

Interestingly, the reverse of lack of access is a major limitation of online recruiting. Many companies find that they are flooded with applicants when they advertise online, most of whom are not really suited to the position advertised. Screening all these applications can be a time-consuming and costly process. However, the use of intelligent agents (see Online File W3.9) offers a solution to this problem for many organizations.

Security and privacy are another limitation. Résumés and other online communications are usually not encrypted, so one's job-seeking activities might not be secure, and thus confidentiality and data protection cannot be guaranteed. It also is possible that someone at a job seeker's current place of employment (possibly even his or her boss) might find out that that person is job hunting. The electronic job market can also create high turnover costs for employers by accelerating employees' movement to better jobs. Finally, finding candidates online is more complicated than most people think, mostly due to the large number of résumés available online.

Section 3.4 ▶ REVIEW QUESTIONS

1. What are the driving forces of the electronic job market?
2. What are the major advantages of the electronic job market to the candidate? To employers?
3. Describe the role of intelligent agents in the electronic job market. (See Online File W3.9.)

3.5 REAL ESTATE, INSURANCE, AND STOCK TRADING ONLINE

Online financial services are exploding on the Internet and are being embraced by customers. According to Dandapani (2004), online financial services essentially altered the industry landscape. Sainsbury's Bank estimated that around 3 million people would take out a financial product, such as a credit card or insurance, online during 2004, 31 percent more than during 2003. This growth rate has continued. The major financial services are presented in this and the following section.

REAL ESTATE ONLINE

The increasing presence and realization of e-commerce possibilities and opportunities in the real estate business is creating a momentum and a readiness for change and slowly adding pressure to transform the old ways of doing things in this previously stable and conservative business. Changes are reaching a tipping point, beyond which the nature of the real estate business will be altered. The changes have been some time in coming, but after a long period of quantitative changes, experts are beginning to see some fundamental qualitative changes in the industry (Knox 2006).

Developers offer "live chat" between sales agents and buyers where very specific questions about the property can be posted. 3D video tours of properties are also offered to buyers who want considerable information before they are willing to see the property itself.

To get some idea of the changes, consider the following statistics. In 2001, when total real estate advertising spending was $11 billion, online real estate advertising spending was $395 million, or 3.5 percent of the total. In 2006, when total advertising spending in real estate was approximately the same, at $11.5 billion, online spending had grown to $2 billion, or 17.7 percent of the total. By 2010, when online spending is predicted to pass $3 billion, online spending is forecast to surpass newspaper print advertising in terms of market share (Borrell Associates 2006). According to the *New York Times News* (2007), in 2007 real estate companies spent 26 percent more on online ads than in 2006.

The increase in Internet real estate advertising is understandably influencing buying behavior. Studies by the National Association of Realtors (NAR) have shown that over 77 percent of real estate buyers begin their searches for properties on the Internet. Further, 24 percent of buyers eventually choose a home they first identified online (Mullaney 2004). Only 6 percent of subprime loans were originated directly over the Internet in the first half of 2007, according to a new survey of subprime lenders by the Mortgage Bankers Association (reported by Carter 2007).

In the face of such increases in consumer knowledge and control of the early parts of the identification and purchase of properties, some U.S. realtors have tried to restrict public access to some of the databases of properties, such as the local Multiple Listing Services. In many localities, local brokers have tried to restrict access to such databases to members of a professional association, such as the NAR.

In summary, e-commerce and the Internet are slowly but surely having an ever increasing impact on the real estate industry. For example, despite the changes that are beginning to emerge, real estate agents have not been disintermediated. Homebuyers today tend to use both real estate agents and the Internet. In 2006, 81 percent of homebuyers who used the Internet to look for a property also used a real estate agent (Knox 2006). Thus, despite the fact that the Internet is shaking up the real estate industry, the emerging pattern is more complex than the simple disintermediation of agents. For examples, see *New York Times News* (2007).

For more about real estate applications and services offered online, see Online File W3.10.

INSURANCE ONLINE

Although the uptake of EC in the insurance industry is relatively slow in some countries, such as New Zealand (Yao 2004), an increasing number of companies use the Internet to offer standard insurance policies, such as auto, home, life, or health, at a substantial discount. Furthermore, third-party aggregators offer free comparisons of available policies. Several large insurance and risk-management companies offer comprehensive insurance contracts online. Although many people do not trust the faceless insurance agent, others are eager to take advantage of the reduced premiums. For example, a visit to insurance.com will show a variety of different policies. At answerfinancial.com customers and businesses can compare car insurance offerings and then make a purchase online. At travel-insurance-online.com, customers can book travel insurance. Another popular insurance site is insweb.com. Many insurance companies use a dual strategy, keeping human agents, but also selling online. Like the real estate brokers, insurance brokers send unsolicited e-mails to millions of people.

ONLINE STOCK TRADING

In the late 1990s, online trading was an exciting innovation in the financial services industry. However, the dot-com crash and increasing competition saw consolidation, cost-cutting, and price reduction become the order of the day (Regan 2005). Major consolidations, involving billions of dollars in total, took place in 2005, with Ameritrade acquiring TD Waterhouse and E*TRADE acquiring BrownCo, Harris Direct, and Kobren Insight Management (Regan 2005). Regarding the cost of trading, CNNMoney.com reported in 2006 that fees are now as low as $1 to $3 per trade. For example, Genesis Securities, through its new unit SogoInvest, offers investors 15 free trades a month for a $15 a month fee with no account minimum required. Investors unwilling to pay the monthly fee can still conduct trades for $3 each.

Since 2004, the majority of stock trading is carried out via the Internet, with 12 brokerage firms handling 75 percent of online trades (Cropper 2004). The top three brokerage firms after the 2005 mergers are Ameritrade, Charles Schwab, and E*TRADE (Regan 2005).

The commission for an online trade is between $1 and $19, compared with an average fee of $100 from a full-service broker and $25 from a non-Internet discount broker. With online trading, there are no busy telephone lines, and the chance for error is small, because there is no oral communication in a frequently noisy environment. Orders can be placed from anywhere, at any time, day or night, and there is no biased broker to push a sale. Furthermore, investors can find a considerable amount of free information about specific companies or mutual funds.

Several discount brokerage houses initiated extensive online stock trading, notably Charles Schwab in 1995. Full-service brokerage companies such as Merrill Lynch followed in 1998–1999. By 2002, most brokerage firms in the United States offered online trading, and the volume of trading has increased significantly in the last 5 years. In 2002, Charles Schwab opened cybertrader.com, charging only $9.95 per trade.

How does online trading work? Let's say an investor has an account with Schwab. The investor accesses Schwab's Web site (schwab.com), enters an account number and password, and clicks stock trading. Using a menu, the investor enters the details of the order (buy, sell, margin or cash, price limit, or market order). The computer tells the investor the current (real-time) "ask" and "bid" prices, much as a broker would do over the telephone, and the investor can approve or reject the transaction. The flow chart of this process is shown in Exhibit 3.8.

Some companies, including Schwab, are now also licensed as exchanges. This allows them to match the selling and buying orders of their own customers for many securities in 1 to 2 seconds.

Some well-known companies that offer online trading are E*TRADE, Ameritrade, and Suretrade. E*TRADE offers many finance-related services using multimedia software.

The most innovative collection of online brokerage services is that of E*TRADE. In 1999, E*TRADE broadened its services by starting its own portfolio of mutual funds. E*TRADE is expanding rapidly into several countries, enabling global stock trading.

With the rapid pace of adoption of mobile handsets, mobile banking will become more and more popular. Mobile banking services enable users to receive information on their account balances via SMS and to settle payments for bills and purchase stocks (Mallat et al. 2004).

See Online File W3.11 for more on investment information available online.

The Risk of Trading in an Online Stock Account

The major risk of online trading is security. Although all trading sites require users to have an ID and password, problems may still occur.

For example, in 2004 it was discovered that hackers could steal users' ID numbers and passwords when they used the Windows operating system. The problem has been

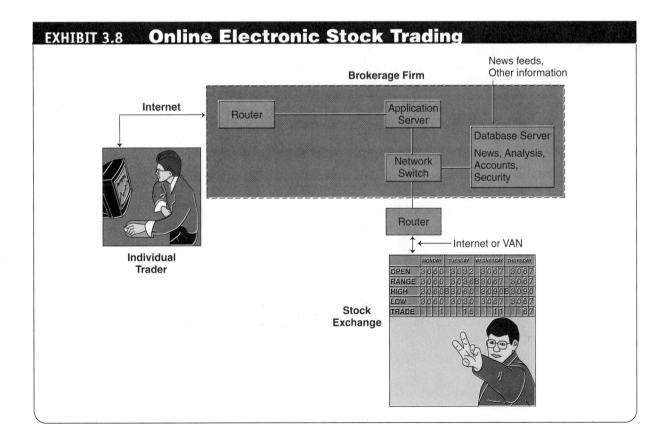

EXHIBIT 3.8   Online Electronic Stock Trading

corrected. Problems of this nature also can occur when conducting online trading or online banking, our next topic.

Section 3.5 ▶ REVIEW QUESTIONS

1. List the major online real estate applications.

2. What are the advantages of online stock tracking?

3. What investment information is available online? (See Online File W3.11.)

4. What are some of the risks of trading stocks online?

3.6 BANKING AND PERSONAL FINANCE ONLINE

electronic (online) banking or e-banking
Various banking activities conducted from home or the road using an Internet connection; also known as cyberbanking, virtual banking, online banking, and home banking.

Online banking, or **electronic banking (e-banking)**, also known as cyberbanking, virtual banking, or home banking, includes various banking activities conducted via the Internet from home, business, or on the road rather than at a physical bank location. Consumers can use e-banking to check their accounts, pay bills online, secure a loan electronically, and much more.

E-banking saves users time and money. For banks, it offers an inexpensive alternative to branch banking and a chance to enlist remote customers. Many physical banks now offer home banking services, and some use EC as a major competitive strategy. One such U.S. bank is Wells Fargo (wellsfargo.com). In Hong Kong, a leading bank is the Bank of East Asia (hkbea-cyberbanking.com). Many banks offer wireless services (see Chapter 9).

An emerging innovation in online banking is peer-to-peer (P2P) online banking. Zopa is a UK Web site offering P2P banking services. People join Zopa as borrowers or lenders. The site has about 90,000 members, and more than $100,000 is being lent every day. The average interest rate on Zopa loans is 7 percent, and uncollectible debts are running at a low 0.05 percent (in mid-2006) (Schonfeld and Borzo 2006).

Pew Internet's December 2005 survey found that 43 percent of all adult Internet users in the United States—63 million adults—were banking online. The users of online banking services were found to be spread across all age groups under the age of 65, with men and women being equally likely to bank online (Fox and Beier 2006).

Online banking has not only been embraced in the developed world; it is becoming an enabling feature of business growth in the developing world. For example, online banking in China is increasing rapidly in popularity, especially among China's new educated middle class in the developed cities. Consequently, the overall turnover of online banking activities is also growing rapidly.

The Bank of China and the China Merchants Bank started their online banking service in 1998. These online service offerings were followed by online offerings by China's other major banks and a number of smaller banks. These services have been enthusiastically embraced by China's new business classes.

Banking online is becoming popular even with small businesses. In 2004, about 16 percent of United States' small businesses banked online, versus 3.3 percent in 2001 (Celent 2004). In 2006, the British Bankers' Association reported that 4 out of 10 small businesses in Britain bank online (Moules 2006).

HOME BANKING CAPABILITIES

Southard and Siau (2004) divide banking applications into the following categories: informational, administrative, transactional, portal, and others (see Exhibit 3.9). They also found that the larger the bank, the more services that were offered online.

EXHIBIT 3.9   Online Banking Capabilities

Informational	General bank information and history
	Financial education information
	Employment information
	Interest rate quotes
	Financial calculators
	Current bank and local news
Administrative	Account information access
	Open new account online
	Applications for services
	Move all banking online
	Personal finance software applications
Transactional	Account transfer capabilities
	Transfer funds housed at different financial institutions
	Bill-pay services
	Corporate services (e.g., cash management, treasury)
	Online insurance services
	Online brokerage services
	Real-time funds transfer
	Online trust services
Portal	Links to financial information
	Links to community information
	Links to local business
	Links to nonlocal businesses (and/or advertisers)
Others	Wireless capabilities
	Search function

Sources: Compiled from Southard and Siau (2004) and *Cashedge.com* (2006).

A description of some of the major e-banking capabilities is provided in Online File W3.12.

Electronic banking offers several of the EC benefits listed in Chapter 1, both to the bank and to its customers, such as expanding the bank's customer base and saving on the cost of paper transactions.

VIRTUAL BANKS

In addition to regular banks' adding online services, *virtual banks* have emerged; these have no physical location but only conduct online transactions. Security First Network Bank (SFNB) was the first such bank to offer secure banking transactions on the Web. Amidst the consolidation that has taken place in the banking industry, SFNB has since been purchased and now is a part of RBC Centura (rbccentura.com). Another representative virtual bank in the United States is First Internet Bank (firstib.com). Virtual banks exist in many other countries (e.g., bankdirect.co.nz). In some countries, virtual banks are involved in stock trading, and some stockbrokers are doing online banking (e.g., see etrade.com). According to Dandapani (2004), 97 percent of the hundreds of pure-play virtual banks failed by 2003 due to lack of financial viability.

A word of caution about virtual banking: Before sending money to any cyberbank, especially those that promise high interest rates for your deposits, make sure that the bank is a legitimate one. Several cases of fraud already have occurred.

INTERNATIONAL AND MULTIPLE-CURRENCY BANKING

International banking and the ability to handle trades in multiple currencies are critical for international trading. Although some international retail purchasing can be done by providing a credit card number, other transactions may require international banking support. Examples of such cross-border support include the following:

- Tradecard and MasterCard have developed a multiple-currency system for global transactions (see tradecard.com). This system is described in Chapter 11.
- Bank of America (bankofamerica.com) and most other major banks offer international capital funds, cash management, trades and services, foreign exchange, risk management investments, merchant services, and special services for international traders.
- Fxall.com is a multidealer foreign exchange service that enables faster and cheaper foreign exchange transactions. Special services are being established for stock market traders who need to pay for foreign stocks (e.g., at Charles Schwab). See *Global Finance* (2004) for more information about foreign exchange banks.

ONLINE FINANCIAL TRANSACTION IMPLEMENTATION ISSUES

As one would expect, the implementation of online banking and online stock trading can be interrelated. In many instances, one financial institution offers both services. The following are some implementation issues for online financial transactions. For an in-depth analysis, see Dandapani (2004). For an example, see Xu et al. (2006).

Securing Financial Transactions

Financial transactions for home banking and online trading must be very secure. In Chapter 11, we discuss the details of secure EC payment systems. In Case 3.2, we give an example of how a bank provides security and privacy to its customers.

Access to Banks' Intranets by Outsiders

Many banks provide their large business customers with personalized service by allowing them access to the bank's intranet. For example, Bank of America allows its business customers access to accounts, historical transactions, and other data, including intranet-based decision-support applications, which may be of interest to large business customers. Bank of America also allows its small business customers to apply for loans through its Web site.

Imaging Systems

Several financial institutions (e.g., Bank of America and Citibank) allow customers to view images of all of their incoming checks, invoices, and other related online correspondence. Image access can be simplified with the help of a search engine.

Fees Online Versus Fees for Offline Services

Computer-based banking services are offered free by some banks, whereas others charge $5 to $10 a month. Also, some banks charge fees for individual transactions (e.g., fee per check, per transfer, and so on). Financial institutions must carefully think through the

CASE 3.2
EC Application
SECURITY FOR ONLINE BANK TRANSACTIONS

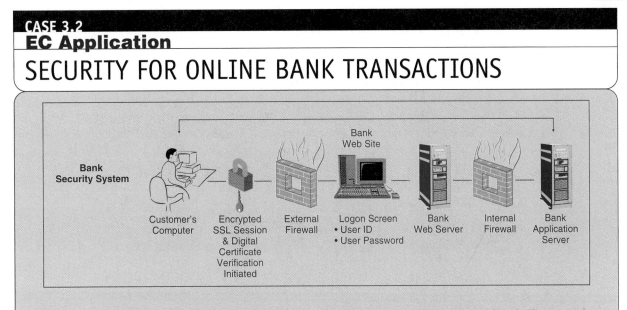

Banks provide extensive security to their customers. The following describes some of the safeguards provided.

Customers accessing the bank system from the outside must go through encryption provided by SSL (Secure Socket Layer) and digital certification verification (see Chapter 11). The certification process assures users each time they sign on that they are indeed connected to their specific bank. The customer inquiry message then goes through an external firewall. Once the log-on screen is reached, a user ID and a password are required. This information flows through a direct Web server and then goes through an internal firewall to the application server.

The bank maintains accurate information. Corrections are made quickly.

Information is shared among the company's family of partners only for legitimate business purposes. Sharing information with outside companies is done with extreme care.

The bank does not capture information provided by customers when it conducts "what-if" scenarios using the bank's planning tools (to assure privacy). The company does use cookies to learn about its customers; however, customers can control both the collection and use of the information. In addition, the bank provides suggestions on how users can increase security (e.g., "Use a browser with 128-bit encryption").

Sources: Compiled from various security statements of online bank Web sites, including *Cooperativebank.co.uk* (2006) and *Thestatebank.com* (2006).

Questions

1. Why is security so important for a bank?
2. Why is there a need for two firewalls?
3. Who is protected by the bank's security system—the customer, the bank, or both? Elaborate.
4. What might be the limitations of such a system?

---

pricing of online and offline services. Fee issues must take into account the costs of providing the different types of services, the organization's desire to attract new customers, and the prices offered by competitors. For further discussion, see Ericson (2004).

Risks

Online banks, as well as click-and-mortar banks, might carry some risks and problems, especially in international banking. The first risk that most people think of is the risk of hackers getting into their account. In addition, some believe that virtual banks carry *liquidity* risk (the risk of not having sufficient funds to pay obligations as they come due) and could be more susceptible to panic withdrawals. Regulators are grappling with the safeguards that need to be imposed on e-banking.

PERSONAL FINANCE ONLINE

Individuals often combine electronic banking with personal finance and portfolio management. Also, brokerage firms such as Schwab offer personal finance services such as retirement planning. However, vendors of specialized personal finance software offer more diversified services. For example, both Intuit's Quicken (Tessler 2004) and Microsoft's Money offer the following capabilities: bill paying and electronic check writing; tracking of bank accounts, expenditures, and credit cards; portfolio management, including reports and capital gains (losses) computations; investment tracking and monitoring of securities; stock quotes and past and current prices of stocks; personal budget organization; record keeping of cash flow and profit and loss computations; tax computations and preparations; and retirement goals, planning, and budgeting.

Although Quicken is the most popular personal finance software, more sophisticated packages such as Prosper (from Ernst & Young) and Captool (captools.com) are available. All of these products are available as independent software programs for use with the Internet or coupled with other services, such as those offered by AOL.

Online Billing and Bill Paying

The era of e-payment is around the corner. The number of checks the U.S. Federal Reserve System processed in 2003 decreased for the fourth consecutive year, dropping 4.7 percent to 15.81 billion checks, while commercial automated clearinghouse (ACH) volume increased 12.1 percent to $95.96 billion in payments (Dernovsek 2004). Many people prefer to pay monthly bills, such as telephone, utilities, rent, credit cards, cable, and so on, online. The recipients of such payments are equally eager to receive money online because online payments are received much more regularly and quickly and have lower processing costs.

Online billing and bill paying can be classified into B2C, B2B, or C2C. This section has focused largely on B2C services, which help consumers save time and payees save on processing costs. However, large opportunities also exist in B2B services, which can save businesses about 50 percent of billing costs. In Hong Kong, for example, CitiCorp enables automatic payments by linking suppliers, buyers, and banks on one platform.

Taxes

One important area in personal finance is advice about and computation of taxes. Dozens of sites are available to help people in their federal tax preparations. Many sites will help people legally cut their taxes. The following list offers some sites worth checking:

▶ irs.gov: The official Web site of the Internal Revenue Service.

▶ webtax.com: A massive directory of tax-related information, research, and services.

▶ fairmark.com: A tax guide for investors.

▶ moneycentral.msn.com/tax/home.asp: A useful reference and educational site.

▶ quicken.com/taxes: Emphasizes tax planning.

▶ taxcut.com/taxtips/hrblock_tips.html: Offers advice on minimizing taxes.

▶ taxaudit.com: Offers advice on minimizing taxes.

▶ taxprophet.com: Provides tax advice in an entertaining manner.

▶ bankrate.com/brm/itax: Contains informative articles about taxation.

▶ 1040.com: Information about deduction rules.

▶ unclefed.com: Offers advice on audits.

Section 3.6 ▶ REVIEW QUESTIONS

1. List the capabilities of online banking. Which of these capabilities would be most beneficial to you?
2. Discuss some implementation issues of financial services.
3. List the major personal finance services available online.
4. Explain online bill paying.

3.7 ON-DEMAND DELIVERY OF PRODUCTS AND DELIVERY OF DIGITAL ITEMS

In this section we deal with the B2C delivery issues related to on-demand items, including perishable ones, as well as the delivery of digitizable items and entertainment.

ON-DEMAND DELIVERY OF PRODUCTS

Most e-tailers use common logistics carriers to deliver products to customers. They might use the postal system within their country or they might use private shippers such as UPS, FedEx, or DHL. Delivery can be made within days or overnight if the customer is willing to pay for the expedited shipment.

Some e-tailers and direct marketing manufacturers own a fleet of delivery vehicles and incorporate the delivery function into their business plan in order to provide greater value to the consumer. These firms will either provide regular deliveries on a daily or other regular schedule or they will deliver items within very short periods of time, usually 1 hour. They might also provide additional services to increase the value proposition for the buyers. An example is Bigboxx.com (bigboxx.com), presented in Online File W5.1. An online grocer, or **e-grocer**, is a typical example of businesses in this category. Home delivery of food from restaurants is another example. In addition, another class of firms (groceries, office supplies, repair parts, and pharmaceutical products) promise virtually instantaneous or at least same-day delivery of goods to consumers.

Whether the delivery is made by company-owned vehicles or is outsourced to a carrier, an express delivery model is referred to as an **on-demand delivery service**. In such a model, the delivery must be done fairly quickly after an order is received. (For more on this topic, see Chapter 11.) A variation of this model is same-day delivery. According to this model, delivery is done faster than "overnight" but slower than the 30 to 60 minutes expected with on-demand delivery. E-grocers often deliver using the same-day delivery model.

The Case of E-Grocers

The U.S. grocery market is valued at over $808 billion annually (Oo 2006). Approximately 1 percent of Americans, or just over 2 million people, buy groceries online (Riseley 2006). It is a very competitive market, and margins are very thin. Online grocery sales are forecast to reach $6.2 billion in 2006, a 17 percent increase on 2005 (McTaggart 2006). Many e-grocers are click-and-mortar retailers that operate in the countries where they have physical stores, such as Woolworths in Australia (woolworths.com.au) and Albertsons (albertsons.com) in the United States. (For statistics on the grocery industry, see retailindustry.about.com/library.)

All e-grocers offer consumers the ability to order items online and have them delivered to their homes. Some e-grocers offer free regular "unattended" weekly delivery (e.g., to the customer's garage), based on a monthly subscription model. Others offer on-demand deliveries (if the customer is at home) with a surcharge added to the grocery

e-grocer
A grocer that takes orders online and provides deliveries on a daily or other regular schedule or within a very short period of time.

on-demand delivery service
Express delivery made fairly quickly after an online order is received.

bill and sometimes an additional delivery charge. One e-grocer sells only nonperishable items shipped via common carrier, a model also adopted by Amazon.com with its recent foray into online grocery sales. Many offer additional services, such as dry-cleaning pickup and delivery. Other add-on features include "don't run out" automatic reordering of routine foods or home office supplies, as well as fresh flower delivery, movie rentals, meal planning, recipe tips, multimedia features, and nutritional information.

Today, it is possible to shop for groceries from cell phones, Blackberries, and PDAs (see Chapter 9). For e-grocery implementation issues see Online File W3.13.

ONLINE DELIVERY OF DIGITAL PRODUCTS, ENTERTAINMENT, AND MEDIA

Certain goods, such as software, music, or news stories, can be distributed in a physical form (such as hard copy, CD-ROM, DVD, and newsprint), or they can be digitized and delivered over the Internet. For example, consumers can purchase shrink-wrapped CD-ROMs containing software (along with the owner's manual and a warranty card) or pay for the software at a Web site and immediately download it onto their computers (usually through File Transfer Protocol [FTP], a fast way to download large files).

As described in Chapter 2, products that can be transformed to digital format and delivered over the Internet are called *digital products*. Exhibit 3.10 provides examples of digital products that can be distributed either physically or digitally. Each delivery method has advantages and disadvantages for both sellers and buyers. Customers, for example, may prefer the formats available through physical distribution. They perceive value in holding a physical CD-ROM or music CD as opposed to a downloaded file. In addition, the related packaging of a physical product can be significant. In some cases, customers enjoy the "liner notes" that accompany a music CD. Paper-based software user manuals and other materials also have value and may be preferred over online help features. However, customers might have to wait days for physical products to be delivered.

For sellers, the costs associated with the manufacture, storage, and distribution of physical products (DVDs, CD-ROMs, paper magazines, etc.) can be enormous. Inventory management also becomes a critical cost issue, and so does delivery and distribution. The need for retail intermediaries requires the establishment of relationships with channel partners and revenue-sharing plans. Direct sales of digital content through digital download, however, allow a producer of digital content to bypass the traditional retail channel, thereby reducing overall costs and capturing greater profits. However, retailers often are crucial in creating demand for a product through in-store displays,

EXHIBIT 3.10 Distribution of Digital Versus Physical Products

Type of Product	Physical Distribution	Digital Distribution
Software	Boxed, shrink-wrapped	FTP, direct download, e-mail
Newspapers, magazines	Home delivery, postal mail	Display on Web, "e-zines"
Greeting cards	Retail stores	E-mail, URL link to recipient
Images (e.g., clip-art, graphics)	CD-ROM, magazines	Web site display, downloadable
Movies	DVD, VHS, NTSB, PAL	MPEG3, streaming video, RealNetwork, AVI, QuickTime, etc.
Music	CD, cassette tape	MP3, WAV, RealAudio downloads, wireless devices, iTunes

advertising, and human sales efforts, all of which are lost when the producer disintermediates the traditional channel.

A major revolution in the online entertainment industry occurred when Napster introduced the P2P file-sharing of music (see Online File W3.14). Another major phenomenon in the online delivery of entertainment is YouTube (see Chapter 8).

ONLINE ENTERTAINMENT

Online entertainment is growing rapidly. A survey by Knowledge Networks/Statistical Research Inc. (Castex 2003) shows that online entertainment is already the most popular medium in the United States among young people between the ages of 8 and 17. Thirty-three percent of these respondents prefer to be entertained online, whereas only 26 percent prefer to watch television. There are many kinds of Internet entertainment. It is difficult to precisely categorize them because there tends to be a mixture of entertainment types, delivery modes, and personal taste and choice in deciding whether something is entertainment or not. Some online entertainment can be regarded as interactive, in that the user can interact, often in a somewhat conversational way, with the software and thus change the outcome or shape the direction of the entertainment activity.

The major forms of traditional entertainment are television, film, radio, music, games, reading, and gambling. All of these are now available over the Internet. However, some have become much more popular in the new environment because the capabilities of modern technology mean that the experience can be enhanced for people who enjoy that activity. For example, online games offer multimedia experiences with colorful animations and sound and allow the player to affect the course and outcome of the game. Examples of online entertainment and services are described in Exhibit 3.11. For a more detailed summary of online entertainment see Online File W3.15. For entertainment in the Web environment see Chapter 8.

Section 3.7 ▶ REVIEW QUESTIONS

1. Explain on-demand delivery service.
2. Describe e-grocers and how they operate.
3. What are the difficulties in shopping online for groceries?
4. Describe digital goods and their delivery.

EXHIBIT 3.11 Examples of Online Entertainment and Services	
Online Entertainment	**Entertainment-Related Services**
Web browsing	Event ticketing
Internet gaming	Restaurant reservations
Fantasy sports games	Information retrieval
Single and multiplayer games	Retrieval of audio and video entertainment
Adult entertainment	
Card games	
Social networking sites	
Participatory Web sites	
Reading	
Live events	

5. What are the benefits and the limitations of digital delivery?

6. What are the major forms of online entertainment? (See Online File W3.15.) Do you think people of different age groups and social classes might be attracted to different types of online entertainment?

3.8   ONLINE PURCHASE-DECISION AIDS

Many sites and tools are available to help consumers with online purchasing decisions. Wal-Mart, for example, equipped its online store with an intelligent search engine. Consumers must decide which product or service to purchase, which site to use for the purchase (a manufacturer site, a general-purpose e-tailer, a niche intermediary, or some other site), and what other services to employ. Some sites offer price comparisons as their primary tool (e.g., pricerunner.com, shopzilla.com, and goodgearguide.com.au); others evaluate services, trust, quality, and other factors. Shopping portals, shopping robots ("shopbots"), business ratings sites, trust verification sites, and other shopping aids also are available.

SHOPPING PORTALS

shopping portals
Gateways to e-storefronts and e-malls; may be comprehensive or niche oriented.

Shopping portals are gateways to storefronts and e-malls. Like any other portal, they can be comprehensive or niche oriented. Comprehensive, or general-purpose, portals have links to many different sellers and present and evaluate a broad range of products. An example of a comprehensive portal is Ecost.com (ecost.com). Several public portals also offer shopping opportunities and comparison aids. Examples are shopping.com, shopping.yahoo.com, shopping.msn.com, and shopping.aol.com. eBay is a shopping portal because it offers shopping at fixed prices as well as auctions. These all have clear shopping links from the main page of the portal, and they generate revenues by directing consumers to their affiliates' sites. Some of these portals even offer comparison tools to help identify the best price for a particular item. Several of these evaluation companies have purchased shopbots (see the following discussion) or other, smaller shopping aids and incorporated them into their portals.

Some shopping portals also offer specialized niche aids with information and links for purchasers of automobiles, toys, computers, travel, or some other narrow area. Such portals also help customers conduct research. Examples include review.zdnet.com and shopper.cnet.com for computer equipment. The advantage of niche shopping portals is their ability to specialize in a certain line of products and carefully track consumer tastes within a specific and relevant market segment. Some of these portals seek only to collect the referral fee from their affiliation with sites they recommend. Others have no formal relationship with the sellers; instead, they sell banner ad space to advertisers who wish to reach the communities who regularly visit these specialized sites. In other cases, shopping portals act as intermediaries by selling directly to consumers, although this might harm their reputation for independence and objectivity.

SHOPBOTS SOFTWARE AGENTS

shopping robots (shopping agents or shopbots)
Tools that scout the Web on behalf of consumers who specify search criteria.

Savvy Internet shoppers may bookmark their favorite shopping sites, but what if they want to find other stores with good service and policies that sell similar items at lower prices? **Shopping robots** (also called shopping agents or shopbots) are tools that scout the Web for consumers who specify search criteria. Different shopbots use different search methods. For example, MySimon (mysimon.com) searches the Web to find the best prices and availability for thousands of popular items. This is not a simple task. The shopbot might have to evaluate different SKU (stock-keeping unit) numbers for the same item, because each e-tailer may have a different SKU rather than a standardized data-representation code. In addition to price, pricegrabber.com includes product details and features, product reviews from merchants and consumers, and additional information about the store selling the item.

Some agents specialize in certain product categories or niches. For example, consumers can get help shopping for cars at autobytel.com, carsdirect.com, autovantage.com, and autos.msn.com. Zdnet.com searches for information on computers, software, and peripherals. A shopping agent at mysimon.com helps consumers find the best price for products from online stores. A shopping agent for books is isbn.nu. In addition, agents such as pricegrabber.com are able to identify customers' preferences. Shopping.com (shopping.com) (now owned by eBay) allows consumers to compare over 1,000 different merchant sites and seeks lower prices on their behalf. Negotiation agents are even available to assist auction bidders (e.g., auctionbid.com) by automating the bid process using the bidder's instructions. For a comparison of shopping bots, refer to Aquino (2005) and Wang (2006).

"SPY" SERVICES

In this context, "spy" services are not the CIA or MI5 (mi5.gov.uk). Rather, they are services that visit Web sites for customers, at their direction, and notify them of their findings. Web surfers and shoppers constantly monitor sites for new information, special sales, ending time of auctions, stock updates, and so on, but visiting the sites to monitor them is time consuming. Several sites will track stock prices or airline special sales and send e-mails accordingly. For example, cnn.com, pcworld.com, and expedia.com will send people personalized alerts. Spectorsoft.com enables users to create a list of "spies" that visit Web sites; the spy sends an e-mail when it finds something of interest. Users can choose predesigned spies or create their own. Special searches are provided by web2mail.com, which responds to e-mail queries. Of special interest is Yahoo! Alerts (alerts.yahoo.com), an index of e-mail alerts for many different things, including job listings, real estate, travel specials, and auctions. Users set up alerts so that they hit their in-boxes periodically or whenever new information is available. The alerts are sent via e-mail and come with commercial ads.

Of course, one of the most effective ways to spy on Internet users is to introduce cookies and spyware in their computers. (See Chapter 4 for details.)

Wireless Shopping Comparisons

Users of mySimon.com (all regular services) and AT&T Digital PocketNet service have access to wireless shopping comparisons. Users who are equipped with an AT&T Internet-ready cell phone can find the service on the AT&T main menu; it enables shoppers to compare prices any time from anywhere, including from any physical store.

BUSINESS RATINGS SITES

Many Web sites rate various e-tailers and online products based on multiple criteria. Bizrate.com (bizrate.com), Consumer Reports Online (consumerreports.org), Forrester Research (forrester.com), and Gomez Advisors (gomez.com) are such well-known sites. At Gomez.com, the consumer can actually specify the relative importance of different criteria when comparing online banks, toy sellers, e-grocers, and so on. Bizrate.com organized a network of shoppers that report on various sellers and uses the compiled results in its evaluations. Note that different raters provide different rankings. Online File W3.16 discusses ResellerRatings.com, an interesting example of a business ratings site.

TRUST VERIFICATION SITES

With so many sellers online, many consumers are not sure whom they should trust. A number of companies purport to evaluate and verify the trustworthiness of various e-tailers. One such company is TRUSTe. The TRUSTe seal appears at the bottom of each TRUSTe-approved e-tailer's Web site. E-tailers pay TRUSTe for use of the seal (which they call a "trustmark"). TRUSTe's 1,300-plus members hope that consumers will use the seal as an assurance and as a proxy for actual research into their conduct of business, privacy policy, and personal information protection.

The most comprehensive trust verification sites are VeriSign, BBBOnline, and WebTrust (cpawebtrust.org). VeriSign (verisign.com) tends to be the most widely used. Other sources of trust verification include Secure Assure (secureassure.com), which charges yearly license fees based on a company's annual revenue. In addition, Ernst and Young, the global public accounting firm, has created its own service for auditing e-tailers in order to offer some guarantee of the integrity of their business practices.

OTHER SHOPPING TOOLS

Other digital intermediaries assist buyers or sellers, or both, with the research and purchase processes. For example, escrow services (e.g., escrow.com and fortis-escrow.com) assist buyers and sellers in the exchange of items and money. Because buyers and sellers do not see or know each other, a trusted third party frequently is needed to facilitate the proper exchange of money and goods. Escrow sites may also provide payment-processing support, as well as letters of credit (see Chapter 11).

Other decision aids include communities of consumers who offer advice and opinions on products and e-tailers. One such site is epinions.com, which has searchable recommendations on thousands of products. Pricescan.com is a price comparison engine, and pricegrabber.com is a comparison shopping tool that covers over 1 million products. Onlineshoes.com specializes in all types of shoes, and askshoppy.com specializes in apparel, health and beauty, and other categories. Other software agents and comparison sites are presented in Online File W3.17.

Another shopping tool is a *wallet*—in this case, an *electronic wallet*, which is a program that contains the shopper's information. To expedite online shopping, consumers can use electronic wallets so that they do not need to reenter the information each time they shop. Although sites such as Amazon.com offer their own specialized wallets, Microsoft has a universal wallet in its Passport program (see Chapter 10 for details).

Section 3.8 ▶ REVIEW QUESTIONS

1. Define shopping portals and provide two examples.
2. What are shopbots?
3. Explain the role of business and Web site rating and site verification tools in the purchase-decision process.
4. Why are escrow services and electronic wallets useful for online purchases?
5. Describe the role of search engines to support shopping.

3.9 PROBLEMS WITH E-TAILING AND LESSONS LEARNED

There are a number of challenges in creating a successful e-tailing business. A few companies do not even try e-tailing, although these numbers are declining. The reasons that retailers give for not going online include: their product is not appropriate for Web sales, lack of significant opportunity, high cost, technological immaturity, online sales conflict with core business, and the like. Others try e-tailing but do not succeed. E-tailing offers some serious challenges and tremendous risks for those who fail to provide value to the consumer, who fail to establish a profitable business model, or who fail to properly execute the model they establish. The road to e-tail success is littered with dead companies that could not deliver on their promises. The shakeout from mid-2000 to late-2002 caused many companies to fail; others learned and adapted. It is fair to say that the much more balanced, analytical, and sober perspective of late offers a much better appreciation of the issues, challenges, risks, and potential benefits of EC.

Online File W3.18 provides a sample of failed B2C companies. Some enduring principles can be distilled from the failures, and these "lessons learned" are discussed next.

SUCCESSFUL CLICK-AND-MORTAR STRATEGIES

Although thousands of companies have evolved their online strategies into mature Web sites with extensive interactive features that add value to the consumer purchase process, many sites remain simple "brochureware" sites with limited interactivity. Many traditional companies are in a transitional stage. Mature transactional systems include features for payment processing, order fulfillment, logistics, inventory management, and a host of other services. In most cases, a company must replicate each of its physical business processes and design many more that can only be performed online. Today's environment includes sophisticated access to order information, shipping information, product information, and more through Web pages, touchtone phones, Web-enabled cell phones, and PDAs over wireless networks. Faced with all of these variables, the challenges to implementing EC can be daunting.

The real gains for traditional retailers come from leveraging the benefits of their physical presence and the benefits of their online presence. Web sites frequently offer better prices and selection, whereas physical stores offer a trustworthy staff and opportunities for customers to examine items before purchasing. Large, efficient established retailers, such as Wal-Mart (walmart.com), Marks & Spencer (marksandspencer.com), and Nordstrom (nordstrom.com), are able to create the optimum value proposition for their customers by providing a complete offering of services.

A traditional brick-and-mortar store with a mature Web site that uses a click-and-mortar strategy is able to do the following:

▶ **Speak with one voice.** A firm can link all of its back-end systems to create an integrated customer experience. The online experience should be an extension of the experience encountered in traditional transactions.

▶ **Leverage the multichannels.** The innovative retailer will offer the advantages of each marketing channel to customers from all channels. Whether the purchase is made online or at the store, the customer should benefit from the presence of both channels.

▶ **Empower the customer.** The seller needs to create a powerful 24/7 channel for service and information. Through various information technologies, sellers can give customers the opportunity to perform various functions interactively, at any time. Such functions include the ability to find store locations, product information, and inventory availability online.

Section 3.9 ▶ REVIEW QUESTIONS

1. Why are virtual e-tailers usually not profitable?

2. What makes click-and-mortar companies successful?

3.10 ISSUES IN E-TAILING

The following are representative issues that need to be addressed when conducting B2C.

DISINTERMEDIATION AND REINTERMEDIATION

disintermediation

The removal of organizations or business process layers responsible for certain intermediary steps in a given supply chain.

reintermediation

The process whereby intermediaries (either new ones or those that had been disintermediated) take on new intermediary roles.

Disintermediation refers to the removal of organizations or business process layers responsible for certain intermediary steps in a given supply chain. As shown in part B of Exhibit 3.12, the manufacturer can bypass the wholesalers and retailers, selling directly to consumers. Also, e-tailers may drive regular retailers out of business. For a vivid case of such disintermediation, see the Blue Nile case in Chapter 2.

However, consumers might have problems selecting an online vendor; vendors might have problems delivering to customers; and both might need an escrow service to ensure the transaction. Thus, new online assistance might be needed, and it might be provided by new or by traditional intermediaries. In such cases, the traditional intermediaries fill new roles, providing *added value* and assistance. This process is referred to as **reintermediation**. It is pictured in part C of Exhibit 3.12. Thus, for the intermediary, the Internet offers new ways to reach new customers, new ways to bring value to customers, and perhaps new ways to generate revenues.

The intermediary's role is shifting to one that emphasizes value-added services, such as assisting customers in comparison shopping from multiple sources, providing

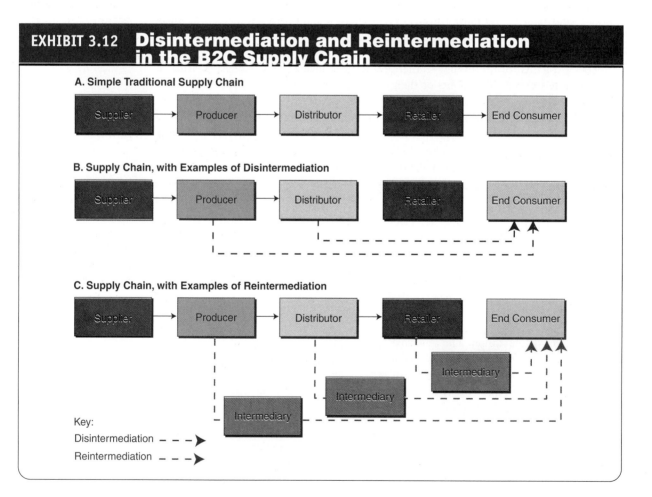

EXHIBIT 3.12 Disintermediation and Reintermediation in the B2C Supply Chain

total solutions by combining services from several vendors, and providing certifications and trusted third-party control and evaluation systems. For instance, in the world of online new and used car sales, electronic intermediaries assist buyers and/or sellers. These are new *reintermediaries*; intermediaries that have restructured their role in the purchase process. An example of the new roles of intermediaries is Edmunds (edmunds.com), which gives consumers a vast amount of information about cars, including price comparisons, ratings, the location of cars for sale, and the dealer's true costs.

Some reintermediaries cooperate with manufacturers or retailers to provide a needed service to the seller or distributor in the online environment. Other reintermediaries are virtual e-tailers that fill a unique niche. Intermediaries such as online retailers and shopping portals can also act as reintermediaries. The evolution and operation of these companies is critical to the success of e-commerce.

Cybermediation

In addition to reintermediation, a completely new role in EC has emerged called **cybermediation**, or **electronic intermediation**. These terms describe special Web sites that use intelligent agents to facilitate intermediation. Cybermediators can perform many roles in EC and can affect most market functions. For example, intelligent agents can find when and where an item that a consumer wants will be auctioned. The matching services described in this chapter are done by *cybermediator agents*. Cybermediator agents also conduct price comparisons of insurance policies, long-distance calls, and other services. Cybermediation services are spreading rapidly around the globe, and with developments in intelligent software are likely to increase in number and capability. Note that some question the risks associated with this (Shoniregun 2004).

cybermediation (electronic intermediation)
The use of software (intelligent) agents to facilitate intermediation.

CHANNEL CONFLICT

Many traditional retailers establish a new marketing channel when they start selling online. Similarly, some manufacturers have instituted direct marketing initiatives in parallel with their established channels of distribution, such as retailers or dealers. In such cases, channel conflict can occur. **Channel conflict** refers to any situation in which direct competition and/or damage caused by bypassing a former existing channel partner is perceived to have resulted from the introduction of a new, often online, channel. The extent of this conflict varies according to the nature of the industry and characteristics of particular firms, but sometimes, a move to sell online can damage old, valued relationships between trading partners. Channel conflict can also be said to occur when a move to online trading simply moves a company's customers from their traditional stores, for example, to an online environment, thus cannibalizing the sales from the former and potentially negatively impacting the traditional outlets by rendering them less profitable. However, careful management and the adoption of sound strategies can deliver a number of synergies for click-and-mortar e-tailers, especially those associated with encouraging cross-channel cooperation and exploiting the unique strengths of each channel to maximize the experience for the customer.

channel conflict
Situation in which an online marketing channel upsets the traditional channels due to real or perceived damage from competition.

DETERMINING THE RIGHT PRICE

Pricing a product or service on the Internet, especially by a click-and-mortar company, is complicated. On the one hand, prices need to be competitive on the Internet. Today's comparison engines will show the consumer the prices at many stores, for almost all commodity products, at almost no cost to the consumer. However, balanced against this is the fact that for some items, transaction costs will decrease, the cost of distribution will decrease, and supply chains may become more efficient and shorter, meaning that e-tailers might be able to compete in the aggressive online market space. On the other hand, prices should be in line with the corporate policy on profitability and, in a click-and-mortar company, in line with the offline channel's pricing strategy. To avoid price conflict, some companies have created independent online subsidiaries.

EC offers companies new opportunities to test prices, segment customers, and adjust to changes in supply and demand. We argue that companies are not taking advantage of these opportunities. Companies can make prices more precise (optimal prices); they can be more adaptable to changes in the environment; and they can be more creative and accurate regarding different prices to different segments. In addition, in one-to-one marketing (Chapter 4) a company can have personalized prices. (For use of price-optimization tools in retailing, see Parks 2004.)

PRODUCT AND SERVICE CUSTOMIZATION AND PERSONALIZATION

One significant characteristic of many online marketing business models is the ability of the seller to create an element of *personalization* for each individual consumer.

The Internet also allows for easy self-configuration ("design it your way"). This creates a large demand for customized products and services. Manufacturers can meet that demand by using a *mass customization* strategy. As indicated earlier, many companies offer customized products from their Web sites (e.g., see the Dell case in Chapter 1).

Although pure-play e-tailing is risky and its future is unclear, e-tailing is growing rapidly as a complementary distribution channel to traditional stores and catalogs. In other words, the *click-and-mortar model is winning currently and all evidence suggests that this trend will continue.* (See the Real-World Case at the end of the chapter.)

FRAUD AND OTHER ILLEGAL ACTIVITIES

A major problem in B2C is the increasing rate of online fraud. This can cause losses to both buyers and sellers. For a more detailed and thorough discussion of online fraud, see the discussion of online fraud in Chapter 10.

HOW TO MAKE CUSTOMERS HAPPY

A critical success factor for B2C is to find what customers want, so the vendor can make them happy. In addition to price, customers want convenience, service, and quality, and they often want to enjoy the experience of online shopping. Merchants can find out what customers want through *market research*, the topic of our next chapter.

Section 3.10 ▶ REVIEW QUESTIONS

1. Define disintermediation.
2. Describe mediation issues, including disintermediation, reintermediation, and cybermediation.
3. Describe channel conflict and other conflicts that may appear in e-tailing.
4. Describe price determination in e-tailing.
5. Explain personalization and mass customization opportunities in e-tailing.

MANAGERIAL ISSUES

Some managerial issues related to this chapter are as follows.

1. **What should our strategic position be?** The most important decision for retailers and e-tailers is the overall *strategic position* they establish within their industry. What niche will they fill? What business functions will they execute internally, and which functions will be outsourced? What partners will they use? How will they integrate brick-and-mortar facilities with their online presence? What are their revenue sources in the short and long run, and what are their fixed and marginal costs? An e-business is still a business and must establish solid business practices in the long run in order to ensure profitability and viability. We discuss such issues in Chapter 12.

2. **Are we financially viable?** The collapse of the dot-com bubble that started in early 2000 provided a wake-up call to many e-tailers. Some returned to business fundamentals, whereas others sought to redefine their business plan in terms of click-and-mortar strategies or alliances with traditional retailers. Because most easy sources of funding have dried up and revenue models are being scrutinized, many e-tailers also are pursuing new partners, and consolidation will continue until there is greater stability within the e-tail segment. Ultimately, there will likely be a smaller number of larger sellers with comprehensive sites and many smaller, specialized niche sites.

3. **How should we introduce wireless shopping?** In some countries (e.g., Japan) shopping from cell phones is very popular (see Chapter 9). However, offering mobile shopping might not be simple or appropriate to all businesses.

4. **Are there international legal issues regarding online recruiting?** Various legal issues must be considered with international online recruiting. For example, online recruitment of people from other countries often involves immigration and legal constraints, and the validity of contracts signed in different countries must be checked by legal experts.

5. **Do we have ethics and privacy guidelines?** Ethical issues are extremely important in an agentless system. In traditional systems, human agents play an important role in assuring the ethical behavior of buyers and sellers. Will online ethics and the rules of etiquette be sufficient to guide behavior on the Internet? Only time will tell. For example, as job-applicant information travels over the Internet, security and privacy become even more important. It is management's job to make sure that information from applicants is secure. Also, e-tailers need to establish guidelines for protecting the privacy of customers who visit their Web sites.

6. **How will intermediaries act in cyberspace?** It will take a few years before the new roles of Internet intermediaries will be stabilized, as well as their fees. Also, the emergence of support services, such as escrow services in global EC, will have an impact on intermediaries and their role.

SUMMARY

In this chapter, you learned about the following EC issues as they relate to the learning objectives.

1. **The scope and characteristics of e-tailing.** E-tailing, the online selling of products and services, is growing rapidly. Computers, software, and electronics are the major items sold online. Books, CDs, toys, office supplies, and other standard commodities also sell well. More successful are services sold online, such as airline tickets and travel services, stocks, and insurance.

2. **E-tailing business models.** The major e-tailing business models can be classified by distribution channel—a manufacturer or mail-order company selling direct to consumers, pure-play (virtual) e-tailing, a click-and-mortar strategy with both online and traditional channels, and online malls that provide either referring directories or shared services.

3. **How online travel/tourism services operate.** Most services available through a physical travel agency also are available online. In addition, customers get much more information, much more

quickly through online resources. Customers can even receive bids from travel providers. Finally, travelers can compare prices, participate in auctions and chat rooms, and view videos and maps.

4. **The online job market and its benefits.** The online job market is growing rapidly, with thousands and thousands of jobs matched with job seekers each year. The major benefits of online job markets are the ability to reach a large number of job seekers at low cost, to provide detailed information online, to take applications, and even to conduct tests. Also, using intelligent agents, résumés can be checked and matches made more quickly. Millions of job offers posted on the Internet help job seekers, who also can post their résumés for recruiters.

5. **The electronic real estate market.** The online real estate market is basically supporting rather than replacing existing agents. However, both buyers and sellers can save time and effort in the electronic market. Buyers can purchase distant properties much more easily and in some places have access to less expensive services. Eventually, commissions on regular transactions are expected to decline as a result of the electronic market for real estate and more sales "by owner" will materialize.

6. **Online trading of stocks and bonds.** One of the fastest growing online businesses is the online trading of securities. It is inexpensive, convenient, and supported by a tremendous amount of financial and advisory information. Trading is very fast and efficient, almost fully automated, and moving toward 24/7 global trading. However, security breaches are possible, so tight protection is a must.

7. **Cyberbanking and personal finance.** Branch banking is on the decline due to less expensive, more convenient online banking. The world is moving toward online banking; today, most routine banking services can be done from home. Banks can reach customers in remote places, and customers can bank with faraway institutions. This makes the financial markets more efficient. Online personal finance applications, such as bill paying, tracking of accounts, and tax preparation, also are very popular.

8. **On-demand delivery service.** On-demand delivery service is needed when items are perishable or when delivering medicine, express documents, or urgently needed supplies. One example of on-demand delivery is e-groceries; these may be ordered online and are shipped or ready for store pickup within 24 hours or less.

9. **Delivery of digital products.** Anything that can be digitized can be successfully delivered online. Delivery of digital products such as music, software, movies, and other entertainment online has been a success. Some print media, such as electronic versions of magazines or electronic books (see Chapter 7), also are having success when digitized and delivered electronically.

10. **Aiding consumer purchase decisions.** Purchase decision aids include shopping portals, shopbots and comparison agents, business rating sites, trust verification sites, and other tools.

11. **Disintermediation and other B2C strategic issues.** Direct electronic marketing by manufacturers results in disintermediation by removing wholesalers and retailers. However, online reintermediaries provide additional value, such as helping consumers make selections among multiple products and vendors. Traditional retailers may feel threatened or pressured when manufacturers decide to sell online; such direct selling can cause channel conflict. Pricing of online and offline products and services is one issue that always needs to be addressed.

KEY TERMS

Brick-and-mortar retailers	93	E-grocer	111	On-demand delivery service	111
Channel conflict	119	E-tailers	85	Reintermediation	118
Click-and-mortar retailers	92	Electronic (online) banking or		Shopping portals	114
Cybermediation (electronic		e-banking	106	Shopping robots (shopping	
intermediation)	119	Electronic retailing (e-tailing)	85	agents or shopbots)	114
Direct marketing	91	Multichannel business model	93	Virtual (pure-play) e-tailers	91
Disintermediation	118				

QUESTIONS FOR DISCUSSION

1. What are Amazon.com's critical success factors? Is its decision not to limit its sales to books, music, and movies but to offer a much broader selection of items a good marketing strategy? With the broader selection, do you think the company will dilute its brand or extend the value proposition to its customers?

2. Discuss the advantages of established click-and-mortar companies such as Wal-Mart over pure-play e-tailers such as Amazon.com. What are the disadvantages of click-and-brick retailers as compared with pure-play e-tailers?

3. Discuss the importance of comparison tools, product reviews, and customer ratings in online shopping.

4. Discuss the advantages of a specialized e-tailer, such as Dogtoys.com (**dogtoys.com**). Can such a store survive in the physical world? Why or why not?

5. Discuss the benefits of build-to-order to buyers and sellers. Are there any disadvantages?

6. Why are online travel services a popular Internet application? Why do so many Web sites provide free travel information?

7. Compare the advantages and disadvantages of online stock trading with offline trading.

8. It is said that the service Zuji.com provides to travel agents will lead to their reintermediation. Discuss.

9. Online employment services make it easy to change jobs; therefore, turnover rates may increase. This could result in total higher costs for employers because of increased costs for recruiting and training new employees and the need to pay higher salaries and wages to attract or keep them. What can companies do to ease this problem?

10. Compare the advantages and disadvantages of distributing digitizable products electronically versus physically.

INTERNET EXERCISES

1. Many consumer portals offer advice and ratings of products or e-tailers. Identify and examine two separate general-consumer portals that look at other sites and compare prices or other purchase criteria. Try to find and compare prices for a digital camera, a microwave oven, and an MP3 player. Visit **clusty.com**. How can this site help you in your shopping? Summarize your experience. Comment on the strong and weak points of such shopping tools.

2. Almost all auto manufacturers allow consumers to configure their cars online. Visit a major automaker's Web site and configure a car of your choice (e.g., **jaguar.com**). Also visit one electronic intermediary (e.g., **autobytel.com**). After you decide what car you want, examine the payment options and figure your monthly payments. Print your results. How does this process compare with visiting an auto dealer? Do you think you found a better price online? Would you consider buying a car this way?

3. Visit **amazon.com** and identify at least three specific elements of its personalization and customization features. Browse specific books on one particular subject, leave the site, and then go back and revisit the site. What do you see? Are these features likely to  encourage you to purchase more books in the future from Amazon.com? Check the 1-Click feature and other shopping aids provided. List the features and discuss how they may lead to increased sales.

4. Visit **landsend.com** and prepare a customized order for a piece of clothing. Describe the process. Do you think this will result in better-fitting clothing? Do you think this personalization feature will lead to greater sales volume for Lands' End?

5. Make your résumé accessible to millions of people. Consult **asktheheadhunter.com** or **careerbuilder. com** for help rewriting your résumé. See **monster. com** for ideas about planning your career. Get prepared for a job interview. Also, use the Web to determine what salary you can get in the city of your choice in the United States.

6. Visit **move.com**, **decisionaide.com**, or a similar site and compute the monthly mortgage payment on a 30-year loan at 7.5 percent fixed interest. Also check current interest rates. Estimate your closing costs on a $200,000 loan. Compare the monthly payments of the fixed rate with that of an adjustable rate for the first year. Finally, compute your total payments if you take the loan for 15 years at the going rate. Compare it with a 30-year mortgage. Comment on the difference.

7. Access the Virtual Trader game at **virtualtrader.co.uk** and register for the Internet stock game. You will be bankrolled with £100,000 in a trading account every month. You also can play investment games at **investorsleague.com**, **fantasystockmarket.com**, and **etrade.com**.

8. Compare the price of a Sony digital camera at **shopping.com**, **mysimon.com**, **bottomdollar.com**, **bizrate.com**, and **pricescan.com**. Which site locates the best deal? Where do you get the best information?

9. Enter **xing.com** and identify its job-related offerings. Prepare a list of support activities offered.

10. Compare the "build-your-own" at Nike (**nike.com**) with Timberland's Boot Studio (**timberland.com**).

11. Enter **jobster.com** and **monster.com** and compare the process used by recruiting companies to find qualified candidates. Comment on the differences between the two sites. Also, compare the sites from a job seeker's perspective.

TEAM ASSIGNMENTS AND ROLE PLAYING

1. Each team will investigate the services of two online car-selling sites from the following list (or other sites). When teams have finished, they should bring their research together and discuss their findings.
   a. Buying new cars through an intermediary (**autobytel.com**, **carsdirect.com**, **autoweb.com**, or **amazon.com**)
   b. Buying used cars (**autotrader.com**)
   c. Buying used cars by auto dealers (**manheim.com**)
   d. Automobile ratings sites (**carsdirect.com** and **fueleconomy.gov**)
   e. Car-buying portals (**thecarportal.com** and **cars.com**)
   f. Buying antique cars (**classiccars.com** and **antiquecars.com**)

2. Each team will represent a broker-based area (e.g., real estate, insurance, stocks, job finding). Each team will find a new development that has occurred in the assigned area over the most recent 3 months. Look for the site vendor's announcement and search for more information on the development with **google.com** or another search engine. Examine the business news at **bloomberg.com**. After completing your research, as a team, prepare a report on disintermediation in your assigned area.

3. Each team will examine fantasy games at various sites. Each team should examine the type of game, the rules, and the cost. Play at least one time. Each team should write a report based on its experiences. (Hint: See Online File W3.15.)

Real-World Case
WAL-MART POWERS ONLINE

Wal-Mart (*walmart.com*) is the largest retailer in the world, with $345 billion in sales for the fiscal year ending January 31, 2007. Wal-Mart employs 1.9 million people, 1.3 million in the United States.

The company has more than 4,000 stores in the United States and more than 2,800 in the rest of the world. Each week, 180 million customers visit Wal-Mart stores worldwide, including 127 million in the United States (see *walmartfacts.com* for current statistics).

Wal-Mart maintains an intense strategic focus on the customer. Its standard company cheer ends with, "Who's number one? The customer." Wal-Mart has also established itself as a master of the retail process by streamlining its supply chain and undercutting competitors with low prices.

Wal-Mart has had an online presence since 1996. However, one problem with its strategy for growing online sales has been the demographics of its primary customer base. Wal-Mart's target demographic is households with $25,000 in annual income, whereas the median income of online consumers is perhaps $60,000. Despite these demographics, online sales (primarily in music, travel, and electronics) through *walmart.com* already account for about 10 percent of Wal-Mart's U.S. sales. Its long-time chief rival, Kmart, Inc., tried to attract its demographic audience to its Web site (*kmart.com*) by offering free Internet access. This appealed to its cost-conscious, lower-income constituency and provided the opportunity for those customers to access the site to conduct purchases. However, this move decreased company profits in the short run and was one of the factors that led Kmart to file for bankruptcy in 2002.

Wal-Mart also has concerns about cannibalizing its in-store sales. Its alliance with AOL is designed to provide cobranded low-cost Internet access to dwellers in both very rural and very urban areas, where there are no Wal-Mart stores nearby. The intent is to lure new market segments and thus cancel the effect of cannibalization. Ultimately, a hybrid e-tailer that can offer a combination of huge selection with the click-and-mortar advantages of nearby stores (e.g., merchandise pickup or returns) might prove to be the 800-pound gorilla of online consumer sales.

In 2002, Walmart.com matured, offering order status and tracking, a help desk, a clear return policy and mechanisms, a store locator, and information on special sales and liquidations. Today, community services, such as photo sharing, are provided.

Wal-Mart only offers some of its merchandise online, but the selection is increasing, including items not available in some or all stores (e.g., spas, mattresses). In 2004, Wal-Mart started selling songs online for 88 cents each, competing with Apple's iTunes. Inexpensive items (e.g., those that sell for less than $5) are not available online. Also in 2004, during a 4-day Thanksgiving special, Wal-Mart began to court more affluent shoppers with new and more expensive items available only online. Products included cashmere sweaters and shiatsu massage chairs. The Web site averaged 8 million visitors each week prior to the promotion.

Wal-Mart had added many new products to its online catalog. International customers can buy Wal-Mart products directly from Wal-Mart (if shipping is available) or from affiliate sites. For example, see ASDA (*asda.co.uk*), a Wal-Mart owned U.K. company.

In 2006, a fake "Wal-Marting Across America" blog—a very rough attempt at teen social networking—became a learning experience for the company. Also in 2006, the company revamped its site for the first time since 2000. The site now features a new four-click checkout process and rich-media, including interactive functions in the toy section.

In 2007, Wal-Mart rolled out its new order online/pick up in store service. "Site to Store," enables customers to buy online and have products shipped for free to their store of choice. The new service also gives customers access to tens of thousands of products, many more than are available in stores. Delivery for such items is 7 to 10 days (*Internetretailer.com* 2007c).

According to Nielsen/NetRatings, in 2007 Wal-Mart recorded the third-largest increase in Web traffic among the top 10 online shopping and travel sites. Site visits to Walmart.com in January 2007 were 23 million, up 25 percent over January 2006. For January 2007, Walmart.com was ranked the third most popular site by Nielsen/NetRatings in terms of the number of visits, behind eBay and Amazon.com (*Internetretailer.com* 2007b).

Sources: Compiled from Bhatnagar (2004), *Internetretailer.com* (2007b), *Internetretailer.com* (2007c), and *walmart.com* (accessed January 2008).

Questions

1. Compare *walmart.com* with *amazon.com*. What features do the sites have in common? Which are unique to Walmart.com? To Amazon.com?

2. Will Wal-Mart become the dominant e-tailer in the world, replacing Amazon.com, or will Amazon.com dominate Wal-Mart online? What factors would contribute to Wal-Mart's success in the online marketplace? What factors would detract from its ability to dominate online sales the way it has been able to dominate physical retail sales in many markets?

3. Check the shopping aids offered at *walmart.com*. Compare them with those at *amazon.com*.

4. What online services can be purchased on Walmart.com?

5. Compare buying a song from Walmart.com versus buying it from Apple's iTunes.

6. Walmart.com sells movies online for a monthly fee. How do similar sellers compare?

7. Visit *walmart.com*, *target.com*, *marksandspencer.com*, and *sears.com*. Identify the common features of their online marketing and at least one unique feature evident at each site. Do these sites have to distinguish themselves primarily in terms of price, product selection, or Web site features?

8. Investigate the options for international customers on the Wal-Mart Web site.

CHAPTER 4

ONLINE CONSUMER BEHAVIOR, MARKET RESEARCH, AND ADVERTISEMENT

Content

Learning Objectives

Upon completion of this chapter, you will be able to:

1. Understand the decision-making process of consumer purchasing online.

2. Describe how companies are building one-to-one relationships with customers.

3. Explain how personalization is accomplished online.

4. Discuss the issues of e-loyalty and e-trust in EC.

5. Describe consumer market research in EC.

6. Describe Internet marketing in B2B, including organizational buyer behavior.

7. Describe the objectives of Web advertising and its characteristics.

8. Describe the major advertising methods used on the Web.

9. Describe various online advertising strategies and types of promotions.

10. Describe permission marketing, ad management, localization, and other advertising-related issues.

NETFLIX INCREASES SALES USING MOVIE RECOMMENDATIONS

Netflix (*netflix.com*) is the world's largest online movie rental subscription company. The company has more than 1,500 employees and over 7 million subscribers. It offers more than 90,000 titles in over 200 categories and more than 55 million DVDs, as well as over 5,000 full-length movies and television episodes that are available for instant viewing on PCs. A typical neighborhood movie store generally has fewer than 3,000 titles and has multiple copies of only a fraction of them. Netflix distributes 1 million DVDs each day.

The Problem

Because of the large number of titles available on DVD, customers often had difficulty determining which ones they would like to rent. In most cases, they picked up the most popular recent titles, which meant that Netflix had to maintain more and more copies of the same title. In addition, some unpopular titles were not renting well, even though they matched certain customers' preferences. For Netflix, matching titles with customers and maintaining the right level of inventory is critical.

A second major problem facing Netflix is the competitive nature of the movie rental business. Netflix competes against Blockbuster and other rental companies, as well as against companies offering downloads of movies and videos.

The Solution

Netflix reacted successfully to the first problem by offering a *recommendation service* called CineMatch. This software agent uses data mining tools to sift through a database of over 1 billion film ratings (which is growing rapidly), as well as through customers' rental histories. Using proprietary formulas, CineMatch recommends rentals to individuals. It is a personalization service, similar to the one offered by Amazon.com that recommends books to customers. The recommendation is accomplished by comparing an individual's likes, dislikes, and preferences against people with similar tastes using a variant of collaborative filtering (described later in this chapter). (Both Blockbuster and Walmart.com are emulating Netflix's model.) With the recommendation system, Netflix tells subscribers which DVDs/CDs they will probably like. CineMatch is like the geeky clerk at a small movie store who sets aside titles he knows you will like.

Netflix subscribers can also invite one another to become "friends" and make movie recommendations to each other, peek at one another's rental lists, and see how other subscribers have rated other movies using a social network called FriendsSM. All these personalized functions make the online rental store very customer-friendly. It is an example of a social network.

To improve CineMatch's accuracy, in October 2006 Netflix began a contest offering $1 million to the first person or team to write a program that would increase the prediction accuracy of CineMatch by 10 percent. The company understands that this will take quite some time; therefore, it is offering a $50,000 Progress Prize each year the contest runs. This prize goes to the team whose solution shows the most improvement over the previous year's accuracy bar (see *netflixprize.com*).

Netflix is advertising extensively on the Web using several methods. For example, to promote its brand, Netflix has placed static banner ads on the Yahoo!, MSN, and AOL Web sites, as well as a number of other sites. Search engine advertisement also is being used (discussed later in this chapter). Netflix also has an affiliate program. It uses almost all online advertising techniques, including permission e-mail, blogs, social networking, classifieds, RSS, and more.

Starting September 13, 2006, Netflix launched a 5-week trivia sweepstakes program with *USA Weekend* magazine. Trivia questions were published each week in *USA Weekend,* directing its 50 million readers to Netflix to enter the sweepstakes and qualify to win weekly prizes. Prizes ranged from $250 to $4,000, costing the company over $140 million.

The Results

As a result of implementing its CineMatch system, Netflix has seen very fast growth in sales and membership. The benefits of CineMatch include the following:

- **Effective recommendations.** According to Netflix, members select 70 percent of their movies based on CineMatch's recommendations.

- **Increased customer satisfaction and loyalty.** The movies recommended generate more satisfaction than the ones customers choose from the new releases page. As a result, between 70 and 80 percent of Netflix rentals come from the company's back catalog of 38,000 films rather than recent releases. It increases customer loyalty to the site and satisfaction for over 90 percent of the customers.

- **Broadened title coverage.** Renters expand their taste. Seventy percent of the movies Netflix customers rent are recommended to them on the site; 80 percent of rental activity comes from 2,000 titles. This decreases demand for popular new releases, which is good for Netflix, whose revenue-sharing agreements require larger payouts for newly released films.

    One example is *Control Room*, a documentary film about Arab television outlet Al Jazeera. Netflix has a 12 percent share of the total movie rental market, and you would expect its share of the rentals for *Control Room* to be in the same range. But Netflix accounted for 34 percent of the title's rental activity in the United States the week it was released on DVD. The difference is primarily due to Netflix's recommendation tools.

- **Better understanding of customer preference.** Netflix's recommendation system collects more than 2 million

ratings forms from subscribers daily to add to its huge database of users' likes and dislikes.

- **Fast membership growth.** Netflix found that the most reliable prediction for how much a customer will like a movie is what the customer thought of other movies. The company credits the system's ability to make automated, yet accurate, recommendations as a major factor in its growth from 600,000 subscribers in 2002 to more than 7 million by the end of 2007.

    CineMatch has become the company's core competence. Netflix's future relies heavily on CineMatch's making accurate recommendations and subscribers' accepting them, which is why the company strives to increase its accuracy.

Sources: Compiled from Flynn (2006), Null (2003), and *Netflix.com* (2006).

WHAT WE CAN LEARN . . .

This case illustrates the use of intelligent agents in movie recommendation system software. Netflix's CineMatch is designed to increase sales, customer satisfaction, and loyalty. The case also identifies some of the most popular market research and advertising methods used in EC. These topics are the subject of Chapter 4.

4.1 LEARNING ABOUT CONSUMER BEHAVIOR AND PURCHASING DECISIONS ONLINE

Companies are operating in an increasingly competitive environment. Therefore, they treat customers like royalty as they try to lure them to buy their goods and services. Finding and retaining customers is a major critical success factor for most businesses, both offline and online. One of the keys to building effective customer relationships is an understanding of consumer behavior online and then influencing it through advertising and promotions. For an overview, see Markellou et al. (2006) and Online File W4.1.

THE CONSUMER PURCHASE DECISION-MAKING PROCESS

Let's clarify the roles people play in the online purchase decision-making process. The major roles are as follows (Armstrong and Kotler 2007):

- ▶ **Initiator.** The person who first suggests or thinks of the idea of buying a particular product or service.
- ▶ **Influencer.** A person whose advice or view carries some weight in making a final purchasing decision.

▶ **Decider.** The person who ultimately makes a buying decision or any part of it—whether to buy, what to buy, how to buy, or where to buy.

▶ **Buyer.** The person who makes an actual purchase.

▶ **User.** The person who consumes or uses a product or service.

If one individual plays all of these roles, the marketer needs to understand and target that individual. When more than one individual plays these different roles, it becomes more difficult to properly target advertising and marketing efforts. How marketers deal with the issue of multiple people in decision-making roles is beyond the scope of this book.

Several models have been developed in an effort to describe the details of the decision-making process that lead up to and culminate in a purchase. These models provide a framework for learning about the process in order to predict, improve, or influence consumer decisions. Here we introduce two relevant models.

A Generic Purchasing-Decision Model

A general purchasing-decision model consists of five major phases. In each phase, we can distinguish several activities and, in some, one or more decisions. The five phases are (1) need identification, (2) information search, (3) evaluation of alternatives, (4) purchase and delivery, and (5) postpurchase behavior. Although these phases offer a general guide to the consumer decision-making process, one should not assume that every consumer's decision-making process will necessarily proceed in this order. In fact, some consumers may proceed to a point and then revert back to a previous phase, or they may skip a phase altogether.

The first phase, *need identification*, occurs when a consumer is faced with an imbalance between the actual and the desired states of a need. A marketer's goal is to get the consumer to recognize such imbalance and then convince the consumer that the product or service the seller offers will fill this gap.

product brokering
Deciding what product to buy.

merchant brokering
Deciding from whom (from what merchant) to buy a product.

After identifying the need, the consumer *searches for information* (phase 2) on the various alternatives available to satisfy the need. Here, we differentiate between two decisions: what product to buy (**product brokering**) and from whom to buy it (**merchant brokering**) (see Guan 2006). These two decisions can be separate or combined. In the consumer's search for information, catalogs, advertising, promotions, and reference groups influence decision making. During this phase, online product search and comparison engines, such as can be found at shopping.com, buyersindex.com, and mysimon.com, can be very helpful.

The consumer's information search will eventually generate a smaller set of preferred alternatives. From this set, the would-be buyer will further *evaluate the alternatives* (phase 3) and, if possible, negotiate terms. In this phase, a consumer will use the collected information to develop a set of criteria. These criteria will help the consumer evaluate and compare alternatives. In phase 4, the consumer will make the *purchasing decision*, arrange payment and delivery, purchase warranties, and so on.

The final phase is a *postpurchase* phase (phase 5), which consists of customer service and evaluation of the usefulness of the product (e.g., "This product is really great!" or "We really received good service when we had problems").

In addition, repeat site visits and repeat purchases can be included in the model as decision activities.

A Customer Decision Model in Web Purchasing

The preceding generic purchasing-decision model was widely used in research on consumer-based EC (Cheung et al. 2003). O'Keefe and McEachern (1998) built a framework for a Web purchasing model. As shown in Exhibit 4.1, each of the phases of the purchasing model can be supported by both Consumer Decision Support

EXHIBIT 4.1 Purchase Decision-Making Process and Support System

Steps in the Decision-Making Process	CDSS Support Facilities	Generic Internet and Web Support Facilities
Need recognition	Agents and event notification	Banner advertising on Web sites URL on physical material Discussions in newsgroups
Information search	Virtual catalogs Structured interaction and question/answer sessions Links to (and guidance on) external sources	Web directories and classifiers Internal search on Web site External search engines Focused directories and information brokers
Evaluation, negotiation, selection	FAQs and other summaries Samples and trials Models that evaluate consumer behavior Pointers to and information about existing customers	Discussions in newsgroups Cross-site comparisons Generic models
Purchase, payment, and delivery	Ordering of product or service Arrangement of delivery	Electronic cash and virtual banking Logistics providers and package tracking
After-purchase service and evaluation	Customer support via e-mail and newsgroups	Discussions in newsgroups

Source: O'Keefe and McEachern (1998).

System (CDSS) facilities and Internet and Web facilities. The CDSS facilities support the specific decisions in the process. Generic EC technologies provide the necessary mechanisms as well as enhance communication and collaboration. Specific implementation of this framework and explanation of some of the terms are provided throughout this chapter and the entire text.

Others have developed similar models (e.g., see Jiang et al. 2005; Silverman et al. 2001). The point here is that the planner of B2C marketing needs to consider the Web purchasing models in order to better influence the customer's decision making (e.g., by effective one-to-one advertising and marketing).

MASS MARKETING, MARKET SEGMENTATION, AND ONE-TO-ONE MARKETING

one-to-one marketing
Marketing that treats each customer in a unique way.

One of the greatest benefits of EC is its ability to match products and services with individual consumers. Such a match is a part of **one-to-one marketing**, which treats each customer in a unique way to fit marketing and advertising with the customer's profile and needs. The one-to-one approach evolved from the traditional marketing approaches, as described in Online File W4.2.

Section 4.1 ▶ REVIEW QUESTIONS

1. List the roles people play in purchasing.
2. List the five stages in the generic purchasing-decision model.
3. Describe the Web-based purchasing-decision model.

4.2 PERSONALIZATION, LOYALTY, SATISFACTION, AND TRUST IN EC

Internet marketing facilitates the use of market segmentation and one-to-one marketing (Online File W4.2). Here we will address several key issues related to one-to-one marketing: personalization, collaborative filtering, customer loyalty, permission marketing (Section 4.8), and trust. For details on these and other issues related to implementing EC-based one-to-one marketing, see Kalyanam and Zweben (2005). For discussion of how one-to-one marketing is related to CRM, see Online Appendix B.

PERSONALIZATION IN E-COMMERCE

Personalization refers to the matching of services, products, and advertising content to individuals and their preferences. The matching process is based on what a company knows about the individual user. This knowledge is usually referred to as a **user profile**. The user profile defines customer preferences, behaviors, and demographics. Profiles can be generated in several ways. The major strategies used to compile user profiles include the following:

personalization
The matching of services, products, and advertising content with individual consumers and their preferences.

user profile
The requirements, preferences, behaviors, and demographic traits of a particular customer.

cookie
A data file that is placed on a user's hard drive by a remote Web server, frequently without disclosure or the user's consent, that collects information about the user's activities at a site.

▶ **Solicit information directly from the user.** This is usually done by asking the user to fill in a questionnaire or by conducting an interview with the user.

▶ **Observe what people are doing online.** A common way to observe what people are doing online is through use of a **cookie**—a data file that is stored on the user's hard drive, frequently without disclosure or the user's consent. Sent by a remote Web server over the Internet, the information stored will surface when the user's browser accesses the specific Web server, and the cookie will collect information about the user's activities at the site (see cookiecentral.com). The use of cookies is one of the most controversial issues in EC, as discussed in Insights and Additions 4.1. Other tools, such as spyware and Web bugs, are described in Section 4.3. For an overview of personalization in EC, see Chan (2005) and Anke and Sundaram (2006).

▶ **Build from previous purchase patterns.** For example, Amazon.com builds customer profiles to recommend books, CDs, and other products, based on what customers have purchased before, rather than asking customers or doing market research.

▶ **Perform marketing research.** Firms can research the market using tools described in Section 4.3 and in the Netflix case at the beginning of the chapter.

▶ **Make inferences.** Infer from information provided by customers on other issues or by analyzing similar customers. (See collaborative filtering in Section 4.3.) When the ad matching is based on information collected about the customers' behavior on the Internet, it is called **behavioral targeting**.

behavioral targeting
The use of information collected on an individual's Internet-browsing behavior to select which advertisements to display to that individual.

Once a customer profile is constructed, a company matches the profile with a database of products, services, or ads. Manual matching is time consuming and expensive; therefore, the matching process is usually done by software agents. One-to-one matching can be applied through several different methods. One well-known method is *collaborative filtering* (Section 4.3).

Chellappa and Sin (2005) highlighted the values of online personalization to consumers. For example, some stores send an instant alert to their customers' handheld devices and notify them when prices of particular items in their "watch list" drop to a predefined level or when an auction comes to a close. Some stores also allow users to

Insights and Additions 4.1 Cookies in E-Commerce

Are cookies bad or good? The answer is "both." When users revisit Amazon.com or other sites, they are greeted by their first name. How does Amazon.com know a user's identity? Through the use of cookies! Vendors can provide consumers with considerable personalized information if they use cookies that signal a consumer's return to a site. (A variation of cookies is known as e-sugging—"SUG-ing," from "selling under the guise of research"). For example, consumers who visit travel sites may get more and more unsolicited travel related e-mails and pop-up ads.

Cookies can provide a wealth of information to marketers, which then can be used to target ads to consumers. Thus, marketers get higher rates of "click-throughs," and customers can view the most relevant information. Cookies can also prevent repetitive ads, because vendors can arrange for a consumer not to see the same ad twice. Finally, advanced data mining companies, such as NCR and

Sift, can analyze information in cookie files so companies can better meet the customers' needs.

However, some people object to cookies because they do not like the idea that "someone" is watching their activity on the Internet. Users who do not like cookies can disable them. However, some consumers might want to keep the friendly cookies. For example, many sites recognize a person as a subscriber so that they do not need to reregister. Internet Explorer (IE) 6.09 and higher also gives users control over third-party cookies. (Go to "Internet Options" under "Tools" and select "Private tab," click "Advanced," and put a check mark next to "Override automatic cookie handling." Then, direct IE to accept first-party cookies.) See *en.wikipedia.org/wiki/HTTP_cookie* and *pcworld.com/resource/browse/0,cat,1384,sortIdx,1,00.asp* for more on cookies.

personalize Web site attributes, such as the site's color or the greeting name. However, privacy and trust issues remain a limiting factor for personalization.

According to Sackmann et al. (2006), the Internet offers online retailers different ways to tailor services to their customers, including:

- **Personalized services.** Services built on a one-to-one communication channel requiring personal data from customers.
- **Individual services.** Recommendation services built on the sequence of clicks, page requests, or items that have been added to the shopping cart. This approach improves the shopping experience while also maintaining consumer anonymity.
- **Universal services.** Consumers use the product search function or read customer reviews. This approach does not require personal or context data.

These services are a form of personalization, because a single customer can choose a service that meets his or her needs at any particular time. All three types of personalization strategies will help build customer relationships, increase customer satisfaction, generate a lock-in situation, and realize greater product or service turnover.

CUSTOMER LOYALTY

One of the major objectives of one-to-one marketing is to increase customer loyalty (recall the Netflix case). *Customer loyalty* refers to a deep commitment to rebuy or repatronize a preferred product/service consistently in the future, thereby causing repetitive same-brand or same brand-set purchasing.

Attracting and retaining loyal customers remains the most important issue for any selling company, including e-tailers. Increased customer loyalty can bring cost savings to a company in various ways: lower marketing and advertising costs; lower transaction costs; lower customer turnover expenses; lower failure costs, such as warranty claims; and so on. Customer loyalty also strengthens a company's market position because loyal customers are kept away from the competition. In addition, customer loyalty can lead to enhanced resistance to competitors, a decrease in price sensitivity, and an increase in favorable word-of-mouth (Balabanis et al. 2006).

Loyalty programs were introduced over 100 years ago and are widely used among airlines, hotel chains, casinos, and credit-card companies. Today, loyalty programs are computer-based and have been expanded to all kinds of businesses, as demonstrated by the following examples:

- Octopus Hong Kong (octopuscards.com) is a stored-value-card operator that launched a reward program for consumers aimed at increasing card usage across Hong Kong. Consumers earn reward points by purchasing at a number of leading merchants across the territory, including Wellcome, Watsons, UA Cinemas, and McDonald's. Each Octopus card can store up to 1,000 reward points, which can be redeemed on the next purchase.
- FANCL (fancl.com), a Japanese cosmetics and health-care company, offers the "FANCL point program" where consumers earn FANCL points that are saved for gift redemption.
- Maxwell House Coffee has its own program where consumers earn "House Points" with each can of coffee they buy and redeem for gift awards.

The introduction of EC decreases loyalty in general because customers' ability to shop, compare, and switch to different vendors becomes easier, faster, and less expensive given the aid of search engines and other technologies. However, companies have found that loyal customers end up buying more when they have a Web site to shop from. For example, W. W. Grainger, a large industrial-supply company, found that loyal B2B customers increased their purchases substantially when they began using Grainger's Web site (grainger.com).

E-Loyalty

e-loyalty
Customer loyalty to an e-tailer or loyalty programs delivered online or supported electronically.

E-loyalty refers to a customer's loyalty to an e-tailer or a manufacturer that sells directly online or to loyalty programs delivered online or supported electronically. Customer acquisition and retention is a critical success factor in e-tailing. The expense of acquiring a new customer can be over $100; even for Amazon.com, which has a huge reach, it is more than $15. In contrast, the cost of maintaining an existing customer at Amazon.com is $2 to $4.

Companies can foster e-loyalty by learning about their customers' needs, interacting with customers, and providing superb customer service. A major source of information about e-loyalty is e-loyaltyresource.com. One of its major services is an online journal, the *e-Loyalty Resource Newsletter*, which offers numerous articles describing the relationships among e-loyalty, customer service, personalization, CRM, and Web-based tools. Another source of information is colloquy.com, which concentrates on loyalty marketing. Comprehensive reviews of the use of the Web and the Internet to foster e-loyalty are provided by Harris and Goode (2004) and Yeo and Chiam (2006).

One of the most publicized computer-based loyalty programs is the one used by Harrah's, the largest casino chain in the world. The casino industry is extremely competitive, with more and more gambling channels and new physical casinos opening to the public. Standing out from the competition is becoming an increasingly enormous challenge. All casinos employ basic loyalty programs. They record the money spent in the machines, tables, restaurants, and so forth by each player and provide awards to frequent gamblers (e.g., a free night's stay in their hotels). Using data mining and business intelligence, Harrah's was able to learn more accurately about its customers and offer them the rewards on a one-to-one basis the players really like.

Lately, Harrah's moved one step further in order to increase its understanding of its customers and their loyalty by moving to a real-time rewards system (Evans 2006; SAS.com 2006). For example, if the casino knows who is playing on each slot machine and the birthdays of each player, it can arrange for a manager to come to the player with a birthday cake and a gift while on the casino floor. And each player might prefer a different gift. Using a teradata data warehouse as well as SAS and Cognos software, an analysis of millions of customers becomes feasible and economical. This enables Harrah's to deliver the best in one-to-one marketing and to do it in real time. Customers feel that the company knows them and their needs, so they keep coming back.

According to Floh and Treiblmaier (2006), satisfaction and trust are the two most important factors in determining customer e-loyalty. More discussion on satisfaction and trust can be found in the following sections. In addition, e-loyalty is a major barrier that customers must cross when deciding to exit to a competitor.

SATISFACTION IN EC

Given the changing dynamics of the global marketplace and the increasingly intense competition, delivering world-class customer online experience becomes a differentiating strategy. Satisfaction is one of the most important consumer reactions in the B2C online environment. Maintaining customer satisfaction in the online shopping experience is as important as the high level of satisfaction associated with several key outcomes (e.g., repeat purchase, positive word-of-mouth, and so on).

Satisfaction has received an enormous amount of attention in studies of consumer-based EC. ForeSee Results, an online customer satisfaction measurement company, developed the American Customer Satisfaction Index (ACSI) (theasci.org) for measuring customer satisfaction with EC. For example, in the fourth quarter of 2005 the ACSI for e-commerce category had increased 1.3 percent over the previous quarter to an aggregate score of 79.6 on a 100-point scale (Tode 2006), below its all-time high of 80.8 in 2003. The Customer Respect Group (customerrespect.com) also provides an index to measure the customer's online experience. The Customer Respect Index (CRI) includes the following components: simplicity, responsiveness, transparency, principles, attitude, and privacy.

Researchers have proposed several models to explain the formation of satisfaction with online shopping. For example, Cheung and Lee (2005a) proposed a framework for consumer satisfaction with Internet shopping by correlating the end-user satisfaction perspective with the service quality viewpoint. The framework has been updated and is shown in Exhibit 4.2.

The ability to predict consumer satisfaction can be useful in designing Web sites as well as advertising and marketing strategies. Shih and Fang (2006) developed a predictive model of customer satisfaction. However, Web site designers should also pay attention to the nature of Web site features. Different features have different impacts on customer (dis)satisfaction. If certain Web site features, such as reliability of content, loading speed, and usefulness, fail to perform properly, customer satisfaction will drop dramatically. In contrast, if features such as those that make the usage enjoyable, entertaining, and fun perform well, they will surprise customers and result in a radical jump in customer satisfaction. The discussion of these two types of features on Web site satisfaction can be found in Cheung and Lee (2005b).

More discussion on EC satisfaction can be found in Collier and Bienstock (2006).

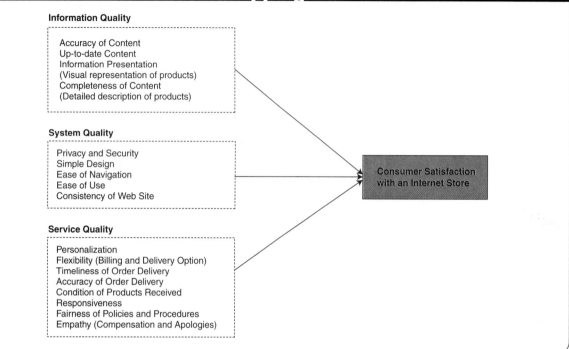

EXHIBIT 4.2   Research Framework for Consumer Satisfaction with Internal Shopping

Information Quality

Accuracy of Content
Up-to-date Content
Information Presentation
(Visual representation of products)
Completeness of Content
(Detailed description of products)

System Quality

Privacy and Security
Simple Design
Ease of Navigation
Ease of Use
Consistency of Web Site

Service Quality

Personalization
Flexibility (Billing and Delivery Option)
Timeliness of Order Delivery
Accuracy of Order Delivery
Condition of Products Received
Responsiveness
Fairness of Policies and Procedures
Empathy (Compensation and Apologies)

Consumer Satisfaction with an Internet Store

TRUST IN EC

trust

The psychological status of willingness to depend on another person or organization.

Trust is the psychological status of depending on another person or organization to achieve a planned goal. When people trust each other, they have confidence that as transaction partners they will keep their promises. However, both parties in a transaction assume some risk. In the electronic marketplace, sellers and buyers do not meet face to face. The buyer can see a picture of the product, but not the product itself. Promises of quality and delivery can be easily made—but will they be kept? To deal with these issues, EC vendors need to establish high levels of trust with current and potential customers. Trust is particularly important in global EC transactions due to the difficulty of taking legal action in cases of a dispute or fraud and the potential for conflicts caused by differences in culture and business environments.

In addition to sellers and buyers trusting each other, both must have trust in the EC computing environment and in the EC infrastructure. If people do not trust the security of the EC infrastructure, they will not feel comfortable about using credit cards to make EC purchases.

EC Trust Models

Several models have been put forth to explain the EC–trust relationship. For example, Lee and Turban (2001) examined the various aspects of EC trust and developed the model shown in Exhibit 4.3. According to this model, the level of trust is determined by numerous variables (factors) shown on the left side and in the middle of the figure. The exhibit illustrates the complexity of trust relationships, especially in B2C EC. Paravastu and Gefen (2006) distinguished between initial and ongoing trust and developed a model accordingly.

EXHIBIT 4.3   EC Trust Model

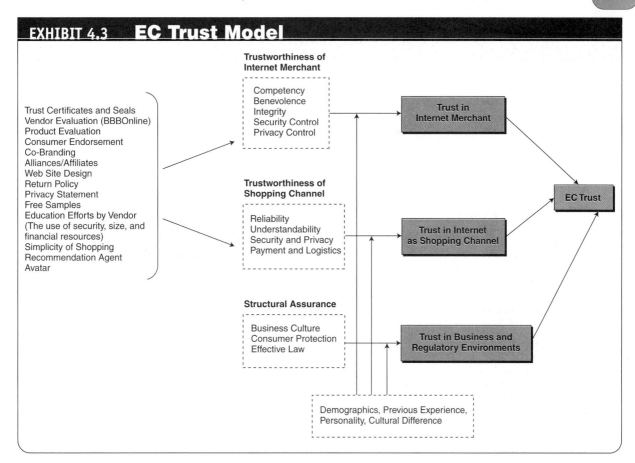

For a more comprehensive treatment of EC trust, see Jeanson and Ingham (2006) and Hoffman et al. (2006). For how to increase trust, see Online File W4.3.

Section 4.2 ▶ REVIEW QUESTIONS

1. Explain how personalization (matching people with goods/services) is done.
2. Define loyalty and describe e-loyalty.
3. Describe the issue of trust in EC and how to increase it.
4. What influences consumer satisfaction online? Why do companies need to monitor it?

4.3 MARKET RESEARCH FOR EC

The goal of market research is to find information and knowledge that describe the relationships among consumers, products, marketing methods, and marketers. Its aim is to discover marketing opportunities and issues, to establish marketing and advertising plans, to better understand the purchasing process, and to evaluate marketing performance. On the Web, the objective is to turn browsers into buyers. Market research includes gathering information about topics such as the economy, industry, firms, products, pricing, distribution, competition, promotion, and consumer purchasing behavior. Here we focus on the latter.

Businesses, educational institutions, and governments use various tools to conduct consumer market research both *offline* and *online*. The major ones that are used in e-commerce are described later in this section.

METHODS FOR CONDUCTING MARKET RESEARCH ONLINE

EC market research can be conducted through conventional methods, or it can be done with the assistance of the Internet. Although telephone or shopping mall surveys will continue, interest in Internet research methods is on the rise. Market research that uses the Internet frequently is faster and more efficient and allows the researcher to access a more geographically diverse audience than those found in offline surveys (see FAQs at casro.org and accutips.com). Also, on the Web market researchers can conduct a very large study much more cheaply than with other methods. The larger the sample size, the larger the accuracy and the predictive capabilities of the results. Telephone surveys can cost as much as $50 per respondent. This may be too expensive for a small company that needs several hundred respondents. An online survey will cost a fraction of a similarly sized telephone survey and can expedite research considerably, as shown in Case 4.1.

CASE 4.1
EC Application

INTERNET MARKET RESEARCH EXPEDITES TIME-TO-MARKET AT PROCTER & GAMBLE

For decades, Procter & Gamble (P&G) and Colgate-Palmolive have been competitors in the market for personal care products. Developing a major new product from concept to market launch used to take over 5 years. First, a concept test was conducted: The companies sent product photos and descriptions to potential customers, asking whether they might buy the product. If the feedback was negative, they tried to improve the product concept and then repeated previous tasks. Once positive response was achieved, sample products were mailed out, and the customers were asked to fill out detailed questionnaires. When customers' responses met the companies' internal hurdles, the companies would start with mass TV advertising.

However, thanks to the Internet, it took P&G only $3^1/_2$ years to get Whitestrips, the teeth-brightening product, onto the market and to a sales level of $200 million a year—considerably quicker than other oral care products. In September 2000, P&G threw out the old marketing test model and instead introduced Whitestrips on the Internet, offering the product for sale on P&G's Web site. The company spent several months studying who was coming to the site and buying the product and collecting responses to online questionnaires, which was much faster than the old mail-outs.

The online research, which was facilitated by data mining conducted on P&G's huge historical data (stored in a data warehouse) and the new Internet data, revealed the most enthusiastic groups. These included teenage girls, brides-to-be, and young Hispanic Americans. Immediately, the company started to target these segments with appropriate advertising. The Internet created a product awareness of 35 percent, even before any shipments were made to stores. This buzz created a huge demand for the product by the time it hit the shelves.

In 2006, P&G began using on-demand solutions from RightNow Technologies (*rightnow.com*), including survey tools that execute opinion polls among selected segments of consumers who have opted into the company's market research programs. From these experiences, P&G learned important lessons about flexible and creative ways to approach product innovation and marketing. The whole process of studying the product concept, segmenting the market, and expediting product development has been revolutionized.

Sources: Compiled from *RightNow.com* (2006), Buckley (2002), and *pg.com* (accessed January 2008).

Questions

1. How did P&G reduce time-to-market?
2. What was data mining used for?
3. What research methods were used?

Hewson et al. (2003) provide a comprehensive review of online market research technologies, methods, tools, and issues, including ethical ones. As you may recall, marketers concentrate on market segmentation and one-to-one. Let's see how this is accomplished.

WHAT ARE MARKETERS LOOKING FOR IN EC MARKET RESEARCH?

By looking at a personal profile that includes observed behaviors on the Web, it is possible for marketers to explain and predict online buying behavior. For example, companies want to know why some customers are online shoppers whereas others are not. Major factors that are used for prediction are (in descending order of importance): product information requested, number of related e-mails, number of orders made, products/services ordered, and gender.

Typical questions that online market research attempts to answer are: What are the purchase patterns for individuals and groups (market segmentation)? What factors encourage online purchasing? How can we identify those who are real buyers from those who are just browsing? How does an individual navigate—does the consumer check information first or do they go directly to ordering? What is the optimal Web page design? Knowing the answers to questions such as these helps a vendor to advertise properly, to price items, to design the Web site, and to provide appropriate customer service. Online market research can provide such data about individuals, about groups, and even about the entire Internet.

Internet-based market research is often done in an interactive manner, allowing personal contact with customers, and it provides marketing organizations with a greater ability to understand the customer, the market, and the competition. For example, it can identify early shifts in product and customer trends, enabling marketers to identify products and marketing opportunities and to develop those products that customers really want to buy. It also tells management when a product or a service is no longer popular. To learn more about market research on the Web, see the tutorials at webmonkey.com.

The following discussion describes some online market research methods.

Market Segmentation Research

Because EC also has to identify an appropriate customer group for specific products and services, it is important first to understand how groups of consumers are classified. This classification is called *market segmentation* (see Online File W4.4).

MARKET RESEARCH FOR ONE-TO-ONE

The major one-to-one marketing approaches are:

▶ Direct solicitation of information from customers and experts (surveys, focus groups)
▶ Observing what customers are doing on the Web
▶ Collaborative filtering

Direct Solicitation of Information

Online direct solicitation methods range from one-to-one communication with specific customers, usually by e-mail, to moderated focus groups conducted in chat rooms, to questionnaires placed on Web sites, to tracking of customers' movements on the Web. Professional pollsters and marketing research companies frequently conduct online voting polls (e.g., see cnn.com and acnielsen.com). For an overview of online market research methods, see Hewson et al. (2003). A typical Internet-based market research process is shown in Exhibit 4.4.

EXHIBIT 4.4   Online Market Research Process

Steps in Collecting Market Research Data

1. Define the research issue and the target market.
2. Identify newsgroups and Internet communities to study.
3. Identify specific topics for discussion.
4. Subscribe to the pertinent groups; register in communities.
5. Search discussion group topic and content lists to find the target market.
6. Search e-mail discussion group lists.
7. Subscribe to filtering services that monitor groups.
8. Read FAQs and other instructions.
9. Visit chat rooms.

Content of the Research Instrument

1. Post strategic queries to groups.
2. Post surveys on a Web site.
3. Offer rewards for participation.
4. Post strategic queries on a Web site.
5. Post relevant content to groups, with a pointer to a Web site survey.
6. Post a detailed survey in special e-mail questionnaires.
7. Create a chat room and try to build a community of consumers.

Target Audience of the Study

1. Compare audience with the target population.
2. Determine editorial focus.
3. Determine content.
4. Determine what Web services to create for each type of audience.

Sources: Compiled from Vassos (1996) and Moisander and Valtonen (2006).

Implementing Web-Based Surveys. Web-based surveys are becoming popular with companies and researchers. For example, Mazda North America used a Web-based survey to help design its Miata line. Web surveys may be passive (a fill-in questionnaire) or interactive (respondents download the questionnaires, add comments, ask questions, and discuss issues). For more information and additional software tools, see supersurvey.com, surveymonkey.com, websurveyor.com, and clearlearning.com. For an introduction on how to conduct Web-based surveys, see Faught et al. (2004).

Online Focus Groups. Several research firms create panels of qualified Web regulars to participate in online focus groups. For example, Research Connections (researchconnections.com), recruits participants in advance by telephone and takes the time to help them connect to the Internet, if necessary. Use of preselected focus group participants helps to overcome some of the problems (e.g., small sample size and partial responses) that sometimes limit the effectiveness of Web-based surveys.

Hearing Directly from Customers. Instead of using focus groups, which are costly and possibly slow, customers can be asked directly what they think about a product or service. Toymaker LEGO used a market research vendor to establish a survey on an electronic bulletin board where millions of visitors read each other's comments and share opinions about LEGO toys. The research vendor analyzed the responses daily and submitted the information to LEGO. In addition, companies can use chat rooms, newsgroups, blogs, wikis, podcasts, and electronic consumer forums to interact with consumers.

Software tools that can be used to hear directly from customers include Brand Advocacy Insights (used by LEGO) from Informative, Inc. (informative.com), Betasphere (voc-online.com), InsightExpress (insightexpress.com), and Survey.com (survey.com).

Observing Customers

To avoid some of the problems of online surveys, especially the giving of false information, some marketers choose to learn about customers by observing their behavior rather than by asking them questions. Many marketers keep track of consumers' Web movements using methods such as transaction logs (log files) or cookie files.

Transaction Logs. A **transaction log** records user activities at a company's Web site. A transaction log is created by a *log file*, which is a file that lists actions that have occurred. The transaction-log approach is especially useful if the visitors' names are known (e.g., when they have registered with the site). In addition, data from the shopping cart database can be combined with information in the transaction log.

Note that as customers move from site to site, they establish their **clickstream behavior**, a pattern of their movements on the Internet, which can be seen in their transaction logs. Both ISPs and individual Web sites are capable of tracking a user's clickstream.

Cookies, Web Bugs, and Spyware. Cookies and Web bugs can be used to supplement transaction-log methods. As discussed earlier, cookies allow a Web site to store data on the user's PC; when the customer returns to the site, the cookies can be used to find what the customer did in the past. Cookies are frequently combined with **Web bugs**, tiny graphics files embedded in e-mail messages and on Web sites. Web bugs transmit information about the user and his or her movements to a monitoring site.

Spyware is software that gathers user information through an Internet connection without the user's knowledge (see en.wikipedia.org/wiki/Spyware). Originally designed to allow freeware authors to make money on their products, spyware applications are typically bundled together with freeware for download onto users' machines. Many users do not realize that they are downloading spyware with the freeware. Sometimes the freeware provider may indicate that other programs will be loaded onto the user's computer in the licensing agreement (e.g., "may include software that occasionally notifies users of important news"). Spyware stays on the user's hard drive and continually tracks the user's actions, periodically sending information on the user's activities to the owner of the spyware. It typically is used to gather information for advertising purposes. Users cannot control what data are sent via the spyware, and unless they use special tools they often cannot uninstall the spyware, even if the software it was bundled with is removed from the system. Effective tools for fighting spyware include Ad-aware (lavasoftusa.com/software/adaware), Spykiller (spykiller.com), and Webwasher Spyware from Secure Computing (securecomputing.com). For more on spyware and banners, see Online File W4.5.

Representative vendors that provide tools for tracking customers' movements are Tealeaf Technology, Inc. (tealeaf.com, log files), Acxiom Corp. (acxiom.com, data warehousing), and Stat Counter (statcounter.com, real-time tracking).

The use of cookies and Web bugs is controversial. Many believe that they invade the customer's privacy (see privacyfoundation.org). Tracking customers' activities *without their knowledge or permission* may be unethical or even illegal.

Analysis of B2C Clickstream Data. Large and ever-increasing amounts of B2C data can be collected on consumers, products, and so on. Such data come from several sources: internal data (e.g., sales data, payroll data, etc.), external data (e.g., government and industry reports), and clickstream data. **Clickstream data** are data generated in the Web environment; they provide a trail of a user's activities (the user's clickstream behavior) in a

transaction log
A record of user activities at a company's Web site.

clickstream behavior
Customer movements on the Internet.

Web bugs
Tiny graphics files embedded in e-mail messages and in Web sites that transmit information about users and their movements to a Web server.

spyware
Software that gathers user information over an Internet connection without the user's knowledge.

clickstream data
Data that occur inside the Web environment; they provide a trail of the user's activities (the user's clickstream behavior) in the Web site.

Web site. These data include a record of the user's browsing patterns: every Web site and every page of every Web site the user visits, how long the user remains on a page or site, in what order the pages were visited, and even the e-mail addresses of mail that the user sends and receives. By analyzing clickstream data, a firm can find out, for example, which promotions are effective and which population segments are interested in specific products.

According to Inmon (2001), B2C clickstream data can reveal information such as the following:

▶ What goods the customer has looked at
▶ What goods the customer has purchased
▶ What goods the customer examined but did not purchase
▶ What items the customer bought in conjunction with other items
▶ What items the customer looked at in conjunction with other items but did not purchase
▶ Which ads and promotions were effective and which were not
▶ Which ads generate a lot of attention but few sales
▶ Whether certain products are too hard to find and/or too expensive
▶ Whether there is a substitute product that the customer finds first
▶ Whether there are too many products for the customer to wade through
▶ Whether certain products are not being promoted
▶ Whether the products have adequate descriptions

Several companies offer tools that enable such an analysis. For example, WebTrends Marketing Lab 2 features several advanced tools for analyzing clickstream data (e.g., see webtrends.com).

Web mining refers to the use of data mining techniques for discovering and extracting information from Web documents. Web mining explores both *Web content* and *Web usage*. The usage analysis is derived from clickstream data. According to Gregg and Walczak (2006), Web mining has the potential to dramatically change the way we access and use the information available on the Web.

Web mining
Web mining explores both Web content data mining techniques for discovering and extracting information from Web documents and Web usage.

Collaborative Filtering

Once a company knows a consumer's preferences (e.g., music, movie, or book preferences), it would be useful if the company could predict, without asking the customer directly, what other products or services this consumer might enjoy. One way to do this is through **collaborative filtering**, which uses customer data to infer customer interest in other products or services. Similarly, if you know what certain customers like, you may want to infer what customers with similar profiles will prefer. These predictions are based on special formulas derived from behavioral sciences. For more on the methods and formulas used to execute collaborative filtering, see Chen and McLeod (2006). Many personalization systems (recall the Netflix case) are based on collaborative filtering (e.g., backflip.com and choicestream.com).

The following are some variations of collaborative filtering:

collaborative filtering
A market research and personalization method that uses customer data to predict, based on formulas derived from behavioral sciences, what other products or services a customer may enjoy; predictions can be extended to other customers with similar profiles.

▶ **Rule-based filtering.** A company asks consumers a series of yes/no or multiple-choice questions. The questions may range from personal information to the specific information the customer is looking for on a specific Web site. Certain behavioral patterns are predicted using the collected information. From this information, the collaborative filtering system derives behavioral and demographic rules such as,

"If customer age is greater than 35, and customer income is above $100,000, show Jeep Cherokee ad. Otherwise, show Mazda Protégé ad."

▶ **Content-based filtering.** With this technique, vendors ask users to specify certain favorite products. Based on these user preferences, the vendor's system will recommend additional products to the user. This technique is fairly complex, because mapping among different product categories must be completed in advance.

▶ **Activity-based filtering.** Filtering rules can also be built by watching the user's activities on the Web.

For more about personalization and filtering, see knowledgestorm.com.

Legal and Ethical Issues in Collaborative Filtering. Information often is collected from users without their knowledge or permission. This raises several ethical and legal questions, including invasion-of-privacy issues (see Chen and McLeod 2006). Several vendors offer *permission-based* personalization tools. With these, companies request the customer's permission to receive questionnaires and ads (e.g., see knowledgestorm.com). See Section 4.8 for information on permission marketing.

LIMITATIONS OF ONLINE MARKET RESEARCH AND HOW TO OVERCOME THEM

One problem with online market research is that too much data may be available. To use data properly, one needs to organize, edit, condense, and summarize it. However, such a task may be expensive and time consuming. The solution to this problem is to automate the process by using data warehousing and data mining. The essentials of this process, known as *business intelligence*, are provided in Online File W4.6 and Turban et al. (2008).

Some of the limitations of online research methods are accuracy of responses, loss of respondents because of equipment problems, and the ethics and legality of Web tracking. In addition, focus group responses can lose something in the translation from an in-person group to an online group. A researcher may get people online to talk to each other and play off of each other's comments, but eye contact and body language are two interactions of traditional focus group research that are lost in the online world. However, just as it hinders the two-way assessment of visual cues, Web research can actually offer some participants the anonymity necessary to elicit an unguarded response. Finally, a major limitation of online market research is the difficulty in obtaining truly representative samples.

Concerns have been expressed over the potential lack of representativeness in samples of online users. Online shoppers tend to be wealthy, employed, and well educated. Although this might be a desirable audience for some products and services, the research results might not be extendable to other markets. Although the Web-user demographic is rapidly diversifying, it is still skewed toward certain population groups, such as those with convenient Internet access (at home or work). Another important issue concerns the lack of clear understanding of the online communication process and how online respondents think and interact in cyberspace.

To overcome some of the limitations of online market research, companies can outsource their market research needs. Only large companies have specialized market research departments. Most other companies use third-party research companies, such as AC Nielsen.

BIOMETRIC MARKETING

One problem with Web analytics, Web mining, clickstream data, and so on is that we observe and follow a *computer*, not knowing who is actually moving the mouse. Many households have several users; thus, the data collected may not represent any one person's preferences (unless of course, we are sure that there is one and only one user, as in the case of smart cell phones). A potential solution is suggested by Pons (2006) in the form of *biometric marketing*.

biometrics

An individual's unique physical or behavioral characteristics that can be used to identify an individual precisely (e.g., fingerprints).

A **biometric** is one of an individual's unique physical or behavioral characteristics that can be used to identify an individual precisely (e.g., fingerprints; see list at en.wikipedia.org/wiki/Biometrics). By applying the technology to computer users, we can improve both security and learn about the user's profile precisely. The question is how to do it? Indeed, there are programs by which users identify themselves to the computer by biometrics, and these are spreading rapidly. To utilize the technology for marketing involves social and legal acceptability. For these reasons, advertisers are using methods that target individuals without knowing their profiles. An example is search engine-based methods such as Google's Adwords (see Section 4.6).

Some researchers are wildly optimistic about the prospects for market research on the Internet; others are more cautious.

Section 4.3 ▶ REVIEW QUESTIONS

1. Describe the objectives of market research.

2. Define and describe market segmentation (see Online File W4.4).

3. Describe how market research is done online and the major market research methods.

4. Describe the role of Web logs and clickstream data.

5. Relate cookies, Web bugs, and spyware to market research.

6. Describe the limitations of online market research and how to overcome them.

4.4 INTERNET MARKETING IN B2B

B2B marketing is completely different from B2C marketing, which was introduced in Chapter 3 and in Sections 4.1 through 4.3. Major differences also exist between B2B and B2C with respect to the nature of demand and supply and the trading process. Here we discuss the corporate purchaser's buying behavior and the marketing and advertising methods used in B2B. More discussion is provided in Chapter 5.

ORGANIZATIONAL BUYER BEHAVIOR

Organizations buy large quantities of *direct materials* that they consume or use in the production of goods and services and in the company's operations. They also buy *indirect materials*, such as PCs, delivery trucks, and office supplies, to support their production and operations processes.

Although the number of organizational buyers is much smaller than the number of individual consumers, their transaction volumes are far larger, and the terms of negotiations and purchasing are more complex. In addition, the purchasing process itself, as will be seen in Chapter 5, usually is more complex than the purchasing process of an individual customer. Also, the organization's buyer might be a group. In fact, decisions to purchase expensive items are usually decided by a group. Therefore, factors that affect individual consumer behavior and organizational buying behavior are quite different (e.g., see Bridges et al. 2006).

A Behavioral Model of Organizational Buyers

The behavior of an organizational buyer can be described by a model similar to that of an individual buyer, which was shown in Online Exhibit W4.1.1. A behavioral model for organizational buyers is shown in the exhibit in Online File W4.7. Compare the two models. Note that some independent variables differ; for example, in the organizational model, the family and Internet communities may have no influence. Also, an *organizational influences module* is added to the B2B model. This module includes the organization's purchasing guidelines and constraints (e.g., contracts with certain suppliers) and the purchasing system used. Also, interpersonal influences, such as authority, are added. Finally, the possibility of group decision making must be considered. For a detailed discussion of organizational buyers, see Armstrong and Kotler (2007).

THE MARKETING AND ADVERTISING PROCESSES IN B2B

The marketing and advertising processes for businesses differ considerably from those used for selling to individual consumers. For example, traditional (offline) B2B marketers use methods such as trade shows, advertisements in industry magazines, paper catalogs, and salespeople who call on existing customers and potential buyers.

In the digital world, these approaches may not be effective, feasible, or economical. Therefore, organizations use a variety of online methods to reach business customers. Popular methods include online directory services, matching services, the marketing and advertising services of exchanges (Chapter 5), cobranding or alliances, affiliate programs, online marketing services (e.g., see digitalcement.com), or e-communities (see Chapter 8 and b2bcommunities.com). Several of these methods are discussed next.

METHODS FOR B2B ONLINE MARKETING

When a B2C niche e-tailer seeks to attract its audience of skiers, musicians, or cosmetic customers, it may advertise in traditional media targeted to those audiences, such as magazines or television shows. The same is true in B2B when trade magazines and directories are used. But when a B2B vendor wants to grow by adding new customers or products, it may not have a reliable, known advertising channel. How can it reach new customers?

Targeting Customers

A B2B company, whether a provider of goods or services, an operator of a trading exchange, or a provider of digital real-time services, can contact all of its targeted customers individually when they are part of a well-defined group. For example, to attract companies to an exchange for auto supplies, one might use information from industry trade association records or industry magazines to identify potential customers.

Another method of bringing new customers to a B2B site is through an affiliation service, which operates just as a B2C affiliate program does. A company pays a small commission every time the affiliate company "drives traffic" to its site. For more on online B2B marketing, see Harrison-Walker and Neeley (2004) and b2bmarketingtrends.com.

An important part of any marketing effort is advertising. Several of the advertising methods that will be presented later in this chapter are applicable both to B2C and B2B. For example, an *ad server network provider*, such as DoubleClick (doubleclick.com), can be used to target customers in B2B2C EC.

Electronic Wholesalers

One of the interesting B2B ventures is the e-wholesaler. Like click-and-mortar e-tailer Sam's Club, this kind of intermediary sells directly to businesses, but does so exclusively online. An example is Bigboxx.com, described in Online File W5.1.

Other B2B Marketing Services

Several other B2B marketing services exist. See Online File W4.8 for details.

One of the major objectives of market research is to provide tactics and strategies for EC advertisement, the topic of Section 4.5.

Section 4.4 ▶ REVIEW QUESTIONS

1. Distinguish between organizational buyers and individual consumers.

2. Describe a behavioral model of an organizational buyer.

3. Describe B2B marketing and advertising methods.

4.5 WEB ADVERTISING

Advertising on the Web by all types of organizations plays an extremely important role in e-commerce. According to Delaney (2006), Internet advertising is growing by about 20 to 30 percent annually, reaching $20 billion in 2007 (Sutel 2007). Therefore, companies are changing their advertisement strategies.

OVERVIEW OF WEB ADVERTISING

Advertising is an attempt to disseminate information in order to affect buyer–seller transactions. In *traditional* marketing, advertising was impersonal, one-way mass communication that was paid for by sponsors. Telemarketing and direct mail ads were attempts to personalize advertising to make it more effective. These *direct marketing* approaches worked fairly well, but were expensive and slow and seldom truly one-to-one interactive. For example, say a direct mail campaign costs about $1 per person and has a response rate of only 1 to 3 percent. This makes the cost per responding person in the range of $33 to $100. Such an expense can be justified only for high-ticket items (e.g., cars).

One of the problems with direct mail advertising was that the advertisers knew very little about the recipients. Market segmentation by various characteristics (e.g., age, income, gender) helped a bit but did not solve the problem. The Internet introduced the concept of interactive marketing, which has enabled marketers and advertisers to interact directly with customers. In **interactive marketing**, a consumer can click an ad to obtain more information or send an e-mail to ask a question. Besides the two-way communication and e-mail capabilities provided by the Internet, vendors also can target specific groups and individuals on which they want to spend their advertising dollars. The Internet enables truly one-to-one advertising. A comparison of mass advertising, direct mail advertising, and interactive online advertising is shown in Online File W4.9.

Companies use Internet advertising as one of their advertising channels. At the same time, they also may use TV, newspapers, or other traditional channels. In this respect, the Web competes on a budget with the other channels.

This chapter deals with Internet advertising in general. For additional resources on Internet advertising, see adage.com and webmonkey.com.

interactive marketing
Online marketing, facilitated by the Internet, by which marketers and advertisers can interact directly with customers and consumers can interact with advertisers/vendors.

The Advertising Cycle

With *closed-loop campaign management*, companies are treating advertisement as a cyclical process, as shown in Exhibit 4.5. The cyclical process entails carefully planning a campaign to determine who the target is and how to reach that consumer. Analyzing the campaign after its completion assists a company in understanding the

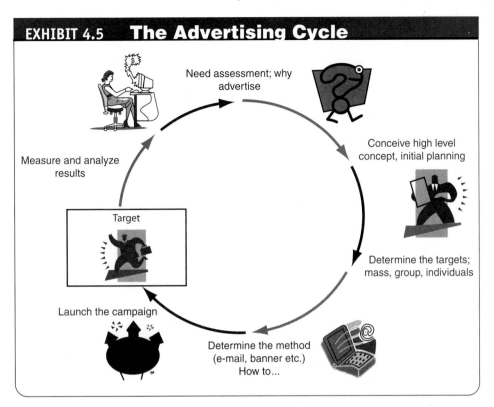

EXHIBIT 4.5   The Advertising Cycle

Need assessment; why advertise

Conceive high level concept, initial planning

Determine the targets; mass, group, individuals

Determine the method (e-mail, banner etc.) How to...

Launch the campaign

Target

Measure and analyze results

campaign's success and why it succeeded. This new knowledge is then used when planning future campaigns.

Before we describe the various steps of the cycle as it is implemented in Web advertising, let's learn some basic advertising terminology and technology.

SOME INTERNET ADVERTISING TERMINOLOGY

The following list of terms and marginal glossary will be of use as you read about Web advertising.

▶ **Ad views**
▶ **Button**
▶ **Page**
▶ **Click** (**click-through** or **ad click**)
▶ **CPM** (**cost per thousand impressions**)
▶ **Conversion rate**
▶ **Click-through rate** (or **ratio**)
▶ **Hit**
▶ **Visit**
▶ **Unique visit**
▶ **Stickiness**

ad views
The number of times users call up a page that has a banner on it during a specific period; known as impressions or page views.

button
A button is a small banner that is linked to a Web site. It can contain downloadable software.

page
A page is an HTML (Hypertext Markup Language) document that may contain text, images, and other online elements, such as Java applets and multimedia files. It can be generated statically or dynamically.

click (click-through or ad click)
A count made each time a visitor clicks on an advertising banner to access the advertiser's Web site.

CPM (cost per thousand impressions)
The fee an advertiser pays for each 1,000 times a page with a banner ad is shown.

conversion rate
The percentage of clickers who actually make a purchase.

click-through rate
The percentage of visitors who are exposed to a banner ad and click on it.

click-through ratio

The ratio between the number of clicks on a banner ad and the number of times it is seen by viewers; measures the success of a banner in attracting visitors to click on the ad.

hit

A request for data from a Web page or file.

visit

A series of requests during one navigation of a Web site; a pause of a certain length of time ends a visit.

unique visits

A count of the number of visitors entering a site, regardless of how many pages are viewed per visit.

stickiness

Characteristic that influences the average length of time a visitor stays in a site.

WHY INTERNET ADVERTISING?

The major traditional advertising media are television (about 36 percent), newspapers (about 35 percent), magazines (about 14 percent), and radio (about 10 percent) (Boswell 2002). Although Internet advertising is a small percentage of the $120-billion-a-year advertising industry (7.4 percent in 2007), it is growing rapidly (InPage 2008). By most accounts, the online ad market has largely remained untapped. Online ad spending, which represents only 5 percent of total media spending, is projected to grow 24.4 percent in 2007, whereas all media, including television, radio, billboards, newspapers and direct mail, are projected to grow only 4.2 percent (Mills 2006).

By 2010, online ad spending in the United States is expected to increase to $25 billion to $30 billion (up from $14 billion in 2006), according to market research and consulting firm Parks and Associates. Worldwide, online ad spending is forecast to grow from $19.5 billion in 2005 to more than $55 billion in 2010, according to Piper Jaffray (reported by Mills 2006).

Search advertising is by far the most lucrative area, accounting for 40 percent of total online ad spending in the United States. Search advertising is expected to grow from $4.2 billion in 2005 to $7.5 billion in 2010, and display advertising is forecasted to grow 10 percent between 2005 and 2010 to $7.5 billion (reported by Mills 2006).

Today, online-advertising technology has advanced to the point where marketers can see how and if their ads result in increased sales, even for target ads based on demographics, location, and other factors. Such analysis of offline advertising is not nearly as fast, easy, or inexpensive.

Companies advertise on the Internet for several reasons. To begin with, television viewers are migrating to the Internet. The UCLA Center for Communication Policy (2004) found that Internet users are spending time online that they previously spent viewing television. Worldwide, Internet users are spending significantly less time watching television and more time using the Internet at home. This trend will continue, especially as Internet-enabled cell phones become commonplace. In addition, many Internet users are well educated and have high incomes. These Internet surfers are a desired target for advertisers.

According to Hallerman (2006), the major advantages of using the Internet over mass advertising are the precise targeting, interactivity, rich media (grabs attention), cost reduction, and rapid customer acquisition.

Advertisers are limited (by cost and space) in the amount of information they can gather about the television and print ads they place. Advertisers are not able to track the number of people who actually view an ad in a print publication or on TV. Print ads cannot be rotated when a person opens the same page multiple times. Print and television ads cannot be filtered only to female readers who earn over $50,000, own a home, and work in a university. Of the people who do look at the ad, the traditional advertiser cannot even record the length of time viewers spent looking at it. The only piece of hard data available for traditional advertising is the total number of print copies sold or the estimated viewing audience of the TV program. Everything else is guesswork.

Much more information and feedback is possible with Internet advertising. Special tracking and ad management programs enable online advertisers to do all of the things mentioned here and more (see Sections 4.6 and 4.7).

The Internet is the fastest growing communication medium by far. Worldwide, the number of Internet users surpassed 1 billion in 2005; the 2 billion Internet users milestone is expected in 2011 (*Computer Industry Almanac* 2006). Of course, advertisers are interested in a medium with such potential reach, both locally and globally.

Other reasons why Web advertising is growing rapidly include:

▶ **Cost.** Online ads are sometimes cheaper than those in other media. In addition, ads can be updated at any time with minimal cost.

▶ **Richness of format.** Web ads can effectively use the convergence of text, audio, video, graphics, and animation. In addition, games, entertainment, and promotions can be easily combined in online advertisements. Also, services such as MySimon.com enable customers to compare prices and, using PDA or cell phone, do it at any time from anywhere.

▶ **Personalization.** Web ads can be interactive and targeted to specific interest groups and/or individuals; the Web is a much more focused medium.

▶ **Timeliness.** Internet ads can be fresh and up-to-the-minute.

▶ **Location-basis.** Using wireless technology and GPS, Web advertising can be location based; Internet ads can be sent to consumers whenever they are in a specific time and location (e.g., near a restaurant or a theater).

▶ **Linking.** It is easy to link from an online ad to a storefront—one click does it.

▶ **Digital branding.** Even the most price-conscious online shoppers are willing to pay premiums for brands they trust. These brands may be click-and-mortar brands (e.g., P&G) or dot-coms such as Amazon.com. British Airways places many Internet banner ads. However, these ads are not for clicking on to buy; they are all about branding, that is, establishing British Airways as a brand.

As of 1998, these factors began to convince large consumer-products companies, such as P&G, to shift an increasing share of their advertising dollars away from traditional media to Web advertising.

Of course, each advertising medium, including the Internet, has its advantages and limitations. Online File W4.10 compares the advantages and limitations of Internet advertising against traditional advertising media. For a comprehensive comparison of the effectiveness of Internet ads versus traditional methods, see Yoon and Kim (2001).

ADVERTISING NETWORKS

One of the major advantages of Internet advertising is the ability to customize ads to fit individual viewers. Specialized firms have sprung up to offer this service to companies that wish to locate customers through targeted advertising. Called **advertising networks** (or *ad server networks*), these firms offer special services such as brokering banner ads for sale, bringing together online advertisers and providers of online ad space, and helping target ads to consumers who are presumed to be interested in categories of advertisements based on technology-based consumer profiling. DoubleClick is a premier company in this area. DoubleClick created an advertising network for 1,500 companies. It prepares thousands of ads for its clients every week.

advertising networks
Specialized firms that offer customized Web advertising, such as brokering ads and targeting ads to select groups of consumers.

Section 4.5 ▶ REVIEW QUESTIONS

1. Define Web advertising and the major terms associated with it.
2. Describe the reasons for the growth in Web advertising.
3. List the major characteristics of Web advertising.
4. Explain the role of ad networks in Web advertising.

4.6 ONLINE ADVERTISING METHODS

A large number of online advertising methods exist. The major ones are covered in this section.

BANNERS

banner
On a Web page, a graphic advertising display linked to the advertiser's Web page.

A **banner** is a graphic display that is used for advertising on a Web page. The size of the banner is usually 5 to 6.25 inches in length, 0.5 to 1 inch in width, and is measured in pixels. A banner ad is linked to an advertiser's Web page. When users "click" the banner, they are transferred to the advertiser's site. Advertisers go to great lengths to design a banner that catches consumers' attention. Banners often include video clips and sound. Banner advertising including pop-up banners is the most commonly used form of advertising on the Internet.

There are several types of banners. **Keyword banners** appear when a predetermined word is queried from a search engine. This is an example of targeted, one-to-one advertising. Other methods of targeted advertising are the behavioral-based approaches, such as collaborative filtering. They are effective for companies that want to narrow their target audience. **Random banners** appear randomly, not as a result of some action by the viewer. Companies that want to introduce new products (e.g., a new movie or CD) or promote their brand use random banners. *Static banners* are always on the Web page. Finally, *pop-up banners* appear when least expected, as will be described later.

keyword banners
Banner ads that appear when a predetermined word is queried from a search engine.

random banners
Banner ads that appear at random, not as the result of the user's action.

If an advertiser knows something about a visitor, such as the visitor's user profile, it is possible to *match* a specific banner with that visitor. Obviously, such targeted, personalized banners are usually most effective.

In the near future, banner ads will greet people by name and offer travel deals to their favorite destinations. Such personalized banners are being developed, for example, by dotomi.com. It delivers ads to consumers who opt in to its system. Initial results show a 14 percent click-through rate versus 3 to 5 percent with nonpersonalized ads.

Benefits and Limitations of Banner Ads

The major benefit of banner ads is that by clicking on them users are transferred to an advertiser's site, frequently directly to the shopping page of that site. Another advantage of using banners is the ability to customize them for individual surfers or a market segment of surfers. Also, viewing of banners is fairly high, because in many cases customers are forced to see banner ads while waiting for a page to load or before they can get the free information or entertainment that they want to see (a strategy called *forced advertising*). Finally, banners may include attention-grabbing multimedia.

The major disadvantage of banners is their cost. Also, a limited amount of information can be placed on the banner. Hence, advertisers need to think of a creative but short message to attract viewers.

Because of these drawbacks, it is important to decide *where* on the screen to place banners. For example, a study of Web ads conducted by the University of Michigan found that ads placed in the lower-right-hand corner of the screen, next to the scrollbar, generate a 228 percent higher click-through rate than ads at the top of the page (Doyle et al. 1997).

Banner Swapping and Banner Exchanges

banner swapping
An agreement between two companies to each display the other's banner ad on its Web site.

Banner swapping means that company A agrees to display a banner of company B in exchange for company B's displaying company A's banner. This is probably the least expensive form of banner advertising, but it is difficult to arrange. A company must locate a site that will generate a sufficient amount of relevant traffic. Then, the company must contact the owner/Webmaster of the site and inquire if the company would be interested in a reciprocal banner swap. Because individual swaps are difficult to arrange, many companies use banner exchanges.

Banner exchanges are markets where companies can trade or exchange placement of banner ads on each other's Web sites. A multicompany banner match may be easier to arrange than a two-company swap. For example, company A can display B's banner effectively, but B cannot display A's banner optimally. However, B can display C's banner, and C can display A's banner. Such bartering may involve many companies. Banner exchange organizers arrange the trading, which works much like an offline bartering exchange. Firms that are willing to display others' banners join the exchange. Each time a participant displays a banner for one of the exchange's other members, it receives a credit. After a participant has "earned" enough credits, its own banner is displayed on a suitable member's site. Most exchanges offer members the opportunity to purchase additional display credits.

Examples of exchanges are click4click.com, unitedbanners.com, and exchange-it.com. For auctions related to banners, see thefreeauction.com/exchange.

banner exchanges
Markets in which companies can trade or exchange placement of banner ads on each other's Web sites.

POP-UP AND SIMILAR ADS

One of the most annoying phenomena in Web surfing is the increased use of pop-up, pop-under, and similar ads. A **pop-up ad**, also known as *ad spawning*, is the automatic launching of new browser windows with an ad when a visitor enters or exits a site, on a delay (see interstitials), or on other triggers. A pop-up ad appears in front of the active window. A **pop-under ad** is an ad that appears underneath (in back of) the current browser window; when users close the active window, they see the ad. (A number of pop-under exchanges function much like banner exchanges.) Pop-ups cover the user's current screen and may be difficult to close. Pop-up and pop-under ads are controversial: Many users strongly object to this advertising method, which they consider intrusive.

Several related tactics, some of which are very aggressive, are used by advertisers, and their use is increasing. Some of these tactics are accompanied by music, voice, and other rich multimedia.

pop-up ad
An ad that appears in a separate window before, after, or during Internet surfing or when reading e-mail.

pop-under ad
An ad that appears underneath the current browser window, so when the user closes the active window the ad is still on the screen.

Interstitials

An **interstitial**, a type of pop-up ad, is a page or box that appears after a user clicks a link. These ads remain while content is loading. (The word *interstitial* comes from *interstice*, which means "a small space between things.") An interstitial may be an initial Web page or a portion of one that is used to capture the user's attention for a short time, either as a promotion or a lead-in to the site's homepage or to advertise a product or a service. They pop onto the PC screen, much like a TV commercial.

interstitial
An initial Web page or a portion of it that is used to capture the user's attention for a short time while other content is loading.

How to Deal with Unsolicited Pop-Ups, Pop-Unders, and Interstitials

If viewers do not want to see these ads, they can remove them by simply closing them or by installing software to block them. Several software packages are available on the market to assist users in blocking these types of ads. Protection against pop-ups is offered by ISPs (e.g., AOL), by software security vendors (e.g., STOPzilla at stopzilla.com and Pop-up Stopper from panicware.com), and by portals (e.g., Yahoo!, Google). In summer 2004, Microsoft introduced a built-in blocker in Internet Explorer.

E-MAIL ADVERTISING

A popular way to advertise on the Internet is to send company or product information to people or companies listed in mailing lists via e-mail. E-mail messages may be combined with brief audio or video clips promoting a product and provide on-screen links that users can click to make a purchase. The Direct Marketing Association reports that e-mail has the second highest return on investment (ROI) index for direct response marketing (reported by Firstfold.com 2006).

However, an Atlantic Media Company (2006) trend analysis suggests that the growth of e-mail advertising is slowing, growing from 8 percent in 2005 to 11 percent in 2006. It forecasts that it will only be 13 percent in 2010. In contrast, rich-media advertising will increase from 11 percent in 2006 to 18 percent in 2010.

The advantages of e-mail advertising are its low cost and the ability to reach a wide variety of targeted audiences. Also, e-mail is an *interactive* medium, and it can combine advertising and customer service. It can include a direct link to any URL, so it acts like a banner. Most companies have a database of customers to whom they can send e-mail messages. However, using e-mail to send ads (sometimes floods of ads) without the receivers' permission is considered *spamming*.

Undoubtedly, the quantity of e-mail that consumers receive is exploding. In light of this, marketers employing e-mail must take a long-term view and work toward motivating consumers to continue to read the messages they receive. As the volume of e-mail increases, consumers' tendency to screen and block messages will rise as well. Most e-mail services (e.g., see mail.live.com, Microsoft's Hotmail) permit users to block messages from specific sources. Also, the automatic filtering of junk mail by Yahoo!, Gmail, and other e-mail services is becoming more effective in moving such mail to the "junk box" or "bulk" areas.

A list of e-mail addresses can be a very powerful tool with which a company can target a group of people it knows something about. For information on how to create a mailing list, consult groups.yahoo.com (the service is free) or topica.com.

E-mail also can be sent to PDA devices and to mobile phones. Mobile phones offer advertisers a real chance to advertise interactively and on a one-to-one basis with consumers, anytime, any place. In the future, e-mail ads will be targeted to individuals based not only on their user profiles but also on their physical location at any point in time. See Chapter 9 for a description of this concept, known as l-commerce.

E-Mail Advertising Management

Although sending e-mail ads sounds simple, it is not. Preparing mailing lists, deciding on content, and measuring the results are some of the activities that are part of e-mail advertising management. One important area is getting reliable mailing lists. Companies such as Worldata.com can help supply lists for both B2C and B2B EC. Worldata.com also provides ad management services. (See the demo of the e-mail tracking system at worldata.com.)

Given the new e-marketing technologies, consumer frustration over spam, and new regulations, marketers should reevaluate how their e-mail advertisements are created, deployed, and measured. The Peppers and Rogers Group (2004) suggests four guidelines that marketers should consider to leverage customer insights throughout the e-mail marketing campaign life cycle: (1) thinking about customer experience, (2) making privacy protection a part of their brand promise, (3) ensuring their recipients know about their privacy protection, and (4) measuring impact. By applying these guidelines, companies can enhance customer experiences and create long-term and loyal relationships. More guidelines are offered by Chase (2006).

E-mail Hoaxes. E-mail hoaxes are very popular; some of them have been going on for years (e.g., Neiman Marcus's cookie recipe, the Nigerian treasure, the Koran and the Iraq invasion). Some of these are scams. For details, see ftc.gov.

Fraud. Fraud also is a danger. For example, a person might get an e-mail stating that his or her credit card number is invalid or that his or her AOL service or newspaper delivery will be terminated unless another credit card number is sent as a reply to the e-mail. For protection against such hoaxes, see scambusters.org.

E-Mail Advertising Methods and Successes

E-mail advertising can be done in a number of different ways (see McDougall and Malykhina 2006 and Mordkovich and Mordkovich 2005), as shown in Online File W4.11.

NEWSPAPER-LIKE AND CLASSIFIED ADS

In 2001, the Internet Advertising Bureau, an industry trade group, adopted five standard ad sizes for the Internet. These standardized ads are larger and more noticeable than banner ads. They look like the ads in a newspaper or magazine, so advertisers like them. Tests found that users read these ads four times more frequently than banners (Tedeschi 2001). The ads appear on Web sites in columns or boxes. Some of these ads are interactive; users can click on a link inside the ad for more information about a product or service.

Classified Ads

Another newspaper-like ad is the *classified* ad. These ads can be found on special sites (e.g., craigslist.org, kijiji.com, infospace.com), as well as on online newspapers, exchanges, portals, and so on. In many cases, posting regular-size classified ads is free, but placing them in a larger size or with some noticeable features is done for a fee. For examples, see traderonline.com and advertising.msn.com. For the capabilities and effectiveness of Craigslist.org see Case 2.2 (Chapter 2).

SEARCH ENGINE ADVERTISEMENT

Most search engines allow companies to submit their Internet addresses, called URLs (Universal Resource Locators), for free so that these URLs can be searched electronically. Search engine spiders crawl through each site, indexing its content and links. The site is then included in future searches. Because there are several thousand search engines, advertisers who use this method should register URLs with as many search engines as possible. In some cases, URLs may be searched even if they are not submitted. For details, see Chase (2006).

The major advantage of using URLs as an advertising tool is that it is *free*. Anyone can submit a URL to a search engine and be listed. By using URLs, it is likely that searchers for a company's products will receive a list of sites that mention the products, including the company's own site. Search engine advertisement has become the most popular online advertising method, mainly thanks to Google.

However, the URL method has several drawbacks. The major one has to do with location: The chance that a specific site will be placed at the top of a search engine's display list (say, in the first 10 sites) is very slim. Furthermore, even if a company's URL makes it to the top, others can quickly displace the URL from the top slot. Second, different search engines index their listings differently; therefore, it is difficult to make the top of several lists. The searcher may have the correct keywords, but if the search engine indexed the site listing using the "title" or "content description" in the meta tag, then the effort could be fruitless. A *meta tag* is a coding statement (in HTML) that describes the content of a Web page and is used by search engines to index content so it can be found.

Improving a Company's Search-Engine Ranking (Optimization)

By simply adding, removing, or changing a few sentences, a Web designer can alter the way a search engine's spider ranks its findings (see Kent 2006) and therefore improve a company's ranking on the search engine's list. Several companies have services that *optimize* Web content so that a site has a better chance of being discovered by a search engine (e.g., Web Position from WebTrends webtrends.com). More tips for improving a site's listing in various search engines can be found at searchenginewatch.com. For further details see Online Chapter 13.

Another way to improve the search-engine ranking is via link partnerships. For example, tucsonproperties.net, a real estate company, contacts other real estate companies and proposes placing links on each other's Web sites. The more links made, the higher the exposure may be. For more on search engine marketing, see Mordkovich and Mordkovich (2005).

Paid Search-Engine Inclusion

Several search engines charge fees for including URLs at or near the top of the search results. For example, Google and Overture charge firms for "sponsor matching." The more the company pays, the closer it will be to the top of the sponsor's list. Overture works with several search engines.

Advertising in Social Networks. Companies are starting to advertise to members of social networks (Chapter 8). Sites such as MySpace.com and CyWorld.com offer targeted advertising opportunities, and some vendors offer discounts on the advertised products to members. Ads also link users to other sites that might be of interest to community members. Finally, extensive brand advertisement, similar to TV commercials are available now on YouTube and other sites that offer video clips. For example, in the YouTube inVideo program viewers of certain videos will see animated overlays while they watch the video. The overlay is animated, interactive, entertaining, and relevant to the original clip. (The video you were watching is temporarily paused. If you choose not to click on the overlay, it will simply disappear.) The video owner shares the income from the sponsors. Advertisers also use online fantasy sports (e.g., available at Yahoo!) to send ads to the fans of specific sports (e.g., National Football League [NFL] and Major League Baseball [MLB]). According to eMarketer.com, online fantasy sports attract millions of visitors every month (reported by Nucifera 2004).

Google—The Online Advertising King

No other EC company can match the success of Google and its meteoric rise. Google is considered by many to be not only changing the Internet, but also the world. Google is using several search engine advertising methods to generate billions of dollars in revenue and profits. Two of these methods are described in Insights and Additions 4.2.

Related to AdSense is the use of traffic arbitrage in ads. This method is used by individuals and companies to capitalize on the inefficiencies in the ad market. According to Sloan (2007), the process is as follows:

1. You create a Web site and fill it with ads from Google's AdSense or similar companies at no cost to you.

2. You place your own ads on Microsoft's search engine, which is relatively inexpensive, or on similar sites.

Insights and Additions 4.2 Google's Advertisement Methods

Google uses several methods to perform online advertisements. The major methods are AdWords and AdSense.

AdWords

AdWords is a self-service ad server that uses *relevance-ranking algorithms* similar to the ones that make the search engine so effective. Advertisers tell Google how much they want to spend and then "buy" pertinent keywords. When Web surfers type in a term that matches the advertiser's keyword, the advertiser is listed in a banner near the search results with the heading "Sponsored Links." Each time a user clicks the advertiser's banner ad, Google subtracts the cost-per-click for the advertiser's prepaid account. When the account's daily ad budget is depleted, Google stops displaying the ad. For details, see Goodman (2005).

The system is easy to use and remarkably effective. The click-through rate is about 15 percent, which is more than 10 times the rate of the average banner ad. According to industry experts, many Google advertisers have experienced a 20 to 25 percent increase in online sales.

Each time a visitor clicks on an ad (which takes the visitor to the advertiser's site) the site owner shares the commission paid by the advertiser with Google. The advertisers also participate in the AdWords program.

Despite its success, AdWords by itself does not provide the best one-to-one targeting. This is achieved in many cases through a complementary program—AdSense.

AdSense

Google's *AdSense* is an *affiliate program* in which Google offers Web site owners a chance to earn a commission for their willingness to place ads of other advertisers on their sites for free. AdSense automatically delivers an advertiser's text and image ads that are precisely matched to each affiliate site. This is a major improvement over matching individuals based on their preferences, which is less accurate in many cases and much more expensive. The matching (called *contextual matching*) is based on a proprietary algorithm (Google filed for over 60 patents on these and other innovations). The key is the quality and appearance of both the pages and the ads, as well as the popularity of the site. Google even provides affiliates with analytics that help convert visitors to customers.

Example

AdSense uses Google's relevance-scoring algorithms to find the best match of an ad to a surfer by analyzing the content of the Web pages of the affiliates' sites and advertisers' keywords. Upon clicking a banner ad, which includes a short sentence describing the advertiser's product (service), the user is transferred to the advertiser's site. All this is done automatically. When a visitor clicks on the ad, Google collects a commission from the advertiser and shares it with the affiliate site.

An affiliate site owner agrees to allow Google to place banners of its clients. Visit google.com/services/adsense_tour/index.htm to see a demo involving PetSmart. For another example of a site using AdSense, see *rtcmagazine.com*.

Google's success is attributed to the quality of the matches of ads to people's profiles, the large number of advertisers in its network, the ability to use ads in many languages, and the ability to understand the content of affiliate Web sites. Any characteristics and demographics of the visitors that Google knows are considered in the match. This is also true of Google's competitors (e.g., MSN, with its AdCenter methodology). Yahoo! and eBay offer similar programs (e.g., see eBay AdContext and Yahoo's Content Match). The closer the match, the less intrusive the ad is to the visitor, and the better the chance of the visitor's clicking on the ad.

Sources: Compiled from *adwords.google.com/select*, *google.com/adsense*, *en.wikipedia.org/wiki/AdSense* (all sites accessed October 2007) and Goodman (2005).

3. When users of your site click on advertisers' ads at AdSense (or similar programs), you are paid by Google.

4. The difference between your cost in Step 2 and your income from Step 3 is your net profit.

The key to success is to select the right topic, to design the ads on your site properly (e.g., with the help of AdSense), and to arbitrage your costs against income properly.

ADVERTISING IN CHAT ROOMS, BLOGS, AND SOCIAL NETWORKS

A chat room can be used to build a community, promote a political or environmental cause, support people with medical problems, or enable hobbyists to share their interest. It can be used for advertising and viral marketing as well (e.g., see Gelb and Sundaram 2002).

Vendors frequently sponsor chat rooms. The sponsoring vendor places a chat link on its site, and the chat vendor does the rest (e.g., **talkcity.com**), including placing the advertising that pays for the session. The advertising in a chat room merges with the activity in the room, and the user is conscious of what is being presented.

The main difference between an advertisement that appears on a static Web page and one that comes through a chat room is that the latter allows advertisers to cycle through messages, analyze them, and target the chatters again and again. Also, advertising can become more thematic in a chat room.

Chat rooms also are used as one-to-one connections between a company and its customers. For example, Mattel (**mattel.com**) sells about one-third of its Barbie dolls to collectors. These collectors use the chat room to make comments or ask questions that are then answered by Mattel's staff.

As described in Chapter 1, advertisers are using social networks to deliver messages to the network's members. Google and MySpace have an agreement on revenue sharing when MySpace members click on Google's ads. Google purchased YouTube for the same reason. Popular blogs contain ads that are based on the bloggers being affiliates of advertisers. A major issue is the disclosure of payments by paid bloggers (e.g., see Covel 2007). For further details, see Chapter 8.

Advertise in Videos

The popularity of YouTube and the hundreds of other sites that offer video clips and movies has attracted the attention of advertisers.

Companies are replacing static banner ads with video clips and placing them on YouTube and other sites, including their own. A new trend is to mine consumers' videos on YouTube and other sites and then use them as new material to create both Internet and TV ads. For example, Howard (2007) reports that KFC and Geico, both large advertisers, have used snippets of consumer Web videos to create 15- to 30-second TV ads. Consumer-generated content, which is a major characteristic of Web 2.0, enables advertisers to create appealing ads cheaper and faster. Howard (2007) reports that this kind of ad is 75 percent cheaper than those created using conventional methods and 66 percent faster. Obviously, this approach might not work in all cases, and the Screen Actors Guild is concerned that the demand for talented actors and actresses will decline due to the use of these videos, according to Howard (2007).

According to Schonfeld (2007), Web TV series such as *Diggnation*, draw millions of viewers and have *Fortune* 500 corporate sponsors. Such series complement the 2-minute video ads that are placed on YouTube and other sites. Video ads take many innovative forms and are growing rapidly.

OTHER FORMS OF ADVERTISING

Online advertising can be done in several other ways, ranging from ads in newsgroups to ads in computer kiosks. Advertising on *Internet radio* is just beginning, and soon advertising on *Internet television* will commence. In November 2004, Amazon.com launched a series of short films for the holiday season that promoted items that customers could purchase. (BMW promotes its cars with short films as well.) According to Wang (2004), marketers are beginning to use online videos in B2B. *eMarketer* (2004) reports that video ads are increasing more than 50 percent each year, topping $120 million in revenue in 2004. By the end of 2006, the use of video clips in online ads was increasing (see qvc.com [featured products], edmunds.com [cars], and so on). For details, see Ossinger (2006).

Innovative online ad methods have no limit. For example, one innovative method is auctions where the winner is the lowest bidder. Marketers have the opportunity to interact with consumers and build their brands through this interactive auction game at limbo.com (see Petrecca 2006). Another innovation is presented in Insights and Additions 4.3.

Some marketers use advertorials. An **advertorial** looks like editorial content or general information, but it is really an advertisement. This form of advertisement also is used in newspapers.

In addition, a site's *domain name* may be used for brand recognition. This is why some companies pay millions of dollars to keep certain domain names under their control (see alldomains.com) or to buy popular names (e.g., tom.com was purchased for $8 million). Known as *domainers*, some individuals buy thousands of names and then run ads on them with Google, charging advertisers (see Sloan 2005 for details).

advertorial
An advertisement "disguised" to look like editorial content or general information.

Web 2.0 and Advertising

With the increased interest in social networks and blogging, it has become natural for advertisers to use blogging sites. Blogs can use several different business models, and new models are being developed all the time. Some of these models are:

▶ Advertisers post banner ads (either text or video) on well-known bloggers' Web sites.

▶ Advertisers have Web TV shows (e.g., see diggnation.com) that deliver full-length episodes of serialized programs.

▶ *Diggnation* provides special shows supported by sponsors.

Insights and Additions 4.3 Innovation in Targeted Ads

Google, Value Click, 24/7 Real Media, Yahoo!, MSN, and more are competing in the targeted ad market. The winner, so far, is Google. However, according to Schonfeld and Borzo (2006), this situation may soon change. The reason is that the tools currently used for targeting segments of the population look at text advertisements. However, display ads are on the rise. A new company (acquired by Yahoo! in September 2007), BlueLithium (*bluelithium.com*), has developed a method by which it can build a profile of a user's clickstream. The more sites a user visits, the larger that user's surfing history becomes, and the more BlueLithium knows about the user. The profile includes what sites the user visits, what ads the user clicks on, and what ads other people with similar clickstreams have clicked. This method concentrates on banner ads, not on keywords. Having over 100 million clickstream histories (in August 2007), the company can direct any kind of ad to a user, including video clips.

As with similar tracking methods, this method observes a computer, not knowing if one or several users are involved. Privacy issues must also be dealt with. Regardless of these limitations, the company is doing extremely well, generating profit within 3 months of operations and expecting to gross over $100 million by the end of 2007.

Sources: Compiled from Schonfeld and Borzo (2006) and *bluelithium.com* (accessed January 2008).

▸ Several blogger–advertiser matchmakers (e.g., PayPerPost Inc. [paypercost.com]) arrange for bloggers to get paid to write reviews for companies (see Chapter 8). Some companies hire bloggers to write their blogs (e.g., see stonyfield.com). This brings into play the issue of disclosure about fees paid to these individuals.

▸ Classified ads targeted to specific groups (e.g., social networks) are becoming popular.

▸ A new field called *social commerce* (see en.wikipedia.org/wiki/Social_commerce) refers to sharing experiences with others through the creation of social networks where people can get advice from trusted individuals, find goods, read ads, and conduct research about purchases.

▸ Several newspapers are integrating their online and offline ad Web activities. For example, *Forbes* plans to open Forbes business and financial ad blog network in spring 2008 (MixedMarketArts, 2008).

Advertising in Newsletters

Free online newsletters are abundant. An example is the *E-Commerce Times*. This informative newsletter (ecommercetimes.com) solicits ads from companies (see "How to Advertise"). Ads usually are short and have a link to more information. They are properly marked as "Advertisement."

Posting Press Releases Online

Many companies post press releases on news sites, portals, and their own or partners' sites. Indeed, Southwest Airlines was successful in selling $1.5 million in tickets by posting four press releases online. Press releases also are available on RSS feeds, blogs, and podcasts. However, it is not as simple as it sounds. For a discussion of how to place online press releases, see the case study at Marketingsherpa.com (2004).

Advergaming

advergaming

The practice of using computer games to advertise a product, an organization, or a viewpoint.

Advergaming is the practice of using games, particularly computer games, to advertise or promote a product, an organization, or a viewpoint. Advergaming normally falls into one of three categories:

▸ A company provides interactive games on its Web site in the hope that potential customers will be drawn to the game and spend more time on the Web site or simply become more product (or brand) aware. The games themselves usually feature the company's products prominently. Examples are intel.co.uk/itgame and clearahill.com.

▸ Games are published in the usual way, but they require players to investigate further. The subjects might be commercial, political, or educational. Examples include *America's Army* (americasarmy.com/downloads), intended to boost recruitment for the United States Army, and pepsiman.com.

▸ With some games, advertising appears within the actual game. This is similar to subtle advertising in films, whereby the advertising content is within the "world" of the movie or game. An example is cashsprint.com, which puts advertising logos directly on the player's racing vehicle and around the racetrack.

With the growth of the Internet, advergames have proliferated, often becoming the most visited aspect of brand Web sites and becoming an integrated part of brand media planning in an increasingly fractured media environment. LifeSavers started a game site called Candystand that has blossomed to a portal for many different advergames; at its peak it was averaging more than 4 to 5 million unique visitors a month (Graham 2005).

Advergames promote repeat traffic to Web sites and reinforce brands in compelling ways. Users choose to register to be eligible for prizes that can help marketers collect customer data. Gamers may invite their friends to participate, which could assist promotion from word-of-mouth or viral marketing. For further discussion, see en.wikipedia.org/wiki/Advergaming, adverblog.com, and Gurau (2006).

Section 4.6 ▶ REVIEW QUESTIONS

1. Define banner ads and describe their benefits and limitations.
2. Describe banner swapping and banner exchanges.
3. Describe the issues surrounding pop-ups and similar ads.
4. Explain how e-mail is used for advertising.
5. Describe advertising via classified ads.
6. Discuss advertising via URLs and in chat rooms.
7. Discuss advertising in blogs and social networks.
8. Describe the search engine ad strategy.
9. Describe Google's AdWords and AdSense.
10. Define advergaming and describe how it works.

4.7 ADVERTISING STRATEGIES AND PROMOTIONS ONLINE

Several advertising strategies can be used over the Internet. In this section, we will present the major strategies used.

AFFILIATE MARKETING AND ADVERTISING

In Chapters 1 through 3, we introduced the concept of **affiliate marketing**, the revenue model by which an organization refers consumers to the selling company's Web site. Affiliate marketing is used mainly as a revenue source for the referring organization and as a marketing tool for sellers. However, the fact that the selling company's logo is placed on many other Web sites is free advertising as well. Consider Amazon.com, whose logo can be seen on about 1 million affiliate sites! For a comprehensive directory of affiliate programs, see cashpile.com.

affiliate marketing
A marketing arrangement by which an organization refers consumers to the selling company's Web site.

ADS AS A COMMODITY

With the *ads-as-a-commodity* approach, people are paid for time spent viewing an ad. This approach is used at mypoints.com, clickrewards.com, and others. At Mypoints.com, interested consumers read ads in exchange for payment from the advertisers. Consumers fill out data on personal interests, and then they receive targeted banners based on their personal profiles. Each banner is labeled with the amount of payment that will be paid if the consumer reads the ad. If interested, the consumer clicks the banner to read it, and after passing some tests as to its content, is paid for the effort. Readers can sort and choose what they read, and the advertisers can vary the payments to reflect the frequency and desirability of the readers. Payments may be cash (e.g., $0.50 per banner) or product discounts. This method is used with smart phones, too (Chapter 9). For further details, see en.wikipedia.org/wiki/Online_advertising#Payment_conventions.

Ads-as-Commodities in Social Networks

An interesting application is promoted by Intent MediaWorks (intentmediaworks.net). When you download a song from a peer-to-peer file sharing social network or service such as LimeWire (limewire.com), a pop-up asks you to look at a text or video ad in return for a free and legal copy of the music. Advertisers pay the peer-to-peer service per ad view.

VIRAL MARKETING

viral marketing

Word-of-mouth marketing by which customers promote a product or service by telling others about it.

Viral marketing or advertising refers to *word-of-mouth* marketing in which customers promote a product or service by telling others about it. This can be done by e-mails, in conversations facilitated in chat rooms, by posting messages in newsgroups, and in electronic consumer forums. Having people forward messages to friends, asking them, for example, to "check out this product," is an example of viral marketing. This marketing approach has been used for generations, but now its speed and reach are multiplied by the Internet. This ad model can be used to build brand awareness at a minimal cost (*MoreBusiness.com* 2007), because the people who pass on the messages are paid very little or nothing for their efforts.

Viral marketing has long been a favorite strategy of online advertisers pushing youth-oriented products. For example, advertisers might distribute, embedded within a sponsor's e-mail, a small game program that is easy to forward. By releasing a few thousand copies of the game to some consumers, vendors hope to reach hundreds of thousands of others. Viral marketing also was used by the founder of Hotmail, a free e-mail service that grew from zero to 12 million subscribers in its first 18 months and to over 50 million in about 4 years. Each e-mail sent via Hotmail carried an invitation for free Hotmail service. Also known as advocacy marketing, this innovative approach, if properly used, can be effective, efficient, and relatively inexpensive. For further details, see en.wikipedia.org/wiki/Viral_marketing#Types_of_viral_campaigns. Goldsmith (2006) investigated the word-of-mouth process and its relationship to social communication.

One of the downsides of this strategy is that several e-mail hoaxes have been spread this way (see Fleitas 2003). Another danger of viral advertising is that a destructive virus can be added to an innocent advertisement-related game or message.

Viral Marketing in Social Networks

One of the major characteristics of social networks is the speed with which word-of-mouth spreads. For example, the membership of YouTube exploded just because members told their friends about the site. For how viral marketing works in social networks, see Chapter 8.

CUSTOMIZING ADS

Webcasting

A free Internet news service that broadcasts personalized news and information, including seminars, in categories selected by the user.

The Internet has too much information for customers to view. Filtering irrelevant information by providing consumers with customized ads can reduce this information overload. BroadVision (broadvision.com) provides a customized ad service platform called BroadVision eMarketing. The heart of eMarketing is a customer database, which includes registration data and information gleaned from site visits. The companies that advertise via One-to-One use the database to send customized ads to consumers. Using this feature, a marketing manager can customize display ads based on users' profiles. The product also provides market segmentation.

Another model of personalization can be found in **Webcasting**, a free Internet news service that broadcasts personalized news and information as well as e-seminars. Users sign into the Webcasting system and select the information they would like to receive, such as sports, news, headlines, stock quotes, or desired product promotions. The users receive the requested information along with personalized ads based on their expressed interests and general ads based on their profile.

ONLINE EVENTS, PROMOTIONS, AND ATTRACTIONS

Today, online promotions are regular events on thousands of Web sites. Contests, quizzes, coupons (see coolsavings.com), and giveaways designed to attract visitors are as much a part of online marketing as they are of offline commerce (see Clow and Baack 2004).

Live Web Events

Live Web events (concerts, shows, interviews, debates, videos), if properly done, can generate tremendous public excitement and bring huge crowds to a Web site. According to Akamai Technologies, Inc. (2000a), the best practices for successful live Web events are:

▶ Carefully planning content, audience, interactivity level, preproduction, and schedule
▶ Executing the production with rich media if possible
▶ Conducting appropriate promotion via e-mails, affinity sites, and streaming media directories, as well as conducting proper offline and online advertisement
▶ Preparing for quality delivery
▶ Capturing data and analyzing audience response so that improvements can be made

Admediation

Conducting promotions, especially large-scale ones, may require the help of vendors who specialize in promotions, such as those listed in Online File W4.12. Gopal et al. (2005) researched this area and developed a model that shows the role of such third-party vendors (such as Mypoints.com), which they call **admediaries.** Their initial model is shown in Exhibit 4.6. The exhibit concentrates on e-mail and shows the role of the admediaries (in the box between the customers and sellers).

admediaries
Third-party vendors that conduct promotions, especially large-scale ones.

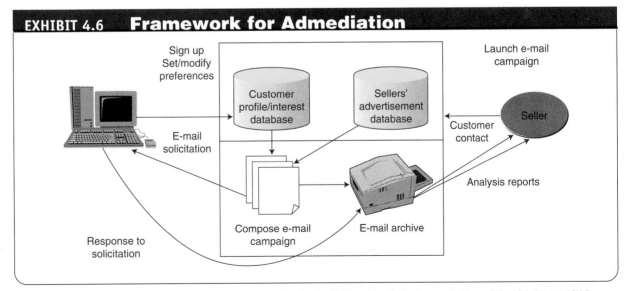

EXHIBIT 4.6   Framework for Admediation

Source: Gopal, R. D., et al. "Admediation: New Horizons in Effective Email Advertising." *The Communications of the ACM.* © 2001 ACM Inc. Used with permission.

Running promotions on the Internet is similar to running offline promotions. According to Clow and Baack (2004), some of the major considerations when implementing an online ad campaign include the following:

▶ The target audience needs to be clearly understood and should be online surfers.
▶ The traffic to the site should be estimated, and a powerful enough server must be prepared to handle the expected traffic volume.
▶ Assuming that the promotion is successful, what will the result be? This assessment is needed to evaluate the budget and promotion strategy.
▶ Consider cobranding; many promotions succeed because they bring together two or more powerful partners.

Companies combine several advertising methods as a result of market research. And if they have several Web sites, they may use different methods on each site. For example, P&G is experimenting with several methods to increase brand recognition (see Online File W4.13).

Selling Space by Pixels: The Case of Million Dollar Homepage

Million Dollar Homepage (milliondollarhomepage.com) was created by 21-year-old student Alex Tew in the U.K. The Web site sold advertising space on a one-page grid, much as real estate is sold, displaying a total of 1 million pixels at $1 per pixel. The site was launched in August 2005 and sold out by January 13, 2006. Within a short time, people started to sell pixels in other countries (e.g., milliondollarhomepage.com.au, one of several Australian sites). Also, people who bought pixels at $1 each were selling them at higher prices through auctions. This is an innovative way of owning space, because once you buy it, it is there forever.

Malicious hackers have targeted MillionDollarHomepage.com with distributed denial-of-service (DDoS) attacks (see Chapter 10). The attacks caused the site to load extremely slowly or be completely unavailable for a few days. Blackmailers at first asked for $5,000 to avert an attack on the site. The DDoS attack was launched after Tew declined to pay, and the hackers then demanded $50,000 to stop it. A further refusal to pay prompted the attackers to deface the site, replacing the regular page with a message stating: "don't come back you sly dog!" For details, see Sanders (2006).

Advertising in Second Life and Other Virtual Worlds

In virtual worlds, consumers have the ability to experience things not currently possible in the real world. For example, product trials in virtual settings provide a low-risk environment for testing features and benefits. Advertisers can create or hire avatars to be product ambassadors and answer common questions while demonstrating the product or service with 3D technology. Live videos and pictures can add to the experience to help educate the user (Nissim 2007).

Section 4.7 ▶ REVIEW QUESTIONS

1. Discuss the process and value of affiliate marketing.
2. How does the ads-as-a-commodity strategy work?
3. Describe viral marketing.
4. How are ads customized?
5. List some typical Internet promotions.
6. Define admediaries and describe their roles.

4.8 SPECIAL ADVERTISING TOPICS

The following are major representative topics related to Internet advertisement.

PERMISSION ADVERTISING

One of the major issues of one-to-one advertising is the flooding of users with unwanted (junk) e-mail, banners, pop-ups, and so on. The problem of flooding users with unsolicited e-mails is called spamming. **Spamming** typically upsets consumers and can keep useful advertising from reaching them.

One solution used by advertisers is **permission advertising** (**permission marketing**, or the *opt-in approach*) in which users register with vendors and *agree* to accept advertising (see returnpath.net). For example, the authors of this book agreed to receive a large number of e-commerce newsletters knowing that some would include ads. This way we can keep abreast of what is happening in the field. We also agree to accept e-mail from research companies, newspapers, travel agencies, and more. These vendors push, for free, very valuable information to us. The accompanying ads pay for such services. One way to conduct permission advertisement is to provide incentives. Note that Netflix asks permission to send users recommendations, but it does not ask whether it can use historical purchasing data to create them (see Team Assignment 4).

ADVERTISEMENT AS A REVENUE MODEL

Many of the dot-com failures in 2000 to 2002 were caused by a revenue model that contained advertising income as the major, or only, revenue source. Many small portals failed, but several large ones are dominating the field: Google, AOL, Yahoo!, and MSN. However, even these heavy-traffic sites only started to show a significant profit in 2004. Too many Web sites are competing for advertising money. Therefore, almost all portals are adding other sources of revenue.

However, if careful, a small site can survive by concentrating on a niche area. For example, playfootball.com is doing well. It pulls millions of dollars in advertising and sponsorship by concentrating on NFL fans. The site provides comprehensive and interactive content, attracting millions of visitors. For more on ad payments (see en.wikipedia.org/wiki/Online_advertising).

MEASURING ONLINE ADVERTISING'S EFFECTIVENESS

One managerial issue is how to measure the effectiveness of online advertisement. A related topic is how to charge for ads. These two topics are presented as a complete section in Online File W4.14. Ad effectiveness depends on ad management and ad localization (see Online File W4.15). A related issue is the assessment of the number of visitors to sites where ads are placed. According to Sutel (2007), there are major disagreements among rating agencies regarding audience measurement.

WIRELESS ADVERTISING

As will be seen in Chapter 9, the number of applications of m-commerce in marketing and advertising is growing rapidly, with advertising on cell phones and PDAs on the rise. Also, a mobile device can be connected to a network of other devices. An interesting application of this is digital ads atop 12,000 taxis in various U.S. cities. The ads also include public service announcements. The technology comes from Vert Inc. (vert.net).

spamming
Using e-mail to send unwanted ads (sometimes floods of ads).

permission advertising (permission marketing)
Advertising (marketing) strategy in which customers agree to accept advertising and marketing materials (known as "opt-in").

Source: Courtesy of Vert Incorporated.

Vert displays live content and advertising messages very effectively by targeting specific zip codes, neighborhoods, and individual city blocks. Ads can be scheduled for specific times during the day (e.g., promote coffee during the morning commute). Ads are beamed to Vert-equipped taxis like a cell phone signal. GPS satellites pinpoint where the cab is traveling, allowing ads to change from block to block (*Vert.net* 2006).

As advertisers look for the best business model, 2006 was a year of experimentation for the emerging mobile advertising market. Between 2006 and 2011, major brands will transition from simple SMS mobile marketing to multimedia advertising. Brands are beginning to identify what works in the mobile device market, and mobile advertising will continue to improve. Mobile marketing and advertising in the United States and Europe are predicted to exceed $1 billion in 2009 (Anywhere You Go 2006).

AD CONTENT

The content of ads is extremely important, and companies use ad agencies to help in content creation for the Web just as they do for other advertising media. A major player in this area is Akamai Technologies, Inc. (akamai.com). In a white paper (Akamai Technologies, Inc. 2000b), the company points out how the right content can drive traffic to a site. Akamai also describes how to evaluate third-party vendors and determine what content-related services are important.

Content is especially important to increase *stickiness*. Customers are expensive to acquire; therefore, it is important that they remain at a site, read its content carefully, and eventually make a purchase. The writing of the advertising content itself is, of course, important (see adcopywriting.com). Finding a good ad agency to write content and shape the advertising message is one of the key factors in any advertising campaign, online or offline.

SOFTWARE AGENTS IN MARKETING AND ADVERTISING APPLICATIONS

As the volume of customers, products, vendors, and information increases, it becomes uneconomical, or even impossible, for customers to consider all relevant information and to manually match their interests with available products and services. The practical solution to handling such information overload is to use software (intelligent) agents. In Chapter 3, we demonstrated how intelligent agents help online shoppers find and compare products, resulting in significant time savings.

In Online File W4.16, we concentrate on how software agents can assist customers in the online purchasing decision-making process as well as in advertisement. Depending on their level of intelligence, agents can do many things.

Section 4.8 ▶ REVIEW QUESTIONS

1. Describe permission advertising.
2. What is localization? What are the major issues in localizing Web pages?
3. How is wireless advertising practiced?
4. What is the importance of ad content?
5. Describe the role of software agents in advertising.

MANAGERIAL ISSUES

Some managerial issues related to this chapter are as follows.

1. **Do we understand our customers?** Understanding customers, specifically what they need and how to respond to those needs, is the most critical part of consumer-centered marketing. To excel, companies need to satisfy and retain customers, and management must monitor the entire process of marketing, sales, maintenance, and follow-up service.

2. **Who will conduct the market research?** B2C requires extensive market research. This research is not easy to do, nor is it inexpensive. Deciding whether to outsource to a market research firm or maintain an in-house market research staff is a major management issue.

3. **Are customers satisfied with our Web site?** This is a key question, and it can be answered in several ways. Many vendors are available to assist you; some provide free software. For discussion on how to improve customer satisfaction, see astea.com/ben_increase_satisfaction.asp. For Web site improvements, see futurenowinc.com.

4. **How can we use social networks for advertising?** A company can capitalize on segmented audiences in a social network in a number of different ways. Companies can create their own social networks, pay to place banner ads on existing networks, do affiliate marketing, and more. See Weber (2007) for guidelines and examples.

5. **How do we decide where to advertise?** Web advertising is a complex undertaking, and outsourcing its management should seriously be considered for large-scale ads. Some outsourcers specialize in certain industries (e.g., ebizautos.com for auto dealers). Companies should examine the adage.com site, which contains an index of Web sites, their advertising rates, and reported traffic counts, before selecting a site on which to advertise. Companies also should consult third-party audits.

6. **What is our commitment to Web advertising, and how will we coordinate Web and traditional advertising?** Once a company has committed to advertising on the Web, it must remember that a successful program is multifaceted. It requires input and vision from marketing, cooperation from the legal department, and strong technical leadership from the corporate information systems (IS) department. A successful Web advertising program also requires coordination with non-Internet advertising and top management support.

7. **Should we integrate our Internet and non-Internet marketing campaigns?** Many companies are integrating their TV and Internet marketing campaigns. For example, a company's TV or newspaper ads direct the viewers/readers to the Web site, where short videos and sound ads, known as *rich media*, are used. With click-through ratios of banner ads down to less than 0.5 percent at many sites, innovations such as the integration of offline and online marketing are certainly needed to increase click-throughs.

8. **What ethical issues should we consider?** Several ethical issues relate to online advertising. One issue that receives a great deal of attention is spamming. Another issue is the selling of mailing lists and customer information. Some people believe not only that a company needs the consent of the customers before selling a list, but also that

the company should share with customers the profits derived from the sale of such lists. Using cookies without an individual's consent is considered by many to be an ethical issue. The negative impacts of advertising need to be considered (see Gao et al. 2006).

9. **Are any metrics available to guide advertisers?** A large amount of information has been developed to guide advertisers as to where to advertise, how to design ads, and so on. Specific metrics may be used to assess the effectiveness of advertising and to calculate the ROI from an organization's online advertising campaign.

10. **Which Internet marketing/advertising channel to use?** An increasing number of online methods are available from which to choose. These include banners, search engines, blogging, social networks, and more. Angel (2006) proposed a methodology to assess these alternatives with a matrix for selection and implementation.

SUMMARY

In this chapter, you learned about the following EC issues as they relate to the learning objectives.

1. **The online consumer decision-making process.** The goal of marketing research efforts is to *understand* the consumers' online decision-making process and formulate an appropriate strategy to *influence* their behavior. For each step in the process, sellers can develop appropriate strategies.

2. **Building one-to-one relationships with customers.** EC offers companies the opportunity to build one-to-one relationships with customers that are not possible in other marketing systems. Product customization, personalized service, and getting the customer involved interactively (e.g., in feedback, order tracking, and so on) are all practical in cyberspace. In addition, advertising can be matched with customer profiles so that ads can be presented on a one-to-one basis.

3. **Online personalization.** Using personal Web pages, customers can interact with a company, learn about products or services in real time, or get customized products or services. Companies can allow customers to self-configure the products or services they want. Customization also can be done by matching products with customers' profiles.

4. **Increasing loyalty and trust.** Customers can switch loyalty online easily and quickly. Therefore, enhancing e-loyalty (e.g., through e-loyalty programs) is a must. Similarly, trust is a critical success factor that must be nourished.

5. **EC customer market research.** Several fast and economical methods of online market research are available. The two major approaches to data collection are: (1) soliciting voluntary information from the customers and (2) using cookies, transaction logs, or clickstream data to track customers' movements on the Internet and find what their interests are. Understanding market segmentation by grouping consumers into categories also is an effective EC market research method. However, online market research has several limitations, including data accuracy and representation of the statistical population by a sample.

6. **B2B Internet marketing methods and organizational buyers.** Marketing methods and marketing research in B2B differ from those of B2C. A major reason for this is that the buyers must observe organizational buying policies and frequently conduct buying activities as a committee. Organizations use modified B2C methods such as affiliate marketing.

7. **Objectives and characteristics of Web advertising.** Web advertising attempts to attract surfers to an advertiser's site. Once at the advertiser's site, consumers can receive information, interact with the seller, and in many cases, immediately place an order. With Web advertising, ads can be customized to fit groups of people with similar interests or even individuals. In addition, Web advertising can be interactive, is easily updated, can reach millions at a reasonable cost, and offers dynamic presentation by rich multimedia.

8. **Major online advertising methods.** Banners are the most popular online advertising method. Other frequently used methods are pop-ups and similar ads (including interstitials), e-mail (including e-mail to mobile devices), classified ads, registration of URLs

with search engines, and advertising in chat rooms. Some of these are related to search results obtained through search engines (especially Google).

9. **Various advertising strategies and types of promotions.** The major advertising strategies are ads associated with search results (text links), affiliate marketing, pay incentives for customers to view ads, viral marketing, ads customized on a one-to-one basis, and online events and promotions. Web promotions are similar to offline promotions. They include giveaways, contests, quizzes, entertainment,

coupons, and so on. Customization and interactivity distinguish Internet promotions from conventional ones.

10. **Permission marketing, ad management, and localization.** In permission marketing, customers are willing to accept ads in exchange for special (personalized) information or monetary incentives. Ad management deals with planning, organizing, and controlling ad campaigns and ad use. Finally, in localization, attempts are made to fit ads to local environments.

KEY TERMS

QUESTIONS FOR DISCUSSION

1. Discuss the similarities and differences between data mining and Web mining. (Hint: To answer this question, you will need to read Online File W4.6.)

2. Discuss why B2C marketing and advertising methods might not fit B2B.

3. Relate banner swapping to a banner exchange.

4. Discuss why banners are popular in Internet advertising.

5. Explain how Google generates targeted ads.

6. Discuss the relationship between market research and advertisement (see Atlas Solutions at atlassolutions.com for a start).

7. Discuss the advantages and limitations of listing a company's URL with various search engines.

8. Is it ethical for a vendor to enter a chat room operated by a competitor and pose queries?

9. Examine some Web avatars and try to interact with them (e.g., secondlife.com). Discuss the potential benefits and drawbacks of using avatars as an advertising medium.

10. When you buy a banner ad, you lease space for a specific time period. In milliondollarhomepage.com, you buy space forever. Compare and discuss.

INTERNET EXERCISES

1. Enter **netflix.com/Affiliates?hnjr=3**. Describe the value of the program as a marketing channel.

2. Examine a market research Web site (e.g., **acnielsen.com** or **claritas.com**). Discuss what might motivate a consumer to provide answers to market research questions.

3. Enter **mysimon.com** and share your experiences about how the information you provide might be used by the company for marketing in a specific industry (e.g., the clothing market).

4. Enter **marketingterms.com** and conduct a search by keywords as well as by category. Check the definitions of 10 key terms in this chapter.

5. Enter **2020research.com**, **infosurv.com**, and **marketingsherpa.com** and identify areas for market research about consumers.

6. Enter **nielsenmedia.com** and view the demos on e-market research. Then go to **clickz.com** and find its offerings. Summarize your findings.

7. Enter **selfpromotion.com** and find some interesting promotion ideas for the Web.

8. Enter **hotwired.com** and **espn.com**. Identify all of the advertising methods used on each site. Can you find those that are targeted advertisements? What revenue sources can you find on the ESPN site? (Try to find at least seven.)

9. Visit **adweek.com**, **wdfm.com**, **ad-tech.com**, **iab.com**, and **adage.com** and find new developments in Internet advertisement. Write a report based on your findings.

10. Enter **clairol.com** to determine your best hair color. You can upload your own photo to the studio and see how different shades look on you. You can also try different hairstyles. It also is for men. How can these activities increase branding? How can they increase sales?

11. What resources do you find to be most useful at **targetonline.com**, **clickz.com**, **admedia.org**, **marketresearch.com**, and **wdfm.com**?

12. Enter **doubleclick.com** and examine all of the company's products. Prepare a report.

13. Enter **zoomerang.com** and learn how it facilitates online surveys. Examine the various products, including those that supplement the surveys. Write a report.

14. Enter **pewinternet.org** and **pewresearch.org**. What research do they conduct that is relevant to B2C? To B2B? Write a report.

TEAM ASSIGNMENTS AND ROLE PLAYING

1. Enter **harrisinteractive.com**, **infosurv.com**, and similar sites. Have each team member examine the free marketing tools and related tutorials and demos. Each team will try to find a similar site and compare the two. Write a report discussing the team's findings.

2. Each team will choose one advertising method and conduct an in-depth investigation of the major players in that part of the ad industry. For example, direct e-mail is relatively inexpensive. Visit **the-dma.org** to learn about direct mail. Then visit **ezinedirector.com**, **venturedirect.com**, and similar sites. Each team will

prepare and present an argument as to why its method is superior.

3. In this exercise, each team member will enter **uproar.com** or similar sites to play games and win prizes. What could be better? This site is the destination of choice for game and sweepstakes junkies and for those who wish to reach a mass audience of fun-loving people. Relate the games to advertising and marketing.

4. Netflix, Amazon.com, and others view historical purchases as input available for use in their recommendation systems. Some believe that this is an invasion of privacy. Debate this issue.

5. Enter **autonlab.org** and download tools for conducting data mining analysis (these downloads are free). Get data on customer shopping and analyze it and write a report.

6. Create two teams. One will investigate advertising practices on **craigslist.org** and the other on **kijiji.com**. Each team will prepare a list of practices used by the sites. The differences should then be summarized.

Real-World Case

TOYOTA SCION'S INNOVATIVE ADVERTISING STRATEGIES

Toyota is becoming the number one car manufacturer while locked in aggressive competition with GM, Honda, and other car manufacturers. Toyota has been known for decades for its manufacturing innovations. Now it is becoming an innovative leader on the Web. Here we look at one of its newest brands, the Scion, which is geared toward Generation Y (consumers 35 years of age and younger).

Scion is using segmented advertising as its major strategy. The company also uses mass advertising and one-to-one targeted advertising, all of which are aimed at increasing brand recognition. Its efforts have been successful; according to MarketingVox News (2007a), Scion has 80-percent brand recognition. As of April 2007, Scion was the number one click-and-mortar e-tailer among consumers 35 and younger. Scion did not even make the top 27 sites in 2006; the jump to its number one ranking has been due to the interactive and community-oriented nature of the Scion online experience. The Scion Web site is highly personalized. Consumers can use sophisticated customization tools to build their own cars on the site and save their work. This online information is then integrated offline—a local dealership locates the desired vehicle (or a similar vehicle) and prepares it for a test drive. Other frills, such as a social network for Scion car owners and a Web site that plays music and lists concert information, make for a brand experience that tries to match its target audience. Let's look at some of Scion's specific advertising activities:

▶ According to a Clickz report (2007), Scion uses display ads and more on sites such as Blastro (*blastro.com*) and HipHopDX (*hiphopdx.com*) that reach urban audiences. It also works with these sites to make the ads attractive to their site readership.

▶ In August 2007, Scion launched Club Scion, a three-story virtual nightclub with dance floors, music, and hot tubs in a virtual world site. Each level reflects a different Scion model, which include xA, xB, and tC.

▶ Scion also has a presence in other large virtual worlds, including Second Life (*secondlife.com*), Whyville (*whyville.com*), There (*there.com*), and Gaia (*Gaia.com*). Scion tracks virtual return on investment (ROI) through online chatter. The brand's Scion City in Second Life generated 10,000 blog posts between April and June of 2007 and is the third most recognized brand behind Reuters in Second Life awareness. Each virtual world lends itself to a different marketing strategy. In Whyville, where users tend to fall between ages 8 and 15, the company launched a kind of virtual driver's education. And because There is populated by older teens, Scion made sure to create a more provocative social environment.

▶ Another strategy is the use of live chats. Toyota made effective use of the Internet by using live chat to attract the 18-to-24-year-old audience. Also, part of the campaign is the use of microapplication ads that allow consumers to stencil designs over the picture of the Scion.

The onsite chat gets hundreds of conversations per week. Prior to the chat, users are asked a few questions, one of which is where they live. Interestingly, Toyota found that many of the

Real-World Case: Scion

Source: *scion.com/#tCPhotoGallery_modified*

chatters reside in areas where Scion is not even available, providing valuable information for dealer expansion plans.

▶ In the wireless area, in 2004 Toyota launched a mobile advergame called "Scion Road Trip." Players accrued virtual miles by sending e-cards to friends and getting back responses. The campaign lasted for several months.

▶ For the 2008 xB car, Scion created a special Web site, *want2bsquare.com*. The site allows users to earn points by playing games, watching videos, and e-mailing others about the site. The site features eight microsites, including user community features. Each microsite has a unique theme, with one focusing on music. Each microsite also has its own design. One resembles a Monty Python set, another a haunted house. Other microsites include a town square and an urban zoo.

▶ Toyota targets children to influence their parents. In April 2007, Toyota began paying to place its Scion on Whyville, an online interactive community populated almost entirely by children and young teens. Toyota hopes Whyvillians will do two things: influence their parents' car purchases and that the children grow up to buy a Toyota themselves. Ten days into the campaign, the *New York Times* reported that visitors to the site had used the word "Scion" in online chats more than 78,000 times; hundreds of virtual Scions were purchased using "clams," the currency of Whyville; and the community meeting place, "Club Scion" was visited 33,741 times. The power of younger consumers has grown stronger in recent years. According to *MediaBuyerPlanner.com* (2007) a study by Packaged Facts showed that 39 percent of parents of 10- and 11-year-olds say their children have a significant impact on brand purchases.

▶ Finally, like several other automakers, Scion is creating its own broadband channel. These channels are viewed as a way to make the move from push to pull marketing where the consumer decides what materials to view and when. A content-rich, broadband-friendly site is seen as an always-on marketing channel to which people will return.

Sources: Compiled from *scion.com* (accessed February 2008), Bosman (2006), *MediaBuyerPlanner.com* (2007), and *MarketingVox.com* (2007a, 2007b, and 2007c).

Questions

1. Identify all marketing research activities cited in this case.

2. Enter *scion.com* and check into "Little Deviant." Check the content of two chapters and explain your experience with the advergame.

3. What mass targeted and one-to-one activities can you identify in this case?

4. Is the strategy to target children worthwhile? Find additional research on this topic.

5. Examine Scion's presence in two different virtual worlds. Summarize your experience from an advertising point of view.

6. Relate chat to advertising on *scion.com*.

7. Relate social network advertising (Chapter 8) to Scion.

B2B E-COMMERCE

Learning Objectives

Upon completion of this chapter, you will be able to:

1. Describe the B2B field.
2. Describe the major types of B2B models.
3. Discuss the characteristics of the sell-side marketplace, including auctions.
4. Describe the sell-side models.
5. Describe the characteristics of the buy-side marketplace and e-procurement.
6. Explain how reverse auctions work in B2B.
7. Describe B2B aggregation and group purchasing models.
8. Describe other procurement methods.
9. Define exchanges and describe their major types.
10. Describe B2B portals.
11. Describe third-party exchanges.
12. Describe partner relationship management (PRM).

Content

GENERAL MOTORS' B2B INITIATIVES

The Problem

General Motors (GM) is the world's second largest vehicle manufacturer. The company sells autos in 190 countries and has manufacturing plants in about 50. Because the automotive industry is very competitive, GM is always looking for ways to improve its effectiveness. Its most publicized new initiative is a futuristic project with which GM expects to custom build the majority of its cars in a few years. The company hopes to use the system to save billions of dollars by reducing its inventory of finished cars.

In the meantime, GM sells custom-designed cars online through its dealers' sites. Because such online sales are not considered direct marketing to the final consumers, GM is able to avoid *channel conflict* with the non–company-owned dealers. This collaboration requires sharing information with dealers for online marketing and service on cars and on warranties. Both GM and its many dealers also need to collaborate with GM's suppliers. These suppliers work with other automakers as well. Therefore, a good communications system is needed.

GM faces many other operational problems that are typical of large companies. One of these is an ongoing financial challenge of what to do with manufacturing machines that are no longer sufficiently productive and eventually must be replaced. GM traditionally has sold these assets through intermediaries at physical auctions. The problem was that these auctions took weeks, even months, to conclude. Furthermore, the prices obtained at the auctions seemed too low, and a 20 percent commission had to be paid to the third-party auctioneers.

Another operational problem for GM relates to procurement of both *direct* materials that go into the vehicles and *indirect* materials, such as light bulbs or office supplies. GM buys about 200,000 different products from 20,000 suppliers, spending over $100 billion annually. The company was using a manual bidding process to negotiate contracts with potential suppliers. Specifications of the needed materials were sent by mail to the potential suppliers, the suppliers would then submit a written bid, and GM would select a winner if a supplier offered a low enough price. If all the bids were too high, second and third rounds of bidding were conducted. In some cases, the process took weeks, even months, before GM was confident that the best deal, from both price and quality standpoints, had been achieved. The preparation costs involved in this process kept some bidders from submitting bids, so a less than optimal number of suppliers participated, resulting in higher prices paid by GM.

The Solution

To solve the problem of *connecting dealers and suppliers*, GM established an extranet infrastructure called ANX (Automotive Network eXchange). ANX, which was supported by other automakers, evolved into a B2B exchange, Covisint. This exchange, as most other exchanges, was not successful (see Section 5.8). To address the *capital assets problem*, in early 2000 GM implemented its own electronic market on *covisint.com* from which *forward auctions* were conducted. The first items put up for bid were eight 75-ton stamping presses. GM invited 140 certified bidders to view the pictures and

service records of the presses online. After only 1 week of preparation, the auction went live online, and the presses were sold in less than 2 hours.

For the *resource procurement problem*, GM automated the bidding process using *reverse auctions* on its e-procurement site. Qualified suppliers used the Internet to bid on each item GM needed to purchase. Bids were "open," meaning that all bidders could see the bids of their competitors. GM was able to accept bids from many suppliers concurrently and, using predetermined criteria, such as price, delivery date, and payment terms, awarded jobs quickly to the most suitable bidder.

The Results

Within just 89 minutes of the opening of the first *forward auction*, eight stamping presses were sold for $1.8 million. With the old offline method, a similar item would have sold for less than half of its online price, and the process would have taken 4 to 6 weeks. Since 2001, GM has conducted hundreds of other electronic auctions. Other sellers were encouraged to put their items up for sale at the site as well, paying GM a commission on the final sales price.

In the first online *reverse auction*, GM purchased a large volume of rubber sealing packages for vehicle production. The price GM paid was significantly lower than the price the company had been paying for the same items previously negotiated by manual tendering. The administrative costs per order were reduced by 40 percent or more.

Sources: Compiled from Ward's Auto World (2000) and miscellaneous press releases at *gm.com* (accessed August 2002).

WHAT WE CAN LEARN . . .

The GM case demonstrates the involvement of a large company in three EC activities: (1) electronically auctioning used equipment to buyers; (2) conducting purchasing via electronic bidding; and (3) using an extranet to bolster communication and collaboration. The auctioning (selling) and purchasing activities were conducted from GM's *private e-marketplace*, and the transactions were B2B. In B2B transactions, the company might be a seller, offering goods or services to many corporate buyers, or it might be a buyer, seeking goods or services from many corporate sellers (suppliers). When conducting such trades, a company can employ electronic auctions, as GM did, or it can use electronic catalogs or other market mechanisms. These mechanisms and methods and the private and public markets that support B2B trades are the subject of this chapter.

5.1 CONCEPTS, CHARACTERISTICS, AND MODELS OF B2B EC

B2B EC has some special characteristics as well as specific models and concepts. The major ones are described next.

BASIC B2B CONCEPTS

business-to-business e-commerce (B2B EC)
Transactions between businesses conducted electronically over the Internet, extranets, intranets, or private networks; also known as eB2B (electronic B2B) or just B2B.

Business-to-business e-commerce (B2B EC), also known as *eB2B* (*electronic B2B*), or just B2B, refers to transactions between businesses conducted electronically over the Internet, extranets, intranets, or private networks (see Mockler et al. 2006 and Papazoglou and Ribbers 2006). Such transactions may take place between a business and its supply chain members, as well as between a business, its customers, and any other business. In this context, a *business* refers to any organization, private or public, for profit or nonprofit. The major characteristic of B2B is that companies attempt to electronically automate trading or communication and collaboration processes in order to improve them. Note that B2B commerce can also be done without the Internet.

Key business drivers for B2B are the availability of a secure broadband Internet platform and private and public B2B e-marketplaces; the need for collaborations between suppliers and buyers; the ability to save money, reduce delays, and improve collaboration; and the emergence of effective technologies for intra- and interorganizational integration. (See en.wikipedia.org/Wiki/B2B_ecommerce.)

MARKET SIZE AND CONTENT OF B2B

Market forecasters estimate that by 2008 the global B2B market (online and offline) could reach $10 trillion. Harris (2006) reports an Interactive Data Corporation (IDC) estimate of $1 trillion B2B online sales, approaching 10 percent of the total B2B market. Chemicals, computer electronics, utilities, agriculture, shipping and warehousing, motor vehicles, petrochemicals, paper and office products, and food are the leading items in B2B. According to *eMarketer* (2003), the dollar value of B2B comprises at least 85 percent of the total transaction value of e-commerce. (Note: This figure is considered current in 2008.)

The B2B market, which went through major consolidation in 2000–2001, is growing rapidly. Different B2B market forecasters use different definitions and methodologies. Because of this, predictions frequently change and statistical data often differ. Therefore, we will not provide any more estimates here. Data sources that can be checked for the latest information on the B2B market are provided in Chapter 3 (Exhibit 3.1).

EXHIBIT 5.1   Generations of B2B E-Commerce

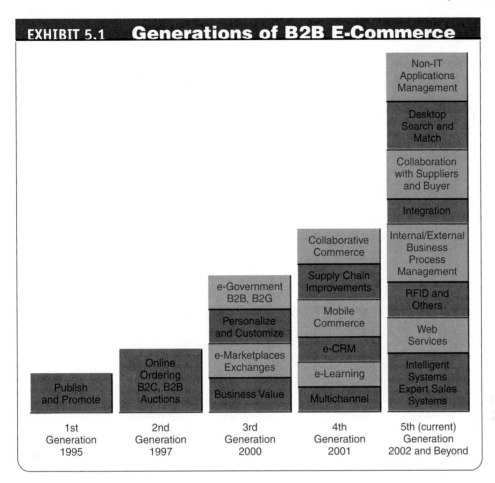

1st Generation 1995	2nd Generation 1997	3rd Generation 2000	4th Generation 2001	5th (current) Generation 2002 and Beyond
Publish and Promote	Online Ordering B2C, B2B Auctions	e-Government B2B, B2G / Personalize and Customize / e-Marketplaces Exchanges / Business Value	Collaborative Commerce / Supply Chain Improvements / Mobile Commerce / e-CRM / e-Learning / Multichannel	Non-IT Applications Management / Desktop Search and Match / Collaboration with Suppliers and Buyer / Integration / Internal/External Business Process Management / RFID and Others / Web Services / Intelligent Systems Expert Sales Systems

B2B EC is now in its fifth generation, as shown in Exhibit 5.1. This generation includes collaboration with suppliers, buyers, and other business partners (see Chapter 6), internal and external supply chain improvements (Chapter 6), and expert (intelligent) sales systems. Note that older generations coexist with new ones. Also, some companies are still using only EC from early generations. In this chapter, we mainly describe topics from the second and third generations. Topics from the fourth and fifth generations are presented in Chapters 6 through 9.

THE BASIC TYPES OF B2B TRANSACTIONS AND ACTIVITIES

The number of sellers and buyers and the form of participation used in B2B determine the basic B2B transaction types:

▶ **Sell-side.** One seller to many buyers
▶ **Buy-side.** One buyer from many sellers
▶ **Exchanges.** Many sellers to many buyers
▶ **Supply chain improvements and collaborative commerce.** Activities other than buying or selling among business partners, for example, supply chain improvements, communicating, collaborating, and sharing of information for joint design, planning, and so on (covered in Chapter 6)

Exhibit 5.2 illustrates these four B2B types.

EXHIBIT 5.2   Types of B2B E-Commerce

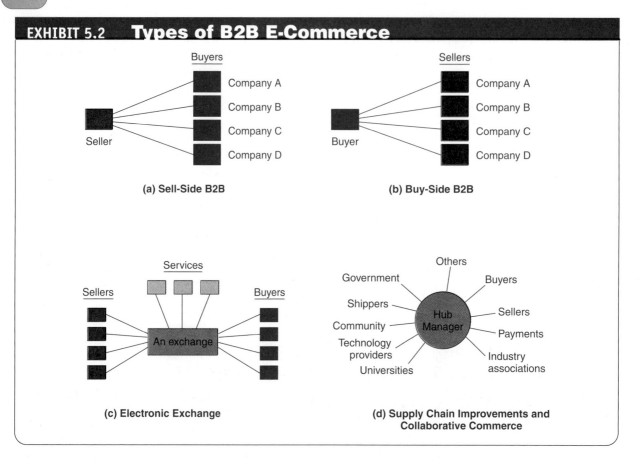

(a) Sell-Side B2B

(b) Buy-Side B2B

(c) Electronic Exchange

(d) Supply Chain Improvements and Collaborative Commerce

THE BASIC TYPES OF B2B E-MARKETPLACES AND SERVICES

The following are the basic types of B2B e-marketplaces.

company-centric EC
E-commerce that focuses on a single company's buying needs (many-to-one, or buy-side) or selling needs (one-to-many, or sell-side).

One-to-Many and Many-to-One: Private E-Marketplaces

In one-to-many and many-to-one markets, one company does either all of the selling (*sell-side market*) or all of the buying (*buy-side market*). Because EC is focused on a single company's buying or selling needs in these transactions, this type of EC is referred to as **company-centric EC**. Company-centric marketplaces—both sell-side and buy-side—are discussed in this chapter.

In company-centric marketplaces, the individual sell-side or buy-side company has complete control over who participates in the selling or buying transaction and the supporting information systems. Thus, these transactions are essentially private. Therefore, sell-side and buy-side markets are considered **private e-marketplaces**. They may be at the sellers' Web sites or hosted by a third party (intermediary).

private e-marketplaces
Markets in which the individual sell-side or buy-side company has complete control over participation in the selling or buying transaction.

Many-to-Many: Exchanges

In many-to-many e-marketplaces, many buyers and many sellers meet electronically for the purpose of trading with one another. There are different types of such e-marketplaces, which are also known as **exchanges**, **trading communities**, or **trading exchanges**. We will use the term *exchanges* in this book. Exchanges are usually owned and run by a third party or by a consortium. They are described in more detail in Sections 5.8 and 5.9. Exchanges are open to all interested parties (sellers and buyers), and thus are considered **public e-marketplaces**.

Supply Chain Improvers and Collaborative Commerce

B2B transactions are segments in the supply chain. Therefore, B2B initiatives need to be examined in light of other supply chain activities such as manufacturing, procurement of raw materials and shipments, and logistics (Chapter 11). Supply chain activities usually involve communication and collaboration.

Businesses deal with other businesses for purposes beyond just selling or buying. One example is that of *collaborative commerce*, which is communication, design, planning, and information sharing among business partners. To qualify as collaborative commerce, the activities that are shared must represent far more than just financial transactions. For example, they might include activities related to design, manufacture, or management. Supply chain issues and collaborative commerce are described in Chapter 6.

B2B CHARACTERISTICS

Here we examine various qualities by which B2B transactions can be characterized.

Parties to the Transaction: Sellers, Buyers, and Intermediaries

B2B commerce can be conducted *directly* between a *customer* and a *manufacturer* or it can be conducted via an **online intermediary.** The intermediary is an online third party that brokers the transaction between the buyer and seller; it can be a virtual intermediary or a click-and-mortar intermediary. See Papazoglou and Ribbers (2006) for details. Some of the electronic intermediaries for consumers mentioned in Chapter 3 also can be referenced for B2B by replacing the individual consumers with business customers. Consolidators of buyers or sellers are typical B2B intermediaries (Section 5.3).

Types of Transactions

B2B transactions are of two basic types: spot buying and strategic sourcing. **Spot buying** refers to the purchasing of goods and services as they are needed, usually at prevailing market prices, which are determined dynamically by supply and demand. The buyers and the sellers may not even know each other. Stock exchanges and commodity exchanges (oil, sugar, corn, etc.) are examples of spot buying. In contrast, **strategic (systematic) sourcing** involves purchases based on *long-term contracts.*

Spot buying can be conducted most economically on the public exchanges. Strategic purchases can be supported more effectively and efficiently through direct buyer–seller offline or online negotiations, which can be done in private exchanges or private trading rooms in public exchanges.

Types of Materials Traded

Two types of materials and supplies are traded in B2B: direct and indirect. **Direct materials** are materials used in making the products, such as steel in a car or paper in a book. The characteristics of direct materials are that their use is usually scheduled and planned for. They usually are not shelf items, and they are frequently purchased in large quantities after extensive negotiation and contracting.

---

exchanges (trading communities or trading exchanges) Many-to-many e-marketplaces, usually owned and run by a third party or a consortium, in which many buyers and many sellers meet electronically to trade with each other.

public e-marketplaces Third-party exchanges open to all interested parties (sellers and buyers).

online intermediary An online third party that brokers a transaction online between a buyer and a seller; may be virtual or click-and-mortar.

spot buying The purchase of goods and services as they are needed, usually at prevailing market prices.

strategic (systematic) sourcing Purchases involving long-term contracts that usually are based on private negotiations between sellers and buyers.

direct materials Materials used in the production of a product (e.g., steel in a car or paper in a book).

indirect materials
Materials used to support production (e.g., office supplies or light bulbs).

MRO (maintenance, repair, and operation)
Indirect materials used in activities that support production.

vertical marketplaces
Markets that deal with one industry or industry segment (e.g., steel, chemicals).

horizontal marketplaces
Markets that concentrate on a service, material, or a product that is used in all types of industries (e.g., office supplies, PCs).

Indirect materials are items, such as office supplies or light bulbs, that support production. They are usually used in **maintenance, repair, and operation (MRO)** activities. Collectively, they are known as *nonproduction materials*.

Direction of Trade

B2B marketplaces can be classified as vertical or horizontal. **Vertical marketplaces** are those that deal with one industry or industry segment. Examples include marketplaces specializing in electronics, cars, hospital supplies, steel, or chemicals. **Horizontal marketplaces** are those that concentrate on a service or a product that is used in all types of industries. Examples are office supplies, PCs, or travel services.

The various characteristics of B2B transactions are presented in summary form in Insights and Additions 5.1.

SUPPLY CHAIN RELATIONSHIPS IN B2B

In the various B2B transaction types, business activities are usually conducted along the supply chain of a company. The supply chain process consists of a number of interrelated subprocesses and roles. These extend from the acquisition of materials from suppliers, to the processing of a product or service, to packaging it and moving it to distributors and retailers. The process ends with the eventual purchase of a product by the end consumer. B2B can make supply chains more efficient and effective or it can change the supply chain completely, eliminating one or more intermediaries.

Historically, many of the segments and processes in the supply chain have been managed through paper transactions (e.g., purchase orders, invoices, and so forth). B2B applications are offered online so they can serve as supply chain enablers that offer distinct competitive advantages. Supply chain management also encompasses the

Insights and Additions 5.1 Summary of B2B Characteristics

Parties to Transactions	Types of Transactions
Direct, seller to buyer or buyer to seller	Spot buying
Via intermediaries	Strategic sourcing
B2B2C: A business sells to a business, but delivers to individual consumers	
Types of Materials Sold	**Direction of Trade**
Direct	Vertical
Indirect (MROs)	Horizontal
Number and Form of Participation	**Degree of Openness**
One-to-many: Sell-side (e-storefront)	Private exchanges, restricted
Many-to-one: Buy-side	Private exchanges, restricted
Many-to-many: Exchanges	Public exchanges, open to all
Many, connected: Collaborative, supply chain	Private (usually), can be public

coordination of order generation, order taking, and order fulfillment and distribution (see Chapters 6 and 11 for more discussion of supply chain management).

VIRTUAL SERVICE INDUSTRIES IN B2B

In addition to trading products between businesses, services also can be provided electronically in B2B. Just as service industries such as banking, insurance, real estate, and stock trading can be conducted electronically for individuals, as described in Chapter 3, so they can be conducted electronically for businesses. The major B2B services are:

- **Travel and hospitality services.** Many large corporations arrange their travel electronically through corporate travel agents. To further reduce costs, companies can make special arrangements that enable employees to plan and book their own trips online. For instance, American Express Business Travel (formerly Rosenbluth International) offers several tools to help corporate travel managers plan and control employee travel. In addition to traditional scheduling and control tools, in 2006 it started offering the following EC-based tools:
  - *TrackPoint* enables travel managers, as well as security and risk professionals, to pinpoint a traveler's whereabouts at any time.
  - *Travel Alert* and *Info Point* are information services that provide details about specific travel destinations. They are available free of charge to American Express Business Travel clients.
  - *Travel Insight Plus* consulting service identifies specific opportunities for savings in air travel expenditure for a given organization. The consulting study compares the client company's air travel expenditure against that of its true peers—other organizations that travel similar routes, over similar periods, with comparable volumes. Savings are identified through two key comparisons: the difference between the client and peer group's average spending on a route as well as highlighting the number of peers that are paying a lower average fare than the client's.

  Expedia, Travelocity, Orbitz, and other online travel services provide B2B service as well.

- **Real estate.** Commercial real estate transactions can be large and complex. Therefore, the Web might not be able to completely replace existing human agents. Instead, the Web can help businesses find the right properties, compare properties, and assist in negotiations. Some government-run foreclosed real estate auctions are open only to corporate real estate dealers and are conducted online.

- **Financial services.** Internet banking is an economical way of making business payments, transferring funds, or performing other financial transactions. For example, electronic funds transfer (EFT) is popular with businesses. Transaction fees over the Internet are less costly than any other alternative method. To see how payments work in B2B, see Chapter 11. Businesses can also purchase insurance online, both from pure online insurance companies and from click-and-mortar ones.

- **Online financing.** Business loans can be solicited online from lenders. Bank of America, for example, offers its commercial customers a matching service on IntraLoan (the bank's global loan syndication service), which uses an extranet to match business loan applicants with potential lending corporations. Several sites, such as garage.com, provide information about venture capital. Institutional investors use the Internet for certain trading activities.

▶ **Other online services.** Consulting services, law firms, health organizations, and others sell knowledge and special services online. Many other online services, such as the purchase of electronic stamps (similar to metered postage, but generated on a computer), are available online (see stamps.com). Also, recruiting and staffing services are done online.

THE BENEFITS OF B2B

The benefits of B2B depend on which model is used. In general, though, the major benefits of B2B are that it:

> ▶ Creates new sales (purchase) opportunities
> ▶ Eliminates paper and reduces administrative costs
> ▶ Expedites processing and reduces cycle time
> ▶ Lowers search costs and time for buyers to find products and vendors
> ▶ Increases productivity of employees dealing with buying and/or selling
> ▶ Reduces errors and improves quality of services
> ▶ Makes product configuration easier
> ▶ Reduces marketing and sales costs (for sellers)
> ▶ Reduces inventory levels and costs
> ▶ Enables customized online catalogs with different prices for different customers
> ▶ Increases production flexibility, permitting just-in-time delivery
> ▶ Reduces procurement costs (for buyers)
> ▶ Facilitates customization via configuration (e.g., at Cisco)
> ▶ Provides for efficient customer service
> ▶ Increases opportunities for collaboration

B2B EC has limitations as well, especially regarding channel conflict and the operation of public exchanges. These will be discussed later in this chapter.

The introduction of B2B might eliminate the distributor or the retailer, which could be a benefit to the seller and the buyer (though not a benefit to the distributor or retailer). In previous chapters, such a phenomenon is referred to as *disintermediation* (Chapters 2 and 3).

In the remainder of the chapter, we will look at the company-centric B2B models, public exchanges, and other B2B topics.

Section 5.1 ▶ REVIEW QUESTIONS

1. Define B2B.
2. Discuss the following: spot buying versus strategic sourcing, direct materials versus indirect materials, and vertical markets versus horizontal markets.
3. What are company-centric marketplaces? Are they public or private?
4. Define B2B exchanges.
5. Relate the supply chain to B2B transactions.
6. List the B2B online services.
7. Summarize the benefits of B2B.

5.2 ONE-TO-MANY: SELL-SIDE E-MARKETPLACES

Many B2B activities involve direct selling.

SELL-SIDE MODELS AND ACTIVITIES

In Chapter 3, we introduced the direct-selling B2C model in which a manufacturer or a retailer sells electronically directly to consumers from a *storefront*. In a B2B **sell-side e-marketplace** a business sells products and services to business customers, frequently over an extranet. The seller can be a manufacturer selling to a wholesaler, to a retailer, or to an individual business. Intel, Cisco, and Dell are examples of such sellers. Or the seller can be a distributor selling to wholesalers, to retailers, or to businesses (e.g., W. W. Grainger). In either case, sell-side e-marketplaces involve one seller and many potential buyers. In this model, both individual consumers and business buyers might use the same sell-side marketplace (e.g., dell.com), or they might use different marketplaces. Exhibit 5.3 shows the architecture of sell-side B2B marketplaces, as compared to that of B2C (left side of figure).

The architecture of this B2B model is similar to that of B2C EC. The major differences are in the process (see Jakovljevic 2004). For example, in B2B, large customers might be provided with customized catalogs and prices. Usually, companies will separate B2C orders from B2B orders. One reason for this is that B2C and B2B orders have different *order-fulfillment processes* (see Chapter 11) and different pricing models (i.e., wholesale vs. retail pricing). Technology supports the ability to identify the customer and determine whether it is a business or consumer customer.

The one-to-many model has three major marketing methods: (1) selling from *electronic catalogs*; (2) selling via *forward auctions* (as GM does with its old equipment); and (3) one-to-one selling, usually under a *negotiated* long-term contract. Such one-to-one

sell-side e-marketplace
A Web-based marketplace in which one company sells to many business buyers from e-catalogs or auctions, frequently over an extranet.

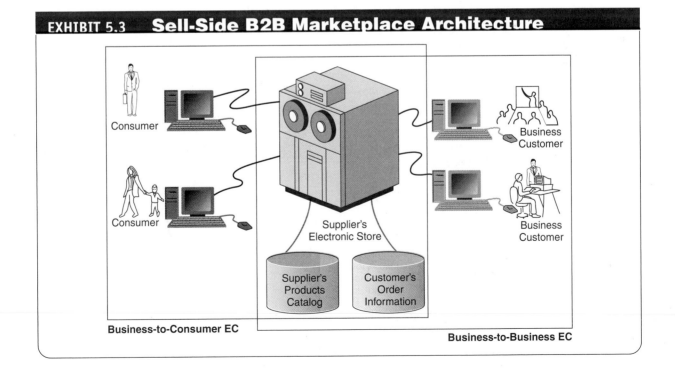

EXHIBIT 5.3   Sell-Side B2B Marketplace Architecture

Consumer

Consumer

Supplier's Electronic Store

Supplier's Products Catalog

Customer's Order Information

Business Customer

Business Customer

Business-to-Consumer EC

Business-to-Business EC

negotiating is familiar: The buying company negotiates price, quantity, payments, delivery, and quality terms with the selling company. We describe the first method in this section and the second in Section 5.3. For methods of improving B2B selling, see Hancock et al. (2005).

B2B Sellers

Sellers in the sell-side marketplace may be click-and-mortar manufacturers or intermediaries (e.g., distributors or wholesalers). The intermediaries may even be online pure companies (virtual), as in the case of Bigboxx.com, described in Online File W5.1.

Customer Service

Online sellers can provide sophisticated customer services. For example, General Electric receives over 20 million calls a year regarding appliances. Although most of these calls come from individuals, many come from businesses. By using the Internet and automatic-response software agents (autoresponders), GE has reduced the cost of handling calls from $5 per call when done by phone to $0.20 per electronically answered call. Patton (2006) estimated that a call handled by a human agent costs $2 to $10. If answered automatically (e.g., autoresponder, IVR), the cost is between $.02 and $.20.

We now turn our attention to the first of the sell-side methods—selling online from electronic catalogs.

DIRECT SALES FROM CATALOGS

Companies can use the Internet to sell directly from their online catalogs. A company may offer one catalog for all customers or a *customized catalog* for each large customer (usually both).

In Chapter 2, we presented the advantages of e-catalogs over paper catalogs. However, this model may not be convenient for large and repetitive business buyers because the buyer's order information is stored in the supplier's server and is not easily integrated with the buyer's corporate information system. To facilitate B2B direct sales, the seller can provide the buyer with a buyer-customized shopping cart (such as Bigboxx.com offers), which can store order information that can be integrated with the buyer's information system.

Many sellers provide separate pages and catalogs to their major buyers. For example, Staples.com, an office-supply vendor, offers its business customers personalized software catalogs of about 100,000 products and pricing at stapleslink.com.

Another example of B2B direct sales from catalogs is Microsoft, which uses an extranet to sell about $10 billion of software annually to its channel partners (distributors). Using Microsoft's extranet-based order-entry tool (MOET), distributors can check inventory, make transactions, and look up the status of orders. The online orders are automatically fed into the customer's SAP applications. The extranet handles about 1 million transactions per year. The system significantly reduces the number of phone calls, e-mails, and incorrect product shipments (Microsoft 2006).

In selling directly, manufacturers might encounter a similar problem to that of B2C, namely conflict with the regular distributors, including corporate dealers (channel conflict). An interesting solution is illustrated in Case 5.1, where Gregg's Cycles sells online (both B2B and B2C). It sells peripheral products, such as parts and accessories, to consumers and provides a store locator where customers can buy its core product—bicycles—at brick-and-mortar distributors.

CASE 5.1
EC Application
GREGG'S CYCLES GOES ONLINE

Reputable bicycle manufacturers such as Gregg's Cycles do not sell their products online, nor do they allow their bicycles to be sold online by others. The manufacturer tries to avoid channel conflicts with its dealers and the independent bike shops that sell bikes. Gregg's Cycles believes that selling bikes is as much as about customer service as it is about the product.

Each bike sold in one of Gregg's stores is custom fitted to the customer. This type of customer service cannot be done online. Therefore, when Gregg's Cycles decided to build a Web site, it decided to display all its bikes online so that customers could see the huge selection as well as use the site as a resource to learn about the bikes. As a bonus, the software Gregg's chose, CartGenie (from J Street Technology), made it easy to sell online peripheral products, such as parts, clothing, accessories, and complementary products, such as snowboards and inline skates.

With the CartGenie software the company is able to show the specs of each bike so that viewers can compare up to three bikes on one screen. Oftentimes, customers come into the company's physical stores armed with printouts from the Web site, knowing exactly what they want. In addition, the site displays inventory availability. If a store has the bike that the customers are looking for, they will quickly come to the store to get their bike.

The online store now carries over 7,000 SKUs and caters to customers across the United States. Gregg's makes sure to mention its Web site address in all of its print ads and promotions. It also publishes an online newsletter to keep in touch with customers.

CartGenie enables bulk import of products to the corporate catalog, a most useful feature. Another useful feature is CartGenie Connect, which automatically updates pricing and availability. CartGenie Connect also takes information directly from the point-of-sale database and syncs it with the online database. With over 7,000 SKUs, it would be close to impossible for a person to keep the site up-to-date.

CartGenie is available in the Standard, Pro, and Enterprise Editions. Key features include:

▶ Full support for B2B and B2C selling
▶ Multiple retail and wholesale price levels
▶ A built-in comparison engine for doing side-by-side product comparisons
▶ A complete inventory control module
▶ Integrated UPS shipping calculator
▶ Volume discount pricing (for retailers, clubs, etc.)
▶ Search engine friendly product catalog system
▶ Integration with PayPal
▶ Built-in product import utilities
▶ Full support for real-time credit card processing

The Web site also offers information on customizing bikes, bicycle repair, bike rental, blogging, store locations, job opportunities, coupons, bike events, and more. Customers love the Web site; the company gets favorable responses from most who send comments.

Sources: Compiled from Rincon (2006), from *greggcycles.com* (accessed January 2008), and from *jstreettech.com* (accessed January 2008).

Questions

1. Why is this a B2B sell-side case?
2. What are the benefits of this type of Web site for the company?
3. Relate the case to social networks.
4. How does CartGenie support the site?

Configuration and Customization

As with B2C EC, B2B direct sales offer an opportunity for efficient customization (e.g., see Dell case in Chapter 1 and the Cisco case in Online File W5.2 later in this chapter). As we will see in the case of Cisco, manufacturers can provide online tools for self-configuration, pricing, ordering, and so on. Business customers can self-configure customized products, get price quotes, and submit orders, all online.

Many click-and-mortar companies use a *multichannel distribution system*, in which the Internet is a supplemental channel that enables greater efficiency in the ordering process, as shown in the case of Whirlpool in Case 5.2.

WHIRLPOOL B2B TRADING PORTAL

Whirlpool (*whirlpool.com*) is a $18-billion global corporation based in Benton Harbor, Michigan. It is in the company's best interest to operate efficiently and to offer as much customer service for the members (partners) of its selling chain as possible. It is a complex job, because the partners are located in 170 countries. Middle-tier partners, who comprise 25 percent of the total partner base and 10 percent of Whirlpool's annual revenue, were submitting their orders by phone or fax because they were not large enough to have system-to-system computer connections direct to Whirlpool.

To improve customer service for these dealers, Whirlpool developed a B2B trading partner portal (Whirlpool Web World), using IBM e-business solutions. The technologies enable fast, easy Web self-service ordering processes. Using these self-service processes, Whirlpool was able to cut the cost per order to under $5—a savings of 80 percent.

The company tested ordering via the Web by developing a portal for low-level products. It was so successful that Whirlpool created a second-generation portal, which allows middle-tier trade partners to place orders and track their status through a password-protected site.

Simultaneously, the company implemented SAP R/3 for order entry, which is utilized by the middle-tier partners on the second-generation portal. The company also is using IBM's Application Framework for e-business, taking advantage of its rapid development cycles and associated cost reductions.

Whirlpool's global platform provides its operations with resources and capabilities few other manufacturers can match. Whirlpool's global procurement, product development, and information technology organizations help the company's operations reduce costs, improve efficiencies, and introduce a continuous stream of relevant innovation to consumers.

Using the same IBM platform, Whirlpool launched a B2C site for U.S. customers for ordering small appliances and accessories. The site was so successful that the company realized a 100 percent ROI in just 5 months.

Sources: Compiled from IBM (2000) and *whirlpoolcorp.com* (accessed January 2008).

Questions

1. How do Whirlpool's customers benefit from the portal?
2. What are the benefits of the trading portal for Whirlpool?
3. Relate the B2B sell-side to a B2C storefront.

Benefits and Limitations of Direct Sales from Catalogs

Successful examples of the B2B direct sales model include manufacturers, such as Dell, Intel, IBM, and Cisco, and distributors, such as Ingram Micro (which sells to value-added retailers; the retailer adds some service along with the product). Sellers that use this model can be successful as long as they have a superb reputation in the market and a large enough group of loyal customers.

Although the benefits of direct sales are similar to that of B2C, there also are limitations. One of the major issues facing direct sellers is how to find buyers. Many companies know how to advertise in traditional channels but are still learning how to contact would-be buyers online. Also, B2B sellers may experience channel conflicts with their existing distribution systems. Another limitation is that if traditional EDI (the computer-to-computer direct transfer of business documents) is used, the cost to the customers can be high, and they will be reluctant to go online. The solution to this problem is the transfer of documents over the extranets (see Online File W5.3) and an Internet-based EDI (see Online File W5.4). Finally, the number of business partners online must be large enough to justify the system infrastructure and operation and maintenance expenses.

DIRECT SALES: THE EXAMPLE OF CISCO SYSTEMS

Cisco Systems (cisco.com) is the world's leading producer of routers, switches, and network interconnection services. Cisco's portal has evolved over several years, beginning with technical support for customers and developing into one of the world's largest direct sales EC sites. Today, Cisco offers about a dozen Internet-based applications to both end-user businesses and reseller partners. For details of the example see Online File W5.2.

Section 5.2 ▶ REVIEW QUESTIONS

1. List the types of sell-side B2B transaction models.
2. Distinguish between the use and nonuse of intermediaries in B2B sell-side transactions.
3. What are buy-side and sell-side transactions? How do they differ?
4. Describe customer service in B2B systems.
5. Describe direct B2B sales from catalogs.
6. Discuss the benefits and limitations of direct B2B sales from catalogs.

5.3 SELLING VIA INTERMEDIARIES AND DISTRIBUTORS

Manufacturers frequently use intermediaries to distribute their products to a large number of buyers. The intermediaries (known as distributors) usually buy products from many vendors and aggregate them into one catalog from which they sell. Now, many of these distributors also are selling online.

As in B2C, many distributors (including retailers) also offer their products online via storefronts. Some well-known online distributors for businesses are Sam's Club (of Wal-Mart), Avnet, and W. W. Grainger (Case 5.3). Most e-distributors sell in horizontal markets, meaning that they sell to businesses in a variety of industries. However, some specialize in one industry (vertical market), such as Boeing PART (see Online File W5.5). Most intermediaries sell at fixed prices; however, some offer quantity discounts.

Section 5.3 ▶ REVIEW QUESTIONS

1. What are the advantages of using intermediaries in B2B sales?
2. What special services are provided to buyers by Boeing Parts? (Online File W5.5)
3. Compare an e-distributor in B2B to Amazon.com. What are the similarities? What are the differences?

5.4 SELLING VIA AUCTIONS

Auctions are gaining popularity as a B2B sales channel (see Dasgupta et al. 2006). Some major B2B auction issues are discussed in this section.

USING AUCTIONS ON THE SELL SIDE

As you read in the opening case study, GM used *forward auctions* to sell its unneeded capital assets. In such a situation, items are displayed on an auction site (private or public) for quick disposal. Forward auctions offer a number of benefits to B2B sellers:

▶ **Revenue generation.** Forward auctions support and expand online and overall sales. Forward auctions also offer businesses a new venue for quickly and easily disposing of excess, obsolete, and returned products (e.g., liquidation.com).

CASE 5.3
EC Application
W. W. GRAINGER AND GOODRICH CORPORATION

W. W. Grainger has a number of Web sites, but its flagship is *grainger.com*. In 2007, of Grainger's $6 billion in annual sales, more than $600 million was done over the Web, with the majority of those sales placed through *grainger.com*.

More than 800,000 brand-name MRO supplies from more than 1,000 suppliers are offered at *grainger.com*, and a growing number of Grainger's 2.2 million customers are ordering online. The Web site continues the same kind of customer service and wide range of industrial products provided by Grainger's traditional offline business with the additional convenience of 24/7 ordering, use of search engines, and additional services.

This convenience is what first attracted BFGoodrich Aerospace (now called Goodrich Corporation) in Pueblo, Colorado. It found *grainger.com* to be one of the most convenient and easy purchasing sites to use. The purchasing agent of this relatively small Goodrich plant of approximately 250 employees used to call in an order to a supplier, give the salesperson a part number, and wait until the price could be pulled up. Goodrich's purchaser now can place orders online in a matter of minutes, and the purchaser's display has Goodrich's negotiated pricing built in.

Goodrich can get just about anything it needs from *grainger.com*. Grainger interfaces with other suppliers, so if Goodrich needs something specific that Grainger does not normally carry, Grainger will research and find the items through its *findmro.com* site. With Grainger's buying power, Goodrich can get better prices.

Goodrich has achieved additional savings from the tremendous decrease in paperwork that has resulted from buying through *grainger.com*. Individuals in each department now have access to purchasing cards, which allow them to do some of their own ordering. Before, the central purchasing department had to issue purchase orders for every single item. Now, employees with purchasing cards and passwords can place orders according to the spending limits that have been set up based on their positions.

In 2002, the Goodrich Pueblo operation spent $200,000 for purchases from *grainger.com*, which reflected a 10 to 15 percent savings on its purchases. Goodrich has now signed a company-wide enterprise agreement that allows every Goodrich facility in the country to order through *grainger.com*, with an expected savings of at least 10 percent.

Sources: Compiled from *Fortune* (2000), *grainger.com* (accessed 2006), and Lucas (2005).

Questions

1. Enter *grainger.com* and review all of the services offered to buyers. Prepare a list of these services.
2. Explain how Goodrich's buyers save time and money.
3. What other benefits does Goodrich enjoy by using *grainger.com*?
4. How was desktop purchasing implemented at Goodrich Corporation?

▶ **Cost savings.** In addition to generating new revenue, conducting auctions electronically reduces the costs of selling the auctioned items. These savings also help increase the seller's profits.

▶ **Increased "stickiness."** Forward auctions give Web sites increased "stickiness." As discussed in Chapter 4, stickiness is a characteristic that describes customer loyalty to a site, demonstrated by the number and length of visits to a site.

▶ **Member acquisition and retention.** All bidding transactions result in additional registered members, who are future business contacts. In addition, auction software aids enable sellers to search and report on virtually every relevant auction activity for future analysis and use.

Forward auctions can be conducted in two ways. A company can conduct its forward auctions from its own Web site or it can sell from an intermediary auction site, such as ebay.com or asset-auctions.com. Let's examine these options.

AUCTIONING FROM THE COMPANY'S OWN SITE

For large and well-known companies that frequently conduct auctions, such as GM, it makes sense to build an auction mechanism on the company's own site. Why should a company pay a commission to an intermediary if the intermediary cannot provide the company with added value? Of course, if a company decides to auction from its own site, it will have to pay for infrastructure and operate and maintain the auction site. However, if the company already has an electronic marketplace for selling from e-catalogs, the additional cost for conducting auctions might not be too high. However, a significant added value that could be provided by intermediaries is the attraction of many potential buyers to the auction site.

USING INTERMEDIARIES IN AUCTIONS

Several intermediaries offer B2B auction sites (e.g., see asset-auctions.com). An intermediary might conduct private auctions for a seller, either from the intermediary's or the seller's site. Or a company might choose to conduct auctions in a public marketplace, using a third-party hosting company (e.g., eBay, which has a special "business exchange" for small companies).

Using a third-party hosting company for conducting auctions has many benefits. The first is that no additional resources (e.g., hardware, bandwidth, engineering resources, or IT personnel) are required. Nor are there any hiring costs or opportunity costs associated with the redeployment of corporate resources. B2B auction intermediary sites also offer fast time-to-market: They enable a company to have a robust, customized auction up and running immediately. Without the intermediary, it can take a company weeks to prepare an auction site in-house.

Another benefit of using an intermediary relates to who owns and controls the auction information. In the case of an intermediary-conducted private auction, the intermediary sets up the auction to show the branding (company name) of the merchant rather than the intermediary's name. Yet, the intermediary does the work of collecting data on Web traffic, page views, and member registration; setting all the auction parameters (transaction fee structure, user interface, and reports); and integrating the information flow and logistics. Of course, if a company wants to dispose of unwanted assets without advertising to the public that it is doing so, an intermediary-conducted public auction would be the logical choice.

Another benefit of using intermediaries relates to billing and collection efforts, which are handled by the intermediary rather than the selling company. For example, intermediaries calculate merchant-specific shipping weights and charge customers for shipping of auctioned items. These services are not free, of course. They are provided as part of the merchant's commission to the intermediary; a cost often deemed worth paying in exchange for the ease of the service.

For an example of using an intermediary to liquidate old equipment, see Case 5.4.

EXAMPLES OF B2B FORWARD AUCTION

The following are examples of B2B auctions:

▶ Whirlpool Corp. sold $20 million in scrap metal in 2003, increasing the price received by 15 percent (*Asset-auctions.com* 2006).
▶ Sam's Club (samsclub.com) auctions thousands of items (especially electronics) at auctions.samsclub.com. Featured auctions include the current bid, the number of bids, and the end date.

CASE 5.4
EC Application

HOW THE STATE OF PENNSYLVANIA SELLS SURPLUS EQUIPMENT

For many years, the Pennsylvania Department of Transportation (DOT) used a traditional offline auction process. As of October 2003 the state is holding online auctions to sell its surplus heavy equipment. The old, live in-person auction system generated about $5 million a year. Using the Internet, the DOT is generating at least a 20 percent increase in revenue.

The Commonwealth of Pennsylvania conducted its initial online sale of surplus DOT items in October 2003. The sale consisted of 77 items (including 37 dump trucks). Onsite inspection was available twice during the 2-week bidding period. The online sale allowed the Commonwealth of Pennsylvania to obtain an average price increase of 20 percent, while reducing labor costs related to holding a traditional on-site sale. On high-value specialty items (i.e., a bridge inspection crane and a satellite van), results exceeded the estimated sale prices by over 200 percent.

The auction was conducted by Asset-auctions.com. The results of the auction were as follows:

▶ Total sales: $635,416.03.
▶ Half of the bidding activity occurred in the final 2 days.
▶ Every lot received multiple bids.

▶ Overtime bidding occurred in 39 lots.
▶ 174 bidders from 19 states and Mexico made about 1,500 bids in 5 days.
▶ 47 different buyers participated.

The Commonwealth of Pennsylvania now sells surplus equipment and properties using both Asset-auctions.com and eBay.

Sources: Material compiled from *asset-auctions.com* (accessed January 2008) and the Commonwealth of Pennsylvania (2006).

Questions

1. Why is heavy equipment amenable to such auctions?
2. Why did the state generate 20 percent more in revenues with the online auction?
3. Why do you need an intermediary to conduct such an auction?
4. Comment on the number of bidders and bids with an online auction as compared to an offline auction.

▶ ResortQuest, a large vacation rental company, uses auctionanything.com to auction rental space.
▶ At GovernmentAuctions.org (governmentauctions.org), businesses can bid on foreclosures, seized items, abandoned property, and more.
▶ Yahoo! conducts both B2C and B2B auctions of many items.

Section 5.4 ▶ REVIEW QUESTIONS

1. List the benefits of using B2B auctions for selling.
2. List the benefits of using auction intermediaries.

5.5 ONE-FROM-MANY: BUY-SIDE E-MARKETPLACES AND E-PROCUREMENT

buy-side e-marketplace
A corporate-based acquisition site that uses reverse auctions, negotiations, group purchasing, or any other e-procurement method.

When a buyer goes to a sell-side marketplace, such as Cisco's, the buyer's purchasing department sometimes has to manually enter the order information into its own corporate information system. Furthermore, manually searching e-stores and e-malls to find and compare suppliers and products can be slow and costly. As a solution, large buyers can open their own marketplaces, as GM did, called **buy-side e-marketplaces**, and invite sellers to browse and offer to fulfill orders. The term *procurement* is used to refer to the purchase of goods and services for organizations. It is usually done by *purchasing agents*, also known as *corporate buyers*.

PROCUREMENT METHODS

Companies use different methods to procure goods and services depending on what and where they buy, the quantities needed, how much money is involved, and more. The major procurement methods include the following:

▶ Conduct bidding in a system in which suppliers compete against each other. This method is used for large-ticket items or large quantities (Section 5.6).

▶ Buy directly from manufacturers, wholesalers, or retailers from their catalogs, and possibly by negotiation.

▶ Buy at private or public auction sites in which the organization participates as one of the buyers (Section 5.6).

▶ Buy from the catalog of an intermediary (e-distributor) that aggregates sellers' catalogs (Section 5.7).

▶ Buy from an internal buyer's catalog, in which company-approved vendors' catalogs, including agreed-upon prices, are aggregated. This approach is used for the implementation of *desktop purchasing*, which allows the requisitioners to order directly from vendors, bypassing the procurement department (Section 5.7).

▶ Join a group-purchasing system that aggregates participants' demand, creating a large volume. Then the group may negotiate prices or initiate a tendering process (Section 5.7).

▶ Buy at an exchange or industrial mall (Section 5.8).

▶ Collaborate with suppliers to share information about sales and inventory, so as to reduce inventory and stock-outs and enhance just-in-time delivery. (See Chapter 6 on collaborative commerce.)

Some of these activities are done in private marketplaces, others in public exchanges. According to Wikipedia (2006), the six main types of e-procurement are as follow:

▶ **e-sourcing.** Identifying new suppliers for a specific category of purchasing requirements using Internet technology.

▶ **e-tendering.** Sending requests for information and prices to suppliers and receiving the suppliers' responses using Internet technology.

▶ **e-reverse auctioning.** Using Internet technology to buy goods and services from a number of known or unknown suppliers.

▶ **e-informing.** Gathering and distributing purchasing information both from and to internal and external parties using Internet technology.

▶ **Web-based ERP (electronic resource planning).** Creating and approving purchasing requisitions, placing purchase orders, and receiving goods and services by using a software system based on Internet technology.

▶ **e-MRO (maintenance, repair, and operating).** The same as Web-based ERP except that the goods and services ordered are non–product-related MRO supplies.

INEFFICIENCIES IN TRADITIONAL PROCUREMENT MANAGEMENT

procurement management
The planning, organizing, and coordinating of all the activities relating to purchasing goods and services needed to accomplish the organization's mission.

Procurement management refers to the planning, organizing, and coordinating of all the activities pertaining to the purchasing of the goods and services necessary to accomplish the mission of an enterprise. It involves the B2B purchase and sale of supplies and services, as well as the flow of required information and networking systems. Approximately 80 percent of an organization's purchased items, mostly MROs, constitute 20 to 25 percent of the total purchase value. Furthermore, a large portion of corporate buyers' time is spent on non–value-added activities, such as entering data, correcting errors in paperwork, expediting delivery, or solving quality problems.

The traditional procurement process, shown in Exhibit 5.4, often is inefficient. For example, for high-value items, purchasing personnel spend a great deal of time and effort on procurement activities. These activities include qualifying suppliers, negotiating prices and terms, building rapport with strategic suppliers, and carrying out supplier evaluation and certification. If buyers are busy with the details of the smaller items (usually the MROs), they do not have enough time to properly deal with the purchase of the high value items.

Other inefficiencies also may occur in conventional procurement. These range from delays to paying too much for rush orders. One procurement inefficiency is **maverick buying**. This is when a buyer makes unplanned purchases of items needed quickly, which results in buying at non-prenegotiated, usually higher, prices.

maverick buying
Unplanned purchases of items needed quickly, often at non-prenegotiated higher prices.

To correct the situation, companies reengineer their procurement systems, implement new purchasing models, and in particular, introduce e-procurement.

THE GOALS AND BENEFITS OF E-PROCUREMENT

e-procurement
The electronic acquisition of goods and services for organizations.

Improvements to procurement have been attempted for decades, usually by using information technologies. The real opportunity for improvement lies in the use of **e-procurement**, the electronic acquisition of goods and services for organizations. For comprehensive coverage and case studies, see Saryeddine (2004). The general e-procurement process (with the exception of tendering) is shown in Exhibit 5.5.

EXHIBIT 5.4   A Traditional Procurement Process

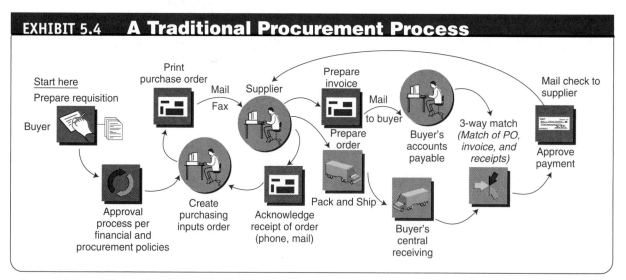

Source: *Ariba.com*, February 2001. Courtesy of Ariba Inc.

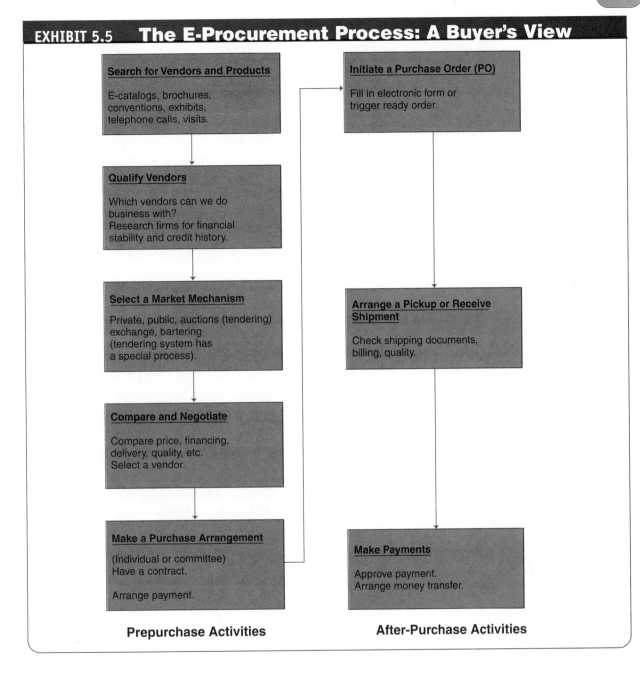

EXHIBIT 5.5   The E-Procurement Process: A Buyer's View

Search for Vendors and Products

E-catalogs, brochures, conventions, exhibits, telephone calls, visits.

Qualify Vendors

Which vendors can we do business with?
Research firms for financial stability and credit history.

Select a Market Mechanism

Private, public, auctions (tendering) exchange, bartering (tendering system has a special process).

Compare and Negotiate

Compare price, financing, delivery, quality, etc.
Select a vendor.

Make a Purchase Arrangement

(Individual or committee)
Have a contract.

Arrange payment.

Initiate a Purchase Order (PO)

Fill in electronic form or trigger ready order.

Arrange a Pickup or Receive Shipment

Check shipping documents, billing, quality.

Make Payments

Approve payment.
Arrange money transfer.

Prepurchase Activities   **After-Purchase Activities**

By automating and streamlining the laborious routines of the purchasing function, purchasing professionals can focus on more strategic purchases, achieving the following goals and benefits:

▶ Increasing the productivity of purchasing agents (providing them with more time and reducing job pressure)
▶ Lowering purchase prices through product standardization, reverse auctions, volume discounts, and consolidation of purchases

- Improving information flow and management (e.g., supplier's information and pricing information)
- Minimizing the purchases made from noncontract vendors (minimizing maverick buying)
- Improving the payment process and savings due to expedited payments (for sellers)
- Establishing efficient, collaborative supplier relations
- Ensuring delivery on time, every time
- Slashing order-fulfillment and processing times by leveraging automation
- Reducing the skill requirements and training needs of purchasing agents
- Reducing the number of suppliers
- Streamlining the purchasing process, making it simple and fast (may involve authorizing requisitioners to perform purchases from their desktops, bypassing the procurement department)
- Streamlining invoice reconciliation and dispute resolution
- Reducing the administrative processing cost per order by as much as 90 percent (e.g., GM achieved a reduction from $100 to $10)
- Finding new suppliers and vendors that can provide goods and services faster and/or cheaper (improved sourcing)
- Integrating budgetary controls into the procurement process
- Minimizing human errors in the buying or shipping processes
- Monitoring and regulating buying behavior

For additional benefits, see Saryeddine (2004). For an example of a successful implementation, see Case 5.3 and Online File W5.6. For implementation process and strategy, see Online File W5.7.

Section 5.5 ▶ REVIEW QUESTIONS

1. Define procurement and list the major procurement methods.
2. Describe the inefficiencies of traditional procurement.
3. Define e-procurement and list its goals.

5.6 BUY-SIDE E-MARKETPLACES: REVERSE AUCTIONS

One of the major methods of e-procurement is through reverse auctions. Recall from our discussions in Chapters 1 and 2 that a *reverse auction* is a tendering system in which suppliers are invited to bid on the fulfillment of an order and the lowest bid wins. In B2B usage of a reverse auction, a buyer may open an electronic market on its own server and invite potential suppliers to bid on the items the buyer needs. The "invitation" to such reverse auctions is a form or document called a **request for quote (RFQ)**. Traditional tendering usually implied one-time sealed bidding, whereas an e-reverse

request for quote (RFQ)
The "invitation" to participate in a tendering (bidding) system.

auction opens the auction to competing sequential bidding. See Smeltzer and Carr (2002) and en.wikipedia.org/wiki/Reverse_auction for a comprehensive overview of reverse auctions.

Governments and large corporations frequently mandate reverse auctions, which may provide considerable savings. To understand why this is so, see Online File W5.8, which compares the pre-Internet tendering process with the Web-based reverse auction process. The electronic process is faster and administratively much less expensive. It also can result in locating the cheapest possible products or services.

CONDUCTING REVERSE AUCTIONS

As the number of reverse auction sites increases, suppliers will not be able to manually monitor all relevant tendering sites. This problem has been addressed with the introduction of online directories that list open RFQs. Another way to solve this problem is through the use of monitoring software agents. Software agents also can aid in the bidding process itself. Examples of agents that support the bidding process are auctionsniper.com and auctionflex.com.

Alternatively, third-party intermediaries may run the electronic bidding, as they do for forward auctions. General Electric's GXS (now an independent company, described in detail in Online File W5.9) is open to any buyer. Auction sites such as govliquidation.com, liquidation.com, and asset-auctions.com also belong to this category. Conducting reverse auctions in B2B can be a fairly complex process. This is why an intermediary may be essential.

The reverse auction process is demonstrated in Exhibit 5.6. As shown in the exhibit, the first step is for the would-be buyer to post bid invitations. When bids arrive, contract and purchasing personnel for the buyer evaluate the bids and decide which one(s) to accept. The details of this process are explained in the General Electric case in Online File W5.9. For further discussion, see Bush (2006).

E-Tendering by Governments

Most governments must conduct tendering when they buy or sell goods and services. Doing this manually is slow and expensive. Therefore, many are moving to e-reverse auctions.

GROUP REVERSE AUCTIONS

B2B reverse auctions are done in a private exchange or at an aggregator's site for a group of buying companies. Such *group reverse auctions* are popular in South Korea and usually involve large conglomerates. For example, the LG Group operates the LG MRO auction for its members, and the Samsung Group operates iMarketKorea, as described in Online File W5.10.

Section 5.6 ▶ REVIEW QUESTIONS

1. Describe the manual tendering system.
2. How do online reverse auctions work?
3. List the benefits of Web-based reverse auctions.
4. Describe the business drivers of GE's TPN now (GXS) and its evolution over time. (See Online File W5.9.)

EXHIBIT 5.6   The Reverse Auction Process

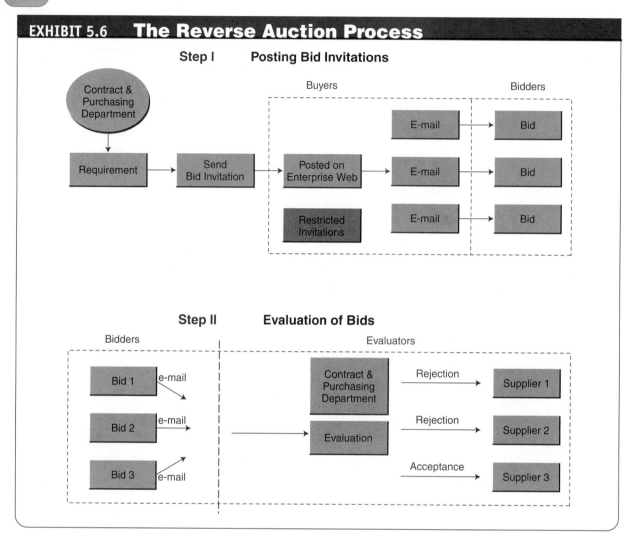

5.7 OTHER E-PROCUREMENT METHODS

Companies also have implemented other innovative e-procurement methods. Some common ones are described in this section.

AN INTERNAL PURCHASING MARKETPLACE: AGGREGATING SUPPLIERS' CATALOGS

Large organizations have many corporate buyers or purchasing agents that are usually located in different departments and locations. For example, Bristol-Myers Squibb Corporation has more than 3,000 corporate buyers located all over the world. These agents buy from a large number of suppliers. The problem is that even if all purchases are made from approved suppliers, it is difficult to plan and control procurement. In many cases, to save time, buyers engage in maverick buying. In addition, an organization needs to control the purchasing budget. This situation is especially serious in government agencies and multinational entities where many buyers and large numbers of purchases are involved.

One effective solution to the procurement problem in large organizations is to aggregate the catalogs of all approved suppliers, combining them into a single internal electronic catalog. Prices can be negotiated in advance or determined by a tendering, so that the buyers do not have to negotiate each time they place an order. By aggregating the suppliers' catalogs on the buyer's server, it also is easier to centralize and control all procurement. Such an aggregation of catalogs is called an **internal procurement marketplace**.

Benefits of Internal Marketplaces

Corporate buyers can use search engines to look through internal aggregated catalogs to quickly find what they want, check availability and delivery times, and complete electronic requisition forms. Another advantage of such aggregation is that a company can reduce the number of suppliers it uses. For example, Caltex, a multinational oil company, reduced the number of its suppliers from over 3,000 to 800. Such reduction is possible because the central catalog enables buyers at multiple corporate locations to buy from remote but fewer sellers. Buying from fewer sellers typically increases the quantities bought from each, lowering the per unit price.

Another example of a successful aggregation of suppliers' catalogs is that of MasterCard International, which aggregates more than 10,000 items from the catalogs of approved suppliers into an internal electronic catalog. The goal of this project is to consolidate buying activities from multiple corporate sites, improve processing costs, and reduce the supplier base. Payments are made with MasterCard's corporate procurement card. By 2006, the system was used by more than 2,500 buyers. MasterCard is continually adding suppliers and catalog content to the system (see MasterCard 2006).

Finally, internal marketplaces allow for easy financial controls. As buyers make purchases, their account balances are displayed. Once the budget is depleted, the system will not allow new purchase orders to go through. Therefore, this model is especially popular in public institutions and government entities. The implementation of internal purchasing marketplaces is frequently done via desktop purchasing.

Desktop Purchasing

Desktop purchasing implies purchasing directly from internal marketplaces without the approval of supervisors and without the intervention of a procurement department. This is usually done by using a *purchasing card (P-card)*. Desktop purchasing reduces the administrative cost and cycle time involved in purchasing urgently needed or frequently purchased items of small dollar value. This approach is especially effective for MRO purchases.

Microsoft built its internal marketplace, named MS Market, for the procurement of small items. The aggregated catalog that is part of MS Market is used by Microsoft employees worldwide, whose purchasing totals over $3.5 billion annually. The system has drastically reduced the role and size of the procurement department.

The desktop-purchasing approach also can be implemented by partnering with external private exchanges. For instance, Samsung Electronics of South Korea, a huge global manufacturer and its subsidiaries, has integrated its iMarketKorea exchange (see Online File W5.10) with the e-procurement systems of its buying agents. This platform can be easily linked with *group purchasing*, which is described later in this section.

BUYING AT E-AUCTIONS

Another popular approach to procurement is e-auctions. As described in Section 5.4, sellers are increasingly motivated to sell surpluses and even regular products via auctions. In some cases, e-auctions provide an opportunity for buyers to find inexpensive or unique items fairly quickly. A prudent corporate buyer should certainly look at both those manufacturers and distributors that conduct auctions periodically (e.g., GM or Dell) and at third-party auctioneers (e.g., eBay or auctions.yahoo.com). Auction aggregators can help purchasers find where and when auctions of needed items are being conducted.

internal procurement marketplace
The aggregated catalogs of all approved suppliers combined into a single internal electronic catalog.

desktop purchasing
Direct purchasing from internal marketplaces without the approval of supervisors and without the intervention of a procurement department.

group purchasing
The aggregation of orders from several buyers into volume purchases so that better prices can be negotiated.

Group Purchasing

Many companies, especially small ones, are moving to group purchasing. With **group purchasing**, orders from several buyers are aggregated into volume purchases so that better prices can be negotiated. Two models are in use: internal aggregation and external (third-party) aggregation.

Internal Aggregation

Large companies, such as GE, spend billions of dollars on MROs every year. Company-wide orders, from GE companies and subsidiaries, for identical items are aggregated using the Web and are replenished automatically. Besides economies of scale (lower prices for large purchases) on many items, GE saves on the administrative cost of the transactions, reducing transaction costs from $50 to $100 per transaction to $5 to $10 (Rudnitsky 2000). With 5 million transactions annually at GE, this is a substantial savings.

External Aggregation

Many SMEs would like to enjoy quantity discounts but have difficulty finding others to join group purchasing to increase the procurement volume. Finding partners can be accomplished by an external third party such as BuyerZone.com (buyerzone.com), HIGPA (higpa.org), or United Sourcing Alliance (usa-llc.com). The idea is to provide SMEs with better prices, selection, and services by aggregating demand online and then either negotiating with suppliers or conducting reverse auctions. The external aggregation group purchasing process is shown in Exhibit 5.7.

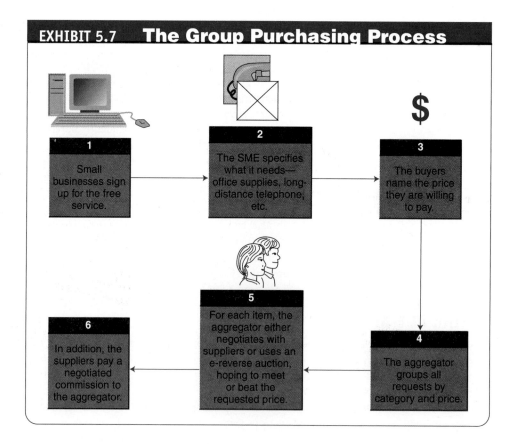

EXHIBIT 5.7   The Group Purchasing Process

1. Small businesses sign up for the free service.
2. The SME specifies what it needs—office supplies, long-distance telephone, etc.
3. The buyers name the price they are willing to pay.
4. The aggregator groups all requests by category and price.
5. For each item, the aggregator either negotiates with suppliers or uses an e-reverse auction, hoping to meet or beat the requested price.
6. In addition, the suppliers pay a negotiated commission to the aggregator.

One can appreciate the importance of this market by taking into consideration some data about small businesses: In the United States, according to the U.S. Department of Commerce, 90 percent of all businesses have fewer than 100 employees, yet they account for over 35 percent of all MRO business volume (Small Business Administration 2002). Therefore, the potential for external aggregators is huge.

Several large companies, including large CPA firms, EDS, and Ariba, are providing similar aggregation services, mainly to their regular customers. Yahoo! and AOL offer such services, too. A key to the success of these companies is a critical mass of buyers. An interesting strategy is for a company to outsource aggregation to a third party. For example, energysolutions.com provides group buying for community site partners in the energy industry.

Group purchasing, which started with commodity items such as MROs and consumer electronic devices, has now moved to services ranging from travel to payroll processing and Web hosting. Some aggregators use Priceline's "name-your-own-price" approach. Others try to find the lowest possible price (see njnonprofits.org/groupbuy.html). Similar approaches are used in B2C, and several vendors serve both markets.

BUYING FROM E-DISTRIBUTORS

Section 5.3 described how companies use e-distributors as a sales channel (recall the case of W. W. Grainger). When buying small quantities, purchasers often buy from an e-distributor. If they buy online, it is considered e-procurement.

PURCHASING DIRECT GOODS

Until 2001, most B2B e-procurement implementations took place in the sell-side of large vendors (Cisco, Intel, IBM) and in the procurement of MROs. In general, MROs comprise 20 to 50 percent of a company's purchasing budget. The remaining 50 to 80 percent of corporate purchases are for *direct materials* and *services*. Therefore, most companies would reap great benefits in using e-purchasing to acquire direct goods: Buyers would be able to purchase direct goods more quickly, reduce unit costs, reduce inventories, avoid shortages, and expedite their own production processes. Sourcing direct materials typically involves more complex transactions requiring negotiation and *collaboration* between the seller and buyer and greater information exchange. This leads us to collaborative commerce, which will be discussed in Chapter 6.

ELECTRONIC BARTERING

Bartering is the exchange of goods or services without the use of money. As described in Chapters 2 and 10, the basic idea is for a company to exchange its surplus for something that it needs. Companies can advertise their surpluses in classified ads and may find a partner to make an exchange, but in most cases a company will have little success in finding an exact match. Therefore, companies usually ask an intermediary to help.

A bartering intermediary can use a manual search-and-match approach or it can create an electronic bartering exchange. With a **bartering exchange**, a company submits its surplus to the exchange and receives points of credit, which the company can then use to buy items that it needs. Popular bartering items are office space, idle facilities and labor, products, and even banner ads. Examples of bartering companies are barteronline.com and itex.com.

Buying in Exchanges and Industrial Malls

Another option for the e-procurer is to buy at a B2B exchange or shop at an industrial e-mall. These options are described in the next section.

bartering exchange
An intermediary that links parties in a barter; a company submits its surplus to the exchange and receives points of credit, which can be used to buy the items that the company needs from other exchange participants.

1. Describe an internal procurement marketplace and list its benefits.
2. Describe the benefits of desktop purchasing.
3. Discuss the relationship of desktop purchasing with internal procurement marketplaces and with group purchasing.
4. Explain the logic of group purchasing and how it is organized.
5. Describe how e-distributors operate and discuss their appeal to buyers.
6. How does B2B bartering work?

5.8 B2B ELECTRONIC EXCHANGES: DEFINITIONS AND CONCEPTS

The term *exchange* implies many-to-many e-marketplaces. In the context of EC, exchanges are online trading venues. Many exchanges support community activities, such as distributing industry news, sponsoring online discussion groups, blogging, and providing research. Some also provide support services such as payments and logistics (see Papazoglou and Ribbers 2006).

Exchanges are known by a variety of names: *e-marketplaces, e-markets,* and *trading exchanges.* Other terms include *trading communities, exchange hubs, Internet exchanges, Net marketplaces,* and *B2B portals.* We will use the term exchange in this book to describe the general many-to-many e-marketplaces, but we will use some of the other terms in more specific contexts (e.g., see epiqtech.com/others-B2B-Exchanges.htm).

Despite their variety, all exchanges share one major characteristic: Exchanges are electronic trading-community meeting places for many sellers and many buyers, and possibly for other business partners, as shown in Exhibit 5.8. At the center of every exchange is a market maker, the third party that operates the exchange and, in many cases, may also own it.

In an exchange, just as in a traditional open-air marketplace, buyers and sellers can interact and negotiate prices and quantities. Generally, free-market economics rules the exchange community, as demonstrated by ChemConnect (see Case 5.5).

DYNAMIC PRICING

dynamic pricing
A rapid movement of prices over time and possibly across customers, as a result of supply and demand matching.

The market makers in both vertical and horizontal exchanges match supply and demand in their exchanges, and this matching determines prices, which are usually *dynamic* and are based on changes in supply and demand. **Dynamic pricing** refers to a rapid movement of prices over time and possibly across customers. Stock exchanges are the prime example of dynamic pricing. Another good example of dynamic pricing occurs in auctions, where prices vary all the time.

The typical process that results in dynamic pricing in most exchanges includes the following steps:

1. A company posts a bid to buy a product or an offer to sell one.
2. An auction (forward or reverse) is activated.
3. Buyers and sellers can see the bids and offers but might not always see who is making them. Anonymity often is a key ingredient of dynamic pricing.
4. Buyers and sellers interact with bids and offers in real time. Sometimes buyers join together to obtain a volume discount price (group purchasing).

EXHIBIT 5.8   The Community of an Exchange: Flow and Access to Information

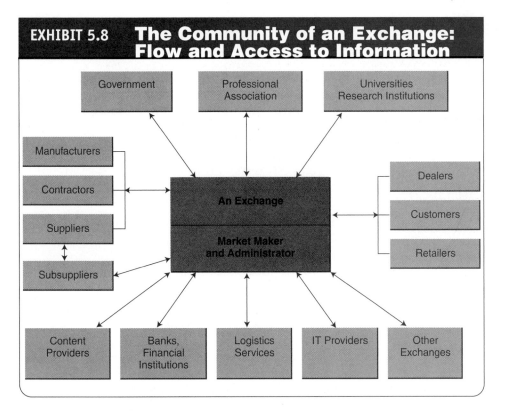

CASE 5.5
EC Application

CHEMCONNECT: THE WORLD COMMODITY CHEMICAL EXCHANGE

Today, buyers and sellers of chemicals and plastics can meet electronically in a large Internet public marketplace (founded in 1995) called ChemConnect (*chemconnect.com*), which was purchased by IntercontinentalExchange in July 2007. Global chemical industry leaders, such as BP, Dow Chemical, BASF, Hyundai, Sumitomo, and many more, make transactions over ChemConnect every day in real time. They save on transaction costs, reduce cycle time, and find new markets and trading partners around the globe. It was the first mover B2B e-market in the chemical industry.

ChemConnect provides a link to the Global eXchange Services (GXS) trading marketplace, which has 100,000 trading partners worldwide. Members are producers, consumers, distributors, traders, and intermediaries involved

in the chemical industry. ChemConnect offers its members a Trading Center with three trading places:

1. **Marketplace for buyers.** In this marketplace, buyers can find suppliers all over the world. They can post RFQs with reverse auctions, negotiate, and more.
2. **Marketplace for sellers.** This marketplace exposes sellers to many potential new customers. It provides automated tools for quick liquidation. More than 1,000 products are negotiated in auctions.
3. **Commodity markets platform.** This platform provides a powerful connection to the global spot marketplaces for chemicals, plastics, and other materials.

ChemConnect members can use the Trading Center to streamline sales and sourcing processes by automating

(continued)

CASE 5.5   (continued)

requests for quotes, proposals, and new suppliers. The center enables a member to negotiate more efficiently with existing business partners as well as with new companies the member may invite to the table—all in complete privacy. The Trading Center is a highly effective way to get the best prices and terms available on the worldwide market. In addition, members can access a database containing more than 63,000 chemicals and plastics—virtually any product members are ever likely to look for. In addition to trading, the exchange provides back-end fulfillment services (e.g., payments, delivery).

All three trading places provide up-to-the-minute market information (via *bloomberg.com*) that can be translated into 30 different languages. Business partners provide several support services. For example, Citigroup and ChemConnect jointly offer several financial services for exchange members. ChemConnect also offers systems for connecting companies' back-end systems with their business partners and with ChemConnect itself.

ChemConnect is linked to GXS (*gxs.com*), which manages a network of tens of thousands of companies.

The overall benefits of ChemConnect to its members are more efficient business processes, lower overall transaction costs, and time saved during negotiation and bidding. For example, conducting a reverse auction in a trading room enables buyers to save up to 15 percent of a product's cost in just 30 minutes. The same process using manual bidding methods would take several weeks or months.

ChemConnect continues to grow, adding members and increasing its trading volume each year. (Transaction volume in 2004 was over $10 billion.) The company hopes to become profitable in 2004. One of the company's success factors is that 40 large chemical companies hold about one-third of the company's stock. Another factor is the fact that about 44 percent of the industry uses the exchange on a regular basis. ChemConnect market data are distributed by Bloomberg (*bloomberg.com*), a major financial information services company.

ChemConnect has expanded its coverage to become a more diversified company, offering midstream energy, such as ethanol, natural gas, and other commodities. It has also added negotiation solutions, collaboration hubs, data integration services, price discovery features, and more. Also, its community has been expanded. Participant companies include most producers, consumers, distributors, traders, and transportation and logistics companies within each product class in addition to banks, hedge funds, and other interested financial institutions.

Sources: Based on information from *chemconnect.com* (accessed January 2008), Angwin (2004), and Rappa (2006).

Questions

1. List the benefits of ChemConnect to trading companies.
2. Describe the different trading platforms.
3. List some of the capabilities of the system.

5. A deal is struck when there is an exact match between a buyer and a seller on price, volume, and other variables, such as location or quality.

6. The deal is consummated, and payment and delivery are arranged.

FUNCTIONS OF EXCHANGES

According to Tumolo (2001), exchanges have three major functions:

1. **Matching buyers and sellers.** The matching of buyers and sellers includes such activities as:
   - Establishing product offerings
   - Aggregating and posting different products for sale
   - Providing price and product information
   - Organizing bids, bartering, and auctions
   - Matching supplier offerings with buyer preferences
   - Enabling price and product comparisons

- Supporting negotiations and agreements between buyers and suppliers
- Providing directories of buyers and sellers

2. **Facilitating transactions.** Facilitating transactions includes the following activities:
   - Providing the trading platform and mechanisms such as arranging logistics of delivering information, goods, or services to buyers
   - Providing billing and payment information, including addresses
   - Defining terms and other transaction values
   - Inputting searchable information
   - Granting exchange access to users and identifying company users eligible to use the exchange
   - Settling transaction payments to suppliers, collecting transaction fees, and providing other escrow services
   - Registering and qualifying buyers and suppliers
   - Maintaining appropriate security over information and transactions
   - Arranging for group (volume) purchasing

3. **Maintaining exchange policies and infrastructure.** Maintaining institutional infrastructure involves the following activities:
   - Ascertaining compliance with commercial code, contract law, export and import laws, and intellectual property law for transactions made within the exchange
   - Maintaining technological infrastructure to support volume and complexity of transactions
   - Providing interface capability to standard systems of buyers and suppliers
   - Obtaining appropriate site advertisers and collecting advertising and other fees

Services Provided by Exchanges

Exchanges provide many services to buyers and sellers. The types of services offered depend on the nature of the exchange. For example, the services provided by a stock exchange are completely different from those provided by a steel or food exchange or by an intellectual property or patent exchange. However, most exchanges provide the services shown in Exhibit 5.9.

ADVANTAGES, LIMITATIONS, AND THE REVENUE MODEL OF EXCHANGES

Exchanges have several benefits, including making markets more efficient, providing opportunities for sellers and buyers to find new business partners, cutting the administrative costs of ordering MROs, and expediting trading processes. They also facilitate global trade and create communities of informed buyers and sellers.

Despite these benefits, beginning in 2001, exchanges started to collapse, and both buyers and sellers realized that they faced the risk of exchange failure or deterioration. In the case of exchange failure, the risk is primarily a financial one—of suddenly losing the market in which one has been buying and selling and, therefore, having to scramble

to find a new exchange or to find buyers and sellers on one's own. In addition, finding a new place to trade is an operational risk. Buyers also risk potentially poor product performance and receipt of incomplete information from degraded exchanges, which is a risk the sellers may face, too. For more on competition among buyers in online exchanges, see Bandyopadhyay et al. (2005).

The potential gains and risks of B2B exchanges for buyers and for sellers are summarized in Exhibit 5.10. As the exhibit shows, the gains outnumber the risks.

EXHIBIT 5.10 Potential Gains and Risks in B2B Exchanges

	For Buyers	For Sellers
Potential gains	• One-stop shopping, huge variety • Search and comparison shopping • Volume discounts • 24/7 ordering from any location • Make one order from several suppliers • Huge, detailed information • Access to new suppliers • Status review and easy reordering • Community participation • Fast delivery • Less maverick buying • Better partner relationship management	• New sales channel • No physical store is needed • Reduced ordering errors • Sell 24/7 • Community participation • Reach new customers at little extra cost • Promote the business via the exchange • An outlet for surplus inventory • Can go global more easily • Efficient inventory management • Better partner relationship management
Potential risks	• Unknown vendors; may not be reliable • Loss of customer service quality (inability to compare all services)	• Loss of direct CRM and PRM • More price wars • Competition for value-added services • Must pay transaction fees (including on seller's existing customers) • Possible loss of customers to competitors

Revenue Models

Exchanges, like all organizations, require revenue to survive. Therefore, an exchange's owners, whoever they are, must decide how they will earn revenue. The following are potential sources of revenue for exchanges:

▶ **Transaction fees.** Transaction fees are basically a commission paid by *sellers* for each transaction they make (see Chapter 1). However, sellers may object to transaction fees, especially when regular customers are involved. Exchanges charge relatively low transaction fees per order in order to attract sellers. Therefore, to cover its expenses the exchange must generate sufficient volume, find other revenue sources, or raise its transaction fees.

▶ **Fee for service.** Some exchanges have successfully changed their revenue model from commission (transaction fee) to "fee for service." Sellers are more willing to pay for value added services than for commissions. Sometimes buyers also pay service charges.

▶ **Membership fees.** A membership fee is a fixed annual or monthly fee. It usually entitles the exchange member to get some services free or at a discount. In some countries, such as China, the government may ask members to pay annual membership fees and then provide the participating sellers with free services and no transaction fees. This encourages members to use the exchange. The problem is that low membership fees might result in insufficient revenue to the exchange. However, high membership fees discourage participants from joining.

▶ **Advertising fees.** Exchanges also can derive income from fees for advertising on the information-portal part of the exchange. For example, some sellers may want to increase their exposure and will pay for special advertisements on the portal (like boxed ads in the yellow pages of telephone books).

▶ **Other revenue sources.** If an exchange is doing auctions, it can charge auction fees. License fees can be collected on patented information or software. Finally, market makers can collect fees for their services.

Section 5.8 ▶ REVIEW QUESTIONS

1. Define B2B exchanges and list the various types of public exchanges.
2. Differentiate between a vertical exchange and a horizontal exchange.
3. What is dynamic pricing? How does it work?
4. Describe the possible revenue models of exchanges.
5. List the potential advantages, gains, limitations, and risks of exchanges.

5.9 B2B PORTALS, DIRECTORIES, AND TRADING EXCHANGES

Three major varieties of B2B marketplaces exist: portals, directories, and trading exchanges.

B2B PORTALS AND DIRECTORIES

B2B portals are information portals for businesses. Some e-marketplaces act as pure information portals. They usually include *directories* of products offered by each seller, lists of buyers and what they want, and other industry or general information. Buyers then visit sellers' sites to conduct their transactions. The portal may get commissions for referrals or only derive revenue from advertisements. Thus, information portals sometimes have a difficult time generating sufficient revenues. Because of this, many information portals are beginning to offer, for a fee, additional services that support trading, such as escrow and shipments. An example of a B2B portal is MyBoeingFleet.com (myboeingfleet.com), which is a Web portal for airplane owners, operators, and MRO operators. Developed by Boeing Commercial Aviation Services, MyBoeingFleet.com provides customers (primarily businesses) direct and personalized access to information essential to the operation of Boeing aircraft.

Like exchanges, information portals may be horizontal (e.g., Alibaba.com, described in the Real-World Case at the end of this chapter), offering a wide range of products to different industries. Or they may be vertical, focusing on a single industry or industry segment. Vertical portals often are referred to as **vortals**.

Some use the word *portal* when referring to an exchange. The reason for this is that many B2B portals are adding capabilities that make them look like exchanges. Also, many exchanges include information portals.

The two examples that follow illustrate some of the differences between *portals* and *exchanges*.

Thomas Global

Thomas Global (thomasglobal.com) is a directory of over 700,000 manufacturers and distributors from 28 countries, encompassing over 11,000 products and service categories in 9 languages. It covers regional guides, such as Thomas Register of America (thomasnet.com), an information portal, which publishes a directory of millions of manufacturing companies. Thomas Register is basically an information portal for buyers using search engines because it does not offer any opportunity for transactions on its site. For example, it does not offer a list of products with quantities needed (requests to buy) or offer what is available from sellers. A similar information-only service is provided by Manufacturing.Net (manufacturing.net).

Alibaba.com Corporation

Another intermediary that started as a pure information portal but that is moving toward becoming a trading exchange is Alibaba.com (alibaba.com). Launched in 1999, Alibaba.com initially concentrated on China. It includes a large, robust community of international buyers and sellers who are interested in direct trade without an intermediary. Initially, the site was a huge posting place for classified ads. Alibaba.com is a portal in transition, showing some characteristics of an information portal plus some services of an exchange. Alibaba.com today has two complementary markets, as described in the Real-World Case at the end of this chapter.

Directory Services and Search Engines

The B2B landscape is huge, with hundreds of thousands of companies online. Directory services can help buyers and sellers manage the task of finding specialized products, services, and potential partners.

According to Killeen (2006), specialized search engines are becoming a necessity in many industries due to the information glut. The most useful search engines are those concentrating on vertical searches. Examples of vertical search engines and their services can be found at globalspec.com. In contrast to vertical searches, products such as Google Search provide search capabilities on many topics within one enterprise or on the Web in general.

THIRD-PARTY AND DIRECTORIES EXCHANGES

Case 5.5 introduced ChemConnect, a neutral, public, third-party-owned vertical market maker. ChemConnect's initial success was well publicized, and dozens of similar third-party exchanges, mostly in specific industries, have been developed since. A thriving example of a third-party exchange is Agentrics.com, which is described in Case 5.6.

Third-party exchanges are electronic intermediaries. In contrast with a portal, such as Alibaba.com, the intermediary not only presents catalogs (which the portal does) but also tries to *match* buyers and sellers and encourages them to make transactions by providing electronic trading floors and rooms (which portals, in general, do not).

Third-party exchanges are characterized by two contradicting properties. On the one hand, they are *neutral* because they do not favor either sellers or buyers. On the other hand, because they do not have a built-in constituency of sellers or buyers, they sometimes have a problem attracting enough buyers and sellers to attain financial viability.

CASE 5.6
EC Application
AGENTRICS: A GIANT RETAIL EXCHANGE

Agentrics (*agentrics.com*) is the world's largest exchange for retail and packaged consumer goods. It was formed from the mergers of several exchanges, including the World Wide Retail Exchange (WWRE) and GNX. As of November 2006, it has 250 members, including 17 of the world's 25 top retailers (e.g., Best Buy, Sears, Safeway, and Tesco). Its primary objective is to enable participating retailers and manufacturers to simplify, rationalize, and automate supply chain processes, thereby eliminating inefficiencies in the supply chain. Today, Agentrics is the premier Internet-based business-to-business (B2B) exchange in the retail e-marketplace. Utilizing the most sophisticated Internet technology available, the exchange enables retailers and manufacturers in the food, general merchandise, textile/home, and drugstore sectors to substantially reduce costs across product development, e-procurement, and supply chain processes. The exchange is used by more than 100,000 suppliers, partners, and distributors worldwide.

The exchange operates as an open, independently managed company that generates benefits for its members and ultimately the consumer. Agentrics is run as a private company with no plans of going public. Rather, it concentrates on bringing value to its members and customers.

Founding Principles
The following six principles guide the exchange's development and growth:

1. Openness
2. Commitment to utilizing the best available technology
3. Focus on improving efficiency and lowering costs for the retail industry
4. Operation as a neutral company
5. Equivalent fee structures for all participants
6. Confidentiality of transaction information

Value Proposition
Members realize value in seven key ways:

1. Low-cost product offerings that are robust, scalable, integrated, and fully supported
2. Shared technology investments and outsourced assets
3. Ability to access a global membership community and network with other retailers/manufacturers

(continued)

CASE 5.6 *(continued)*

4. Value-added services from a trusted source, at competitive costs
5. Participation in collaborative activities
6. Complex transactions and interactions made easy through automation
7. Standard-setting benefits for all B2B activities

The exchange offers about 20 different products and services. They are classified as those related to WWRE (e.g., global data synchronization, trading, sourcing, supply chain solutions) and those related to GNX (e.g., collaboration, performance and life cycle management, CPFR, and negotiation).

An example of one of the exchange's current efforts is its Global Data Synchronization project. Inaccurate product and item information costs the consumer goods industry more than $40 billion each year. Agentrics has developed a solution that enables retailers and suppliers to accurately maintain item information using industry

standards and achieve a single point of entry into the Global Data Synchronization Network. The project is supported by WebMethods Corporation, which provides the necessary integration.

Sources: Compiled from *agentrics.com* (accessed January 2008); WebMethods (2005); WWRE (2005); and *webmethods.com* (accessed January 2008).

Questions

1. Enter *agentrics.com* and find information about services offered, including auctions and negotiations. Note the benefits to retailers and to suppliers. Write a report.

2. Enter *webmethods.com* and find information about the item synchronization project (for WWRE). Summarize the benefits to retailers and to suppliers.

Therefore, to increase their financial viability, these exchanges try to team up with partners, such as large sellers or buyers, financial institutions that provide payment schemes (as ChemConnect did with Citigroup), and logistics companies that fulfill orders.

Consortium Trading Exchanges

consortium trading exchange (CTE)
An exchange formed and operated by a group of major companies in an industry to provide industry-wide transaction services.

A subset of third-party exchanges is a **consortium trading exchange (CTE)**, an exchange formed and operated by a group of major companies in one industry. The major declared goal of CTEs (also called *consortia*) is to provide industry-wide transaction services that support buying and selling. These services include links to the participants' back-end processing systems as well as collaborative planning and design services.

Markets operate in three basic types of environments, shown in the following list. The type of environment indicates which type of exchange is most appropriate.

1. **Fragmented markets.** These markets have large numbers of both buyers and sellers. Examples include the life sciences and food industries. When a large percentage of the market is fragmented, third-party managed exchanges are most appropriate.

2. **Seller-concentrated markets.** In this type of market, several large companies sell to a very large number of buyers. Examples are the plastics and transportation industries. In this type of market, consortia may be most appropriate.

3. **Buyer-concentrated markets.** In this type of market, several large companies do most of the buying from a large number of suppliers. Examples are the automotive, airline, and electronics industries. Here, again, consortia may be most appropriate.

According to Richard and Devinney (2005), CTEs fared much better than independent third-party exchanges during the dot-com shakeout that took place between 2000–2002. Yet, of the hundreds of CTEs that existed all over the world in 2000, by 2002 many had folded or were inactive, including giants such as Covisint (see Online File W5.11). By 2006,

EXHIBIT 5.11 Comparing the Major B2B Many-to-Many Models

Name	Major Characteristics	Types
B2B portals and directories	• Community services, news, information • Communication tools • Classified ads • Employment markets • May support selling (buying) • Fixed prices • May do auctions	• Vertical (vortals), horizontal • Shopping directory, usually with hyperlinks
B2B trading exchanges	• Matches buyer/seller orders at dynamic prices, auctions • Provides trading-related information and services (payment, logistics) • Highly regulated • May provide general information, news, etc. • May provide for negotiations	• Vertical, horizontal • Forward auctions • Reverse auctions • Bid/ask exchanges

CTEs had achieved stability, and some new exchanges arrived on the business scene. An example of a successful CTE is provided in Online File W5.12.

COMPARING THE MANY-TO-MANY B2B MODELS

Exhibit 5.11 summarizes the many-to-many models presented in this chapter.

Section 5.9 ▶ REVIEW QUESTIONS

1. Define B2B portals.
2. Distinguish a vortal from a horizontal portal.
3. Describe some directory services in B2B.
4. What is a third-party owned exchange?
5. Define CTEs.
6. List the major characteristics of portals, directories, and trading exchanges.

5.10 PARTNER AND SUPPLIER RELATIONSHIP MANAGEMENT

In order to succeed in B2B, and particularly in exchanges, it is necessary to have several support services.

PARTNER AND SUPPLIER RELATIONSHIP MANAGEMENT

Successful e-businesses carefully manage partners, prospects, and customers across the entire value chain, most often in a 24/7 environment. For benefits and methods, see Markus (2006). Therefore, one should examine the role of solution technologies, such as call centers and collaboration tools, in creating an integrated online environment for engaging e-business customers and partners. The use of such solutions and technology appears under two names: customer relationship management (CRM) and partner relationship management (PRM).

partner relationship management (PRM)
Business strategy that focuses on providing comprehensive quality service to business partners.

Corporate customers may require additional services. For example, customers need to have access to the supplier's inventory status report so they know what items a supplier can deliver quickly. Customers also may want to see their historical purchasing records, and they may need private showrooms and trade rooms. Large numbers of vendors are available for designing and building appropriate B2B relationship solutions. The strategy of providing such comprehensive, quality e-service for business partners is sometimes called **partner relationship management (PRM)**.

In the context of PRM, business customers are only one category of business partners. Suppliers, partners in joint ventures, service providers, and others also are part of the B2B community in an exchange or company-centric B2B initiative, as illustrated in Exhibit 5.8. PRM is particularly important to companies that conduct outsourcing (Hagel 2004). Companies with many suppliers, such as the automobile companies, may create special programs for them. Such programs are called *supplier relationship management* (SRM) (see Online File W5.13).

E-COMMUNITIES AND PRM

B2B applications involve many participants: buyers and sellers, service providers, industry associations, and others. Thus, in many cases the B2B implementation creates a community. In such cases, the B2B market maker needs to provide community services, such as chat rooms, bulletin boards, and possibly personalized Web pages.

E-communities are connecting personnel, partners, customers, and any combination of the three. E-communities offer a powerful resource for e-businesses to leverage online discussions and interaction in order to maximize innovation and responsiveness (e.g., see the Real-World Case at the end of this chapter). It is therefore beneficial to study the tools, methods, and best practices of building and managing e-communities. Although the technological support of B2B e-communities is basically the same as for any other online community, the nature of the community itself and the information provided by the community are different.

B2B e-communities are mostly communities of transactions or business networks, and, as such, members' major interests are trading and business-related information gathering. Most of the communities are associated with vertical exchanges; therefore, their needs may be fairly specific. However, it is common to find generic services such as classified ads, job vacancies, announcements, industry news, and so on. Communities promote partnering. For further information, see About.com (2006).

Section 5.10 ▶ REVIEW QUESTIONS

1. Define PRM and describe its functions.
2. Define SRM (See Online File W5.13).
3. Describe e-communities in B2B.

MANAGERIAL ISSUES

Some managerial issues related to this chapter are as follows.

1. **Can we justify the cost of B2B applications?** Because there are several B2B models and architectures (see Al Mosawi et al. 2006 and Papazoglou and Ribbers 2006), each of which can be implemented in different ways, it is critical to conduct a cost-benefit analysis of the proposed applications (projects). Such an analysis should include organizational impacts, such as possible channel conflicts, and how to deal with resistance to change within the organization. Also, implementation difficulties

may increase costs (see Langelier and Lapierre 2003). One way to justify B2B is to look at the experiences of successful companies, best practices, and guidelines for success. For justification of reverse auctions see Emiliani (2006).

2. **Which vendor(s) should we select?** Vendors normally develop the B2B applications, even for large organizations. Two basic approaches to vendor selection exist: (1) Select a primary vendor such as IBM, Microsoft, or Oracle. This vendor will use its software and procedures and add partners as needed. (2) Use an integrator that will mix and match existing products and vendors to create "the best of breed" for your needs. See Online Chapter 14 for details.

3. **Which B2B model(s) should we use?** The availability of so many B2B models, especially in e-procurement, means that companies need to develop selection strategies based on preferred criteria. In addition to the company-centric models, several types of exchanges should be considered.

4. **What are the ethical issues in B2B?** Because B2B EC requires the sharing of proprietary information, business ethics are a must. Employees should not be able to access unauthorized areas in the trading system, and the privacy of trading partners should be protected both technically and legally.

5. **Will there be massive disintermediation?** With the increased use of private e-marketplaces, disintermediation and channel conflicts are bound to occur. However, reintermediation may occur with those vendors that can adapt to EC (see Malhotra and Malhotra 2006 and Zeng et al. 2003).

6. **How can trust and loyalty be cultivated in B2B?** As discussed in Chapter 4, trust and loyalty are important in any type of EC in which the partners do not know each other. For a discussion and a case study, see Ratnasingam and Phan (2003).

7. **Will joining an exchange force restructuring?** Joining an exchange may require a restructuring of the internal supply chain, which may be expensive and time consuming. Therefore, this possibility must be taken into consideration when deciding whether to join an exchange.

8. **Which exchange to join?** One of the major concerns of management is selecting exchanges in which to participate. At the moment, most exchanges are not tightly connected, so there may be a substantial start-up effort and cost for joining another exchange. This is a multicriteria decision that should be analyzed carefully. A related issue is whether to join a third-party public exchange or a consortium or to create a private exchange.

9. **What are the benefits and risks of joining an exchange?** Companies must take very seriously the issues listed in Exhibit 5.10. The risks of joining an exchange must be carefully weighed against the expected benefits.

SUMMARY

In this chapter, you learned about the following EC issues as they relate to the learning objectives.

1. **The B2B field.** The B2B field comprises e-commerce activities between businesses. B2B activities account for 77 to 85 percent of all EC. B2B e-commerce can be done using different models.

2. **The major B2B models.** The B2B field is very diversified. It can be divided into the following segments: sell-side marketplaces (one seller to many buyers), buy-side marketplaces (one buyer from many sellers), and trading exchanges (many sellers to many buyers). Intermediaries play an important role in some B2B models.

3. **The characteristics of sell-side marketplaces.** Sell-side B2B EC is the online direct sale by one seller (a manufacturer or an intermediary) to many buyers. The major technology used is electronic catalogs, which also allow for efficient customization, configuration, and purchase by customers. In addition, forward auctions are becoming popular, especially for liquidating surplus inventory. Sell-side auctions can be conducted from the seller's own site or from an intermediary's auction site. Sell-side activities can be accompanied by extensive customer service.

4. **Sell-side intermediaries.** The role of intermediaries in B2B primarily is to provide value-added services to manufacturers and business customers. They can also aggregate buyers and conduct auctions.

5. **The characteristics of buy-side marketplaces and e-procurement.** Today, companies are moving to e-procurement to expedite purchasing, save on item and administrative costs, and gain better control over the purchasing process. Major procurement methods are reverse auctions (bidding system); buying from storefronts and catalogs; negotiation; buying from an intermediary that aggregates sellers' catalogs; internal marketplaces and group purchasing; desktop purchasing; buying in exchanges or industrial malls; and e-bartering. E-procurement offers the opportunity to achieve significant cost and time savings.

6. **B2B reverse auctions.** A reverse auction is a tendering system used by buyers to get better prices from suppliers competing to fulfill the buyers' needs. Auctions can be done on a company's Web site or on a third-party auction site. Reverse auctions can dramatically lower buyers' costs, both product costs and the time and cost of the tendering process.

7. **B2B aggregation and group purchasing.** Increasing the exposure and the bargaining power of companies can be done by aggregating either the buyers or the sellers. Aggregating suppliers' catalogs into an internal marketplace gives buying companies better control of purchasing costs. In desktop purchasing, buyers are empowered to buy from their desktops up to a set limit without the need for additional approval. They accomplish this by viewing internal catalogs with pre–agreed-upon prices with the suppliers. Industrial malls specialize in one industry (e.g., computers) or in industrial MROs. They aggregate the catalogs of thousands of suppliers. A purchasing agent can place an order at an industrial mall, and shipping is arranged by

the supplier or the mall owner. Buyer aggregation through group purchasing is very popular because it enables SMEs to get better prices on their purchases. In addition to direct purchasing, items can be acquired via bartering.

8. **Other procurement methods.** Common procurement methods include: internal marketplaces and desktop purchasing, buying at e-auctions, group purchasing, buying from distributors, bartering, and buying at exchanges.

9. **E-marketplaces and exchanges defined and the major types of exchanges.** Exchanges are e-marketplaces that provide a trading platform for conducting business among many buyers, many sellers, and other business partners. Types of public e-marketplaces include B2B portals, directories, third-party trading exchanges, and consortium trading exchanges. Exchanges may be vertical (industry oriented) or horizontal. They may target systematic buying (long-term relationships) or spot buying (for fulfilling an immediate need).

10. **B2B portals.** B2B portals are gateways to B2B community-related information. They are usually of a vertical structure, in which case they are referred to as *vortals*. Some B2B portals offer product and vendor information and even tools for conducting trades, sometimes making it difficult to distinguish between B2B portals and trading exchanges.

11. **Third-party exchanges.** Third-party exchanges are owned by an independent company and usually operate in highly fragmented markets. They are open to anyone and, therefore, are considered public exchanges. They try to maintain neutral relations with both buyers and sellers.

12. **Good relationship with business partners is critical to the success of B2B.** Similar to CRM in B2C, companies use Internet-based tools to support their relationships with their partners (known as PRM).

KEY TERMS

QUESTIONS FOR DISCUSSION

1. Explain how a catalog-based sell-side e-marketplace works and describe its benefits.
2. Discuss the advantages of selling through online auctions over selling from catalogs. What are the disadvantages?
3. Discuss the role of intermediaries in B2B. Distinguish between buy-side and sell-side intermediaries.
4. Discuss and compare all of the mechanisms that group-purchasing aggregators can use.
5. Should desktop purchasing only be implemented through an internal marketplace?
6. How do companies eliminate the potential limitations and risks associated with Web-based EDI? (See Online File W5.3.)
7. Suppose a manufacturer uses an outside shipping company. How can the manufacturer use an exchange?
8. Compare and contrast a privately owned exchange with a private e-marketplace.
9. How does ChemConnect change the market for commodity chemicals?

INTERNET EXERCISES

1. Enter **gxs.com** and review GXS Express's bidding process. Describe the preparations a company would have to make in order to bid on a job. Also, check how some of its customers are using the company (e.g., Rohm and Haas 2005 case study).
2. Enter **inovis.com** and view the capabilities of BizManager **inovis.com/solutions/software/bizmanager** and BizConnect **inovis.com/trybizconnect/form.jsp**. Write a report.
3. Examine the following sites: **ariba.com**, **trilogy.com**, and **icc.net**. Match a B2B business model with each site.
4. Visit **supplyworks.com** and **procuri.com**. Examine how each company streamlines the purchase process. How do these companies differ from ariba.com?
5. Visit **ebay.com** and identify all of the activities related to its small business auctions. What services are provided by eBay?
6. Enter **ondemandsourcing.com** and view the demo. Prepare a list of benefits to small and midtier organizations.
7. Enter **bitpipe.com** and find recent B2B vendor reports related to e-procurement. Identify topics not covered in this chapter.
8. Visit **iasta.com**, **purchasing.com**, and **cognizant.com** and examine the tools they sell for conducting various types of e-procurement. List and analyze each tool.
9. Enter **bambooweb.com** and find information about EDI. Prepare a report.
10. Enter **thebuyinggroup.com**, **tidewatergpo.com**, and other group purchasing sites. Report on B2B group buying activities.
11. Go to **procurenet.biz**. Prepare a list of resources related to e-procurement.

12. Go to **alibaba.com** and sign up as a member (membership is free). Create a product and post it. Tell your instructor how to view this product.

13. Compare the services offered by **globalsources.com** with those offered by **alibaba.com**. Assuming you are a toy seller, with which one would you register? Why? If you are a buyer of auto parts, which one would you join and why?

14. Enter **chemconnect.com** and view the demos for different trading alternatives. Examine the revenue model. Evaluate the services from both the buyer's and seller's points of view. Also, examine the site policies and legal guidelines. Are they fair? Compare **chemconnect.com** with **chemicalonline.com** and **hubwoo.com**. Which of these do you think will survive? Explain your reasoning.

15. Enter eBay's Business Industrial area (**business. ebay.com** or **ebay.com** and select "wholesale"). What kind of e-marketplace is this? What are its major capabilities?

16. Visit **converge.com**. What kind of exchange is this? What services does it provide? How do its auctions work?

17. Enter **globalspec.com**. Find information about vertical search engines. Summarize in a report.

18. Enter **dir.yahoo.com/Business_and_Economy/ Business_to_Business**. Prepare a list of resources about exchanges and B2B directories.

TEAM ASSIGNMENTS AND ROLE PLAYING

1. Predictions about the future magnitude of B2B and statistics on its actual volume in various countries keep changing. In this activity, each team will locate current B2B predictions and statistics for different world regions (e.g., Asia, Europe, North America). Using at least five sources, each team will find the predicted B2B volume (in dollars) for the next 5 years in its assigned region. Sources statistics are listed in Exhibit 3.1 (page 86).

2. Each team should explore a different e-procurement method and prepare a paper for a class presentation. The paper should include the following about the e-procurement method:
   a. The mechanisms and technologies used
   b. The benefits to buyers, suppliers, and others (if appropriate)
   c. The limitations
   d. The situations for which each method is recommended

3. Form two teams (A and B) of five or more members. On each team, person 1 plays the role of an assembly company that produces television monitors. Persons 2 and 3 are domestic parts suppliers to the assembling company, and persons 4 and 5 play foreign parts suppliers. Assume that the TV monitor company wants to sell televisions directly to business customers. Each team is to design an environment composed of membership in exchanges they can use and present its results. A graphical display is recommended.

4. Enter **isteelasia.com**, **metalworld.com**, and **lme.co.uk**. Compare their operations and services. These exchanges compete in global markets. Examine the trading platforms, portal capabilities, and support services (e.g., logistics, payments, etc.) offered by each. In what areas do these companies compete? In what areas do they not compete? What are the advantages of **isteelasia.com** in dealing with Asian companies? Are regional exchanges needed? If it is good for Asia to have a regional exchange, why not have a Western European exchange, an Eastern European exchange, a Central American exchange, and so on? If regional exchanges are needed, can they work together? How? If there are too many exchanges, which are likely to survive? Research this topic and prepare a report.

5. Enter **gtnexus.com** and examine its offerings. Prepare a report on how exchanges can benefit from its services. How does GT Nexus facilitate supply chains? Can it help e-marketplaces?

Real-World Case

ALIBABA.COM

Alibaba International (*alibaba.com*), Alibaba Group's flagship company, is an English-language Web site primarily serving small and medium-sized enterprises (SMEs) in the international trade community. It is the leading B2B e-commerce company in China, serving SMEs in China and around the world. Alibaba.com has more than 24 million registered users from over 200 countries and territories. More than 500,000 people visit the site every day, most of them global buyers and importers looking to find and trade with sellers in China and other major manufacturing countries. Because it charges for only a small percentage of its services, the venture depends on a tiny core of 22,000 paying "Gold Suppliers" for 71 percent of its earnings. Alibaba is prospering from a business model dedicated to serving a vital, but disadvantaged, segment of China's economy: SMEs. Fewer than 1 million of the nation's 42 million small and medium-sized enterprises have any Internet capability. Alibaba offers simple and efficient Internet solutions for fledgling ventures to such companies.

Alibaba China (*alibaba.com.cn*) is China's largest online marketplace for domestic trade among business people. Using the Internet to connect Chinese suppliers to foreign buyers is the essence of Alibaba's business model. The company's Web platform provides Chinese firms with ready-made online "storefronts" to list their products and services in more than 5,000 categories. With more than 10 million registered users, Alibaba China is a trusted community of members who regularly meet, chat, search for products, and do business online. Customers pay an annual subscription fee for membership, which entitles them to post trade offers and products online. The subscription fee also includes authentication and verification of the member's identity, which is performed by a third-party credit reporting agency.

In addition, Alibaba owns and maintains the following:

▶ *Yahoo.china.cn* is a leading Internet search engine for businesses.

▶ *Japan.alibaba.com* is an Alibaba site for the Japanese market.

▶ *Taobao.com* is a Chinese C2C auction site (see Heilemann 2006).

▶ *AliPay.com* is an online payment services provider that enables individuals and businesses to execute payments online in a safe and secure manner.

▶ *Alisoft.com* develops, markets, and delivers Internet-based business management software to SMEs in China. It offers enterprise management tools, such as e-mail, customer support software, and information management, and basic financial management tools, such as invoicing and bookkeeping.

▶ *Alimama.com* is China's leading online advertising exchange, helping to connect Web publishers to advertisers. The publishers make money on their Web site traffic and advertisers gain an affordable way to reach highly targeted audience groups.

To understand the capabilities of Alibaba.com, we need to explore its marketplace (take the multimedia tour!).

The Database

The center of Alibaba.com is its huge database, which is basically a horizontal information portal with offerings in a wide variety of product categories. The portal is organized into 39 major product categories (as of 2007), including agriculture, apparel and fashion, automobiles, and toys. Each product category is further divided into subcategories (over 700 in total). For example, the toy category includes items such as dolls, electrical pets, and wooden toys. Each subcategory includes classified ads organized into four groups: sellers, buyers, agents, and cooperation. Each group may include many companies. The ads are fairly short. Note that in all cases a user can click an ad for details. In 2007, all postings were still free. Some categories have thousands of postings; therefore, a search engine is provided. The search engine works by country, type of advertiser, and age of the postings.

Reverse Auctions

Alibaba.com also allows buyers to post RFQs. Would-be sellers can then send bids to the buyer, conduct negotiations, and accept a purchase order when one is agreed upon (all via the exchange). As of March 2007, the process was not fully automated. (To see how the process works, go to "My trade activity" and take the tour, initiate a negotiation, and issue a purchase order.)

Features and Services

Alibaba.com provides the following features: free e-mail, Trust Service, FAQs, tutorials for traders, free e-mail alerts, a China club membership, news (basically related to importing and exporting), trade show information, legal information, arbitration, and forums and discussion groups. In addition, a member can create a personalized company Web page as well as a "sample house" (for showing products); members also can post their own marketing leads (where to buy and sell). As of 2006, the site offers its services in English, Chinese, and Korean. Also, the site is doing e-tailing.

For-fee services include business credit reports, AliPay, export/import reports, and a quote center for shipping services. In the future, additional services will be added to increase the company's revenue stream.

Revenue Model

The site's revenue stream has been expanded from advertisements only to include fees for special services. For example, income is generated through paid memberships, online booths, priority listings, and so on. Alibaba.com competes with several global exchanges that provide similar services (e.g., see *asia-links.com* and *globalsources.com*). The advantage of Alibaba.com is its low operational costs. Therefore, it probably will be able to sustain losses much longer than its competitors. Someday in the future, Alibaba.com may be in a position that will enable it to make a great deal of money. Alibaba.com was strong enough to sustain losses until 2003, when it made $12 million profit. As of 2007, company profits were growing very rapidly.

Going Public

Alibaba's founder Jack Ma took the company public in November of 2007 using outside capital to deploy its business model on a full scale in order to show that e-commerce in China can make money. The influx of capital will allow Alibaba to continue building its customer base by offering the bulk of its services at no charge. And that may prove a winning strategy.

Sources: Compiled from *alibaba.com* (accessed January 2008), Heilemann (2006), and Chandler (2007).

Questions

1. When the company's IPO started trading, hundreds of large corporations rushed to invest in it. Why?
2. Trace Alibaba's revenue sources.
3. List the major services provided by Alibaba.

E-SUPPLY CHAINS, COLLABORATIVE COMMERCE, AND CORPORATE PORTALS

Content

Learning Objectives

Upon completion of this chapter, you will be able to:

1. Define the e-supply chain and describe its characteristics and components.

2. List supply chain problems and their causes.

3. List solutions to supply chain problems provided by EC.

4. Describe RFID as a supply chain application.

5. Define c-commerce and list the major types.

6. Describe collaborative planning and Collaboration, Planning, Forecasting, and Replenishing (CPFR) and list the benefits of each.

7. Discuss integration along the supply chain.

8. Understand corporate portals and their types and roles.

9. Describe e-collaboration tools such as groupware and screen sharing.

BOEING'S GLOBAL SUPPLY CHAIN FOR THE DREAMLINER 787

The Problem

Designing and manufacturing an aircraft is an immensely complex undertaking; the 787 Dreamliner project is said to be one of the largest, most complex, and challenging engineering projects being undertaken in the world. The supply chain involved in the design and production of this aircraft involves millions of different parts and component materials and thousands of different suppliers, partners, contractors, and outsourcing vendors scattered across 24 countries working from 135 different sites. Absolute precision and meticulous attention to detail is required, and safety and quality are paramount. In addition to designing and producing a new aircraft, the new production processes had to be designed, tested, and implemented. Close collaboration and communication among thousands of employees, information and knowledge management, and sound management of this complex global supply chain were essential to the project's success. In addition, competitive pressures, rising oil prices, and enhanced security forced Boeing to improve the old methods.

The Solution

Boeing had been increasingly relying on sophisticated information technology (IT) to support its operations for some time and had been a user of CAD/CAM technologies since the early 1980s. The Dreamliner, however, was to be a "paperless airliner," with IT being employed to support many critical activities. Boeing teamed with Dassault Systemes to create a Global Collaboration Environment (GCE), a product management lifecycle solution, to support the virtual rollout of the new aircraft. The GCE enabled Boeing to digitally monitor the design, production, and testing of every aspect of the aircraft and its production processes before the actual production started.

The GCE included the following components:

- **CATIA.** A collaborative 3D-design platform that enabled engineers worldwide to collaborate on the design of each and every part of the 787.

- **ENOVIA.** A system that supported the accessing, sharing, and managing of all information related to the 787 design in a secure environment.

- **DELMIA.** An environment for defining, simulating, and validating manufacturing and maintenance processes and establishing and managing workflows before actually building tools and production facilities.

- **SMARTEAM.** A Web-based system to facilitate collaboration, which included predefined and auditable processes and procedures, project templates, and best-practice methodologies all geared toward ensuring compliance with corporate and industry standards.

In addition, Boeing also decided to integrate all databases associated with the Dreamliner, teaming up with IBM to employ a DB2 Universal Database for this purpose and ensuring partners access to Dassault's suite of systems.

As the Dreamliner moved toward physical production using the new manufacturing processes (Boeing was to become the final assembler and integrator, rather than building much of the aircraft from scratch), excellent supply chain management was required to carefully coordinate the movement of components and systems across multiple tier partners around the world. Boeing teamed with Exostar to provide software to support its supply chain coordination challenges. The Exostar supply chain management solution enables all suppliers access to real-time demand, supply, and logistics information so that crucial components and systems arrive at Boeing's production facilities just in time for assembly over a 3-day period. The Exostar solution includes the following functionalities: planning and scheduling; order placement and tracking purchase order changes; exchanging shipping information; managing inventory consumption across suppliers; managing returns; and providing a consolidated view of all activities in the manufacturing process. Business process exceptions can also be monitored across partners, allowing for informed evaluation of the impacts of these exceptions to take place across affected parties.

RFID applications were deployed in the aircraft to support maintenance activities. By tagging component parts, Boeing reduced maintenance and inventory costs.

The Results

The goal of the Dreamliner project was to produce a fuel-efficient (and less polluting, hence environmentally responsible), cost-effective, quiet, and comfortable midsize aircraft that could travel long distances without stopping. It is a critical innovation for Boeing, which has in recent years struggled in the face of rising competition from Airbus. IT has played a critical role in supporting collaboration throughout this massive project, reducing the need for physical prototyping and testing, and making substantial impacts on the supply chain. IT has enabled faster decision making, better management of critical information and knowledge assets, increased sharing and exchange of product-related information and processes, reduced time-to-market, less rework, and reduced costs of manufacturing by reducing the assembly time for the aircraft from 13 to 17 days to just 3 days.

Boeing has received in excess of 750 orders for the plane to date and commitments in excess of $100 billion. Dreamliner may just be the most successful commercial airplane launch in history.

Sources: Kumar and Gupta (2006), Kidman (2006), *Supply and Demand Chain Executive* (2006), *RFID Gazette* (2006), *CompMechLab* (2006), and *boeing.com* (accessed January 2008).

WHAT WE CAN LEARN . . .

In increasingly global industries, effective communication and collaboration are essential to an organization's success. Modern IT and Web-based systems have made collaboration, both internally and externally with key players along an industry supply chain, simpler, faster, and cheaper than ever before. Boeing recognized this, and implemented a range of technologies to facilitate the access, sharing, and storage of critical information related to the Dreamliner project. This case demonstrates several applications of EC, IT, and a range of Web-enabled collaborative technologies. These and related issues are the major topics of this chapter.

6.1 E-SUPPLY CHAINS

Many people equate e-commerce with selling and buying on the Internet. However, although a company's success is clearly dependent on finding and retaining customers; its success may be far more dependent on what is *behind* the Web page than on what is on the Web page. In other words, the company's internal operations (the *back end*) and its relationships with suppliers and other business partners are as critical, and frequently much more complex, than customer-facing applications, such as taking an order online. In many cases, these non–customer-facing applications are related to the company's supply chain.

It has been well known for generations that the success of many organizations— private, public, and military—depends on their ability to manage the flow of materials, information, and money into, within, and out of the organization. Such a flow is referred to as a *supply chain*. Because supply chains may be long and complex and may involve many different business partners, we frequently see problems in the operation of the supply chains. These problems may result in delays, in products not being where they are required at the right time, in customer dissatisfaction, in lost sales, and in high expenses that result from fixing the problems once they occur. World-class companies, such as Dell and Toyota, attribute much of their success to effective supply chain management (SCM), which is largely supported by IT and e-commerce technologies.

This chapter focuses on supply chain issues related to e-commerce. In addition, it examines several related topics, such as collaboration and integration along the supply chain. The topic of financial supply chains (payment systems) is discussed in Chapter 11, where order fulfillment is also presented.

DEFINITIONS AND CONCEPTS

To understand e-supply chains, one must first understand nonelectronic supply chains. A **supply chain** is the flow of materials, information, money, and services from raw material suppliers through factories and warehouses to the end customers. A supply chain also

supply chain
The flow of materials, information, money, and services from raw material suppliers through factories and warehouses to the end customers.

includes the *organizations* and *processes* that create and deliver products, information, and services to the end customers. The term *supply chain* comes from the concept of how the partnering organizations are *linked* together.

As shown in Exhibit 6.1, a simple linear supply chain links a company that manufactures or assembles a product (middle of the chain) with its suppliers (on the left) and distributors and customers (on the right). The upper part of the figure shows a generic supply chain. The bottom part shows a specific example of the toy-making process. The solid links in the figure show the flow of materials among the various partners. Not shown is the flow of returned goods (e.g., defective products) and money, which are flowing in the reverse direction. The broken links, which are shown only in the upper part (generic) of Exhibit 6.1, indicate the bidirectional flow of information.

A supply chain involves activities that take place during the entire product *life cycle*, "from dirt to dust," as some describe it. However, a supply chain is more than that, because it also includes the movement of information and money and the procedures that support the movement of a product or a service. Finally, the organizations and individuals involved are considered part of the supply chain as well. When looked at very broadly, the supply chain actually ends when the product reaches its after-use disposal—presumably back to Mother Earth somewhere.

The supply chain shown in Exhibit 6.1 is fairly simple. However, supply chains can be much more complex, and they are of different types.

EXHIBIT 6.1   A Simple Supply Chain

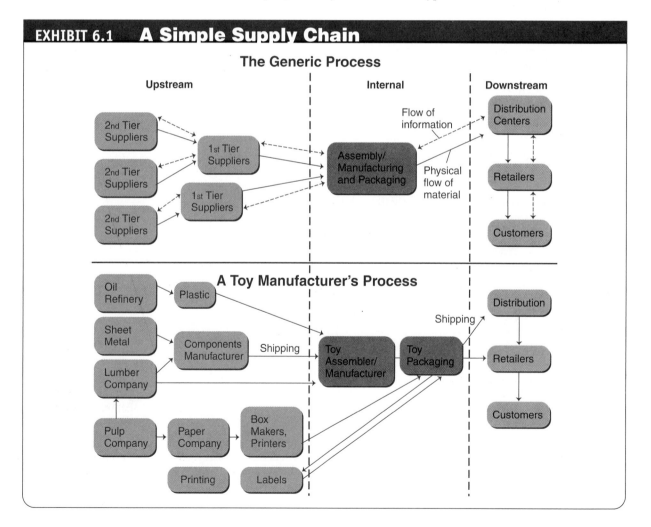

When a supply chain is managed electronically, usually with Internet technologies, it is referred to as an **e-supply chain**. As will be shown throughout this chapter, improvements in supply chains are a major target for EC applications. However, before examining how e-supply chains are managed, it is necessary to better understand the composition of supply chains.

e-supply chain
A supply chain that is managed electronically, usually with Web technologies.

SUPPLY CHAIN PARTS

A supply chain can be broken into three major parts: upstream, internal, and downstream, as was shown in Exhibit 6.1:

▶ **Upstream supply chain.** The upstream part of the supply chain includes the activities of a company with its suppliers (which can be manufacturers, assemblers, or both, or service providers) and their connections with their suppliers (and second-tier suppliers). The supplier relationship can be extended to the left in several tiers, all the way to the origin of the material (e.g., mining ores, growing crops). In the upstream supply chain, the major activity is *procurement*. **Procurement** is the process made up of a range of activities by which an organization obtains or gains access to the resources (materials, skills, capabilities, facilities) they require to undertake their core business activities. Procurement and the technologies now used to support these activities are concerned with the consideration of what is required, where it should be obtained in a timely and cost-effective manner, and issues such as spend analysis, sourcing strategies, supplier relationship management, reverse auctions, and the like, all informed by the organization's supply chain strategy (*Line56.com* 2008).

procurement
The process made up of a range of activities by which an organization obtains or gains access to the resources (materials, skills, capabilities, facilities) they require to undertake their core business activities.

▶ **Internal supply chain and value chain.** The internal part of the supply chain includes all of the in-house processes used in transforming the inputs received from the suppliers into the organization's outputs. It extends from the time the inputs enter an organization to the time that the products go to distribution outside of the organization. In this part of the supply chain, the major concerns are production management, manufacturing, and inventory control. The activities along the internal supply chain are referred to as the company's *value chain* (see Davenport and Brooks 2004). The value chain is composed of a sequential set of primary activities (operations, outbound logistics, after sales support and service, etc.) and support activities (administration, HR, finance, etc.) that an organization undertakes in order to deliver a good or service of value to their customers. The primary objective of the value chain is to add value along the internal supply chain.

▶ **Downstream supply chain.** The downstream part of the supply chain includes all the activities involved in delivering the products to the final customers. In the downstream supply chain, attention is directed at distribution, warehousing, transportation, and after-sale service.

A company's supply chain and its accompanying value chain encompass an array of business processes that create value by delivering goods or services to customers.

MANAGING SUPPLY CHAINS

Supply chain management (SCM) is a complex process that requires the coordination of many activities so that the shipment of goods and services from suppliers through to customers is done efficiently and effectively for all parties concerned. SCM aims to minimize inventory levels, optimize production and increase throughput, decrease manufacturing time, optimize logistics and distribution, streamline order fulfillment, and overall reduce the costs associated with these activities (*SupplyChainManagement101.com* 2006).

supply chain management (SCM)
A complex process that requires the coordination of many activities so that the shipment of goods and services from supplier right through to customer is done efficiently and effectively for all parties concerned.

E-Supply Chains and Their Management

The capabilities of the Internet are having a profound impact on organizations' supply chains. Increasingly, companies are recognizing that the efficient and effective flow of information and materials along their supply chains is a source of competitive advantage and differentiation. According to Norris et al. (2000), **e-supply chain management (e-SCM)** is the collaborative use of technology to enhance B2B processes and improve speed, agility, real-time control, and customer satisfaction. The success of an e-supply chain depends on the following:

e-supply chain management (e-SCM) The collaborative use of technology to improve the operations of supply chain activities as well as the management of supply chains.

▶ **The ability of all supply chain partners to view partner collaboration as a strategic asset.** It is the tight integration and trust among the trading partners that generates speed, agility, and lower cost.

▶ **A well-defined supply chain strategy.** This includes a clear understanding of existing strengths and weaknesses, articulating well-defined plans for improvement, and establishing cross-organizational objectives for supply chain performance.

▶ **Information visibility along the entire supply chain.** Information about inventories at various segments of the chain, demand for products, capacity planning and activation, synchronization of material flows, delivery times, and any other relevant information must be visible to all members of the supply chain at any given time. Therefore, information must be managed properly—with strict policies, discipline, and daily monitoring.

▶ **Speed, cost, quality, and customer service.** These are the metrics by which supply chains are measured. Consequently, companies must clearly define the measurements for each of these four metrics, together with the target levels to be achieved.

▶ **Integrating the supply chain more tightly.** An e-supply chain will benefit from tighter integration, both within a company and across an *extended enterprise* made up of suppliers, trading partners, logistics providers, and the distribution channel.

Activities and Infrastructure of E-SCM

E-supply chain processes and activities include the following.

Supply Chain Replenishment. Companies can use replenishment information to reduce inventories, eliminate stocking points, and increase the velocity of replenishment by synchronizing supply and demand information across the extended enterprise. Real-time supply and demand information facilitates make-to-order and assemble-to-order manufacturing strategies across the extended enterprise. Supply-chain replenishment is a natural companion to Web-enabled customer orders. (For more on this topic, see Stevenson 2004.)

e-procurement The use of Web-based technology to support the key procurement processes, including requisitioning, sourcing, contracting, ordering, and payment.

E-Procurement. E-procurement serves to streamline a firm's purchasing processes and aims to eliminate paper-based documents, such as purchase orders and the like. As described in Chapter 5, e-procurement is the use of Web-based technology to support the key procurement processes, including requisitioning, sourcing, contracting, ordering, and payment. E-procurement supports the purchase of both direct and indirect materials and employs several Web-based functions, such as online catalogs, contracts, purchase orders, and shipping notices. E-procurement can improve the operation of the supply chain in various ways:

▶ Online catalogs can be used to eliminate redesign of components in product development.

▶ Visibility of available parts and their attributes enables quick decision making.

▶ Online purchase orders expedite the ordering process.

▶ Advanced-shipping notifications and acknowledgments streamline delivery.

Supply Chain Monitoring and Control Using RFID. This is one of the most promising applications of RFID. We will return to this topic later in this chapter.

Inventory Management Using Wireless Devices. Many organizations are now achieving improvements in inventory management by using combinations of barcoding technologies and wireless devices. For example, the auto industry is dependent on the supply of spare parts; in 2005, dealerships sold about $48.9 billion worth of spare parts. By combining barcoding and wireless technologies, dealers are now able to electronically scan in parts as they arrive and place them in inventory up to 50 percent faster than previously. This also means that parts are available for technicians to install in cars or for purchase by customers much faster than in the past. Dealers have a much more accurate picture of their inventory levels and are now able to avoid running out of stock.

Collaborative Planning. Collaborative planning is a business practice that combines the business knowledge and forecasts of multiple players along a supply chain to improve the planning and fulfillment of customer demand (*Vics.org* 2006). Collaborative planning requires buyers and sellers to jointly develop demand forecasts and supply plans for how to support demand. These forecasts and supply plans should be updated regularly, based on information shared over the Internet. Such collaborative planning requires B2B workflow across multiple enterprises over the Internet, with data exchanged among partners dynamically. This topic is discussed further in Section 6.4.

collaborative planning
A business practice that combines the business knowledge and forecasts of multiple players along a supply chain to improve the planning and fulfillment of customer demand.

Collaborative Design and Product Development. Collaborative product development involves the use of product design and development techniques across multiple companies to improve product launch success and reduce time-to-market (as demonstrated in the Boeing opening case).

E-Logistics. E-logistics is the use of Web-based technologies to support the material acquisition, warehousing, and transportation processes. E-logistics enables distribution to couple routing optimization with inventory-tracking information. For example, Internet-based freight auctions enable spot buying of trucking capacity. Third-party logistics providers offer virtual logistics services by integrating and optimizing distribution resources. A company may consider collaboration with its competitors to improve its supply chain. For an example of how Land O'Lakes even collaborates with its competitors via an electronic market, see Online File W6.1. This topic will be discussed more fully in Chapter 11.

Use of B2B Exchanges and Supply Webs. The B2B exchanges introduced in Chapter 5 could play a critical role in e-supply chain management. Supply webs, also known as *value nets* and *value webs*, emerge as alternative configurations to traditional supply chains. In a supply web, information, transactions, products, and funds all flow to and from *multiple* nodes.

Infrastructure for e-SCM

The key activities just described use a variety of infrastructure and tools. The following are the major infrastructure elements and tools of e-supply chains:

- ▶ **Electronic Data Interchange.** EDI (see Online File W5.4) is the major tool used by large corporations to facilitate supply chain relationships. Many companies are shifting from traditional EDI to Internet-based EDI.

- ▶ **Extranets.** These are described in Online File W5.3. Their major purpose is to support interorganizational communication and collaboration. For details on success factors for using extranets in e-SCM, see Chow (2004).

- ▶ **Intranets.** These are the corporate internal networks for communication and collaboration.

▶ **Corporate portals.** These provide a gateway for external and internal collaboration, communication, and information search. They are described in Section 6.7.

▶ **Workflow systems and tools.** These are systems that *manage* the flow of information in organizations. They are described in Section 6.8. Also see van der Aalst and van Hee (2004).

▶ **Groupware and other collaborative tools.** A large number of tools facilitate collaboration and communication between two parties and among members of small as well as large groups. Various tools enable such collaboration, as described in Section 6.8.

Section 6.1 ▶ REVIEW QUESTIONS

1. Define the e-supply chain and list its three major parts.
2. Describe success factors of e-supply chain management.
3. List the eight processes or activities of e-supply chains.
4. List the major e-supply chain management infrastructures and enabling tools.

6.2   SUPPLY CHAIN PROBLEMS AND SOLUTIONS

Supply chains have been plagued with problems, both in military and business operations, for generations. These problems have sometimes caused armies to lose wars and companies to go out of business. The problems are most apparent in complex or long supply chains and in cases where many business partners are involved. Complex and long supply chains involving multiple business partners are becoming more common in the contemporary business world as globalization and off shoring of manufacturing operations continue to intensify. Thus, the problems faced by those managing supply chains are becoming both more complex and more critical to company competitiveness and survival (Kotabe and Mol 2006). As this section will show, some remedies are available through the use of IT and EC.

TYPICAL PROBLEMS ALONG THE SUPPLY CHAIN

In the offline world, there are many examples of companies that were unable to meet demand for certain products while having oversized and expensive inventories of other products. Similar situations exist online (see Chapter 11). Typical of the sorts of problems in EC that gain adverse publicity are when there is a supply–demand mismatch of goods or during a period of particularly high demand, such as the holiday period. For example, a shortage of toys due to incorrect demand forecasting might attract negative attention. A demand forecast is influenced by a number of factors, including consumer behavior, economic conditions, competition, prices, weather conditions, technological developments, and so on. Companies can improve their demand forecasting by using IT-supported forecasts, which are done in collaboration with business partners.

Another problem often is related to shipping. A lack of logistics infrastructure might prevent the right goods (say toys) from reaching their destinations on time. Various uncertainties exist in delivery times, which depend on many factors ranging from vehicle failures to road conditions.

Quality problems with materials and parts also can contribute to deficiencies in the supply chain. The worst case is when quality problems create production delays, causing factories and workers to lie idle and disrupting inventories. Some companies grapple with quality problems due to general misunderstandings or to shipments of wrong materials and parts. Sometimes, the high cost of expediting operations or shipments is the unfortunate result.

Pure EC companies may be likely to have more supply chain problems because they may not have a logistics infrastructure and may be forced to use external logistics services. This can be expensive, plus it requires more coordination and dependence on outsiders. For this reason, some large virtual retailers, such as Amazon.com, have developed physical warehouses and logistics systems. Other virtual retailers are creating strategic alliances with logistics companies or with brick-and-mortar companies that have their own logistics systems. Other problems along the EC supply chain mainly stem from the need to coordinate several activities and internal units and business partners.

For further information on the problems, issues, and challenges of contemporary supply chain management, see Chopra and Meindl (2006).

The Bullwhip Effect

One additional supply chain problem, the *bullwhip effect*, is worth noting. The **bullwhip effect** refers to erratic shifts in orders up and down supply chains (see Davies 2004). This effect was initially observed by P&G with their disposable diapers in offline retail stores. Although actual sales in stores were fairly stable and predictable, orders from distributors had wild swings, creating production and inventory problems for P&G and other suppliers. An investigation revealed that distributors' orders were fluctuating because of poor demand forecasts, price fluctuations, order batching, and rationing within the supply chain. All of this resulted in unnecessary inventories in various places along the supply chain, fluctuations in P&G orders to its suppliers, and the flow of inaccurate information.

Firms from HP in the computer industry to Bristol-Myers Squibb in the pharmaceutical field have experienced a similar phenomenon (Davies 2004). Stockpiling may be occurring simultaneously at as many as seven or eight different places along the supply chain as a defense against shortages. Such stockpiling can lead to as many as 100 days of inventory waiting "just in case" (Taylor and Fearne 2006). Companies can avoid the "sting of the bullwhip" if they take steps to share information along the supply chain. For further information and explanation regarding information sharing in supply chains and the consequent impact on the bullwhip effect, see Fiala (2005). Such information sharing is, of course, implemented and facilitated by EDI, extranets, and groupware technologies and is delivered as part of interorganizational EC and *collaborative commerce*, topics discussed elsewhere in this chapter.

bullwhip effect
Erratic shifts in orders up and down supply chains.

THE NEED FOR INFORMATION SHARING ALONG THE SUPPLY CHAIN

Finley and Srikanth (2005) emphasize communication and information sharing as critical imperatives in avoiding the bullwhip effect and achieving successful supply chain management. According to Handfield and Nichols (2002), they represent one of the fundamental elements that link the organizations of the supply chain into a unified and coordinated system.

Case studies of some world-class companies, such as Wal-Mart (see the Real-World Case at the end of this chapter), Dell, and FedEx, show that these companies have created very sophisticated information systems, exploiting the latest technological developments and creating innovative solutions. However, even world-class companies, such as Nike, can suffer from inappropriate information sharing, resulting in poor forecasting and severely underestimating the complexity of automating aspects of the supply chain (see Case 6.1).

CASE 6.1

EC Application

NIKE'S SUPPLY CHAIN: FAILURE AND EVENTUAL SUCCESS

Back in the 1970s, retailers placed orders with Nike 9 months before the required delivery date. These orders were then forwarded to Nike's manufacturing units around the world. Nike guaranteed that 90 percent of their orders would be delivered within a set time period at an agreed-upon fixed price. This system initially worked well.

However, during the 1980s and 1990s, Nike's business expanded and became more and more global. At the same time, customers became more demanding regarding quality, style, and comfort, and, as a result, product sophistication and variety exploded, causing demand forecasting, manufacturing, and distribution to become increasingly complex. Nike's supply chain managers were soon dealing with hundreds of styles of shoes, each offered in both a large number of different color combinations and sizes. Thus, even without considering the raw materials and equipment sides of the business, Nike had an enormously complex global supply chain.

In 1999, supply chain factors, particularly demand and inventory forecasting, manifested themselves in the bottom line: Profits dropped by 50 percent. Nike management's analysis and assessment of the situation led to the launch of NSC, the Nike Supply Chain project. This initiative was aimed at bringing about excellence in supply chain processes. The first element of the initiative was an attempt to improve the somewhat fragmented and failing demand forecasting and order management activities in Nike. In 1998, 27 order management systems led to poor demand forecasting and, hence, ineffective supply chain management overall. To overcome a number of the supply chain management problems, Nike decided to acquire and implement i2 Technologies' demand forecasting system.

The i2 Technologies implementation was begun in 1999 with a projected cost of $40 million. The objectives of the project were ambitious and included detailed forecasting of over 1 million stock keeping units (SKUs). Where the i2 Technologies' standard software did not exactly meet Nike's requirements, extensive customization was undertaken. Further, large amounts of data were fed into the i2 Technologies' system from legacy systems within Nike. From this data, sophisticated and complex algorithms automatically generated thousands of forecasts that were used to drive Nike manufacturing.

In the latter half of 2000, the demand forecasting was found to be faulty, causing Nike to overmanufacture some products, while struggling to meet demand for others. For example, Nike overproduced poorselling shoe lines such as Air Garnett II by $90 million worth of product, while underproducing popular lines such as Air Force One by $80 million to $100 million worth of product. It took about 6 to 9 months for Nike to overcome its inventory imbalance and more than 2 years to make up the financial loss. In setting things right, many shoes were sold at heavily discounted prices.

Nike analyzed its i2 Technologies' demand forecasting application in an effort to correct the problems and move forward. Immediate lessons learned involved the need for more adequate training of users, more comprehensive testing of the application, better data cleansing, and more careful integration of the application with other information systems. The extensive customization of the i2 Technologies' software, which, among other things, broke forecasts down to individual styles, added undue complexity to an already complex project. Generally, the review of the project found that there was altogether too much reliance on automatically generated forecasts rather than a judicious blend of human judgment and intuition together with the statistical analysis.

Looking back over the problematic project, Nike management felt that the initial attempt to bring about supply chain improvements had been too ambitious. Deadlines had been too tight, and the implementation had been rushed. The complexity of the undertaking had been increased and focus had been lost because Nike had, in addition to the i2 Technologies' project, attempted to implement a SAP ERP system and Siebel's CRM system at the same time.

Nike moved to take control of its supply chain project, eventually moving its shoe product lines forecasting application onto SAP, where the forecasting was based more heavily on forward orders and planners' judgment rather than relying on statistical algorithms. After considerable improvements, i2 Technologies' system continued to be used for Nike apparel lines. By 2004, its implementation of i2 Technologies' forecasting system, SAP's ERP system, and Siebel's

(continued)

CASE 6.1   (continued)

CRM system was complete, giving Nike an integrated and efficient supply chain.

Nike had spent 6 years and $800 million on the project. Generally speaking, despite the early problems, Nike management was well satisfied with the project. The project had enabled Nike to shorten its lead time for building footwear from 9 to 6 months, and its enhanced capabilities in planning and tracking inventory resulted in a return on investment of 20 percent in 2004 alone.

Sources: Compiled from Koch (2004) and Chaturvedi and Gupta (2005).

Questions

1. What factors led to Nike's supply chain being such a challenge to manage?

2. What factors led to the i2 Technologies implementation being a highly complex project? Were the increased complexities really necessary?

3. What was wrong with Nike relying heavily on automatic statistical forecasts generated by the i2 Technologies' software?

4. What solutions were employed?

EC SOLUTIONS ALONG THE SUPPLY CHAIN

Information technology, including Web-based EC technologies, provides solutions along the supply chain, as shown throughout this book. Such solutions are beneficial both to brick-and-mortar operations and to online companies (Moody 2006). The following is a representative list of the major solutions provided by an EC approach and technologies:

▶ *Order taking* can be done over the Internet, EDI, EDI/Internet, or an extranet, and it may be fully automated. For example, in B2B, orders are generated and transmitted automatically to suppliers when inventory levels fall below certain levels. The result is a fast, inexpensive, and more accurate (no need to rekey data) order-taking process. In B2C, Web-based ordering using electronic forms expedites the process, makes it more accurate (intelligent agents can check the input data and provide instant feedback), and reduces processing costs (Leonard and Davis 2006).

▶ *Order fulfillment* can become instant if the products can be digitized (e.g., software). In other cases, EC order taking interfaces with the company's back-office systems, including logistics. Such an interface, or even integration, shortens cycle time and eliminates errors. (See Chapter 11 for more on order fulfillment.)

▶ *Electronic payments* can expedite both the order fulfillment cycle and the payment delivery period. Payment processing can be significantly less expensive, and fraud can be better controlled. (See Chapter 11 for more on electronic payments.)

▶ *Managing risk* to avoid supply-chain breakdown (Hillman 2006) can be done in several ways. Carrying additional inventories is effective against the risk of stock-outs, and hence poor customer service, but can be expensive. Also, in certain cases the risk increases because products may become obsolete.

▶ *Inventories can be minimized* by introducing a build-to-order (on demand) manufacturing process as well as by providing fast and accurate information to suppliers. By allowing business partners to electronically track and monitor orders and production activities, inventory management can be improved and inventory levels and the expense of inventory management can be minimized.

▶ *Collaborative commerce* among members of the supply chain can be done in many areas ranging from product design to demand forecasting. The results are shorter cycle times, minimal delays and work interruptions, lower inventories, and lower administrative costs (Cassivi 2006).

CASE 6.2
EC Application

NETAFIM: PROBLEMS AND SOLUTIONS ON THE WAY TO AN AGILE GLOBAL SUPPLY CHAIN

Introduction

Netafim is an Israeli company that markets and sells irrigation solutions based on its irrigation system products. The company's vision is to "expand its presence as the global leader in the field of innovative irrigation-based solutions and water technologies" (*Netafim.com* 2007). The company Web site describes the Netafim mission as meeting the irrigation needs of customers, wherever they are located, through innovative irrigation solutions.

Netafim was the first company to develop drip irrigation technology. Other firms quickly established themselves in this now highly competitive marketplace. The company had a decentralized operational and management structure through its early years and onward through its main period of growth.

Netafim had a significant advantage in the early days in that its early employees were farmers who had an intimate knowledge of farming in the arid and salty soils of Southern Israel. Thus, with the knowledge possessed by such employees, Netafim was able to deliver complete and practical water management solutions to farmers. This led to the firm having remarkable success and growth through the next few decades, expanding its product range to a number of innovative irrigation solutions. By the early 2000s, Netafim was selling its products in 130 countries and had 30 subsidiary companies in different locations around the world, enabling Netafim to offer relevant and practical irrigation solutions tailored to local needs by drawing on local knowledge.

In the 1990s, to deal with the demands of the increasingly large and complex global supply chain, Netafim decided to build extrusion plants in some of its key markets, while keeping the production and assembly of the drippers themselves in Israel, so as to protect key company knowledge. Extrusion plants were built in Australia in 1996 and in Brazil and South Africa in 1998. Further, Netafim began to augment its irrigation pipe and dripper products with irrigation and related crop management products from other vendors in hopes of providing farmers with near-total solutions for water and crop management problems. By 2000, approximately 60 percent of Netafim's 50,000 SKUs were supplied by external vendors.

Supply Chain Problems

Initially, Netafim's decentralized structure allowed it to respond quickly to particular local needs in terms of designing solutions. However, an agile global supply chain was needed to deliver these solutions worldwide. By the early 2000s, the company's outdated, local, and fragmentary information systems were beginning to affect both Netafim's bottom line and its competitiveness.

The company lacked any visibility of its total supply chain material flows. Furthermore, planning, forecasting, procurement, and distribution processes were inefficient, thus lead times were lengthy and variable. Adding to the lack of inventory visibility and the general lack of coordination was the fact that each subsidiary placed orders separately with the outside vendors of irrigation system and related products. In this environment of uncertainty, subsidiary companies, manufacturing plants, and the head office were forced to anticipate future needs without good information about production, orders, and inventories. Unsure of production and inventory status up the line, subsidiaries, when they noticed a slight increase in demand, would order a little extra just in case they had noticed an upward trend. However, once they had received one or two overly large orders they would minimize or cancel the next order. When the manufacturing facilities received such orders they tended to follow similar practices. Given that orders tended to be large and infrequent, the upshot was the bullwhip effect, whereby the supply chain is characterized by infrequent, inappropriate, and fluctuating orders, as described in Section 6.2. Further, in an environment where demanding local customers wanted prompt order fulfillment, subsidiaries tended to cushion themselves against the poorly performing supply chain system by keeping high "safety" stocks. Despite the "safety stocks," out-of-stock instances at the subsidiaries continued to grow. In general, the poorly performing supply chain was threatening the future performance and competitiveness of the company.

The Supply Chain Management Solution

In 2002, a new CEO quickly saw that one of his first priorities was a complete reorganization of the supply chain. He created a supply chain manager position as part of his executive team with two initial objectives. One was to create a uniform set of product codes across the organization. The other was to create information visibility and information sharing across the entire supply chain and to use this to increase efficiency and effectiveness.

To increase information visibility and information sharing in the supply chain, Netafim decided to

(continued)

CASE 6.2 (continued)

implement SAP's ERP system. The idea was to use SAP to move the company to dynamic real-time production management and inventory control based, as much as was possible, on actual forward demand rather than on forecasting. Staff in subsidiaries and headquarters redesigned and modernized the supply chain business processes of order management, procurement, production, and inventory management. Soon inventory levels across the entire supply chain were visible, and efforts could be focused on inventory reduction. Further, order placement and confirmation activities improved dramatically, with the average time for order placement and confirmation decreasing from 10 days to 1 day.

Some strategic structural decisions also were necessary. Regional Logistic Hubs (RLHs) were created in order to maintain customer service while minimizing total inventory in the supply chain. The RLHs would be located at strategic positions in the supply chain in order to be in locations that were in close proximity to the major points of demand. The plan was to get lead times regarding deliveries to subsidiaries and dealers down to under 20 days instead of 2 to 3 months. Further, it was hoped that through a combination of utilizing RLHs effectively and good planning and inventory control local inventories could be reduced by 50 percent or more. To ensure that inventories of external vendors' products were reduced, VMI (vendor managed inventory) was introduced, under which the vendors owned and managed their stock items in the RLHs, the stock becoming Netafim's only when the subsidiary ordered the product. The SAP ERP system assisted in the implementation of VMI because it enabled an authorized individual at Netafim or one of its vendors to see both the Netafim and the vendor inventory at the RLHs.

To further improve supply chain management, a new procurement department was created and authorized to carry out central and strategic purchasing for all of Netafim, including the subsidiaries.

A new planning department also was created that engaged in forecasting and production planning and inventory control in the manufacturing units and the RLHs. Enabling this activity was a new software system called Viva Cadena. This system allowed a blend of statistical forecasting and inventory control, together with both planners' intuitive judgments and real-time information on current inventory status and forward order books. The system essentially made suggestions to planners rather than automatically determining orders and the like.

By 2005, the strategic decisions and information visibility across the entire supply chain began to bring results. Stock levels throughout the Netafim group were reduced significantly, customer service had improved dramatically, and general business competitiveness had been enhanced.

Sources: Compiled from Lee and Michlin (2006) and *netafim.com* (accessed January 2008).

Questions

1. Describe the supply chain challenges the new CEO faced when he took over Netafim in 2002.

2. Describe the strategic and structural changes made to improve supply chain management at Netafim.

3. Discuss the role of SAP's ERP system in the improvements in Netafim's supply chain management.

4. What is the role of RLHs?

For implementation issues related to these technologies, see Singh et al. (2007).

Supply chain problems may become more serious when the supply chain involves global segments. The Netafim example in Case 6.2 reviews some of these problems and describes how they were successfully addressed.

The following section examines RFID applications that may be used to provide supply chain solutions. For implementation issues of different IT/EC tools, see Sing et al. (2007).

Section 6.2 ▶ REVIEW QUESTIONS

1. Describe some typical problems along the supply chain.
2. Describe the reasons for supply-chain-related problems.
3. Describe the bullwhip effect.
4. Describe the benefits of information sharing along the supply chain.
5. List some EC solutions to supply chain problems.

6.3   RFID AS A KEY ENABLER OF SUPPLY CHAINS

A major technology that has the potential to revolutionize supply chain management is RFID.

THE RFID REVOLUTION

radio frequency identification (RFID)
A technology that uses electronic tags (chips) instead of bar codes to identify items. RFID readers use radio waves to interact with the tags.

Radio frequency identification (RFID) is a technology that uses electronic tags (chips) instead of bar codes to identify items. RFID readers use radio waves to interact with the tags. The tags can be attached to or embedded in objects, animals, or humans. The radio waves enable the unique identification of the objects, transmission of data, and/or storage of information about the object (or to locate the item). The technology behind RFID is presented in detail in Online File W6.2. Eventually, RFID tags will be attached to many items. RFID tags are like bar codes, but contain much more information. Also, they can be read from greater distances (up to 30 feet).

Cost has been a real issue and one inhibitor of the uptake of RFID technology. In 2006, a major landmark was reached when Israeli RFID manufacturer SmartCode offered RFID tags for 5 cents per tag, providing orders were placed for 100 million tags at a time! This compares to Avery Dennison in the United States, which is offering tags at 7.9 cents for volumes of 1 million or more tags. Although few would be in a position to take up the SmartCode offer, it is an important signal that the cost of RFID technology is coming close to reaching a point where companies will be willing to invest in RFID because they can be more certain of achieving an ROI on their RFID investments (Roberti 2006).

However, cost is just one issue. Organizations still need to learn exactly how to effectively use the capabilities of RFID technology in their supply chains with the back-office systems and how business processes may need to be redesigned and retooled so that solid business benefits accrue from the use of this technology (for benefits, see Loebbecke 2006).

Given these developments, what effect will RFID have on supply chains? Exhibit 6.2 shows the relationship between a retailer (Wal-Mart), a manufacturer (such as P&G),

EXHIBIT 6.2   How RFID Tags Smooth Supply Chains

1. A special offer causes Wal-Mart shoppers to snap up boxes of Pampers Baby-Dry.

2. Each box of Pampers has the RFID tag. Shelf-mounted scanners alert the stockroom of urgent need for restock.

3. Wal-Mart's inventory management system tracks and links the in-store stock and the warehouse stock, prompting quicker replenishment and providing accurate real-time data.

4. Wal-Mart's systems are linked to the P&G supply chain management system. Demand spikes reported by RFID tags are immediately viable throughout the supply chain.

5. P&G's logistics software tracks the trucks with GPS locators and tracks their contents with RFID tag readers. Request managers can reroute trucks to fill urgent needs.

6. P&G suppliers also use RFID tags and readers for raw materials management, thus giving P&G viability several tiers down the supply chain, and giving suppliers the ability to accurately forecast demand and production.

Source: Heizer, J., and B. Render, *Operations Management*, 7th ed. (pp. 450–452), Upper Saddle River, NJ: Prentice Hall, 2004.

and the manufacturer's suppliers. All of the companies in the exhibit use RFID tags. It is no longer necessary to manually count inventories, and all business partners are able to view inventory information in real time. This transparency can go several tiers along the supply chain. Additional applications, such as rapid store checkout, which eliminates the need to scan each item, will be provided by RFID in the future.

Other applications of RFID are shown in Exhibit 6.3. The upper part of the exhibit shows how the tags are used as merchandise travels from the supplier to the retailer. Note that the RFID transmits real-time information on the location of the merchandise. The lower part of the exhibit shows the use of the RFID at the retailer, mainly to locate merchandise, control inventory, prevent theft, and expedite processing of relevant information.

RFID Applications in the Supply Chain

The following are examples of how RFID can be used in the supply chain.

RFID at Metro. Metro, a huge retailer from Germany, is using RFID tags in an attempt to speed the flow of goods from manufacturers in China to their arrival in Europe

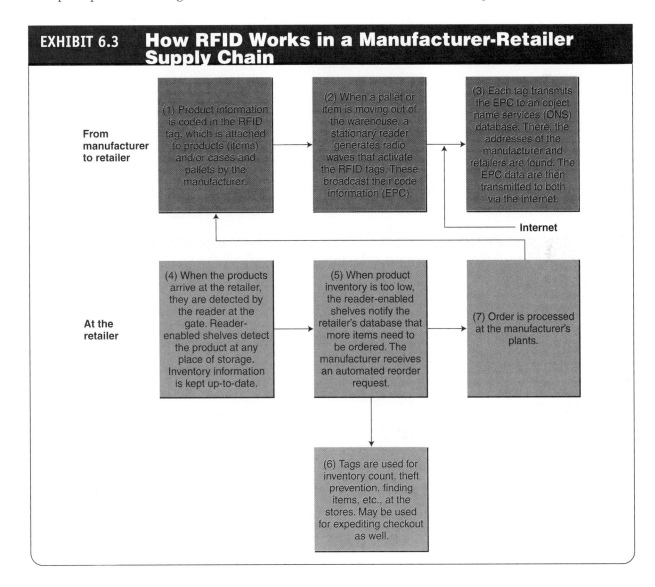

EXHIBIT 6.3   How RFID Works in a Manufacturer-Retailer Supply Chain

at the port of Rotterdam to distribution centers in Germany. Passive tags (see Online File W6.2) are being applied to cartons and cases of goods; active tags also are being applied to the containers in which those goods are packed for shipping. At various points en route to Germany, the active tags are read and record the arrival of the cargo, enabling a record to be kept of where goods are located at any point in time. This gives Metro greater insights into the flow of goods along their supply chain, with bottlenecks or points that slow the delivery of goods becoming quickly evident. This allows for a review of business processes and work practices to ensure speedier handling and delivery. In addition, these RFID tags are equipped with intrusion sensors, which give an indication of whether any attempt has been made to open the sealed containers during the journey. If the container is tampered with, the tags can trigger flashing lights or a siren to alert staff. Thus, Metro is able to detect any attempts to tamper with or pilfer stock (see Heinrich 2005).

The benefits of the RFID system to Metro are substantial. It is calculated that eliminating a single day from the supply chain will save Metro hundreds of thousands of dollars annually by reducing the amount of stock held in inventory. Estimates are that for large retailers (in excess of $1 billion in sales annually) each 1-day reduction in inventory can free up to $1 million in working capital (Sullivan 2006).

RFID at Starbucks. As Starbucks expands its range of fresh foods (such as salads, sandwiches, and the like) available at its outlets, the complexity and demands of managing this supply chain increases. Keeping the food fresh depends on keeping it at a steady cool state and in ensuring timely delivery. Starbucks is requiring its distributors to employ RFID tags to measure the temperature at the delivery trucks. These tags are programmed to record the temperature inside the truck every few minutes, and on return to the depot this temperature data can be downloaded and analyzed. If there are unacceptable readings (i.e., the temperature is deemed to have risen too high), efforts are made to determine the cause and remedy the problem. This can then cause a redesign of critical business processes with regard to the transportation and handling of food (*RFID Journal* 2006). As RFID technology matures, it is conceivable that in the future the tags themselves will be able to detect variation in temperature and send a signal to a thermostat to activate refrigeration fans within the truck.

RFID at Harmon Hospital. Keeping track of relatively small, moveable assets (such as wheelchairs, pulse oximeters, and other medical devices) in hospitals can be time consuming and difficult. Equipment may be stored in cupboards, moved to other wards and not returned, and sometimes sent home with patients and not returned. Studies also suggest that when hospital staff members are unable to find the equipment they need, rather than instigating a full-scale search, they tend to place an order for more equipment. Thus, hospitals incur significant costs in both searching for equipment and in ordering equipment that is not actually necessary. Harmon Hospital in Las Vegas is addressing these concerns by attaching active RFID tags on various medical devices and installing RFID readers at various points throughout the hospital. This enables staff to locate any required item of equipment, with the system providing a text-based report or a map of the hospital indicating the location of the desired piece of equipment (Bacheldor 2006a). Many other organizations in a variety of industries would clearly experience similar problems as those at Harmon Hospital.

RFID at Atlantic Beef Products (Ontario, Canada). At Atlantic Beef Products, cows' ears are tagged with RFID tags. Once a cow is killed, its ear tags are scanned. The carcass goes onto two leg hooks, each equipped with an RFID tag. These are synced to each animal's database record. The RFIDs replace bar codes, which could be contaminated with *E. coli* on the slaughterhouse floor. The RFID helps track the movement of each cow and the meat produced at any time. The system won a gold award from the Canadian IT Organization.

RFID in Pharmaceuticals. MIT and SAP are examining the use of RFID in various industries, including pharmaceuticals, and the necessary IT architecture to support such uses (Boucher-Ferguson 2007). The goal is to be able to know where everything—or anything—is at any given time. The challenge, however, is determining how such a scenario would play out; that is, determining what the actual network would look like once companies up and down the supply chain collaboratively start inputting and exchanging information among trading partners and their partners' partners. The FDA, for example, is interested in using RFID to find counterfeit drugs in the supply chain.

RFID in Philadelphia Cabs. Taxi cabs in Philadelphia, Pennsylvania, are equipped to accept payments using RFID technologies. Passengers can use RFID-enabled credit cards, such as PayPass from MasterCard to pay their cab fares. A terminal is located behind the front seat, facing the passenger. To activate the system, passengers wave their RFID-enabled cards near the reader. The driver can then complete the transaction using either credit or debit facilities. Payments are processed by sending payment information over wireless networks. Such technologies are reducing the time taken to complete a transaction. This system also can be used by the cab driver for routing and navigational information, for work scheduling (signing on and off a shift), for keeping logs of trips, and for tracking items left by mistake by passengers in the cab (O'Connor 2006c).

RFID Use by CHEP. The Asia Pacific Division of CHEP (famous for its pallets and reusable containers, based in Florida) has developed an innovative use of RFID for the automotive industry in Australia. CHEP manufactures and then rents reusable, custom-made, plastic stacking crates for transporting parts and components along the automotive supply chain. In addition to the traditional text tags and bar-coded labels, CHEP has now added RFID tags to the outside of these crates. CHEP is thus able to easily determine which customer has which crate, while it gives the automotive companies much more precise insights into the location of parts both within their manufacturing environment and along their extended supply chains (Bacheldor 2006b).

RFID at Nokia. Security guards employed at Nokia facilities now carry a mobile phone handset with an RFID tag added and an RFID reader in the outer casing. At the start of a shift, guards use the phone to read their RFID-enabled name badges. RFID tags are installed at various points around the facility. As security guards do their rounds, they open the handsets to read the tags as they pass. Details of the phone number and the RFID tag just read are transmitted over cell phone networks. Supervisors are thus given accurate information as to when a particular guard started and finished a shift, whether the guard patrolled all the required locations, and where the guard was at a particular point in time. In addition, supervisors can use the text and phone function to ask guards to recheck an area, vary their route, and the like.

The ability to link mobile phone technologies and RFID opens many more possibilities. For example, JCDecaux is considering using this Nokia application to track the installation and removal of billboards, posters, and rolling paid advertising displays at bus stops, train stations, movie theaters, roadsides, and other public locations (Bacheldor 2006d). Another company, Gentag, is developing technologies that will utilize mobile phones as RFID readers in health-care applications. RFID-enabled skin patches will allow the remote monitoring of pulse rates, temperatures, glucose levels, and the like (Bacheldor 2006c).

RFID at Deutsche Post. Deutsche Post owns 6 million shipping containers that it uses to hold and transport about 70 million letters and other items that pass through its distribution centers daily. In order to process these crates, Deutsche Post prints in excess of 500 million thick paper labels, all of which are thrown away after a single use. It was environmental concerns, rather than purely economic ones, that have driven Deutsche Post's RFID initiative (Wessel 2006).

For other applications and more details, refer to Loebbecke (2006) and Heinrich (2005).

LIMITATIONS OF RFID

RFID does have a number of limitations. For small companies, the cost of the system may be too high (at least for the near future). The lower-frequency systems (300 to 500 KHz) required for passive tags are much cheaper but offer a decreased range. Radio frequency interference and the limited range of passive RFID tags also may be problematic, especially because passive tags are the most economically viable option for some businesses. These limitations should be minimized in the future as the cost of both passive and active RFID decreases and functionality increases. However, to date, many organizations have struggled to demonstrate the ROI of their RFID initiatives, raising the question of how long organizations will continue to invest in such technologies without gaining adequate returns (Schurman 2006).

Another major limitation of RFID currently is the restriction of the environments in which RFID tags are easily read. RFID tags do not work well in "harsh" environments, where reads are required in or around liquids and metals or around corners, for example. This means that RFID cannot readily be used underwater or near items that are largely liquid (such as human beings and livestock, which are mostly water!), nor do they function well in warehouses or areas where large amounts of metals are present (e.g., metal-lined deep freezers or metal shelving). Thus, in environments where foodstuffs must be kept deep frozen in metal-lined freezers (e.g., Sara Lee cakes, pastries, and ice creams), getting accurate reads from RFID tags can be problematic. So, too, can getting reads of tagged items already placed on metal supermarket shelves or in metal supermarket trolleys. Ingenious shoplifters have found that lining handbags with aluminum foil will often render the security RFID tag on items placed in their bags unreadable, and hence they are able to pass out of stores undetected! RFID tags do not work well underground, around corners, through brick, rock, and the like (Johnson 2006b).

Another issue has arisen in real-world implementations of RFID—the accuracy of the reads (Finin 2006). Some organizations have reported achieving only about 70 to 80 percent accuracy in their read rates and, of additional concern, achieving different levels of accuracy at different points along the supply chain (Schuman 2006a). Using active tags with a relatively large read range on individual items can prove problematic when passing through where there are many other items stocked proximate to the reader but not part of the shopping cart (O'Connor 2006a).

Concern over customer privacy is another issue that remains a significant point of contention in arguments about the appropriateness of wide-scale implementation of RFID. First and foremost are security concerns related to the potential of RFID tags to be tracked long after their SCM purpose has been served. The following are some concerns regarding customer privacy and RFID tags:

▶ The customer buying an item with an RFID tag may not be able to remove the tag or may be unaware that an RFID tag is attached to the item.

▶ The presence of a tag might mean that it would still be capable of being read from some distance away without the knowledge of the purchaser or user of that item. These two concerns have lead to comments such as a California state senator's remarking that "one day you realized your underwear was reporting your whereabouts!" (reported in en.wikipedia.org/wiki/RFID).

▶ If a purchase is made using a credit card, then the potential exists for the tag details to be linked directly to the personal details of the credit card holder (en.wikipedia.org/wiki/RFID).

As with most immature technologies, agreeing on universal standards, as well as connecting the RFIDs with existing IT systems is yet another issue. In 2006, however, the Gen 2 standard (a protocol for the exchange of information between the RFID tag and the reader) was announced, and it appears to be the major standard moving forward.

RUBEE: AN ALTERNATIVE TO RFID?

In 2006, a technology emerged that might act as an important complement to RFID in that it excels in situations where RFID has limitations. Known as RuBee, it relies on low-frequency magnetic waves to track products and transfer information. **RuBee** is a bidirectional, on-demand, peer-to-peer radiating transceiver protocol (en.wikipedia.org/wiki/RuBee). It is currently being developed by the Institute of Electrical and Electronics Engineers. Exhibit 6.4 compares RuBee and RFID. Note that RuBee is not intended as a replacement for RFID, but rather as a complement. As suggested in Exhibit 6.4, RFID is excellent for many applications, and indeed better than RuBee for some. However, RuBee tends to excel in areas where RFID has proven problematic; hence, it may prove vital in overcoming some of RFID's limitations. RuBee and RFID together may become partners in helping organizations better manage their global supply chains.

RuBee
Bidirectional, on-demand, peer-to-peer radiating transceiver protocol under development by the Institute of Electrical and Electronics Engineers.

EXHIBIT 6.4 **Comparison of RuBee and RFID**		
	RuBee	**RFID**
Signal type	Magnetic waves (99.9% magnetic, 0.1% radio)	Radio waves (99.9% radio, 0.1% magnetic)
Frequency	Low frequency (below 450 KHz, often 132 KHz)	High and Ultra High Frequency (HF = 13.56 MHz and UHF = 916 MHz)
Read speed	Slower 6 to 10 reads per second	Faster HF = 100 reads/second UHF = 150 to 200 reads/second
Battery life of active tags	Long (10 to 15 years)	Short (1 to 4 years)
Suitable for visibility	Locating items in warehouse	Tracking
	Medical and health-care applications	High-volume scanning
	Livestock applications	Counting inventory moving on conveyor belts
	Obtaining real-time information on full history of item via the Internet	Ensuring inventory is moving along supply chain as planned
	Error detection	
	Creation of smart store by reducing likelihood of stock-outs	
	Theft prevention	
Tagging	Item-level tagging	Pallet, crate, carton tagging
Ability to handle harsh environments	Works underwater, around metal, around corners	Does not always work effectively in harsh environments
Safety issues	Very safe: Not absorbed through human tissue, lower field strength than that of an airport metal detector	Relatively safe
Cost	Infrastructure costs lower than RFID; tag costs may be higher, depending on amount of intelligence built into tag	Infrastructure costs higher; tag costs depend on whether active or passive

Sources: Compiled from *RFID Solutions Online* (2006), Johnson (2006a), Schuman (2006b), Schurman (2006), O'Connor (2006b).

Section 6.3 ▶ REVIEW QUESTIONS

1. Describe how RFID can be used to improve supply chains.
2. Explain how RFID works in a supplier–retailer system.
3. Briefly explain the differences between active and passive RFID tags. (See Online File W6.2.)
4. In what circumstances would it be better to use passive RFID tags? And in what circumstances might it be better to use active RFID tags? (See Online File W6.2.)
5. What are some of the major limitations of RFID technology?
6. What is RuBee?
7. How does RuBee overcome some of the limitations of RFID? (See Exhibit 6.4.)

6.4 COLLABORATIVE COMMERCE

Previous chapters introduced B2B activities related mainly to selling and buying. E-commerce also can be used to improve collaboration within and among organizations along the supply chain.

ESSENTIALS OF COLLABORATIVE COMMERCE

collaborative commerce (c-commerce)
The use of digital technologies that enable companies to collaboratively plan, design, develop, manage, and research products, services, and innovative EC applications.

Collaborative commerce (c-commerce) refers to the use of digital technologies that enable companies to collaboratively plan, design, develop, manage, and research products, services, and innovative EC applications. An example would be a company that is collaborating electronically with a vendor that designs a product or a part for the company, as was shown in the Boeing opening case. C-commerce implies communication, information sharing, and collaborative planning done electronically through tools such as groupware and specially designed EC collaboration tools.

Numerous studies (e.g., *Microsoft.com* 2006) suggest that collaborative relationships result in significant impacts on organizations' performance. Major benefits cited are cost reduction, increased revenue, and better customer retention. These benefits are the results of fewer stock-outs, less exception processing, reduced inventory throughout the supply chain, lower materials costs, increased sales volume, and increased competitive advantage.

COLLABORATION HUBS

collaboration hub
The central point of control for an e-market. A single collaborative-hub (c-hub), representing one e-market owner, can host multiple collaboration spaces (c-spaces) in which trading partners use collaboration enablers (c-enablers) to exchange data with the c-hub.

One of the most popular forms of c-commerce is the *collaboration hub*, which is used by the members of a supply chain. A **collaboration hub** is the central point of control for an e-market. A single collaboration hub (c-hub), representing one e-market owner, can host multiple collaboration spaces (c-spaces) in which trading partners use collaboration enablers (c-enablers) to exchange data with the c-hub.

C-commerce activities usually are conducted between and among supply chain partners. Leightons Opticians, as shown in Case 6.3 uses a hub to communicate among all its business partners, thus improving customer service. Online File W6.3 presents the case of Webcor, a company that uses c-commerce to better collaborate with its partners electronically.

There are several varieties of c-commerce, ranging from joint design efforts to forecasting. Collaboration can be done both between and within organizations. For example, a collaborative platform can help in communication and collaboration between headquarters and subsidiaries or between franchisers and franchisees. The platform provides, for example, e-mail, message boards, chat rooms, and online corporate data access around the globe, no matter what the time zone. The following sections demonstrate some types and examples of c-commerce.

CASE 6.3
EC Application

LEIGHTONS OPTICIANS SEES THE VALUE OF COLLABORATIVE HUBS

Leightons Opticians was founded in 1928 in Southampton, United Kingdom. The business progressed throughout the decades, and a number of branches were opened. In 1996, Leightons launched a franchise business aimed at attracting high-quality and business-focused opticians and optometrists. Leightons now owns 25 branch stores and has 15 franchisees. Leightons still maintains its traditional family values of outstanding personal customer service delivered by highly professional staff offering excellent treatment and advice and the best quality lens and frame technologies. As the business expanded, however, the challenge was to ensure that staff spent time serving customers and not on administrative issues, such as order tracking, filing, and the like.

Leightons decided to implement a collaborative hub from Supply Chain Connect (*supplychainconnect.com*). All of the branches, franchises, and suppliers are able to connect to a single hub and seamlessly exchange information, irrespective of the internal systems operated at the respective sites. Leightons pays a monthly subscription fee for Supply Chain Connect's services, which meant that it was able to avoid making a substantial upfront investment in the technology.

Staff members at any of Leightons' branches are able to send orders electronically to a number of different suppliers. Because orders are sent through the hub, they can now be tracked, so Leightons' staff members are able to check the real-time status of any order at any time. Leightons has been very happy with the direct cost savings generated and

also believes that its staff is now able to spend more time delivering excellent personal customer service.

Leightons' two major suppliers are Luxottica and Marchon; both are enthusiastic users of Supply Chain Connect. They receive hundreds of orders daily from a variety of branches and franchisees, and the collaboration hub enables them to view all orders from a particular buyer very easily. The system is integrated with their back-office systems, eliminating any need for rekeying data, thus saving the status of any particular order, meaning that they are better able to monitor the performance of their critical suppliers.

Future expansion is planned to allow for automated matching of orders against invoices for payment approvals.

Sources: Compiled from *SupplyChainConnect.com* (2005) and *LeightonsOpticians.com* (2008).

Questions

1. Why is this considered to be a collaboration hub?
2. What are the potential risks associated with participation in this collaboration hub?
3. In what other ways could these players utilize the collaboration hub?
4. Think of the various parties involved in this collaboration and identify the benefits that each derives from it.

COLLABORATIVE NETWORKS

Traditionally, collaboration took place among supply chain members, frequently those that were close to each other (e.g., a manufacturer and its distributor or a distributor and a retailer). Even if more partners were involved, the focus was on the optimization of information and product flow between existing nodes in the traditional supply chain. Advanced approaches such as collaboration, planning, forecasting and replenishing (CPFR), which is described in the next section, do not change the basic structure.

Traditional collaboration results in a vertically integrated supply chain. However, as stated in Chapters 1 and 2, EC and Web technologies can *fundamentally* change the shape of the supply chain, the number of players within it, and their individual roles. The new supply chain can be a hub or even a network. A comparison between the traditional supply chain and the new one, which is made possible by Web technologies, is shown in Exhibit 6.5. Notice that the traditional chain in Exhibit 6.5A is

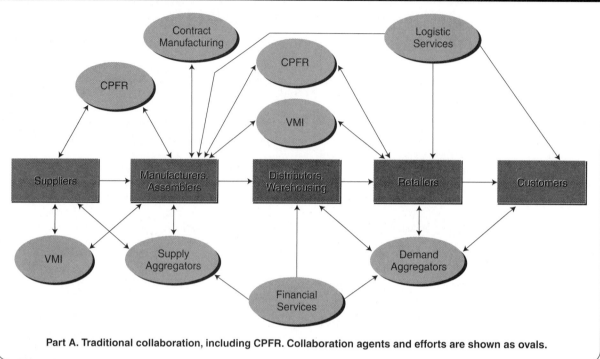

EXHIBIT 6.5A Comparing the Traditional Collaborative Supply Chain and Collaborative Networks

Part A. Traditional collaboration, including CPFR. Collaboration agents and efforts are shown as ovals.

basically linear. The collaborative network in Exhibit 6.5B shows that partners at any point in the network can interact with each other, bypassing traditional partners. Interaction may occur among several manufacturers or distributors, as well as with new players, such as software agents that act as aggregators, B2B exchanges, hubs, or logistics providers.

Mobile Collaborative Networks

As mobile technologies become more and more mature, mobile collaborative networks are gradually coming into being. These networks have the ability to share valuable business information in mobile scenarios with those who are co-located or remote and who are not necessarily from the same enterprise. Mobile workers are able to communicate and share information anytime, anywhere (Divitini et al. 2004).

REPRESENTATIVE EXAMPLES OF E-COLLABORATION

Leading businesses are moving quickly to realize the benefits of c-commerce. Large companies such as Wal-Mart and Toyota have been leaders in the field in this regard for some time. However, smaller companies are now benefiting from the opportunities afforded by e-collaboration. ToySolution (toysolution.com) was established in Hong Kong to support collaboration between the many players in the toy industry. Within 6 months of launching, ToySolution had more than 700 active members in the system. ToySolution enables suppliers, manufacturers, designers, and toy retailers to

EXHIBIT 6.5B

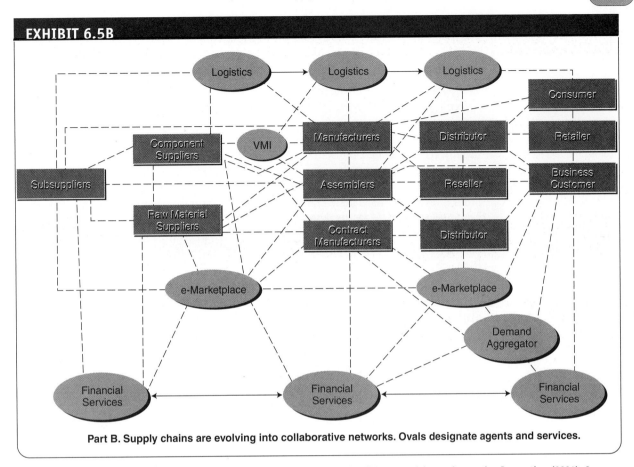

Part B. Supply chains are evolving into collaborative networks. Ovals designate agents and services.

Source: Poirier, C., "Collaborative Commerce: Wave Two of the Cyber Revolution." *Computer Sciences Corporation Perspectives* (2001): 8, pp. 9–8, fig. 1. Used with permission of Computer Sciences Corporation. All rights reserved.

collaborate online and improve process efficiency along the entire supply chain through the use of a variety of applications, including those involving document management, workflow processes, order tracking, online payments, arrangement of cargo inspections, insurance, logistics, and the like. It has successfully met the challenge of allowing small family owned and operated, low-tech companies to collaborate online with the large, sophisticated operators with large corporate ERP applications (*IBM.com* 2006a).

Leading companies such as Dell, Cisco, and HP also use collaborative commerce strategically, enabling sophisticated business models while transforming their value chains. They also have implemented e-procurement and other mature collaboration techniques to streamline operations, reduce overhead, and maintain or enhance margins in the face of intense competition. For example, Dell implemented end-to-end integrated configuration and ordering, a single enterprise middleware backbone, and multitier collaborative planning. This has enabled Dell to support a make-to-order business model with best-in-class speed and efficiency. Cisco chose to support a virtual business model focusing on time-to-market and customer satisfaction. Cisco has integrated its order process with back-end processes, implemented purchase order automation, and enabled collaborative product development.

There are many examples of e-collaboration. Some representative examples follow. For more, see Schram (2004).

Vendor-Managed Inventory

vendor-managed inventory (VMI)
The practice of retailers' making suppliers responsible for determining when to order and how much to order.

With **vendor-managed inventory (VMI)**, retailers make their suppliers responsible for determining when to order and how much to order. The retailer provides the supplier with real-time information (e.g., point-of-sale data), inventory levels, and a threshold below which orders are replenished. The reorder quantities also are predetermined and usually recommended by the supplier. With this approach, the retailer is no longer burdened with inventory management, demand forecasting becomes easier, the supplier can see the potential need for an item before the item is ordered, there are no purchase orders, inventories are kept low, and out-of-stocks become infrequent. This method was initiated by Wal-Mart in the 1980s and was supported by EDI. Today, it can be supported by CPFR and special software. VMI software solutions are provided by Sockeye Solutions (sockeyesolutions.com) and JDA Software (jda.com). For details, see Richardson (2004).

Information Sharing Between Retailers and Suppliers: P&G and Wal-Mart

One of the most notable examples of information sharing is between P&G and Wal-Mart. Wal-Mart provides P&G access to sales information on every item P&G makes for Wal-Mart. The information is collected by P&G on a daily basis from every Wal-Mart store, and P&G uses the information to manage inventory replenishment for Wal-Mart. By monitoring the inventory level of each P&G item in every Wal-Mart store, P&G knows when the inventories fall below the threshold that triggers a shipment. All this is done electronically. The benefit for P&G is accurate demand information; the benefit for Wal-Mart is adequate inventory. P&G has similar agreements with other major retailers. For more on Wal-Mart, see Staff (2004).

Retailer–Supplier Collaboration: Target Corporation

Target Corporation (targetcorp.com) is a large retail conglomerate. It conducts EC activities with about 20,000 trading partners. In 1998, then operating under the name Dayton-Hudson Corporation, the company established an extranet-based system for those partners that were not connected to its VAN-based EDI. The extranet enabled the company not only to reach many more partners but also to use many applications not available on the traditional EDI. The system (based on GE's InterBusiness Partner Extranet platform, geis.com) enabled the company to streamline its communications and collaboration with suppliers. It also allowed the company's business customers to create personalized Web pages that were accessible via either the Internet or GE's private VAN, as shown in Exhibit 6.6. Target now has a Web site called Partners Online (partnersonline.com), which it uses to communicate with and provide an enormous amount of information to its partners.

Reduction of Design Cycle Time: Clarion Malaysia

Clarion Malaysia, part of the global company the Clarion Group, employs approximately 700 people in Malaysia. It manufactures audio electronic systems for cars. Over the years, the Clarion Group has developed an excellent reputation first for car radios (it produced Japan's first car radio in 1951) and more recently for offering a range of audiovisual, multimedia, car navigation, telematics, and automotive electronic

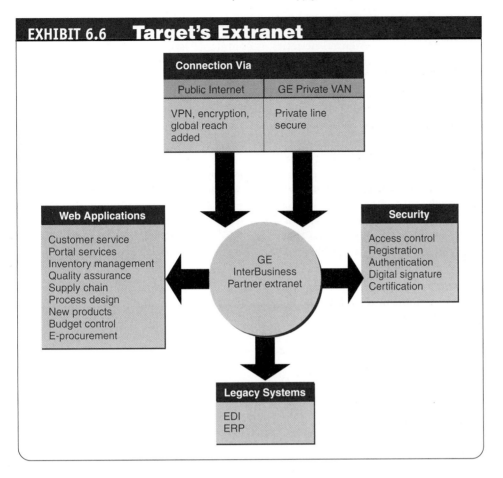

EXHIBIT 6.6   Target's Extranet

Connection Via	
Public Internet	GE Private VAN
VPN, encryption, global reach added	Private line secure

Web Applications
Customer service
Portal services
Inventory management
Quality assurance
Supply chain
Process design
New products
Budget control
E-procurement

GE InterBusiness Partner extranet

Security
Access control
Registration
Authentication
Digital signature
Certification

Legacy Systems
EDI
ERP

components. Approximately 60 percent of its sales come from installing Clarion OEM systems in a range of cars, including Ford, GM, Honda, Mazda, Nissan, BMW, and most of the European manufacturers.

In an increasingly global and competitive market, Clarion recognized a need to improve product innovation, time-to-market, customer loyalty, and profitability. It aimed to align itself more closely with its customers' R&D processes and to dramatically cut lead times through more efficient and effective supply chains, thus forming the basis of strong partnerships with car manufacturers worldwide through outstanding business performance. It also recognized a need to understand collaborative projects with the auto manufacturers in terms of product development and delivery, quality control, and cost management. It also sought to protect its traditional markets in North America, Europe, and Japan while acquiring new customers in the burgeoning markets in China and other ASEAN countries.

Working with IBM through the implementation of CAD systems and collaborative product life cycle management technologies, Clarion has slashed its time-to-market from 14 months to about 9 months, while at the same time improving the quality of the products because more time can be spent in yielding superior designs. The application of the latest information technology has also supported much closer cooperation with and responsiveness to customers throughout the design process, better use of materials through the deployment of 3D modeling, and a 60 percent reduction in tooling preparation time (Clarion Group 2006 and *IBM.com* 2006b).

BARRIERS TO C-COMMERCE

Despite the many potential benefits, c-commerce is moving ahead fairly slowly, and reports in the media and other business publications have been somewhat hyped. Some studies have suggested that most organizations have achieved moderate levels of collaboration (parties can view one another's databases and engage in electronic exchanges of information, but high automated exchanges or tight integration of systems and databases is not the norm). Collaboration is most common in the high-tech manufacturing, financial services, and telecommunications industries (*NerveWire* 2002). Reasons cited in various studies for lack of collaboration include technical reasons involving a lack of internal integration, standards, and networks; security and privacy concerns, and some distrust over who has access to and control of information stored in a partner's database; internal resistance to information sharing and to new approaches; and lack of internal skills to conduct c-commerce (Schram 2004). Gaining agreement on how to share costs and benefits can also prove problematic (*NerveWire* 2002).

A big stumbling block to the adoption of c-commerce has been the lack of defined and universally agreed upon standards. Even early initiatives such as CPFR (see next section) are still in their infancy. New approaches, such as the use of XML and its variants and the use of Web Services, could significantly lessen the problem of standards.

Sometimes collaboration is an organizational culture shock—people simply resist sharing. One reason for this is lack of trust. According to Gibson-Paul (2003), companies such as Boeing are grappling with the trust factor. Some techniques Gibson-Paul suggests to increase trust include starting small (e.g., synchronizing one type of sales data), picking projects that are likely to provide a quick return on investment for both sides, meeting face-to-face in the beginning of a collaboration, and showing the benefits of collaboration to all parties. Despite an initial lack of trust, if potential collaborators judge the benefits of collaboration to be sufficient and distributed fairly among collaborators, they will be more eager to join in.

Finally, global collaboration involves all of the above potential barriers and more. For more on c-commerce barriers, see Schrage (2004).

Specialized c-commerce software tools will break down some of the barriers to c-commerce (see Section 6.8). In addition, as companies learn more about the major benefits of c-commerce—such as smoothing the supply chain, reducing inventories and operating costs, and increasing customer satisfaction and the competitive edge—it is expected that more will rush to jump on the c-commerce bandwagon.

C-commerce is a response to business pressure (Chapter 1). Let's examine the example of a global supply chain in the fashion retailing industry (Insights and Additions 6.1).

Section 6.4 ▶ REVIEW QUESTIONS

1. Define c-commerce.
2. List the major types of c-commerce.
3. Describe some examples of c-commerce.
4. Define collaborative networks and distinguish them from traditional supply chain collaboration.
5. Describe KM–collaboration relationships.
6. List some major barriers to c-commerce. How might these limitations be overcome?
7. How might collaboration support improve industry supply chains?

Insights and Additions 6.1 Using EC in the Retail Industry to Reduce Time and Cost

Retailers, especially those dealing with fashion clothing (apparel), must deal with difficult environmental pressures (Chapter 1). Specifically, they must deliver products very quickly to their stores while cutting costs at the same time. In many cases, cost-cutting is done by moving production to Asia. This means creating a global supply chain because the major retailers are located mostly in Europe and the United States.

The fashion retail supply chain can be complex and long because it includes numerous functions—product design, merchandiser input, procurement of raw materials, manufacturing, and distribution. Therefore, communication and collaboration are critical. If lead time is not compressed, the risk of the product being too late on the shelf or obsolete is increased. All of this is done in an environment in which customer demand changes rapidly. If a retailer is too slow to react, store shelves will be stocked with uninspired fashions—resulting in substantial markdowns and anemic sales growth. As mentioned earlier in this chapter, demand forecasting can be very difficult.

Many retailers have implemented sourcing initiatives such as just-in-time (JIT) manufacturing, quick response (QR), efficient consumer response (ECR), and fast-moving consumer goods (FMCG). However, many retailers are still in trouble. Unfortunately, most solutions involve two contradicting factors: increasing speed and reducing or holding costs. If a company can do both simultaneously, it will be a winner. To do both, a company must change business processes and possibly look to adopt a range of EC tools and other information systems. Changes in business processes may include component-based product design, e-sourcing, and supply chain improvements, all of which are supported electronically.

For example, Web-enabled planning, execution, and optimization tools improve data availability and boost collaborative efforts between retail and brand managers and their suppliers. Product development management (PDM) software allows brand managers to conduct online "what-if" scenarios relating to product design. To expedite cycle time, tools from companies such as Freeborders (*freeborders.com*), Logility (*logility.com*), New Generation Computing (*ngcsoftware.com*), can be utilized. These tools relate demand forecast to supply forecast and support planning in an uncertain environment from an enterprise wide perspective. For example, using optimization techniques, the tools enable performance of supply chain activities in parallel.

These solutions usually are limited to one segment of the internal supply chain. Unfortunately, this may not be sufficient because the supply chain crosses numerous functions, including product design, merchandiser's input, raw material procurement, manufacturing, and distribution. Therefore, collaboration and communication are needed to supplement these tools.

To enhance collaboration and communication, retailers can implement Web-based collaborative product design (CPD) solutions. With CPD tools, different people can work on the same design at the same or different times, from different locations. Yet another set of tools enables brand managers to build an item's design into a system and generate all of the cutting patterns and distribute them to manufacturers in seconds. A major factor in the success of all of these tools is partnership and collaboration. For details, see Reda (2003).

The fashion retail supply chain poses some unique and very challenging decisions for managers, and the adoption of appropriate technologies to support such supply chains is obviously critical. However, some fashion retailers are achieving extraordinary levels of success and are the envy of nearly all other players in this industry, yet have not adopted all the prescriptions we have detailed here. Zara (*zara.com*) is one such example. An examination of Zara and a consideration of how it has achieved success is detailed in Online File W6.4.

6.5 COLLABORATIVE PLANNING, CPFR, AND COLLABORATIVE DESIGN

In *collaborative planning*, business partners—manufacturers, suppliers, distribution partners, and other partners—create initial demand (or sales) forecasts, provide changes as necessary, and share information, such as actual sales, and their own forecasts. Thus, all parties work according to a unified schedule aligned to a common view, and all have access to order and forecast performance that is globally visible through electronic links. Schedule, order, or product changes trigger immediate adjustments to all parties' schedules.

Collaborative planning is designed to synchronize production and distribution plans and product flows, optimize resource utilization over an expanded capacity base, increase customer responsiveness, and reduce inventories. Collaborative planning is a necessity in e-SCM (see Ireland and Crum 2005 and vics.org/committees/cpfr). The planning process is difficult because it involves multiple parties and activities. This section examines several aspects of collaborative planning and collaborative design.

COLLABORATIVE PLANNING, FORECASTING, AND REPLENISHMENT (CPFR)

collaborative planning, forecasting, and replenishment (CPFR)
Project in which suppliers and retailers collaborate in their planning and demand forecasting to optimize flow of materials along the supply chain.

Collaborative planning, forecasting, and replenishment (CPFR) is a business practice in which suppliers and retailers collaborate in planning and demand forecasting in order to ensure that members of the supply chain will have the right amount of raw materials and finished goods when they need them. The goal of CPFR is to streamline product flow from manufacturing plants all the way to customers' homes. Large manufacturers of consumer goods, such as Warner-Lambert (WL), have superb supply chains resulting from their use of CPFR.

As part of a pilot project, WL shared strategic plans, performance data, and market insight with Wal-Mart. The company realized that it could benefit from Wal-Mart's market knowledge, just as Wal-Mart could benefit from WL's product knowledge. In CPFR, trading partners collaborate on making *demand forecasts*. Using CPFR, WL increased its products' shelf-fill rate (the extent to which a store's shelves are fully stocked) from 87 percent to 98 percent, earning the company about $8 million a year in additional sales.

When implementing a CPFR process, the collaborators agree on a standard process, shown in Exhibit 6.7. The process ends with an order forecast. CPFR provides a

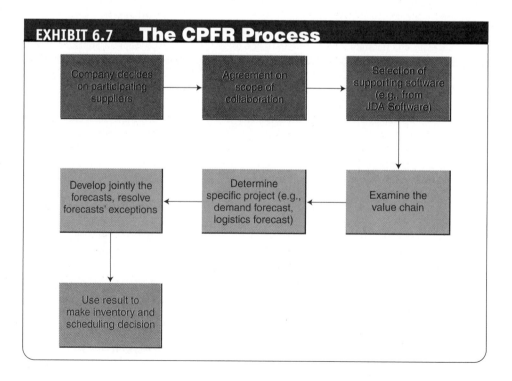

EXHIBIT 6.7   The CPFR Process

Company decides on participating suppliers → Agreement on scope of collaboration → Selection of supporting software (e.g., from JDA Software)

Develop jointly the forecasts, resolve forecasts' exceptions ← Determine specific project (e.g., demand forecast, logistics forecast) ← Examine the value chain

Use result to make inventory and scheduling decision

standard framework for collaborative planning. Retailers and vendors determine the "rules of engagement," such as how often and at what level information will be provided. Typically, they share greater amounts of more detailed information, such as promotion schedules and item point-of-sale history, and use store-level expectations as the basis for all forecasts.

Besides working together to develop production plans and forecasts for stock replenishment, suppliers and retailers also coordinate the related logistics activities (such as shipment or warehousing) using a common *language standard* and new information methodologies (Ireland and Bruce 2000).

The CPFR strategy has been driven by Wal-Mart and various benchmarking partners. After a successful pilot between Wal-Mart and Warner-Lambert involving Listerine products, a VICS (Voluntary Interindustry Commerce Standards) subcommittee was established to develop the proposed CPFR standard for the participating retailing industries (Wal-Mart's suppliers). An interesting application of CPFR is that of West Marine presented in Case 6.4.

CASE 6.4
EC Application
WEST MARINE: A CPFR SUCCESS STORY

West Marine is the largest boating-supply company in the United States. It has 372 stores in 38 states, Puerto Rico, and Canada and annual sales of $685 million. The company sells more than 50,000 different products, ranging from stainless-steel propellers and anchors to life jackets and wet suits, through its stores, Web site, catalog, and commercial sales arm.

West Marine has a dramatic story when it comes to its effective supply chain, which was guided and directed through its deep, intensive, and effective implementation of CPFR. West Marine is now regarded as having a showcase CPFR implementation; however, it was not always that way.

In 1997, West Marine acquired its East Coast competitor E&B Marine. As a result of the challenges of integrating the two companies, sales fell by almost 8 percent, and during the peak season out-of-stock situations rose by more than 12 percent over the previous year. Income dropped from $15 million in 1997 to little more than $1 million in 1998.

The situation was quite different when in 2003 West Marine purchased its largest competitor, BoatUS. West Marine successfully integrated BoatUS's distribution center in just 30 days. BoatUS's in-store systems were integrated into West Marine in just under 60 days. Further, supply chain performance and the bottom-line were not affected.

So why was this second acquisition so much smoother? The difference was that by 2003 the company had an effective IT-enabled supply chain management system driven by CPFR.

In reviewing the CPFR implementation in West Marine, it is clear that a key success factor was West Marine's commitment to technology enablement. Through the CPFR information systems, data such as seasonal forecasts, promotional stock levels, and future assortment changes are calculated automatically. Joint forecasting and order fulfillment are enabled by information systems that are suitably integrated between supply chain partners. As many similar case studies attest, such information sharing through integrated supply chain systems is one factor in successful supply chain management.

However, West Marine's successful CPFR implementation was not simply about the technology. Significant energy and resources were devoted to collaboration among the key supply chain personnel in West Marine and its supply chain partners. Joint skills and knowledge were developed along with the key elements of trust and joint understanding. These elements were built through joint education and training sessions as well as through the standard CPFR joint planning and forecasting sessions.

West Marine's CPFR program now involves 200 suppliers and more than 20,000 stock items, representing more than 90 percent of West Marine's procurement spending. Further, more than 70 of West Marine's top suppliers load West Marine's order forecasts directly into their production planning systems. In-stock rates at West Marine stores are well over 90 percent, forecast accuracy

(continued)

CASE 6.4   *(continued)*

stands at 85 percent, and on-time shipments are now consistently better than 80 percent. Summing up West Marine's collaborative supply chain journey using CPFR, Senior Vice President of Planning and Replenishment Larry Smith, states, "The results, we believe, speak for themselves."

Sources: Compiled from Lee and Denend (2005) and Smith (2006).

Questions

1. What were the major elements of West Marine's CPFR success?
2. What were the benefits of the CPFR implementation for West Marine?

For more on the benefits of CPFR, see cpfr.org/cpfr_pdf/index.html. Also, for comprehensive coverage, see Industry Directions (2000).

ADVANCED PLANNING AND SCHEDULING

advanced planning and scheduling (APS) systems
Programs that use algorithms to identify optimal solutions to complex planning problems that are bound by constraints.

Advanced planning and scheduling (APS) systems are math-based programs that identify optimal solutions to complex planning problems that are bound by constraints, such as limited machine capacity or labor. Using algorithms (such as linear programming), these systems are able to solve a wide range of problems, from operational (e.g., daily schedule) to strategic (e.g., network optimization). For examples, see Gregory (2004).

Basically, APS supplements ERP in revolutionizing a manufacturing or distribution firm's supply chain, providing a seamless flow of order fulfillment information from consumers to suppliers. It helps integrate ERP, CRM, SFA, KM, and more, enabling collaborative fulfillment and an integrated EC strategy.

PRODUCT LIFE CYCLE MANAGEMENT

product lifecycle management (PLM)
Business strategy that enables manufacturers to control and share product-related data as part of product design and development efforts.

Product lifecycle management (PLM) is a business strategy that enables manufacturers to control and share product-related data as part of product design and development efforts and in support of supply chain operations (en.wikipedia.org/wiki/Product_Lifecycle_Management, *IBM.com* 2008). Internet and other new technologies can automate the *collaborative aspects* of product development that even within one company can prove tedious and time consuming if not automated.

PLM can have a significant beneficial impact in engineering change, cycle time, design reuse, and engineering productivity. Studies have shown that electronic-based collaboration can reduce product costs by 20 percent and travel expenses by 80 percent, as well as significantly reduce costs associated with product-change management. Moreover, an explosion of new products that have minimal life cycles, as well as increasing complexity in supply chain management, are driving the need for PLM.

PLM tools are offered by SAP (MYSAP PLM, see Buxmann et al. 2004), Matrix One, EDS, PTC, Dassault Systems, and IBM (IBM PLM).

SUPPORTING JOINT DESIGN

Collaborative efforts are common in joint design, as illustrated in the Boeing opening case. This is one of the oldest areas of electronic collaboration, which is becoming even more popular due to EC tools, as discussed in Online File W6.5 and in the Boeing opening case.

1. Define collaborative planning.
2. Define CPFR and describe its advantages.
3. Describe APS efforts.
4. Describe PLM.

6.6 SUPPLY CHAIN INTEGRATION

Today, many business experts consider that the effective way to view contemporary business is that supply chains compete with other supply chains (Bendoly et al. 2004). This is a more insightful way of assessing business competitiveness than viewing competition as being between individual companies. Thus, supply chains from the suppliers' suppliers to the customers' customers need to be effective and efficient when viewed as a whole and, therefore, should be jointly planned and designed for overall optimality by all of the supply chain partners. Further, the supply chain needs to be operationally integrated so that procurement activities link seamlessly to order management activities, inventory activities link seamlessly to manufacturing activities, and so on. This implies attention to business process design and management that includes not only organizational business process redesign but also *interorganizational* business process redesign (Jeston and Nelis 2006).

Within each organization in the supply chain, the primary value chain activities of inbound logistics, production, and outbound logistics must be integrated with supporting value chain activities such as marketing, customer service, after sales service, procurement, and product design. Further, outsourced elements of the primary value chain need to be integrated efficiently and effectively with the organization's primary value chain activities.

HOW INFORMATION SYSTEMS ARE INTEGRATED

The integration issue can be divided into two parts: internal integration and integration with business partners. Internal integration includes connecting applications with databases and with each other and connecting customer-facing applications (front end) with order fulfillment and the functional information systems (back end). Internal integration is now commonly achieved through the implementation of an ERP and/or Web Services systems. Integration with business partners connects an organization's systems with those of its external business partners; for example, a company's ordering system to its suppliers' fulfillment systems.

Where a company has implemented an ERP system, it is necessary to connect the EC applications to the ERP system (see Siau and Tian 2004). An ERP system automates the flow of routine and repetitive information, such as submission of purchasing orders, billing, and inventory management. An example of the integration of EC applications with an ERP system is provided in Online File W6.6. Increasingly, EC applications are incorporated into an ERP system's basic functionality.

ENABLING INTEGRATION AND THE ROLE OF STANDARDS AND WEB SERVICES

Web Services is an architecture that enables the assembly of distributed applications from software services and ties them together. Integrating EC systems can be a complex task. As described in Online Chapter 14, integration involves connectivity, compatibility, security, and scalability. In addition, applications, data, processes, and interfaces must be integrated. Finally, a major difficulty is the connection of Web-based systems with legacy systems.

Web Services
An architecture enabling assembly of distributed applications from software services and tying them together.

To ease the task of integration, vendors have developed integration methodologies and special software called *middleware* (see Online Chapter 14). In addition, major efforts are being undertaken to develop standards and protocols that will facilitate integration, such as XML. The topic of Web Services, one of the major goals of which is to facilitate seamless integration, is discussed in detail in Online Chapter 14.

INTEGRATION ALONG THE EXTENDED SUPPLY CHAIN

The discussion in Insights and Additions 6.2 provides an illustration of information integration along the extended supply chain—all the way from raw material to the customer's door. Such integration is possible with second-generation ERP systems. Second-generation ERP systems include increasing amounts of SCM and CRM functionality, along with the internal ERP functionality.

A particular technology used in external supply chain integration is EDI. Large corporations have for some years used EDI to support their collaboration with partners. Increasingly, EDI is becoming Internet based.

Insights and Additions 6.2   Seamless Integration of Business Partners' Systems

In Chapter 5, we raised the issue of B2B integration and some of the methods and standards used. One also can use these standards and methods, as well as some special tools that we describe here, to facilitate integration.

Retailers, such as Costco, Wal-Mart, QVC, Sears, Target, and Staples need to talk to their business partners in the "same language." They want to do so without learning "foreign" languages that may be used by their partners' systems. Those different languages are "translated" using special integration software and order management services from CommerceHub (*commercehub.com*). The company's translation platform enables retailers to electronically integrate with all of their suppliers, regardless of differing systems and incompatibilities. In addition to connectivity, the software provides real-time visibility and control over transactions. This enables better performance at a reduced cost.

According to Seideman (2004), QVC and its 200 suppliers tap into CommerceHub's universal translator instead of making separate links. The suppliers can be connected to QVC and to other retailers.

Companies that use traditional EDI have problems if their partners use different EDI standards or messages. Also, EDI runs on expensive VANs and is focused strictly on transactions. CommerceHub's service overcomes traditional EDI deficiencies. CommerceHub's software runs on Web EDI (see Online File W5.4), which is much cheaper, more flexible, and more capable than traditional EDI. The software

also enables performance and expense monitoring, finds abnormalities, and solves order fulfillment problems.

A food distributor, Michael Foods, is using Sterling Commerce's (*sterlingcommerce.com*) Gentran Integration Suite to provide communication and collaboration when it deals with retailers such as Wal-Mart. Michael Foods uses collaboration tools and data synchronization to provide retail partners with assurance that products flow through the supply chain efficiently. The Gentran suite works with the EDI that is used by Michael Food and large retailers, but it also can accommodate new integration standards (e.g., ebXML, Web Services). The business partners can maintain their existing business processes and communication languages.

For example, in 2003 Michael Foods had to comply with Wal-Mart's requirement of moving to *AS2 Communication* (a new B2B protocol). Gentran Integration Suite made the transfer easy and inexpensive. Here is how it works: When a retail customer sends a purchase order EDI data file to Michael Foods, Gentran pulls the order and "wraps" it with the proper Internet elements to ensure security. It then translates the data file into the AS2 protocol and routes the order as a B2B file to the appropriate place at Michael Foods. There, the order is processed and fulfilled quickly and with fewer data errors. For details, see Amato-McCoy (2004).

Sources: Amato-McCoy (2004), Seideman (2004), *commercehub. com* (accessed January 2008), and *sterlingcommerce.com* (accessed January 2008).

As an example of a corporation making extensive use of EDI, one can look at Boeing, which relies on hundreds of internal and external suppliers in dozens of different countries for the several million components needed to build a large airplane. Boeing is using EDI and other systems (e.g., PART, see Online File W5.5) to facilitate collaboration with its partners. For more information and examples, see Davenport and Brooks (2004).

Section 6.6 ▶ REVIEW QUESTIONS

1. Describe internal and external integration.
2. Explain the need to connect to an ERP system.
3. Describe the need for integrating standards and methodologies.

6.7 CORPORATE (ENTERPRISE) PORTALS

Portals and corporate portals were defined in Chapter 2. Corporate portals facilitate collaboration with suppliers, customers, employees, and others. This section provides in-depth coverage of corporate portals, including their support of collaboration and business process management.

CORPORATE PORTALS: AN OVERVIEW

A **corporate (enterprise) portal** is a gateway to a corporate Web site that enables communication, collaboration, and access to company information. Kounadis (2000) more formally defines a corporate portal as a personalized, single point of access through a Web browser to critical business information located inside and outside of an organization. In contrast with commercial portals such as Yahoo! and MSN, which are gateways to general information on the Internet, corporate portals provide a single point of access to information and applications available on the intranets and extranets of a specific organization. Companies may have separate portals for outsiders and for insiders. One of the most pressing reasons for adopting modern portal technologies is to build a framework to host a variety of Web applications, each of which may serve different and distinct audiences and support differing requirements and preferences (BEA Systems 2006).

corporate (enterprise) portal
A gateway for entering a corporate Web site, enabling communication, collaboration, and access to company information.

Corporate portals offer employees, business partners, and customers an organized focal point for their interactions with the firm. Through the portal, these people can have structured and personalized access to information across large, multiple, and disparate enterprise information systems, as well as the Internet. A schematic view of a corporate portal is provided in Exhibit 6.8.

Many large organizations are already implementing corporate portals. The reasons for doing so are to cut costs, to free up time for busy executives and managers, and to add to the bottom line. Corporate portals are especially popular in large corporations, as shown in Insights and Additions 6.3.

TYPES OF CORPORATE PORTALS

Corporate portals are either generic or functional. Generic portals are defined by their audience (e.g., suppliers, employees). Functional portals are defined by the functionalities they offer. Portals are popular both in the private and the public sectors. See BEA Systems (2006) for an interesting array of both generic and functional portal applications in both the public and private sectors.

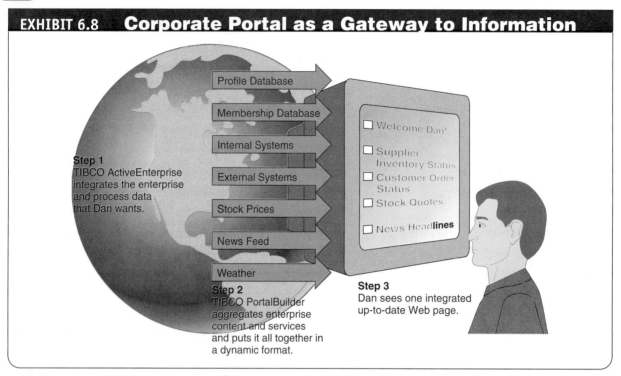

EXHIBIT 6.8   Corporate Portal as a Gateway to Information

Step 1
TIBCO ActiveEnterprise integrates the enterprise and process data that Dan wants.

Profile Database
Membership Database
Internal Systems
External Systems
Stock Prices
News Feed
Weather

Step 2
TIBCO PortalBuilder aggregates enterprise content and services and puts it all together in a dynamic format.

Step 3
Dan sees one integrated up-to-date Web page.

- Welcome Dan'
- Supplier Inventory Status
- Customer Order Status
- Stock Quotes
- News Headlines

Source: Courtesy of TIBCO Software, Inc., *www.tibco.com*.

Types of Generic Portals

The following generic types of portals can be found in organizations.

Portals for Suppliers and Other Partners. Using such portals, suppliers can manage their own inventories online. They can view what they sold to the portal owner and for how much. They can see the inventory levels of the portal owner and send material and supplies when they see that a reorder level is reached, and they can collaborate with corporate buyers and other staff.

Insights and Additions 6.3   Some Large-Company Corporate Portals

Four examples of corporate portals—P&G, DuPont, Staples, and Redback Networks—are presented here to demonstrate how companies use corporate portals.

P&G

The IT division of P&G developed a system for sharing documents and information over the company's intranet. The scope of this system later expanded into a global knowledge catalog to support the information needs of all 98,000 P&G employees worldwide. Although the system helped in providing required information, it also led to

information overload. To solve this problem, P&G developed a corporate portal that provides personalized information to each employee.

P&G's corporate portal, implemented by Plumtree (*plumtree.com*, now a subsidiary of BEA Systems), provides P&G's employees with marketing, product, and strategic information and with industry news documents numbering over 1 million Web pages. The corporate portal can be accessed through a Web browser without having to navigate through all of the different divisions' Web sites.

(continued)

Insights and Additions 6.3 *(continued)*

Employees can gain access to the required information through customized preset views of various information sources and links to other up-to-date information.

DuPont

DuPont implemented an internal portal to organize millions of pages of scientific information stored in information systems throughout the company. The initial version of the portal was intended for daily use by over 550 employees to record product orders, retrieve progress reports for research products, and access customer-tracking information. Today, DuPont uses the portal for its 55,000 employees in 30 business units in 70 countries.

Staples

The corporate portal for Staples, an office supply company, was launched in February 2000. It was immediately used by the company's 3,000 executives, knowledge workers, and store managers; by 2003, over 10,000 users were registered, with the objective to reach most employees by 2005. The portal serves as the interface to Staples' business processes and applications. It offers e-mail, scheduling, headlines on articles about the competition, new-product information, internal news, job postings, and newsletters. The portal is used by top management as well as by managers of contracts, procurement, sales and marketing, human resources, and retail stores and by the company's three B2B Web sites.

Redback Networks

A corporate enterprise portal implementation that is vital to the company's business performance is that of Redback Networks. Redback is meeting the growing demand for its computer networking products via a virtual manufacturing approach that leverages outsourcing to trusted partners and frees the company to focus on sales and product design. Redback's successful manufacturing strategy is based on its very creative and robust partnering strategy and the ICT infrastructure that connects Redback with its partners. Redback's connectivity includes three key portals: the Customer Portal, which connects the company with its customers; the Supplier Portal, which connects it with partners and suppliers; and the Employee Portal for its 600-plus employees.

Sources: Compiled from Konicki (2001), Regan (2006), and from press releases from the companies described (2002–2006).

An example of a partners' portal is that of Samsung Electronic America's Digital IT. The company must keep in touch with 110,000 resellers and distributors. As part of its PRM, Samsung developed a portal that enables it to personalize relationships with each partner (e.g., conduct promotions, provide special pricing, etc.). The portal helped to increase sales by 30 percent; related expenses dropped by 25 percent. For details, see Schneider (2004).

Customer Portals. Portals for customers can serve both businesses and individual customers. Customers can use these *customer-facing portals* to view products and services and to place orders, which they can later track. They can view their own accounts and see what is going on with their accounts in almost real time. They can pay for products and services and arrange for warranties and deliveries.

Employee Portals. Such portals are used for training, dissemination of company news and information, discussion groups, and more. Employee portals also are used for self-service activities, mainly in the human resources area (e.g., change of address forms, tax withholding forms, expense reports, class registration, and tuition reimbursement forms). Employees' portals are sometimes bundled with supervisors' portals in what are known as workforce portals (e.g., Workbrain Enterprise Workforce Management, workbrain.com).

Executive and Supervisor Portals. These portals enable managers and supervisors to control the entire workforce management process—from budgeting to workforce scheduling. For example, Pharmacia (a Pfizer company) built a portal for its executives and managers worldwide, the Global Field Force Action Planner, which provides a single, worldwide view of the company's finances and performance. Business goals and sales figures are readily available on a consistent and transparent basis, allowing corporate management to evaluate and support field offices more effectively. Country managers also can share best practices with their peers and learn from other action plans, helping them to make better decisions.

mobile portals
Portals accessible via mobile devices, especially cell phones and PDAs.

Mobile Portals. **Mobile portals** are portals accessible via mobile devices, especially cell phones and PDAs. Most mobile portals are noncorporate information portals (i.e., they are commercial portals), such as DoCoMo's i-mode. (See the description of i-mode in Chapter 9.) Eventually, large corporations will introduce mobile corporate portals. Alternatively, they will offer access to their regular portals from wireless devices, which many already do (e.g., major airlines, banks, and retailers).

The Functionalities of Portals

information portals
Portals that store data and enable users to navigate and query the data.

collaborative portals
Portals that enable collaboration.

Whoever their audience, the functionalities of portals range from simple **information portals** that store data and enable users to navigate and query those data to sophisticated **collaborative portals** that enable collaboration.

Several types of functional portals exist: *Business intelligence portals* are used mostly by middle- and top-level executives and analysts to conduct business analyses and decision-support activities (Ferguson 2001). For example, a business intelligence portal might be used to generate ad hoc reports or to conduct a risk analysis. *Intranet portals* are used mostly by employees for managing fringe benefits and for self-training (Ferguson 2001). *Knowledge portals* are used for collecting knowledge from employees and for disseminating collected knowledge. (For an example of a business intelligence and knowledge management portal, see Kesner 2003.)

CORPORATE PORTAL APPLICATIONS

According to a 2002 Delphi Group survey (*DM Review* 2003), the top portal applications, in decreasing order of importance, are as follows: knowledge bases and learning tools; business process support; customer-facing (frontline) sales, marketing, and services; collaboration and project support; access to data from disparate corporate systems; personalized pages for various users; effective search and indexing tools; security applications; best practices and lessons learned; directories and bulletin boards; identification of experts; news; and Internet access.

Exhibit 6.9 depicts a corporate portal framework. This framework illustrates the features and capabilities required to support various organizational applications.

JUSTIFYING PORTALS

As with any IT project, management needs to be able to justify the development and use of a corporate portal by comparing its cost with its benefits. Some of the tangible benefits from investment in portal technology include revenue growth, call center productivity increases, and increased customer loyalty and retention. Adopters also report much improved trading relationships with suppliers and business partners (BEA Systems 2006). However, most of the benefits of portals are *intangible*. For example, Reda (2002) claims that employee portals have the potential to fundamentally change and improve employer–employee relationships—a desirable benefit, although somewhat difficult to measure. According to Ferguson (2001), portals offer the following benefits that are difficult to quantify:

▶ They offer a simple user interface for finding and navigating content via a browser.

▶ They improve access to business content and increase the number of business users who can access information, applications, and people.

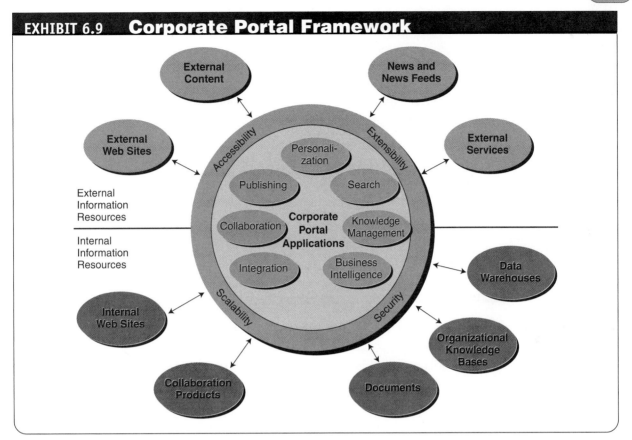

EXHIBIT 6.9   Corporate Portal Framework

Source: Compiled by N. Bolloju, City University of Hong Kong, from Aneja et al. (2000) and Koundadis (2000).

▶ They offer access to common business applications from anywhere in a geographically distributed enterprise and beyond. Using Web-enabled mobile or wireless devices, content can be accessed from anywhere.

▶ They offer the opportunity to use platform-independent software (Java) and data (XML).

However, given that portals are relatively low-cost, low-risk devices, it is not surprising that they are being adopted by thousands of organizations worldwide. A formal approach to justifying portals is offered by Plumtree (2002), which devised a framework for assessing the ROI of portals. BEA Systems offers several white papers and examples on this topic at its Web site (bea.com). For methods of justifying portals and intangible benefits, see Chapter 12.

Section 6.7 ▶ REVIEW QUESTIONS

1. What is a corporate portal?
2. List the types of corporate portals.
3. List five applications of portals.
4. Discuss the issue of justifying enterprise portals.
5. List the major benefits of corporate portals.

6.8 COLLABORATION TOOLS

As mentioned earlier, collaboration, knowledge management, and e-commerce are all vital ingredients in improving the performance of supply chains. A large number of tools and methodologies also are available that facilitate e-collaboration. This section presents groupware and other collaboration-enabling tools. Workflow technologies are discussed in Online File W6.7.

GROUPWARE

groupware

Software products that use networks to support collaboration among groups of people who share a common task or goal.

Groupware refers to software products that support groups of people who share a common task or goal and collaborate on its accomplishment. These products provide a way for groups to share resources and opinions. Groupware implies the use of networks to connect people, even if they are in the same room. Many groupware products are available on the Internet or an intranet, enhancing the collaboration of a large number of people worldwide (e.g., see Henrie 2004).

A number of different approaches and technologies are available for the support of groups on the Internet. Groupware tools and applications that support collaboration and conferencing are listed in Exhibit 6.10.

Synchronous Versus Asynchronous Products

Notice that the features in Exhibit 6.10 may be *synchronous*, meaning that communication and collaboration are done in real time, or *asynchronous*, meaning that communication and collaboration are done by the participants at different times (e.g., by leaving a message on a bulletin board to be read and answered later), potentially from disparate locations. Web conferencing and instant messaging as well as Voice-over-Internet Protocol (VoIP) are associated with synchronous mode. Associated with asynchronous mode are online workspaces where participants can collaborate on joint designs or projects but work at different times. Vignette (vignette.com), Google (google.com), and Groove Networks (groove.net) allow users to set up online workspaces for sharing and storing documents. According to Henrie (2004), many of the tools offered by vendors are converging. This is done with the help of new technologies, such as VoIP.

Groupware products are either stand-alone products that support one task (such as e-mail) or integrated kits that include several tools (such as e-mail and screen sharing). In general, groupware technology products are fairly inexpensive and can be easily incorporated into existing information systems.

The Internet, intranets, extranets, and private communication lines provide the infrastructure needed for groupware. Most of the software products are Web based. The following describes some of the most common groupware collaboration tools.

Electronic Meeting Systems

An important area of virtual collaboration is electronic meetings. For decades, people have attempted to improve face-to-face meetings, which are known to have many potential dysfunctions. Initially, people attempted to better organize group meetings by using a facilitator and established procedures (known as *group dynamics*). Numerous attempts have been made to use information technologies to improve meetings conducted in one room (see Nunamaker et al. 1997 for examples). The advancement of Web-based systems opens the door for improved electronically supported **virtual meetings**, where members are in *different* locations and even in different countries. For example, online meetings and presentation tools are provided by WebEx (webex.com) and by GoToMeeting (gotomeeting.com).

virtual meetings

Online meetings whose members are in different locations, even in different countries.

EXHIBIT 6.10 Major Features in Collaboration and Conferencing Tools

General

- Built-in e-mail, messaging system, instant messaging
- Browser interface
- Joint Web-page creation
- Sharing of active hyperlinks
- File sharing (graphics, video, audio, or other)
- Built-in search functions (by topic or keyword)
- Workflow tools
- Use of corporate portals for communication, collaboration
- Shared screens
- Electronic decision rooms
- Peer-to-peer networks

Synchronous (same-time)

- Webinar
- Webcast
- Videoconferencing, multimedia conferencing
- Audioconferencing
- Shared whiteboard, smart whiteboard
- Text chart
- Brainstorming, polling (voting), and other decision support (consensus builder, scheduler)
- Instant messaging (chatting)

Asynchronous (different times)

- Threaded discussions
- Voice mail
- Users can receive/send e-mail, SMS
- Users can receive activity notification via e-mail
- Users can collapse/expand threads
- Users can sort messages (by date, author, or read/unread)
- Chat session logs
- Bulletin boards, discussion groups
- Use of blogs, wikis
- Web publishing
- Collaborative planning and/or design tools

One of the major benefits of electronic meeting systems are the dramatic reductions in costs associated with business travel (en.wikipedia.org/wiki/Conferencing). In addition, improvements in supporting technology, reductions in the price of the technology, and the acceptance of virtual meetings as a respected way of doing business are fueling their growth (see Austin et al. 2006).

Virtual meetings are supported by a variety of groupware tools, as will be shown in the remainder of this section. An important area is the support provided to decision making (see Online File W6.8).

Real-Time Collaboration Tools

The Internet, intranets, and extranets offer tremendous potential for real-time (synchronous) interaction for people working in groups. *Real-time collaboration (RTC) tools* help companies bridge time and space to make decisions and collaborate on projects. RTC tools support synchronous communication of graphical and text-based information. These tools are being used in distance training, product demonstrations, customer support, e-commerce, and sales applications. RTC tools can be purchased as stand-alone tools or used on a subscription basis (as offered by many vendors). Of special interest is the *Instant Messenger* tool that is used extensively in some companies (see Mamberto 2007) and can be used for teleconferencing as well (e.g., see messenger.yahoo.com).

Mobile Communication and Collaboration Platforms

With millions of employees on the road, it has become necessary to develop mobile support systems. Probably the most important one is mobile e-mail. Ginevan (2007) provides an assessment of the benefits and risks of mobile e-mail, including assessment of the major vendors, their groupware products, and integration platforms and vendors.

Web Collaboration

Web-based online collaboration is growing rapidly with support from most major vendors. For example, Lotus Sametime (from IBM) is an instant messaging system that is integrated with Web conferencing tools from WebDialogs connected with the Lotus Connections communications system. Other products include Microsoft's SharePoint, Cisco's WebEx, and Google's GAPE—a suite that includes instant messaging, e-mail, and related tools.

Electronic Teleconferencing

teleconferencing
The use of electronic communication that allows two or more people at different locations to have a simultaneous conference.

Teleconferencing is the use of electronic communication that enables two or more people at different locations to have a simultaneous conference. It is the simplest infrastructure for supporting a real-time virtual meeting. Several types of teleconferencing are possible. The oldest and simplest is a telephone conference call, wherein several people talk to each other from three or more locations. The biggest disadvantage of this is that it does not allow for face-to-face communication. Also, participants in one location cannot see highly detailed graphs, charts, and pictures at other locations. Although the latter disadvantage can be overcome by using a fax and scanning, this is a time-consuming, expensive, and frequently poor-quality process. One solution is video teleconferencing, in which participants can see each other, as well as the documents.

video teleconference
Virtual meeting in which participants in one location can see participants at other locations on a large screen or a desktop computer.

Video Teleconferencing. In a **video teleconference**, participants in one location can see participants at other locations. Dynamic pictures of the participants can appear on a large screen or on a desktop computer. Originally, video teleconferencing was the transmission of live, compressed TV sessions between two or more points. Today, video teleconferencing (or *videoconferencing*) is a digital technology capable of linking various types of computers across networks. Once conferences are digitized and transmitted over networks, they become a computer application.

data conferencing
Virtual meeting in which geographically dispersed groups work on documents together and exchange computer files during videoconferences.

With videoconferencing, participants can share data, voice, pictures, graphics, and animation. Data can be sent along with voice and video. Such **data conferencing** makes it possible to work on documents and to exchange computer files during videoconferences. This enables several geographically dispersed groups to work on the same project and to communicate by video simultaneously. Vendors of data conferencing tools include Microsoft, IBM (Lotus), NetSpoke, and WebEx.

Video teleconferencing offers various benefits. Two of them—providing the opportunity for face-to-face communication for individuals in different locations and supporting several types of media during conferencing—have already been discussed. Video teleconferencing may also improve employee productivity, cut travel costs, conserve the time and energy of key employees, and increase the speed of business processes (such as product development, contract negotiation, and customer service). It improves the efficiency and frequency of communications and saves an electronic record of a meeting, enabling specific parts of a meeting to be reconstructed for future purposes. Video teleconferencing also makes it possible to hold classes at different locations. Finally, the tool can be used to conduct meetings with business partners as well as to interview candidates for employment.

Web Conferencing. *Web conferencing* is conducted on the Internet for as few as two and for as many as thousands of people. It allows users to simultaneously view something on their computer screens, such as a sales presentation in Microsoft PowerPoint or a product drawing; interaction takes place via messaging or a simultaneous phone teleconference. Web conferencing is much cheaper than videoconferencing because it runs over the Internet.

The latest technological innovations support both B2B and B2C Web conferencing applications. For example, banks in Alaska use *video kiosks* in sparsely populated areas instead of building branches that will be underutilized. The video kiosks operate on the banks' intranet and provide videoconferencing equipment for face-to-face interactions. A variety of other communication tools, such as online polls, whiteboards, and question-and-answer boards may also be used. Such innovations can be used to educate staff members about a new product line or technology, to amplify a meeting with investors, or to walk a prospective client though an introductory presentation. People can use Web conferencing to view presentations, seminars, and lectures, and to collaborate on documents.

Web conferencing is becoming very popular. Almost all Web conferencing products provide whiteboarding and polling features and allow users to give presentations and demos and share applications. Popular Web conferencing products are Centra EMeeting, Genesys Meeting Center, Microsoft Office Live Meeting, and WebEx Meeting Center. Yahoo! messenger offers conferencing capabilities (see Team Assignment 5).

Voice-over-IP

Voice-over-IP (VoIP) refers to communication systems that transmit voice calls over Internet-Protocol–based networks. Corporations are moving their phone systems to Internet standards to cut costs and boost efficiency. Strategies for how to do this are described in Sturdevant (2004) and by Blickstein (2004). VoIP also is known as *Internet telephony*. Most browsers provide for VoIP capabilities. Users use their browsers to receive telephone calls initiated on the Internet (with a microphone and special VoIP software, which may be provided with the sender's browser). The market leader in VoIP is Skype, the world's fastest-growing Internet communication offering. Skype offers unlimited free voice, video, and instant messaging communication between users provided they also use the Skype software, which is available for free download over the Web (Skype.com 2007). VoIP is available in Yahoo! messenger and other instant messaging tools.

According to Intel (2005), the following are the benefits of VoIP communications.

For the business:

▶ Allows chief information officers to explore different deployment options for company's communications needs

▶ Lowers total cost of ownership through voice/data convergence

Voice-over-IP (VoIP)
Communication systems that transmit voice calls over Internet–Protocol-based networks.

- Lowers operational costs through use of integrated applications
- Reduces hardware requirements on the server side for certain applications (e.g., VoIP)
- Provides a holistic approach to security, enhanced by encryption and identity management
- Helps streamline workflows by empowering companies to communications-enable different business processes
- Enables optimized conferencing tools to replace business travel

For the user:

- Eliminates unwanted interruptions and unproductive actions by intelligently filtering communications
- Provides access to real-time presence information, which helps decisions get made faster
- Initiates ad hoc conferencing/collaboration sessions without the need to prearrange separate audio or videoconferencing bridges
- Enables participation in conferencing sessions quickly and easily via a variety of mobile devices

Interactive Whiteboards

Whiteboards are another type of groupware. Computer-based whiteboards work like real-world whiteboards with markers and erasers, except for one big difference: Instead of one person standing in front of a meeting room drawing on the whiteboard, all participants can join in. Throughout a meeting, each user can view and draw on a single document "pasted" onto the electronic whiteboard on a computer screen. Users can save digital whiteboarding sessions for future use. Some whiteboarding products let users insert graphics files that can be annotated by the group. Interactive whiteboards also enable the display of video clips, which can be frozen and then annotated and "cut" into PowerPoint presentations and the like.

Take, for example, an advertisement that needs to be cleared by a senior manager. Once the proposed ad has been scanned into a PC, both parties can see it on their screens. If the senior manager does not like something, she highlights what needs to be changed using a stylus pen. This tool makes communication between the two parties easier and clearer. The two parties also can share applications. For example, if party A works with Excel, party B does not have to have Excel in order to work with it in the whiteboarding tool.

Besides being used to support people working on the same task, whiteboards also are used for training and learning. An example of whiteboarding products is Digital Wall Display from 3M Corp. (3m.com). This tool is a multifunction whiteboard. It shows whatever is written on it, as well as anything—text, charts, still and moving pictures—that is stored in a computer and loaded onto the whiteboard. With a remote mouse, presenters or teachers can edit and move the material around on the touch-screen board. All of this, including audio, can be transmitted instantaneously to any connected board, anywhere in the world, making it useful for virtual, long-distance teaching or training. The system also is used for sharing research among colleagues.

screen-sharing software
Software that enables group members, even in different locations, to work on the same document, which is shown on the PC screen of each participant.

Screen Sharing

In collaborative work, members frequently are in different locations. Using **screen-sharing software**, group members can work on the same document, which is shown on the PC screen of each participant. For example, two authors can work on a single manuscript. One can suggest a correction and execute it so that the other author can view the change. Collaborators can work together on the same spreadsheet or on the resultant graphics. Changes can be done by using the keyboard or by touching the screen. This capability can expedite the design of products, the preparation of reports and bids, and the resolution of conflicts.

A special screen-sharing capability is offered by Groove Networks (groove.net). Its product enables the joint creation and editing of documents on a PC (see Team Assignment 1).

Instant Video

The spread of instant messaging and Internet telephony has naturally led to the idea of linking people via both voice and audio. Called *instant video*, the idea is for a kind of video chat room. It allows users to chat in real time and see the person(s) they are communicating with. A simple way to do this is to add video cameras to the participants' computers. A more sophisticated and better-quality approach is to integrate an existing online videoconferencing service with instant messaging software, creating a service that offers the online equivalent of a videophone.

This idea is still in the early stages. One instant video pioneer is CUworld (cuworld.com). Users get free software (CUworld 6.0) that can compress and decompress video signals sent over an online connection.

Integration and Groupware Suites

Because groupware technologies are computer based, with the same objectives of supporting group work, it makes sense to integrate them among themselves and/or with other computer based technologies. A *software suite* is created when several products are integrated into one system. Integrating several technologies can save time and money for users. For example, Polycom (polycom.com) is a market leader in combining video, voice, data, and Web conferencing capabilities into a single solution. Polycom has formed an alliance with Microsoft to deliver collaborative solutions across a range of communication devices and applications to allow participants to connect and share information both inside and between organizations worldwide. The alliance offers seamless real-time communication across a range of media, including video, instant messaging, business applications, business processes, Web Services, and Web collaboration.

Lotus Notes/Domino. The Lotus Notes/Domino suite includes a document management system, a distributed client/server database, a basis for intranet and e-commerce systems, and a communication support tool. It enhances real-time communications with asynchronous electronic connections (e.g., e-mail and other forms of messaging).

Lotus Notes provides online collaboration capabilities, workgroup e-mail, distributed databases, bulletin whiteboards, text editing, (electronic) document management, workflow capabilities, instant virtual meetings, application sharing, instant messaging, consensus building, voting, ranking, and various application development tools. All of these capabilities are integrated into one environment with a graphic-menu-based user interface. In 2007, Lotus added wikis, blogs, and other Web 2.0 tools to Domino Notes.

OTHER COLLABORATIVE TOOLS AND WIKIS

Many different collaborative tools are available. A sampler of these tools is provided in Online File W6.9. Consult that resource for information about collaborative tools in addition to those already discussed. Before closing this discussion of collaborative tools, however, we need to mention another tool—wikis (or wikilogs). Wikis, which were described in Chapter 2, enable people to work on the same files and documents, making changes in a very rapid way.

IMPLEMENTATION ISSUES FOR ONLINE COLLABORATION

This chapter has presented numerous online collaboration issues of one sort or another. The following are a few implementation issues that must be addressed when planning online collaboration. First, to connect business partners, an organization needs an effective collaborative environment. Such an environment is provided by groupware suites such as Lotus Notes/Domino or Cybozu Share360 (share360.com). Another issue is the need to connect collaborative tools with file management products on an organization's intranet. Two products that offer such connection capabilities are e/pop Web conferencing and online meeting software (wiredred.com) and eRoom's server (documentum.com).

In addition, protocols are required to create a truly collaborative environment. Protocols are needed to integrate different applications and for standardizing communication. One such protocol is WebDAV (Web Distributed Authoring and Versioning protocol; see webdav.org).

Finally, note that online collaboration is not a panacea for all occasions or all situations. Oftentimes, a face-to-face meeting is a must. People sometimes require the facial cues and the physical closeness that no computer system can currently provide. (A technology called *pervasive computing* attempts to remove some of these limitations by interpreting facial cues. For more, see Chapter 9.) However, face-to-face meetings may sometimes be improved by collaborative technologies, such as groupware, described earlier.

Section 6.8 ▶ REVIEW QUESTIONS

1. Define workflow systems and management.
2. Explain the types of workflow systems and the benefits of such systems.
3. List the major groupware tools.
4. Describe groupware and electronic meeting systems.
5. Describe the various types of electronic teleconferencing, including Web-based conferencing.
6. Describe whiteboards and screen sharing.
7. Describe integrated suites and their benefits.

MANAGERIAL ISSUES

Some managerial issues related to this chapter are as follows.

1. **How difficult is it to introduce e-collaboration?** Dealing with the technology may be the easy part. Tackling the behavioral changes needed within an organization and its trading partners may be the greater challenge. Change management requires an understanding of the new interdependencies being constructed and the new roles and responsibilities that must be adapted in order for the enterprise and its business partners to collaborate. Finally, e-collaboration costs money and needs to be justified. This may not be an easy task due to the intangible benefits involved.

2. **How much can be shared with business partners?** Can they be trusted? Many companies are sharing forecast data and actual sales data. But when it comes to allowing real-time access to product design, inventory, and ERP systems, there may be some hesitation. It is basically a question of trust. The more information that is shared, the better the collaboration. However, sharing information can lead to the giving away of trade secrets. In some cases, there is a cultural resistance against sharing (some employees do not like to share information even within their own organization).

The value of sharing needs to be carefully assessed against its risks.

3. **Who is in charge of our portal and intranet content?** Because content is created by many individuals, two potential risks exist. First, proprietary corporate information may not be secure enough, so unauthorized people may have access to it. Second, appropriate intranet "netiquette" must be maintained; otherwise unethical, or even illegal, behavior may develop. Therefore, managing content, including frequent updates, is a must (see Online Chapter 13).

4. **Who will design the corporate portal?** Corporate portals are the gateways to corporate information and knowledge. Appropriate portal design is a must, not only for easy and efficient navigation but also because portals portray the corporate image to employees and to business partners who are allowed access to it. Design of the corporate portal must be carefully thought out and approved by management.

5. **Should we conduct virtual meetings?** Virtual meetings can save time and money and if properly planned can bring as good or even better results than face-to-face meetings. Although not all meetings can be conducted online, many can. The supporting technology is getting cheaper and better with time.

SUMMARY

In this chapter, you learned about the following EC issues as they relate to the learning objectives.

1. **The e-supply chain, its characteristics, and its components.** Digitizing and automating the flow of information throughout the supply chain and managing it via the Web results in an entity called the *e-supply chain*. The major parts of the e-supply chain are the upstream (to suppliers), internal (in-house processes), and downstream (to distributors and customers) components. E-supply chain activities include replenishment, procurement, collaborative planning, collaborative design/development, e-logistics, and use of exchanges or supply webs—all of which can be Internet based.

2. **Supply chain problems and their causes.** The major supply chain problems are too large or too small inventories, lack of supplies or products when needed, the need for rush orders, deliveries of wrong materials or to wrong locations, and poor customer service. These problems result from uncertainties in various segments of the chain (e.g., in transportation), from mistrust of partners and a lack of collaboration and information sharing, and from difficulties in forecasting demand (e.g., the bullwhip effect). Also, lack of appropriate logistics infrastructure can result in problems.

3. **Solutions to supply chains problems provided by EC.** EC technologies automate and expedite order taking, speed order fulfillment, provide for e-payments, properly control inventories, provide for correct forecasting and thus better scheduling, and improve collaboration among supply chain partners. Of special interest is the emerging RFID and RuBee technologies that could revolutionize supply chain management.

4. **RFID Applications.** Replacing bar codes with RFID can greatly improve locating items along the supply chain quickly, help in taking inventory, reduce misplaced and stolen items, and expedite transportation. RFID has many other potential benefits that can be much larger as the cost of tags is reduced and privacy protection is assured. RFID could revolutionize supply chain management.

5. **C-commerce: Definitions and types.** Collaborative commerce (c-commerce) refers to a planned use of digital technology by business partners. It includes planning, designing, researching, managing, and servicing various partners and tasks, frequently along the supply chain. Collaborative commerce can be between different pairs of business partners or among many partners participating in a collaborative network.

6. **Collaborative planning and CPFR.** Collaborative planning concentrates on demand forecasting and on resource and activity planning along the supply chain. Collaborative planning tries to synchronize partners' activities. CPFR is a business

strategy that attempts to develop standard protocols and procedures for collaboration. Its goal is to improve demand forecasting by collaborative planning in order to ensure delivery of materials when needed. In addition to forecasting, collaboration in design is facilitated by IT, including groupware. Product lifecycle management (PLM) enables manufacturers to plan and control product-related information.

7. **Integration along the supply chain.** Integration of various applications within companies and between business partners is critical to the success of companies. To simplify integration, one can use special software as well as employ standards such as XML. Web Services is a promising new approach for facilitating integration.

8. **Types and roles of corporate portals.** The major types of corporate portals are those for suppliers, customers, employees, and supervisors. There also are mobile portals (accessed by wireless devices). Functional portals such as knowledge portals and business intelligence portals provide the gateway to specialized knowledge and decision making. Corporate portals provide for easy information access, communication, and collaboration.

9. **Collaborative tools.** Hundreds of different collaboration tools are available. The major groups of tools are workflow and groupware (including conferencing tools). In addition, specialized tools ranging from wikis to devices that facilitate product design also are available.

KEY TERMS

QUESTIONS FOR DISCUSSION

1. Define *e-supply chain*. In the light of your definition, discuss the difference between an IT-enabled supply chain and an e-supply chain.

2. Discuss the benefits of e-supply chains.

3. Does a company's supply chain include the activities involving the movement of materials and information within the company? Discuss the difference between a value chain, an extended value chain, and a supply chain.

4. Discuss the relationship between c-commerce and corporate portals.

5. Compare and contrast a commercial portal (such as Yahoo!) with a corporate portal.

6. Describe how the advent of the Internet has affected supply chain management. Include in your answer the contribution of the Internet to the following aspects and challenges:

  ▶ Globalization

  ▶ Outsourcing, including business process outsourcing

  ▶ Increasingly demanding customers

  ▶ Diminishing product life cycles

7. Discuss the importance of taking a holistic view of supply chain management rather than simply approaching supply chain management from a business process and IT viewpoint.

8. Discuss the major considerations that must be taken into account when implementing vendor-managed inventory (VMI).

9. Discuss the difference between a portal, a marketplace, and an e-hub. Do you think that there are any significant differences?

10. Explain the need for groupware to facilitate collaboration.

11. Discuss the relationship between portals and intranets at the same organization.

12. It is said that c-commerce signifies a move from a transaction focus to a relationship focus among supply chain members. Discuss.

13. Discuss the need for virtual meetings.

14. Discuss how CPFR can lead to more accurate forecasting and how it can resolve the bullwhip effect.

15. Describe the advantages of RFID over a regular bar code in light of supply chain management.

16. Compare a collaborative hub and a collaborative network.

INTERNET EXERCISES

1. Enter **ca.com/products** and register. Take the Clever Path Portal Test Drive. (Flash Player from Macromedia is required.) Then enter **ibm.com** and **bea.com**. Prepare a list of the major products available for building corporate portals.

2. Enter **bea.com**. Find the white papers about corporate portals and their justification. Prepare a report based on your findings.

3. Enter **doublediamondsoftware.com/product_overview.htm**. Identify all potential B2B applications and prepare a report about them.

4. Investigate the status of CPFR. Start at **vics.org/committees/cpfr**, **google.com**, and **yahoo.com**. Also enter **supply-chain.org** and find information about CPFR. Write a report on the status of CPFR.

5. Enter **mysap.com** and **bea.com** and find the key capabilities of their enterprise portals. List the benefits of using five of the capabilities of portals.

6. Enter **nokia.com**, **mdsi.com**, and **symbolic.com**. Identify the business-to-enterprise (B2E) products you find at these sites. Prepare a list of the different products.

7. Enter **i2.com** and review its products. Explain how some of the products facilitate collaboration.

8. Enter **collaborate.com** and read about recent issues related to collaboration. Prepare a report.

9. Enter **kolabora.com** or **mindjet.com**. Find out how collaboration is done. Summarize the benefits of this site to the participants.

10. Enter **vignette.com** or **cybozu.com** and read the company vision for collaborative commerce. Then view the demo. Explain in a report how the company facilitates c-commerce.

11. Enter **lotus.com** and find the collaboration-support products. How do these products support groups?

12. Enter **supplyworks.com** and **worldchain.com**. Examine the functionalities provided for supply chain improvements (the inventory management aspects).

13. Enter **3m.com** and **smarttech.com**. Find information about their whiteboards. Compare the products.

14. Enter **electronicssupplychain.org**, then click "Resources." Find new information on supply chain automation.

15. Enter **epiqtech.com** and find information about products related to this chapter.

TEAM ASSIGNMENTS AND ROLE PLAYING

1. Have each team download a free copy of Groove from **groove.net**. Install the software on the members' PCs and arrange collaborative sessions. What can the free software do for you? What are its limitations?

2. Each team is assigned to an organization. The team members will attempt to identify several supply chains, their components, and the partners involved. Draw the chains and show which parts can be treated as e-supply chain parts.

3. Each team is assigned to a major vendor of corporate portals, such as BEA, TIBCO, IBM, or Oracle. Each team will check the capabilities of the corporate portal tools and try to persuade the class that its product is superior.

4. Each team is assigned to one area of collaborative commerce. The mission is to find recent applications and case studies in that area. Present the findings to the class.

5. All members sign onto Yahoo! Messenger. Try all the tools offered including Webcam and voice. Relate the experience to the tools described in this chapter. Conduct a chat with voice and vision and comment on your experience.

Real-World Case

WAL-MART LEADS RFID ADOPTION

In the first week of April 2004, Wal-Mart (*walmart.com*) launched its first live test of RFID tracing technology. Using one distribution center and seven stores, 21 products from participating vendors were used in the pilot test.

In the pilot application, passive RFID chips with small antennae were attached to cases and pallets. When passed near an RFID "reader," the chip activated, and its unique product identifier code was transmitted back to an inventory control system. Cases and pallets containing the 21 products featuring RFID tags were delivered to the distribution center in Sanger, Texas, where RFID readers installed at the dock doors notified both shippers and Wal-Mart what products had entered the Wal-Mart distribution center and where the products were stored. RFID readers were also installed in other places, such as conveyor belts, so that each marked case could be tracked. The readers used by Wal-Mart have an average range of 15 feet. The major objectives of the RFID is to lower operating costs and reduce out-of-stock incidents.

Wal-Mart set a January 2005 target for its top 100 suppliers to place RFID tags on cases and pallets destined for Wal-Mart stores. Wal-Mart believed that the implementation of the pilot scheme would pave the way for achieving this goal. According to Linda Dillman, then CIO at Wal-Mart, the company's RFID strategy was a success in that by the end of January the required RFID systems were in place and many of Wal-Mart's suppliers were collecting data on the delivery of their products (*IDTechEX* 2005). The system is expected to improve flows along the supply chain, reduce theft, increase sales, reduce inventory costs (by eliminating both overstocking and understocking), and provide visibility and accuracy throughout Wal-Mart's supply chain. By January 2007, Wal-Mart had 600 suppliers on the system (nearly doubling the 330 in January 2006; see Duvall 2007).

Although some of Wal-Mart's suppliers have been late in implementing the system, it is clear that if the pilot is successful (and so far it is) RFID will become an industry standard. After all, nearly $70 billion is lost in the retail sector in the United States every year due to products getting lost in the supply chain or being stored in wrong places.

In addition to requiring RFID from its suppliers, Wal-Mart is installing the technology internally. According to Scherago (2006), more than 2,000 Wal-Mart stores were RFID-enabled with gate readers and handhelds at loading docs, the entrance, stockrooms, and the sales floor by the end of 2006.

The next step in Wal-Mart's pilot is to mark each individual item with a tag. This plan raises a possible privacy issue: What if the tags are not removed from the products? People fear that they will be tracked after leaving the store. Wal-Mart also can use RFIDs for many other applications. For example, it could attach tags to shoppers' children, so if they are lost in the megastore they could be tracked in seconds.

According to Songini (2007), Wal-Mart had to shift its original plan to emphasize RFID at stores rather than distribution centers. Also, the strategy was changed to provide more benefits to the suppliers.

Retailers such as Wal-Mart believe that the widespread implementation of RFID technology marks a revolutionary change in supply chain management, much as the introduction of bar codes was seen as revolutionary two decades ago.

The RFID initiative is an integral part of improving the company's supply chain (Scherago 2006). The RFID, along with a new EDI, will improve the collaboration with the suppliers and help reduce inventories. According to Ferguson (2006), Wal-Mart's new CIO has said that he will stand behind the RFID technology.

Sources: Condensed from Songini (2007), *BusinessWeek Online* (2004), *IDTechEX* (2005), Ferguson (2006), Scherago (2006), and Duvall (2007).

Questions

1. Assuming that the cost of RFID is low (less than $0.05 per item), what advantages can you see for tagging individual items in each store? Is it necessary to do so?

2. Find some information regarding the advantages of RFIDs over regular bar codes.

3. Is this an e-business application? Why or why not? If it is, what business model is being used?

4. What are some of the business pressures driving the use of RFID in retailing?

INNOVATIVE EC SYSTEMS: FROM E-GOVERNMENT AND E-LEARNING TO CONSUMER-TO-CONSUMER COMMERCE

Learning Objectives

Upon completion of this chapter, you will be able to:

1. Describe various e-government initiatives.
2. Describe G2C, G2B, G2G, and IEE activities.
3. Describe e-learning, virtual universities, and e-training.
4. Describe online publishing and e-books.
5. Describe knowledge management and dissemination as an e-business.
6. Describe C2C activities.

Content

Henkels & McCoy Inc. Improves Bottom Line with E-Training

HENKELS & MCCOY INC. IMPROVES BOTTOM LINE WITH E-TRAINING

Henkels & McMcoy (H&M) is a large engineering network development and construction firm with 4,600 employees in 80 permanent sites in the United States.

The Problem

H&M competes with other companies via bids for large-scale projects. If it wins the bid, H&M needs to manage the project, which might last many months and involve subcontracting. Until recently, the company did not have a uniform company-wide project management system.

This resulted in delays and/or extra costs. The company decided to develop a standard project management methodology for increasing internal efficiency and improving communication with its many contracting partners. To teach the methodology to all employees at different locations was going to require considerable time and money.

The Solution

H&M decided to use ESI International to implement e-learning (training). ESI understood H&M's special requirements and constraints. Almost everyone needed training, including the CEO, COO, and CFO. The company wanted to create a project management culture. A variety of skills at different managerial and staff levels was needed. The training courses were customized for H&M's needs using ESI's project management

methodology. A special unit at H&M developed all the materials, standards, terminology, and processes. The material was carefully checked for fit with the corporate needs and strategy before it was delivered.

The courses were designed with George Washington University and ESI International. All the participants, including top executives, received Associate's Certificates in Project Management.

The Results

The company's bottom line has consistently improved since the beginning of e-training. The e-training also contributed to a project management culture and improved decision making on deciding on which projects to bid. The corporate climate and attitudes toward both project management and e-training improved drastically, and many employees now take other e-training courses.

The new methodology helped H&M take on more complex projects that have helped the company to grow and to cement its reputation as an industry leader. H&M also provides training programs for customers both offline and online (for both adults and youth participants).

Sources: Compiled from ESI International (2007) and *henkels.com* (accessed January 2008).

WHAT WE CAN LEARN . . .

Although the initial drivers of the e-learning (training) program were to overcome the difficulties of teaching people in many locations, a major benefit was the creation of a project management methodology and a better decision-making climate. More benefits of e-learning are provided later in this chapter. The chapter also examines the topic of e-government. Finally, the topic of consumer-to-consumer e-commerce is presented.

7.1 E-GOVERNMENT: AN OVERVIEW

Electronic government, or e-government, is a growing e-commerce application that encompasses many topics (see U.S. Government 2003; Lee et al. 2005; and U.S. Department of the Interior 2007). This section presents the major e-government topics.

DEFINITION AND SCOPE

e-government

E-commerce model in which a government entity buys or provides goods, services, or information to businesses or individual citizens.

As e-commerce matures and its tools and applications improve, greater attention is being given to its use to improve the business of public institutions and governments (country, state, county, city, etc.). **E-government** is the use of information technology in general, and e-commerce in particular, to electronically provide citizens and organizations with more convenient access to government information and services and to provide delivery of public services to citizens, business partners, and those working in the public sector. It also is an efficient and effective way of conducting government business transactions with citizens and businesses and within governments themselves. See Scholl (2006) and Marchioni et al. (2003) for details.

In the United States, the use of e-government by the federal government was driven by the 1998 Government Paperwork Elimination Act and by former President Clinton's December 17, 1999, Memorandum on E-Government, which ordered the top 500 forms used by citizens (such as tax forms) to be placed online by December 2000. The memorandum also directed agencies to construct a secure e-government infrastructure. Other drivers of e-government were increased computing power, the reduced cost of computing, the increased number of businesses and individuals on the Internet, and the need to make governments more efficient.

In this book, the term *e-government* will be used in its broader context—the bringing together of governments, citizens, and businesses in a network of information, knowledge, and commerce.

Several major categories fit within this broad definition of e-government: government-to-citizens (G2C), government-to-business (G2B), government-to-government (G2G), Internal Efficiency and Effectiveness (IEE), and government-to-employees (G2E). The performance objectives of the first four categories are provided in Exhibit 7.1. For a comprehensive listing of e-government resources, tutorials, and more, see egov.gov. For a description of the range of e-government activities in the United States, see Moon (2004), U.S. Government (2003), and whitehouse.gov/egov/index.html.

GOVERNMENT-TO-CITIZENS

government-to-citizens (G2C)

E-government category that includes all the interactions between a government and its citizens.

The **government-to-citizens (G2C)** category includes all of the interactions between a government and its citizens that can take place electronically. See U.S. Government (2003) or Siau and Long (2006) for an overview of G2C. As described in the Real-World Case about Hong Kong at the end of the chapter, G2C can involve dozens of different initiatives. The basic idea is to enable citizens to interact with the government from their homes. G2C applications enable citizens to ask questions of government agencies and receive answers, pay taxes, receive payments and documents, and so forth. For example, citizens can renew driver's licenses, pay traffic tickets, and make appointments for vehicle emission inspections and driving tests. Governments also can disseminate information on the Web, conduct training, help citizens find employment, and more. In California, for example, drivers' education classes are offered online and can be taken anytime, anywhere.

EXHIBIT 7.1   Categories of E-Government Performance Objectives

G2C

Create easy-to-find single points of access to government services for individuals.

Reduce the average time for citizens to find benefits and determine eligibility.

Reduce the number of clicks to access relevant loan information.

Increase the number of citizens who use the Internet to find information on recreational opportunities.

Meet the high public demand for information.

Improve the value of government to citizens.

Expand access to information for people with disabilities.

Make obtaining financial assistance from the government easier, cheaper, quicker, and more comprehensible.

G2B

Increase the ability for citizens and businesses to find, view, and comment on rules and regulations.

Reduce burden on business by enabling online tax filing.

Reduce the time to fill out export forms and locate information.

Reduce time for businesses to file and comply with regulations.

Make transactions with the government easier, cheaper, quicker, and more comprehensible.

G2G

Decrease response times for jurisdictions and disciplines to respond to emergency incidents.

Reduce the time to verify birth and death entitlement information.

Increase the number of grant programs available for electronic application.

Share information more quickly and conveniently between the federal, state, local, and tribal governments.

Improve collaborations with foreign partners, including governments and institutions.

Automate internal processes to reduce costs within the federal government by disseminating best practices across agencies.

Plan IT investments more effectively.

Secure greater services at a lower cost.

Cut government operating costs.

Internal Efficiency and Effectiveness (IEE)

Increase availability of training programs for government employees.

Reduce the average time to process clearance forms.

Increase use of e-travel services within each agency.

Reduce the time for citizens to search for federal jobs.

Reduce time and overhead cost to purchase goods and services throughout the federal government.

Sources: U.S. Government (2003), Lee et al. (2005), and *Hyperion* (2007).

Government services to citizens are provided via citizen portals. The services will vary depending on the country, on the level (city, county, country), and on the level of users' skills in using computers. An example of representative services in municipalities in Denmark is provided in Online File W7.1.

According to *Emarketer* (2002), the major features of government Web sites are phone and address information (96 percent), links to other sites (71 percent), publications (93 percent), and databases (57 percent). The major areas of G2C activities are tourism and recreation (77 percent), research and education (70 percent), downloadable forms (63 percent), discovery of government services (63 percent), information about public policy (62 percent), and advice about health and safety issues (49 percent).

Use by Politicians

An interesting recent application is the use of the Internet by politicians, especially during election periods (Mark 2007). For example, the French political parties pursued millions of voters in the blogosphere for the 2008 presidential election. In the United States, during the 2004 presidential election both major-party candidates sent e-mail messages to potential voters and had comprehensive information portals. The major debates were delivered on YouTube, and blogging for and against candidates was extensive. In South Korea, politicians log onto the Internet to recruit voters because many people who surf the Internet rarely read newspapers or watch TV. The target audience of these politicians is 20- to 30-year-olds, the vast majority of whom surf the Internet. Pasdaq, the Seoul-based over-the-counter stock exchange, offers an Internet game that simulates the stock market and measures the popularity of some 300 politicians by allowing players to buy "stocks" in a politician. In one year, over 500,000 members signed up. It became a necessity in South Korea, as in several other countries, for politicians to have a Web site. Involved citizens even make donations over the Internet using credit cards. Some politicians make decisions based on citizens' opinions collected on the Internet. All major candidates for the U.S. 2008 presidential election had hundreds of thousands of supporters at MySpace and Facebook and used video feeds on their own YouTube sites (see Mark 2007).

Another area of G2C activity is in solving constituents' problems. The government (or a politician) can use CRM-type software to assign inquiries and problem cases to the appropriate staff member.

Yet another common G2C use is the broadcasting of city council meetings, press conferences, and public addresses. In many municipalities, delivering training and educational courses both to citizens and to employees is a very popular Internet activity. For more on G2C, see Paskaleva-Shapira (2006) and govbenefits.gov.

Note that over 20 countries block Web sites for political, social, or other reasons (e.g., China, Iran, Myanmar, and Syria).

Electronic Voting

Voting processes are inherently subject to error and also are historically subject to manipulation and fraud. In many countries, there are attempts to "rig" the votes; in others, the losers want to count and recount. Voting may result in major political crises, as happened in the Ukraine in November 2004. Problems with the U.S. 2000 and 2004 presidential elections have accelerated the trend toward electronic voting.

The voting process requires extraordinary integrity (particularly for any computerized systems involved), as well as honesty and experience among the people involved in administering elections.

electronic voting
Voting process that involves many steps ranging from registering, preparing, voting, and counting (voting and counting are all done electronically).

Voting encompasses a broad spectrum of technological and social problems that must be systematically addressed—from registration and voter authentication to the casting of ballots and subsequent tallying of results. Because of this, **electronic voting** means different things to different people.

Each of the current voting technologies has its own set of vulnerabilities; none are infallible. However, fully electronic voting systems have raised considerable controversy because of a variety of factors, such as the proprietary nature of the software, the weakness of the certification criteria, the inability of black-box testing to provide full assurances of correctness, the general secrecy of the evaluation process, vendor-commissioned evaluations, and the lack of any mechanism whereby independent recounting of the ballots and auditing of the vote totals can be performed. Several of these issues are the subject of a special issue of the *Communications of the ACM* (see Neumann 2004). Also see several papers in Khosrow-Pour (2006).

The first country to use fully computerized balloting was Brazil followed by Australia. In the United States, electronic systems have been in use since 1980 (mainly for counting the results); large-scale implementation of touch-screen systems started in 2008. It is interesting to note that several states (e.g., California, Nevada) require that touch-screen machines be able to produce a printed record. A good voting machine should show the voter what he or she has entered and ask for confirmation, much like when purchasing a book online from Amazon.com, transferring funds, or selling stocks.

From a technology point of view, voting machines make electronic fraud simple. Election fraud could easily be carried out by changing a program to count votes for X twice or not to count votes for Y at all (see Rash and Hines 2006 and Gibson and Brown 2006). Therefore, security and auditing measures are key to the success of e-voting. However, considering the amount of fraud that occurs with traditional, non–e-voting systems and the fact that e-security is improving, e-voting eventually could become the norm. For more information on e-voting, see fcw.com.

Many believe that with the ever-increasing percentage of Internet users who get information about governments and politics online, also known as **Netizens**, the manner in which elections are conducted will change drastically in the not-so-distant future. For further discussion of online voting, and why it may take years to *fully* implement it in the United States, see Neumann (2004) and Epstein (2007).

Netizen
A citizen surfing the Internet.

Politicians to Citizens. Aspiring politicians are using blogs to promote themselves, and many use blogs after getting elected. As of 2006, social networks, especially MySpace, Facebook, and YouTube (see Chapter 8) are being used to reach voters directly, especially young voters. For example, Keen (2006) reported that facebook.com had 1,400 candidate profiles for the November 2006 U.S. elections. Politicians use social networks not only to promote themselves, but also to trash their opponents.

Electronic Benefits Transfer

One e-government application that is not new is *electronic benefits transfer* (EBT), which has been available since the early 1990s. The U.S. government, for example, transfers around $1,000 billion in benefits to its citizens annually. In 1993, the U.S. government launched an initiative to develop a nationwide EBT system to deliver government benefits electronically. Initially, the attempt was made to deliver benefits to recipients' bank accounts. However, more than 20 percent of these transfers go to citizens who do not have bank accounts. To solve this problem, the government is initiating the use of smart cards. Benefit recipients will be able to load electronic funds onto the cards and use the cards at automated teller machines (ATMs), point-of-sale locations, and grocery and other stores, just like other bank card users do. When the smart card systems are in place, recipients will either get electronic transfers to their bank accounts or be able to download money to their smart cards. The advantage is not only the reduction in processing costs (from about 50 cents per paper check to 2 cents for electronic payment), but also the reduction of fraud. With biometrics (see Chapter 10) coming to smart cards and PCs, officials expect fraud to be reduced substantially.

The smart card system is part of a nationwide EBT system for miscellaneous payments, such as those for Social Security and welfare. Agencies at the federal, state, and local levels are expanding EBT programs into new areas, including health, nutrition, employment, and education. Also, many states operate EBT systems for state-provided benefits. Governments also use smart cards as purchasing media for G2B procurement. For more information on EBT in government, see nfc.usda.gov/dcia.

GOVERNMENT-TO-BUSINESS

government-to-business (G2B)

E-government category that includes interactions between governments and businesses (government selling to businesses and providing them with services and businesses selling products and services to government).

Governments seek to automate their interactions with businesses. Although we call this category **government-to-business (G2B)**, the relationship works two ways: government-to-business and business-to-government. Thus, G2B refers to e-commerce in which government sells products to businesses or provides them with services as well as to businesses selling products and services to government (see Lee 2005). Two key G2B areas are e-procurement and the auctioning of government surpluses. For other U.S. G2B initiatives, see nbc.gov/g2b.html.

Government E-Procurement

Governments buy large amounts of MROs and other materials directly from suppliers. In many cases, RFQ (or tendering) systems are mandated by law. For years, these tenderings were done manually; the systems are now moving online. These systems employ *reverse auctions* (buy-side auction systems), such as those described in Chapter 5. An example of a reverse auction used for G2B procurement in Hong Kong is described in the Real-World Case at the end of the chapter and at info.gov.hk. For additional information about such reverse auctions, see gsa.gov. In the United States, for example, the local housing agencies of HUD (Housing and Urban Development), which provides housing to low-income residents, are moving to e-procurement (see Kumar and Peng 2006 and U.S. Department of Housing and Urban Development 2006). Governments provide all the support for such tendering systems, as shown in Case 7.1.

Procurement Marketing and Access Network (Small Business Administration). This service (pro-net.sba.gov) presents PRO-Net, a searchable database that contracting officers in various U.S. government units can use to find products and services sold by small, disadvantaged, or women-owned businesses.

Group Purchasing

The U.S. government also uses online group purchasing, which was described in Chapters 1 and 5. For example, the eFAST service conducts reverse auctions for aggregated orders (see gsa.gov). Suppliers post group-purchasing offers, and the prices fall as more orders are placed. Alternatively, government buyers can post product requests that other buyers may review and join in on. Pooled orders are then forwarded to suppliers for reverse auction bidding. Also, government hospitals and public schools actively purchase in groups online.

Forward E-Auctions

Many governments auction equipment surpluses or other goods, ranging from vehicles to foreclosed real estate. Such auctions used to be done manually and then were done electronically over private networks. These auctions are now moving to the Internet. Governments can auction from a government Web site, or they can use third-party auction sites such as ebay.com, bid4assets.com, or governmentauctions.org for this purpose. In January 2001, the U.S. General Services Administration (GSA) launched a property auction site online (auctionrp.com) where real-time auctions for surpluses and seized goods are conducted. Some of these auctions are restricted to dealers; others are open to the public (see governmentauctions.org).

Tax Collection and Management

Every year millions of individuals file tax reports. Similarly, hundreds of thousands of businesses do the same. Businesses in the United States and other countries must file

CASE 7.1
EC Application
CONTRACT MANAGEMENT IN AUSTRALIA

The focus of the Western Australian (WA) government agency Contract and Management Services (CAMS) is to develop online contract management solutions for the public sector. CAMS Online allows government agencies to search existing contracts to locate commonly used ones. It also assists suppliers that want to sell to the government. Suppliers can view the current tenders (bids) on the Western Australia Government Contracting Information Bulletin Board and download tender documents from the site.

CAMS Online also provides government departments and agencies with unbiased expert advice on e-commerce, Internet, and satellite services as well as on building bridges between the technological needs of the public sector and the expertise of the private sector. The center offers various types of support for government procurement activities.

Support of E-Commerce Activities

WA's e-commerce activities include electronic markets for government purchasing. Government clients can purchase goods and services on the *CAMS Internet Marketplace*, which provides services ranging from sending a purchase order to receiving an invoice and paying for an item. The *WA Government Electronic Market* provides online supplier catalogs, electronic purchase orders, electronic invoicing, EFT, and check and credit card payments. The Victoria government and the New South Wales government in WA are spending over $500 million on e-procurement systems under the Government Electronic Market system.

Other WA e-commerce functions are *ProcureLink*, a CAMS service that sends electronic purchase orders to suppliers via EDI, EDI Post (an online hybrid mail service),

fax, and the Internet; *SalesNet*, by which the government secures credit card payments for the sale of government goods and services across the Internet; and *DataLink*, which enables the transfer of data using a secure environment for message management. DataLink is an ideal solution for government agencies that need to exchange large volumes of operational information.

Online Training

In addition to G2B functions, the site also offers online training to citizens. A service called *Westlink* delivers adult training and educational programs to remote areas and schools, including rural and regional communities. A videoconferencing service offers two-way video and audio links, enabling government employees to meet together electronically from up to eight sites at any one time.

Access to the Online Services Centre is given to government employees and businesses that deal with the government via the CAMS Web site at *doir.wa.gov.au/80.aspx*.

Sources: Compiled from *e-start.sbdc.com.au* (accessed February 2008) and *sbdc.com.au/drilldown/drilldown.asp?refid=7* (accessed February 2008).

Questions

1. How is contract management in WA facilitated by e-commerce tools?
2. What other e-commerce activities does the government perform?
3. Describe the WA online training program.

---

quarterly reports. Electronic filing of taxes is now available in over 100 countries, from Thailand to Finland to the United States. In addition to personal and income taxes, it also is possible to pay online sales taxes and value-added taxes. For a case study of successful online tax implementation in Thailand, see Hopfner (2002).

GOVERNMENT-TO-GOVERNMENT

The **government-to-government (G2G)** category consists of EC activities between units of government, including those within one governmental body. Many of these are aimed at improving the effectiveness or the efficiency of the government. Here are a few examples from the United States:

▶ **Intelink.** Intelink is an intranet that contains classified information that is shared by the numerous U.S. intelligence agencies.

government-to-government (G2G)
E-government category that includes activities within government units and those between governments.

▶ **Procurement at GSA.** The GSA's Web site (gsa.gov) uses technologies such as demand aggregation and reverse auctions to buy for various units of the federal government. (See also governmentauctions.org and liquidation.com). The agency seeks to apply innovative Web-based procurement methods to government buying. The site offers many services (see lvanj.org/government/directory.php?offset= 0&searchterm=Government%20Sales%20and%20Auctions).

▶ **Federal Case Registry (Department of Health and Human Services).** This service helps state governments locate information about child support, including data on paternity and enforcement of child-support obligations. It is available at acf.hhs.gov/programs/cse/newhire/fcr/fcr.htm.

For more examples of G2G services, see the Real-World Case at the end of the chapter, govexec.com, and govbenefits.gov. For implementation of G2G, see Joia (2006).

GOVERNMENT-TO-EMPLOYEES AND INTERNAL EFFICIENCY AND EFFECTIVENESS

government-to-employee (G2E)
E-government category that includes activities and services between government units and their employees.

Governments employ large numbers of people. Therefore, governments are just as interested as private-sector organizations are in electronically providing services and information to their employees. Indeed, because employees of federal and state governments often work in a variety of geographic locations, **government-to-employee (G2E)** applications can be especially useful in enabling efficient communication. One example of G2E is the Lifelines service provided by the U.S. government to U.S. Navy employees and their families, described in Case 7.2.

CASE 7.2
EC Application

G2E IN THE U.S. NAVY

The U.S. Navy uses G2E to improve the flow of information to sailors and their families. Because long shipboard deployments cause strains on navy families, in 1995 the navy began seeking ways to ensure that quality-of-life information reaches navy personnel and their loved ones all over the world. Examples of quality-of-life information include self help, deployment support, stress management, parenting advice, and relocation assistance.

Lifelines (*lifelines.navy.mil*) uses the Internet, simulcasting, teleconferencing, cable television, and satellite broadcasting to reach overseas personnel. The navy has found that certain media channels are more appropriate for different types of information. Lifelines regularly features live broadcasts, giving forward-deployed sailors and their families welcome information and, in some cases, a taste of home. On the Web, thousands of people, access the Lifelines portal each day. In 2008, the portal covered dozens of topics ranging from jobs to recreation.

The government provides several other e-services to navy personnel. Notable are online banking, personal finance services, and insurance. Education and training also are provided online. In 2001, the navy started issuing mobile computing devices to sailors while they are deployed at sea. The handheld devices offer both entertainment and information to navy personnel on active duty.

Sources: Compiled from *GovExec.com* (2000), Dean (2000), and *lifelines.navy.mil* (accessed January 2008).

Questions

1. Why is the U.S. Navy using multiple media channels?
2. Compare the G2E services provided by the navy with the employee portal services discussed in Section 7.3.

Internal Efficiency and Effectiveness

These internal initiatives provide tools for improving the effectiveness and efficiency of government operations, and the processes are basically intrabusiness applications implemented in government units. The U.S. Office of Management and Budget (2002) provides the following examples:

- ▶ **E-payroll.** Consolidate systems at more than 14 processing centers across government.
- ▶ **E-records management.** Establish uniform procedures and standards for agencies in converting paper-based records to electronic files.
- ▶ **E-training.** Provide a repository of government-owned courseware.
- ▶ **Enterprise case management.** Centralize justice litigation case information.
- ▶ **Integrated acquisition.** Agencies share common data elements to enable other agencies to make better informed procurement, logistical, payment, and performance-assessment decisions.
- ▶ **Integrated human resources.** Integrate personnel records across government.
- ▶ **One-stop recruitment.** Automate federal government information on career opportunities, résumé submission and routing, and assessment. Streamline the federal hiring process and provide up-to-the-minute application status for job seekers.

For more on using EC to improve the efficiency and effectiveness of government, see govbenefits.gov.

FACILITATING HOMELAND SECURITY

A major responsibility of the government is homeland security. We introduced this topic briefly in Chapter 1. The government is using different electronic and other information technology systems to improve security. For more information on security in e-government, see Wang and Wang (2004). A list of such systems is provided in Online File W7.2.

Example: Ilan County in Taiwan Promotes Tourism on a Portal

Situated on Taiwan's east coast, Ilan County is known for its quality agricultural and fishery products. The county government launched an online supermarket (agrishop.ilfa.org.tw) to showcase a wide array of products from its 10 township farmers' associations and 2 fishermen's association. Almost 2 million people visit the county's portal each year, mainly to buy agricultural products, generating about $60 million. The portal's objective is to promote the image of Ilan's agricultural produce, boosting the farmers and fishermen's business.

As of 2006, the site offered 150 fresh and processed products, as well as souvenirs. Buyers must register as members. The shoppers pay by credit card or at convenience stores. Most of the buyers are from Taipei (30 minutes driving time) and other large cities where they can pick up the merchandise at their nominated supermarkets. For further details, see Lin (2006) and agrishop.ilfa.org.tw.

Section 7.1 ▶ REVIEW QUESTIONS

1. Define e-government.
2. What are the four major categories of e-government services?
3. Describe G2C.
4. Describe how EBT works.
5. Describe the two main areas of G2B activities.
6. Describe IEE in e-government activities.

7.2 IMPLEMENTING E-GOVERNMENT

Like most other organizations, government entities want to move into the digital era and become click-and-mortar organizations. Therefore, one can find a large number of EC applications in government organizations. For information on the difficulties of implementing e-government, see Chen et al. (2006) and Rowe and Bell (2005). This section examines some of the issues involved in *implementing* e-government. Huang et al. (2006) review many implementation issues and trends in e-government. These are summarized in Online File W7.3.

THE TRANSFORMATION TO E-GOVERNMENT

The transformation from traditional delivery of government services to full implementation of online government services can be a lengthy process. The business consulting firm Deloitte and Touche conducted a study (see Wong 2000) that identified six stages in the transformation to e-government. These stages are shown in Exhibit 7.2 and described in the following list.

▶ **Stage 1: Information publishing/dissemination.** Individual government departments set up their own Web sites. These provide the public with information about the specific department, the range of services it offers, and contacts for further assistance. In stage 1, governments may establish an electronic brochure, the purpose of which is to reduce the number of phone calls customers need to make to reach the employee who can fulfill their service requests. These online resources also help reduce paperwork and the number of help-line employees needed.

▶ **Stage 2: "Official" two-way transactions with one department at a time.** With the help of legally valid digital signatures and secure Web sites, customers are able to

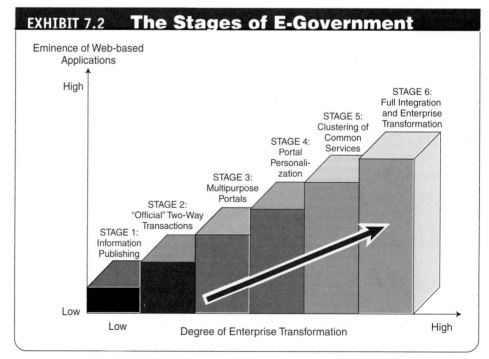

EXHIBIT 7.2   The Stages of E-Government

Source: Wong, W. Y. *At the Dawn of E-Government.* New York: Deloitte Research, Deloitte & Touche, 2000.

submit personal information to and conduct monetary transactions with single government departments. For example, the local government of Lewisham in the United Kingdom lets citizens claim income support and housing benefits by filing an electronic form and then receiving benefits online. In Singapore, payments to citizens and from citizens to various government agencies can be performed online. In many countries (e.g., United States, United Kingdom, Hong Kong), tax returns are filed online with attached payments, if needed. At this stage, customers must be convinced of the department's ability to keep their information private and free from piracy.

▶ **Stage 3: Multipurpose portals.** At this stage, customer-centric governments make a big breakthrough in service delivery. Based on the fact that customer needs can cut across department boundaries, a portal enables customers to use a single point of entry to send and receive information and to process monetary transactions across multiple departments. For example, in addition to acting as a gateway to its agencies and related governments, the government of South Australia's portal (sa.gov.au) features a "business channel" and a link for citizens to pay bills (utilities, automotive), manage bank accounts, and conduct personal stock brokering. The portal described in the Real-World Case at the end of this chapter is such a portal, as are Singapore's portals. See (ecitizen.gov.sg and gov.sg). The design of one-stop e-government sites is explored by Wimmer (2002), who developed a model for integrating multiple services in one location.

▶ **Stage 4: Portal personalization.** Through stage 3, customers can access a variety of services at a single Web site. In stage 4, government puts even more power into customers' hands by allowing them to customize portals with their desired features. To accomplish this, government sites require much more sophisticated Web programming that permits interfaces that can be manipulated by the users. The added benefit of portal personalization is that governments get a more accurate read on customer preferences for electronic versus nonelectronic service options. This allows for true CRM in government. Government use of such portals began in spring 2001. Many state and county governments in the United States (e.g., U.S. Department of Education at ed.gov and the Internal Revenue Service at irs.gov), Australia, Denmark, United Kingdom, and several other countries have now implemented such portals.

▶ **Stage 5: Clustering of common services.** Stage 5 is where real transformation of government structure takes shape. As customers now view once-disparate services as a unified package through the portal, their perception of departments as distinct entities will begin to blur. They will recognize groups of transactions rather than groups of agencies. To make this happen, governments will cluster services along common lines to accelerate the delivery of shared services. In other words, a business restructuring will take place. Initial stage 5 implementations were started in Australia, Canada, New Zealand, the United Kingdom, and the United States in late 2004.

▶ **Stage 6: Full integration and enterprise transformation.** Stage 6 offers a full-service center, personalized to each customer's needs and preferences. At this stage, old walls defining silos of government services have been torn down, and technology is integrated across the new structure to bridge the shortened gap between the front and back offices. In some countries, new departments will be formed from the remains of predecessors. Others will have the same names, but their interiors will look nothing like they did before the e-government implementation. Full electronic collaboration among government agencies and between governments, citizens, and other partners will occur during this phase, which is in its planning stage. Many countries, such as the United States, Norway, and Sweden, are experimenting with this stage or are in the early phases of implementation.

For more on e-transformation in government, see Malkia et al. (2004).

IMPLEMENTATION ISSUES OF E-GOVERNMENT

The following implementation issues depend on which of the six stages of development a government is in and on its plan for moving to higher stages.

▶ **Transformation speed.** The speed at which a government moves from stage 1 to stage 6 varies, but usually the transformation is very slow. Some of the determining factors are the degree of resistance to change by government employees, the rate at which citizens adopt the new applications (see the following section), the available budget, and the legal environment.

▶ **G2B implementation.** G2B is easier to implement than G2C. In some countries, such as Hong Kong, G2B implementation is outsourced to a private company that pays all of the start-up expenses in exchange for a share of future transaction fees. As G2B services have the potential for rapid cost savings, they can be a good way to begin an e-government initiative.

▶ **Security and privacy issues.** Governments are concerned about maintaining the security and privacy of citizens' data. According to *Emarketer* (2002), the number of U.S. government Web sites with *security policies* increased from 5 percent in 2000 to 63 percent in 2004. The percentage of those with *privacy policies* increased from 7 percent in 2000 to 43 percent in 2002 and 54 percent in 2003 (West 2004). An area of particular concern is health care. From a medical point of view, it is necessary to have quick access to people's data, and the Internet and smart cards provide such capabilities; however, the protection of such data is very expensive. Deciding on how much security to provide is an important managerial issue. In the United States, the 2002 E-Government Act requires all federal agencies to conduct privacy assessments of all government information systems.

▶ **Wireless applications.** Several wireless applications suitable for e-government will be presented in Chapter 9. Notable are B2E applications, especially for field employees, and B2C information discovery. Another example is the city of Bergen, Norway, which provides wireless portable tourism services. An interesting wireless application in the city of Manchester (United Kingdom) is provided by Davies et al. (2002). Many more applications are expected in the future.

▶ **Business aspects.** Andersen (2006) points to the strategic management value of such initiatives. The author claims that the transformation of government to act "like business" requires internal analysis from a business point of view.

See Chao and Tong (2005), and Association for Federal Information Resources Management (2002), for additional implementation issues.

CITIZEN ADOPTION OF E-GOVERNMENT

One of the most important issues in implementing e-government is its adoption and usage by citizens. Warkentin et al. (2002) constructed a model that attempts to explore this issue. They believe that the adoption rate depends on many variables. One of the major variables is "trust in e-government," which is itself mediated by several variables. Other variables, such as perceived ease of use and perceived usefulness, may influence EC adoption. Moderating variables, such as culture, also are important.

Section 7.2 ▶ REVIEW QUESTIONS

1. List and briefly describe the six stages of e-government development.

2. Describe some e-government implementation issues.

7.3 E-LEARNING

The topic of e-learning is gaining much attention, especially because world-class universities such as MIT, Harvard, and Stanford in the United States and Oxford in the United Kingdom are implementing it. Exhibit 7.3 shows the forces that are driving the transition from traditional education to online learning in the academic setting. E-learning also is growing as a method for training and information delivery in the business world and is becoming a major e-business activity. In this section, we will discuss several topics related to e-learning.

THE BASICS OF E-LEARNING: DEFINITIONS AND CONCEPTS

E-learning is the online delivery of information for purposes of education, training, or knowledge management. (See Aldrich 2006 and elearnmag.org.) It is a Web-enabled system that makes knowledge accessible to those who need it, when they need it, anytime, anywhere.

E-learning can refer to any method of computer enhanced learning. This could be as simple a meaning as an extension of traditional mail-order distance learning where CD-ROMS are used for interactive and media-rich interaction with the student. Alternatively, the meaning can be extended all the way to fully interactive, institution-wide

e-learning
The online delivery of information for purposes of education, training, or knowledge management.

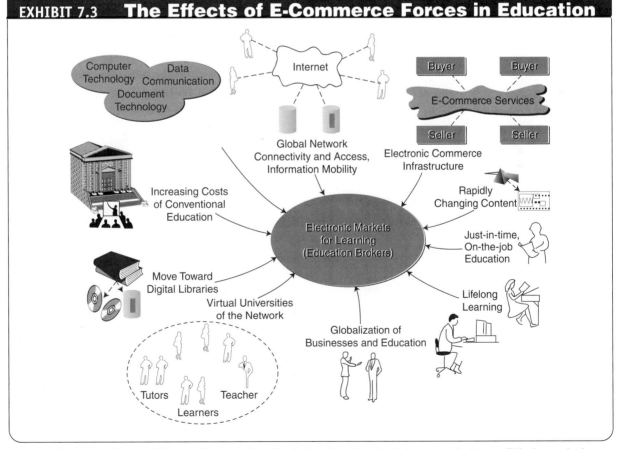

EXHIBIT 7.3   The Effects of E-Commerce Forces in Education

Source: Hamalainen, M. and A. Whinston. "Electronic Marketing for Learning: Education Brokerages on the Internet." *The Communications of the ACM,* © 1996, ACM, Inc.

"managed learning environments" in which students communicate with professors and classmates, much like in a face-to-face delivered course (see en.wikipedia.org/wiki/Electronic_learning). E-learning may include the use of Web-based teaching materials and hypermedia in general, multimedia CD-ROMs, Web sites, discussion boards, collaborative software, e-mail, blogs, wikis, chat rooms, computer-aided assessment, educational animation, simulations, games, learning management software, electronic voting systems, and more, with possibly a combination of different methods being used (see Ng 2006 for details).

The term *e-learning* is broader than *online learning*, which generally refers to purely Web-based learning. The term *m-learning* has been proposed when the material is delivered wirelessly to cell phones or PDAs.

E-learning can be useful both as an environment for facilitating learning at schools and as an environment for efficient and effective corporate training, as shown in Case 7.3.

CASE 7.3
EC Application

E-LEARNING AT CISCO SYSTEMS

The Problem

Cisco Systems (*cisco.com*) is one of the fastest growing high-tech companies in the world, selling devices that connect computers to the Internet and to other networks. Cisco's products continuously are being upgraded or replaced, so extensive training of employees and customers is needed. Cisco recognizes that its employees, business partners, and independent students seeking professional certification all require training on a continuous basis. Traditional classroom training was flawed by its inability to scale rapidly enough. Cisco offered in-house classes 6 to 10 times a year, at many locations, but the rapid growth in the number of students, coupled with the fast pace of technological change, made the training both expensive and ineffective.

The Solution

Cisco believes that *e-learning* is a revolutionary way to empower its workforce and its partners with the skills and knowledge needed to turn technological change to an advantage. Therefore, Cisco implemented e-learning programs that enable students to learn new software, hardware, and procedures. Cisco believes that once people experience e-learning, they will recognize that it is the fastest, easiest way to get the information they need to be successful.

To implement e-learning, Cisco created the Delta Force, which was made up of its CEO John Chambers, the IT unit, and the Internet Learning Solution Group. The group's first project was to build two learning portals, one for 40 partner companies that sell Cisco products and one for 4,000 systems engineers who deploy and service the products after the sale.

Cisco also wants to serve as a model of e-learning for its partners and customers, hoping to convince them to use its e-learning programs. To encourage its employees to use e-learning, Cisco:

- Makes e-learning a mandatory part of employees' jobs.
- Offers easy access to e-learning tools via the Web.
- Makes e-learning nonthreatening through the use of an anonymous testing and scoring process that focuses on helping people improve rather than on penalizing those who fail.
- Gives those who fail tests precision learning targets (remedial work, modules, exercises, or written materials) to help them pass and remove the fear associated with testing.
- Enables managers to track, manage, and ensure employee development, competency change, and, ultimately, performance change.
- Offers additional incentives and rewards such as stock grants, promotions, and bonuses to employees who pursue specialization and certification through e-learning.
- Adds e-learning as a strategic top-down metric for Cisco executives, who are measured on their deployment of IT in their departments.

For its employees, partners, and customers, Cisco operates E-Learning Centers for Excellence. These centers offer training at Cisco's office sites as well as at customers' sites via intranets and the Internet. Some of the training requires the use of partnering vendors.

(continued)

CASE 7.3 *(continued)*

Cisco offers a variety of training programs supported by e-learning. For example, in 2001 Cisco converted a popular four-and-a-half-day, instructor-led training (ILT) course on Cisco's signature IOS (internetwork operating system) technologies into an e-learning program that blends both live and self-paced components. The goal was to teach seasoned systems engineers (SEs) how to sell, install, configure, and maintain those key IOS technologies and to do so in a way that would train more people than the 25 employees the on-site ILT course could hold.

The Results

With the IOS course alone, Cisco calculated its ROI as follows:

▶ It cost $12,400 to develop the blended course.
▶ The course saved each SE 1 productivity day and 20 percent of the travel and lodging cost of a 1-week training course in San Jose. Estimating $750 for travel and lodging and $450 for the productivity day, the savings totaled $1,200 per SE.
▶ Seventeen SEs attended the course the first time it was offered, for a total savings of $20,400. Therefore, in the first offering of the course, Cisco recovered the development costs and saved $8,000 over and above those costs.

▶ Since March 2001, the IOS Learning Services team has presented two classes of 40 SEs per month. At that rate, Cisco saves $1,152,000 net for just this one course every 12 months.

In 2004, over 12,000 corporate salespeople, 150,000 employees of business partners, and 200,000 independent students were taking courses at Cisco learning centers, many using the e-learning courses. By 2004, Cisco had developed over 100 e-learning courses and was planning to develop many more. According to Galagan (2002), e-learning is a major underpinning of Cisco's economic health.

Sources: Compiled from *cisco.com* (accessed January 2008), Galagan (2002), and Delahoussaye and Zemke (2001).

Questions

1. Use examples from the Cisco case to discuss the differences between e-learning and e-training.

2. What measures has Cisco adopted to encourage its employees to use e-learning?

3. Comment on the effectiveness of the e-learning programs of Cisco.

Aldrich (2006) surveyed the technological changes, such as simulations, open-source software, and content management that have reshaped the e-learning landscape. Boehle (2005) describes rapid development tools that enable organizations to create e-learning environments quickly and easily. This resource also compares e-learning with traditional classroom teaching. Comprehensive sites about e-learning, including videos and PowerPoint presentations, are available at e-learningcenter.com and e-learningcentre.co.uk.

BENEFITS AND DRAWBACKS OF E-LEARNING

E-learning has many benefits. However, it also has several drawbacks, thus making it a controversial topic.

Benefits of E-Learning

E-learning can be a great equalizer: By eliminating barriers of time, distance, and socioeconomic status, it can enable individuals to take charge of their own lifelong learning. In the information age, skills and knowledge need to be *continually updated* and refreshed to keep up with today's fast-paced business environment. E-learning of new content will help organizations and countries adapt to the demands of the Internet economy by training their workers and educating their citizens. E-learning can save money, reduce travel time, increase access to experts, enable large numbers of students to take classes simultaneously, provide on-demand education, and enable self-paced learning. It also may make learning less frustrating by making it more interactive and engaging (e.g., see Kim and Ong 2005).

More specific benefits of e-learning are as follows:

▶ **Time reduction.** As shown in the Cisco case, e-learning can reduce training time by 50 percent.

▶ **Large volume and diversity.** E-learning can provide training to a large number of people from diverse cultural backgrounds and educational levels even though they are at different locations in different time zones.

▶ **Cost reduction.** One study reported that the cost of providing a learning experience can be reduced by 50 to 70 percent when classroom lectures are replaced by e-learning sessions (see Urdan and Weggen 2000).

▶ **Higher content retention.** E-learning students usually are self-initiated and self-paced. Their motive for acquiring more knowledge may be to widen their scope of view or to develop career skills. Urdan and Weggen (2000) contend that such self-motivation results in content retention that could be 25 to 60 percent higher than that of lecturer-led training.

▶ **Flexibility.** E-learners are able to adjust the time, location, content, and speed of learning according to their own personal schedules. For example, if necessary, they can refer back to previous lectures without affecting the learning pace of other students.

▶ **Updated and consistent material.** It is almost impossible to economically update the information in textbooks more frequently than every 2 or 3 years; e-learning can offer just-in-time access to timely information. In addition, as Urdan and Weggen (2000) reported, e-learning may be 50 to 60 percent more consistent than material presented in traditional classroom learning because variations between teachers are eliminated.

▶ **Fear-free environment.** E-learning can facilitate learning for students who may not wish to join a face-to-face group discussion or participate in class. This kind of behavior usually is attributed to their reluctance to expose their lack of knowledge in public. E-learning can provide a fear-free and privacy-protected environment in which students can put forth any idea without fear of looking stupid.

These benefits, according to Resta et al. (2007), may enable remote learners to outperform traditional classroom students. Tutoring services that once required face time can also now be profitably handled online and offshored to low-cost countries such as India. For more discussion of the benefits of e-learning, see e-learningguru.com/articles/art1_3.htm and elearnmag.com.

E-learning provides a new set of tools that can add value to traditional learning modes. It might not replace the classroom, but it can enhance it, taking advantage of new content and delivery technologies. The better the match of the content and delivery vehicle to an individual's learning style, the greater the content retention and the better the learning results. Advanced e-learning support environments, such as Blackboard and WebCT, add value to traditional learning. See Insights and Additions 7.1 for descriptions of these e-learning tools.

As the Cisco case showed, e-learning also can be used in the business environment. Besides increasing access to learning and reducing costs, e-learning equips employees with the knowledge needed to help increase customer satisfaction, expand sales, and accelerate technology adoption. In short, e-learning enables companies to prepare their workforces for an increasingly competitive world marketplace.

Insights and Additions 7.1 Blackboard and WebCT

Blackboard Inc. ("Blackboard"), the world's largest supplier of course management system software to educational institutions, acquired rival WebCT Inc. ("WebCT") in early 2006 for $180 million. The merger has created an e-learning company with 3,700 customers, including colleges, universities, and corporate and government users. There is a good chance that you will use the Blackboard or WebCT framework when using this text. These products provide the Internet software needed for e-learning, thus serving one of the fastest-growing industry segments in the world.

How do these products work? A publisher places a book's content, teaching notes, quizzes, and other materials on Blackboard or WebCT in a standardized format. Instructors can access modules and transfer them into their own specific Blackboard or WebCT sites, which can be accessed by their students.

Blackboard offers a complete suite of enterprise software products and services that power a total "e-education infrastructure" for schools, colleges, universities, and other education providers. Blackboard's two major lines of business are Course & Portal Solutions and Commerce & Access Solutions.

WebCT provides a similar set of tools but with a different vision and strategy. It uses advanced pedagogical tools to help institutions of higher education make distance-learning courses possible. Such courses enable schools to expand campus boundaries, attract and retain students and faculty, and continually improve course and degree program quality.

Textbook publishers are embracing these tools by making their major textbooks Blackboard and/or WebCT enabled. Thus, a professor can easily incorporate a book's content into the software that is used by thousands of universities worldwide. As of 2007, Blackboard/WebCT delivers corporate and government employee training programs that increase productivity and reduce costs in every major region of the world.

Sources: Compiled from *webct.com* (accessed January 2007) and *blackboard.com* (accessed January 2008).

Drawbacks and Challenges of E-Learning

Despite the numerous benefits, e-learning does have some drawbacks. The following issues have been cited as possible drawbacks of e-learning:

- **Need for instructor retraining.** Some instructors are not competent in teaching by electronic means and may require additional training. It costs money to provide such training.
- **Equipment needs and support services.** Additional funds are needed to purchase multimedia tools to provide support services for e-learning creation, use, and maintenance.
- **Lack of face-to-face interaction and campus life.** Many feel that the intellectual stimulation that takes places through instruction in a classroom with a "live" instructor cannot fully be replicated with e-learning.
- **Assessment.** In the environment of higher education, one criticism is that professors may not be able to adequately assess student work completed through e-learning. There is no guarantee, for example, of who actually completed the assignments or exams.
- **Maintenance and updating.** Although e-learning materials are easier to update than traditionally published materials, there are practical difficulties (e.g., cost, instructors' time) in keeping e-learning materials up-to-date. The content of

e-learning material can be difficult to maintain due to the lack of ownership of and accountability for Web site material. In addition, no online course can deliver real-time information and knowledge in the way a "live" instructor can.

▶ **Protection of intellectual property.** It is difficult and expensive to control the transmission of copyrighted works downloaded from the e-learning platform.

▶ **Computer literacy.** E-learning cannot be extended to those students who are not computer literate or who do not have access to the Internet.

▶ **Student retention.** Without some human feedback, it may be difficult to keep some students mentally engaged and enthusiastic about e-learning over a long period of time.

Some of these drawbacks can be reduced by advanced technologies. For example, some online products have features that help stimulate student thinking. Offsetting the assessment drawback, biometric controls can be used to verify the identity of students who are taking examinations from home. However, these features add to the costs of e-learning.

In addition to these drawbacks, e-learning faces challenges that threaten its acceptance (e.g., see Resta et al. 2007). From the learner's perspective, the challenge is simply to change the mind-set of how learning typically takes place. Learners must be willing to give up the idea of traditional classroom training, and they must come to understand that continual, lifelong learning will be as much a part of normal work life, past the college years, as voice mail and e-mail. From the teaching perspective, all learning objects must be converted ("tagged") to a digital format. This task can be challenging. Finally, another challenge for e-learning systems is the updating of the knowledge in them—who will do it and how often? Also, how will the cost of the updating be covered? For more on the strengths and weaknesses of e-learning, see Bach et al. (2007).

PREVENTING E-LEARNING FAILURES

Many of those who have tried e-learning have been pleased with it. In many cases, self selection ensures that those who are likely to benefit from e-learning choose e-learning opportunities. For example, students who live at a great distance from school or who have family responsibilities during traditional school hours will be motivated to put in the time to make e-learning work. Similarly, employees for whom a training course at a distant site is a problem, either because of budget or personal constraints, are likely to be enthusiastic about e-learning programs.

E-learning does not work for everyone, though. It is believed that e-learning failures are due to the following issues (*Impact-information.com* 2006 and Weaver 2002):

▶ **Believing that e-learning is always a cheaper learning or training alternative.** E-learning can be less expensive than traditional instruction, depending on the number of students. However, if only a few students are to be served, e-learning can be very expensive because of the high fixed costs.

▶ **Overestimating what e-learning can accomplish.** People sometimes do not understand the limitations of e-learning and, therefore, may expect too much.

- **Overlooking the shortcomings of self-study.** Some people cannot do self-study or do not want to. Others may study incorrectly.
- **Failing to look beyond the course paradigms.** The instructor needs to look at the entire problem in the area of teaching and at material creation and delivery as well.
- **Viewing content as a commodity.** This results in a lack of attention to quality and delivery to individuals.
- **Ignoring technology tools for e-learning or fixating too much on technology as a solution.** A balanced approach is needed.
- **Assuming that learned knowledge will be applied.** This is difficult to accomplish successfully.
- **Believing that because e-learning has been implemented, employees and students will use it.** This is not always the case.

To prevent failure, companies and schools need to address these issues carefully and systematically. Balancing the benefits and the drawbacks of e-learning, many people remain enthusiastic about its potential.

DISTANCE LEARNING AND ONLINE UNIVERSITIES

The term **distance learning** refers to formal education that takes place off campus, often from home. The concept is not new. Educational institutions have been offering correspondence courses and degrees for decades. What is new, however, is the application of IT in general and the Web in particular to expand the opportunities for distance learning to the online environment (see Lagoio 2007). Neal (2007) describes the role of the Web 2.0 tools in distance learning in higher education, surveying implementation issues in terms of technology, course content, and pedagogy.

distance learning
Formal education that takes place off campus, usually, but not always, through online resources.

The concept of **virtual universities**, online universities from which students take classes from home or an off-site location via the Internet, is expanding rapidly. Hundreds of thousands of students in dozens of countries, from the United Kingdom to Israel to Thailand, are studying in such institutions. A large number of existing universities, including Stanford University and other top-tier institutions, offer online education of some form. Some universities, such as University of Phoenix (phoenix.edu), California Virtual Campus (cvc.edu), and the University of Maryland (umuc.edu/distance), offer hundreds of courses and dozens of degrees to students worldwide, all online See distancelearn.about.com for more resources of distance learning and online universities. For a list of distance learning MBA programs see *Financial Times* (2007).

virtual university
An online university from which students take classes from home or other off-site locations, usually via the Internet.

The virtual university concept allows universities to offer classes worldwide. Moreover, integrated degrees may soon appear by which students can customize a degree that will best fit their needs and take courses at different universities. Several other virtual schools include eschool.com, waldenu.edu, and trainingzone.co.uk.

Social Networks, E-Learning, and the Second Life Experience

Many universities combine e-learning and social networks. Many professors have blogs and wikis for their classes. According to Lagorio (2007), more than 100 universities have set up campuses on Second Life's islands where classes meet and students interact in real time. They hold chat discussions and create multimedia presentations. The Second Life experience is particularly enhanced for distance learning. Of special interest is Harvard

University's Extension School. For more details see simteach.com/wiki/index.php?title=Campus:Second_Life.

ONLINE CORPORATE TRAINING

Like educational institutions, a large number of business organizations are using e-learning on a large scale (e.g., see Neal 2007). Many companies offer online training, as Cisco does. Some, such as Barclays Bank, COX Industries, and Qantas Airways, call such learning centers "universities." New employees at IBM Taiwan Corp. are given Web-based "electronic training," and KPMG Peat Marwick offers e-learning to its customers.

Corporate training often is done via intranets and corporate portals. However, in large corporations with multiple sites and for studies from home, the Internet is used to access the online material. For discussion of strategies for implementing corporate e-learning, see Mahapatra and Lai (2005). Vendors of online training and educational materials can be found at convergys.com and deitel.com.

For examples of successful corporate training, see Insights and Additions 7.2.

Insights and Additions 7.2 Examples of Corporate Training

The following are a few examples of successful e-training:

▶ Sheetz operates approximately 300 convenience stores across 5 states. It uses e-training via a corporate portal to train and certify store associates in the proper procedures for alcohol sales. It uses a compliance-tracking tool from Compliance Solutions of Arlington, Virginia, to monitor employee participation in the classes. The employees must know both government and corporate policies and regulations. The program helped to train about 1,000 employees in 2003, saving the company a considerable amount of money. Compliance Solutions prepares teaching materials for the entire industry. For details, see Korolishin (2004a).

▶ Tweeter Home Entertainment Group must continuously train its 2,600 sales associates in the new technologies of electronic entertainment products, such as HDTV or surround sound. To help with its traditional classroom training, the company is using two e-learning products from OutStart (an e-learning software company). E-learning has been especially useful for people who are experts in the field. These people can log into the system from anywhere and do a quick brush-up. Two OutStart products are in use: Evolution (for content) and Evolution Learner Management (for course administration). The course content can be paced to fit the learners' time availability. For details, see Korolishin (2004b).

▶ Shoney's Restaurant chain (over 400 restaurants) needs to provide training continuously to its thousands of employees, from busboys to managers. A multicasting solution (RemoteWare from XcelleNet) is used to offer computer-based training. With multicasting, files are sent by telephone line or satellite from a server to many remote computers at the same time. The system helps both in communication and information dissemination as well as in training. These capabilities have allowed Shoney's to use PCs located at the chain's sites for computer-based training (CBT). Each restaurant has one computer (with speakers) used exclusively for staff training. Training files containing video clips, animation, and spot quizzes are easily transferred to the restaurants' computers. The solution also offers management and evaluation tools (e.g., which employees have completed which courses and how they scored on tests). Course evaluation also is done online. Test results provide indications that aid in improving content. The cost is much lower than training offered via videotape or CD-ROM. Training material is kept up-to-date and is consistent across the corporation. High-quality training has helped the company reduce employee attrition, which means people stay longer at their jobs and provide better customer service. For details, see McKinley (2003).

▶ British Airways is the world's largest international airline. Training and development are a critical part of

(continued)

Insights and Additions 7.2 (continued)

the company's business strategy, but with a huge and diverse global workforce that is constantly on the move and typically working irregular hours, delivering training is a continuous and costly challenge. E-learning was proven to be the most effective and efficient solution (Summerfield 2005).

▶ Nestlé Foods upskilled its global workforce with e-learning. Since 1999, Nestlé has worked in partnership with Thomson NETg to provide a consistent learning solution to staff worldwide. Thomson NETg's expertise and dedication to developing innovative and tailored learning, which delivers fast, tangible results, ensures that Nestlé

optimizes productivity, and therefore business performance (*NestleUSA.com* 2008).

▶ The Royal Bank of Scotland Group is the second largest bank in the United Kingdom and Europe. As of March 2000, the company completed the acquisition of NatWest, one of the largest takeovers in British banking history. With this acquisition came a dramatic increase in staff—the group now employs around 100,000 staff worldwide. Training employees, especially tellers, has been considerably improved with e-learning (*Fastrak-Consulting.com* 2000).

The Drivers of E-Training

The business forces that are driving the transition from traditional education to online learning are described next. See elearnmag.org for more information on drivers and justification.

Technological Change. Technological changes and global network connectivity have increased the complexity and velocity of the work environment. Today's workforce has to process more and more information in a shorter amount of time. New products and services are emerging with accelerating speed. As product life cycles and life spans shorten, today's knowledge quickly will become obsolete. In the age of just-in-time (on demand) production, just-in-time training becomes a critical element to organizational success.

Competition and Cost Pressures. Fierce competition in most industries leads to increasing cost pressures. In today's competitive environment, organizations can no longer afford to inflate training budgets with expensive travel and lodging. Time spent away from the job, traveling or sitting in a classroom, tremendously reduces per-employee productivity and revenue.

Globalization. Globalization is resulting in many challenges. Today's businesses have more locations in different time zones and employ larger numbers of workers with diverse cultural backgrounds and educational levels than ever before. Corporations worldwide are seeking innovative and efficient ways to deliver training to their geographically dispersed workforces in other countries. E-learning is an effective way to achieve just this. Companies do not need to bring employees to a trainer or training facility (or even send a trainer to the employees); online classes can run anywhere in the world.

Continual Learning. In the new economy, corporations face major challenges in keeping their workforces current and competent. Learning has become a continual process rather than a distinct event. To retain their competitive edge, organizations have started to investigate which training techniques and delivery methods enhance motivation, performance, collaboration, innovation, and a commitment to lifelong learning.

Network Connectivity. The Internet provides an ideal delivery vehicle for education. The emergence of online education relates not only to economic and social change, but also to access. Through its increasing penetration and simplicity of use, the Internet has opened the door to a global market where language and geographic barriers for many training products have been erased. Because of the popularity of the Internet, Web-based e-learning is perhaps the most effective way to deliver training electronically.

Fueling the boom in Internet-based management education are corporations hungry for better-trained executives. General Motors pays for its employees to earn an MBA through an Internet-based school launched in 2003 by the New York Institute of Technology and Cardean University. Ingersoll-Rand has a deal with the University of Indiana to customize an online MBA program for its employees. Capella offers tuition discounts to *Fortune* 500 companies, such as Boeing, Johnson & Johnson, and Wells Fargo, for putting the school on "preferred provider" lists. Online MBAs serve "a real market need," says Trace Urdan, an analyst with Robert W. Baird's equity research unit. "It's a win-win for companies and employees" (Crawford 2005).

Examples of top traditional MBA programs that are introducing e-learning are MIT, Kellogg (Northwestern), INSEAD, University of Chicago, Duke, Berkeley, Purdue, Wharton (University of Pennsylvania), and Cornell. Examples of joint ventures of MBA programs with industry can be seen at Duke, Darden (University of Virginia), UCLA, INSEAD (partners with Pensure), Columbia, Stanford, University of Chicago (partners with UNext), and Wharton (partners with FT Knowledge). Of special interest is the Harvard/Stanford Joint Venture in developing e-learning materials for executives. The materials are delivered in a combination of classroom teaching and e-learning known as Leading Change and Organizational Renewal. A similar venture is that of MIT (Sloan School) and IMD of Switzerland. As of 2007, more than 150 accredited business schools offer online versions of their curricula, according to *GetEducated.com*, which tracks online education trends. For more information, see Watts (2007).

IMPLEMENTING E-LEARNING AND E-TRAINING IN LEARNING CENTERS

Most schools and industries use e-learning as a *supplementary* channel to traditional class-rooms. One facility that is used in the integration of the two approaches is the learning center. A *learning center* is a focal point for all corporate training and learning activities, including online ones. Some companies have a dedicated online learning center. However, most companies combine online and offline activities, as done by W. R. Grace and described in Case 7.4.

Learning center facilities may be run by a third party rather than connected to any particular corporation; these are referred to as *electronic education malls* (see Langenbach and Bodendorf 1999–2000). For example, Turbolinux (turbolinux.com), in collaboration with Hong Kong University, developed such a mall for primary and secondary schools in Hong Kong. For additional information about e-learning, see trainingmag.com, elearnmag.org, and learningcircuits.org.

EDUTAINMENT

edutainment
The combination of education and entertainment, often through games.

Edutainment is a combination of education and entertainment, often through games. One of the main goals of edutainment is to encourage students to become active rather than passive learners. With active learning, a student is more involved in the learning process, which makes the learning experience richer and the knowledge gained more memorable. Edutainment embeds learning in an entertaining environment to help students learn almost without their being aware of it.

Edutainment covers various subjects, including mathematics, reading, writing, history, and geography. It is targeted at various age groups, ranging from preschoolers to adults, and it is also used in corporate training over intranets. Software Toolworks

CASE 7.4
EC Application

ONLINE GLOBAL LEARNING CENTER AT W. R. GRACE

The newest concept for training and development is the *online learning center*. Online learning centers combine the Internet, intranets, and e-delivered courses with conventional learning media, such as books, articles, instructor-led courses, and audio and videotapes.

W. R. Grace, a global specialty chemicals company (*grace.com*), initiated its online learning center in 2001. The company's human resources leaders were looking for a solution that would provide fast and easy access to a wide selection of tools for developing employee skills. Surveys indicated a need for self-paced professional and personal training support for employees. Strategic Partners' learning center concept provided the solution. A pilot program was initiated in March 2001. Within 6 months, the center was available 24/7 to 6,000 employees worldwide.

The learning center is organized around the core competencies that characterize the knowledge, skills, and abilities all W. R. Grace employees are expected to achieve. It offers internal classroom training; external courses; CD-ROM courses; self-paced learning tools; streaming video; Internet learning conferences; e-learning courses; coaching tips for managers and mentors; audio and video-tapes; books and articles; information about the corporate mission, values, and strategy; strategy guides suggesting specific development actions, on-the-job and in the community; and corporate and industry news. Employees can access resources on a particular topic; they can search a range of appropriate tools and action alternatives specific to their needs, including training sessions, recommended readings, a rental library, and a strategy guide.

The center's Global Steering Committee, made up of representatives from all the functional areas of the business from around the world, keeps the center in tune with the development needs of employees and encourages the use of the center in all regions. The committee also provides human resources management with feedback on how the center is meeting identified needs.

Every 6 weeks, the center's electronic newsletter lands on each employee's desktop. The publication keeps employees up-to-date on the offerings of the center,

reports on how employees are using the center, and encourages all employees to use the center as a source for learning and development. Corporate news also is included in the newsletter, keeping the company's initiatives and communications visible to all employees.

Based on its experience, W. R. Grace offers the following suggestions for the successful implementation of a learning center:

- Line up strong senior management support.
- Build gradually—start with a modest center, get it running smoothly, gather feedback from the users, make needed adjustments, and develop a more extensive center over time.
- Invite involvement—people support what they help to create.
- Provide a variety of learning tools, mixing in-house and external resources.
- Keep the learning center visible.
- Ensure the content is fresh and up-to-date.

W. R. Grace's Global Learning Center supports employee growth in a cost-effective manner while relating learning to performance and talent management, strategic communication, and individual development planning. It has proved to be a powerful learning and communications channel for the entire corporation.

Sources: Compiled from Boxer and Johnson (2002) and press releases at *grace.com* (accessed January 2008).

Questions

1. List the factors that drive e-learning at W. R. Grace.
2. How is e-learning integrated with other learning methods?
3. List the e-learning offerings of W. R. Grace's learning center.
4. Describe the critical success factors of e-learning offered by W. R. Grace.

(toolworks.com, now a part of the Learning Company at broderbund.com) is a major vendor of edutainment products.

For over a decade, educational games have been delivered mostly on CD-ROMs. However, since 1998, increasing numbers of companies now offer online edutainment in a distance learning format (e.g., Knowledge Adventure products at sunburst.com and education.com).

E-LEARNING TOOLS

Many e-learning tools are available (e.g., see Zhang and Nunamaker 2003). WebCT and Blackboard, described earlier, are two such tools. One of the facilitators of e-learning is Web 2.0 technology such as Wikipedia.org (see Chapter 8). The following are several other examples:

- IBM Workplace Collaborative Learning 2.6 (and higher) software (ibm.com/software/workplace/collaborativelearning) is a Web-based tool that can be customized to fit a company's training needs. It uses customer-supplied job profile information to deliver role-based learning resources right to the users' desktops.
- ComputerPREP (computerprep.com) offers almost 400 e-learning products, including a comprehensive library of Web-based classroom, distance-learning, and self-study curricula. Students can even combine products from different categories to customize their learning environments.
- Adobe offers tools for e-learning at adobe.com/resources/elearning.
- eCollege (ecollege.com) offers an e-learning platform that includes free collaboration tools.
- Artificial Life, Inc., launched an e-learning portal based on intelligent agents for teaching English and basic sciences in China. This is done in collaboration with Extempo Systems, Inc., which offers an interactive character-based e-learning portal for teaching English as a second language.

For more e-learning tools, see Online File W7.4. For the use of intelligent agents see Li (2007).

E-learning content can be facilitated with the aid of online publishing and e-books (Section 7.4), wikis and blogs (Chapter 2), and knowledge management (Section 7.5). The first two topics and their relationship to e-training are discussed by Weinstein (2006).

Section 7.3 ▶ REVIEW QUESTIONS

1. Define e-learning and describe its benefits.
2. List some of the major drawbacks of e-learning.
3. Describe virtual universities.
4. Define e-training and describe its drivers and how it is done.
5. List some e-learning tools and describe WebCT and Blackboard.
6. Describe learning centers in industry.

7.4 ONLINE PUBLISHING AND E-BOOKS

online publishing
The electronic delivery of newspapers, magazines, books, news, music, videos, and other digitizable information over the Internet.

Moving paper information to electronic form has revolutionized both the dissemination of information and learning. **Online publishing** is the electronic delivery of newspapers, magazines, books, news, music, videos, and other digitizable information over the Internet (see Spanbauer 2006). Initiated in the late 1960s, online publishing was designed to provide online bibliographies and to sell knowledge that was stored in online commercial databases. Publicly funded online publishing was established for the purpose of disseminating medical, educational, and aerospace research information. It initially was conducted over private communication lines.

Today, online publishing has additional purposes. It facilitates e-learning, provides entertainment, disseminates knowledge, and supports advertising (because it is sometimes provided for free to attract people to sites where advertising is conducted). Publishers of traditional hard-copy media have expanded to add online operations. Magazine and newspaper publishers such as *Time, PC Magazine,* the *Wall Street Journal,* and *Ad Week* all use online publishing to disseminate information online. Many magazines are offered only online; they are referred to as **e-zines** (e.g., technewsworld.com). Online publishing includes materials supplied for free or by subscription or per item fees; sometimes such material may be customized for the recipient. The potential of new interactive technologies and other Internet applications is expected to aid the growth of online publishing.

e-zines
Electronic magazine or newsletter delivered over the Internet via e-mail.

APPROACHES AND METHODS TO ONLINE PUBLISHING

Several online publishing methods are in use. The following are common methods:

- **Online-archive approach.** The online-archive approach is a digital archive. Such an archive may be a library catalog or a bibliographic database. With this approach, paper publications are converted to a digitized format, without any changes, and are offered electronically.

- **New-medium approach.** The new-medium approach is used by publishers that seek to use the publication capabilities of the Web to create new material or add content and multimedia to paper publications. With this approach, publishers may provide extra analysis or additional information on any issue or topic online, offering more information than a traditional magazine or newspaper can offer. For example, chicagotribune.com (the online version of the *Chicago Tribune*) provides information from the paper's hard-copy issue plus additional news details, job ads, housing listings, and community service information. It also has an archive of past issues. One way of offering additional content is to offer integrated hypertext links to related stories, topics, and graphics. The Web medium also allows for easy customization or personalization, which old publishing media do not. Major journal publishers, such as Taylor and Francis Publishing Co., have placed many of their journals online. The publisher provides, at no charge, abstracts, search engines, and more. Users who want the full version article are asked to pay. Subscribers are provided with research services, hypertext links, summaries, and more. The new-medium approach also offers up-to-date material, including breaking news. Examples of the new-medium approach include wired.com, which complements a paper version of *Wired* magazine, and the *Wall Street Journal Online* (wsj.com). The student companion Web site (prenhall.com/turban) for this book is another example.

- **Publishing-intermediation approach.** The publishing-intermediation approach can be thought of as an online directory for news services. Publishing intermediation is an attempt to help people locate goods, services, and products online. Yahoo!, MSN Network, and other portals provide publishing-intermediation services.

- **Dynamic approach.** The dynamic approach personalizes content in *real time* and transmits it on the fly in the format best suited to the user's location, tastes, and preferences. This approach also is referred to as the *just-in-time* approach, *print-on-demand,* or *point casting.*

Publishing of Music, Videos, Games, and Entertainment

The Internet is an ideal medium for publishing music, videos, electronic games, and related entertainment. As with content providers, a major issue here is the payment of intellectual property fees (see Chapter 12).

One of the most interesting new capabilities in this area is peer-to-peer networks over which people swap digital files, such as music or video files. When such swapping is managed by a third-party exchange (e.g., Napster or KaZaa), the third party may be in violation of copyright law. For a discussion of the social and legal impacts of online music sharing activities, see Bhattacharjee et al. (2006). More and more people are willing to pay for digital music, as shown by the success of Apple's iTunes and others. For a survey, examples, and discussion, see Dahl (2003).

Webcasting

One way that new or obscure musicians promote their work on the Web is by using **Webcasting**, or "live Webcasting shows." For example, onlineevents.com.au broadcasts Webcasts to inform clients about Australian and international entertainment activities. Affiliate clubs and artists get royalty payments based on how many people purchase and download a performance. House of Blue's hob.com has been a pioneer, offering pay-per-view Webcasts.

Webcasting also can be used to broadcast public lectures. For example, *DM Review* (dmreview.com) offers Webcast Direct, a series of Webcast seminars, known as **Webinars**, or e-seminars, on topics related to business intelligence, data warehousing and mining, and data quality. Many other sites offer e-seminars.

ELECTRONIC BOOKS

An electronic book, or **e-book**, is a book in digital form that can be read on a computer screen, including handheld computers and special readers. A major event in electronic publishing occurred on March 24, 2000, when Stephen King's book *Riding the Bullet* was published exclusively online. For $2.50, readers could purchase the e-book at simonsays.com/content/book.cfm?isbn=0743204670&sid=33 and other e-book providers. Several hundred thousand copies were sold in a few days. However, the publishing event did not go off without some problems. Hackers breached the security system and distributed free copies of the book.

Publishers of e-books have since become more sophisticated, and the business of e-publishing has become more secure. E-books can be delivered and read in various ways:

- ▶ **Via Web access.** Readers can locate a book on the publisher's Web site and read it there. The book cannot be downloaded. It may be interactive, including links and rich multimedia.
- ▶ **Via Web download.** Readers can download the book to a PC.
- ▶ **Via a dedicated reader.** The book must be downloaded to a special device (an e-book reader).
- ▶ **Via a general-purpose reader.** The book can be downloaded to a general-purpose device, such as a Palm Pilot.
- ▶ **Via a Web server.** The contents of a book are stored on a Web server and downloaded for print-on-demand (see later discussion).

Most e-books require some type of payment. Readers either pay when they download a book from a Web site or when they order the special CD-ROM or DVD edition of the book.

Depending on the method by which the book is delivered, software and hardware may be needed to read the book. For example, e-book software such as Adobe Acrobat eBook Reader or Microsoft Reader may be required to read an e-book. These readers can be downloaded *for free* from Amazon.com or from other e-book sites. A portable hardware device such as Softbook or Rocket e-book also may be necessary. E-books can

Webcasting
A free Internet news service that broadcasts personalized news and information, including seminars, in categories selected by the user.

Webinars
Seminars on the Web (Web-based seminars).

e-book
A book in digital form that can be read on a computer screen or on a special device.

be downloaded in PDF, HTML, XML, JPEG, or MP3 formats (Miller 2005). After installing the software, the user downloads the e-book and within minutes can enjoy reading it. The books may be portable (e.g., see Pocket PC store at amazon.com) and convenient to carry. The Sony E-Book Reader (see Arar 2006) has a 64MB user-accessible memory and can hold approximately 80 (800KB or 500- to 800-page) books. The 2008 Sony PRS 500 is very powerful with many capabilities. More content can be loaded onto special memory cards that (in 2007) can store up to 100GB (see tigerdirect.com). Books also can be read online, in which case no special hardware is needed. Amazon's Kindle is a portable reader that can be used without a computer. It can hold more than 200 books.

Several aids are available to help readers who want to read large amounts of material online. For example, ClearType from Microsoft and CoolType from Adobe can be used to improve screen display, colors, and font sizes.

Types of E-Books

Several types of e-books are available:

- **Traditional book format.** This type of e-book is a classic or new book that is presented in traditional linear format, usually without special features, such as hyperlinks or search mechanisms. With the right software (Adobe Portable Document Format), a reader can print the book.
- **Online bookshelf.** This is a *collection* of books (rather than just a single book) that can be read online or downloaded. They are simple in format and do not have hyperlinks.
- **The download.** This is an e-book in simple text files, HTML source documents, or Adobe Acrobat files that *can be downloaded* once the viewer has paid a fee.
- **The Rubics-cube hyperlink book.** This is a truly multimedia, online-only book. It has hyperlinks and provides three-dimensional text and display, employing graphics, audio, and video in a dramatically supportive manner. It supports nonlinear exploration of topics. It is especially useful in supporting learning.
- **The interactive, build-your-own (BYO) decision book.** This kind of book puts the reader "in the driver's seat." Combined with multimedia and VRML (a 3D version of HTML), this e-book leads to dramatic engagement with content, plot, destiny, and responsibility. More information about BYO decision books can be found at From Now On (fno.org).
- **The online reference book model.** Safari (safaribooksonline.com), a joint venture of technical publishing giants O'Reilly and Pearson Technologies, provides online reference book services. Users search across the content of the Safari e-books, get relevancy ranked search results to answer their specific query, and then view the content immediately in a Web browser (see Miller 2005).

In addition to regular books, electronic *technical* documents and manuals are available from the eMatter division of Fatbrain (now a Barnesandnoble.com company). In addition to all the major publishers that sell e-books directly from their Web sites, readers also can buy e-books at electronic bookstores. All major textbook publishers (e.g., Pearson Education, the publisher of this text) are creating electronic companion textbooks that feature audio, video, and other interactive elements (see Spanbauer 2006).

Advantages and Limitations of E-Books

For e-books to make an impact, they must offer advantages to both readers and publishers. Otherwise, there would be little incentive to change from the traditional format. E-books, like any other books, can be used for pleasure reading and as textbooks to support learning (see Chu and Lam 2006).

The major advantage of e-books to readers is portability. As noted earlier, readers can carry as many as 200 books wherever they go (and more when portable memory drives are used). Other advantages are easy search capabilities and links; easy downloading; the ability to quickly and inexpensively copy material, including figures; easy integration of content with other text; no wear and tear on a physical book; ability to find out-of-print books; and books can be published and updated quickly, so they can be up-to-the-minute.

E-books also can reduce some of the physical burdens of traditional books. A number of studies have shown that 6 out of 10 students ages 9 to 20 report chronic back pain related to heavy backpacks filled with books. Some schools have eliminated lockers for safety reasons, causing students to carry heavy backpacks not only to and from school but all day long. A number of schools are experimenting with eliminating textbooks altogether and using an Internet-based curriculum or school materials on CD-ROMs (*Ergonomics Today* 2004).

The primary advantage that e-books offer publishers is lower production, marketing, and delivery costs, which have a significant impact on the price of books. E-textbooks cost about half the price of regular textbooks. Other advantages for publishers are lower updating and reproduction costs; the ability to reach many readers; the ease of combining several books, so professors can customize textbooks by using materials from different books by the same publisher; and lower advertising costs (see Chu and Lam 2006).

Of course, e-books have some limitations: They require hardware and software that may be too expensive for some users; some people have difficulty reading large amounts of material on a screen; batteries may run down; there are multiple, competing standards; and finally, only a few books are available as e-books.

E-Book Issues

The functionality of e-books is increasing rapidly. Software providers are supplying tools that make e-books easier to use—tools that search like search engines and that enable easy annotation and bookmarks that enable readers to expedite research of large volumes of information. According to the Association of American Publishers (2006), e-book sales were up 26.2 percent for the year 2006. Despite persistent growth in the use of e-books and their advantages, e-books generally are not selling well in relation to the overall size of the book market. Although e-books are easy to read, are generally platform independent, have high-resolution displays, and can be read using long-lasting batteries, customers are still reluctant to change their habits. The following issues, when resolved, will contribute to the ease of use and popularity of e-books:

▶ How to protect the publisher's/author's copyright.
▶ How to secure content (e.g., use encryption, employ Digital Rights Management [DRM]; see en.wikipedia.org/wiki/Digital_rights_management).
▶ How to distribute and sell e-books.
▶ How much to charge for an e-book versus a hard copy.

- How to collect payment for e-books.
- How to best support navigation in an e-book.
- Which standards to use (e.g., see the Online Information Exchange Standard [ONIX] developed by EDItEUR [editeur.org/onix.html]).
- How to increase reading speed. On the average screen, reading is 25 percent slower than hard-copy reading.
- How to transform readers from hard-copy books to e-books; how to deal with resistance to change.
- How to design an e-book (e.g., how to deal with fonts, typefaces, colors, etc., online).
- How publishers can justify e-books in terms of profit and market share.

Free e-books and white papers on e-publishing are available from a number of different sites (e.g., free-ebooks.net, fictionwise.com). For more information on e-books, see netlibrary.com.

Digital Libraries

Many organizations are building digital libraries of e-books, journals, periodicals, and other materials. In fact, most universities no longer subscribe to paper periodicals. Electronic library items (books, journals, and periodicals) are cheaper, easier to handle, do not require storage space, and are amenable to electronic searches.

The problem, according to Thong et al. (2004), is that millions of potential users are still ignoring these digital libraries. The search engine giant Google has been digitizing millions of print volumes to add to the Google Print database. Partnering with Google on this project are universities, including Harvard, Stanford, and Oxford, as well as the New York Public Library (Price 2004). The British Library in London has partnered with Microsoft, digitizing around 25 million pages of its books (Schuman 2005).

PRINT-ON-DEMAND

A recent trend in publishing is *print-on-demand*, which refers to customized printing jobs, usually in small quantities, possibly only one document or book. The process is especially attractive for small print jobs because both the total fixed setup cost and the per unit setup cost can be very low.

The print-on-demand process has three steps:

1. A publisher creates a digital master, typically in Adobe Systems' Acrobat format, and sends it to a specialized print-on-demand company. The files are stored on the printing company's network.
2. When an order is placed, a print-on-demand machine prints out the text of the document or book and then covers, binds, and trims it. The entire process can take about a minute for a 300-page book.
3. The book is packaged and shipped to the publisher or the consumer.

Most textbook publishers now offer print-on-demand textbooks, including Pearson Education, the publisher of this book. Tarnoff (2007) suggests that print-on-demand technology has shifted students' financial responsibilities from traditional textbooks to other learning resources. For some issues related to the topic of print-on-demand, see Metz (2004).

Section 7.4 ❯ REVIEW QUESTIONS

1. Define online publishing and list some of the advantages it offers over traditional media.
2. List the major methods of online publishing.
3. What issues are involved in content creation and distribution?
4. Describe e-books and list their advantages and limitations.
5. List five e-books issues.
6. Describe print-on-demand.

7.5   KNOWLEDGE MANAGEMENT AND E-COMMERCE

The term *knowledge management* frequently is mentioned in discussions of e-learning. Why is this? To answer this question, one first needs to understand what knowledge management is.

Knowledge management and e-learning both use the same "coin of the realm"—knowledge. Whereas e-learning uses that "coin" for the sake of *individual* learning, knowledge management uses it to improve the functioning of an *organization*. Knowledge is one of the most important assets in any organization, and thus it is important to capture, store, and apply it. These are the major purposes of knowledge management. Thus, **knowledge management (KM)** refers to the process of capturing or creating knowledge, storing and protecting it, updating it constantly, and using it whenever necessary. For a comprehensive discussion of KM, see Naka (2007), Holsapple (2003), and kmworld.com. For KM resources, see en.wikipedia.org/wiki/knowledge_management.

Knowledge is collected from both external and internal sources. Then it is examined, interpreted, refined, and stored in what is called an organizational knowledge base, the repository for the enterprise's knowledge. A major purpose of an **organizational knowledge base** is to allow for *knowledge sharing*. Knowledge sharing among employees, with customers, and with business partners has a huge potential payoff in improved customer service, the ability to solve difficult organizational problems, shorter delivery cycle times, and increased collaboration within the company and with business partners. Furthermore, some knowledge can be sold to others or traded for other knowledge.

KM promotes an *integrated* approach to the process of handling an enterprise's information assets, both those that are documented and the tacit expertise stored in individuals' heads. The integration of information resources is at the heart of KM. EC implementation involves a considerable amount of knowledge—about customers, suppliers, logistics, procurement, markets, and technology. The integration of that knowledge is required for successful EC applications. These applications are aimed at increasing organizational competitiveness (see Putnik and Cunha 2007 and Holsapple 2003).

The KM–EC connection is described in Online File W7.5. First, though, let's examine KM types and activities.

KM TYPES AND ACTIVITIES

According to Lai and Chu (2002), organizational knowledge is embedded in the following resources: (1) *human capital*, which includes employee knowledge, competencies, and creativity; (2) *structured capital* (organizational capital), which includes organizational structure and culture, processes, patents, and the capability to leverage knowledge through sharing and transferring; and (3) *customer capital*, which includes the relationship between organizations and their customers and other partners.

---

knowledge management (KM)
The process of capturing or creating knowledge, storing it, updating it constantly, interpreting it, and using it whenever necessary.

organizational knowledge base
The repository for an enterprise's accumulated knowledge.

This organizational knowledge must be properly managed, and this is the purpose of KM. According to Davenport and Prusak (2000), KM has four tasks: (1) creating knowledge repositories where knowledge can be stored and retrieved easily; (2) enhancing a knowledge environment in order to conduct more effective knowledge creation, transfer, and use; (3) managing knowledge as an asset so as to increase the effective use of knowledge assets over time; and (4) improving knowledge access to facilitate its transfer between individuals. The knowledge access and transfer between individuals is part of knowledge usage and sharing. For a comprehensive list of KM activities and tools, see Naka (2007) and kmworld.com.

Knowledge Sharing

Knowledge is of limited value if it is not shared. The Web 2.0 boom discussed in Chapter 8 is based in part on online knowledge sharing (see Howe 2007). The ability to share knowledge decreases its cost and increases its effectiveness for greater competitive advantage. Thus, another major purpose of KM is to increase knowledge sharing. Song (2002) demonstrated that through effective knowledge sharing, organizations can reduce uncertainty and risk, improve efficiency, reduce training costs, and more. Roberts-Witt (2002) noted that KM used to be about sharing company databases but that increasingly it is also about sharing the information stored in people's heads.

Song (2002) proposed a framework for organizing and sharing knowledge gleaned from the Internet. According to this framework, organizations promote knowledge sharing via the use of rewards or incentives, through the use of different sharing mechanisms according to the type of knowledge, and by appropriately codifying knowledge. An example knowledge sharing system at Xerox is provided in Case 7.5.

The KM discussion thus far has been fairly generic. For additional material regarding major KM activities, see the discussion of KM activities in Online File W7.6.

KNOWLEDGE PORTALS

Knowledge portals are single-point-of-access software systems intended to provide easy and timely access to knowledge and to support communities of knowledge workers who share common goals. Knowledge portals can be used for either external or internal use. A knowledge portal also can be defined as an information portal that will be used by knowledge workers.

Knowledge portals support various tasks performed by knowledge workers: gathering, organizing, searching for, and analyzing information; synthesizing solutions with respect to specific task goals; and then sharing and distributing what has been learned with other knowledge workers. These tasks are illustrated in Online File W7.7. In this example, Mack et al. (2001) illustrate how a knowledge portal was used to support the work of knowledge-work consultants at IBM and what technologies can be used to support each category of tasks. For further details on how knowledge portals are related to collaborative and intellectual capital management, see Jones et al. (2006) and Wimmer (2006).

Information Intelligence

Information intelligence refers to information, data, knowledge, and the semantic infrastructure that enables organizations to create more business applications. It creates a platform that leverages information analytics, patterns, and associations to extract business value from internal and external knowledge. For details, see Delphi Group (2004).

knowledge portal
A single-point-of-access software system intended to provide timely access to information and to support communities of knowledge workers.

information intelligence
Information, data, knowledge, and semantic infrastructure that enable organizations to create more business applications.

CASE 7.5
EC Application
ONLINE KNOWLEDGE SHARING AT XEROX

In the early 1990s, Xerox Corporation had a nationwide database that contained information that could be used to fix its copiers, fax machines, and high-speed printers. However, the information was not readily available to the 25,000 service and field employees and engineers whose job it is to repair the machines at customer sites. Satisfaction with customer service was low.

The engineers at Xerox's Palo Alto Research Center (PARC) spent 6 months observing repair personnel, watching how they worked, noting what their frustrations were, and identifying what kind of information they needed. They determined that the repair personnel needed to share their knowledge with their peers. PARC engineers developed Eureka, an online knowledge-sharing system created to assist the service people with time-consuming and complicated repair problems.

Ray Everett, program manager for Eureka, describes the powerful impact the program has had on service: "You went from not knowing how to fix something to being able to get the answer instantly. Even better, you could share any solutions you found with your peers around the globe within a day, as opposed to the several weeks it used to take."

Since its inception in 1996, Eureka has been implemented in 71 countries. It has helped solve 350,000 problems and has saved $3 to $4 million in parts and labor every year.

The system is available to all of Xerox's service engineers via notebook computers and is accessed through the Internet. Product fixes (50,000 of them), documentation updates, and product-update bulletins are delivered over the Web. Individual service employees and engineers can enter possible new solutions to problems into the system. The solution will appear in Eureka, giving credit to the author and noting the service employee's country of origin. An alert about a new solution is sent to validators who test the solution; if it works consistently, it is sent to all engineers via Eureka updates.

The 2006 version is designed to work over wireless Internet connections. Eureka is a constantly evolving and growing system that connects and shares the collective knowledge of Xerox's service force.

Sources: Compiled from Roberts-Witt (2002) and Xerox (2007).

Questions

1. What knowledge is shared via Eureka? How is it shared?
2. What EC technologies are described in this case?
3. Classify the EC transactions.
4. What were the drivers of the program?
5. What advantages may be provided by the wireless system?

Online Advice and Consulting

Another use of knowledge online is offering advice and consulting services. The online advice and consulting field is growing rapidly as tens of thousands of experts of all kinds sell or provide for free or for fee, their expertise over the Internet. The following are some examples:

▶ **Medical advice.** Companies such as WebMD (webmd.com) (see Chapter 2) and others (see liveperson.com) provide health-advice consultations with top medical experts. Consumers can ask specific questions and get an answer from a specialist in a few days. Health sites also offer specialized advice and tips for travelers.

▶ **Management consulting.** Many consultants are selling their accumulated expertise from organizational knowledge bases. A pioneer in this area was Andersen Consulting (now Accenture at accenture.com). Other management consultants that sell knowledge online are Aberdeen (aberdeen.com) and Forrester Research (forresterresearch.com). Because of their high consultation fees, such services mainly are used by corporations.

▶ **Legal advice.** Delivery of legal advice to individuals and businesses by consultation services has considerable prospects. For example, Atlanta-based law firm Alston & Bird coordinates legal counseling with 12 law firms for a large health-care company and for many other clients. The company created an organizational knowledge base that contains information from some of the best law firms in the country. This information is then made available to all 12 of the law firms in the consultation group. Also, many lawyers offer inexpensive consulting services online. Linklaters, a leading law firm in the United Kingdom, created a separate company (blueflag.com) to sell its legal services online. The company offers several products and also sells support technology to other law firms.

▶ **Gurus and answers to questions.** Several sites provide diversified expert services, some for free. One example is guru.com, which offers general advice and a job board for experts on legal, financial, tax, technical, lifestyle, and other issues. As of 2007, it has aggregated over 480,000 professional "gurus." Expertise is advertised at elance.com, where one can post a required service for experts to bid on. Of special interest is sciam.com, which offers advice from science experts at *Scientific American.*

Some of the most popular services that offer information from experts are answers.com (previously GuruNet), answers.yahoo.com, catholic.com, muslim-answers.com, healthanswers.com, wineanswers.com, and many, many more. These companies provide free answers and some charge fees for premium services. Answers.com (with its teachers.answers.com) provides free access to over 4 million answers and generates income from advertisements.

▶ **Financial advice.** Many companies offer extensive financial advice. For example, Merrill Lynch Online (askmerrill.ml.com) provides free access to some of the firm's research reports and analyses.

▶ **Other advisory services.** Many other advisory services are available online—some for free and others for a fee. For example, guestfinder.com makes it easy for people who work in the media to find guests and interview sources.

One word of caution about advice: It is not wise to risk your health, your money, or your legal status on free or even for-fee online advice. Always seek more than one opinion, and carefully check the credentials of any advice provider.

EMPLOYEES' KNOWLEDGE NETWORKS AND EXPERT ADVICE WITHIN ORGANIZATIONS

Expert advice can be provided within an organization in a variety of ways. Human expertise is rare; therefore, companies attempt to preserve it electronically in corporate knowledge bases. Alternatively, electronic expert systems may be used. Although such systems are very useful and they can be used directly by nonexperts, they cannot solve all problems, especially new ones. For such cases, human experts are needed. In large organizations, it may be difficult to locate experts quickly.

Finding Experts Electronically

Companies know that information technology can be used to find experts. People who need help may post their problem on the corporate intranet, on blogs or wikis, and ask for help. Similarly, companies may ask for advice on how to exploit an opportunity. IBM frequently uses this method. Sometimes it obtains hundreds of useful ideas within a few days. It is a kind of brainstorming. The problem with this approach is that it may take days to get an answer if an answer is even provided, and the answer may not be from the top experts. Therefore, companies employ expert location systems.

Expert Location Systems

expert location systems
Interactive computerized systems that help employees find and connect with colleagues who have expertise required for specific problems—whether they are across the country or across the room—in order to solve specific, critical business problems in seconds.

Expert location systems are interactive computerized systems that help employees find and connect with colleagues with expertise required for specific problems—whether they are across the country or across the room—in order to solve specific, critical business problems in seconds. Such software is made by companies such as AskMe, RightNow Technologies, and Tacit Knowledge Systems Inc. For example, AskMe Enterprise, a software solution for deploying employee knowledge networks, enables organizations to fully leverage employee knowledge and expertise to drive innovations and improve bottom-line performance. The solution is the result of AskMe's collaboration, experience, and success with real-world customer deployments and many companies. For benefits, features, and demonstrations, see askmecorp.com. Most expert location systems work similarly, exploring knowledge bases for either an answer to the problem (if it exists there) or locating qualified experts. The generic process is shown in Exhibit 7.4. Case 7.6 demonstrates how such a system works for the U.S. government.

Desktop Search

With all of the challenges facing organizations, knowledge management is an essential function for capturing data that resides in a myriad of formats, systems, and locations. Although today's $12 billion knowledge management software market offers a variety of solutions for such obstacles, successful implementation of these solutions is highly

---

EXHIBIT 7.4   How Expert Location Systems (Save) Work

Step 1:
An employee submits a question into the expertise location management system.

Step 2:
The software searches its database to see if an answer to the question already exists. If it does, the information (research reports, spreadsheets, etc.) is returned to the employee. If not, the software searches documents and archived communications for an "expert."

Step 3:
Once a qualified candidate is located, the system asks if he is able to answer a question from a colleague. If so, he submits a response. If the candidate is unable (perhaps he is in a meeting or otherwise indisposed), he can elect to pass on the question. The question is then routed to the next appropriate candidate until one responds.

Step 4:
After the response is sent, it is reviewed for accuracy and sent back to the querist. At the same time, it is added to the knowledge database. This way, if the question comes up again, it will not be necessary to seek real-time assistance.

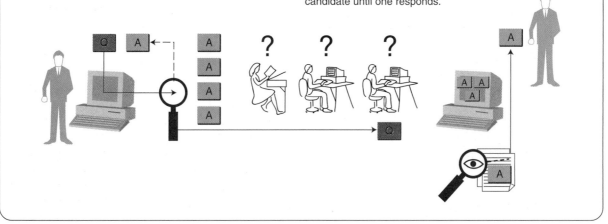

Source: D'Agostino D. "Expertise Management: Who Knows About This?" *CIO Insight*, July 1, 2004. Used with permission of artist, David Falherty.

CASE 7.6
EC Application

HOW THE U.S. DEPARTMENT OF COMMERCE USES AN EXPERT LOCATION SYSTEM

The U.S. Commercial Service Division at the Department of Commerce (DOC) conducts approximately 200,000 counseling sessions a year involving close to $40 billion in trade. The division employs many specialists who frequently need to do research or call on experts to answer a question posed by a U.S. corporation.

For example, in May 2004 a U.S.–based software company called Brad Anderson, a DOC specialist, for advice. The software company wanted to close a deal with a customer in Poland, but the buyer wanted to charge the U.S. company a 20 percent withholding tax, a tax it attributed to Poland's recent admission into the European Union. Was the tax legitimate?

To find out, Anderson turned to the DOC Insider, an *expertise location system* (from AskMe). After typing in his question, Anderson first found some documents that were related to his query, but they did not explain the EU tax code completely. Anderson next asked the system to search the 1,700-strong Commercial Service for a real "live" expert, and within seconds, he was given a list of 80 people in the DOC who might be able to help him. Of those, he chose the six people he felt were most qualified and then forwarded his query.

Before the DOC Insider was in place, Anderson says, it would have taken him about 3 days to answer the same question. "You have to make many phone calls and deal with time zones," he says. Thanks to the expertise location system, however, he had three responses within minutes, a complete answer within an hour, and the sale went through the following morning. Anderson estimates that he now uses the system for roughly 40 percent of the work he does.

The DOC Insider is an invaluable tool. Anderson thinks the tool is vital enough to provide it to other units at the agency. In the first 9 months the system was in place, it saved more than 1,000 man hours.

Sources: Compiled from D'Agostino (2004) and *AskMe.com* (2008).

Questions

1. What are the benefits of the expertise location system to the DOC? To U.S. companies?
2. Review Exhibit 7.4 and relate it to this case.
3. What in your opinion are the limitations of this system? Can they be overcome? How?

---

dependent upon organizations' willingness and ability to pledge considerable resources as well as adaptation of employees. The inability to supply or control those factors often causes knowledge management efforts not to provide their desired effect.

Desktop search is the name for the field of search tools that search the contents of a user's or organization's own computer files rather than searching the Internet. The emphasis is on finding all the information that is available on users' computers, including Web browser histories, e-mail archives, and word-processor documents, as well as in all internal files and databases. For applications, see en.wikipedia.org/wiki/Desktopsearch.

One of the main advantages of desktop search programs is that search results come up in a few seconds, much faster than was possible with previous tools such as Windows XP's search companions. A variety of desktop search programs are available. Examples are Google Desktop, Copernic Desktop Search, and X1 Enterprise (see Insights and Additions 7.3).

desktop search
Search tools that search the contents of a user's or organization's computer files rather than searching the Internet. The emphasis is on finding all the information that is available on the user's PC, including Web browser histories, e-mail archives, and word-processor documents, as well as in all internal files and databases.

Section 7.5 ▶ REVIEW QUESTIONS

1. Define knowledge management.
2. Discuss the relationship between KM and EC.

Insights and Additions 7.3 X1 Enterprise Software Searches for Knowledge

X1 Enterprise is a major *desktop search tool* from Yahoo! and X1 (*desktop.yahoo.com*). X1's knowledge management model is based on the intelligent indexing and searching of a company's data, no matter where it is stored or how it is organized. This solution acknowledges the fundamental truth that traditional knowledge management solutions do not: People have various organization skills and work in different ways. Many knowledge workers have too much information and not enough time to find it, so they generally use some business rules and their intuition.

X1 provides a state-of-the-art, customizable search interface that returns an entire data set of matching items, allows access to any element in the results, presents high-quality previews of each data item, allows real-time modification of multiple search parameters, and frees the IT department from management tasks required by other knowledge management systems.

One product is X1 Government Edition, which has been implemented at secure installations in both military and agency accounts. This is certainly a positive step, because a user-centric approach in knowledge management will support faster response times, especially in times of crisis. Because the actions of the government affect us all, we should be concerned about the knowledge management issues that government agencies face. Through user-centric technologies such as X1.com, the government will be better equipped to meet the needs of the people.

Sources: Compiled from Nenov (2005), *kmworld.com* (accessed January 2008), and *x1.com* (accessed January 2008).

3. Describe knowledge portals.
4. Describe online advisory services.
5. Describe expert location systems and their benefits.
6. Describe software support to information discovery in organizations.

7.6 CUSTOMER-TO-CUSTOMER E-COMMERCE

customer-to-customer (C2C)
E-commerce model in which consumers sell directly to other consumers.

The section examines e-commerce transactions between individual consumers. **Customer-to-customer (C2C)** e-commerce refers to e-commerce in which both the buyer and the seller are individuals, not businesses. C2C is conducted in several ways on the Internet; the best-known C2C activities are auctions. Millions of individuals are buying and selling on eBay and hundreds of other auction sites worldwide. In addition to the major C2C activity of auctions, other C2C activities include classified ads, personal services, exchanges, selling virtual properties, and support services.

C2C AUCTIONS

In dozens of countries, selling and buying on auction sites is exploding. Most auctions are conducted by intermediaries (e.g., eBay). Consumers can select general sites such as ebay.com or auctionanything.com or they can use specialized sites such as ubid.com. In addition, many individuals are conducting their own auctions with the use of special software. For example, greatshop.com provides software to create C2C reverse auction communities online.

CLASSIFIED ADS

People sell to other people every day through classified ads. Internet-based classified ads have several advantages over newspaper classified ads. They offer a national, rather than a local, audience. This greatly increases the supply of goods and services available and the number of potential buyers. One of the most successful C2C classified ad sites is Craigslist (see Chapter 2). It also includes apartments for rent across the United States (powered by rent.com) and personal ads (powered by match.com). Another example is freeclassified.com. Both Google and Yahoo! are expanding their online classifieds. Many newspapers also offer their classified ads online. In many cases, placing an ad on one Web site brings it automatically into the classified sections of numerous partners. This increases ad exposure at no additional cost. To help narrow the search for a particular item, on some sites shoppers can use search engines. In addition, Internet-based classifieds often can be placed for free by private parties, can be edited or changed easily, and in many cases can display photos of the product offered for sale.

The major categories of classified ads are similar to those found in a newspaper: vehicles, real estate, employment, general merchandise, collectibles, computers, pets, tickets, and travel. Classified ads are available through most ISPs (AOL, MSN, etc.), in some portals (Yahoo!, etc.), and from Internet directories, online newspapers, and more. Once a person finds an ad and gets the details, he or she can e-mail or call the other party to find out additional information or to make a purchase. Most classified ads are provided for free. Some classified ad sites generate revenue from advertisers who pay for larger ads, especially when the sellers are businesses. Classified ad Web sites accept no responsibility for the content of any advertisement.

PERSONAL SERVICES

Numerous personal services are available on the Internet (lawyers, handy helpers, tax preparers, investment clubs, dating services). Some are in the classified ads, but others are listed in specialized Web sites and directories. Some are free, some charge a fee. Be very careful before purchasing any personal services. Fraud or crime could be involved (e.g., a lawyer online may not be an expert in the area professed or may not deliver the service at all). Online advising and consulting, described in Section 7.5, also are examples of personal services.

C2C EXCHANGES

C2C exchanges are of several types. They may be *consumer-to-consumer bartering exchanges* (e.g., targetbarter.com) in which goods and services are exchanged without monetary transactions. Or they may be *consumer exchanges* that help buyers and sellers find each other and negotiate deals. Another form of C2C exchange is one in which consumers exchange information about products (e.g., consumerdemocracy.com and epinions.com).

SELLING VIRTUAL PROPERTIES

Believe it or not, millions of online game players in Asia, and especially in China, are selling and buying online virtual properties. Here is how it works: With popular multi-player online role playing games (MMORPG), such as Jianxia Qingyuan or Legend of MIR, players own virtual properties that are registered under their names. The players can buy or sell these virtual properties via auctions when playing the game. According to Ding (2004), who quoted an IDC report, 26.7 percent of the 13.8 million

MMORPG players (or about 3.7 million) have bought or sold virtual a property, for about $120 million a year.

The trading platform is provided by companies such as Intelligence Dragon Software Technology. People win items in MMORPG games, such as rings or shields, and then they can sell them in e-auctions or classified ads. Of course, there are risks. Hackers may steal items, and even market organizers can sell them. Because the industry is not regulated, the player may have little chance of recovering the virtual property. In addition, there is the risk of the buyer's not paying for the item.

However, MMORPGs are very popular throughout the world, with combined global memberships in both subscription and nonsubscription games exceeding 15 million as of 2006 (see mmogchart.com). Revenues for MMORPGs exceeded half a billion dollars in 2005 (Parks Associates 2007) and are expected to reach over a billion dollars by 2009.

Virtual properties also are being traded in virtual worlds such as Second Life (Chapter 1). As of January 2008, some legal and tax issues regarding payments for virtual properties have yet to be resolved.

SUPPORT SERVICES FOR C2C

When individuals buy products or services from other individuals online, they usually buy from strangers. The issues of assuring quality, receiving payments, and preventing fraud are critical to the success of C2C. One service that helps C2C is payments by intermediary companies such as PayPal (paypal.com) (see Chapter 12). Other innovative services and technologies that support C2C are described in Chapter 8.

Section 7.6 ❭ REVIEW QUESTIONS

1. List the major C2C applications.
2. Describe how C2C works in classified online ads.
3. Describe C2C personal services, exchanges, and other support services.

MANAGERIAL ISSUES

Some managerial issues related to this chapter are as follows.

1. **What are the e-learning and e-training opportunities?** Adding an e-learning component to a company's activities is useful when employees require retraining to keep up with new knowledge. Organizations can cut retraining costs and shorten the learning period. Also, companies can help customers train their employees in new products.

2. **Can we capitalize on C2C?** Businesses cannot capture much C2C activity unless they are providers of some innovative service, such as   . Businesses may consider using P2P to support C2C.

3. **How well are we managing our knowledge?** Connecting e-commerce initiatives with a KM program, if one exists, is a very viable strategy. The knowledge is needed for the operation and implementation of EC projects, as well as for e-training.

4. **What are the e-government opportunities?** If an organization is doing business with the government, eventually some or all of it may be moved online. Organizations may find new online business opportunities with the government because governments are getting serious about going online. Some even mandate it as the only way to conduct B2G and G2B.

SUMMARY

In this chapter, you learned about the following EC issues as they relate to the learning objectives.

1. **E-government activities.** Governments, like any other organization, can use EC applications for great savings. Notable applications are e-procurement using reverse auctions, e-payments to and from citizens and businesses, auctioning of surplus goods, and electronic travel and expense management systems. Governments also conduct electronic business with other governments. Finally, governments can facilitate homeland security with EC tools.

2. **E-government to citizens, businesses, and its own operations.** Governments worldwide are providing a variety of services to citizens over the Internet. Such initiatives increase citizens' satisfaction and decrease government expenses in providing customer service applications including electronic voting. Governments also are active in electronically trading with businesses. Finally, EC is done within and between governments.

3. **E-learning and virtual universities.** E-learning is the delivery of educational content via electronic media, including the Internet and intranets. Degree programs, lifelong learning topics, and corporate training are delivered by thousands of organizations worldwide. A growing area is distance learning via online university offerings. Some are virtual; others are delivered both online and offline. Online corporate training also is increasing and is sometimes conducted at formal corporate learning centers.

4. **Online publishing and e-books.** Online publishing of newspapers, magazines, and books is growing rapidly, as is the online publishing of other digitizable items, such as software, music, games, movies, and other entertainment.

5. **Knowledge management and dissemination as an e-business.** Knowledge has been recognized as an important organizational asset. It needs to be properly captured, stored, managed, and shared. Knowledge is critical for many e-commerce tasks. Knowledge can be shared in different ways; expert knowledge can be provided to nonexperts (for fee or free) via a knowledge portal or as a personal service (e.g., via e-mail).

6. **C2C activities.** C2C consists of consumers conducting e-commerce with other consumers, mainly in auctions (such as at eBay).

KEY TERMS

Customer-to-customer (C2C)	300	Expert location systems	298	Information intelligence	295
Desktop search	299	Government-to-business		Knowledge management (KM)	294
Distance learning	283	(G2B)	270	Knowledge portal	295
E-book	290	Government-to-citizens		Netizen	269
E-government	266	(G2C)	266	Online publishing	288
E-learning	277	Government-to-employees		Organizational knowledge base	294
E-zines	289	(G2E)	272	Virtual university	283
Edutainment	286	Government-to-government		Webcasting	290
Electronic voting	268	(G2G)	271	Webinars	290

QUESTIONS FOR DISCUSSION

1. Some say that G2B is simply B2B. Explain.

2. Compare and contrast B2E with G2E.

3. Which e-government EC activities are intrabusiness activities? Explain why they are intrabusiness.

4. Identify the benefits of G2C to citizens and to governments.

5. How can e-government enhance homeland security?

6. How can online publishing support paper-based publications?

7. Discuss the advantages and disadvantages of e-books.

8. Will paper-based books and magazines be eliminated in the long run? Why or why not?

9. Check an online version of a newspaper or magazine you are familiar with and discuss the differences between the print and online versions.

10. Discuss the advantages of e-learning for an undergraduate student.

11. Discuss the advantages of e-learning in the corporate training environment.

12. Discuss the relationship between KM and a portal.

13. In what ways does KM support e-commerce?

14. Why do you think people trade online virtual properties? (Check how it is accomplished at **secondlife.com**.)

15. Discuss the advantages of expert location systems over corporate knowledge bases that contain experts' knowledge. What are the disadvantages? Can they be combined? How?

16. Compare desktop searches to expert location systems.

INTERNET EXERCISES

1. Enter **secondlife.com**. Identify some e-government, e-learning, and property-trading activities.

2. Enter **pcmag.com**, **fortune.com**, or other online versions of popular magazines. How would you compare reading the electronic magazine against the print version?

3. Enter **e-learningcentre.co.uk** and evaluate its resources and activities.

4. Enter **elearnmag.org** and **elearningpost.com**. Identify current issues and find articles related to the effectiveness of e-training. Write a report.

5. Identify a difficult business problem. Post the problem on **elance.com** and on **answers.com**. Summarize the offers to solve the problem.

6. Enter **kmworld.com** and find recent developments in KM. Prepare a report.

7. Enter **whitehouse.gov/government** and review the "Gateway to Government." Based on the stages presented in Exhibit 7.2, what stage does this site

represent? Review the available site tours. Suggest ways the government could improve this portal.

8. Enter **oecd.org** and identify the studies conducted by the Organization for Economic Cooperation and Development (OECD) on the topic of e-government. What are the organization's major concerns?

9. Enter **fcw.com** and read the latest news on e-government. Identify initiatives not covered in this chapter. Check the G2B corner. Then enter **gcn.com**. Finally, enter **estrategy.gov**. Compare the information presented on the three Web sites.

10. Enter **procurement.com** and **govexec.com**. Identify recent e-procurement initiatives and summarize their unique aspects.

11. Enter **sbdc.com.au** and **fcw.com** and find the specific G2C information provided. Prepare a list.

TEAM ASSIGNMENTS AND ROLE PLAYING

1. Assign each team to a different country. Each team will explore the e-government offerings of that country. Have each team make a presentation to convince the class that its country's offerings are the most comprehensive. (Exclude Hong Kong.)

2. Create four teams, each representing one of the following: G2C, G2B, G2E, and G2G. Each team will prepare a plan of its major activities in a small country, such as Denmark, Finland, or Singapore. A fifth team will deal with the coordination and

collaboration of all e-government activities in each country. Prepare a report based on the activity.

3. Have teams search for virtual universities (e.g., the University of Phoenix, **pheonix.edu**; Liverpool University in the United Kingdom **liv.ac.uk**; or **ecollege.com**). Write a summary of the schools' e-learning offerings.

4. Have each team represent one of the following sites: **netlibrary.com**, **ebooks.com**, and **librarydepot.com**.

Each team will examine the technology, legal issues, prices, and business alliances associated with its site. Each team will then prepare a report answering the question, "Will e-books succeed?"

5. Have teams investigate various homeland security activities and how they are facilitated electronically. Write a report that expands on the material in Section 7.1. Investigate several countries.

Real-World Case

A DECADE OF E-GOVERNMENT DEVELOPMENT IN HONG KONG (1998 TO 2007)

Since 1998, the Hong Kong (HK) Special Administrative Region (SAR) government has implemented territory-wide e-government initiatives, which are pursuant to the Digital 21 Information Technology Strategy (*info.gov.hk/digital21*). Subsequently, the years 1998 to 2007 marked the initial stages of e-government development in HKSAR as information and services were made available online (refer to stages 1 to 4 of e-government in Exhibit 7.2). As a result, an infrastructure where citizens, business organizations, and the government can perform electronic transactions was established by February 2007. Moreover, the city of Hong Kong is now regarded as a "mature city" in terms of e-government development (Accenture 2003). The following are some of the key e-government projects in HKSAR that were developed from 1998 to 2007.

Electronic Service Delivery (ESD) Scheme

Since 2001, the Electronic Service Delivery Scheme, or ESD, has provided a central electronic platform through which the Hong Kong public can transact business with the government. ESDlife (*esdlife.com*), a Web portal launched under the ESD scheme, hosts over 200 e-government applications for more than 50 bureaus, departments, and agencies as of February 2007. Moreover, the average monthly number of visits to all government Web sites is 280 million, and over 90 percent of HKSAR government services are provided to the public with an e-option. Some examples of the ESD services include the following:

▶ Booking for leisure and sports facilities

▶ Performing civic duties, such as filing tax returns, paying tax bills, and purchasing tax reserve certificates

▶ Applying and subsequent registration for public examinations

▶ Searching for job vacancies

▶ Renewing driving and vehicle licenses

▶ Selling of statistical data and government publications

▶ Booking appointments for registration of identity card

▶ Booking appointments for giving marriage notice

▶ Registering to vote

▶ Applying for a senior citizen card

▶ Paying government bills

▶ Serving as a one-stop venue for changing one's address with multiple government departments

ESD employs a variety of CRM characteristics. For example, the 200 interactive and transactional services made available to the public are organized around their daily needs under the categories of "Health," "Personal Growth," "Leisure," "Household," and the like. A life event service index is also made available to facilitate the search for services under categories such as "Building a Career," "Establishing a Family," "Having a Baby," "Retiring," and so on. Some public services, such as the weather reports, air pollution index, and a government telephone directory, also are available through the mobile network.

The GovHK Web Portal

Between 2001 to late 2006, the HKSAR government provided online government information and services through two Web portals—ESDlife (*esdlife.com*) and the Government Information Centre (GIC) (*info.gov.hk*).

The former Web portal is controlled and operated by a private company and hosts all e-government applications. As a separate function, the GIC operated by the HKSAR Government provides easy access to some 200 departmental/thematic Web sites administered through different bureaus/departments (B/Ds). A new government Web portal GovHK (*gov.hk*) was launched in early 2007 to replace the government-centric GIC, and this new portal serves as the one-stop shop for online government information and services. For instance, related information and services provided by different B/Ds are brought together in service clusters on GovHK, the purpose of which is to serve one or more target customer groups with needs and interests within a particular subject (e.g., environment, employment, education, and transportation) or in a particular age range or role (e.g., business and trade, visitors, and residents). The goal is to migrate e-government applications hosted on ESDlife to GovHK by January 2008. In its inception, the GovHK portal was developed to provide a citizen-centric way of e-government services delivery.

Smart Identity Card

The HKSAR government started issuing smart identity cards to its citizens in June 2003. By March 2007, Hong Kong's 7 million residents acquired the new generation of smart ID cards. This project has effectively made Hong Kong one of the largest populations in the world to use smart ID cards. The smart ID facilitated the formation of a community-wide information infrastructure for the government and the private sectors to introduce value-added e-applications.

The following are some applications provided on Smart ID cards:

▶ **E-certificates.** The embedding of a free e-Cert in the smart ID card presents Hong Kong citizens with an option to possess an "electronic-ID" that can be used for identity authentication and for ensuring confidentiality, integrity, and nonrepudiation of data transmitted in electronic transactions.

▶ **E-channels.** The Immigration Department of HKSAR introduced an automated passenger clearance system (e-channels) in December 2004. The e-channel system performs mutual authentication with the smart identity card key and then deploys fingerprint verification technology for the authentication of a person's identity. This way, HKSAR residents can use their smart identity cards to perform self-service immigration clearance.

▶ **E-library card.** Cardholders have the option to use their smart ID card as a library card.

▶ **E-driving licenses.** Smart ID card holders have the option not to carry their driving licenses when driving.

Hong Kong Education City

Set up in 2000, the Hong Kong Education City (HKedCity) provides an interactive electronic platform with rich e-learning resources for students, teachers, and parents. Users can exchange experiences and promote effective practices through the portal. As of February 2007, over 1.4 million registered users were on the platform.

Electronic Tendering System (ETS)

The Electronic Tendering System (ETS) enables international suppliers to do business with the HKSAR government online. Approximately 3,000 suppliers from over 30 countries were registered to use ETS in 2005.

Government Electronic Trading Service

The Government Electronic Trading Service (GETS) enables the trading community to submit official trade related documents to the government through electronic means. Commercial service providers enable value-added services creating opportunities for the further enhancement of the local e-commerce service industry. Between 1998 and 2007, HKSAR moved to the established stages of e-government, placing emphasis on the clustering of common services and full-enterprise reform and collaboration (refer to stages 5 and 6 of Exhibit 7.2). Refer to Online File W7.8 for the e-government activities of Hong Kong SAR that are subject to implementation from 2007 to 2010.

Sources: Compiled from Accenture (2003); OGCIO (2005); and *govhk.com*, *esdlife.com*, and *smartid.com* (all accessed February 2007).

Questions

1. Identify each initiative as G2C, G2B, C2G, or G2E.

2. Visit *info.gov.hk/digital21* and identify the goals of the five e-government initiatives.

3. Section 7.1 and Exhibit 7.2 discuss the stages of e-government development. Specifically, the HKSAR government is at what stage of transformation?

4. How will the role of the HK government change when the initiatives mature and are fully utilized?

5. Compare the services offered by Hong Kong with those offered in other Asian cities, such as Taiwan (*gov.tw*) and Singapore (*ecitizen.gov.sg*). What are the major differences among these e-governments?

CHAPTER 8

SOCIAL NETWORKS AND INDUSTRY DISRUPTORS IN THE WEB 2.0 ENVIRONMENT

Content

Wikipedia and Its Problems of Content Quality and Privacy Protection

Learning Objectives

Upon completion of this chapter, you will be able to:

1. Understand the Web 2.0 revolution, social and business networks, and industry and market disruptors.

2. Understand the concept, structure, types, and issues of virtual communities.

3. Understand social networks and describe MySpace, Flickr, Facebook, Cyworld, and similar sites.

4. Understand person-to-person video sharing and describe YouTube and its competitors.

5. Describe business networks.

6. Describe how the entertainment industry operates in the Web 2.0 environment.

7. Describe some of the enablers of the Web 2.0 revolution.

8. Understand the relationship between Web 2.0 and e-commerce.

9. Describe Web 3.0.

WIKIPEDIA AND ITS PROBLEMS OF CONTENT QUALITY AND PRIVACY PROTECTION

The Problem

Wikipedia is the largest free online pop culture collaborative encyclopedia that Web 2.0 communities have created. In 2008, it had over 7 million articles in over 250 languages, generating some 80 million hits per day. By comparison, Wikipedia is 42 times larger than the *Encyclopedia Britannica*, which only contains 120,000 articles (reported by McNichol 2007a and Wikipedia 2008). However, Wikipedia's greatest strength is also its biggest weakness. Its content is user created; therefore, sometimes people with no special expertise on their chosen topics or people with malicious agendas post so-called "facts." For instance, a contributor to a Pope Benedict article substituted the Pontiff's photo with that of Emperor Palpatine from the *Star Wars* films. Another example was an accusation made by a contributor against distinguished journalist and long-time civil rights advocate John Seigenthaler that alleged Seigenthaler was involved in the assassinations of President John Kennedy and his brother Bobby Kennedy. The contributor practically fabricated the entire article. Seigenthaler pursued legal action against the anonymous Wikipedia contributor through a lawsuit using the poster's IP address and charged the unidentified accuser with defamation. For Seigenthaler, Wikipedia is "populated by volunteer vandals with poison-pen intellects," and should not be permitted to exist in its current form. According to Farrell (2007), Microsoft paid experts to write information about the company. This information was found to be inaccurate. (For more about the inaccuracy issue, see McNichol 2007a.)

Another problem is invasion of privacy. Even if information about a certain individual or company is correct (i.e., no defamation), the individuals might not want the information to become public. Because most contributors do not ask permission from those they are writing about, an invasion of privacy occurs.

The Solution

In order to avoid false or misleading entries, the Wikimedia Foundation, which operates Wikipedia along with several other wiki initiatives (such as Wikibooks), is evaluating alternatives to improve the quality. The first step was the creation of a formal advisory board. The second step was to empower system administrators to block access to the site to certain users who repeatedly vandalized entries. Next, the complaint-handling process was improved.

Ultimately, the Wikimedia Foundation plans to change the site to Wikipedia 2.0 and are considering the following three options:

1. Experts in specific fields will edit mediocre Wikipedia articles. More qualified art editors will be used to improve Wikipedia's humanities coverage.

2. Articles will be created from the ground up. According to Larry Sanger, one of the founders and owners of Wikipedia, this could provide a more distinctive culture and authors would take pride in their articles. In this case, the name of the site would change to *citizendium*.

3. Make the users' policy more interactive. Wikipedia is asking readers to notify the company whenever they read inaccurate or incomplete content.

The Results

While the Seigenthaler issue was debated in fall 2005, early quality measures were instituted. When the site founder, Jimmy Wales, appeared on CNN with Seigenthaler in December 2005, traffic to Wikipedia nearly tripled (Martens 2006). Yet problems still exist, with complaints against both content and privacy invasion online. And, after years of enormous growth, the rate of editing articles, new account registration, user block, article protection and deletion, and uploads have all declined (Riley 2007).

Sources: Compiled from Martens (2006), Cone (2007a), Flynn (2006), and McNichol (2007a).

WHAT WE CAN LEARN . . .

The Wikipedia case illustrates a *wiki implementation*, a collaborative online encyclopedia that is primarily written by volunteers. Murray-Buechner (2006) lists it as one of the 25 sites "we cannot live without" and labeled it as a "real Web wonder." It is a typical Web 2.0 application, done for people by people. It illustrates both the benefits to society and the problems of content accuracy by volunteers. It also illustrates the potential of invasion of privacy, potential of litigation against the site, and the need for financial viability, especially when money is needed to check what people contribute for the online publishing.

In this chapter, we present several of the Web 2.0 applications (see the basics of Web 2.0 in Chapter 1) and examine their impact on the way we live and do business, relating it to the experience of Wikipedia and other companies. We also introduce social networks that may change markets or even whole industries. We also present specific companies, such as YouTube, Facebook, and Flickr, that have already changed the lives of millions of people.

8.1 THE WEB 2.0 REVOLUTION, SOCIAL NETWORKS, INNOVATIONS, AND INDUSTRY DISRUPTORS

This chapter of the text deals with the newest areas of e-commerce—social networks and other Web 2.0 applications.

THE WEB 2.0 REVOLUTION

Time's 2006 Person of the Year was "You," reflecting the Web's digital democracy (Grossman 2006–2007). Today, ordinary people control, use, and are immersed in the information age. What makes this possible is the phenomenon known as Web 2.0 (defined and described briefly in Chapter 1). It has become the framework for bringing together the contributions of millions of people. Web 2.0 applications make everyone's work, thoughts, opinions, and essentially their identity, matter (see rheingold.com). If Web 1.0 was organized around pages, software, technology, and corporations, Web 2.0 is organized around ordinary people and services. Ordinary people created Web 2.0: hobbyists, diarists, armchair pundits, and those just sharing their two cents' worth through blogs, wikis, social networks, and videos. By 2007, no one had more power to influence society than Web 2.0 communities (see Gillin 2007a). Yet, does this influence truly benefit us, or do we suffer because of it (*Business 2.0* 2007)?

According to *The Economist* (2007), Tim Berners-Lee, the creator of the Web, regards Web 2.0 as a movement that encompasses a range of technologies, including blogs, wikis, and podcasts, and that represents the Web adolescence. It has all the hallmarks of youthful rebellion against the conventional social order and is making many traditional media companies tremble.

Web 2.0 can be viewed as a large-scale and global social experiment. Like any other experiment, it may fail. What could cause Web 2.0 to ultimately fail? As seen in the Wikipedia case, some have serious concerns regarding the quality and integrity of user-created content on the Web. In addition, there also are security problems.

WHAT IS WEB 2.0?

Web 2.0

The popular term for advanced Internet technology and applications, including blogs, wikis, RSS, and social bookmarking. One of the most significant differences between Web 2.0 and the traditional World Wide Web is greater collaboration among users, content providers, and enterprises.

Web 2.0 is the popular term for advanced Internet technology and applications, including blogs, wikis, RSS, and social networks. One of the most significant differences between Web 2.0 and the traditional Web is greater collaboration among Internet users and other users, content providers, and enterprises. As an umbrella term for an emerging core of technologies, trends, and principles, Web 2.0 is not only changing what's on the Web, but also how it works. Many believe that companies that understand these new applications and technologies—and apply the benefits early on—stand to greatly improve internal business processes and marketing. Among the biggest advantages is better collaboration with customers, partners, and suppliers, as well as among internal users (see the Real-World Case at the end of this chapter and McAfee 2006).

As you may recall from Chapter 1, O'Reilly (2005) cited the following as being important Web 2.0 tools:

- Google AdSense (Chapter 4)
- Flickr (Section 8.3)
- Blogs (Chapter 2 and Section 8.7)
- Web Services (Online Chapter 14)
- RSS and podcasting (Chapter 2)
- Search engines (Online File W8.1)
- Napster (P2P, Online File W8.2)

Innovations (2006) adds social networks (Section 8.3), service-oriented architecture (Online Chapter 14), and software as a service (Online Chapter 14). And there are more products available.

According to *Innovations* (2006), 12 percent of all U.S. consumers use RSS, and 12 million U.S. households will regularly subscribe to podcasts by 2010. Microsoft Office Outlook 2007, Yahoo! Mail Beta, and possibly GMail will allow subscription to and interaction with RSS feeds right from e-mail, which will certainly increase the use of this technology (MacManus 2006).

The following are some key Web 2.0 statistics as of April 2007 (Sifrey 2007):

- There are 70 million blogs.
- About 120,000 new blogs are created each day, or 1.4 every second.
- 3,000 to 7,000 new splogs (fake, or spam blogs) are created every day, with a peak of 11,000 splogs per day last December.
- Each day, approximately 1.5 million posts are made to blogs, or 17 posts per second.
- Growth from 35 to 75 million blogs took 320 days.
- 22 blogs among the top 100 blogs were among the top 100 sources linked to in the fourth quarter of 2006—up from 12 in the prior quarter.
- Japanese is the most popular blogging language, at 37 percent; English is second at 33 percent; Chinese is third at 8 percent; Italian fourth at 3 percent; and Farsi, a newcomer in the top 10, is at 1 percent.
- English is the most popular even in postings around-the-clock.
- 230 million posts that use tags or categories are tracked.
- 35 percent of all February 2007 posts used tags.
- 2.5 million blogs posted at least one tagged post in February.

FOUNDATION OF WEB 2.0

Proponents of the Web 2.0 approach believe that Web usage has been increasingly moving toward interaction and rudimentary social networking, which can serve content that exploits the network effect with or without creating a visual, interactive Web page. Web 2.0 sites sometimes act more as user-dependent Web portals than as traditional Web sites. Access to consumer-generated content facilitated by Web 2.0 brings the Web closer to the concept of the Web as a democratic, personal, and do-it-yourself medium of communication.

REPRESENTATIVE CHARACTERISTICS OF WEB 2.0

The following are representative characteristics (O'Reilly 2005):

- The ability to tap into the collective intelligence of users. The more users contribute, the more popular and valuable a Web 2.0 site becomes.
- Making data available in new or never-intended ways. Web 2.0 data can be remixed or "mashed up," often through Web-service interfaces, much the way a dance-club DJ mixes music.
- The presence of lightweight programming techniques and tools that lets nearly anyone act as a developer.
- The virtual elimination of software-upgrade cycles makes everything a *perpetual beta*, or work in progress, and allows rapid prototyping using the Web as a platform.

    Other characteristics are:

- Networks as platforms, delivering and allowing users to use applications entirely through a browser.
- Users own the data on the site and exercise control over that data.
- An architecture of participation and digital democracy encourages users to add value to the application as they use it.
- New business models are created (Chesbrough 2006).
- A major emphasis on social networks.

    Many Web 2.0 sites feature a rich interactive, user-friendly interface based on Ajax or similar frameworks. Ajax (Asynchronous JavaScript and XML) is a Web development technique for creating interactive Web applications. The intent is to make Web pages feel more responsive by exchanging small amounts of data with the server behind the scenes so that the entire Web page does not have to be reloaded each time the user makes a change. This is meant to increase the Web page's interactivity, speed, and usability.

Web 2.0 Companies

O'Reilly (2005) explained what Web 2.0 is and listed some typical Web 2.0 companies, such as Google. Dozens of companies have emerged as providers of infrastructure and services to social networks. In addition, many companies provide the technology for Web activities (see lists in Section 8.7). A large number of Web 2.0-related star-tups appeared in 2005–2007. Sloan (2007) provides a guide to the 25 hottest Web 2.0 companies and the powerful trends that are driving them (others are described in Gillin 2007a):

- Social media: StumbleUpon (stumbleupon.com), Slide (slide.com), Bebo (bebo.com), Meebo (meebo.com), and Wikia (wikia.com).

▶ Video: Joost (joost.com), Metacafe (metacafe.com), Dabble (dabble.com), Revision3 (revision3.com), and Blip TV (blip.tv).

▶ Mobile: Mobio (getmobio.com), Soonr (soonr.com), TinyPicture (tinypic.com), Fon (fon.com), and Loopt (loopt.com). (For 20 companies in this area, see Longino 2006.)

▶ Advertising: Adify (adify.com), Admob (admob.com), Turn (turn.com), Spotrunner (spotrunner.com), and Vitrue (vitrue.com).

▶ Enterprise: SuccessFactors (successfactors.com), Janrain (janrain.com), Logowork (logowork.com), Simulscribe (simulscribe.com), and ReardenCommerce (rearden commerce.com).

Several of these companies are described in this chapter.

Web 2.0 Going Global

Schonfeld (2006a) believes a major characteristic of Web 2.0 is the global spreading of innovative Web sites. As soon as a successful idea is deployed as a Web site in one country, other sites appear around the globe. He presents 23 Web 2.0–type sites in 10 countries. This section presents some of these sites. Others appear in different sections of this chapter. Another excellent source for material on Web 2.0 is "CIO's Executive Guide: Web 2.0" (see searchcio.techtarget.com/general/0,295582,sid19_gci1244339,00.html#glossary).

SOCIAL MEDIA

social media

Online platforms and tools that people use to share opinions and experiences, including photos, videos, music, insights, and perceptions.

One of the major phenomena of Web 2.0 is the emergence and rise of mass social media. **Social media** refers to the online platforms and tools that people use to share opinions and experiences including photos, videos, music, insights, and perceptions with each other. Social media can take many different forms including text, images, audio, or video clips. Section 8.6 describes popular social media. The most important feature of social media is that they are controlled by the users rather than by organizations. Furthermore, people can use these media with ease at little or no cost. It is a powerful force of democratization; the network structure enables communication and collaboration on a massive scale. For details see Hinchcliffe (2007). Exhibit 8.1 illustrates the emergence and rise of mass social media.

Note that with traditional media content is pushed from a company or content provider, whereas with social media the users create and control the content.

INDUSTRY AND MARKET DISRUPTORS

disruptors

Companies that introduce significant changes in their industries.

In this book, we have described several cases of companies that introduced e-commerce innovations that could disrupt and reorder markets, or even entire industries. These companies introduced a major change in the way companies do business (see Schonfeld and Borzo 2006). For example, Blue Nile (Chapter 2) displaced hundreds of jewelers and is changing the jewelry retail industry. *Business 2.0* refers to such companies as **disruptors**. Another example of a potential disruptor is ZOPA. ZOPA facilitates person-to-person lending, which might lead to changes in the banking industry (Online File W8.2).

Business 2.0 created The Disruption Group and an accompanying blog (e.g., see Urlocker 2006 and Schonfeld 2006b). The Disruption Group developed a series of questions to help identify successful disruptors (see the Disruption Scorecard at ondisruption.com):

1. Is the service or product simpler, cheaper, or more accessible?
2. Does the disruptor change the basis of competition with the current suppliers?

EXHIBIT 8.1 The Emergence and Rise of Mass Social Media

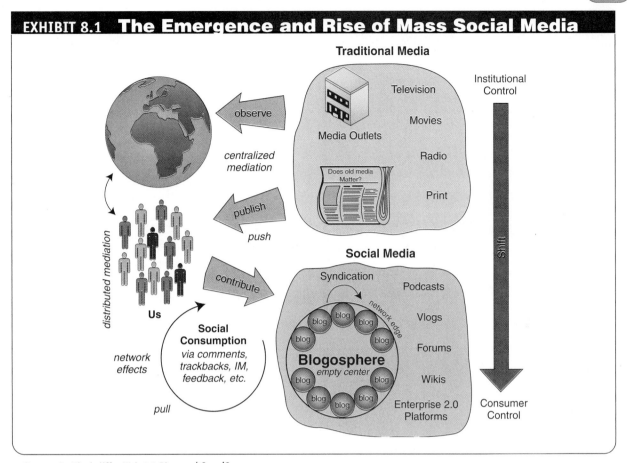

Source: D. Hinchcliffe, *Web 2.0 Blog, web2.wsj2.com.*

3. Does the disruptor have a different business model?
4. Does the product or service fit with what customers value and pay for?

The following can help to identify possible problems with would-be disruptors:

1. Is the disruptor trying to beat the mainstream supplier at its own game?
2. Is the disruptor choosing growth ahead of profits?
3. Does the disruptor need to change consumer behavior or to "educate" the customer?
4. Is the disruptor saddled with old business processes or an outdated business model?

Exhibit 8.2 illustrates how consumer-generated content swamping is disrupting traditional media. Additional examples of disruptors can be found in the wedding services industry, as traditional providers face competition from online vendors and Web 2.0 tools, as described in Insights and Additions 8.1.

Another example of disruption is in the real estate brokerage industry. For example, companies such as Zillow (zillow.com) and Homegain (homegain.com) provide more services and information than Web 1.0 companies, such as realtor.com, realtytrack.com, and similar sites, provide. According to O'Brien (2007), sellers can use zillow.com to obtain an approximation of their home's market value based on recent sales in their

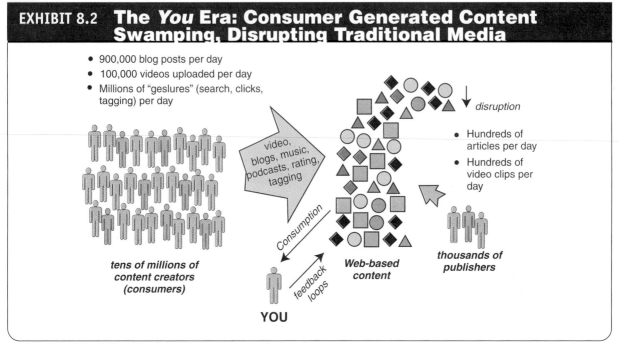

EXHIBIT 8.2 The *You* Era: Consumer Generated Content Swamping, Disrupting Traditional Media

- 900,000 blog posts per day
- 100,000 videos uploaded per day
- Millions of "geslures" (search, clicks, tagging) per day

video, blogs, music, podcasts, rating, tagging

Consumption

feedback loops

YOU

tens of millions of content creators (consumers)

Web-based content

↓ *disruption*

- Hundreds of articles per day
- Hundreds of video clips per day

thousands of publishers

Source: D. Hinchcliffe, *Web 2.0 Blog, web2.wsj2.com.*

neighborhood. The seller than adds extra features to the home's profile and a new estimate is generated (see Team Exercise 1 at the end of this chapter). Sellers can list their homes for free after they come up with a selling price. The service also is helpful for home buyers. Buyers can use Zillow to buy a house that is not even on the market—without open houses, bidding wars, or buyer's remorse—and get it cheaper by avoiding the commission that is paid to the realtor. Will real estate agents be made extinct? Some will. More likely the 6 percent commission that most realtors earn in the United States will drop toward the 1 percent commission that is common in other countries.

Insights and Additions 8.1 Weddings Are Going High Tech with Web 2.0

Technology in the United States and some other countries has shaken up the traditional wedding. Today, many couples create their own wedding sites to keep their guests informed of wedding plans. Many couples use the Internet for bridal registries. Guests can buy gifts online from major department stores. Wedding Webcasts are becoming popular too: Couples can broadcast the wedding ceremony on the Web for people who are not able to attend, as well as post wedding videos on YouTube and pictures on Flickr. Friends can start a blog or a wiki, too.

Next is the use of digital music. Couples create their own playlists on their iPods and use them for both wedding ceremony and reception music, especially for small, intimate weddings. This is noninteractive, but it is original and less costly. Couples also save money by using the Internet to compare items they need to buy (e.g., see *theknot.com*). Finally, couples can design and buy their wedding rings online (e.g., see *bluenile.com*). The result is that competition has increased among those vendors serving the approximately 2.4 million weddings that take place annually in the United States.

Section 8.1 ❱ REVIEW QUESTIONS

1. Define Web 2.0.
2. List the major characteristics of Web 2.0.
3. List the Web 2.0 technologies.
4. Define social media.
5. Define disruptors.

8.2 VIRTUAL COMMUNITIES

A community is a group of people with some interest in common who interact with one another. A **virtual (Internet) community** is one in which the interaction takes place over the Internet. Virtual communities parallel physical communities, such as neighborhoods, clubs, and associations, but people do not meet face-to-face. Instead, they meet online. Virtual communities offer several ways for members to interact, collaborate, and trade (see Exhibit 8.3). Similar to the click-and-mortar e-commerce model, many physical communities have a Web site for Internet-related activities.

virtual (Internet) community
A group of people with similar interests who interact with one another using the Internet.

CHARACTERISTICS OF COMMUNITIES AND CLASSIFICATION

Pure-play Internet communities may have thousands or even millions of members. This is one major difference with purely physical communities, which usually are smaller. Another difference is that offline communities frequently are confined to one geographic location, whereas only a few online communities are geographically confined.

Many thousands of communities exist on the Internet. Several communities are independent and are growing rapidly. For instance, GeoCities grew to 10 million members in less than 2 years and had over 50 million members in 2004 (GeoCities 2007).

EXHIBIT 8.3 Elements of Interaction in a Virtual Community	
Category	**Element**
Communication	Bulletin boards (discussion groups)
	Chat rooms/threaded discussions (string Q&A)
	E-mail and instant messaging and wireless messages
	Private mailboxes
	Newsletters, "netzines" (electronic magazines)
	Blogging, wikis, and mashups
	Web postings
	Voting
Information	Directories and yellow pages
	Search engine
	Member-generated content
	Links to information sources
	Expert advice
EC Element	Electronic catalogs and shopping carts
	Advertisements
	Auctions of all types
	Classified ads
	Bartering online

MySpace (see Case 1.4) grew to 100 million members in about a year. GeoCities members can set up personal home pages on the site, and advertisers buy ad space targeted to community members. Insights and Additions 8.2 presents a number of examples of online communities. Sections 8.3 through 8.6 present in-depth descriptions of various social networking communities.

Virtual communities can be classified in several ways. One possibility is to classify members as *traders, players, just friends, enthusiasts*, or *friends in need*. A more common classification is the one proposed by Hagel and Armstrong (1997). This classification recognizes the five types of Internet communities shown in Exhibit 8.4. For a different, more complete classification, see the classification proposed by Schubert and Ginsburg (2000).

Cashel (2004) proposed another classification of communities, identifying 10 specific niches within the online community space that are bucking the trend and demonstrating

Insights and Additions 8.2 Types of Online Communities

The following are examples of some of the various types of online communities:

▶ **Associations.** Many associations have a Web presence. These range from Parent–Teacher Associations (PTAs) to professional associations. An example of this type of community is the Australian Record Industry Association (*aria.com.au*).

▶ **Ethnic communities.** Many communities are country or language specific. An example of such a site is *elsitio.com*, which provides content for the Spanish- and Portuguese-speaking audiences mainly in Latin America and the United States. A number of sites, including *china.com, hongkong.com, sina.com*, and *sohu.com*, cater to the world's large Chinese-speaking community.

▶ **Gender communities.** *Women.com* and *ivillage.com*, the two largest female-oriented community sites, merged in 2001 in an effort to cut losses and become profitable.

▶ **Affinity portals.** These are communities organized by interest, such as hobbies, vocations, political parties, unions (e.g., *workingfamilies.com*), and many more. Many communities are organized around a technical topic (e.g., a database), a product (e.g., Lotus Notes), or a company (e.g., Oracle Technology news at *oracle.com/technology*). A major subcategory here is medical- and health-related portals. According to Johnson and Ambrose (2006), almost 30 percent of the 90 million members who participated in communities in 2005 were in this category.

▶ **Catering to young people (teens and people in their early 20s).** Many companies see unusual opportunities here. Three community sites of particular interest are *alloy.com, bolt.com*, and *blueskyfrog.com*. Alloy.com is based in the United Kingdom and claims to have over 10 million members. Bolt.com claims to have 4.5 million members and operates from the United States. Blueskyfrog.com operates from Australia, concentrating on cell phone users, and claims to have more than 2.5 million devoted members.

▶ **Megacommunities.** Megacommunities combine numerous smaller communities under one "umbrella" (under one name). GeoCities is one example of a megacommunity with many subcommunities. Owned by Yahoo!, it is by far the largest online community.

▶ **B2B online communities.** Chapter 6 introduced many-to-many B2B exchanges. These often are referred to as communities. B2B exchanges support community programs such as technical discussion forums, blogs, interactive Webcasts, user-created product reviews, virtual conferences and meetings, experts' seminars, and user-managed profile pages. Classified ads can help members to find jobs or employers to find employees. Many also include industry news, directories, links to government and professional associations, and more.

▶ **Social networks.** These are megacommunities, such as MySpace and YouTube, in which millions of unrelated members can express themselves, find friends, exchange photos, view video tapes, and more (Section 8.3).

EXHIBIT 8.4 Types of Virtual Communities

Community Type	Description
Transaction and other business	Facilitates buying and selling (e.g., *ausfish.com.au*). Combines an information portal with an infrastructure for trading. Members are buyers, sellers, intermediaries, and so on who are focused on a specific commercial area (e.g., fishing).
Purpose or interest	No trading, just exchange of information on a topic of mutual interest. Examples: Investors consult The Motley Fool (*fool.com*) for investment advice; rugby fans congregate at the Fans Room at *nrl.com.au*; music lovers go to *mp3.com*; *geocities.yahoo.com* is a collection of several areas of interest in one place.
Relations or practices	Members are organized around certain life experiences. Examples: *ivillage.com* caters to women and *seniornet.com* is targeted to senior citizens. Professional communities also belong to this category. For example, *isworld.org* is for information systems faculty, students, and professionals.
Fantasy	Members share imaginary environments. Examples: sport fantasy teams at *espn.com*; GeoCities members can pretend to be medieval barons at *dir.yahoo.com/Recreation/games/role_playing_games/titles*. See *games.yahoo.com* for many more fantasy communities.
Social networks	Members communicate, collaborate, create, share, form smaller groups, entertain, and more. MySpace.com is the leader.

Sources: Compiled from Hagel and Armstrong (1997) and Rheingold (2000).

strong revenues. These 10 important trends include: (1) search communities, (2) trading communities, (3) education communities, (4) scheduled events communities, (5) subscriber-based communities, (6) community consulting firms, (7) e-mail-based communities, (8) advocacy communities, (9) CRM communities, and (10) mergers and acquisitions activities. See Cashel (2004) for details.

COMMERCIAL ASPECTS OF COMMUNITIES

A logical step as a community site grows in members and influence may be to turn it into a commercial or revenue-generating site. Examples of such community-commercial sites include ivillage.com and wikia.com. The following are suggestions on how to make the transformation from a community site to a commercial one:

▶ Understand a particular niche industry, its information needs, and the step-by-step process by which it does the research needed to do business, and try to match the industry with a potential or existing community.

▶ Build a site that provides that information, either through partnerships with existing information providers or by gathering it independently, or identify a community that can be sponsored.

▶ Set up the site to mirror the steps a user goes through in the information-gathering and decision-making process (e.g., how a chip designer whittles down the list of possible chips that will fit a particular product).

▶ Build a community that relies on the site for decision support (or modify an existing one).

▶ Start selling products and services that fit into the decision-support process (such as selling sample chips to engineers who are members of the community).

Social Commerce

According to Wikipedia, **social commerce** is a subset of e-commerce in which the active participation of customers and their personal relationships are at the forefront. The main element is the involvement of a customer in the marketing of products being sold (e.g., recommendations and comments from customers). For instance, this happens when customers publish Weblogs with their shopping lists. The term has been expanded to include a variety of collaborative commerce activities, where the social participation may extend beyond recommendation to collaborative purchasing, such as BountyUp (bountyup.com), or fundraising. Social commerce includes many EC activities conducted in social networks, such as purchasing or trading information or content.

Electronic communities can create value in several ways. Members input useful information to the community in the form of comments and feedback, elaborating on their attitudes, beliefs, and information needs. This information can then be retrieved and used by other members or by marketers. The community organizers may also supply their own content to communities, as AOL does.

KEY STRATEGIES FOR SUCCESSFUL ONLINE COMMUNITIES

The model of self-financing communities (i.e., those without a sponsor) has not worked very well. Several communities that were organized for profit sustained heavy losses and some are still struggling. Examples include ivillage.com, china.com, and elsitio.com. Several other communities ceased operations in 2000 and 2001 (e.g., esociety.com and renren.com). The trend toward mergers and acquisitions among communities that started in 2001 is expected to improve the financial viability of some communities. For financial viability of social networks, see Section 8.8.

The management consulting company Accenture outlined the following eight critical factors for community success (see details in Duffy 1999):

1. Increase traffic and participation in the community.
2. Focus on the needs of the members; use facilitators and coordinators.
3. Encourage free sharing of opinions and information—no controls.
4. Obtain financial sponsorship. This factor is a must. Significant investment is required.
5. Consider the cultural environment.
6. Provide several tools and activities for member use; communities are not just discussion groups.
7. Involve community members in activities and recruiting.
8. Guide discussions, provoke controversy, and raise sticky issues. This keeps interest high.

Leimeister and Krcmar (2004) add the following top six success factors based on their own 2004 survey:

1. Handle member data sensitively.
2. Maintain stability of the Web site with respect to the consistency of content, services, and types of information offered.
3. Provide fast reaction time of the Web site.
4. Offer up-to-date content.
5. Offer continuous community control with regard to member satisfaction.
6. Establish codes of behavior (netiquette or guidelines) to contain conflict potential.

Examples of some communities that use one or more of these principles of success include the following: earthweb.com, icollector.com, webmd.com, terra.es, ivillage.com, icq.com, letsbuyit.com, paltalk.com, radiolinja.fi, and projectconnections.com. For more details and discussion of communities, see Dholakia et al. (2004).

The virtual communities described here have evolved into one of the major phenomena of e-commerce, the *social networks*, as described in Section 8.3.

Section 8.2 ▶ REVIEW QUESTIONS

1. Define virtual (Internet) communities and describe their characteristics.
2. List the major categories of virtual communities.
3. Describe the commercial aspects of virtual communities.
4. Describe the critical success factors for virtual communities.

8.3 ONLINE SOCIAL NETWORKS

A **social network** is a place where people can create their own spaces, or homepages, on which they can create blogs; post pictures, videos, or music; share ideas; and link to other Web locations they find interesting. Users can tag the content they post with keywords of their own choosing, which makes the content searchable. In effect, they create online communities of people with similar interests.

CONCEPTS AND DEFINITIONS

Social network theory views social relationships in terms of *nodes* and *ties*. Nodes are the individual actors within the networks, and ties are the relationships between the actors. The social network indicates the ways in which individuals are connected through various social familiarities, ranging from casual acquaintance to close familial bonds. There can be many kinds of ties between the nodes. In its most simple form, a social network is a map of all the relevant ties between the nodes being studied. The network can also determine the social assets of individuals. Often, a social network diagram displays these concepts, where nodes are the points and ties are the lines.

The shape of the social network helps determine a network's usefulness to its individuals. Smaller, tighter networks can be less useful to their members. This is one reason for the large size of most social networks.

Social networking also refers to a category of Internet applications to help connect friends, business partners, or other individuals together using a variety of tools. These applications, known as *online social networks,* are becoming increasingly popular (e.g., see *Read/WriteWeb* 2006 and en.wikipedia.org/wiki/Social_marketplace). The companies that provide these services are known as *social networking services.*

Social Network Analysis

Social network analysis (SNA) is the mapping and measuring of relationships and flows between people, groups, organizations, animals, computers or other information or knowledge-processing entities. The nodes in the network are the people and groups, whereas the links show relationships or flows between the nodes. SNA provides both a visual and a mathematical analysis of relationships.

SNA has emerged as a key technique in modern sociology, anthropology, geography, social psychology, information science, and organizational studies, as well as a popular topic of speculation and study. Research in a number of academic fields has demonstrated that social networks operate on many levels, from families up to the level of nations.

---

social network
A special structure composed of individuals (or organizations) that is based on how its members are connected through various social familiarities.

social network analysis (SNA)
The mapping and measuring of relationships and flows between people, groups, organizations, animals, computers, or other information or knowledge processing entities. The nodes in the network are the people and groups, whereas the links show relationships or flows between the nodes. SNA provides both a visual and a mathematical analysis of relationships.

SNA has the potential to play a critical role in determining the way problems are solved, organizations are run, and the degree to which individuals succeed in achieving their goals. For an example of the benefits of communities in health care, see Johnson and Ambrose (2006).

Social Networking Services

Social networking services are Web sites that allow anyone to build a homepage for free. People can list personal information, communicate with others, upload files, communicate via IM, or create blogs. The homepages may also contain links to user-generated content. Although blogs and wikis are influential social networking tools, IM, RSS, and Internet forums also are considered social networking tools. Some of these tools are discussed in Section 8.7.

REPRESENTATIVE SOCIAL NETWORKS: FROM FACEBOOK TO CLASSMATES.COM

There are thousands of social networks online, with many added each week. (For a list of the major communities, including the number of users, see en.wikipedia.org/wiki/ List_of_social_networking_websites). Here we provide a short discussion of the major social networking Web sites. Wikipedia (wikipedia.org) provides more in-depth information on many of these companies.

Representative Social Networking Web Sites

The following are some popular social networking Web sites.

Flickr. Flickr (flickr.com) is a photo-sharing Web site, Web services suite, and an online community platform. In addition to being a popular Web site for users to share personal photographs, the service is widely used by bloggers as a photo repository. Its most innovative feature is that users can tag and browse photos by folksonomic means. Flickr provides a search engine (based on keywords). It has limits on contacts (3,000) and tags (75) for photos. Flickr is owned by Yahoo!, and the service is free to users.

Flickr has two goals: (1) to help people make their photos available to the people who matter to them and (2) to enable new ways to organizing photos.

Facebook. Facebook (facebook.com) is a social networking Web site that is popular among college students. It was originally developed for university students, faculty, and staff, but has since expanded to include everyone, including high school, corporate, and geographic communities.

As of December 2007, the Web site had the largest number of registered users among college-focused sites (at over 50 million college students worldwide). It is the number one site for photos, ahead of sites such as Flickr, with 2.3 million photos uploaded daily (see en.wikipedia.org/wiki/Facebook).

Some are concerned that Facebook could be used as a means of surveillance and data mining. For other concerns, see Wikipedia.org.

Classmates Online. Classmates Online (classmates.com) helps members find, connect, and keep in touch with friends and acquaintances from throughout their lives—including kindergarten, primary school, high school, college, work, and the U.S. military. Classmates Online has more than 40 million active members in the United States and Canada.

It is free for people to register as a Basic member of Classmates Online in order to list themselves to be found and to search the entire database for friends. Members can also post photographs, announcements, and biographies, read community message boards, and receive information about upcoming reunions. Gold members, who pay a fee, can also send e-mail to any member, use Web site tools for planning reunions and events, form private groups, and use My Network to communicate with friends. Classmates Online is owned by United Online, the company that also owns social networking companies in Germany and Sweden. The site is profitable.

Friendster. Friendster (friendster.com) is based on the Circle of Friends technique for networking individuals in virtual communities and demonstrates the small-world phenomenon.

Friendster was considered the top online social network service until around April 2004, when it was overtaken by MySpace. Other competitors include all-in-one sites (sites that offer a diversity of services), such as Windows Live Spaces and Facebook. Friendster is most popular among young adults in Europe, North America, and Asia between the ages of 21 and 30.

Orkut. Orkut (orkut.com) is Google's social network service offering. Google claims that it is designed to help users meet new friends and maintain existing relationships. Similar to Friendster and MySpace, Orkut goes a step further by permitting the creation of easy-to-set-up simple forums (called "communities") of users. Until October 2006, Orkut was available by invitation only, but it now permits users to create accounts without an invitation.

Orkut's use as a social tool is complex, because people frequently try to add strangers to their pool of friends in an effort to increase the number next to their name in their profile that indicates the number of friends they have. Many "add-me" communities exist solely for this purpose. A large number of bogus, cloned, fake, invisible, and "orphaned" profiles also exist.

Users can rate their friends, and profile information is available to all. It is popular mostly in Brazil (almost 55 percent of about 70 million members), and Portuguese is the first default language (McCarthy 2007).

Xanga. Xanga (xanga.com) is a Web site that hosts Weblogs, photoblogs, and social networking profiles. It is operated by Xanga.com, Inc. Users of Xanga are referred to as "Xangans." Xanga's origins can be traced back to 1998, when it began as a site for sharing book and music reviews. It has since then evolved into one of the most popular blogging and networking services on the Web, with an estimated 27 million users worldwide (see en.wikipedia.org/wiki/Xanga).

A blogring connects a circle of Weblogs with a common focus or theme. All Xanga users are given the ability to create a new blogring or join an existing one. Blogrings are searchable by topic. A list of blogrings that the user is associated with appears in a module typically on the left side of the Web site. Each user is allowed a maximum of eight blogrings.

Digg. Digg (digg.com) is a community-based Web site with an emphasis on technology and science articles (see en.wikipedia.org/wiki/Digg). The site has recently expanded to provide a variety of other categories, such as politics and videos. It combines social bookmarking, blogging, and syndication with a form of nonhierarchical, democratic editorial control. Users submit news stories and Web sites, and then a user-controlled ranking system promotes these stories and sites to the front page. This differs from the hierarchical editorial system employed by many other news sites. When users read a news item they have the option to "digg it" or "digg that."

Readers can view stories that fellow users have submitted in the "Digg Upcoming" section of the site. Once a story has received enough "diggs," it appears on Digg's front page. Should the story not receive enough diggs, or if enough users report a problem with the submission, the story will remain in the "Digg All" area, where it may eventually be removed. For further details, see en.wikipedia.org/wiki/Digg and Heilemann (2006b).

Cyworld. Cyworld (cyworld.com) is a South Korean Web community site operated by SK Telecom. Literally translated, "Cyworld" can mean "cyberworld," but it's also a play on the Korean word for "relationship," so it could also mean "relationship world." It uses "virtual rooms," similar to those on MySpace and CokeMusic.

Members cultivate on- and offline relationships by forming Ilchon buddy relationships with each other through a service called "minihompy," which encompasses a photo gallery, message board, guestbook, and personal bulletin board (see en.wikipedia.org/wiki/Cyworld). A user can link his or her minihompy to another user's minihompy to form a buddy relationship. It is similar to U.S.–based Facebook and MySpace Web sites. Reports show that as many as 90 percent of South Koreans in their 20s and 25 percent of the total population of South Korea are registered users of Cyworld, and as of September 2005 daily unique visitors numbered about 20 million. Cyworld's revenue comes from the sale of over 300,000 items, which supplement the revenue from ads.

Today, Cyworld serves users in the United States, China, Japan, Taiwan, Vietnam, and South Korea. For analysis, see Schonfeld (2006a).

Some Other Social Networking Sites. The following social networking sites also are of interest:

- Bebo.com is popular in the United Kingdom, Ireland, and New Zealand; it is similar to MySpace.
- Piczo.com is popular in Canada and the United Kingdom; it is a teen-friendly site designed to deter perverts.
- His.com is most popular in Mexico and Spain; it is one of MySpace's major competitors.
- Reunion.com serves alumni of schools and organizes reunions; it owns several related Web sites.
- Friendsreunited.co.uk is the UK version of Reunion.com.
- Iwiw.net is a Hungarian social network with a multilingual interface.
- Migente.com focuses on the America Latino community.
- Blackplanet.com focuses on the African American community.
- Grono.net is a Polish social network.

One of the most popular social networks, YouTube, is described next. This network is changing the media and advertising industries.

Section 8.3 ▶ REVIEW QUESTIONS

1. Define social network.
2. Define social network analysis and services.
3. Describe Flickr, Facebook, Classmates, and Friendster.
4. Describe Digg.
5. What is Cyworld?

8.4 YOUTUBE AND COMPANY—A WHOLE NEW WORLD

Free video-sharing Web sites (where users can upload, view, and share video clips) became very popular after the inception of YouTube in February 2005. Many startups have tried to compete with YouTube, which was named by *Time* magazine as the "Invention of the Year 2006." In this section, we will present the company and some of its competitors.

YOUTUBE: THE ESSENTIALS

YouTube is a consumer media company where people can watch and share original videos worldwide via the Web. People can see firsthand accounts of current events, find videos about their hobbies and interests, and discover the quirky and unusual. As more people capture special moments on video, YouTube is empowering them to become the broadcasters of tomorrow. Users can rate videos, and the site shows the average rating and the number of times users have watched a video.

YouTube originally started as a personal video-sharing service. It has grown into an entertainment destination: about 70 million people viewed more than 2.5 billion videos in September 2007 alone (comScore 2007). It is a prime example of a social network. With YouTube, users can:

▶ Upload, tag, and share videos worldwide
▶ Browse millions of original videos uploaded by community members
▶ Find, join, and create video groups to connect with people who have similar interests
▶ Customize the experience by subscribing to member videos, saving favorites, and creating play lists
▶ Integrate YouTube videos on Web sites using video embeds or APIs
▶ Elect to broadcast their videos publicly or share them privately with specified friends and family upon upload

YouTube is building a community that is highly motivated to watch and share videos. The service is free for everyone. The company always encourages users to contact YouTube with thoughts, suggestions, feedback, or otherwise random ramblings. The site advises users to check out YouTube's blog in order to keep up-to-date on all the latest developments.

BRIEF HISTORY AND TECHNOLOGY

YouTube's video playback technology is based on Macromedia's (an Adobe company) Flash Player 7 (or newer) and uses the Sorenson Spark H.263 video codec. This technology allows users to display videos (including movies, TV clips, music videos, videoblogging, etc.) with quality comparable to more established video playback technologies that generally require user to download and install a small piece of software (called a browser plug-in) in order to watch video. Flash itself requires a plug-in, but the Flash 7 (or newer) plug-in is generally considered to be present on approximately 90 percent of Internet-connected computers. Alternatively, users can use a number of Web sites to download the videos to their own computers. The use of Flash video was most likely a key component of YouTube's success, allowing viewers to watch video instantly without installing software or dealing with a common problem experienced with other Web video technologies, such as incompatible or varying versions of video players.

YouTube was one of the fastest-growing Web sites on the Internet during January 2008 and was ranked as the third most popular Web site on Alexa (a popular rating company, see Section 8.7), far outpacing even MySpace's growth. YouTube's preeminence in the online video market is staggering. By July 2006, 100 million clips were viewed daily on YouTube, with an additional 65,000 new videos uploaded each day (en.wikipedia.org/wiki/YouTube). The site has about 20,000,000 visitors per month.

Like many startups, YouTube began as an angel-funded enterprise in a small office in San Mateo, California. Later on, Sequoia Capital, a venture capital firm, invested more money (see the process in Online Chapter 13). Google purchased YouTube for

$1.65 billion in stock on October 9, 2006. The purchase agreement between Google and YouTube came after YouTube entered into three agreements with media companies in an attempt to escape the threat of copyright-infringement lawsuits. YouTube continues to operate independently.

It is interesting to note that much of the site's early publicity was based on the frequent demands from copyright holders to remove material from the site. NBC, which initially demanded the removal of copyrighted material, has created a strategic alliance with YouTube. An official NBC channel on YouTube now showcases promotional clips of its videos.

THE SOCIAL IMPACT OF YOUTUBE

YouTube's popularity has led to the creation of many YouTube Internet celebrities, popular individuals who have attracted significant publicity in their home countries through their videos. The most-subscribed to YouTube member in fall 2006 was Geriatric 1927, an 80-year-old pensioner from England who gained widespread recognition within a week of making his debut on the site. He is still on the top subscribed list (see en.wikipedia.org/wiki/Peter_Oakley). For these users, Internet fame has had various unexpected effects. As an example, a YouTube user and former receptionist, Brooke Brodack, from Massachusetts was signed by NBC's Carson Daly for an 8-month development contract. Another example is the blogger known as lonely girl15, who ended up being the fictitious character created by New Zealand actress Jessica Rose and some film directors. In 2007, a Dutch vocalist and songwriter named Esmée Denters announced that she would be traveling to the United States for professional recording sessions on the strength of her YouTube appearances. For a representative list of others who became Internet phenomena, see en.wikipedia.org/wiki/YouTube.

YouTube has also become a means of promoting bands and their music. One such example is OK Go, which received a huge radio hit and an MTV Video Music Awards performance out of the treadmill video for "Here It Goes Again." In the same light, a video broadcasting the Free Hugs Campaign with accompanying music by the Sick Puppies led to instant fame for both the band and the campaign. The main character of the video, Juan Mann, who also achieved fame, is now being interviewed on Australian news programs and even has appeared on *The Oprah Winfrey Show*.

YouTube's voter education initiative YouTube You Choose 08 is designed to allow political candidates to communicate with voters about their campaigns. It features campaign videos, speeches, informal chats and behind-the-scenes footage. The platform allows potential voters to participate in dialogue with candidates using video responses, text comments, and ratings (Sachoff 2007).

THE BUSINESS AND REVENUE MODELS

Before being bought by Google, YouTube had an advertising-based business model. Some industry commentators speculated that YouTube's running costs—specifically the bandwidth required—might be as high as $1 million per month, thereby fueling criticisms that, like many Internet startups, it did not have a viable business model (see en.wikipedia.org/wiki/YouTube).

The site launched advertisements in March 2006. In April 2006, YouTube started using Google's AdSense. Given its traffic levels, video streams, and page views, some have calculated YouTube's potential revenues could be in the millions per month.

Strategic Advantages of the Business Model

The growth of YouTube has been extremely rapid, depending largely on referrals from users who alert their friends and family to a favorite video. That many viewers who discover the site and then decide to share their own videos continually expands YouTube's content pool. A steady increase in high-speed Internet connections at home has propelled YouTube's success, making the distribution and consumption of online video more effective. Online File W8.3 and Case 8.1 show typical applications of YouTube.

CASE 8.1
EC Application

HOW YOUTUBE CAPITALIZES ON MAJOR EVENTS AND COMMERCIAL VIDEOS

The following are some examples of how YouTube collaborates with both advertisers and media companies.

The Sundance Channel

The Sundance Channel announced a strategic alliance with YouTube on January 17, 2007, (YouTube 2007) for coverage of the 2007 Sundance Film Festival that included a video blog on YouTube. YouTube showed special clips from the festival throughout 2007 (see *youtube.com/sundancechannel*). It also featured profiles of competing filmmakers, clips from past festivals, and in-depth daily coverage by YouTube users Arin Crumley and Susan Buice. The partnership also provided advertising for YouTube partners, including Sundance.

The Sundance Channel syndicated a video blog created by Crumley and Buice exclusively for YouTube. Crumley and Buice served as Sundance Channel correspondents during the 2007 Sundance Film Festival and documented their daily experiences from a festival-attendee and independent-filmmaker perspective. They pioneered new strategies for independent film distribution through digital technology, including podcasts, custom Google maps, and a 2007 screening of their film *Four Eyed Monster* at Second Life in the virtual world.

The Sundance Channel's Festival's minisite includes all content available on YouTube, plus exclusive photos and a blog hosted by Peter Bowen, senior editor of *Filmmaker Magazine*, who follows the buzz around films and acquisitions. Sundance pays fees for the advertisements on YouTube.

Coca-Cola

YouTube and Coca-Cola introduced video cards for the 2006 and 2007 holiday seasons (YouTube 2006a). People were able to send their own personal videos as a holiday greeting card online. Visitors were also able to share their holiday spirit by uploading their own videos or using video greetings created by popular YouTube personalities, including Geriatric 1927, Boh3m3, TerraNaomi, Renetto, TheWineKone, and LisaNova. Holiday-themed videos also were available to share from Coca-Cola, including clips from vintage Coke advertisements. Selected video greetings that users chose to share with the world were featured as part of a video play list on Coca-Cola.com called the Holiday WishCast and were seen by people around the world.

The Coca-Cola Holiday WishCast gave friends and families a new way to communicate during the 2006 and 2007 holiday seasons. WishCast was a unique way for people to connect, whether it was helping loved ones keep in touch, creating a last-minute holiday card, or enabling bands to send personalized greetings to their fans. It was the latest evolution in the development of Coca-Cola.com following the relaunch of the site in 2006, which included user-generated content and digital music downloads.

The partnership with Coca-Cola gave the YouTube community the ability to send holiday wishes in a way that truly harnesses the creativity of the users. To send a holiday video greeting, people visited either *youtube.com/wishcast* or *coca-cola.com/wishcast*.

Warner Music Group

According to YouTube (2006b), the YouTube Community and Warner Music Group (WMG) artists created "Special New Year's Messages to Share with the World" (sponsored by Chevrolet). The first-ever YouTube New Year's Eve Countdown celebrated New Year's as it happened around the world with new videos featured every hour from dozens of locations worldwide.

(continued)

CASE 8.1   *(continued)*

SuperDotComAdsXLI

Starting January 31, 2007, Plaxo, RockYou.com, Technorati, and three other small companies are putting their versions of Super Bowl-style ads on the Web. The companies have bundled their ads together in a YouTube channel called SuperDotComAdsXLI, hoping to use their various social networks and corporate blogs to generate audiences for all the commercials.

The various start-ups involved began kicking the idea around January 15, 2007. Plaxo is home to some budding filmmakers, so McCrea (vice president of marketing at Plaxo) let a small team of employees put something together. He was so impressed with the results that he decided to use the spot to launch Plaxo's new logo and tagline. Now he's considering doing even more

video ads solely for the online medium. Because these ads are inexpensive to produce it makes sense that Web-based companies use that platform to promote themselves.

Sources: YouTube (2006a, 2006b, 2007).

Questions

1. How does the Sundance Channel benefit from its relationship with YouTube?

2. How did Coca-Cola benefit from YouTube's greeting card program?

3. YouTube collects money from its partners. Why are the partners willing to pay?

IMPLEMENTATION DIFFICULTIES: THE COPYRIGHT PROBLEM

YouTube policy does not allow content to be uploaded by anyone not permitted by U.S. copyright law to do so, and the company frequently removes infringing content. Nonetheless, a large amount of copyrighted videos continue to be uploaded. Generally, YouTube only discovers these videos via self-policing within its community. YouTube has a flagging feature, intended as a means for reporting questionable content, including that which might constitute copyright infringement. However, the feature can be susceptible to abuse; for a time, some users were flagging other users' original content for copyright violations purely out of spite. YouTube then proceeded to remove copyright infringement from the list of offenses flagable by members. The primary way in which a user identifies the content of a video is through the search terms that are associated with clips. However, some users have created alternative words as search terms when uploading files with copyrighted content. This makes it difficult to find the files.

TV journalist Robert Tur filed the first lawsuit against YouTube in summer 2006, alleging copyright infringement for hosting a number of famous news clips without permission. In August 2007, Tur dropped his individual suit and joined a class action suit led by England's Premier Soccer League. That suit is unresolved as of January 2008 (Baage 2007).

The Brazilian Court Case

Consider the following example of the complexity of the legal issues faced by YouTube. In early January 2007, a Brazilian court ordered (for the second time) YouTube to block footage of supermodel Daniela Cicarelli and her boyfriend in intimate scenes along a beach in Spain. YouTube removed the clip in September 2006, but the clip still appears periodically on YouTube under different titles. The judge said YouTube must find a way to use filters so the clip stops popping up in Brazil. Lawyer Rubens Decousseau Tilkian, who represents Cicarelli's boyfriend, said YouTube had not gone *far enough* to prevent access to the clip because people succeeded in posting it using different names for the video. Can YouTube comply with the court order? And at what cost? The Brazilian court has the authority to fine YouTube about $120,000 for each day the video is viewable.

In 2007, big media, such as Viacom, NBC, and News Corp., all took shots at YouTube (see La Monica 2007).

THE COMPETITION

The success of YouTube spawned a large number of competitors. Several of these startups were dedicated to video sharing. In addition, several social networks (e.g., MySpace) added video sharing as one of their offerings. Online File W8.4 offers a comparison of several of YouTube's competitors. Additional details on YouTube's competitors are available at dvguru.com (posting by Bilsborrow-Koo 2006).

Meetcafe (meetcafe.com), a potential YouTube rival, launched a new forum for online video content by putting amateur contributors together with professional film makers. Known as Café Confidential, the new channel is an attempt to introduce higher standards to the often chaotic user-generated content. Meetcafe rewards amateurs who use the channel.

According to Media Metrix, in September 2006 MySpace accounted for 20 percent of the 7.2 billion video streams across the Web (comScore 2006), making MySpace YouTube's strongest competitor. Five major media companies joined MySpace in 2007 (see Lashinsky 2007) to offer free, legitimate videos in an effort to "kill" YouTube.

To counter the competition, YouTube is offering innovative applications such as video awards to most creative and popular original videos (youtube.com/YTAwards). However, YouTube remains the powerhouse when it comes to video. YouTube's market share was 50 percent greater than 64 other video sites combined (Prescott 2007).

Section 8.4 ▶ REVIEW QUESTIONS

1. Define video sharing and describe how it is done at YouTube.
2. What can users do on YouTube?
3. How can YouTube create Internet celebrities?
4. How can YouTube promote music and artists?
5. What are YouTube's revenue sources? How are these revenue models related to Google?

8.5 BUSINESS AND ENTREPRENEURIAL NETWORKS

In Chapter 1, we introduced Xing.com, a business-related network. Here, we describe some other business and entrepreneurial networks.

BUSINESS NETWORKS

A **business network** is a group of people that have some kind of commercial or business relationship—for example, the relationships between sellers and buyers, buyers among themselves, buyers and suppliers, and colleagues and other colleagues. They also are referred to as *business social networks*. Business networking functions best when individuals offer to help others to find connections rather than "cold-calling" on prospects themselves (see en.wikipedia.org/wiki/Business_network). Business networking can take place outside of traditional business physical environments. For example, public

business network
A group of people that have some kind of commercial relationship; for example, the relationships between sellers and buyers, buyers among themselves, buyers and suppliers, and colleagues and other colleagues.

places such as airports or golf courses provide opportunities to make new business contacts if an individual has good social skills. The Internet also is proving to be a good place to network.

Example: LinkedIn

The main purpose of LinkedIn is to allow registered users to maintain a list of contact details of people they know and trust in business (see en.wikipedia.org/wiki/LinkedIn). The people in the list are called *connections*. Users can invite anyone, whether they are a LinkedIn user or not, to become a connection.

A contact network is built up consisting of a user's direct connections, his or her connections' connections (called second-degree connections), and the connections of second-degree connections (called third-degree connections). These connections can then be used to gain introductions through mutual, trusted contacts (see Copeland 2006 and linkdin.com).

Users can use LinkedIn to learn about jobs, people, and business opportunities recommended by contacts in their contact network. Employers can list jobs and search for potential candidates. Job seekers can review the profile of hiring managers and discover which of their existing contacts can introduce them.

The "gated-access approach," whereby contact with another professional requires either a preexisting relationship or the intervention of a contact, is intended to build trust among the service's users. LinkedIn participates in the EU Safe Harbor Privacy Framework.

LinkedIn also features "LinkedIn Answers." As the name suggests, the service is similar to Answers.com or Yahoo! Answers. The service allows LinkedIn users to ask questions for the community to answer. "LinkedIn Answers" is free, and the questions are generally more business oriented.

For more on LinkedIn and its capabilities and successes see Copeland (2006).

Entrepreneurial Network

In business, *entrepreneurial networks* are social organizations that offer resources to start or improve entrepreneurial projects or startups. Entrepreneurial networks can help their members in properly running a business or project as well as differentiating the business from similar ones.

The goal of most entrepreneurial networks is to bring together a broad selection of professionals and resources that complement each others' endeavors (see en. wikipedia.org/wiki/Entrepreneurial_network). One of their priorities is to aid in successful business launches. The networks also provide motivation, direction, and increased access to opportunities and other skill sets. Promotion of members' talents and services, both within the network and in the broader market, increases opportunities for all participants. One of the key needs of any startup is capital, and entrepreneurial networks often focus on helping entrepreneurs obtain financial resources. Entrepreneurial networks may also become online communities involved in endorsing reforms, legislation, or other municipal drives that accommodate the organization's goals.

The following are examples of entrepreneurial networks:

▶ Ecademy (ecademy.com) is a global social network for businesspeople. Members can build relationships with other business professionals; share contacts and knowledge; provide support; locate jobs, prospects, and clients; attend networking events; and trade across the globe.

▶ Young European professionals can join European Young Professionals (eyplondon.org), which promotes links between European business professionals.

Both organizations conduct offline activities as well.

COOPERATE SOCIAL NETWORKS

An increasing number of companies are creating their own social networks for their employees, former employees, and/or customers.

For example, Wachovia (wachovia.com), a large financial holding company, introduced its social networking service to its 110,000 workers in early 2008. Like the popular Facebook service, the network allows users to upload photos of themselves—not just corporate ID mug-shots either—and personal information. One of the site's goals is to build a sense of community across the vast company.

However, the primary purpose of Wachovia's network is all business. Think of it as a nervous system for the enterprise, one that gets more valuable the more it's used. Wachovia envisions that the network will evolve into a sophisticated knowledge-management platform integrated with multiple applications that will enable workers to locate information—and the people who use it—simply and intuitively. When users look up coworkers, they can see their relationships to other employees and departments and determine their availability at any given moment. A search for best practices on a particular topic will find blogs and wikis written by informed employees, along with an in-house encyclopedia of all things Wachovia. People use it in many imaginative ways.

Many large corporations, including IBM, Coca-Cola, Cisco, and Deloitte Touche, have developed innovative in-house social networks. Others have created groups within MySpace or other social networks (see Weber 2007, Demopoulas 2007, and Cone 2007b for many examples). One innovative application used for recruiting is described in Online File W8.5.

SOCIAL MARKETPLACE

The term **social marketplace** is derived from the combination of *social networking* and *marketplaces*, such that a social marketplace acts like an online community, harnessing the power of social networks for introducing, buying, and selling products, services, and resources, including people's own creations.

Ideally, a social marketplace should support members' own creations as much as they blog, link, and post. Section 8.6 describes a market for musicians, filmmakers, authors, designers, and other creative individuals.

Examples of social marketplaces include (per en.wikipedia.org/wiki/Social_marketplace):

▶ **Windows Live Expo.** Windows Live Expo (expo.live.com) is an online social marketplace that is similar to Craigslist in that it provides online classifieds. A major feature of the site is that users choose the listings they want to search based on friends and contacts or by geographic proximity.

▶ **Fotolia.** Fotolia (fotolia.com) is a social marketplace that supports a huge community of creative people who enjoy sharing, learning, and expressing themselves through forums and blogs. Users can legally buy and share stock images and illustrations.

▶ **Flipsy.** Anyone can use Flipsy (flipsy.com) to list, buy, and sell books, music, movies, and games. It was created to fill the need for a free and trustworthy media marketplace. Flipsy sells products by identification using bar codes. In order to foster increased trading, it does not charge commissions. Payment processing is handled by a third party, such as PayPal.

social marketplace
An online community that harnesses the power of social networks for the introduction, buying, and selling of products, services, and resources, including people's own creations.

1. What is a business network?
2. Describe LinkedIn and its capabilities.
3. What is an entrepreneurial network?
4. What is a social marketplace?

8.6 ENTERTAINMENT WEB 2.0 STYLE: FROM COMMUNITIES TO ENTERTAINMENT MARKETPLACES

The rich media of Web 2.0 technologies, the involvement of millions of young people who are interested in online entertainment, the availability of innovative tools, and the creative and collaborative nature of Web 2.0 all facilitate entertainment. Also, Web 2.0 tools facilitate the proliferation of entertainment on demand (Tynan 2006). In this section, we describe entertainment-centered communities as well as other issues related to Web 2.0 entertainment.

ENTERTAINMENT AND BUSINESS COMMUNITIES

A large number of social networks and communities are fully or partially dedicated to entertainment. Here are a few examples:

Last.FM

Last.fm (last.fm) is an Internet radio station and music recommendation system that merged with sister site Audioscrobbler in August 2005. In May 2007, CBS purchased Last.fm in order to extend its online reach (*New York Times* 2007). The system builds a detailed profile of each user's musical preferences. Based on this profile, Last.fm recommends artists similar to members' favorites, features their favorite artists and songs on a customizable Web page comprising the songs played on its stations selected via a collaborative filter or recorded by a Last.fm plug-in installed into its users' music playing application.

Last.fm users can build their musical profiles in two ways: by listening to their personal music collection on a music player application with an Audioscrobbler plug-in or by listening to the Last.fm Internet radio service. Songs played are added to a log from which musical recommendations are calculated. Last.fm calls this automatic track logging *scrobbling*. The user's page also displays recently played tracks, which are available via Web services, allowing users to display them on blogs or as forum signatures.

Regular membership is free; premium membership is $3 per month. The site won Best Community Music Site at the BT Digital Music Awards in October 2006, and in January 2007 it was nominated for Best Web site in the NME Awards. The site operates in 10 major languages.

Mixi

Mixi, Inc. (mixi.co.jp) is an invitation-only social networking service site in Japan. The focus of mixi is "community entertainment"; that is, meeting new people by way of common interests. Users can send and receive messages, write in a diary, read and comment on others' diaries, organize and join communities, and invite their friends to join. Mixi Station, a client program that detects songs being played in iTunes and Windows Media Player, uploads songs automatically to a communally accessible list in the "Music" section.

The site had more than 12.4 million members and 490,000 small communities of friends and interests as of November 2007 (see en.wikipedia.org/wiki/Mixi). The word *mixi* is a combination of *mix* and *I*, referring to the idea that the user, "I," "mixes" with other users through the service.

ADVERTISING MOVIES AND EVENTS IN COMMUNITIES

Communities are a natural place to advertise events such as movies. For example, *Clerks II* was released in August 2006 by Kevin Smith, the producer. Smith used MySpace to promote the film in a true "Indy Guerilla style." The movie characters (e.g., Dante Hicks, Randall Graves) have their own pages at MySpace linked to the movie's hub pages as biographies.

Each week, starting in May 2006 and running until the release of *Clerks II* on August 18, 2006, users went into the "Our Friends" list and picked out fellow MySpacers at random to participate in a contest. Those who had the *Clerks II* MySpace page in their top 8 sites won a prize shipped directly from the View Askew offices in Red Bank, New Jersey (Smith 2006).

By word-of-mouth, information about the contest and the movie was spread across MySpace, enabling Smith to stay within his limited advertising budget and gross millions from the movie.

ONLINE MARKETPLACE FOR MOVIES

The startup company InDplay Inc. (indplay.com) has a mission to connect films with professional buyers through an online marketplace. It can be viewed as occupying the middle ground between the user-generated videos on YouTube and the select world of theatrical distribution. It uses databases, such as those from IMD6 Inc.

In the InDplay marketplace, owners of any video can register as sellers and upload preview clips and any other information. Buyers representing theaters, DVD, TV networks, cable networks, Internet sites, and other outlets, register and make e-mail offers to the sellers. Purchases and payments are made via PayPal or wire transfer. InDplay gets an 8 percent standard commission. According to Woyke (2006), more than 10 million films and TV programs from around the world are available for sale (or license), and more than 100,000 professional buyers are registered.

The site includes community features such as ratings and reviews (similar to eBay) and connects people at all stages of a film project via wikis and blogs. For more on movie downloading, see the Netflix Opening Case in Chapter 4.

Startups such as Lulu (lulu.com) and Zatto (zato.com) offer similar online markets for music, TV shows, and books.

THE HYPE MACHINE

The Hype Machine (hypem.com) is a new concept (Heilemann 2006a). Here is how it works: A server scans music blogs for postings with links to MP3 files. When a file is found, it is indexed, and the file is added to a database. The title is posted on the Hype Machine directory. Users can listen to tracks through the site's built-in player or buy music through links to Amazon.com or iTunes. Users can also search the database for their favorite bands.

INTERNET SERIES

Internet series are similar to soap operas on TV. There is an increasing number of Internet series, and some are already on DVD. Examples include *Broken Trail*, *Soup of the Day*, and *Floaters*. For details, see Arnold (2006).

MOBILE WEB 2.0 DEVICES FOR ENTERTAINMENT AND WORK

Several mobile devices were designed with blogs, wikis, and other P2P services in mind. Here are some examples.

iPhone

The iPhone (from apple.com), introduced in 2007, is an *all-in-one* smartphone (see photo below). It is considered a disruptor in the cell phone market. Soon after iPhone's release, Samsung announced a competitor phone.

The iPhone has all the functionalities of BlackBerry (Chapter 9). It is also a personal media player, offering all the capabilities of an iPod, with music and video playback, plus the benefits of a high-resolution widescreen display for watching movies and videos. It is a touch-screen smartphone with full-blown Internet communication capabilities; a quad-band, EDGE-capable mobile phone; and it has a brain (i.e., PAD capabilities), making it simple and easy to use. It also has a camera, a headset jack, and a built-in speaker.

The iPhone also has a sleep/wake button, and a proximity sensor turns off the screen when users hold the phone to their heads. It features automatic-orientation adjustment, switching between portrait and landscape modes on-the-fly. The iPhone boasts virtually no dedicated controls; instead, everything is driven using a new (patented) multitouch touch screen that Apple claims is far more accurate than

Apple iPhone

Source: *apple.com/iphone*

previous touch-sensitive displays. For additional details, see apple.com/iphone and Metz (2007).

The iPhone lets companies such as Apple and Google "merge without merging" by delivering Google services through Apple hardware. Yahoo! offers free "push" e-mail capabilities to Yahoo! Mail users.

YAHOO! GO

Yahoo! Go is optimized for a mobile phone's "small screen," making it easy and fun to access the Internet. Everything about the Yahoo! Go interface is designed to be both visually striking and give users what they want with the fewest clicks possible. E-mail, news, photos, and more are "pushed" to users' phones. It includes Yahoo! oneSearch, a new mobile search that provides answers on the spot.

At its core is the *carousel*, which enables users to navigate intuitively among the various Yahoo! Go *widgets*—personal channels for e-mail, local information and maps, news, sports, finance, entertainment, weather, Flickr photos, and search. Using the carousel, users scroll over the widget they want. Because Yahoo! Go uses advanced caching and background loading technology, the widget content is automatically and continuously "pushed" to the phone. For details see mobile.yahoo.com/go.

Nokia's N800 Internet Tablet

Nokia's N800 Internet Tablet (see photo), which is about the size of a paperback novel, lets users surf the Internet, send and receive e-mail and instant messages, download audio and video, and get RSS feeds. The new model adds a Webcam for videoconferencing and a microphone for Internet phone calls.

As a media player, the N800 handles MP3 and Windows Media files and other common formats, displaying images on a 4.1-inch color screen and playing audio through built-in stereo speakers or a headphone jack. It uses Wi-Fi networking when available, but it can also connect to a compatible Nokia phone via Bluetooth and be used as a wireless modem.

The Internet Tablet, available from retailers and nokiausa.com, has an on-screen keyboard that automatically adjusts its key size and spacing for finger or stylus operation. It recognizes text written on the screen with a stylus, as shown in the photo.

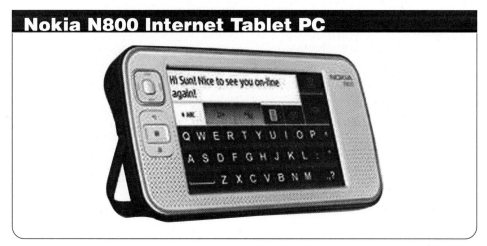

Nokia N800 Internet Tablet PC

Source: *mobilewhack.com/reviews/nokia_n800_internet_tablet_pc.html*

Section 8.6 ▶ REVIEW QUESTIONS

1. Describe entertainment communities and provide an example.
2. Describe online marketplaces for music.
3. What is an Internet series?
4. Describe the iPhone.
5. What is unique to the Nokia N800 Internet Tablet?

8.7 TECHNOLOGY SUPPORT: FROM BLOGGER.COM TO INFRASTRUCTURE SERVICES

A large number of software tools is used to facilitate the various Web 2.0 activities. Here are some representative examples.

WEB 2.0 AND SOCIAL SOFTWARE

Social software enables people to rendezvous, connect, and collaborate through computer-mediated communication. Many advocates of these tools believe that they help to create actual communities.

The more specific term *collaborative software* applies to cooperative work systems and is usually narrowly applied to software that enables work functions (see Chapter 6). Distinctions between the usage of the terms *social* and *collaborative* are in the applications, not the tools, although there are some tools that are only rarely used for work collaboration. Exhibit 8.5 shows the major categories of social software tools.

Carr (2007a) provides the following examples of Web 2.0 technologies used by a toy manufacturer:

▶ **Ratings.** Consumers create profiles and rate and comment on the company's products.
▶ **Forums.** Consumers create their own topic areas and build communities around shared interests.
▶ **Blogs.** Staff editors lead company-formatted essays and discussions that allow (but do not drive) customer comments.
▶ **E-newsletters.** Available on an opt-in basis; flow of information to customers, partners, and employees.
▶ **Streaming video.** Videos created by consumers showing the use of the company's toys and the company's TV commercials are all available for viewing.
▶ **Contests.** Sweepstakes, do-it-yourself challenges, incentives, and other initiatives involve customers from product development to marketing campaigns.
▶ **Search engine.** Using search engines (e.g., Google AdWords and Google Desktop) attract even more customers and traffic.

Here, we describe some of these tools. A complete list of free tools is available in the May 2006 issue of *PCWorld* (see find.pcworld.com/52516) and Gillin (2007b).

TOOLS FOR BLOGGING AND WIKIS

Many tools are available for bloggers and wiki writers.

Tools for Blogging

Problogger (problogger.net) lists dozens of blog tools, including statistical packages, blog editors, news aggregators, e-mail subscription and newsletter services, blog poll tools, and others. For details, see Rowse (2006).

EXHIBIT 8.5 Social Software Tools

Communication Tools
- Instant messaging
- VoIP and Skype
- Text chat
- Internet forums
- Blogs
- Wikis
- Collaborative real-time editor
- Prediction markets

Services
- Search engines
- Social guides
- Social bookmarking
- Social citations
- Social libraries
- Virtual worlds and massively multiplayer online games (MMOGs)
- Other specialized social applications
- Politics and journalism features
- Content management tools

Emerging Technologies
- Peer-to-peer social networks
- Virtual presence
- Mobile tools for Web 2.0

Tools for Individuals
- Personalization
- Customization
- Search
- RSS
- File-sharing tools

Web 2.0 Development Tools
- Mashups
- Web Services (Online Chapter 14)

Sources: Compiled from *en.wikipedia.org/wiki/Social_software*, Hinchcliffe (2007), and *Weblogsinc.com* (2007).

Notable tools include Blogger, Digg, and Del.icio.us. Blogger (offered free from Google) is a blog publishing system. For details, see blogger.com, en.wikipedia.org/wiki/Blogger, and Weber (2007). Digg (digg.com) and Del.icio.us (del.icio.us) are social bookmarking tools for sourcing stories and linking to get traffic.

Wiki Tools

Representative wiki tools include EditMe (editme.com), Seed Wiki (seedwiki.com), Socialtext (socialtext.com), Eurekster Swiki (swiki.net), TeamFlux (teamflux.com), and OpenWiki (openwiki.com). For more on the use of these tools, see Tapscott and Williams (2006), Online File W8.6, and Hinchcliffe (2007).

Tools for RSS and Podcasting

RSS and podcasting were introduced in Chapter 2. These Web 2.0 tools are now entering use in enterprises (see the Real-World Case at the end of this chapter and Gibson [2007]). Representative companies in this area are NewsGator (NewsGator.com) and KnowNow, Inc. (KnowNow.com), which boast integration with Microsoft's Exchange e-mail platform and Microsoft's Outlook.

Will Wikis, Blogs, and RSS Replace E-Mail or Just Supplement It?

E-mail has proven itself to be an indispensable form of communication, but it has limits as a collaborative tool. Enterprise content-management systems are important for codifying and organizing important corporate data, but they can be expensive and inflexible.

The point-to-point nature of e-mail limits its use as a collaborative tool. In addition, the CC and BCC fields in an e-mail can be dangerous. Oftentimes, the wrong person gets a copy of the message, and many people ignore a message with a wide distribution. Most important, the one person who might have a key insight on an issue may be left off the recipient list. Poor decisions often are made regarding to whom an e-mail should be forwarded. In theory, a blog or wiki can be seen by everyone, as can readers' responses and edits. No one is left out of the loop. Blogs and wikis have the potential to fill e-mail's collaborative gap (e.g., see Weber 2007 and Tapscott and Williams 2006).

E-mail was never designed to be a news source. An increasing number of companies are providing RSS–based tools to their employees in order to manage news feeds that they pick from the outside and distribute inside the enterprise (Gibson 2007). For benefits and corporate applications of RSS, see Gibson (2007).

Enterprise Wiki and Blog Tools

Companies such as Traction Software (tractionsoftware.com) and Socialtext Enterprise (socialtext.com) offer enterprise versions of wiki and blog software that include security controls, archiving, and identity management tools. Many companies with grassroots adoption of wikis and blogs use open-source versions of the technology, but CIOs may prefer deploying tools developed specifically for the enterprise. For a detailed case, see McGillicuddy (2006b).

Blogging for Business

According to Sloan and Kaihla (2006), enterprises are now experimenting with blogs. Team members now can publish items to the blog that were formerly sent as e-mail and copied to "My Whole Division." Newsreader clients can capture these feeds using RSS or ATOM, two simple text formats published by many Web sites, blogging tools, and wikis. Users subscribe to the feeds and receive results in a common Web browser or customized reader application. Feed subscribers can be more selective about what they receive than users of traditional e-mail. For example, rather than downloading entire articles, users can first see headlines and summaries only. (For a discussion and examples of blog marketing, see Demopoulos 2007 and Weber 2007).

For SAP, blogging has been a change for the better. Until 2006, SAP paid a clipping service to collect relevant news stories and then e-mailed the articles to large groups. Now, the Six Apart's Movable Type Weblog system is used to send news articles to field staff. SAP's blog also acts as a central source for competitive data, with field personnel contributing content. Their comments, tags, and data create a virtual conversation around the way the team works. It is much better than a stream of "FYI" e-mailed articles. Because the blog is field generated, the content is highly relevant. The blog's value is not so much about saving money, but rather improving the depth of competitive news. Many companies are using wikis and blogs to facilitate online training (see Weinstein 2006 and Wright 2006 for details).

PERSONALIZATION TOOLS: FROM MY YAHOO! TO NETVIBES

Users can create highly personalized pages that are constantly updated with information, such as news articles and stock prices, view photos, use a calculator, and perform similar actions, all in one page. Users can also post necessary tools as modules, which appear as small square or rectangular objects, with the content or functionality inside. Users can arrange the modules on their sites. Users also produce a wide variety of modules, and they upload them on My Yahoo! and similar software and make them available for free. Pages can be personalized online or offline.

One such personalization tool is My Yahoo! Users can use My Yahoo! to combine page segments featuring Yahoo!'s own news and information with segments containing RSS feeds. Microsoft's My MSN is another tool (both sites were revised in 2007).

On the desktop, the best known mini-application is Apple's Dashboard, which allows Macintosh users to install tiny programs called Widgets that perform searches, display photo slideshows, track stocks, play music, and more. Microsoft's Windows Vista operating system has a comparable system called Sidebar. Netvibes (netvibes.com) offers the best features of My Yahoo! and Dashboard. Modules can be added easily and are arranged in a menu (for details see Mossberg 2007). For graphics-rich content, users can use Pageflakes (pageflakes.com).

DEVELOPMENT TOOLS

To implement Web 2.0 applications, users sometimes need a development framework for building rich media Internet applications—Web-based programs that run like they are on a desktop, refreshing page views without resetting the page through the server (see Online Chapter 14 for details.) These frameworks come in different styles, including Flash, a multimedia development platform, and JavaScript, a Web-development language. Organizations are using these tools to build Web applications faster and cheaper than ever before. Several other tools exist.

One example of the use of Web 2.0 development tools is that of the American Cancer Society. The American Cancer Society (cancer.org) redesigned its online bookstore using Adobe Systems' Flex 2, a development environment based on Flash that lets visitors read book descriptions and drag selections into a shopping cart without waiting for a server to refresh the page. Before the redesign, the society's Web presence—built on HTTP—was inefficient, because it was necessary to call back to the server each time a user clicked a different link. The process was cumbersome. The new solution is flashy, catches attention, and makes an emotional impression, as well as an educational one, for the user. For details see Watson (2007a).

Social Bookmarking

Social bookmarking is a Web Service for sharing Internet bookmarks. Social bookmarking is a popular way to store, classify, share, and search links through folksonomy techniques on the Internet and intranets. Examples of such sites are Reddit, Digg, and Del.icio.us. For details see en.wikipedia.org/wiki/Social_bookmarking and Hammond et al. (2005).

social bookmarking
Web service for sharing Internet bookmarks. The sites are a popular way to store, classify, share, and search links through the practice of folksonomy techniques on the Internet and intranets.

Intel's Web 2.0 Software Suite

Intel offers a collaboration software suite for SMEs. Called SuiteTwo, the package includes software from Six Apart (a free blogging service that lets bloggers decide who gets to see what—if anything—on their blogs), Socialtext (an enterprise wiki systems), NewsGator (an RSS platform and readers), and SimpleFeed (RSS-based feed parsing that enables users to subscribe to topics of interest). These are small software companies that provide applications for blogs, RSS feeds, wikis, and social networking.

All of these so-called Web 2.0 applications are more commonly associated with and used by consumers. However, corporations are increasingly using blogs, wikis, and social networking applications. By partnering with these software providers, Intel hopes to have Intel-optimized programs in the emerging Web 2.0 area. Intel envisions other software bundles in the future.

TOOLS THAT SUPPORT APPLICATIONS

A large number of tools support Web 2.0 applications. The following are a few examples.

File-Sharing Tools

According to Schonfeld (2006b), several new services let people exchange large digital files (some for free, some for a fee):

- AllPeers (allpeers.com) enables users to easily transfer files.
- Glide Presenter from TransMedia (transmediacorp.com) can be used to store and share digital media.
- MediaMax (mediamax.com) can be used to store digital photos and movies on the Web.
- Myfabrik (myfabrik.com) can be used to send links to shared files stored on the Web.
- Pando (pando.com) bypasses e-mail attachment limits for P2P transfers.
- YouSendit (yousendit.com) enables users to send links to uploaded files.
- Zapr (zapr.net) turns any file on a PC into a shareable Web link.

For details see Schonfeld (2006b).

Alexa: Web Traffic Information Provider

Alexa Internet (alexa.com) is a Web site owned by Amazon.com that provides information on Web traffic to other Web sites. Alexa collects information from users who have installed an "Alexa Toolbar," allowing them to provide statistics on Web site traffic, as well as lists of related links. Alexa ranks sites based on visits from users of its Alexa Toolbar for Internet Explorer and from integrated sidebars in Mozilla and Netscape.

Some question how representative Alexa's user base is of typical Internet behavior (see en.wikipedia.org/wiki/Alexa_Internet). If Alexa's user base is a fair statistical sample of the Internet user population (e.g., a random sample of sufficient size), Alexa's ranking should be quite accurate. In reality, not much is known about the sample, and it might or might not have many sources of sampling bias. Another concern is whether Alexa ratings are easily manipulated. Some Webmasters claim that they can significantly improve the Alexa ranking of less popular sites by making them the default page, by exchanging Web traffic with other Webmasters, and by requiring their users to install the Alexa toolbar; however, such claims are often anecdotal and are offered without statistics or other evidence.

Competitors in the Internet market research space include Complete Inc., ComScore, Hitwise, Nielsen/NetRatings, and Netcraft.

Mobile Phones and Social Networks

Mobile phones are heavily used by members of social networks. Thus, the e-commerce opportunities are enormous. For example, in 2007 the mobile phone company Vodafone disclosed a deal that will allow its customers to access the popular online video service YouTube. The launch initially will focus on the United Kingdom and involve YouTube providing a daily selection of videos. Vodafone says that customers will also be able to forward links of their favorite clips and upload their own content from the phones. Vodafone also said it will roll out a service with MySpace. That deal will allow its customers to access the social network via cell phones. Vodaphone also offers its users access to eBay via their phones.

Similarly, Verizon has made a deal with YouTube to bring popular videos from YouTube to cell phones using Verizon's V-cast service.

INFRASTRUCTURE SUPPORT

With millions of members, and in the case of MySpace, close to 200 million members, heavy traffic demands stress the social networks' computing infrastructure. The problem is becoming even more serious as sites add more functionalities, becoming all-in-one communities. In addition, many companies are adding Web 2.0 tools, which also increases demand. Companies need to analyze the data that add more demand on information infrastructure and processing.

The Real-World Case at the end of this chapter discusses how one social network has added blogs and wikis. To overcome the demand more servers that handle higher power are being installed. Also, the use of content delivery networks such as akamai.com, which are systems of computers networked together across the Internet, are helpful in delivering the massive amount of multimedia information being posted and accessed.

The heavy traffic has caused other problems. For example, Universal Tube (Toledo, Ohio) filed a lawsuit against YouTube, claiming that the company had to shut down its Web site, utube.com, because millions of people mistook it for youtube.com. Utube received 68 million hits in August 2006 (Zappone 2006).

Luckily, social network growth is slow enough to enable appropriate infrastructure upgrades. Carr (2007b) describes how MySpace has adopted new technologies as it has grown. MySpace has managed to scale its Web site infrastructure to meet booming demand by using a mix of time-proven and leading-edge information technologies. By 2007, MySpace was able to support 140 million accounts and more than 38 billion page views a month.

The Need for Very Rich Media

MySpace was successful with its infrastructure upgrades because the site is not rich media. CondéNet Inc. has launched flip (flip.com) a rich media, social network for teens. The new, rich-media style might make MySpace's two-dimensional static pages obsolete as users migrate toward Flash-heavy slideshows. VUVOX (VUVOX.com) offers special authoring tools that enable users to turn amateur Web page creators into Adobe Photoshop experts. How MySpace and others will deal with this emergence of media-rich features is yet to be seen (*Fortune* Technology Staff 2007).

Other Tools

Other examples of infrastructure support tools include (Gillin 2007b):

- ▶ A number of companies will monitor online chats and provide subscribers with reports on topics such as the opinions, preferences, issues, and coming trends that are being discussed. Companies offering such services include Nielsen BuzzMetrics—BrandPulse (nielsenbuzzmetrics.com), Cymfony—Orchestra (cymphony.com), Nstein—NtelligentEnterpriseSearch (nstein.com), and Factiva (factiva.com).
- ▶ Google Alerts can be used to monitor what the media has to say about any topic.
- ▶ Advanced search features, such as the linkdomain and allinanchor commands at Yahoo! provide useful information, as does Amazon's AG search engine.
- ▶ Popular RSS-based search engines include Technorati (technorati.com), IceRocket (icerocket.com), Feedster (feedster.com), and BlogPulse (blogpulse.com). These can be used to search blogs as well (e.g., Technorati's Top 100 blogs monitor the links from these for other bloggers). Monitoring over 2 million blogs is not an easy task.
- ▶ Podcasts are difficult to search because the content is hard to index. Some interesting search engines are Podscope (podscope.com) and Podzinger (podzinger.com).
- ▶ Several companies, including Nielsen's BuzzMetrics—BrandPulse, track comments on blogs in order to assess their popularity.
- ▶ Aggregation engines analyze link blogs, topical blogs, and community news sites. Sites such as Boing Boing (boingboing.net), Metafilter (metafilter.com), Waxy.org (waxy.org), and ScienceBlogs (scienceblogs.com) are all link blogs and are major influencers in social media.

For details on these tools, see Gillin (2007a). For other tools, see Online Chapter 14.

WHERE IS WEB 2.0 SOFTWARE GOING?

By 2007, several hundred Web 2.0 products were on the market, with little agreement on standards (Watson 2007b). Many of these products will probably disappear, and others will be purchased by large companies (such as the purchases of Groove by Microsoft and Blogger by Google).

Large companies like to embed Web 2.0 tools in their existing collaboration products (see Raman 2006). For example, IBM is adding such tools to its Lotus/Domino Collaboration Suite (Taft 2007, Hoover 2007). IBM is adding the following products to Lotus to make it easier for people to collaborate: Lotus Connection (social networking software for the enterprise including Activities, Communities, Dogear for social bookmarking, and Profiles and Blog), Lotus Quickr, and Lotus Sametime. IBM WebSphere also has been redesigned to support collaboration. (See Taft 2007 for details.) Oracle has an extensive collaboration suite that includes Web 2.0 tools. Another example is Intel's Web 2.0 software suite. Even Acrobat 8.0 (from Adobe Systems) has collaboration capabilities in its professional version.

Section 8.7 ▶ REVIEW QUESTIONS

1. Describe some tools for blogging and wikis.
2. Define social software and list some examples.
3. What is social bookmarking?

4. Describe suites of Web 2.0 tools and the integration of tools.

5. Describe the need for IT infrastructure with regard to the Web 2.0 revolution.

6. Describe the future direction of Web 2.0 software.

8.8 WEB 2.0, SOCIAL NETWORKS, AND E-COMMERCE

Implementing Web 2.0 sites, especially social networks and similar communities, attracts a large number of visitors. This opens the door to several e-commerce initiatives. These are sometimes referred to as *social commerce*.

Virtual communities are closely related to EC. For example, Zetlin and Pfleging (2002) describe online, consumer-driven markets in which most of the consumers' needs, ranging from finding a mortgage to job hunting, are arranged from a community Web site. This gathering of frequently segmented needs in one place enables vendors to sell more and community members to get discounts. Internet communities will eventually have a massive impact on almost every company that produces consumer goods or services, and they could change the nature of corporate advertising and community sponsorship strategies and the manner in which business is done. Although this process of change is slow, we can see some of the initial commercial development changes.

Also, some communities charge members content fees for downloading certain articles, music, or pictures, thus producing sales revenue for the site. Finally, because many community members create their own homepages, it is easy to learn about them and reach them with targeted advertising and marketing. For more on this topic, see Lee et al. (2003).

WHY IS THERE AN INTEREST?

Web 2.0 applications, and especially social networks, attract a huge number of users. Furthermore, they are spreading rapidly, and many of them cater to a specific segment of the population (e.g., music lovers, travelers, game lovers, car fans, etc.). Finally, many of the visitors are young, and they will grow up and have more money to spend (see Regan 2006 for a discussion). For these reasons, many believe that social networks, blogging, and other Web 2.0 activities will play a major role in the future of e-commerce. In the following sections, we will cover a few areas where success is already evidenced.

Retailers stand to benefit from online communities in several important ways:

▶ Consumers can be a source of feedback (similar to a focus group) on existing product features and new product design, on marketing and advertising campaigns, and on customer service and support, which can lead to innovation for a retailer.

▶ Word-of-mouth (i.e., viral marketing) is free advertising that increases the visibility of niche retailers and products.

▶ Increased Web site traffic, a common effect of viral marketing, inevitably brings with it more ad dollars.

▶ Increased sales can come from harnessing techniques based on personal preferences, such as collaborative filtering. At a more advanced level, retailers strive for a higher degree of relevance in matching the knowledge of one person to someone of like interests who has a need to know (the "twinsumer" concept).

Case 8.2 demonstrates some of the potential of EC social networks.

CASE 8.2
EC Application
REVENUE SOURCES AT YOUTUBE

Some people think that Google paid too much for YouTube, especially in light of its legal problems. The opposite may be true. Consider the following examples.

Two-Minute YouTube Clips Are Just the Start

As television comes to the Internet, dozens of companies are gunning to become the networks of tomorrow. Where viewers go, advertisers are expected to follow. Citigroup pegged YouTube's ad-revenue potential in 2007 alone at $200 million. Wherever there's video programming, viewers will be seeing more video ads. One forecast from research firm eMarketer calls for overall video advertising on the Web (including video ads replacing banners on regular Web pages) to hit $2.9 billion in 2010, a sevenfold leap from the 2006 tally of $410 million (Schonfeld 2007).

Brand-Created Entertainment Content

In 2005, Nike produced a pseudo-home-video of soccer star Ronaldinho practicing while wearing his new Nike Gold shoes. In 1 week, the clip was downloaded 3.5 million times on YouTube, providing Nike with tremendous exposure to its core audience of young males. The younger generation is moving away from traditional TV and toward online video content, such as that found on YouTube.

User-Driven Product Advertising

User-generated videos could be leveraged in a similar fashion to product placement on TV. Although unintentional, the use of Logitech's Webcam featured on a short clip on YouTube by a 17-year-old girl talking about the breakup with her boyfriend greatly increased consumers' awareness of Logitech's offering. The product-placement trend also is

expanding across the blogosphere. For example, Nokia is promoting its N90 phone through the 50 most influential bloggers in Belgium and by establishing a blogger-relationship blog.

Multichannel Word-of-Mouth Campaigns

When Chevrolet decided to combine its *Apprentice* Tahoe Campaign with an online consumer-generated-media (CGM) campaign, it did not anticipate the additional viral impact of YouTube. On the Chevrolet site, users could create their own customized video commercial, complete with text and background music. Environmentalists took the opportunity to produce spoof videos and published them on YouTube. However, the word-of-mouth advertising Chevrolet got on YouTube was ultimately beneficial to Chevrolet and contributed to the 4 million page views, 400,000 unique visitors, and 22,000 ad submissions on Chevrolet's site. This has been one of the most creative and successful promotions.

Users are integral to the success of these methods, and YouTube has announced that it will share revenue with users who have helped to generate ad revenues.

Sources: Compiled from Sandoval and Borzo (2006), Sandoval (2006b), and Schonfeld (2007).

Questions

1. List the different advertising models on YouTube.
2. List the critical success factors from these cases.
3. How do advertisers benefit from YouTube?

ADVERTISING

Several advertisers are placing ads on MySpace and YouTube or are using Google AdSense with user searches in community sites. The following areas are developing.

Viral Marketing

Young adults are especially good at viral marketing. What they like can spread very quickly, sometimes to millions of people at a minimal cost to companies (e.g., see Weber 2007). One example is YouTube. The company conducted almost no advertising in the first months of its inception, but millions joined. Similarly, if members like a certain product or service, word-of-mouth advertising works rapidly. At SpiralFrog (spiralfrog.com), cell phone users can download songs for free in exchange for watching advertisements. The free music site is passed on from user to user.

An example of viral marketing on social networks is provided by McNichol (2007b), who describes the story of Stormhoek Winery (see the Real-World Case in Chapter 2).

The company first offered a free bottle of wine to bloggers. About 100 of the bloggers posted voluntary comments about the winery on their own blogs within 6 months. Most of the comments were positive.

MyPickList (mypicklist.com) is a viral marketing program that uses the usual loyalty-program mechanisms without the worries of loyalty erosion or the perception that the program is only a discount scheme. MyPickList helps consumers make purchase decisions by creating a social commerce network Web site that drives word-of-mouth commerce by leveraging the community aspects of a social network. MyPickList integrates user profiles and their favorite product recommendations (hence, the name "pick list") into a networked community. Once a user creates a pick list, the user can share it with family, friends, or the public at large.

Any product can be added to the pick list, but only products sold through a retailer in MyPickList's network are eligible for a commission when someone purchases an item off a member's pick list. Members can receive their commission once they have accumulated $25 or more in their account. All payments are made via PayPal; therefore, members must have a PayPal account. Once a user creates a pick list, it can be viewed and distributed in several different ways. For details, see *Revenue News* (2006).

According to Megna (2007) and Goldsmith (2006), many retailers are capitalizing on word-of-mouth marketing by bloggers. This brings up an interesting question: Can bloggers be bought? According to Wagnar (2006), companies pay bloggers to endorse products via an intermediary such as PayPerPost.

PayPerPost (payperpost.com) runs a marketplace where advertisers can find bloggers, video bloggers, online photographers, and podcasters willing to endorse advertisers' products. A company that wants to advertise a product or service registers with PayPerPost and describes what it wants. A sneaker company, for example, might post a request for people willing to write a 50-word blog entry about their sneakers or upload a video of themselves playing basketball in the sneakers. The company might also be willing to pay for the posting.

Bloggers and other content creators sign up with PayPerPost and shop for opportunities they like. They create the blog post (or whatever content is requested) and then inform PayPerPost, which checks to see that the content matches what the advertiser asked for and arranges payment.

The criticism is that bloggers are not required to disclose that they are being paid for the endorsements (see Wagner 2006). When viral marketing is done by bloggers it is referred to as **viral blogging**. For details, see Demopoulos (2007).

viral blogging
Viral marketing done by bloggers.

Classifieds and Job Listing

MySpace has provided classifieds and job listings since fall 2005, competing with Craigslist and CareerBuilder. According to O'Malley (2006), MySpace is already a major e-commerce force: It sends more traffic to shopping and classifieds sites than MSN, and it is fast closing in on Yahoo! According to Hitwise, MySpace accounted for 2.53 percent of all visits to EC sites for the last week of August 2006—up from 1.28 percent the last week of February 2006 (reported by Phillips 2006).

Google partnered in 2006 with eBay to roll out "click-to-call" advertising across Google and eBay sites—a deal that is expanding to MySpace's giant network.

Mobile Advertising

Mobile advertising is a rapidly developing area (Sharma 2007). The competition for online ad revenue is intensifying, especially with the increasing use of Internet-enabled cell phones. Recently, watching video clips has become popular on cell phones. Advertisers are starting to attach ads to these video clips.

SHOPPING

Shopping is a natural area for social networks to be active, and although by 2007 it was only beginning to grow, it has enormous potential. MySpace offers many examples of how social networks are trying to capitalize on e-commerce:

▶ According to Kafka (2007), many of MySpace's most popular pages came from e-tailers who stock the site with low-cost cosmetics, other Web site ads, and the like. The value is $140 million or more in sales revenue per year.

▶ MySpace lets brand owners create profile pages. For example, Burger King has a page devoted to its mascot, "The King."

▶ MySpace is planning its own behavioral targeting, which is similar to collaborative filtering (Chapter 4). Based on the members' voluntary information on their likes and dislikes, MySpace will serve up its users to relevant advertisers. For example, DaimlerChrysler's Jeep already has its own MySpace page. In the future, it will be able to target sales campaigns to specific individuals.

▶ MySpace's music-download service allows the site's independent and signed musicians to sell their work directly from their profile pages. Snocap, a copyright-services company cofounded by Napster creator Shawn Fanning, supports the relationship. MySpace and Snocap get a cut of every track sold. By allowing users to self-publish, MySpace has become a launching pad for about 3 million musicians, from garage bands to big names.

▶ In 2006, Google signed an agreement to pay more than $900 million in ad revenue over 5 years to MySpace for the right to serve searches inside MySpace. The deal includes offering MySpace members access to Google's checkout payment service, which allows customers to pay several vendors at once.

FEEDBACK FROM CUSTOMERS

Companies are starting to utilize Web 2.0 tools to get feedback from customers.

Conversational Marketing

Web 2.0 opens the feedback loop. In Chapter 4, we described customer feedback via questionnaires, focus groups, and other methods. However, Web 2.0 brings in feedback via blogs, wikis, online forums, chat rooms, and social networking sites. Companies are finding that these "conversational marketing" outlets not only generate faster and cheaper results than traditional focus groups, but also foster closer relationships with customers. For example, Macy's quickly removed a metal toothbrush holder from its product line after receiving several complaints about it online (see Gogoi 2007).

Companies such as Dell also are learning that conversational marketing is less expensive and yields quicker results than focus groups. The computer maker recently launched a feedback site called IdeaStorm, where it allows customers to suggest and vote on improvements to its offerings (see Scable and Israel 2006).

Known also as *enterprise feedback management*, companies are interested not only in collecting information, but also in interaction between customers and company employees and in properly distributing customer feedback throughout the organization.

According to Gogoi (2007), retailers know that customers, especially the younger and more Net-savvy ones, want to be heard, and they also want to hear what others like them think. In response, retailers increasingly are opening up their Web sites to customers, letting them post product reviews and ratings and in some cases photos and videos. The result is that *customer reviews* are emerging as a prime stop for online shoppers.

Marketing companies have longed for years to have a window on how consumers use their products in order to develop product innovations and improve marketing. Customer reviews have long been part of cutting-edge sites such as Amazon.com and Netflix, but by the end of 2006, 43 percent of e-commerce sites offered customer reviews and ratings. As many as 50 percent of customers 18 to 34 years old have posted a comment or review on products they have bought or used (Gogoi 2007). A large part of the reason for this achievement is the confluence of social computing and the success of sites such as MySpace, Facebook, and YouTube.

Consider the example of PETCO, a click-and-mortar pet supply company that operates 800 pet supply stores nationally. The PETCO Web site (petco.com) launched customer reviews in October 2005, and within a week PETCO noticed that customers who clicked on the highest-customer-rated products were 49 percent more likely to buy something.

PETCO also noticed that top customer-rated pet toys and items draw customers, even if the customers were not necessarily planning on buying them; people trust someone else's opinion when it is independent of the manufacturer or retailer (Gogoi 2007).

PETCO's experience is not unique. According to an eVoc Insights study, 47 percent of consumers consult reviews before making an online purchase, and 63 percent of shoppers are more likely to purchase from a site if it has ratings and reviews. Negative reviews not only help the retailer address a defect or poorly manufactured item, they also help decrease the number of returns. People are less likely to return an item due to personal expectation, because reviews give realistic views of a product and its characteristics (see Gorgoi 2007 for details).

Risks

Organizations do face some risks in opening up their marketing and advertising to social networks. For example, according to Regan (2006) aligning a product or company with sites where the content is user-generated and often not edited or filtered has its downsides. A company needs to be willing to have negative reviews and feedback. If a company has really positive customer relationships and strong feedback, and it is willing to have customers share the good, the bad, and the ugly, then it might be a good candidate for a relationship with a social network. However, if the company worries about what its customers might say if they were alone in a room with prospective customers—the product or business might not be ready for Web 2.0.

Another thing to consider is the 20–80 rule; that is, that a minority of individuals contributes most of the content material in some Web 2.0 blogs, wikis, and similar sites. For example, about 1,000 of the millions of contributors write most of the content for Wikipedia. According to *Business 2.0* (2007), in an analysis of thousands of submissions over a 3-week period on audience voting sites such as Digg and Reddit the *Wall Street Journal* reported that one-third of the stories that made it to Digg's home page were submitted by 30 users (out of 900,000 registered), and that one single person on Netscape, who goes by the online handle "Stoner," was responsible for 13 percent of the top posts on that site.

Any social media site that relies on the contributions of its users will find a similar distribution curve, with a relatively small number of top contributors representing the bulk of submissions. For instance, user-submitted stock photography site iStockphoto has more than 35,000 contributing photographers, but only about 100 have sold more than 100,000 images (at about $1 to $5 a pop). The difference is that with iStockphoto, users submit work in hopes of getting paid. Companies such as BuzzMetrics offer services that tell companies what their customers are saying on the Internet and what it means to their brands and markets. For details, see *Taipei Times* (2006).

Finally, according to *Innovations* (2006), 74 percent of all CIOs surveyed said that Web 2.0 applications will significantly increase their security risk over the next 3 years. For more on security and other Web 2.0 implementation issues, see Ricadela (2006) and D'Agostino (2006).

OTHER REVENUE-GENERATION STRATEGIES IN SOCIAL NETWORKS

The following are some interesting ways social networks generate revenue:

▶ The social network offers a premium service for a monthly or per service fee.

▶ Organizations partner with the social network, paying it a monthly service fee.

▶ Some social networks have a network of thousands of local physical venues where members can meet (e.g., meetup.com). Venues, such as coffee shops, might choose to pay a fee to be affiliated with the social network.

According to Millard (2004), Tickle Inc. implemented an integrated advertising campaign with Fox TV studio's program *North Shore*. The site created social networking profiles for some of the key characters on the show and promoted them on the site as "featured members." To learn how a blog can bring in big money, see Sloan and Kaihla (2006) and Wright (2006).

Hinchcliffe (2007) provides Exhibit 8.6, which illustrates revenue generation from Web 2.0 applications. Hinchcliffe (2007) identifies three direct ways to make the most of Web 2.0 applications: advertising, subscriptions, and commissions. In addition, he identifies the following indirect strategies that lead to revenue growth, user growth, and

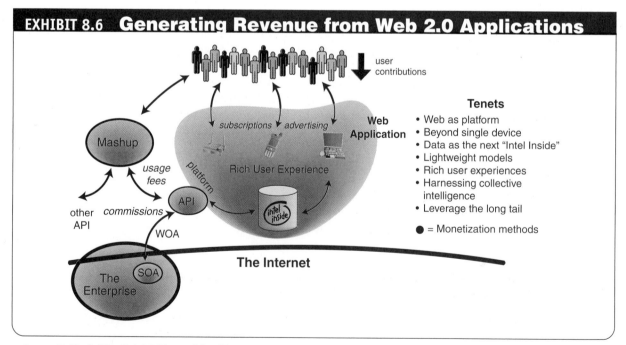

EXHIBIT 8.6 Generating Revenue from Web 2.0 Applications

Source: D. Hinchcliffe, *Web 2.0 Blog, web2.wsj2.com.*

increased resistance to competition, which in turn lead to increased subscriptions, advertising, and commission revenue:

- **Strategic acquisition.** Identifying and acquiring Web 2.0 companies on the exponential growth curve before the rest of the market realizes what they are worth.
- **Maintaining control of hard to re-create data sources.** Let users access everything, but do not let them keep it, such as Google's providing access to their search index only over the Web.
- **Building attention trust.** By being patently fair with customer data and leveraging users' loyalty, users will share more information about themselves, which in turn leads to much better products and services tailored to them.
- **Turning applications into platforms.** One single use of an application is simply a waste of software. Online platforms are actually easy to monetize, but having compelling content or services is a prerequisite.
- **Fully automated online customer self-service.** Let users get what they want, when they want it, without help.

WEB 2.0 COMMERCE ACTIVITIES INSIDE THE ENTERPRISE

Whereas many companies use Web 2.0 technology for supporting B2C and B2B e-commerce by building up their brand online, advertising, and selling, other companies use these technologies inside the enterprise. McGillicuddy (2006a) offers the following guidelines for Web 2.0 activities within the larger enterprise:

- Allow employees to collaborate and communicate in an employee-driven system (e.g., see Real-World Case at the end of this chapter).
- Promote the use of enterprise wikis via demonstrations.
- Set up internal blogs and incorporate them into internal directories so users can see who has a blog.
- Set up enterprise social bookmarking systems so users can see what sort of content their colleagues are tagging.
- CIOs should be involved from the beginning to make sure the right infrastructure and tools are in place.

For an example of how T. Rowe Price Group Inc. is using internal Web 2.0 technology, see McGilicuddy (2006). For tutorials, see Hinchcliffe, (2007) and web2.0central.com.

Section 8.8 ▶ REVIEW QUESTIONS

1. Why is there so much interest in e-commerce via social communities?
2. How can a social network facilitate viral marketing?
3. Why is there so much interest in classifieds on social networks?
4. How can social networks support shopping?
5. How is customer feedback solicited in social networks?

8.9 THE FUTURE: WEB 3.0

Web 2.0 is here. What's next? This unknown entity is referred to as *Web 3.0*. Some of its characteristics are already in the making. Based on nontechnological success factors (see Online File W8.7) and technological factors and trends (see Online File W8.8), there is general optimism about the future of the Web and e-commerce. This future is described by some as Web 3.0. For a discussion, see Stafford (2006).

WEB 3.0: WHAT'S NEXT?

Web 3.0 will not be just about shopping, entertainment, and searching. It also will deliver a new generation of business applications that will see business and social computing converge on the same fundamentals as on-demand architecture has for consumer applications. Web 3.0 is not something that is of merely passing interest to those who work in enterprise IT. The Web 3.0 era will radically change individuals' career paths as well as the organizations where they work (see Rouch 2006).

According to Stafford (2006), the next-generation Internet will not only just be more portable and personal, it will also harness the power of people. It will be even easier for people to zero in on precisely what they are looking for. Web 3.0 will be characterized by

- Faster and wider-ranging connectivity
- New Web Services that will work entirely within a browser window
- More powerful search engines
- More clout for everyday people

Web 3.0 Structure

The topology of Web 3.0 can be divided into four distinct layers: API services, aggregation services, application services, and serviced clients.

Application Program Interface (API) Services. API services are the hosted services that have powered Web 2.0 and that will become the engines of Web 3.0. Google's search and AdWords APIs; Amazon.com's affiliate APIs; a large number of RSS feeds; a multitude of functional services, such as those included in the StrikeIron Web Services Marketplace (strikeiron.com) (Wainewright 2005) are just some examples. One of the most significant characteristics of this foundation layer is that it is a commodity layer. As Web 3.0 matures, an almost perfect market will emerge and squeeze out virtually all the profit margin from the highest-volume services.

Aggregation Services. These services are the intermediaries that take some of the hassle out of locating all those raw API services by bundling them together in useful ways. Representative examples are the various RSS aggregators and emerging Web Services marketplaces, such as the StrikeIron service.

Application Services. This layer is where the biggest, most durable profits should be found. These services will not be like the established enterprise application categories, such as CRM or ERP, but a new class of composite applications that bring together functionality from multiple services to help users achieve their objectives in a flexible, intuitive way. An example of an area that is expected to grow is **voice commerce (v-commerce)**, which is an umbrella term for the use of speech recognition to enable voice-activated services, including Internet browsing and e-mail retrieval.

Serviced Clients. There is a role for client-side logic in the Web 3.0 landscape, but users will expect it to be maintained and managed for them.

From the billions of documents that form the Web and the links that weave them together, computer scientists and a growing number of startups are finding new ways to mine human intelligence. Their goal is to add a layer of meaning on top of the existing Web that will make it less of a catalog and more of a guide—and even provide the foundation for systems that can reason in a human fashion. That level of artificial intelligence, with machines doing the thinking instead of simply following commands, has eluded researchers for more than half a century. One of the major Web 3.0 technologies is the Semantic Web.

voice commerce (v-commerce)
An umbrella term for the use of speech recognition to support voice-activated services, including Internet browsing and e-mail retrieval.

Web 3.0 and the Semantic Web

One potential area for Web 3.0 is the increased use of the Semantic Web (see en.wikipedia.org/wiki/Semantic_Web). According to *The Economist* (2007), a Semantic-Web browser soon will be available in which people will be able to display data, draw graphs, and so on. An example would be "friend-of-a-friend" networks, where individuals in online communities provide data in the form of links between themselves and their friends. The Semantic Web could help to visualize such complex networks and organize them to allow deeper understanding of the communities' structures.

The **Semantic Web** is an evolving extension of the Web in which Web content can be expressed not only in natural language but also in a form that can be understood, interpreted, and used by intelligent computer software agents, permitting them to find, share, and integrate information more easily (see en.wikipedia.org/wiki/semantic_web). The technology is derived from W3C director Tim Berners-Lee's vision of the Web as a universal medium for data, information, and knowledge exchange. At its core, the Semantic Web comprises a philosophy, a set of design principles, collaborative working groups, and a variety of enabling technologies.

Borland (2007) views the Semantic Web as a core tool for Web 3.0 which is coming soon. Borland believes that the new tools of Web 3.0 (some of which are already helping developers "stitch" together complex applications) will improve and automate database searches, help people choose vacation destinations, and sort through complicated financial data more efficiently. For more on Web 3.0 and the Semantic Web, see Markoff (2006).

Web 3.0 will be characterized by an explosion of mobile social networks.

Semantic Web
An evolving extension of the Web in which Web content can be expressed not only in natural language, but also in a form that can be understood, interpreted, and used by intelligent computer software agents, permitting them to find, share, and integrate information more easily.

Mobile Social Networks

An explosive growth of mobile social networks is predicted by ABI Research (see Mello 2006), tripling the 50 million members in 2006 to 174 million in 2011. The explosion of wireless Web 2.0 services and companies (see Longino 2006) enables many social communities to be based on the mobile phone and other portable wireless devices. This extends the reach of social interaction to millions of people who do not have regular or easy access to computers. For example, MySpace can be accessed via Cingular's mobile system. At minimum, existing members who use PCs will supplement their activities with wireless devices. Thus, wireless would be the environment of choice for the Web 3.0 users.

Future Threats

According to Stafford (2006) the following four trends may slow EC and Web 3.0 and even cripple the Internet:

- **Security concerns.** Both shoppers and users of e-banking and other services worry about online security. The Web needs to be made safer.
- **Lack of Net neutrality.** If the big telecom companies are allowed to charge companies for a guarantee of faster access, critics fear that small innovative Web companies could be crowded out by the Microsofts and Googles that can afford to pay more.
- **Copyright complaints.** The legal problems of YouTube, Wikipedia, and others might result in a loss of vital outlets of public opinion, creativity, and discourse.
- **Choppy connectivity.** Upstream bandwidths are still constricted, making uploading of video files a time-consuming task. Usable mobile bandwidth still costs a lot, and some carriers impose limitations on how Web access can be employed.

Section 8.9 ▶ REVIEW QUESTIONS

1. Describe nontechnological EC trends. (See Online File W8.7.)
2. Describe technological EC trends. (See Online File W8.8.)
3. What is Web 3.0, and how will it differ from Web 2.0?
4. Describe the future of mobile social networks.
5. List the major potential inhibitors of e-commerce and Web 3.0.

MANAGERIAL ISSUES

Some managerial issues related to this chapter are as follows.

1. **How will e-commerce impact the business environment?** The impacts of e-commerce and the Internet are so strong that the entire manner in which companies do business will change, with significant impacts on procedures, people, organizational structure, management, and business processes. (Read "The Economic and Social Impact of Electronic Commerce" at oecd.org/subject/e_commerce.)

2. **What are the impacts of the Web 2.0 boom?** With the push toward Web 2.0 technologies, *Time* magazine (Grossman 2006–2007) named "you" as the person of the year for 2006. In the new information age, no one has more power to influence society than Web 2.0 communities. Yet does this influence truly benefit us, or will we suffer because of it?

3. **Should we explore Web 2.0 collaboration?** Managers should consider whether its corporate culture is ready to experiment with public collaboration (Web 2.0) tools. The corporate-learning or organization-development department is a good start to find areas for experimentation.

4. **How shall we start?** Start small: Determine whether a collaborative tool would benefit a team or group working on a specific project. Marketing groups often are good first targets for information sharing, because they are usually the ones tasked with sharing corporate information. Try establishing a wiki for a team's collaborative project. Some wikis are hosted on an internal server, whereas others are available as open source or via a hosted service.

5. **Do we need a community?** Although sponsoring a community might sound like a good idea, it might not be simple to execute. Community members need services, which cost money to provide. The most difficult task is to find a community that matches your business.

6. **How should we deal with Web 2.0 risks?** Several risks are possible depending on the applications. Consult with internal security experts and get some outside legal advice. Use a consultant for large projects to examine the risks.

SUMMARY

In this chapter you learned about the following EC issues as they relate to the learning objectives.

1. **Web 2.0, social media, and disruptors.** Web 2.0 is about the innovative application of existing technologies. Web 2.0 has brought together the contributions of millions of people and made their work, opinions, and identity matter. The consequences of the rapid growth of person-to-person computing, such as blogging, are currently hard to understand and difficult to estimate. User-created content is a major characteristic of Web 2.0, as is the emergence of social networking. One impact of Web 2.0 has been the creation of industry disruptors.

2. **The structure and role of virtual communities.** Virtual communities create new types of business opportunities—people with similar interests that congregate at one Web site are a natural target for advertisers and marketers. Using chat rooms,

members can exchange opinions about certain products and services. Of special interest are communities of transactions, whose interest is the promotion of commercial buying and selling. Virtual communities can foster customer loyalty, increasing sales of related vendors that sponsor communities and facilitating customer feedback for improved service and business.

3. **Online social networks.** These are very large Internet communities that enable the sharing of content, including videos and photos, and virtual socialization and interaction. Hundreds of networks are popping up around the world, some of which are global, competing for advertising money. Notable are MySpace, Facebook, Flickr, and Cyworld.

4. **YouTube and others.** Sharing videos, movies, and TV shows is becoming a major activity of social networks, including YouTube and dozens of its competitors. Despite litigation, these companies are growing rapidly, along with other social networks (e.g., My Space also offers video sharing).

5. **Business networks.** These communities concentrate on business issues both in one country and around the world (e.g., recruiting, finding business partners). Social marketplaces meld social networks and some aspects of business networks. Notable are LinkedIn and Xing.

6. **Web 2.0 and entertainment.** The entertainment industry is embracing Web 2.0 tools. Many communities provide entertainment, and others are fully dedicated to it. Wonderful innovations bring user created entertainment to others. Videos and movies are at the forefront of this area, as well as mobile entertainment.

7. **Web 2.0 enablers.** Blogs and wikis are popular Web 2.0 tools. Web services and open source tools are used in the infrastructure, as well as rich media and sharing tools.

8. **Social networks and e-commerce.** The major areas of interface are online shopping, online advertising, online market research, and innovative revenue models. The major attraction is the volume of social networks and the hope that the young people in the communities will become online buyers in the future.

9. **Web 3.0.** Web 3.0, the next generation of the Web, will combine social and business computing. It will be more portable and personal, with powerful search engines, clout to the people, greater connectivity in the wireless environment, and more on-demand applications. The Semantic Web will play a major role in Web 3.0 applications.

KEY TERMS

Business network	327	Social marketplace	329	Viral blogging	343
Disruptors	312	Social media	312	Virtual (Internet) community	315
Semantic Web	349	Social network	319	Voice commerce (v-commerce)	348
Social bookmarking	337	Social network analysis (SNA)	319	Web 2.0	310
Social commerce	318				

QUESTIONS FOR DISCUSSION

1. Discuss the differences between Web 2.0 and the traditional Web.

2. Discuss the major characteristics of Web 2.0. What are some of its major advantages?

3. Discuss the relationship between virtual communities and e-commerce.

4. Explain why Cyworld might pull users from other social networks.

5. Discuss why a social marketplace is a Web 2.0 instrument.

6. What are the advantages and disadvantages of social bookmarking?

7. Discuss the infrastructure required for Web 2.0 services and tools.

8. What are the benefits of conversational marketing?

9. Discuss the nature of industry disrupters.

INTERNET EXERCISES

1. Enter the Web site of an Internet community (e.g., **myspace.com** or **geocities.yahoo.com**). Build a homepage. Add a chat room and a message board using the free tools provided. Describe the other capabilities that are available.

2. Investigate the community services provided by Yahoo! to its members (**groups.yahoo.com**). List all the services available and assess their potential commercial benefits to Yahoo!

3. Enter **calastrology.com**. What kind of community is this? Check the revenue model. Then enter **astrocenter.com**. What kind of site is this? Compare the two sites.

4. Enter **ediscovery.com** and describe its functionalities. (See also Carr 2006.) Write a report.

5. Enter **classmates.com, myspace.com,** and **linkedin.com**. Describe how each site generates revenue.

6. Enter **xing.com** and **linkedin.com** and compare their functionalities. Write a report.

7. Enter **flip.com** and compare its rich media with that of **myspace.com** and **cyworld.com**. Prepare a report.

8. Enter **gnomz.com** through **google.com** (translate the page). What is the purpose of this site?

9. Enter **advertising.com**. Identify any innovative methods it uses. Relate it to Web 2.0 and search.

10. Enter the **paulgillin.com** blog and find information related to enterprise applications of Web 2.0 technologies. Write a report.

11. Enter **pandora.com**. Check how you can create and share music with friends. Why is this a Web 2.0 application?

12. Enter **webkinz.com** and compare its activities to that of **facebook.com**. Enter **netratings.com** and find the average stay time in both social network sites.

13. Enter **smartmobs.com**. Go to blogroll. Find three blogs related to Web 2.0 and summarize their major points.

14. Enter **oreilly.com** and find its latest conferences on Web 2.0. Look for topics not covered in this chapter. Write a summary. Find their RSS and Atom products. Discuss their capabilities.

15. Enter **mashable.com** and review the latest news regarding social networks and network strategy. Briefly summarize three of each.

TEAM ASSIGNMENTS AND ROLE PLAYING

1. Each group member selects a single-family home where he or she lives or where a friend lives. Next, enter **zillow.com** and find the value of a house in the neighborhood. Then, add any improvements and reprice the house. Find out how to list the house for sale on Zillow and other sites (e.g., **craigslist.org**). Write a summary. Compare each members' experiences.

2. Assign each team member a different type of community, per Exhibit 8.4. Identify the services offered by that type of community. Have each team compare the services offered by each type of community. Prepare a report.

3. Enter **web2.wsj2.com, web2.0central.com,** and other sites dedicated to Web 2.0. Each team member selects one area of Web 2.0 (e.g., social media, development tools, strategies, etc.) and prepares a presentation.

4. Debate the following: Should bloggers who endorse products or services be required to disclose whether they received payment for their endorsement or comment?

Real-World Case

WEB 2.0 AT EASTERN MOUNTAIN SPORTS

Eastern Mountain Sports (EMS) (*ems.com*) is a medium-sized specialty retailer (annual sales $200 million) selling via over 80 physical stores, a mail-order catalog, and an online storefront. Operating in a very competitive environment, the company uses leading-edge IT technologies and lately has introduced a complementary set of Web 2.0 tools in order to increase collaboration, information sharing, and communication among stores and their employees, suppliers, and customers.

The Business Intelligence Strategy and System

During the last few years, the company implemented a business intelligence (BI) system that includes business performance management and dashboards. A BI system collects raw data from multiple sources, processes them into a data warehouse (or data mart), and conducts analyses that include comparing performance to operational metrics in order to assess the health of the business (see details in Turban et al. 2008).

The following exhibit illustrates how the system works. Point-of-sale information and other relevant data, which are available on an IBM AS/400 computer, is loaded into Microsoft's SQL Server and into a data mart. The data are then analyzed with Information Builders' WebFOCUS 7.12 platform. The results are presented via a series of dashboards that users can view via their Web browsers. This way users can access a unified, high-level view of key performance indicators (Chapter 12), such as sales, inventory, and margin levels, and drill down to granular details that analyze specific transactions.

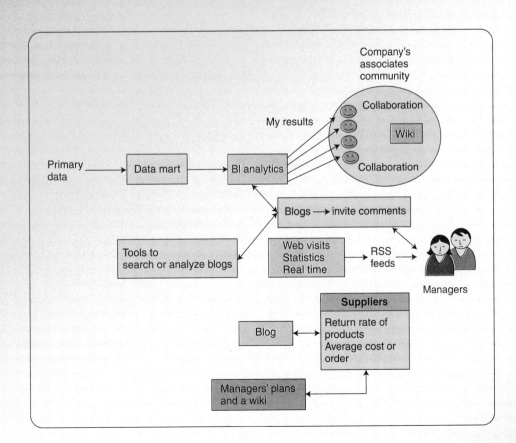

The Web 2.0 Collaboration, Sharing, and Communication System

The company created a multifunction employee workbench called E-Basecamp. It contains all the information relevant to corporate goals integrated with productivity tools (e.g., Excel) and role-based content, customized to each individual user. Then, it added a set of Web 2.0 tools (see exhibit). The system facilitates collaboration among internal and external stakeholders. EMS is using 20 operation metrics (e.g., inventory levels and turns). These also include e-tailing; e-commerce managers monitor hour-by-hour Web traffic and conversion rates (Chapter 4). The dashboard shows deviations from targets with a color code.

The EMS dashboard uses the following Web 2.0 tools:

▶ **RSS feeds.** These are embedded into the dashboard to drive more-focused inquiries. These feeds are the base for information sharing and online conversations. For example, by showing which items are selling better than others, users can collectively analyze the transaction characteristics and selling behaviors that produce the high sales. The knowledge acquired then cascades throughout the organization. For instance, one manager observed an upward spike in footwear sales at store X. Investigating "why" revealed that store X employees had perfected a multistep sales technique that included recommending (both online and in stores) special socks designed for specific uses along with an inner sole. The information was disseminated using the RSS feed. As a result, sales of footwear increased 57 percent in a year.

▶ **Wikis.** The wikis are used to encourage collaborative interaction throughout the company. Dashboard users are encouraged to post a hypothesis or requests for help and invite commentary and suggestions, almost like a notepad alongside the dashboard.

▶ **Blogs.** Blogs were created around specific data or a key metric. The blogs are used to post information and invite comment. Tools are used to archive, search, and categorize blogs for easy reference. For example, store managers post an inquiry or explanation regarding sale deviations (anomalies). Keeping comments on blogs lets readers observe patterns they might have overlooked using data analysis alone.

Going to Business Partners Externally

EMS has also added its suppliers to the system. For example, suppliers can monitor the return rate of their product on the dashboard and invite store managers to provide explanations and suggestions using wikis or blogs. Suppliers can get almost real-time data about how well their products sell, resulting in a better production plan.

EMS's goal is to build a tighter bond with its partners. For example, by attaching a blog to the suppliers' dashboard, the suppliers can view current sales information and post comments to the blogs. Product managers use a wiki to post challenges for the next season, such as a proposed percentage increase in sales, and then ask vendors to suggest innovative ways to achieve these goals. Several business partners subscribe to the RSS feed.

Blogs called Extreme Deals (big discounts for a limited time) also are embedded into the EMS product management lifecycle (PLM) tool. This allows vendors to have virtual conversations with the product development managers.

The major impact of the Web 2.0 collaboration tools is that instead of having conversations occur in the hallway (where you need to be in the right place at the right time), conversations take place on blogs and wikis where all interested parties can participate.

Sources: Compiled from Nerille (2007) and from *ems.com* (accessed January 2008).

Questions

1. Why not just have regular meetings and send e-mails rather than using blogs, wikis, and RSS feeds?
2. What are the benefits to EMS of combining its BI system and Web 2.0 tools?
3. In what ways does the system bolster corporate performance?
4. How can customers of the retail stores utilize the Web 2.0 tools?
5. Can the company use any other Web 2.0 technologies? Describe.
6. What information on *ems.com* is typical for what you find in Internet communities?

MOBILE COMPUTING AND COMMERCE

Content

Learning Objectives

Upon completion of this chapter, you will be able to:

1. Discuss the value-added attributes, benefits, and fundamental drivers of m-commerce.

2. Describe the mobile computing environment that supports m-commerce (i.e., devices, software, services).

3. Describe the four major types of wireless telecommunications networks.

4. Discuss m-commerce applications in finance.

5. Describe m-commerce applications in shopping, advertising, and provision of content.

6. Discuss the application of m-commerce within organizations and across the supply chain.

7. Describe consumer and personal applications of m-commerce.

8. Understand the technologies and potential application of location-based m-commerce.

9. Describe the major inhibitors and barriers of m-commerce.

THE BLOOMING OF FOOD LION

The Problem

Food Lion is a U.S. supermarket chain with approximately 1,300 stores in the Southeast and Mid-Atlantic states. Like other chains, Food Lion has found it increasingly difficult to compete on price against Wal-Mart. Trying to seek an advantage against low-price competitors, such as Wal-Mart, Food Lion decided in 2004 to open a new upscale chain called "Bloom." From the beginning, Bloom stores have focused on providing "a more hassle-free shopping experience that would help consumers find products and check out quicker." This hassle-free experience rests on the creative use of "technology touch points that improved the level of convenience for the shopper."

The Solution

At the heart of the shopping experience at Bloom is a variety of m-commerce technologies. For the moment, we define *m-commerce* as the ability to conduct commerce using a mobile device (i.e., a mobile device or cell phone). Although Bloom utilizes a variety of information technologies, the following are critical to customer convenience:

- **Handheld scanners.** Shoppers are given a handheld device (from Symbol Technology) that emulates the system used at checkout. When customers pick an item off the shelf, they scan the item with the device and then place the item in their cart as they shop. The device shows the price of the item and the running total of all items placed in the cart. Food Lion can also use the personal scanner to send messages, such as special marketing offers, to customers while they are shopping. When they complete their shopping, shoppers hand the scanner to a store associate and settle their bill using their preferred method of payment. To deter shoplifting or cheating, customers are picked at random to check whether items placed in the shopping cart have been scanned. Shoplifting has not been a serious problem.

- **Self-service produce scales.** These scales with specialized printers enable customers to create a bar-coded tag for vegetables, fruits, and other produce items that do not have price tags. Once the bar code is created, the item can be scanned like any other item in the store.

- **Information kiosks.** The meat and liquor departments provide kiosks that shoppers can use to scan items for nutritional and recipe information. The kiosks also enable shoppers to do party planning by generating shopping lists that indicate how much to buy based on the number of people expected to attend.

- **Wireless checkouts.** This is a mobile checkout point-of-sale (POS) terminal equipped with wheels that can be moved to any location in the store as well as outside (e.g., storefront for special sales). This brings flexibility and the ability to expedite checkout time. These devices can be added whenever checkout lines are becoming too long.

The Results

Food Lion began the Bloom chain as an experiment with five stores. During the initial rollout, approximately 20 percent of regular Bloom shoppers used the handheld scanners. Based on success of the pilot stores, the Bloom chain had expanded to 54 locations by October 2007. The handheld scanners are available in 26 of these stores.

Overall, Bloom customers indicate that the scanners, and implicitly the associated technologies such as the bar-code printer, help them keep a running total against their budget and make it easier and faster to shop and checkout. It also helps the company control costs, reduce prices, and increase revenue. Those customers who enjoy chatting with cashiers can still shop the old fashion way. But most customers, especially those in high-traffic locations, would rather use the scanners to save time.

Food Lion is not the only retailer experimenting with wireless devices. METRO Group in Germany (2,400 stores) is experimenting with in-store mobile devices at its "Future Store" in Rheinberg, Germany. At the Future Store, touch-screen PCs mounted on shopping carts serve as "Personal Shopping Assistants" (PSAs) providing shopping lists downloaded from METRO Group's Web site, product descriptions and pictures, pricing information, and store maps. The PSAs also enable shoppers to scan items as they are placed in the cart and to keep a running list and total cost of the items. Finally, the PSA allows shoppers to "pay in passing" by using the PSA's checkout function, which passes the scanned data to a payment terminal. METRO has measured the reactions and satisfaction of Future Store shoppers. The results indicate that customers are more satisfied (20 percent increase), that they visit the store more often, that the percentage of new customers has increased by approximately 30 percent, and that they spend on average 65 more Euros per month.

Sources: Compiled from Bonkoo (2007), and *Intel* (2006b).

WHAT WE CAN LEARN . . .

From a retail perspective, this case illustrates that mobile devices have the potential to enhance the shopping experience for in-store customers and to increase the overall financial performance of retailers employing those technologies. This is only one example of the impact of emerging mobile and wireless technologies on commerce and EC. In this chapter, we will explore a number of these emerging mobile and wireless technologies as well as their potential applications in the commercial arena.

9.1 MOBILE COMMERCE: ATTRIBUTES, BENEFITS, AND DRIVERS

Mobile commerce (m-commerce), also known as **m-business,** includes any business activity conducted over a wireless telecommunications network. This includes B2C and B2B commercial transactions as well as the transfer of information and services via wireless mobile devices. Like regular EC applications, m-commerce can be done via the Internet, via private communication lines, or over other computing networks. M-commerce is a natural extension of e-commerce. Mobile devices create an opportunity to deliver new services to existing customers and to attract new customers. However, the small screen size and limited bandwidth of most computing devices have limited consumer interest. So even though the mobile computing industry recognizes the potential for B2C m-commerce applications, the number of existing applications is still emerging and consumer uptake has been slow. Instead, it is intrabusiness and B2B applications that are receiving most of the attention and offer the best short-range benefits for businesses. In this chapter, we consider some of the distinguishing attributes and key drivers of m-commerce, its technical underpinnings, and some of the major m-commerce applications.

mobile commerce (m-commerce, m-business) Any business activity conducted over a wireless telecommunications network or from mobile devices.

ATTRIBUTES OF M-COMMERCE

Generally speaking, many of the EC applications described in this book also apply to m-commerce. For example, online shopping, Internet banking, e-stock trading, and online gambling are gaining popularity in wireless B2C. Auction sites are starting to use m-commerce (e.g., sending a text-message alert when an auction is about to close), and wireless collaborative commerce in B2B EC is emerging. There are, however, some key attributes that offer the opportunity for development of new applications that are possible only in the mobile environment. These include:

▶ **Ubiquity.** Ubiquity means being available at any location at any time. A wireless mobile device such as a smartphone or tablet PC can deliver information when it is needed, regardless of the user's location. Ubiquity creates easier information access in a real-time environment, which is highly valued in today's business and consumer markets.

▶ **Convenience.** It is very convenient for users to operate in the wireless computing environment. Mobile computing devices are increasing in functionality and usability while remaining the same size or becoming smaller. Unlike traditional computers, mobile devices are portable, can be set in a variety of monitoring modes, and most feature instant connectivity (i.e., no need to wait for the device to boot up). Mobile devices enable users to connect easily and quickly to the Internet, intranets, other mobile devices, and online databases. Thus, the new wireless information.

▶ **Interactivity.** In comparison with the desktop computing environment, transactions, communications, and service provision are immediate and highly interactive in the mobile computing environment. Businesses in which customer support and delivery of services require a high level of interactivity with the customer are likely to find a high value-added component in mobile computing.

▶ **Personalization.** Mobile devices are truly personal computing devices. Whereas a computer in a home, library, or Internet café might be used by a number of people, mobile devices are almost always owned and operated by a single individual. This enables consumer personalization—the delivery of information, products, and services designed to meet the needs of individual consumers. For example, users planning a trip can be sent travel-related information for retrieval when and where they want. Consumer personalization applications on mobile devices are still limited. However, the personal nature of the computing device, the increasing availability of personalized services, and transaction feasibility via mobile portals means that the mobile computing device could become the primary EC tool for delivering personalized information, products, and services.

▶ **Localization.** Knowing where a user is physically located at any particular moment is key to offering relevant mobile services in real-time. Such services are known as location-based m-commerce (see Section 9.8). Localization can be general; for example, targeting everyone in a certain location (e.g., all shoppers at a shopping mall). Or, even better, it can be targeted so that users get messages that depend both on where they are and what their preferences are, thus combining personalization and localization. For instance, if it is known that a person likes Italian food and that person is strolling in a mall that has an Italian restaurant, the device owner could receive a text message that displays the restaurant's menu offerings and offers a 10 percent discount.

Vendors and carriers can differentiate themselves in the competitive marketplace by offering new, exciting, and useful services based on these attributes. These value-adding attributes can be the basis for businesses to better deliver the value proposition they offer to customers. The services these attributes represent will help e-businesses attract and keep customers and grow their revenues.

DRIVERS OF M-COMMERCE

In addition to the value-added attributes just discussed, the development of m-commerce is being driven by the following technological, business, social, and economic factors:

▶ **Widespread availability of more powerful mobile devices.** At the end of 2007, 26 years after the first cellular network was launched, worldwide mobile telephone subscriptions had reached 3.3 billion—equivalent to half the global population (Virki 2007). These devices are increasing in power, functionality, and features (e.g., color screens, GPS locators, Internet access) that support m-commerce. Thus, a potential mass market for conducting m-commerce is emerging.

▶ **The handset culture.** A closely related driver is the widespread use of cell phones among the 15- to 25-year-old age group. These users will constitute a major market of online buyers once they begin to make and spend reasonable amounts of money.

▶ **The service economy.** The transition from a manufacturing to a service-based economy is encouraging the development of mobile-based services, especially when customer service is a differentiator in highly competitive industries. Time-starved, but resource-rich, individuals will pay for mobile services that perform a range of tasks (e.g., locating a restaurant or dry cleaner in close proximity to the user's position and mobile banking allowing users to pay bills online from their cell phones) at their convenience.

▶ **Vendors' push.** Both mobile communication network operators and manufacturers of mobile devices are advertising the many potential applications of m-commerce so that they can push new technologies, products, and services to buyers. The advertising expenditure by these companies to encourage businesses to "go mobile" or "mobilize your business" is huge.

▶ **The mobile workforce.** Some workers, such as salespeople and field service employees, have always worked away from an office. Increasingly, other sectors of the workforce also are "going mobile." This is being driven by work trends such as telecommuting, employers' concerns about security, employees' desires for improved work-life balance, and a general questioning of where knowledge workers need to be located to conduct their work.

▶ **Increased mobility.** The most widely recognized benefit of increased mobility is the productive use of travel time. Workers who commute long distances, and especially executives who travel frequently, want to make more productive use of time they spend in public transportation vehicles or in airport lounges. However, there also are spatial, temporal, and contextual aspects of increased mobility that introduce business and personal benefits.

▶ **Improved price and performance.** The price of wireless devices and the per-minute pricing of mobile services continues to decline even as available services and functionality are increasing. This is leading to improvements in the price/performance ratio. This is enticing new owners into the market and encouraging existing owners to increase consumption of services and to upgrade their handsets.

▶ **Improvement of bandwidth.** To properly conduct m-commerce, it is necessary to have sufficient bandwidth to transmit the desired information via text, picture, voice, video, or multimedia. The 3G communications technology is providing a data rate of up to 2 Mbps.

The drivers and attributes of m-commerce underlie most of the applications discussed in later sections of the chapter.

Section 9.1 ▶ REVIEW QUESTIONS

1. Briefly describe the value-added attributes of m-commerce.
2. List and briefly describe eight major drivers of m-commerce.

9.2 MOBILE COMPUTING COMPONENTS AND INFRASTRUCTURE

In the traditional computing environment, users require a desktop computer and cabled connections to networks, servers, and peripheral devices, such as printers. This situation has limited the use of computers to fixed locations and has created difficulties for people

wireless mobile computing (mobile computing)
Computing that connects a mobile device to a network or another computing device, anytime, anywhere.

who either want or need to be connected anytime, anywhere. For instance, salespeople, field-service employees, law enforcement agents, inspectors, utility workers, and executives who travel frequently can be more effective if they can use information technology while at their jobs in the field or in transit. A solution to this situation is **wireless mobile computing** (or just **mobile computing**) which enables a real-time connection between a mobile device and computing networks or to another computing device, anytime, anywhere. Mobile computing offers a computing environment suitable for workers who travel outside the boundaries of their workplace or for anyone on the move.

An extensive hardware and software infrastructure underlies mobile computing. First are the mobile devices that enable a user to connect to a mobile network. Next are those components (e.g., network access points) that support the wireless connection, as well as parts of the infrastructure (e.g., GPS locators) that support the delivery of services over the connection. Finally, are the components that support m-commerce activities in the same way they support typical e-commerce activities. For example, a Web server, database server, and enterprise application server offer the same services to a wireless device as they do to a wired computer, with one significant exception. Certain characteristics of mobile devices—small screens, reduced memory, limited bandwidth, and restricted input capabilities—means that hardware and software designers need to anticipate special requirements and design the system accordingly. For example, a Web server might need two versions of the same Web page—a "normal" page with full graphics for desktop computers and a "mobile" page for PDAs and cell phones—as well as a way to distinguish between devices requesting the Web page.

This section and the next briefly discuss the major components of the mobile computing infrastructure. A more extensive discussion is available in Hu et al. (2006).

MOBILE DEVICES

A few years ago a computer was basically a computer, a cell phone was basically a phone, and a PDA was essentially a stand-alone personal information manager (calendar, contacts, calculator, and the like). Today, all of these devices are converging so that it is difficult from a functional perspective to tell them apart.

Mobile computers come in all shapes and sizes—laptops, thin-and-light notebooks, ultra portables, and ultra-mobile PCs (UMPCs). Most of these have the same basic capabilities (e.g. support for audio and video, e-mail, Internet browsers, and Wi-Fi connections) and run essentially the same operating system (i.e., some form of Microsoft Windows). What distinguishes one type of mobile computer from another is its physical footprint. Thin notebooks weigh between 4 and 6 pounds and have 14-inch displays. Ultra portables weigh less than 4 pounds and have smaller screens. Most of the major computer manufactures (e.g., HP, Dell, Toshiba, and Lenovo) produce thin notebooks and ultra portables. In contrast, few of the major computer makers produce UMPCs. UMPCs are full-blown computers, but they tend to have much smaller footprints and either no standard keyboard (like the Samsung Q1P SSD) or much smaller keyboards (like the Vulcan FlipStart or OQO Model 2). At a minimum a UMPC must include an LCD with 800 × 480-pixel resolution, 256MB to 1GB of RAM, a 30GB hard drive, 2.5 hours of battery life, and a 900-MHz Intel Celeron M, Pentium M, Core Solo, or Via C7-M processor. UMPCs usually weigh around 1 pound and have small screens (5 to 6 inches).

personal digital assistant (PDA)
A stand-alone handheld computer principally used for personal information management.

Originally, a **personal digital assistant (PDA)**, also known as palmtop, was a stand-alone handheld computer that provided access to a user's address book and calendar and supported calculation and desktop applications such as word processing and spreadsheets.

Most of the original PDAs could also be synchronized with a user's desktop computer. This enabled a user to read e-mail offline. Most PDAs now have added support for wireless connectivity to the Internet through Wi-Fi. In this way, a PDA can be used to browse the Web and read and send e-mail in real time. Most PDAs also provide multimedia support for audio and video.

The leading producers of PDAs are Palm, Inc., (palm.com) and HP. From a hardware perspective, most PDAs have small screens (2.5 to 4 inches), small memories (64 MB of RAM), either small keyboards with thumb wheels or virtual keyboards on the screen, and expansion slots for memory cards (SD or compact flash) that offer additional storage or access to other applications. From a software perspective, most PDAs either run the Palm Operating System (OS) or Microsoft's Windows Mobile operating system.

In recent years, sales of standalone PDAs have declined precipitously, dropping over 40 percent from 2006 to 2007 (Anderson 2007). However, the sales of cell phones with PDA capabilities have increased substantially over the same period. For this reason, PDA manufacturers have created PDA models with cell phone capabilities or have started producing devices such as the Palm Treo.

A **smartphone** is a mobile phone with PDA-like or PC-like functionality including e-mail, Web browsing, multimedia capabilities, address book, calendar, calculator, support for reading Word and PDF documents, a digital camera, and so on. Unlike PDAs, there are a wide variety of smartphone manufacturers. These devices are supported by a variety of operating systems, including Symbian, Linux, Palm OS, Windows Mobile, Apple OS/X, and RIM Blackberry. Like PDAs, smartphones have small screens, keyboards, memory, and storage.

smartphone
A mobile phone with PC-like capabilities.

In addition to the full-function mobile devices, such as smartphones and UMPCs, specialized devices such as Internet tablets and multimedia players provide wireless access to the Web. The Nokia N800 series is an example of the former, whereas the Apple iPod and Archos 604 are examples of the latter. The Nokia N800, for instance, runs a modified version of the Linux operating system, has 128 MG of RAM and 256 MG of flash memory, a virtual keyboard, a 4-inch screen, a Web cam, and expansion slots. The device also supports a broad range of applications, including multimedia players and Skype (skype.com).

Clearly, PDAs, smartphones, Internet appliances, and multimedia players appear to be converging toward the same endpoint—a handheld mobile device with a small footprint that combines all the capabilities of these devices in one package. The future of laptops, notebooks, and UMPCs is a little less clear, although these mobile computers will continue to support a broad span of capabilities in a shrinking footprint.

MOBILE COMPUTING SOFTWARE

Developing software for wireless devices is challenging for several reasons. First, there are a number of competing standards for application development on various devices. This means that software applications must be customized for each type of device with which the application might communicate. Second, software applications have to adapt to match the requirements of the device, not the other way around. Specifically, all software must deal with the technological challenges of small display screens, reduced bandwidth, limited input capabilities, and restricted memory that are common on most mobile devices. In the desktop computing world, the inability of a computer to properly load an application due to insufficient memory is solved by adding more memory. In the mobile computing world, the solution is to redesign the application.

The following are the major software components associated with mobile computing.

Mobile Operating System

Microsoft, Symbian, Linux, and other, more specialized, operating systems are available for most mobile devices. For example, PDA manufacturers have a choice of operating systems: Palm OS from Palm Computing, Windows CE (PocketPC) from Microsoft, and EPOC from the Symbian consortium.

Mobile Application User Interface

The interface is the application logic in a PDA, smartphone, Wintel notebook, or other device. Small handheld computing devices use a variety of interface approaches, including a touch screen, mini-joystick, jog dial, and thumb wheel.

Microbrowsers

microbrowser
Wireless Web browser designed to operate with small screens and limited bandwidth and memory requirements.

Microbrowsers, as the name implies, resemble standard Internet browsers on desktop computers and are used to access the Web. However, they have been adapted to deal with the special requirements of mobile devices, especially small screens, limited bandwidth, and minimal memory. A case in point is the mobile version of Microsoft's Internet Explorer, which is called Internet Explorer Mobile. Similarly, Opera (opera.com), a company that provides browsers for a wide variety of computing platforms, offers Opera Mobile and Opera Mini for smartphones running either the Symbian or Windows Mobile operating systems.

Wireless Application Protocol

Wireless Application Protocol (WAP)
A scripting language used to create content in the WAP environment; based on SML, minus unnecessary content to increase speed.

The **Wireless Application Protocol (WAP)** is a suite of network protocols designed to enable different kinds of wireless devices (e.g., mobile phones, PDAs) to access WAP-readable files on an Internet-connected Web server. The central part of the WAP architecture (see Exhibit 9.1.) is a WAP gateway server that sits between the mobile device and the Internet. The gateway server is responsible for translating information requests from the device into an HTTP request that the Web server can understand. The server also checks ("parses") the WAP-compatible file from the Web server to ensure that it is correct for the device and then forwards the file to the device. WAP was the first standard for accessing data from the Internet, but today WAP is being challenged by several other competing standards, including Java-based applications (the J2ME platform), which offer better graphics and security.

Markup Languages

Wireless Markup Language (WML)
A scripting language used to create content in the WAP environment; based on XML, minus unnecessary content to increase speed.

In the wired world, HTML and XML are used extensively to create Internet content and applications. In the wireless world, currently there is no single standard. Originally, the **Wireless Markup Language (WML)** was being promoted as the scripting language to be used for the WAP environment. WML is based on XML, and pages written in WML are usually abbreviated versions of their HTML counterparts, sometimes offering only the most relevant text-based content. The uptake of WML has been minimal. Instead, xHTML has gained more traction among mobile application developers. **Extensible Hypertext Markup Language (xHTML)** is a subset of the extensible markup language (XML). xHTML is compatible with and considered by many to be a successor to HTML, which means that normal Web browsers can view pages developed in xHTML without any modification. Unlike WML, xHTML is a standard markup language set by the World Wide Web Consortium, the most widely recognized standards-setting organization for the Web. A third alternative is the Compact Hypertext Markup Language (cHTML). cHTML is the scripting language used in i-mode, an extremely popular

Extensible Hypertext Markup Language (xHTML)
A general scripting language; compatible with HTML; a standard set by W3Consortium.

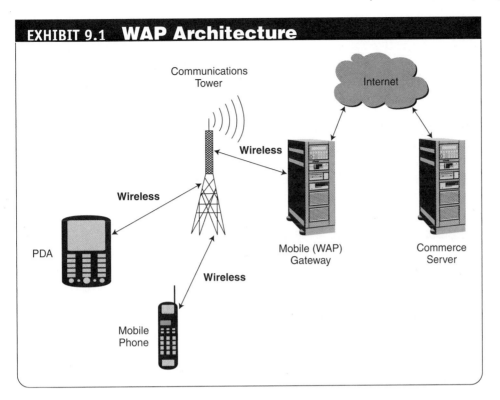

EXHIBIT 9.1 WAP Architecture

mobile Internet service that originated in Japan (i-mode is described in more detail in Online File W9.1).

MOBILE COMPUTING SERVICES

In a separate category all their own—software-enabled but not truly applications—are a range of mobile computing services primarily developed for mobile phones. These services fulfill the needs of mobile device users, but they also provide a foundation for supporting many applications described later in this chapter. For example, SMS is the underlying service that supports communication.

Messaging Services

Short Message Service (SMS), frequently referred to as *text messaging*, or simply *texting*, is a service that supports the transmittal of short text messages (up to 160 characters) between mobile phones on a cellular telephone network. The limited message length means users often use acronyms to convey the message in shorthand text. For example, "how are you" becomes "how r u," and "great" becomes "gr8." Texting has been wildly popular in Asia and Europe for some time. The Network for Online Commerce (2006) reported an increase in text messages of 30 to 40 percent in 2005 compared to 2004 in many European countries and in Asia, especially on New Year's Day. The adoption of SMS in the United States has been much slower, although it is increasing in popularity.

Enhanced Messaging Service (EMS) is an extension of SMS that can send tiny pictures, simple animations, sounds, and formatted text. EMS is sometimes referred to as *picture texting* or *pictxt*.

Short Message Service (SMS)
A service that supports the sending and receiving of short text messages on mobile phones.

Enhanced Messaging Service (EMS)
An extension of SMS that can send simple animation, tiny pictures, sounds, and formatted text.

Multimedia Messaging Service (MMS)
The emerging generation of wireless messaging; MMS is able to deliver rich media.

Multimedia Messaging Service (MMS) is the emerging generation of wireless messaging, delivering rich media, including video and audio, to mobile phones and other devices. MMS enables the convergence of mobile devices and personal computers because MMS messages can be sent between PCs, PDAs, and MMS-enabled cell phones.

Location-Based Services

global positioning system (GPS)
A worldwide satellite-based tracking system that enables users to determine their position anywhere on the earth.

Another support service that can be built into many m-commerce applications, is location-based services that use the **global positioning system (GPS)**, a worldwide satellite-based tracking system that enables advertisers and sellers to determine the position of potential customers anywhere on the earth. This supports localization of products and services and location-based m-commerce (see Section 9.8).

Voice-Support Services

The most natural mode of human communication is voice. Voice recognition and voice synthesization in m-commerce applications offer advantages such as hands- and eyes-free operation, better operation in dirty or moving environments, faster input (people talk about two-and-a-half times faster than they type), and ease-of-use for disabled people. Most significantly, increased use of voice-support services exploits the built-in audio capabilities of many mobile devices and reduces their dependence on less-than-satisfactory input solutions, such as handwriting recognition, keypads, or virtual touch-screen keyboards.

interactive voice response (IVR)
A voice system that enables users to request and receive information and to enter and change data through a telephone to a computerized system.

Voice support applications such as **interactive voice response (IVR)** systems enable users to interact with a computerized system to request and receive information and to enter and change data using a telephone. These systems have been around since the 1980s but are becoming more functional and widespread as artificial intelligence and voice recognition capabilities continue to improve.

voice portal
A Web site with an audio interface that can be accessed through a telephone call.

The highest level of voice support services is a **voice portal**, a Web site with an audio interface that can be accessed through a telephone call. A visitor requests information by speaking, and the voice portal finds the information on the Web, translates it into a computer-generated voice reply, and provides the answer by voice. For example, tellme.com and bevocal.com allow callers to request information about weather, local restaurants, current traffic, and other handy information. IVR and voice portals are likely to become important ways of delivering m-commerce services over audio-enabled computing devices.

Mobile services are a rapidly developing area in mobile computing, and additional services can be expected to be offered as mobile computing devices become more powerful, increased bandwidth (e.g., 3G and WiMax) becomes widespread, and m-commerce becomes more commonplace.

Section 9.2 ▶ REVIEW QUESTIONS

1. Define mobile computing.
2. Identify two user needs that have propelled the development of wireless mobile devices.
3. List and describe the major mobile devices used in m-commerce.
4. List the major software components of mobile computing.
5. Distinguish between WML, cHTML, and xHTML.
6. List and briefly describe the major mobile computing services.

9.3 WIRELESS TELECOMMUNICATIONS NETWORKS

All mobile devices need to connect with a telecommunications network or with another device. How they do this depends on the purpose of the connection, the capabilities and location of the device, and what connection options are available at the time. This section explores four levels of telecommunication networks: (1) personal area networks for device-to-device connections up to 30 feet; (2) wireless local area networks for medium-range connections, typically up to 300 feet; (3) wireless metropolitan area networks for connections up to 31 miles; and (4) wireless wide area networks for connecting to a network from anywhere with cellular phone coverage.

PERSONAL AREA NETWORKS

A good place to begin a discussion of mobile wireless networks is at the personal level. A **personal area network (PAN)** is suitable for mobile users who need to make very short-range device-to-device wireless connections within a small space, typically a single room. The most common way to establish a PAN is with Bluetooth.

Bluetooth is a set of telecommunications standards that enables wireless devices to communicate with each other over short distances of up to 20 meters (60 feet). Bluetooth uses low-power radio technology in the 2.4GHz radio spectrum, and up to seven simultaneous connections can be made to link individual devices. Bluetooth operates under the IEEE (Institute of Electrical and Electronic Engineers) 802.15 standard. (Bluetooth gets its curious name from the heroic tenth-century Viking king who united Denmark and conquered Norway.) More information about Bluetooth technology is available from bluetooth.com.

Why would someone want to create a PAN? Suppose a mobile worker with a cell phone and a wireless laptop needs to connect to the Internet from a rural area. The laptop has a Web browser, but it is unable to connect to the Internet without a wireless network signal, which is unavailable in this remote location. The cell phone can make a dial-up connection to the Internet, but it does not have a Web browser. If both devices are Bluetooth enabled, the worker can pair the devices ("introduce" one device to another through a shared profile) to establish a communication link between them. Now the mobile user can dial up an ISP on the cell phone and wirelessly pass the information to the laptop, where it is displayed on the Web browser.

Another common PAN is Bluetooth-enabled headsets that some people use with their cell phones. Once the Bluetooth-enabled headset is paired with the cell phone, the wearer can answer a call, speak, listen, and terminate a call through the headset; the wearer can do everything except place an outgoing call (at least not until speech recognition becomes commonplace in cell phones). The cell phone can be on the person, in a purse, in a briefcase, in a docking station, or some other location as long as it is within Bluetooth's radio range.

Bluetooth can be used to pair a number of different devices—wireless keyboards with tablet PCs, PDAs with computers for easy data synchronization, and digital cameras with printers. Bluetooth also can link more than two devices, as is done in connectBlue's (connectblue.se) operating-room control system. Equipment that monitors a patient's heartbeat, ECG, respiration, and other vital signs all can be linked via Bluetooth, eliminating obstructive and dangerous cables and increasing the portability of the equipment.

Bluetooth does have some limitations, however, other than the obvious one of its short range. First, the communication is very directional, and objects located between paired devices can interrupt the connection. Similarly, because 2.4GHz is a commonly

personal area network (PAN)
A wireless telecommunications network for device-to-device connections within a very short range.

Bluetooth
A set of telecommunications standards that enables wireless devices to communicate with each other over short distances.

used radio range, interferences can arise from microwave ovens, cordless phones, and similar sources. Security can be a problem, too, especially if the default low-level security setting is used. Finally, first-time and infrequent users sometimes have difficulty finding the right configurations and doing the necessary setup procedures to make the initial pairing.

For additional information, see Wikipedia (2008) and bluetooth.org.

WIRELESS LOCAL AREA NETWORKS AND WI-FI

In the past few years, the fastest-growing area of wireless connectivity has been in making short-range network connections inside a building or a house. As its name implies, a **wireless local area network,** or **WLAN,** is equivalent to a wired LAN, but without the cables. Most WLANs run on a telecommunications standard known as IEEE 802.11 or, more commonly, as **Wi-Fi** (for **wireless fidelity**). IEEE 802.11 comes in four forms:

- ▶ **802.11b** is the most widely used standard. WLANs employing this standard have communication speeds of 11 Mbps for ranges up to 100 meters (300 feet) for indoor use and up to 275 meters (900 feet) for open space or outdoor use. The 802.11b standard operates in the 2.4GHz range, and microwave ovens, cordless phones, and other devices using this same range cause interference.
- ▶ **802.11a,** which was issued at the same time as 802.11b, offers faster transfer rates (54 Mbps) but a weaker signal range (maximum of 30 meters or 100 feet) indoors.
- ▶ **802.11g** is a standard that attempts to combine the best of both of the other standards. 802.11g offers the high transfer rate (54 Mbps) of 802.11a, a strong signal range like 802.11b, and is backward compatible with 802.11b. 802.11g is fast becoming the new 802.11 standard.
- ▶ A standard currently under development, 802.11n, promises bandwidth transfer rates of 200 to 540 Mbps. Although currently not very practical because it exceeds the limits of most broadband connections used by homes and businesses, as Internet connections move from cable or DSL to fiber-optic cables, the need for Wi-Fi connections at these high speeds will grow.

Increasingly, 802.11g is being used in commercial environments where cost is not a major issue and where laptop computers can take advantage of the 54 Mbps transfer rate. 802.11b remains the Wi-Fi standard of choice for inexpensive installations in most public areas and homes.

Physically, the heart of a WLAN is a wireless access point that connects wireless devices to the desired network (see Exhibit 9.2). The access point is analogous to the network cable plugged into a desktop computer, but without the wires. On the back end, the wireless access point makes a wired connection to the Internet, an intranet, or any other network in the same manner as a wired LAN cable. Mobile devices send and receive signals from the access point via a wireless network card, installed by the user or built into the device by the manufacturer.

WLANs provide fast and easy Internet or intranet broadband access from public hotspots located in airports, hotels, restaurants, and conference centers. A California vineyard is using Wi-Fi to monitor field conditions (see the Real-World Case at the end of the chapter). Wi-Fi has residential applications, too. Many homeowners install a WLAN to enable Internet connectivity throughout their homes without the need to retrofit the house with cables. However, security is sometimes lacking in these residential installations. Unprotected WLANs in homes and small businesses can be discovered via war driving, with unanticipated consequences for the homeowner (see Online File W9.2).

Sidebar definitions

wireless local area network (WLAN)
A telecommunications network that enables users to make short-range wireless connections to the Internet or another network.

Wi-Fi (wireless fidelity)
The common name used to describe the IEEE 802.11 standard used on most WLANs.

802.11b
The most popular Wi-Fi standard; it is inexpensive and offers sufficient speed for most devices; however, interference can be a problem.

802.11a
This Wi-Fi standard is faster than 802.11b but has a smaller range.

802.11g
This fast but expensive Wi-Fi standard is mostly used in businesses.

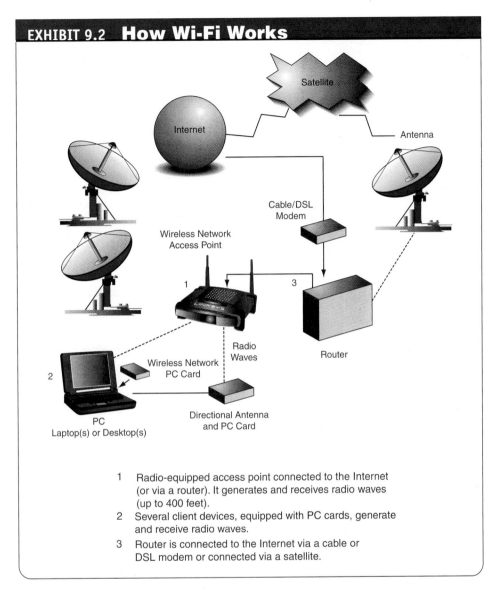

EXHIBIT 9.2   How Wi-Fi Works

1   Radio-equipped access point connected to the Internet
    (or via a router). It generates and receives radio waves
    (up to 400 feet).
2   Several client devices, equipped with PC cards, generate
    and receive radio waves.
3   Router is connected to the Internet via a cable or
    DSL modem or connected via a satellite.

One wireless access point or hotspot can provide service to between 4 and 16 users within a small geographic area. Several wireless access points can be used to support a larger number of users across a larger geographic area. Multiple hotspots can operate simultaneously in any given area, providing overlapping coverage. The hotspots do not interfere with each other as long as they are operating on different radio channels. A sample application of Wi-Fi is provided in Insights and Additions 9.1.

MUNICIPAL WI-FI NETWORKS

By using a large number of connected hot spots, one can create a wireless city. This is known as a city-wide or municipal Wi-Fi network. Wi-Fi signals are irregular and hard to predict, so coverage varies depending on the user's location, the proximity of a node, and what the user's house is made of. However, users experiencing weak signals can purchase inexpensive repeater devices to strengthen the reception in their homes.

Insights and Additions 9.1 Wi-Fi Takes Off

Perhaps nowhere else in the world is there a more compelling case for Wi-Fi connectivity than in the travel industry. Airports, airplanes, and hotels are the places that travelers are most likely to have spare time on their hands. Business travelers are keen to make productive use of this "dead" time by answering e-mail or conducting business research on the Web. Recreational travelers frequently want to send e-mail to or read e-mail from friends and family, catch up with fellow travelers through instant messaging, or investigate activities at their next destination. Both types of travelers may need to book accommodations, alert contacts at their destination of expected arrival times, or reserve taxis or shuttles.

The air transport and travel industries know this, and Wi-Fi is taking off in airports and hotels around the world. According to a report by IT-industry research firm IDC, Wi-Fi hotspots doubled at U.S. airports in 2004 (compared to 2003) and will nearly triple again by 2008, exceeding their growth rate at hotels, cafés, and restaurants.

Not only is the number of airport-based hotspots increasing faster than in other locations, but the number of users using Wi-Fi is expected to grow faster because of the nature of the target audience—travelers need Internet connectivity more than restaurant patrons or even hotel visitors.

Airport hotspots are being installed in a number of ways. Terminal-wide access is available at most major U.S. airports. At Kennedy and La Guardia airports in New York City and Newark Liberty in Newark, New Jersey, access is restricted to certain terminals or gate areas. In other airports, airport authorities have left it to restaurants (e.g., McDonald's, Starbucks) or airlines to offer Wi-Fi services to their customers.

Like a number of airports in the United States, the Minneapolis–St. Paul International airport is served by Wi-Fi. The fee is $7.95 for unlimited daily access. Northwest Airlines has 570 hotspots in the United States.

Wi-Fi access usually is free in the business-class lounges of all major airlines. However, most airport authorities, restaurants, and airlines view Wi-Fi access as something travelers are willing to pay for and charge for it. Rates usually are set by the Wi-Fi provider (e.g., T-Mobile) and tend to be $7 to $10 per day or $20 to $40 per month. Business centers in some airports offer Wi-Fi connections as well.

Of course, another source of unproductive travel time is in the airplane itself, and Wi-Fi is beginning to take off into the skies as well. In the past, Lufthansa offered in-flight Wi-Fi service on its long-haul fleet. The hotspots were connected to the Internet via satellites, and the user paid fees similar to other Wi-Fi access services. However, Lufthansa discontinued the service in 2006 due to low usage.

As of 2008, a number of airlines are poised to introduce a new set of Wi-Fi services. The services vary from one airline to the next. American Airlines will provide nationwide in-flight broadband Internet access on its Boeing 767–200 aircraft. Passengers can use any device that has 802.11a/b/g capabilities. This service is based on AirCell's (*aircell.com*) air-to-ground broadband service. Like American Airlines, Virgin America will also offer Internet access based on AirCell's service. Alaska Airlines is relying on Row 44's (*row44.com*) satellite service to supply 802.11 b/g Wi-Fi connections on its Boeing 737 aircraft. Unlike AirCell's service, Row 44 is not limited by international borders and is available throughout the North American continent.

Sources: Compiled from Fleishman (2006) and Reed (2007).

For example, on August 16, 2006, Google created a network of 380 access points posted on light poles throughout the city of Mountain View, California. Residents of Mountain View just have to choose the "GoogleWiFi" signal and sign into their Google accounts with their user ID and password in order to access the Web through the free Wi-Fi service. These networks also are known as *mesh networks* (see Online File W9.3).

Many municipal Wi-Fi projects have run into substantial barriers. As a consequence, most of the projects are way behind schedule or have been dropped. Portland Oregon's "Personal TelCo" project (*Fox News* 2007) and Philadelphia Pennsylvania's "Wireless Philadelphia" project (*Philadelphia Inquirer* 2007) are cases in point. Neither project has provided anywhere near the city-wide coverage that was originally envisioned and both have experienced cost overruns. Fortunately, in both instances the build out and the cost of the networks has been shouldered by third-party providers. In the case of Portland, the network is being built by MetroFi. In Philadelphia, EarthLink is the third-party provider.

Municipal Wi-Fi networks compete with a related technology called WiMax.

WiMax

WiMax (Worldwide Interoperability for Microwave Access) is a wireless standard (IEEE 802.16) for making broadband network access widely available for data and voice over a medium-sized area of up to 50 kilometers (31 miles). WiMax, which is a technology for *wireless metropolitan area networks (WMANs)*, was released in 2005. The WiMax Forum (wimaxforum.org) describes WiMax as "a standards-based technology enabling the delivery of last mile wireless broadband access as an alternative to cable and DSL." WiMax does not require a clear line of sight to function, as satellites do.

WiMax uses the same technology as Wi-Fi, but its potential is more like the fast data communications services being developed by cell phone companies. WiMax uses a radio-based, ultrawide bandwidth, offering normal data transfer speeds of 70 Mbps and peaks of up to 268 Mbps. The first step of WiMax is the installation and support of fixed rooftop antennas. The second phase is the rollout of indoor antennas, greatly reducing installation costs. The third step moves wireless connectivity down to mobile devices such as notebooks, PDAs, and 3G phones, allowing connectivity anywhere within range of an antenna. Intel integrated WiMax into its Centrino wireless chip beginning in late 2006. The architecture of WiMax is illustrated in Exhibit 9.3.

WiMax
A wireless standard (IEEE 802.16) for making broadband network connections over a medium-sized area such as a city.

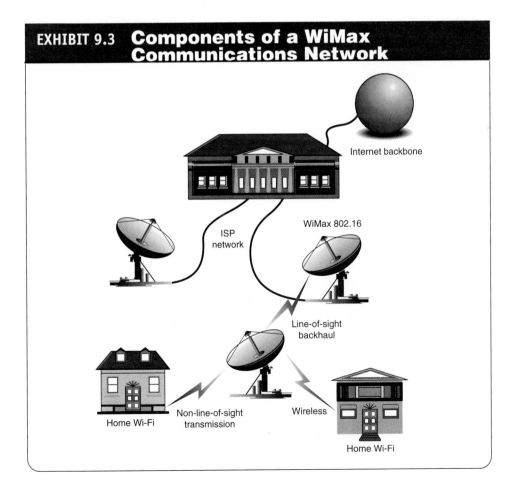

EXHIBIT 9.3   Components of a WiMax Communications Network

WiMax is still an evolving telecommunications standard, and its eventual impact on m-commerce is speculative. As with other aspects of rapidly developing wireless technologies, the only sure thing that can be said is "watch this space."

WIRELESS WIDE AREA NETWORKS

The broadest wireless coverage is offered by the world's most well-established wireless communications network—cellular networks operated by telecommunications companies. A **wireless wide area network (WWAN)** offers widespread wireless coverage over a large geographical area. Most WWANs are cellular phone networks.

Physical Topology of a WWAN

A WWAN achieves its widespread coverage through a set of overlapping cells that collectively form a cell cluster. At the center of each cell is a base station transceiver or cell tower that is used to send and receive signals to and from mobile devices operating within the cell. These signals are, in turn, communicated to a base station controller (BSC) that is connected to a mobile switching center (MSC) that is connected to the land-based public switched telephone network.

A unique feature of a WWAN is how the mobile switching station tracks a cell phone user as the user moves from cell to cell. When a device is turned on, a **subscriber identification module (SIM) card** inside the device identifies itself to the network. This SIM card is an extractable memory storage card that is used for identification, customer location information, transaction processing, secure communications, and the like. A SIM card also makes it possible for a handset owner to change phone numbers.

As the mobile phone user changes physical location, the *mobility management protocol* in the mobile switching station directs each base station controller to make the handoff from one transceiver to the next as the user moves from cell to cell and cell cluster to cell cluster.

The size of a cell is determined by the number of objects that may interfere with the signal and the traffic volume. For both of these reasons, a cell in a dense urban area is likely to be small, perhaps a few hundred feet wide, whereas a cell in a rural area may be over 6 miles (10 kilometers) in size.

WWAN Communication Bandwidths

All WWANs are not equal. Currently, four generations of communications technology can be distinguished:

▶ **1G.** This was the first generation of wireless technology. It was an analog-based technology in effect from 1979 to 1992 and was used exclusively for voice.

▶ **2G.** This second generation of digital wireless technology is in widespread existence today. 2G is based on digital radio technology and is able to accommodate text messages (SMS).

▶ **2.5G.** This is an interim technology based on new cell phone protocols such as GPRS (General Packet Radio Service) and CDMA2000 (Code Division Multiple Access). This generation can communicate limited graphics, such as in picture text messages.

▶ **3G.** The third generation of digital wireless technology supports rich media, such as video. 3G utilizes packet switching in the high 15 to 20 MHz range. 3G started in Japan in 2001, reached Europe in 2002, and the United States and much of Asia in 2003. As of 2004, the number of 3G-enabled devices was only a tiny fraction of the cell phone market. However, sales are projected to increase gradually as more 3G networks and applications become available.

wireless wide area network (WWAN)
A telecommunications network that offers wireless coverage over a large geographical area, typically over a cellular phone network.

subscriber identification module (SIM) card
An extractable storage card used for identification, customer location information, transaction processing, secure communications, etc.

1G
The first generation of wireless technology, which was analog based.

2G
The second generation of digital wireless technology; accommodates voice and text.

3G
The third generation of digital wireless technology; supports rich media such as video.

▶ **3.5G.** This generation is expected to be about seven times better than 3G. It promises data download speeds of 14 Mbps and upload speeds of up to 1.8 Mbps. This means major improvement in mobile voice telephony, video telephony, mobile TV, and other media. For details, see softpedia.com.

▶ **4G.** The next generation after 3.5G. The arrival of 4G, which will provide faster display of multimedia, is expected between 2008 and 2010.

Exhibit 9.4 compares 2G and 3G on a number of important variables. Of most interest for m-commerce are the faster download speeds and the extension of cellular connectivity to mobile devices other than phones.

In addition to the high data transmission rates illustrated in Exhibit 9.4, all 3G networks aim to offer efficient spectrum utilization (see the following discussion on communication protocols) and worldwide connectivity or global roaming (see the discussion of network systems later in this chapter). These benefits come at a cost, however. A fairly complete new infrastructure has to be built on top of the existing one, and telecommunications providers have already paid high prices for 3G frequencies in frenzied auctions at the height of the dot-com boom. The rollout of 3G has been slow, and large profits remain uncertain. However, the potential is there for 3G to change the way mobile devices are used and dramatically increase m-commerce applications and activities.

4G
The expected next generation of wireless technology that will provide faster display of multimedia.

WWAN Communication Protocols

A second way WWANs differ is in the communication protocols they use. These multiplexing communication protocols are used to provide service to large numbers of users with limited communication bandwidth. In today's mobile world, there are three main multiplexing protocols:

▶ **Frequency Division Multiple Access (FDMA).** This protocol divides the available bandwidth into different frequency channels, and each device is given its own frequency on which to operate. Although easy to implement and necessary in the circuit-switched analog world of 1G, it is terribly wasteful of limited bandwidth.

▶ **Time Division Multiple Access (TDMA).** Widely used in 2G networks, TDMA assigns different users different time slots on a communications channel (e.g., every

EXHIBIT 9.4 Comparison of 2G and 3G Communication Bandwidth

	2G	3G
Bandwidth	30 to 200 KHz	15 to 20 MHz
Connectivity	Dial up	Always on
Hardware	Telephone handset	Mobile computing device
Speed	9.6 to 384 Kbps	144 Kbps to 2 Mbps
Download delivery times:		
E-mail file (10 Kb)	8 seconds	0.04 second
Web page (9 Kb)	9 seconds	0.04 second
Text file (40 Kb)	33 seconds	0.2 second
Large report (2 Mb)	28 minutes	7 seconds
Video clip (4 Mb)	48 minutes	14 seconds
TV quality movie (6 Gb)	1,100 hours	5 hours (approximately)

Sources: Hansmann et al. (2003), p. 278; Burkhardt et al. (2002), p. 94.

one-eighth time slot). TDMA is sometimes used in conjunction with FDMA; the available bandwidth is divided into frequencies, and each frequency is divided into time slots.

▶ **Code Division Multiple Access (CDMA).** Designed for 3G networks, this protocol divides data into small packets that are distributed across the frequency spectrum in a set pattern. CDMA is very reliable and efficient (Hansmann et al. 2003).

Even more advanced communications protocols, such as orthogonal frequency-division multiplexing (OFDM), are emerging.

WWAN Network Systems

A third way WWANs differ is in the network standards they use. These competing standards resulted from the simultaneous development of cellular networks in different countries (e.g., Global System for Mobile Communications [GSM] in Europe, Personal Digital Cellular [PDC] in Japan, both IS-95 and IS-136 in the United States). The differences among these systems have been the primary cause for incompatibility of handsets between different countries, and even within countries, in the first decade of cellular networks.

Global System for Mobile Communications (GSM)
An open, nonproprietary standard for mobile voice and data communications.

The **Global System for Mobile Communications (GSM)** has emerged as the most popular standard. According to the GSM Association, one-fourth of the world's population uses GSM. This represents about 85 percent of the world's mobile phone users (*GSM Association* 2007). To learn more about GSM, visit gsmworld.com.

This concludes our overview of the technological foundations upon which mobile commerce is based. Mobile computing—devices, infrastructure, software, and services—and wireless telecommunications networks—personal, local, metropolitan, and wide area—have been presented and discussed. These two sections explored the mobile part of mobile commerce. Next we turn our attention to an in-depth exploration of the commerce aspect.

Section 9.3 ▶ REVIEW QUESTIONS

1. What is a personal area network?
2. Describe a scenario in which Bluetooth might be used.
3. Define Wi-Fi and list some of its applications.
4. List the distinguishing characteristics of each of the three Wi-Fi standards.
5. What is war driving? List at least two reasons why someone would war drive. (See Online File W9.2.)
6. What distinguishes WiMax from the other telecommunication networks discussed in this section?
7. Describe WWAN and list its communication bandwidth.
8. Define 3G and list some potential uses of 3G technology.

9.4 MOBILE FINANCIAL APPLICATIONS

Most mobile financial applications are simply a mobile version of their wireline counterparts, but they have the potential to turn a mobile device into a business tool, replacing bank branches, ATMs, and credit cards by letting a user conduct financial transactions with a mobile device, anytime, anywhere. In this section, we will look at some of the most popular mobile applications in financial services.

MOBILE BANKING AND FINANCIAL SERVICES

Throughout Europe, the United States, and Asia, an increasing percentage of banks are offering mobile access to financial and account information. Customers of such banks can use their mobile handsets to access account balances, pay bills, and transfer funds using SMS. The Royal Bank of Scotland, for example, uses a mobile payment service, and Banamex, one of Mexico's largest banks, is a strong provider of wireless services to customers. Many banks in Japan, Korea (Infobank), and Hong Kong allow for banking transactions to be done via cell phone. Banks in Germany, Switzerland, Sweden, Finland, and Austria offer several mobile financial services. Of special interest to banking customers is financial-alert applications (e.g., a loan payment is due, a scheduled rental payment has not been made, a bank balance has fallen below a specified amount).

To date, though, the uptake of mobile banking is still low. However, surveys indicate a strong latent demand for these offerings; customers may be waiting for the technology and transmission speeds to improve (e.g., mobile banking support is now offered in the United States by Cingular and other major carriers). The same can be said for other mobile financial applications, such as those supporting the real estate and insurance industries and stock trading.

WIRELESS ELECTRONIC PAYMENT SYSTEMS

Wireless payment systems transform mobile phones into secure, self-contained purchasing support tools capable of instantly authorizing payments over the cellular network. A recent survey by VISA USA of 800 consumers found that over 75 percent of respondents indicated that it would be hard for them to get through the day without their mobile phones and over 50 percent wanted electronic payment options so they would not have to carry cash. The percentages were higher for the 18-to-34 age group, which industry experts feel will play a key role in the adoption of wireless payments (Becker 2007).

Two types of wireless payment systems are available: (1) remote payment systems that allow payments to be made anytime and anywhere and (2) proximity payment systems that require near-field communication between the mobile device and a special point of sale (POS) reader.

Today, remote mobile payments are used quite frequently in Asia. In 2004, Japan's NTT DoCoMo initiated a service called FeliCa that enables customers to pay for goods in retail stores, to buy items from vending machines, and to pay transit fares. Similar sorts of capabilities are offered in Singapore and Malaysia by TeleMoney.

Even though there has been widespread adoption in Asia, the adoption in other parts of the world has been weak. The technology certainly exists in most countries, because many remote wireless payment systems are based on SMS text messages. However, various obstacles are impeding its adoption. Of critical importance is the "chicken and egg problem" that faces most forms of electronic payments that are not based on credit cards. Essentially, without a critical mass of merchants accepting wireless payments consumers will not adopt the payment system and vice versa.

Proximity wireless payments are still in their infancy. One example that was piloted in 2007 was MasterCard's "Tap-and-Go" mobile payment system (*MasterCard* 2006). This mobile system, which was part of MasterCard's larger Tap-and-Go system, was based on a partnership among Citi, MasterCard, Cingular, and Nokia. Basically, a special MasterCard PayPass chip was embedded in a particular Nokia phone model. When the consumer tapped the phone to a Merchant's PayPass card reader, it was the same as using a standard credit card with the PayPass reader. The phones were given to a select sample of card holders to use for a short period of time. It is unclear what MasterCard plans to do with the system in the coming years.

Wireless Bill Payments

A number of companies are now providing their customers with the option of paying their bills directly from a cell phone. HDFC Bank of India (hdfcbank.com), for example, allows customers to pay their utility bills using SMS. An example of how bill payments can be made using a mobile device is shown in Online File W9.4. This service is offered by Nordea, a pioneering provider of wireless banking services in Scandinavia.

According to *Payment News* (2006), mobile payments are set to rise to $10 billion in total revenue by 2010, thanks to the entrance of new players offering m-payment schemes and subsequent consumer demand. The expansion of PayPal services into the micropayment and m-retail sector will serve to facilitate a fundamental shift in global consumer payment services now and into the future.

Closing the Digital Divide

Mobile devices, especially smartphones and even regular cell phones, are closing the digital divide in developing countries such as China, India, and the Philippines. These developing countries do not have the money to implement wireline phone systems, but they can afford WWANs. As a result, people can afford telephones, and with declining Internet access fees, they can do m-commerce. Even if they do not have Internet access, they can still pay bills, as is the case in China.

SmartPay Jieyin, working with banks and utility companies, provides a service for people in Shanghai and Beijing to pay their utility bills by cell phone. Most people in China do not have checking accounts, and very few have credit cards, so bills must be paid by standing in a long line at a bank. The system sends an SMS message on a subscriber's cell phone when a payment is due. The user then types in a PIN number to authorize the money transfer from his or her bank account.

Section 9.4 ▶ REVIEW QUESTIONS

1. Describe some of the services provided by mobile banking.
2. Discuss remote and proximity-based wireless payments.
3. Briefly describe how wireless bill payment works.

9.5   MOBILE SHOPPING, ADVERTISING, AND CONTENT PROVISION

As in e-commerce, m-commerce B2C applications are concentrated in three major areas: retail shopping for products and services, advertising, and providing content for a fee.

WIRELESS SHOPPING

An increasing number of online vendors allow customers to shop from mobile devices, especially cell phones and PDAs (see pilotzone.com for more information on how this is done). Customers can use their wireless devices to perform quick searches, compare prices, use a shopping cart, order, and view the status of their order. Wireless shoppers are supported by services similar to those available for wireline shoppers. For example, mobile shoppers have access to shopping carts, as well as product search and price comparison tools. Japan has the highest number of 3G service users of any country in the world. Eighty percent of e-commerce by teenagers between 15 and 19 was done on mobile phones in 2005 (Belew 2006).

An example of restaurant shopping from wireless devices is those restaurant chains that enable consumers to place an order for pickup or delivery virtually anytime, anywhere. For example, some of the major U.S. pizza chains—Pizza Hut, Domino's, and Papa John's—allow customers to order pizza via SMS text messaging (Horowitz 2008).

Cell phone users also can participate in online auctions. For example, eBay offers "anywhere wireless" services. Account holders at eBay can access their accounts, browse, search, bid, and rebid on items from any Internet-enabled phone or PDA. The same is true for participants in Amazon.com Auctions.

MOBILE AND TARGETED ADVERTISING

Knowing the real-time location of mobile users and their preferences or surfing habits, marketers can send user-specific advertising messages to wireless devices. Location-sensitive advertising (using GPS) to find where a customer is can inform a potential buyer about shops, malls, and restaurants close to where the mobile device owner is. This topic is discussed in more detail in Section 9.8. Examples of companies capitalizing on targeted advertising, including paying users to listen to advertising, are included in Online File W9.5.

Currently SMS and e-mails are the principal technologies used to deliver advertisements to cell phones. However, as more wireless bandwidth becomes available, content-rich advertising involving audio, pictures, and video clips will be generated for individual users with specific needs, interests, and inclinations.

For example, Expedia (expedia.com, the largest online travel company) sends SMS messages to targeted segments of frequent travelers, offering incentives to enter the Expedia Web site. Cell phone users can opt-in for free services and for information to be delivered to their phones.

A mobile advertising campaign should be pursued with some caution, however. The number of ads pushed to an individual customer should be limited, to avoid overwhelming a user with too much information and also to avoid the possibility of congestion over the wireless networks. Wireless network managers might consider ad traffic to be of a lower priority compared with purchases or customer interaction. Finally, because advertisers need to know a user's current location, a third-party vendor might need to be used to provide location services. This would require the sharing of revenues with a location service provider. Mobile advertisements can also be unrelated to location. For details, see 3GNewsroom.com (2006). For permission-based m-advertising and factors affecting mobile advertisements, see Salo and Tahtinen (2006). For other topics, see Pierre (2006).

MOBILE PORTALS

A **mobile portal** is a customer access and interaction channel, optimized for mobility, that aggregates and provides content to and services for mobile users. Zed (zed.com) from Sonera in Finland is Europe's leading mobile portal. Nordea's Solo banking portal is described in Online File W9.4. Vodafone offers its customers Vodafone Live! The world's best-known mobile portal, with over 40 million members, mostly in Japan, is i-mode, which is described in Online File W9.1.

Mobile portals offer news, sports, entertainment, and travel information; restaurants and event information; leisure-related services (e.g., games, videos, and movies); e-mail; community services; and stock trading. A sizeable percentage of the portals also provides downloads and messaging, music-related services, and health, dating, and job information. Mobile portals often charge a monthly fee to access basic information services and a per-service fee for premium content, such as location-based weather reports and downloads.

mobile portal
A customer interaction channel that aggregates content and services for mobile users.

Specifically designed for m-commerce, mobile portals plan their pages to supply a limited amount of information and very few graphics. Examples are MSN and Yahoo!'s mobile portals, which offer short menus of popular topics (e.g., news, sports, finance, e-mail, instant messenger, and search capabilities).

Section 9.5 ▶ REVIEW QUESTIONS

1. Describe how mobile devices can be used to shop.
2. Explain targeted advertising in the wireless environment.
3. Describe mobile portals and the types of information they provide.

9.6 MOBILE ENTERPRISE AND SUPPLY CHAIN

Although B2C m-commerce gets considerable publicity in the media and first mention in most discussions of m-commerce, for most organizations the greatest short-term benefit from mobile commerce is likely to come from intrabusiness applications, especially B2E (business-to-employee) ones. This section looks at how mobile devices and technologies can be used within organizations.

SUPPORT OF MOBILE EMPLOYEES

Mobile workers are employees who work outside the corporate premises. Examples of mobile workers are members of sales teams, traveling executives, telecommuters, employees working in corporate yards or warehouses, and repair or installation employees who work at customers' sites or in the field. These mobile workers need the same corporate data available to employees working inside the company's offices. However, it may be inconvenient or impossible for these off-site employees to use wireline-based devices, even portable ones.

The solution is smaller, simpler wireless devices such as tablet PCs, PDAs, and smartphones. Increasingly, companies are realizing that equipping their mobile employees with mobile computing devices increases employee productivity, improves customer service, and bolsters employee morale and job satisfaction. According to *Intel* (2006a), a new wireless notebook PC can provide nearly 100 hours of additional productivity per employee per year. That is what Intel's IT department found when it began migrating users from mobile Pentium III processor-based notebooks to Intel Centrino mobile-technology-based notebooks in early 2003. In short, the company received considerable gains from its investment. Perhaps in no area is this truer than in the use of mobile devices in mobile offices and sales force mobilization and automation.

According to Malykhina (2006b), the major enterprise mobile applications are e-mail, cell phone contacts, calendaring, customer relations, sales force automation, field service, logistics and supply chain, human resources management, and financial support (in descending order of frequency). Let's look at some of these applications in more detail.

Mobile Office

The most obvious application of supporting employees is the ability to work from the car, at airports, hotels, and so on. The simplest form is that of communication (e.g., via SMS) or connection to the Web for downloading or uploading data. In the following applications, both technologies are used. For details, see Pierre (2006).

Sales Force Mobilization and Automation

Many employees who sell must travel. Whether making a sales pitch to a potential customer, demonstrating a new product to an existing customer, checking inventory in the customer's store, or maintaining a close working relationship with customers, salespeople spend a lot of time away from the office. Mobile computing devices can keep these employees better informed about new product launches, product information, pricing schedules, order status, manufacturing schedules, inventory levels, and delivery schedules. Popular devices used by salespeople are the Palm Treo and RIM Blackberry. For details, see Chen (2006) and Malykhina (2006a).

The business case for sales force mobilization—equipping sales force employees with wireless Internet-enabled computing devices—is a compelling one. Sales staff can enter sales meetings with the most current and accurate information, perhaps even checking sales and product information during the meeting itself. When it is time to close the deal, the salesperson can wirelessly check production schedules and inventory levels to confirm product availability, and even specify a delivery date. This available-to-promise/capacity-to-promise (ATP/CTP) capability means no more "I will have to check on that" promises that can sometimes delay or cancel a sale. It also can mean more competitive and realistic offers to customers.

By enabling sales force employees to record orders in real time, the organization benefits through improved manufacturing and delivery scheduling, fewer data entry errors, less clerical and administrative overhead, and better decision making. Case 9.1 provides a clear example of these organizational benefits.

CASE 9.1
EC Application

MOBILE SALES SOLUTION RESULTS IN £1 MILLION REVENUE BOOST

Formed in 1971, Hillarys is one of the United Kingdom's leading made-to-measure blinds manufacturers, with revenues of over $165 million a year and a 23 percent share of the domestic made-to-measure blinds market. Hillarys employs 800 self-employed advisors who visit customers in their homes to provide guidance on the company's range of blinds, awnings, and canopies. The advisors take orders and measure the windows. Once the blinds have been manufactured, the advisor returns to customers' homes to fit them. Each week 8,500 orders are processed and 25,000 individual blinds are sold, manufactured, and fitted.

In the past, orders were done manually by completing a paper form and submitting the form to Hillarys' head office. This resulted in a 4-day delay from the time an order was taken to the time that it was manually entered into the system at the head office. Because the forms were handwritten, details were sometimes prone to errors and misinterpretation. It is well known that manual order entry and processing often leads to inaccurate information. It

also requires a substantial amount of extra work to chase down the correct information. Hillarys was processing approximately 10,000 handwritten orders a week, and about 20 percent of those orders required correction. The amount of time required to correct the entries averaged about 4 days, thus customers often experienced delays in their orders.

Hillarys recognized that it needed a cost-effective solution that would improve the efficiency and accuracy of ordering and that was integrated with its existing SAP system. The solution also had to be easy to use and fit with Hillarys' existing sales cycle and processes.

After a thorough review of the situation, Hillarys responded to a proposal from Fujitsu Services to develop a mobile solution. The solution was based on Microsoft Windows Mobile-based Pocket PC Phone Edition technology running on handheld PDAs. Fujitsu Services developed a solution running on Vodafone Qtek 2020 devices. Hillarys called the solution Sales Advisory Mobilisation (SAM).

(continued)

CASE 9.1   (continued)

SAM offers real-time, two-way communications from the PDAs to the back office. It also integrated seamlessly with the organization's existing SAP ordering and diary-management system.

Using SAM, advisors access their daily schedules on their PDAs. This gives them customer details, timing, and the nature of appointments. Customer and appointment information, which is gathered centrally in Hillarys' call center, is sent to the advisors' devices daily. The automated allocation is based on an advisor's location, availability, and skills.

The device leads the sales advisor through the sales process. Using a series of dropdown menus and pick lists, the advisor captures order information about window size, product type, and other special instructions. Complex pricing and promotions information is retrieved from a pocket edition of Microsoft's SQL Server database running on the PDA. This ensures that the customer gets the best deal. The advisor can then give the customer a quote, which can be printed out on a portable printer, or support payment with a credit or debit card. The device submits credit card information to the bank for on-the-spot authorization. The order is sent to the head office in real time and automatically uploaded into the SAP ordering system, eliminating the risk of processing errors associated with handwritten forms.

The advisors helped Fujitsu design the screens, the application flow, and the language used. As a result, the solution mimics their sales process. By the time the project is complete, 700 advisors will be using the device, which is about 85 percent of Hillarys' sales force.

The mobile solution provided by Fujitsu has resulted in a number of benefits for Hillarys:

▶ **Increased efficiency and productivity.** Through the electronic capture of data and its immediate transmission to the ordering system the need for time-consuming, unproductive work has been dramatically reduced. Better customer service is achieved by field advisors getting to their appointments promptly, pricing is more accurate, debit and credit card transactions are more secure, and blinds are fitted on time. Hillarys was able to redeploy resources into more productive areas. Queries are resolved much earlier in the sales cycle. If an order changes, the information is automatically uploaded from the device to the back office.

▶ **Increased revenue.** Results from the pilot demonstrated sales opportunities of around $215 million a year as a result of improved accuracy in the pricing of blinds. The system calculates the price automatically, which is more effective than a manual system.

▶ **Reduced costs.** Hillarys expected to achieve return on investment (ROI) in the first year of rollout and deliver net cost savings of around $.5 million a year thereafter. Hillarys has greater visibility of incoming orders and the organization can more effectively balance income with advertising and direct-labor costs. The increased accuracy of advisors' diary information means fewer wasted journeys and considerably less paperwork for them to complete at the end of each day.

Not only does the system impact the companies overall revenues, but it also impacts the costs and earnings of individual advisors. The company estimated that SAM would save the average advisor around $1,380 a year and would increase his or her incremental commission by approximately $3,950 a year.

Sources: Compiled from Fujitsu (2005) and Microsoft (2005).

Questions

1. Why did Hillarys need a mobile order entry system?
2. What were some of the key technical features of the mobile solution provided by Fujitsu?
3. What benefits did the mobile system provide for Hillarys?

Worker Support in Retailing

Symbol Technology (symbol.com) provides rugged handheld, small computers that enable data capture applications, collaboration, and price markdowns. The Symbol MC series, for example, can facilitate inventory taking and management. Warehouse management systems are greatly improved with software that is combined with the device (e.g., from M-Netics). Wild Oats employees use handheld computers to reorder. When an employee scans a product's bar code, the handheld recommends how much to order. All the employee has to do is accept or modify the recommendation and press "execute."

Support in Operations

Many devices are available to facilitate different tasks of mobile employees. For example, Driscoll Strawberry Associates uses wireless data collection devices, mobile printers, and handheld devices to accelerate transactions, increase accuracy, and enable real-time receiving and inventory management. The company arranges the delivery of berries to market. The company achieved a 25-percent reduction in transaction processing time, a 30-percent reduction in account reconciliation errors, and improved employee feedback on ease of use. For details, see the Driscoll's Berries case study at symbol.com.

Home Depot equipped close to 12,000 service agents with the Wi-Fi–based Enfo Trust system. The system can take photos as well. See Nobel (2005) for details.

Job Dispatch

Another group of inherently mobile employees are those involved in delivery and dispatch services, including transportation (e.g., delivery of food, oil, newspapers, and cargo; courier services; tow trucks; taxis), utilities (e.g., gas, electricity, phone, water), field services (e.g., computer, office equipment, home repair), health care (e.g., visiting nurses, doctors, social services), and security (e.g., patrols, alarm installation). Mobile devices are becoming an integral part of the groupware and workflow applications that support these employees. Mobile computing can assist in dispatch functions—assigning jobs to mobile employees—and provide workers with detailed information about the task.

A dispatching application for wireless devices enables improved response with reduced resources, real-time tracking of work orders, increased dispatcher efficiency, and a reduction in administrative work. For example, AirIQ's OnLine system (airiq.com) combines Internet, wireless, GPS, digital mapping, and intelligent information technologies. The system collects information about a vehicle's direction, speed, and location from a device housed in each vehicle. Managers can view and access information about the fleet on digital maps, track vehicles on the Internet, and monitor the fleet's operating condition. AirIQ promises savings of about 30 percent in communication costs and increases in workforce efficiency of about 25 percent. Online File W9.6 provides a detailed description of a job-dispatching system that a truck service company has used to provide benefits to both itself and its customers.

Maintenance and Repair at Remote Sites

Many companies have maintenance and repair people in their own field or at customers' sites. These employees need to be in constant contact with the office, the warehouse, engineering, and so on. Cell phones are useful but not sufficient in all cases. Tablet PCs, PDAs, smartphones, and cameras that can be connected to the corporate intranets are useful as well. One category of devices of particular interest for maintenance and repair at remotes sites is wearable devices.

SUPPORTING OTHER TYPES OF WORK

There are many other examples of how wireless devices can support workers. The applications will surely grow as the technology matures and as workers discover new ways to apply the functions of wireless devices to their jobs. Consider the following examples:

▶ Wireless devices can be used to support traveling executives, managers, or other employees. The iPaq Travel Companion is not only a smartphone, it even has a GPS receiver. With Windows Mobile, it offers business travelers effective navigation, connectivity, and entertainment options.

▶ Tractors equipped with sensors, onboard computers, and GPS units help farmers save time, effort, and money. GPS determines the precise location of the tractor and can direct its automatic steering. Because the rows of planting resulting from GPS-guided plowing are more exact, farmers save both on seeds and on fertilizers due to minimized overlapping and spillage. Farmers also can work longer hours (at dark) with the satellite-controlled steering to take advantage of good weather. Another savings is due to the instant notification to the service department of any machine that breaks down.

▶ Like e-mail, SMS can be used to bolster collaboration. According to Kontzer (2003), the following are 10 applications of SMS for mobile workers: (1) alerting mobile technicians to system errors; (2) alerting mobile executives to urgent voice messages; (3) confirming with mobile sales personnel that a faxed order was received; (4) informing travelers of delays and changes; (5) enabling contract workers to receive and accept project offers; (6) keeping stock traders up to date on urgent stock activity; (7) reminding data services subscribers about daily updates; (8) alerting doctors to urgent patient situations; (9) enabling mobile sales teams to input daily sales figures into corporate databases; and (10) sending mobile sales representatives reminders of appointments and other schedule details.

▶ Companies are using mobile devices to locate items in warehouses.

▶ In some amusement parks (e.g., LEGO/Denmark), children are tagged so they can be found if they become lost.

CUSTOMER AND PARTNER SUPPORT

Mobile access extends the reach of customer relationship management (CRM) to both employees and business partners on a 24/7 basis to any place where recipients are located. In large software suites, such as Siebel's CRM (from Oracle), the two CRM functions that have attracted the most interest are sales force mobilization and field service, both discussed earlier. Two illustrations of the use of mobile technologies for sales support and customer service support are provided in Online File W9.7.

Voice portals also can be used to enhance customer service or to improve access to data for employees. For example, customers who are away from the office could use a vendor's voice portal to check on the status of deliveries to a job site. Salespeople could check on inventory status during a meeting to help close a sale. There are a wide variety of CRM applications for voice portal technology. The challenge is in learning how to create the navigation and other aspects of interaction that makes customers feel comfortable with voice-access technology.

B2B M-COMMERCE AND SUPPLY CHAIN MANAGEMENT

Timely access to accurate information is critical for B2B EC success. Companies must be able to respond to business partner requirements in real time, and speedy response is especially important in managing the supply chain. Mobile computing solutions enable organizations to respond faster to supply chain disruptions by proactively adjusting plans or by shifting resources related to critical supply chain events as they occur.

The two greatest opportunities in B2B mobile commerce are to use wireless communication to share information along the supply chain and to collaborate with partners. By integrating the mobile computing device into supply chain communications, it is possible to make mobile reservations of goods, remotely check availability of a particular item in the warehouse, order a customized product from the manufacturing department, or provide secure access to confidential financial data from a management information system.

One way to share information with supply chain partners is wireless telemetry, which is the science of measuring physical phenomena such as temperature, volume, or an on/off condition at a remote point and transmitting the value to a distant recorder or observer. (Telemetry is described further in Section 9.8.) This technology enables automated data capture, improved timeliness and accuracy of billing, lower overheads, and increased customer satisfaction through faster and more complete service responsiveness.

Mobile devices also can facilitate collaboration among members of the supply chain. It is no longer necessary for a company to call a partner company to find its offsite employees. Instead, managers can contact these employees directly on their mobile devices.

Finally, many of the organizational benefits of sales force mobilization mentioned earlier flow up and down the supply chain, too. Direct, remote, real-time entry of sales into ERP systems can improve supply chain operations because today's ERP systems tie into broader supply chain management solutions that extend visibility across multiple tiers in the supply chain. Mobile supply chain management (mSCM) empowers the workforce to leverage these broader systems through improved inventory management and ATP/CTP functionality that extends across multiple supply chain partners and takes into account logistics considerations.

Section 9.6 ▶ REVIEW QUESTIONS

1. In what ways does an organization benefit from providing mobile wireless devices to its sales employees?
2. Describe wireless job dispatch.
3. Briefly describe two ways wireless communications can support B2B e-commerce and supply chain management.
4. What are the benefits of mSCM?

9.7 MOBILE CONSUMER SERVICES

A large number of wireless applications exist that support consumers and provide personal services (see Kou and Yesha 2006). As an example, consider the situation of a traveler taking an international flight: 48 hours before the flight, the traveler checks-in via the airline's SMS messaging system. Before leaving home, the traveler is advised by that same system about any flight delays. Upon arrival at the airport, entering the flight number into the device returns a message from the airline indicating the correct check-in desk and confirming the flight time. The traveler checks in his or her luggage at the designated desk and picks up his or her boarding pass. After check-in, a GPS-enabled device could be used to determine the nearest washroom or restaurant and provide directions. Information about today's specials at a duty free store can be requested through an SMS number posted on advertising in the terminal's lobby. A text message from the airline alerts the traveler when boarding is about to commence. Finally, the traveler can make a taxi reservation at the destination while waiting in the airport lounge for boarding. Although some of these services are fictitious, most of the flight-related services are supported by a number of airlines, including Singapore Airlines (singaporeair.com/saa/en_UK/content/before/travelfaq/index.jsp).

Similar scenarios can be created for hotels, a day at a theme park, conference attendance, an entertainment facility, or a night out on the town.

Many other mobile computer services in a variety of service categories are available to consumers. Examples include services providing news, weather, and sports reports; language translators; information about tourist attractions (hours, prices); currency, time zone, and other converters for travelers; and emergency services. At CVS Pharmacy, customers can print photos directly from their mobile phones to store kiosks (*Pmai.org* 2005). For more examples, see the case studies at mobileinfo.com/case_study/index.htm.

MOBILE ENTERTAINMENT

Mobile entertainment is available on many mobile devices, ranging from smartphones to iPods. Notable applications are music, videos, games, adult entertainment, sports, gambling, and more.

Music and Video

For quite some time, Apple has offered consumers the ability to download songs and videos from the Apple iTunes store. Recently, Amazon.com has begun offering similar capabilities via its Amazon MP3 and Amazon unBox digital download services. In both cases, the consumer downloads the music and videos to their PCs. The media can then be played directly on the PC or transferred through a USB cable or Wi-Fi to a mobile device with multimedia capabilities (e.g., an Apple iPod or a Microsoft Zune). The major difference between content downloaded from Apple iTunes and Amazon.com is that the Amazon.com downloads are not controlled by digital rights management technologies, which restrict access, copying, or conversion of the downloaded material.

There is no doubt that Apple's iTunes has been wildly successful. There is a strong chance that Amazon's MP3 and unBox services will also enjoy success. The success of both will certainly be bolstered when mobile devices can simply bypass the PC and use their built in Wi-Fi capabilities to download music and videos directly. Although the Apple iPod provides end users with the ability to download music directly, the strain on the battery is pretty substantial.

Mobile Games

Worldwide, one of the largest mobile application areas for consumers is mobile gaming. For instance, according to *Telephia Research* (2006), nearly 13.5 million mobile subscribers in the United States downloaded a game in the second quarter of 2006, representing average monthly revenues for the major U.S. vendors of $46.9 million for the quarter. Since the third quarter of 2005, the number of subscribers who have downloaded mobile games from game portals has increased by 15 percent. During the same time period, revenues for game providers jumped 63 percent.

With more than 2 billion cell phones in use by the end of 2006 (Goodman 2006), the potential audience for mobile games is substantially larger than the market for other platforms, such as PlayStation and Gameboy. This explains why the number of companies involved in creating, distributing and running mobile games is so large. According to the Multimedia Research Consultancy (multimedia-research.com/Global-DAPP-database-2008.html), the number of developers, aggregator-distributors, publishers and portals (DAPPs) is close to 2,000. Approximately 40 percent of these mobile game enterprises reside in Europe, although the United States has more than any other single country (Olsder 2008). Although most games are fairly simple in nature, a number have 3D capabilities and a large percentage support multiple players. Recently, some of the games have started to incorporate motion sensing similar to Nintendo's Wii. In such cases, the handset's camera is used to detect movement.

Because of the market potential, cell phone manufacturer Nokia decided a few years back to enter the mobile-gaming world by introducing a special mobile telephone and game system called N-Gage. Essentially, N-Gage failed. As a consequence, Nokia decided in 2007 to move its N-Gage gaming capabilities onto a series of Nokia smartphones. These capabilities will appear sometime in 2008.

In July 2001, Ericsson, Motorola, Nokia, and Siemens established the Mobile Games Interoperability Forum to define a range of technical standards that would make it possible to deploy mobile games across multigame servers, wireless networks, and different mobile devices. This organization became part of the Open Mobile Alliance (cms.openmobilealliance.org), which is now called the Games Services Working Group.

A number of blogs are devoted to mobile gaming. One of the best is mobilegames. blogs.com.

Mobile Gambling

Mobile gambling refers to gambling done on remote wireless devices. Market analysts such as Gartner and Jupiter put the overall market space at around $1 billion in 2006. It is expected to grow substantially to around $20 billion by 2010.

One of the largest gambling sites is Microgaming (microgaming.com). Microgaming is a privately held company located on the Isle of Man. Microgaming software forms the basis for over 120 online casinos and 40 poker rooms. The same software also runs the world's largest poker and progressive jackpot networks.

The market for mobile gambling can be divided into three segments: style gambling (e.g. mobile poker), lotteries, and sports betting. According to an earlier report by *Jupiter* (2005), the growth of the lottery segment will be the strongest and reach approximately $9 billion by 2009, followed by sports betting at approximately $7 billion and casino-style gambling at around $4.5 billion.

Given the legal prohibitions against online gambling in countries such as the United States and China, the growth of mobile gambling will be driven first by various Asian Pacific countries followed closely in uptake by various European countries. The estimated share of the growth in the Asian Pacific regions is around 40 percent, followed very closely by Europe at approximately 35 percent (*Jupiter* 2005).

Section 9.7 ▶ REVIEW QUESTIONS

1. List a few ways wireless communications can assist a traveler.

2. Briefly describe the markets for mobile gaming and mobile gambling.

9.8 LOCATION-BASED MOBILE COMMERCE

As discussed earlier in this chapter, the use of GPS enables localization of mobile services, a value-added attribute of mobile commerce (Section 9.1). Formally, **location-based m-commerce (l-commerce)** refers to the use of GPS-enabled devices or similar technologies (e.g., triangulation of radio- or cell-based stations) to find where a customer is and deliver products and services based on the customer's location. Location-based services are attractive to both consumers and businesses alike. From a consumer or business user's viewpoint, localization offers safety (emergency services can pinpoint the mobile device owner's exact location), convenience (a user can locate what is nearby without consulting a directory, pay phone, or map), and productivity (time can be optimized by determining points of interest within close proximity). From a business supplier's point of view, location-based m-commerce offers an opportunity to provide services that more precisely meet a customer's needs.

The services provided through location-based m-commerce focus on five key factors:

1. **Location.** Determining the basic position of a person or a thing (e.g., car or boat)

2. **Navigation.** Plotting a route from one location to another

3. **Tracking.** Monitoring the movement of a person or a thing (e.g., a package or vehicle)

location-based m-commerce (l-commerce) Delivery of m-commerce transactions to individuals in a specific location, at a specific time.

4. **Mapping.** Creating maps of specific geographical locations

5. **Timing.** Determining the precise time at a specific location

THE TECHNOLOGY FOR L-COMMERCE

The ability of a location-based service to identify where a mobile consumer is located depends on the global positioning system and geographical information system.

Global Positioning System

The global positioning system (GPS) is based on a worldwide satellite-based tracking system that enables users to determine exact positions anywhere on the earth. GPS was developed by the U.S. Defense Department for military use, but its high value for civilian use was immediately recognized, and the technology was released into the civilian domain, originally for use by commercial airlines and ships. In recent years, GPS locators have become a part of the consumer electronics market and are used widely for business and recreation (e.g., see geocaching.com).

GPS is supported by 24 U.S. government satellites. Each satellite orbits the earth once every 12 hours on a precise path at an altitude of 10,900 miles. At any point in time, the exact position of each satellite is known, because the satellite broadcasts its position and a time signal from its onboard atomic clock, which is accurate to one-billionth of a second. Receivers on the ground also have accurate clocks that are synchronized with those of the satellites.

GPS locators may be stand-alone units or embedded into a mobile device. Using the fast speed of the satellite signals (186,272 miles, or 299,775 kilometers, per second; the speed of light) the system can determine the location (latitude and longitude) of any GPS locator, to within 50 feet (15 meters) by triangulation, using the distance from the GPS locator to three satellites to make the computation. Advanced forms of GPS can pinpoint a location within a centimeter. GPS software then computes the latitude and longitude of the receiver. More information on how the GPS system works is available in Online File W9.8. An online tutorial on GPS is available at trimble.com/gps.

GEOGRAPHICAL INFORMATION SYSTEM AND GPS

Geographical information system (GIS)
A computer system capable of integrating, storing, editing, analyzing, sharing, and displaying geographically referenced (spatial) information.

The location provided by GPS is expressed in terms of latitude and longitude. To make that information useful to businesses and consumers, these measures need to be related to a specific place or address. This is done by inserting the latitude and longitude onto an electronic map, which is known as *a geographical information system (GIS)*. A **geographical information system (GIS)** is a computer system capable of integrating, storing, editing, analyzing, sharing, and displaying geographically referenced (spatial) information. The GIS data visualization technology integrates GPS data into digitized map displays (see idelix.com for an explanation of how this is done). Companies such as mapinfo.com and navteq.com provide the GIS core spatial technology, maps, and other data content needed in order to deliver location-based services such as emergency assistance, restaurant locators, buddy finders, and service-call routing.

An interesting application of GPS/GIS is now available from several car manufacturers (e.g., Toyota, Cadillac) and car rental companies (e.g., Hertz, Avis). Some cars have a navigation system that indicates how far away the driver is from gas stations, restaurants, and other locations of interest. The GPS knows where the car is at any time, so the application can map the route for the driver to a particular destination. Another example of a location-based application in the transportation industry is NextBus, as described in Online File W9.9. Any GPS application can be classified as telemetry, a topic discussed later in this section. Other examples are provided next.

GPS/GIS Applications

The following are illustrative examples of various GPS/GIS applications:

▶ UltraEx, a West Coast company that specializes in same-day deliveries of items such as emergency blood supplies and computer parts, equips all of its vehicles with @Road's GPS receivers and wireless modems. In addition to giving dispatchers a big-picture view of the entire fleet, @Road helps UltraEx keep clients happy by letting them track the location and speed of their shipments on the Web in real time. This service shows customers a map of the last place the satellite detected the delivery vehicle and how fast it was traveling. Drivers use AT&T's Mobile Data Service to communicate with dispatch, and drivers who own their vehicles are unable to falsify mileage sheets because @Road reports exact mileage for each vehicle.

▶ The Mexican company Cemex is the third largest cement producer in the world. Concrete is mixed en route to construction sites and must be delivered within a certain time period or it will be unusable. Rather than waiting for orders, preparing delivery schedules, and then sending out the deliveries as most companies do, Cemex has trucks fitted with GPSs patrolling the road at all times, waiting for orders; this allows the company to guarantee delivery within 20 minutes of the agreed time. Real-time data on each truck's position are available not only to company managers but also to clients and suppliers, enabling them to plan their schedules to fit in with the next available truck. Digital maps help locate the customers and the trucks, allowing the use of shortcut routes.

▶ CSX Transportation Inc. has equipped all its 3,700 locomotives with a GPS. The Union Pacific Railroad has installed satellite-based monitoring devices on thousands of its freight cars so they can be tracked. By combining GIS with a GPS, a freight company can identify the position of a railroad car or truck within 100 meters at any time. For example, it can identify locomotives that have left their route and the specific cars that have been left behind or sent with the wrong locomotive. Further benefits include the ability to minimize accidents.

▶ The city of Beijing, China, is preparing a network of intelligent transportation systems for the 2008 Summer Olympics. A major portion of the system is a real-time traffic control based on GPS/GIS technology.

LOCATION-BASED ADVERTISING

Imagine that you are walking near a Starbucks, but you do not even know that one is there. Suddenly your cell phone beeps with a message: "Come inside and get a 15 percent discount." Your wireless device was detected, and similar to the pop-up ads on your PC, advertising was directed your way (Pierre 2006). You could use permission marketing to shield yourself from location-based advertising; if the system knows that you do not drink coffee, for example, you would not be sent a message from Starbucks.

Another method of location-based advertising involves putting ads on the top of taxicabs. The ads change based on the taxi's location. For example, a taxi cruising in the theater district in New York City might show an ad for a play or a restaurant in that area; when the cab goes to another neighborhood, the ad might be for a restaurant or a business in that part of the city.

Yet another method of location-based advertising is discussed in Insights and Additions 9.2.

Insights and Additions 9.2 The Eyes Have It

Advertising firms have long relied on the Nielsen Ratings to help them determine which media ads to run and how much to spend on those ads. In the case of television, the Nielsen Ratings have been around since the 1950s. Nielsen determines ratings in one of two ways: via surveys or with Set Meters. In the case of surveys, a sample of viewers with certain demographic characteristics are asked to keep diaries of what they watch. In the case of Set Meters, a small meter is attached to the TV sets of a sample of households. The meters collect information about the shows being watched in the household. Each night, this information is transmitted back to Nielsen, enabling Nielsen to generate a minute-by-minute analysis of the households' viewing habits. Nielsen employs similar techniques to measure audience size and composition for a variety of media, including radio, films, theater and newspapers.

One area where advertisers have been in the dark is billboard advertising. Unlike other media, there are no well-established methods for determining the size of the audience exposed to a billboard ad, much less the number of people who have viewed the ad. About the only information available to billboard advertisers has been the count of the traffic passing by the billboard. This is one of the reasons that media buyers offer for the anemic spending for outdoor ads in the United States. In the United States, billboard advertising accounts for only around 2 percent of total advertising spending.

A few years back Nielsen Media Research, the firm that produces the Nielsen Ratings, decided to develop a new billboard rating system for the Outdoor Advertising Association of America (OAAA). The system was based on the use of GPS to track consumers as they drive. The system was piloted in Chicago with a sample of adults who for a small fee allowed their minute-by-minute movements to be recorded on a small GPS receiver. Obviously, the demographic characteristics of the sample were well known, which was something missing from the standard traffic counts.

The GPS receivers were designed to transmit the latitude and longitude of each driver every 20 seconds. These measurements were then correlated with computer scans for intersections with visible billboards. Of course, just because someone drives by a billboard does not mean that they looked at it. To account for this fact, Nielsen adjusted its audience measurements based on third-party research about the likelihood that someone will actually look at a billboard ad based on the size and placement of the ad.

Last year, the OAAA decided that using the GPS system would be too impractical and costly. By some estimates, using GPS would require a sizeable panel of drivers, something on the order of 25,000 participants in a given market. The cost of supplying the systems would be prohibitive and would still require questionable adjustments to the actual measures.

In place of Nielsen's GPS system, the association has opted for a system developed by the Traffic Audit Bureau (TAB) for Media Measurement called Eyes On. The system, which has received not only the endorsement of the OAAA, but also most every outdoor company and media buying agency, utilizes a mathematical formula that takes existing traffic counts and parses them into demographic groups. The system has the ability to report on a board-by-board basis the number of people and their demographic characteristics who pass a board and view it in an average week. Media buyers have indicated that the system is more credible and easier to use than the GPS system or raw traffic counts.

The system is being rolled out gradually over next year.

Sources: Downey (2007) and Raskin (2003).

TELEMATICS AND TELEMETRY APPLICATIONS

telematics

The integration of computers and wireless communications to improve information flow using the principles of telemetry.

Telematics refers to the integration of computers and wireless communications in order to improve information flow (see *Cybit* 2006). It uses the principles of telemetry, the science that measures physical phenomena at a remote point and transfers the value to a receiving station. For example, Wireless Matrix (wirelessmatrix.com) tracks and monitors trucks and containers for fleet management, driver communication, environmental changes, and intrusion detection, all while the vehicle or container is in motion.

Using *mobile telemetry*, technicians can diagnose maintenance problems in equipment from a remote distance. Car manufacturers use the technology for remote vehicle diagnosis and preventive maintenance. Finally, doctors can use mobile telemetry to monitor patients and control medical equipment from a distance.

Imagine the following scenario, an example of *mobile inventory* (Pierre 2006): As soon as a store (e.g., 7-Eleven) requires a certain item, the wireless system can automatically locate a truck that carries the item, preferably one in the area, and obtain just-in-time (or on-demand) delivery. Similar applications can be used in hospitals. This reduces the storage space and the inventory holding costs as well.

One of the major problems in many cities is the lack of sufficient parking spaces. This is the situation in Paris, France, where as many as 20 to 25 percent of all vehicles may circulate the city looking for a parking space at certain times of the day. This causes traffic jams and wastes gasoline.

As of December 2006, relief is in sight. Orange, a large mobile telecommunications company, and its partners organized a system that allows drivers to find the empty parking spaces quickly in one of the nearest parking garages. Here is how it works: The 120 participating garages collect information electronically about open parking spaces and send the information to a central server at Orange. The messages are transmitted over the Internet. As soon as an open space is occupied, the information is updated. Drivers call Orange for help in finding a parking space using their cell phones. Orange knows their location by the location of the antenna being used to make the cell phone call. As of 2007, the system will find the location of those with GPS embedded in their cell phones. The system matches drivers with available spaces. Those who have GPSs are guided to the available space. As a bonus, the system tells the drivers when they approach a speed camera (*Taipei Times* 2006; Mullen 2006).

General Motors popularized automotive telematics with its OnStar system (see Online File W9.10). Nokia has set up a business unit, Smart Traffic Products, which focuses solely on telematics. Nokia believes that every vehicle will be equipped with at least one Internet Protocol (IP) address by the year 2010.

OTHER APPLICATIONS OF LOCATION-BASED SYSTEMS

New and innovative applications of location-based systems (LBS) appear almost daily. The following are some examples:

- In Las Vegas, the Luxor preregisters guests when their airplane lands and they turn on their cell phones. Also, the hotel can determine when guests leave the hotel, luring them back (to gamble) with mobile incentives and pitches.

- Jewel Chaser from TikGames (tikgames.com) is a GPS-based cops-and-robbers game that puts players in the role of detective, deciphering location clues sent to their mobile phones and navigating their way through the real world in order to capture runaway thieves. Loc-Aid (loc-aid.net) has unveiled a location-based treasure hunt game played on a mobile phone.

- GlobalPetFinder (globalpetfinder.com) is a small device that pet owners can snap onto their pet's collar. If a pet wanders outside the "virtual fence," the pet's owner will receive a text alert of the pet's whereabouts.

- KnowledgeWhere's Mobile Pooch (knowledgewhere.ca), Kamida's Socialight (socialight.com), and Proxpro (proxpro.com) are applying LBS to social networking. Socialight lets users publish pictures, words, sound, and video tagged to specific locales.

BARRIERS TO LOCATION-BASED M-COMMERCE

What is holding back the widespread use of location-based m-commerce? Several factors come into play, including the following:

▶ **Accuracy of devices.** Some of the location technologies are not as accurate a people expect them to be. A good GPS provides a location that is accurate up to 15 meters (50 feet). Less expensive, but less accurate, locators can be used to find an approximate location within 500 meters (1,640 feet).

▶ **The cost-benefit justification.** For many potential users, the benefits of location-based services do not justify the cost of the devices or the inconvenience and time required to utilize the service (e.g., Bial and Mayhew 2005). After all, many seem to feel that they can just as easily obtain information the old-fashioned way.

▶ **Limited network bandwidth.** Wireless bandwidth is currently limited; it will be improved as 3G technology spreads. As bandwidth improves, applications will improve, which will attract more customers.

▶ **Invasion of privacy.** When "always-on" cell phones are a reality, many people will be hesitant to have their whereabouts and movements tracked throughout the day, even if they have nothing to hide. This issue will be heightened when our cars, homes, appliances, and all sorts of other consumer goods are connected to the Internet and have a GPS device embedded in them.

Section 9.8 ▶ REVIEW QUESTIONS

1. Describe some of the potential uses of location-based m-commerce.
2. Discuss the technologies used in providing location-based services.
3. Describe GPS and GIS.
4. Discuss telematics.
5. List some of the barriers to location-based m-commerce.

9.9 SECURITY AND OTHER IMPLEMENTATION ISSUES IN M-COMMERCE

Despite the vast potential for mobile commerce to change the way many companies do business, several barriers are either slowing the spread of mobile commerce or leaving many m-commerce businesses and their customers disappointed or dissatisfied. According to Malykhina (2006b), the following are the major barriers to enterprise mobile computing (based on the percentage of companies experiencing them): high cost (59 percent), inadequate security (48 percent), lack of integration (46 percent), insufficient broadband (41 percent), inadequate mobile applications development (36 percent), not a high IT priority (34 percent), short battery life (32 percent), management requirements (32 percent), small screens (30 percent), lack of industry standards (21 percent), and inadequate device memory (18 percent). In this section we examine some of these barriers, starting with the issue of the security of mobile communications and mobile computing systems.

M-COMMERCE SECURITY ISSUES

In 2004, Cabir became the first known worm capable of spreading through mobile phones (Laudermilch 2006). Technically, Cabir is a Bluetooth worm that only runs on Series 60 Symbian mobile phones. The worm arrives in the phone's messaging inbox in the guise of a file named caribe.sis. When an unsuspecting recipient clicks on the file, the worm activates and is sent to other devices via Bluetooth. To date, the worm has not been launched on a widespread basis. The same is true for other malicious codes, such as Brador and Redbrowser (Laudermilch 2006). Brador is a backdoor utility for PocketPCs based on Windows CE or Windows Mobile. Like Cabir, Brador appeared in 2004. Unlike Cabir, when Brador is launched it creates a special file that enables a malicious user to gain control of the device. Every time the device is connected to the Internet, the malicious user is informed and knows that the backdoor is ready for action. At this point the backdoor will respond to commands such as "list the directory contents," "download a file," and so on. In contrast to Cabir and Brador, RedBrowser is a Trojan horse that infects mobile phones running Java (J2ME). It was first identified in August 2006. Redbrowser comes in the form of a Java JAR file and is delivered via the Internet or Bluetooth. Once installed, the Trojan sends SMSs to premium rate numbers resulting in charges of $5 to $6 per SMS.

These three cases are indicative of the type of malicious code threat that may someday plague mobile computing as much as it does desktop computing. Most Internet-enabled cell phones in operation today have their operating systems and other functional software "burned" into the hardware. This makes them incapable of storing applications and, in turn, incapable of propagating a virus, worm, or another rogue program from one phone to another. However, as the capabilities of cell phones increase and the functionality of PDAs and cell phones converge, the threat of attack from malicious code will certainly increase. However, although m-commerce shares some of the same security issues as general e-commerce, there are some differences between the two.

The basic security goals of confidentiality, authentication, authorization, and integrity are just as important for m-commerce as they are for e-commerce, but are more difficult to ensure. Specifically, m-commerce transactions almost always pass through several networks, both wireless and wired. An appropriate level of security must be maintained on each network, in spite of the fact that interoperability among the various networks is difficult. Similarly, post-transaction security issues of auditing and nonrepudiation are more difficult because cell phones do not yet have the capability to store the digital equivalent of a receipt.

Other m-commerce security challenges are unique to mobile computing because of the nature of the mobile computing environment. First, the open-air transmission of signals across multiple networks opens up new opportunities for compromising security. Interception of a communication in a wired network requires physical access to the wires in which the signal is being carried. Interception of a communication in a wireless network can be done with a carefully aimed, even crude, antenna (e.g., a legendary war-driving tip is how to use a Pringles potato chip can to find a rogue Wi-Fi signal). Second, because of their small size, mobile devices are easily lost or stolen. Similarly, because they are mobile, cell phones, PDAs, Blackberries, and other devices are sometimes dropped, crushed, or damaged by water and extreme temperature. A stolen device can provide the thief with valuable data and digital credentials that can be used to compromise an m-commerce network. A lost or damaged device is a security threat because of the loss of any stored data or device settings.

In general, many of the processes, procedures, and technologies used for e-commerce security and for general organizational computer security also apply to m-commerce security. Passwords, encryption, active tokens, and user education are cases in point. However, given the unique nature of mobile security, special security measures for m-commerce might also be required. For example, to prevent the theft of a mobile device, a user might carry a "wireless tether" that sounds a warning if a device is left behind or carried away. Wi-Fi networks have their own built-in security system known as Wired Equivalent Privacy (WEP), which is, as the name suggests, similar to encryption protocols used on wired networks. Similarly, WAP networks depend on the Wireless Transport Layer Security (WTLS), and cell phones can be protected by SIM-based authentication. These three approaches to m-commerce security are discussed in more detail in the Online File W9.11. Additional information about mobile commerce security is available in *Commonwealth Telecommunications Organization* (2006).

TECHNOLOGICAL BARRIERS TO M-COMMERCE

When mobile users want to access the Internet, the *usability* of the site is critical to achieve the purpose of the visit and to increase user stickiness (the degree to which users remain at a site). However, current devices have limited usability, particularly with respect to pocketsize screens or data-input devices. In addition, because of the limited storage capacity and information access speed of most smartphones and PDAs, it is often difficult or impossible to download large files to these devices.

Mobile visitors to a Web site are typically paying premium rates for Internet connections and are focused on a specific goal (e.g., conducting a stock trade). For visitors to find exactly what they are looking for easily and quickly, the navigation systems have to be fast and designed for mobile devices. Similarly, the information content needs to meet the user's needs. For example, many WAP screens are text based and have only simple black-and-white graphics. This means that mobile users cannot browse an online picture-based catalog, which makes mobile shopping difficult. This situation is improving as devices become more powerful and as 3G bandwidth becomes more commonplace.

Other technical barriers related to mobile computing technology include limited battery life and transmission interference with home appliances. These barriers and others are listed in Exhibit 9.5.

ETHICAL, LEGAL, AND HEALTH ISSUES IN M-COMMERCE

The increasing use of mobile devices in business and society raises new ethical, legal, and health issues that individuals, organizations, and society will have to resolve.

One workplace issue is the isolation that mobile devices can impose on a workforce. The introduction of desktop computing invoked a profound change on social interaction in the workplace, illustrated by the walled cubicles featured in Dilbert cartoons. Some workers had difficulty adjusting to this new environment and sought to replace face-to-face interactions with e-mail interactions, prompting organizational policies against the forwarding of non-business-related e-mail and IM messages.

Equipping the workforce with mobile devices may have similar impacts. Field service employees dispatched remotely and who acquire replacement parts from third-party sources will visit "the office" only briefly at the start and end of each day, if at all. The result could be a reduction in organizational transparency, making it difficult for employees to know what other employees do, how the organization is evolving, and how they fit into it. These changes have powerful implications for individuals and the organization for which they work. Whether the results are good or bad depends on how the change is managed.

The truly personal nature of the mobile device also raises ethical and legal issues in the workplace. Most employees have desktop computers both at home and at work, and separate business and personal work accordingly. However, it is not so easy to separate work and personal life on a cell phone, unless one is willing to carry two phones or two

EXHIBIT 9.5 Technical Limitations of Mobile Computing

Limitation	Description
Insufficient bandwidth	Sufficient bandwidth is necessary for widespread mobile computing, and it must be inexpensive. It will take a few years until 3G and WiMax are available in many places. Wi-Fi solves some of the problems for short-range connections.
Security standards	Universal standards are still under development. It may take 3 or more years for sufficient standards to be in place.
Power consumption	Batteries with long life are needed for mobile computing. Color screens and Wi-Fi consume more electricity, but new chips and emerging battery technologies are solving some of the power-consumption problems.
Transmission interferences	Weather and terrain, including tall buildings, can limit reception. Microwave ovens, cordless phones, and other devices on the free, but crowded, 2.4GHz range interfere with Bluetooth and Wi-Fi 802.11b transmissions.
GPS accuracy	GPS may be inaccurate in a city with tall buildings, limiting the use of location-based m-commerce.
WAP limitations	Many mobile phone users find that WAP is expensive and difficult to access.
Potential health hazards	Potential health damage from cellular radio frequency emission is not known yet. Known health hazards include cell phone addiction, thumb-overuse syndrome, and accidents caused by people using cell phones while driving.
Human–computer interface	Screens and keyboards are too small, making mobile devices uncomfortable and difficult for many people to use.
Complexity	Too many optional add-ons are available (e.g., battery chargers, external keyboards, headsets, microphones, cradles). Storing and using the optional add-ons can be a problem.

PDAs. And if an organization has the right to monitor e-mail communications on its own network, does it also have the right to monitor voice communications on a company-owned cell phone?

A widely publicized health issue is the potential, but not yet proven, health damage from cellular radio frequency emissions. Cell phone addiction also is a problem. A study by Seoul National University found that 30 percent of South Korean high school students reported addiction effects, such as feeling anxious when they did not have their phones with them. Many also displayed symptoms of repetitive stress injury from obsessive text messaging.

Other ethical, legal, and health issues include the ethics of monitoring staff movements based on GPS-enabled devices or vehicles, maintaining an appropriate work–life balance when work can be conducted anywhere at anytime, and the preferred content of an organizational policy to govern use and control of personal mobile computing devices in and out of the workplace.

Section 9.9 ▶ REVIEW QUESTIONS

1. Discuss how m-commerce security is similar to e-commerce security.
2. Identify three unique security challenges for mobile devices.
3. Discuss the role that usability plays in the adoption of m-commerce.
4. Discuss a couple of the technical limitations of m-commerce.
5. Discuss the potential impact of mobile devices on the workplace.
6. Describe the potential health hazards of mobile devices.

MANAGERIAL ISSUES

Some managerial issues related to this chapter are as follows.

1. **What's our timetable?** Although there has been a great deal of hype about m-commerce in the last few years, only a small number of large-scale m-commerce applications have been deployed to date. This means that companies still have time to carefully craft an m-commerce strategy. This will reduce the number of failed initiatives and bankrupt companies.

2. **Is it real or just a buzzword?** In the short run, m-commerce and location-based m-commerce may be just buzzwords due to the many limitations they now face. However, in the long run, both concepts will fly. Management should monitor technological developments and make plans accordingly.

3. **Is an all-in-one device a winner?** It looks like it. Almost all vendors are moving in this direction. PDAs now include cell phones, Internet access, GPS, and more, and smartphones (by definition) have PDA and often GPS capabilities.

4. **Which system to use?** The multiplicity of standards, devices, and supporting hardware and software can confuse a company planning to implement m-commerce. An unbiased consultant can be of great help. Researching the vendors and products carefully is important. Making sure an m-commerce strategy fits into the organization's overall business strategy is most critical of all.

5. **Which will win the wireless race: WiMax, Wi-Fi, or 3G?** It is difficult to say at this time. WiMax is cost-effective, but some issues regarding its use have not been resolved. Each technology will probably prosper in certain areas and applications.

6. **Which applications first?** Finding and prioritizing applications is part of an organization's e-strategy. Although location-based advertising is logically attractive, its effectiveness may not be known for several years. Therefore, companies should be very careful in committing resources to m-commerce. For the near term, applications that enhance the efficiency and effectiveness of mobile workers are likely to have the highest payoff as well as advertisement-related applications. For adoption issues, see Petrova (2006).

SUMMARY

In this chapter, you learned about the following EC issues as they relate to the learning objectives.

1. **What is m-commerce, its value-added attributes, and its fundamental drivers?** M-commerce is any business activity conducted over a wireless telecommunications network. M-commerce is a natural extension of e-commerce. M-commerce can help a business improve its value proposition to customers by utilizing its unique attributes: ubiquity, convenience, interactivity, personalization, and localization. Currently, m-commerce is being driven by large numbers of users of mobile devices; a developing "cell phone culture" among youth; demands from service-oriented customers; vendor marketing; declining prices; a mobile workforce; improved performance for the price; and increasing bandwidth.

2. **What is the mobile computing environment that supports m-commerce?** Mobile computing refers to computing done with mobile devices, usually in a wireless environment. Mobile computing devices vary in size and functionality. One limitation of m-commerce is the poor usability of mobile devices with small screens, reduced memory, limited bandwidth, and restricted input capabilities. A range of support services, principally SMS, micropayments, voice, and location-based services, at present, are used to support mobile computing and the implementation of m-commerce applications.

3. **Wireless telecommunications networks.** Mobile computing devices connect to networks or other devices at a personal, local, metropolitan, or wide-area

level. Bluetooth (personal) and especially cellular phone networks (wide area) are known technologies and are well established in the marketplace. Wi-Fi (local) is new but increasingly popular. WiMax (metropolitan) is emerging as an important technology.

4. **Finance applications.** Many EC applications in the financial service industries (e.g., banking and electronic bill payment) can be conducted with wireless devices. Most mobile financial applications are simply a mobile version of their wireline counterparts, but they have the potential to turn a mobile device into a business tool, replacing bank branches, ATMs, and credit cards by letting a user conduct financial transactions with a mobile device, anytime, anywhere.

5. **Shopping, advertising, and content-providing applications.** Shopping can be done from mobile devices. Location-based advertising and advertising via SMSs is expected to increase. Mobile portals aggregate and provide content and services for mobile users.

6. **Enterprise and SCM applications.** Business applications such as sales force mobilization, inventory management, and wireless job dispatch offer

the best opportunities for high return on investment for most organizations, at least in the short term. Emerging B2B applications are being integrated with the supply chain and are facilitating cooperation between business partners.

7. **Consumer applications.** M-commerce is being used to provide applications in travel, general entertainment (music and video), online games, and gambling.

8. **Location-based commerce.** The delivery of services based on the location of a device, as determined by GPS, is emerging in the advertising, emergency response, and transport industries. These applications utilize the localization attribute of m-commerce.

9. **Security and other implementation issues.** The mobile computing environment offers special challenges for security, including the need to secure transmission over open air and through multiple connecting networks. The biggest technological changes relate to the usability of devices. Finally, ethical, legal, and health issues can arise from the use of m-commerce, especially in the workplace.

KEY TERMS

QUESTIONS FOR DISCUSSION

1. Discuss how m-commerce can solve some of the problems of the digital divide (the gap within a country or between countries with respect to people's ability to access the Internet).

2. Discuss how m-commerce can expand the reach of EC.

3. Explain the role of wireless telecommunications networks in m-commerce.

4. How are GIS and GPS related?

5. What sells best in m-commerce? Make a list of products and services that offer the best opportunity for the development of m-commerce.

6. List three to four major advantages of wireless commerce to consumers presented in this chapter and explain what benefits they provide to consumers.

7. Location-based services can help a driver find his or her car or the closest gas station. However, some people view location-based services as an invasion of privacy. Discuss the pros and cons of location-based services.

8. Based on what you know about Internet services and wireless technology in your own country, what success and risk factors should DoCoMo consider if it wanted to offer i-mode services in your country?

9. What is the relationship between sales force mobilization and mobile supply chain management?

10. Discuss the benefits of telemetry-based systems.

11. Discuss the ways in which Wi-Fi is being used to support m-commerce. Describe the ways in which Wi-Fi is affecting the use of cell phones for m-commerce.

12. Which of the m-commerce limitations listed in this chapter do you think will have the biggest negative impact on m-commerce? Which ones will be minimized within 5 years? Which ones will not?

13. If a company monitors desktop e-mails, should it monitor company-owned cell phones? Debate this issue.

INTERNET EXERCISES

1. Learn about smartphones by visiting vendors' sites such as Nokia, RIM, Apple, Motorola, and others. List the capabilities the various devices from these vendors offer for supporting m-commerce.

2. Research the status of 3G and the future of 4G by visiting **3gnewsroom.com** (you can find information on 4G by searching for the term at the site). Prepare a report on the status of 3G and 4G based on your findings.

3. Go to **wi-fihotspotlist.com** and **hotspot-locations.com** to determine whether there are any Wi-Fi hotspots in your area. Enter **wardriving.com**. Based on information provided at this site, what sorts of equipment and procedures could you use to locate hotspots in your area?

4. Enter **mapinfo.com** and download the white paper on Location Intelligence. Based on the white paper, discuss the role that location intelligence plays in retail, financial applications, insurance, government and communications.

5. Enter **packetvideo.com**. Who are its customers? What sorts of products and services does it provide to its customers? Select one of the customers and discuss how PacketVideo's products are used by the customer to deliver a mobile application or solution.

6. Enter **gpshopper.com**. What sorts of products and services does it provide? One of its products is Slifter. Go to **slifter.com** and run the demo. Enter **nearbynow.com**. Compare the products and services it provides with those offered by GPShopper.

7. Enter **hp.com** and find information about iPaq rx5900. Why is it called the travel companion? View the demo. Find a competing device and compare the two.

8. Find information about Google Maps for mobile devices. Also review the capabilities of Google SMS and other Google applications. Write a report based on your findings.

TEAM ASSIGNMENTS AND ROLE PLAYING

1. Each team should examine a major vendor of mobile devices (Nokia, Kyocera, Motorola, Palm, Blackberry, etc.). Each team will research the capabilities and prices of the devices offered by each company and then make a class presentation, the objective of which is to convince the rest of the class why they should buy that company's products.

2. Each team should explore the commercial applications of m-commerce in one of the following areas: financial services, including banking, stocks, and insurance; marketing and advertising; manufacturing; travel and transportation; human resources management; public services; and health care. Each team will present a report to the class based on their findings. (Start at **mobiforum.org**.)

3. Each team will investigate a global organization involved in m-commerce, such as **gsmworld.com**, **wimaxforum.com**, and **openmobilealliance.com**. The teams will investigate the membership and the current projects each organization is working on and then present a report to the class based on their findings.

4. Each team will investigate a standards-setting organization and report on its procedures and progress in developing wireless standards. Start with the following: **atis.org**, **etsi.org**, and **tiaonline.org**.

5. Each team should take one of the following areas—homes, cars, appliances, or other consumer goods, such as clothing—and investigate how embedded microprocessors are currently being used and will be used in the future to support consumer-centric services. Each team will present a report to the class based on its findings.

Real-World Case

WI-FI SENSOR NET AIDS WINE MAKERS

The Problem

Pickberry, a California vineyard, is using a sensor network to answer an age-old question: how to grow better grapes. Grapes that produce good wine sell at a premium, so getting the right conditions for good growth can mean the difference between profit and loss for small vineyards.

One problem Pickberry faces is that the Sonoma County vineyard is spread over a hill, and growing conditions vary over the different parts of the slope. In order to monitor key growing conditions, such as temperature, humidity, and soil moisture, measurements need to be taken at various points throughout the vineyard. Field monitor sensors have been available for some time, but it has been prohibitively expensive and impractical to run data cables through the vineyard.

Pickberry's viticulturists also want information that can help them work out what grape-growing conditions produce good quality grapes. In the past, they have had to retrospectively speculate why vines growing in one part of the vineyard in one year produced better grapes than vines in another part of the vineyard in another year.

The Solution

The solution is a sensor net that uses Wi-Fi for data connectivity. Sensors that monitor the conditions known to be key influences on grape quality have been placed throughout the vineyard. A sensor communicates its data to a central server by hopping from one Wi-Fi access point to another. The analysis engine on the server has a series of alerts built in that tells the growers when particular levels of indicators, such as soil moisture or temperature, are reached. Then corrective action can be taken.

Wireless was a natural choice for the grape growers, according to Bill Westerman, an associate partner at Accenture who worked on the project. "We are able to get data from 30 acres back to home base without having to run cables and without having to have radio transmitters that are powerful enough to make the leap from one end of the field to the other," said Westerman.

The Remote Sensor Network provides Pickberry with the ability to:

- **Make calculated decisions.** Decisions can be made on an almost vine-by-vine basis thanks to the granular level of the data obtained in near real time. For example, Pickberry can use the data to adjust watering schedules for a specific area.

- **Combine vineyard data with other data sources.** This enables Pickberry to manage operations and resources, such as water usage, more scientifically. Live data on soil moisture and air humidity can be correlated with weather forecast data to match estimated water demand with well supply.

- **Detect potentially devastating events such as frost, disease, and pests early on.** This enables Pickberry to take immediate action, which leads to more effective crop management, low costs, and higher product quality.

The Results

What are the results? Obviously the data are helping the Pickberry grape growers know much more about the health of their vines in different parts of the vineyard. They better understand how water is being retained and how much water needs to be applied, promoting both healthy vines and water conservation. The analysis also has been used to reduce the application of fungicides to control mildew. Now fungicides are applied only when and where they are needed rather than blanket coverage on a regular schedule, as was done before the sensor net.

The data also are helping the viticulturists work out the conditions that produce the best grapes. According to Westerman, "They are using this data in part to verify what they did before and to get details they never had before."

Armed with insight provided from sensor applications, Pickberry can take immediate action. These capabilities lead to more effective crop management, lowering costs while raising product quality.

Sources: Compiled from Ward (2004) and *Accenture.com* (2006).

Questions

1. How is the Wi-Fi sensor net contributing to Pickberry's core competency of grape production?

2. Why is Wi-Fi such an important part of this solution?

3. What are the benefits for Pickberry, the environment, and for the wine industry?

E-COMMERCE SECURITY

Content

Learning Objectives

Upon completion of this chapter, you will be able to:

1. Explain EC-related crimes and why they cannot be stopped.

2. Describe an EC security strategy and why a life cycle approach is needed.

3. Describe the information assurance security principles.

4. Describe EC security issues from the perspective of customers and e-businesses.

5. Identify the major EC security threats, vulnerabilities, and risks.

6. Identify and describe common EC threats and attacks.

7. Identify and assess major technologies and methods for securing EC communications.

8. Identify and assess major technologies for information assurance and protection of EC networks.

9. Describe types of fraud on the Internet and how to protect against it.

CYBER CRIMES CUT INTO E-TAILERS' PROFITABILITY

The Problem

Statistics reported by the National Retail Federation (*nrf.com*) indicated that 72 million consumers visited online shopping sites on *Cyber Monday*, the day officially starting the holiday season for e-tailers. Online sales hit $733 million on Cyber Monday in 2007, a 21 percent increase over that day in 2006. In the United Kingdom, the Interactive Media in Retail Group (*imrg.org*) estimated that 27 million people in Britain bought online and spent nearly $14 billion during the season, an increase of 40 percent over the previous holiday season. The holiday shopping season also is hunting season for those committing fraud. **Fraud** is any business activity that uses deceitful practices or devices to deprive another of property or other rights. Online consumers can be victims or perpetrators of fraud, with both situations cutting into the profits of Web merchants.

fraud
Any business activity that uses deceitful practices or devices to deprive another of property or other rights.

According to 2007 estimates, cyber crimes against consumers cost more than $100 billion annually in the United States, and $350 billion annually worldwide. With less than 5 percent of those who attack via the Internet ever getting caught, fear of prosecution is not a deterrent. In many cases, hackers do not run up exorbitant charges when they get hold of credit card information, but rather take a few hundred dollars from each person to avoid getting caught.

E-tailers risk selling to identity thieves who use stolen credit card numbers as payment. Web merchants are usually the ones to take the loss from online credit card fraud. In 2006, Web merchants in the United States and Canada lost an estimated $3 billion to online payment fraud. While the volume of online fraud is increasing, its percentage of online retail sales is decreasing. In 2006, the value of online fraud was 1.4 percent of total online sales, down from 1.6 percent in 2005 and 3.6 percent in 2000.

Not only do fears of cyber cons stunt EC growth, defending against cons and compensating for damages significantly increase the costs of EC. As companies try to expand their e-business in countries where consumers have limited purchasing power and legal systems are underdeveloped, opportunities for fraud expand with it.

Another security risk facing e-tailers is return fraud, which cost all retailers $3.7 billion for the 2007 holiday season, up from $3.5 billion in 2006. Return fraud falls into the category of consumer fraud and includes the return of items that were bought with stolen credit cards or used and later returned as being defective.

The Solution

Security solutions involve some form of authentication and/or verification. To protect against losses due to fraud and identity theft, online retailers check for and reject suspicious orders. They try to strike a balance between accepting fraudulent orders and rejecting valid ones that will maximize their sales and profits. Overall, online retailers' order-rejection rates were 5.9 percent in 2004, 3.9 percent in 2005, and 4.1 percent in 2006. The fall in rejection rates since 2004 is due in large part to retailers' concern that too much fraud control was lowering their sales and profits.

To protect against return fraud, e-tailers have imposed stricter return policies. They have tightened rules covering what merchandise they will take back, when, and under what conditions. By providing buyers the ability to view their order histories and the option for gift receipts, Web merchants can require receipts to minimize return fraud.

Both consumers and merchants need to invest the time and effort to authenticate the identity of buyers and sellers. Users can no longer trust Web sites or e-mails without the extra effort of verifying their authenticity. Likewise, EC retailers cannot trust buyers without authentication processes.

The Results

Profit-driven cyber crimes are increasing with EC. In 2007, the estimated median ratio of fraud management expenses to sales was 0.3%, with merchants in high-risk categories spending significantly more. Fraud-detection tools to assess online fraud risks have helped reduce losses due to fraud. For example, one commonly used tool, the Address Verification Service (AVS), compares address data with data on file from the cardholder's card-issuing bank. AVS is generally available for U.S. cardholders and for limited numbers of cardholders in Canada and the United Kingdom. However, managing online fraud continues to be a significant and growing cost.

Sources: Compiled from *CyberSource* (2008), Ellis (2007), Grau (2006), Lopez (2007), O'Donnell (2008), and Richtel (2007).

Electronic transactions and Web sites create business risks. Criminals around the world are stealing credit card information, bank account passwords, and other personal information in greater numbers than ever before. An **EC security strategy** consisting of multiple layers of defense is needed. This strategy views EC security as the process of preventing and detecting unauthorized use of the organization's brand, identity, Web site, e-mail, information, or other assets and attempts to defraud the organization, its customers, and employees. Making sure that a shopping experience is a safe and secure one is a crucial part of improving the buyer experience and maximizing profit.

In this chapter, you will learn about EC security strategies, prevention and detection measures, and the need for a defense-in-depth security approach. Firewalls protecting business networks, for example, cannot prevent an attack if the company lacks **human firewalls** that limit employees' access to critical business documents and enforce strict security policies. Companies also need disaster recovery and business continuity plans. You will also learn how EC companies should prepare for security risks and fraud that will occur.

EC security strategy
A strategy that views EC security as the process of preventing and detecting unauthorized use of the organization's brand, identity, Web site, e-mail, information, or other asset and attempts to defraud the organization, its customers, and employees.

human firewalls
Methods that filter or limit people's access to critical business documents.

10.1 STOPPING E-COMMERCE CRIMES

Why is it so difficult for e-tailers to stop cyber criminals and fraudsters? The following are six major reasons:

1. **Strong EC security makes online shopping inconvenient for customers.** The EC industry does not want to enforce safeguards that add friction to the profitable wheels of online commerce. It is possible, for example, to demand passwords or PINs for all credit card transactions, but that could discourage customers from completing their purchase. It also is possible to demand delivery only to the billing address for a credit card, but that would eliminate an important convenience for gift senders.

2. **Lack of cooperation from credit card issuers and foreign ISPs.** The incentives are insufficient for credit card issuers to share leads on criminal activity with each other or law enforcement. It is much cheaper to block a stolen card and move on than to invest time and money in a prosecution with an uncertain outcome.

3. **Online shoppers do not take necessary precautions to avoid becoming a victim.** Some shoppers rely too heavily on fraud protection provided by credit card issuers ignoring the bigger risk of identity theft. Phishing is rampant because some people respond to it—making it profitable. Although phishing gets most of the media attention, equally dangerous are risks that users expose themselves to by using debit cards on online gambling sites or revealing themselves in online communities such as MySpace (myspace.com), Facebook (facebook.com), and France's Skyblog (skyblog.com).

4. **IS design and security architecture are vulnerable to attack.** It is well known that preventing vulnerability during the EC design and pre-implementation stage is far less expensive than mitigating problems later. The IS staff needs to plan security from the design stage because simple mistakes, such as not ensuring that all traffic into and out of a network pass through a firewall, often are to blame for letting in hackers.

EXHIBIT 10.1   General Security Issues at EC Sites

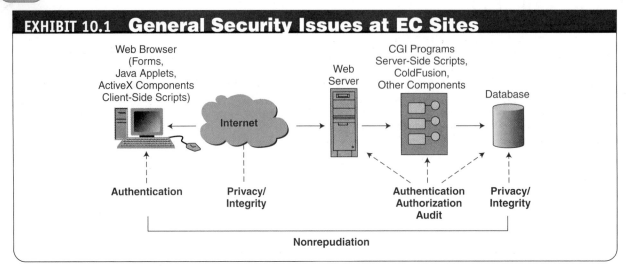

Source: Scambray, J. et al. *Hacking Exposed*, 2d ed. New York: McGraw-Hill, 2000. Copyright ©The McGraw-Hill Companies.

If companies do not invest the resources needed to ensure that their applications are secure, they may as well forget about security elsewhere on the Web site. Web applications that provide access to back-end databases or banking applications can provide an attack vector. Exhibit 10.1 shows some of the major components involved in EC applications and indicates where security issues come into play.

5. **Software vulnerabilities (bugs) are a huge security problem.** The well-documented weaknesses in the wireless 802.11 standard were built into the protocols (Berghel and Uecker 2005). These weaknesses give hackers access to a system or network. Vulnerabilities need to be managed with patches. The challenge is for EC systems designers and network administrators to integrate risk management into the system development life cycle (SDLC).

6. **Managers sometimes ignore due standards of care.** If managers ignore the standard of due care in business practices, hire criminals, outsource to fraudulent vendors, or partner with unsecured companies, they put their EC business and confidential data at risk exposing themselves to legal problems. **Due care** in EC are those actions that a company is reasonably expected to take based on the risks affecting its EC business and online transactions. Violators of the Foreign Corrupt Practices Act (FCPA) and the Sarbanes-Oxley Act face lawsuits and fines from regulators, such as the Federal Trade Commission (FTC) and Securities and Exchange Commission (SEC). See Online File W10.1 for a discussion of the impacts on ChoicePoint for its negligence for not following reasonable information security and privacy practices. For a description of **Payment Card Industry** (PCI) requirements and guidelines for data security, see pcistandard.com. The PCI data security standard was developed by major credit card companies to help companies that process card payments to protect against credit card fraud and other security vulnerabilities and threats.

Every EC business knows that the threat of bogus credit card purchases, data breaches, phishing, malware, and identity theft never end—and that these threats must be addressed comprehensively and strategically. Cyber crime will not be adequately deterred until there are strict international EC laws and an international task force to enforce them.

due care
Care that a company is reasonably expected to take based on the risks affecting its EC business and online transactions.

1. List one technology-related reason why it is difficult to halt cyber crime.
2. List one nontechnology reason why it is difficult to halt cyber crime.
3. What security risks do people expose themselves to on social networks?
4. In what ways can managers ignore the standards of due care for EC?

10.2 E-COMMERCE SECURITY STRATEGY AND LIFE CYCLE APPROACH

Information security departments with big workloads and small budgets are not able to optimize their EC security program for efficiency. Endless worms, spyware, data privacy vulnerabilities, and other crises keep them working reactively rather than strategically. In addition, they address security concerns according to attackers' schedules instead of their own. As a result, their security costs and efforts from reacting to crises and paying for damages are greater than if they had an EC security strategy. The reasons why a comprehensive EC security strategy is needed are discussed next.

THE INTERNET'S VULNERABLE DESIGN

The Internet, or more specifically the Internet and network protocols, was never intended for use by untrusted users or components. It was designed to accommodate computer-to-computer communications in a closed, trustworthy community. However, the Internet has evolved into an any-to-any means of communication in an open community. Furthermore, the Internet was designed for maximum efficiency without regard for security or the integrity (or malicious intent) of a person sending a message or requesting access. Error checking to ensure that the message was sent and received correctly was important at that time, but not user authentication or access control. The Internet is still insecure.

THE SHIFT TO PROFIT-MOTIVATED CRIMES

In the early days of e-commerce, many hackers simply wanted to gain fame or notoriety by defacing Web sites or "gaining root"; that is, gaining root access to a network. Criminals and criminal gangs are now profit oriented, and their tactics are not limited to the online world. For example, in June 2006 international insurance company AIG, with operations in over 130 countries, admitted that the personal data of almost 1 million people had been stolen a month earlier. Firewalls and intrusion detection systems were irrelevant in this breach. Thieves physically broke into an AIG Midwestern regional office through the ceiling and carried off a server and laptop. That server contained detailed personal data from 930,000 prospective AIG customers.

Continuing e-business security crises prove that a company needs to have in place a risk management process to methodically assess potential risks and vulnerabilities and incident-response processes when compromises occur. Such processes are crucial, as the intrusion to access corporate data at conglomerate TJX illustrates. See Online File W10.2 to read about the network intrusion at TJX.

IGNORING EC SECURITY BEST PRACTICES

Companies of all sizes fail to implement basic IT security management best practices, business continuity plans, and disaster recovery plans. In its survey of information security

Computing Technology Industry Association (CompTIA)
Nonprofit trade group providing information security research and best practices.

information assurance (IA)
The protection of information systems against unauthorized access to or modification of information whether in storage, processing, or transit, and against the denial of service to authorized users, including those measures necessary to detect, document, and counter such threats.

and the workforce released in April 2007, the **Computing Technology Industry Association (CompTIA)**, a nonprofit trade group, said that more than three-quarters of respondents allow data access for remote/mobile employees, yet only 32 percent have implemented security awareness training for these workers. The study also revealed that more than half of breaches related to human error had happened because staff did not follow security procedures (CompTIA 2007). In the next section, you will learn about reasonable EC security strategies and the information assurance (IA) model.

Section 10.2 ▶ REVIEW QUESTIONS

1. How have the motives of cyber criminals changed?
2. Why do companies need a risk management approach to EC security?
3. What did CompTIA's survey results reveal?

10.3 INFORMATION ASSURANCE

Information assurance (IA) is the protection of information systems against unauthorized access to or modification of information that is stored, processed, or being sent over a network. The importance of the IA model to EC is that it represents the processes for protecting information by ensuring its confidentiality, integrity, and availability. This model is referred to as the CIA security triad, or simply the CIA triad.

EXHIBIT 10.2	Encryption Components	
Component	**Description**	**Example or Description**
Plaintext	The original message or document is created by the user, which is in human-readable form.	Credit card number 5342 8765 3652 9982
Encryption algorithm	The set of procedures or mathematical functions to encrypt or decrypt a message. Typically, the algorithm is not the secret piece of the encryption process.	Add a number (the key) to each number in the card. If the number is greater than 9, wrap around the number to the beginning (i.e., modulus arithmetic). For example, add 4 to each number so that 1 becomes 5, 9 becomes 3, etc.
Key or Key Value	The secret value used with the algorithm to transform the message.	The key dictates what parts (functions) of the algorithm will be used, in what order, and with what values.
Keyspace	The large number of possible key values (keys) created by the algorithm to use when transforming the message.	The larger the keyspace, the greater the number of possibilities for the key, which makes it harder for an attacker to discover the correct key.
Ciphertext	Message or document that has been encrypted into unreadable form.	The original 5342 8765 3652 9982 becomes 9786 2109 7096 3326.

CONFIDENTIALITY, INTEGRITY, AND AVAILABILITY

The success and security of EC depends on the confidentiality, integrity, and availability of information and the business Web site:

1. **Confidentiality** is the assurance of data privacy. The data or transmitted message is encrypted so that it is readable only by the person for whom it is intended, as shown in Exhibit 10.2.
2. **Integrity** is the assurance that data is accurate or that a message has not been altered.
3. **Availability** is the assurance that access to data, the Web site, or other EC data service is timely, available, reliable, and restricted to authorized users.

Security concepts relating to users, rather than data, are authentication, authorization, and nonrepudiation. Confidentiality, integrity, availability, authentication, authorization, and nonrepudiation are all assurance processes.

AUTHENTICATION, AUTHORIZATION, AND NONREPUDIATION

All CIA functions depend on authentication. **Authentication** is a process to verify (assure) the real identity of an entity, which could be an individual, computer, computer program, or EC Web site. For transmissions, authentication verifies that the sender of the message is whom the person or organization claims to be.

Authorization is the process of determining what the authenticated entity is allowed to access and what operations it is allowed to perform. Authorization of an entity occurs after authentication. Closely associated with authentication is **nonrepudiation**, which is assurance that online customers or trading partners cannot falsely deny (repudiate) their purchase, transaction, and so on. For EC and other electronic transactions, including ATMs, all parties in a transaction must be confident that the transaction is secure, that the parties are who they say they are (authentication), and that the transaction is verified once it has been completed.

Authentication and nonrepudiation are potential defenses against phishing and identity theft. To protect and ensure trust in EC transactions, **digital signatures**, or **digital certificates**, often are used to validate the sender and time stamp of the transaction so that it cannot later be claimed that the transaction was unauthorized or invalid. Exhibit 10.3 shows how digital signatures work. A technical overview of digital signatures and certificates and how they provide verification is presented in Section 10.7.

E-COMMERCE SECURITY TAXONOMY

EC security strategy needs to address the three IA metrics and three user assurance metrics. In Exhibit 10.4, an EC security taxonomy is presented that defines the high-level categories the six assurance metrics map to and their controls. The three major categories are regulatory, financial, and marketing and operations.

Being proactive by setting the IA requirements correctly as a first step in the EC security life cycle and following a strategy to meet regulatory, financial, and marketing and operations is the most cost-effective security approach. That approach requires significant investments, inconvenience, and commitment, as you will learn in the next section.

confidentiality
Assurance of data privacy and accuracy. Keeping private or sensitive information from being disclosed to unauthorized individuals, entities, or processes.

integrity
Assurance that stored data has not been modified without authorization; and a message that was sent is the same message that was received.

availability
Assurance that access to data, the Web site, or other EC data service is timely, available, reliable, and restricted to authorized users.

authentication
Process to verify (assure) the real identity of an individual, computer, computer program, or EC Web site.

authorization
Process of determining what the authenticated entity is allowed to access and what operations it is allowed to perform.

nonrepudiation
Assurance that an online customer or trading partner cannot falsely deny (repudiate) their purchase or transaction.

digital signature or **digital certificate**
Validates the sender and time stamp of a transaction so it cannot be later claimed that the transaction was unauthorized or invalid.

EXHIBIT 10.3 Digital Signatures

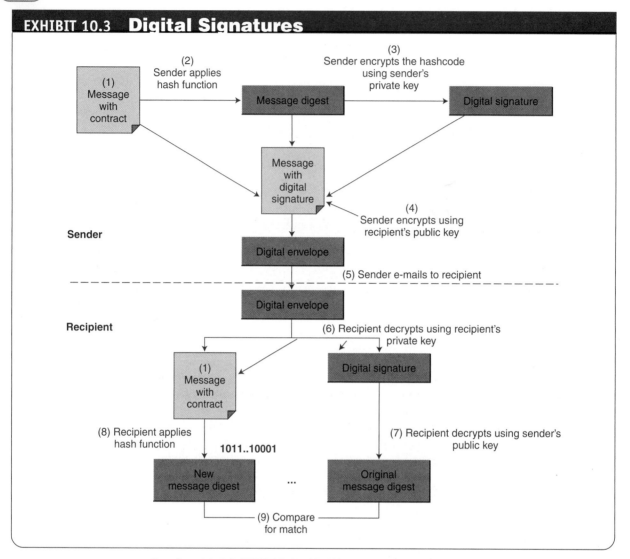

Section 10.3 ▶ REVIEW QUESTIONS

1. What is information assurance (IA)?

2. What are the six assurances for information and people (i.e., senders and receivers of information)?

3. Why is authentication so difficult in an EC transaction?

10.4 ENTERPRISEWIDE E-COMMERCE SECURITY AND PRIVACY MODEL

An EC security strategy and program begins with the commitment and involvement of executive management, as shown in Exhibit 10.5. This model views EC security as a combination of commitment, people, processes, and technology. A well-communicated executive commitment is needed to convince users that insecure practices, risky or unethical methods, and mistakes due to ignorance will not be tolerated. Security practices tend not to be a priority unless they are mandatory and there are negative consequences for noncompliance.

EC security programs consist of all the policies, procedures, documents, standards, hardware, software, training, and personnel that work together to protect

EC security program
Set of controls over security processes to protect organizational assets. All the policies, procedures, documents, standards, hardware, software, training, and personnel that work together to protect information, the ability to conduct business, and other assets.

EXHIBIT 10.4   E-Commerce Security Taxonomy

E-Commerce Security Strategy

Regulatory (External)	Financial (Internal)	Marketing & Operations (Internal)
Control: Database and network security **Assurance metrics:** Confidentiality, integrity, authorization **Protect against:** Unauthorized access by hackers, former employees, malware, and crimeware Privacy violations	**Control:** Fraud; embezzlement, bad debt expense **Assurance metrics:** Authentication and integrity **Protect against:** Transactions using stolen identities, debit or credit cards, and checks. Unauthorized transactions and overrides Pretexting	**Control:** Web site functions, customer transactions, electronic documents, intellectual property **Assurance metrics:** Availability, nonrepudiation. **Protect against:** Phishing Spoofing Denial of service attacks Industrial espionage

information, the ability to conduct business, and other assets. Regulators and government agencies are imposing harsh penalties to deter weak security programs that allow confidential data to be compromised. For further information about management accountability and standards of the attorneys general, see naag.org.

SECURITY TOOLS: HARDWARE AND SOFTWARE

After the EC security program and policies are defined and risk assessment completed, then the software and hardware needed to support and enforce them can be put in place. Decisions regarding data encryption are implemented at this stage. Although encryption to protect moving or static data is not foolproof, it helps protect a company from customer outrage and public outcry if it suffers a data breach.

Neither hardware nor software security defenses protect against irresponsible business practices or corruption. Managers and employees are potential attack vectors like hackers and criminal communities. For more information on the reasons for a multilayered security approach, read Online File W10.3.

PRIVACY

Why should EC companies comply with ethical privacy practices? Customers need to trust that the online marketplace and its businesses will not violate the right to privacy. Unethical privacy practices can have immediate and long-term negative business consequences. Violators expose themselves to harsh penalties from various government agencies and victimized customers, as well as bloggers and consumer interest groups, such as privacy

EXHIBIT 10.5   Enterprisewide EC Security and Privacy Model

Senior Management Commitment & Support > Security Policies & Training > Security Procedures & Enforcement > Security Tools: Hardware & Software

CASE 10.1
EC Application

FACEBOOK SOCIAL ADVERTISING VIOLATED PRIVACY

Facebook is one of the most popular social networking sites, providing free services to over 59 million members. Like all social networks, Facebook's profitability depends on advertisers. To increase advertising revenues, in November 2007 Beacon technology was used to attract advertisers by giving those companies access to Facebook's members' personal information. In addition, the Beacon program notified friends when someone purchased a product from a participating company. This was done without the member's knowledge or permission.

Using Beacon, advertisers and EC sites can capture and publish a person's detailed activities to that person's newsfeed, which in turn reveals those movements to friends. These newsfeeds can identify, among other things, what a Facebook member has bought, from where, and a link to the item and its price, all without the member's consent. Tens of thousands of Facebook consumers were outraged when they learned that their online holiday shopping was exposed in their Facebook newsfeed. Exposing what they had purchased not only spoiled surprises, it was an intolerable violation of online privacy. An estimated 46,000 users felt that this level of advertising was intrusive and signed a petition called "Facebook! Stop invading my privacy!" On November 29, 2007, Facebook made modifications to this controversial advertising system.

Social networkers, security experts, and privacy watchdogs complained that Facebook was gathering data surreptitiously about people who used Facebook or services from its many partner companies. Facebook claimed that the purpose of collecting this information was to be able to present highly targeted ads to its members. Letting advertisers capitalize on data helps Web companies increase sales, but sharing too much data can result in backlash.

Sources: Compiled from Hodgkinson (2008), Musthaler (2008), and Tsai (2008).

Questions

1. What sorts of precautions should Facebook have taken to avoid abusing members' privacy?

2. What problems could Beacon have created for members whose shopping purchases were exposed to friends?

3. If a customer purchases an item from an online store, what are some of the security concerns that might arise?

groups, as Case 10.1 illustrates. The integrity of EC depends on people's knowing and obeying the letter and spirit of laws that apply to business and advertising.

Section 10.4 ▶ REVIEW QUESTIONS

1. If senior management is not committed to EC security, how might that impact the e-business?

2. What are the components of an EC security program?

3. What risks cannot be mitigated with hardware or software?

10.5 BASIC E-COMMERCE SECURITY ISSUES AND PERSPECTIVES

EC security involves more than just preventing and responding to cyber attacks and intrusion. Consider, for example, the situation in which a user connects to a Web server at a marketing site to obtain some product literature. In return, the user is asked to fill out a Web form providing information about herself and her employer before receiving the literature. In this situation, what kinds of security questions arise?

From the user's perspective:

▶ How can the user know whether the Web server is owned and operated by a legitimate company?

▶ How does the user know that the Web page and form have not been compromised by spyware or other malicious code?

▶ How does the user know that an employee will not intercept and misuse the information?

From the company's perspective:

▶ How does the company know the user will not attempt to break into the Web server or alter the pages and content at the site?

From both parties' perspectives:

▶ How do both parties know that the network connection is free from eavesdropping by a third party "listening" on the line?

▶ How do they know that the information sent back and forth between the server and the user's browser has not been altered?

These questions illustrate the types of security issues that arise in an EC transaction. For transactions involving e-payments, additional types of security issues must be confronted.

Section 10.5 ▶ REVIEW QUESTIONS

1. If a customer purchases an item from an online store, what are some of the security concerns that might arise?

2. What security issues may be faced by the provider of information?

10.6 THREATS AND ATTACKS

It is helpful to distinguish between two types of attacks: nontechnical and technical. **Nontechnical attacks** are those in which a perpetrator uses some form of deception to trick people into revealing information or performing actions that harm the security of a network. **Social engineering** is a type of nontechnical attack to circumvent technological security measures by manipulating people to disclose crucial authentication information. Like hacking, the goals of social engineering are to gain unauthorized access to systems or information. Phishing relies on social engineering. **Phishing** refers to techniques to steal the identity of a target company to get the identities of its customers. Even though most people are aware of phishing scams, phishers still remain a serious threat because they change their tactics and too many users are easily tricked by the scams.

In contrast, software and systems knowledge are needed to carry out technical attacks. A computer worm is an example of a technical attack. Most attacks involve a combination of the two types. For instance, an intruder may use an automated tool to post a message to an instant messaging service offering the opportunity to download software of interest to the reader (e.g., software for downloading music or videos). When an unsuspecting reader downloads the malicious software, it automatically runs on his or her computer, enabling the intruder to turn the machine into a zombie to perpetrate a technical attack.

The time-to-exploitation of today's most sophisticated spyware and worms has shrunk from months to days. **Time-to-exploitation** is the elapsed time between when a vulnerability is discovered and the time it is exploited. For more on spyware, see **SpywareGuide**, a public reference site, at spywareguide.com. New vulnerabilities are continuously being found in operating systems, applications, and networks. Left undetected or unpatched, these vulnerabilities provide an open door for attacks—and business interruptions and their financial consequences.

nontechnical attack
An attack that uses chicanery to trick people into revealing sensitive information or performing actions that compromise the security of a network.

social engineering
A type of nontechnical attack that uses some ruse to trick users into revealing information or performing an action that compromises a computer or network.

phishing
A crimeware technique to steal the identity of a target company to get the identities of its customers.

time-to-exploitation
The elapsed time between when a vulnerability is discovered and the time it is exploited.

SpywareGuide
A public reference site for spyware.

zero-day incidents
Attacks through previously unknown weaknesses in their computer networks.

denial of service (DoS) attack
An attack on a Web site in which an attacker uses specialized software to send a flood of data packets to the target computer with the aim of overloading its resources.

botnet
A huge number (e.g., hundreds of thousands) of hijacked Internet computers that have been set up to forward traffic, including spam and viruses, to other computers on the Internet.

malware
A generic term for malicious software.

virus
A piece of software code that inserts itself into a host, including the operating systems, in order to propagate; it requires that its host program be run to activate it.

worm
A software program that runs independently, consuming the resources of its host in order to maintain itself, that is capable of propagating a complete working version of itself onto another machine.

The SANS Institute publishes a report on the "Top 20 Internet Security Vulnerabilities" (SANS 2007). The SANS top 20 is a consensus list of vulnerabilities that require immediate remediation. Organizations use this report to prioritize their security efforts so they fix the most dangerous vulnerabilities first. The SANS Institute noted that companies were seeing an increasing number of **zero-day incidents**, or attacks through previously unknown weaknesses in their computer networks.

DENIAL OF SERVICE, ZOMBIES, AND PHISHING

A **denial of service (DoS)** is an attack in which a server gets so many requests for service or access that it crashes and cannot respond. In a DoS attack, an attacker uses specialized software to send a flood of data packets to the target computer, with the aim of overloading it. Zombied PCs—and the spyware that controls them—can be used to launch DoS attacks or spread adware. Connecting wireless laptops and palmtops to insecure networks in airport Wi-Fi facilities, hotels, and Internet cafés totally exposes data to threats.

BOTNETS

A **botnet** is a huge number (e.g., hundreds of thousands) of hijacked Internet computers that have been set up to forward traffic, including spam and viruses, to other computers on the Internet. An infected computer is referred to as a *computer robot*, or *bot*. Botmasters, or bot herders, control botnets. The combined power of these coordinated networks of computers can scan for other computers, compromise them, and then perpetrate DoS attacks.

MALICIOUS CODE: VIRUSES, WORMS, AND TROJAN HORSES

Malicious code, also known as **malware**, is classified by how it spreads. A **virus** is a piece of software code that inserts itself into a system to take control of it or steal or destroy data. A virus has two components: a propagation mechanism so it can spread and a payload that does the damage.

Unlike a virus, a **worm** can spread itself without any human intervention. Worms use networks to propagate and infect a computer or handheld device (e.g., cell phone) and can even spread via instant messages. A worm's ability to self-propagate can degrade network performance. A **macro virus** or **macro worm** is executed when the application object that contains the macro is opened or a particular procedure is executed.

A **Trojan horse** is a program that appears to have a useful function but contains a hidden function that presents a security risk. There are many types of Trojan horse programs. The programs of interest are those that make it possible for someone else to access and control a person's computer over the Internet. This type of Trojan horse has two parts: a server and a client. The server is the program that runs on the computer under attack. The client program is the program used by the person perpetrating the attack.

Malware is used to commit new computer crimes. For example, spyware researchers at Webroot Software uncovered a stash of tens of thousands of stolen identities from 125 countries that they believe were collected by a new variant of a Trojan program the company named **Trojan-Phisher-Rebery** (Roberts 2006). The Rebery malicious software is an example of a **banking Trojan**, which is programmed to come to life when computer owners visit one of a number of online banking or EC sites.

Bank of America has 19 million customers online and processes more transactions online than it does in all its physical banking centers. In February 2005, a customer, Ahlo, a Miami wholesaler of ink and toner cartridges, sued Bank of America (Gage 2006). Ahlo held the bank responsible for an unauthorized transfer of more than $90,000 from Ahlo's account to a bank in Latvia. A Trojan infected the company's PC. The Trojan was spread by a phishing attack—fraudulent e-mails that tricked bank customers into giving up their account information and infecting their computers with malware that logged keystrokes. (The bank does not discuss individual phishing attempts but posted information on its Web site, bofa.com/privacy, to educate customers about online fraud.) Bank of America's battle against phishing shows how hard it is for businesses that have grown by acquiring companies with incompatible information systems to protect gullible and sometimes lazy or "can't happen to me" mentality customers from cyber crime.

The best way to defend against Trojan horses is to implement strict policies and procedures for installing new software. In an organization, end users should be forbidden from installing unauthorized programs. Administrators need to check the integrity of programs and patches that are installed. In the same vein, new programs and tools should be installed in a test environment before putting them into a production environment.

Section 10.6 ▶ REVIEW QUESTIONS

1. Describe the difference between a nontechnical and a technical cyber attack.
2. How has the time-to-exploitation changed, and what is the impact of that change?
3. How are DoS attacks perpetrated?
4. What are the major forms of malicious code?
5. What are some of ways to defend against Trojan horses?

10.7 SECURING E-COMMERCE COMMUNICATIONS

Most organizations rely on multiple technologies to secure their networks. These technologies can be divided into two major groups: those designed to secure communications across the network and those designed to protect the servers and clients on the network. This section considers the first of these technologies.

ACCESS CONTROL

Network security depends on access control. **Access control** determines who (person, program, or machine) can legitimately use a network resource and which resources he, she, or it can use. A resource can be anything—Web pages, text files, databases, applications, servers, printers, or any other information source or network component. Typically, access control lists (ACLs) define which users have access to which resources and what rights they have with respect to those resources (i.e., read, view, write, print, copy, delete, execute, modify, or move). Each resource needs to be considered separately, and the rights of particular users or categories of users (e.g., system administrators, northwest sales representatives, marketing department, trading partners, etc.) need to be established.

After a user has been identified, the user must be authenticated. As noted earlier, authentication is the process of verifying that the user is who he or she claims to be. Verification usually is based on one or more characteristics that distinguish the individual from others. Traditionally, authentication has been based on passwords. Passwords are insecure because people write them down in easy-to-find places, choose values that are guessed easily, and willingly tell others their passwords when asked.

Biometric Systems

Two-factor authentication, which requires two pieces of information to authenticate the user, also can be based on a biological or physical trait. The two factors are often a password and a biometric. Fingerprint scanners, facial recognition systems, and voice recognition all are examples of **biometric systems** that recognize a person by some physical trait. Biometric verification is the process used in two-factor authentication. See Case 10.2.

---

macro virus (macro worm)
A virus or worm that executes when the application object that contains the macro is opened or a particular procedure is executed.

Trojan horse
A program that appears to have a useful function but that contains a hidden function that presents a security risk.

Trojan-Phisher-Rebery
A new variant of a Trojan program that stole tens of thousands of identities from 125 countries that the victims believed were collected by a legitimate company.

banking Trojan
A trojan that comes to life when computer owners visit one of a number of online banking or e-commerce sites.

access control
Mechanism that determines who can legitimately use a network resource.

biometric systems
Authentication systems that identify a person by measurement of a biological characteristic, such as fingerprints, iris (eye) patterns, facial features, or voice.

CASE 10.2

EC Application

THE EYES HAVE IT

With increasing concerns over terrorism, air safety, and fraud, the United Kingdom has turned to biometric identification and authentication for both security and commercial purposes. In one pilot project, British Airways and Virgin Atlantic tested an iris-scanning system from EyeTicket Corporation at Heathrow Airport in London, JFK Airport in New York City, and Dulles Airport outside Washington, D.C. The 6-month pilot, which occurred in 2002, was arranged by the UK's Simplifying Passenger Travel Project (SPT) of the International Air Transport Association (IATA). The major goal of the project was to determine whether iris scanning could be used with passports to speed the authentication process for international travelers entering the United Kingdom.

The two airlines chose participants from among their frequent-flyer programs, focusing on passengers who made frequent trips between the United States and the United Kingdom. Potential participants registered for the program via e-mail. The UK Immigration Service interviewed them to ensure that there were no security issues. Approximately 900 people registered for the program.

The actual tests involved iris-scanning enrollment stations at Heathrow, JFK, and Dulles, as well as video cameras and a recognition station at Heathrow. Passengers who participated in the program enrolled only once. This was done at the enrollment stations by taking a close-up digital image of the passenger's iris. The image was then stored as a template in a computer file. When a passenger landed at Heathrow, the passenger's iris was scanned at the recognition station and compared to the stored template. If a match occurred, the passenger passed through immigration. On average, the scan and match took about 12 seconds. If the match failed, the passenger had to move to the regular immigration line. The failure rate was only 7 percent. Watery eyes and long eyelashes were some of the major sources of failure.

According to the IATA's SPT regional group in charge of the project, the initial findings of the pilot project were encouraging. Not only did the biometric system simplify and speed the arrival process, but the system also successfully verified passengers, maintained border integrity, and was well received by the participants.

Despite the success of the pilot project, there are barriers to using the system for larger populations of passengers. One of the major barriers is the initial registration. According to the Immigration Service, the most difficult and time-consuming aspect of the pilot program was working through the processes and procedures for registration and risk assessment. As noted, the pilot only involved around 900 passengers. It would be much more difficult to register thousands, or millions, of passengers. Likewise, it would be a much slower process to compare a scanned iris against thousands or millions of iris templates.

Another barrier to wider deployment is the lack of technical and procedural standards. On the technical front, there are no standards for iris scanning. The EyeTicket system is based on an iris-scanning algorithm originally created by Jeffrey Daugman, a professor at Cambridge University. Other iris enrollment and scanning devices use other algorithms. This makes it difficult to share templates across systems and across borders. Standard procedures are needed. Without common enrollment, authentication, and identification procedures, there is little basis for trust among different government agencies or different governments.

According to the TSSI Biometrics in Britain Study 2006, undertaken by TSSI Systems, Britain's document and identity security specialists, the UK public is now overwhelmingly in favor of wider biometrics use. Seventy-six percent are more in favor of biometrics than they were in 2005. The striking opinion change came after the United Kingdom thwarted an airline terrorist plot and the London transport bombings of July 2005. Personal safety was identified as the biggest driver for the change: three-quarters of the respondents believe it is important for combating terrorism.

Sources: Compiled from Emigh (2004) and TSSI (2006).

Questions

1. What are the major components of the EyeTicket iris scanning system?

2. What are some of the difficulties in using iris scanning to verify passengers for passport control?

3. Is it reasonable to use iris scanning or any other biometric to identify terrorists at airports?

Interest in biometric security is increasing, spurred by declining prices in biometric systems and the worldwide focus on terrorism, fraud, and identity theft. Many financial institutions, for instance, are interested in using a combination of smartcards and biometrics to authenticate customers and ensure nonrepudiation for online banking, trading, and purchasing transactions.

PUBLIC KEY INFRASTRUCTURE

Authentication can be based on the **public key infrastructure (PKI)**. PKI has become the cornerstone for secure e-payments. It refers to the technical components, infrastructure, and practices needed to enable the use of public key encryption, digital signatures, and digital certificates with a network application. PKI also is the foundation of a number of network applications, including SCM, VPNs, secure e-mail, and intranet applications.

Private and Public Key Encryption

PKI is based on encryption. **Encryption** is the process of transforming or scrambling data in such a way that it is difficult, expensive, or time-consuming for an unauthorized person to unscramble (decrypt) it. All encryption has five basic parts (see Exhibit 10.2 p. 402): plaintext, ciphertext, an encryption algorithm, a key, and a key space. **Plaintext** is a human-readable text or message. **Ciphertext** is not human-readable text, because it has been encrypted. The **encryption algorithm** is the set of procedures or mathematical functions to encrypt or decrypt a message. Typically, the algorithm is not the secret piece of the encryption process. The **key** (or **key value**) is the secret value used with the algorithm to transform the message. The **key space** is the large number of possible key values (keys) created by the algorithm to use when transforming the message. The two major classes of encryption systems are *symmetric systems*, with one secret key, and *asymmetric systems*, with two keys.

Symmetric (Private) Key System

In a **symmetric (private) key system**, the same key is used to encrypt and decrypt the plaintext (see Exhibit 10.6). The sender and receiver of the text must share the same key without revealing it to anyone else, making it a so-called private system.

Because the algorithms used to encrypt a message are well known, the confidentiality of a message depends on the key. It is possible to guess a key simply by having a computer try all the encryption combinations until the message is decrypted. High-speed and

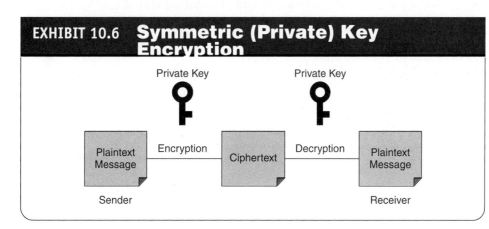

EXHIBIT 10.6 Symmetric (Private) Key Encryption

Private Key   Private Key

Plaintext Message → Encryption → Ciphertext → Decryption → Plaintext Message

Sender   Receiver

---

public key infrastructure (PKI)
A scheme for securing e-payments using public key encryption and various technical components.

encryption
The process of scrambling (encrypting) a message in such a way that it is difficult, expensive, or time-consuming for an unauthorized person to unscramble (decrypt) it.

plaintext
An unencrypted message in human-readable form.

ciphertext
A plaintext message after it has been encrypted into a machine-readable form.

encryption algorithm
The mathematical formula used to encrypt the plaintext into the ciphertext, and vice versa.

key (key value)
The secret code used to encrypt and decrypt a message.

key space
The large number of possible key values (keys) created by the algorithm to use when transforming the message.

symmetric (private) key system
An encryption system that uses the same key to encrypt and decrypt the message.

parallel-processing computers can try millions of guesses in a second. This is why the length of the key (in bits) is the main factor in securing a message. If a key were 4 bits long (e.g., 1011), there would be only 16 possible combinations (i.e., 2 raised to the fourth power). However, a 64-bit encryption key would take 58.5 years to be broken at 10 million keys per second.

Public (Asymmetric) Key Encryption

Imagine trying to use one-key encryption to buy something offered on a particular Web server. If the seller's key was distributed to thousands of buyers, then the key would not remain secret for long. This is where public key (asymmetric) encryption comes into play. **Public (asymmetric) key encryption** uses a pair of matched keys—a **public key** that is publicly available to anyone and a **private key** that is known only to its owner. If a message is encrypted with a public key, then the associated private key is required to decrypt the message. If, for example, a person wanted to send a purchase order to a company and have the contents remain private, he or she would encrypt the message with the company's public key. When the company received the order, it would decrypt it with the associated private key.

The most common public key encryption algorithm is **RSA** (rsa.com). RSA uses keys ranging in length from 512 bits to 1,024 bits. The main problem with public key encryption is speed. Symmetrical algorithms are much faster than asymmetric key algorithms. In practice, a combination of symmetric and asymmetric encryption encrypts messages.

Digital Signatures and Certificate Authorities

In effect, a digital signature is the electronic equivalent of a personal signature that cannot be forged. Digital signatures are based on public keys for authenticating the identity of the sender of a message or document. They also can ensure that the original content of an electronic message or document is unchanged. Digital signatures have additional benefits in the online world. They are portable, cannot be easily repudiated or imitated, and can be time-stamped.

See Exhibit 10.3 (p. 404) to review how a digital signature works. Suppose a person wants to send the draft of a financial contract to a company with whom he or she plans to do business as an e-mail message. The sender wants to assure the company that the content of the draft has not been changed en route and that he or she really is the sender. To do so, the sender takes the following steps:

1. The sender creates the e-mail message with the contract in it.
2. Using special software, a mathematical computation called a **hash** function is applied to the message, which results in a special summary of the message, converted into a string of digits called a **message digest (MD)**.
3. The sender uses his or her private key to encrypt the hash. This is the sender's digital signature. No one else can replicate the sender's digital signature because it is based on the sender's private key.
4. The sender encrypts both the original message and the digital signature using the recipient's public key. This is the **digital envelope**.
5. The sender e-mails the digital envelope to the receiver.
6. Upon receipt, the receiver uses his or her private key to decrypt the contents of the digital envelope. This produces a copy of the message and the sender's digital signature.

public (asymmetric) key encryption
Method of encryption that uses a pair of matched keys—a public key to encrypt a message and a private key to decrypt it, or vice versa.

public key
Encryption code that is publicly available to anyone.

private key
Encryption code that is known only to its owner.

RSA
The most common public key encryption algorithm; uses keys ranging in length from 512 bits to 1,024 bits.

hash
A mathematical computation that is applied to a message, using a private key, to encrypt the message.

message digest (MD)
A summary of a message, converted into a string of digits, after the hash has been applied.

digital envelope
The combination of the encrypted original message and the digital signature, using the recipient's public key.

7. The receiver uses the sender's public key to decrypt the digital signature, resulting in a copy of the original message digest.

8. Using the same hash function employed in step 2, the recipient then creates a message digest from the decrypted message.

9. The recipient compares this digest with the original message digest.

10. If the two digests match, then the recipient concludes that the message is authentic.

In this scenario, the company has evidence that the sender sent the e-mail because (theoretically) the sender is the only one with access to the private key. The recipient knows that the message has not been tampered with because if it had been, the two hashes would not have matched.

According to the U.S. Federal Electronic Signatures in Global and National Commerce Act that went into effect in October 2000, digital signatures in the United States have the same legal standing as a signature written in ink on paper.

Third parties called **certificate authorities (CAs)** issue digital certificates. A certificate contains things such as the holder's name, validity period, public key information, and a signed hash of the certificate data (i.e., hashed contents of the certificate signed with the CA's private key). There are different types of certificates, namely those used to authenticate Web sites (site certificates), individuals (personal certificates), and software companies (software publisher certificates).

There is a large number of third-party CAs. VeriSign (verisign.com) is the best known of the CAs. VeriSign issues three classes of certificates: Class 1 verifies that an e-mail actually comes from the user's address. Class 2 checks the user's identity against a commercial credit database. Class 3 requires notarized documents. Companies such as Microsoft offer systems that enable companies to issue their own private, in-house certificates.

certificate authorities (CAs)
Third parties that issue digital certificates.

Secure Socket Layer (SSL)

If the average user had to figure out how to use encryption, digital certificates, digital signatures, and the like, there would be few secure transactions on the Web. Web browsers and servers handle many of these issues in a transparent fashion. Given that different companies, financial institutions, and governments in many countries are involved in EC, it is necessary to have generally accepted protocols for securing e-commerce. One of the major protocols is Secure Socket Layer (SSL).

Secure Socket Layer (SSL) was invented by Netscape to use standard certificates for authentication and data encryption to ensure privacy or confidentiality. SSL makes it possible to encrypt credit card numbers and other transmissions between a Web server and a browser. In the case of credit card transactions, there is more to making a purchase on the Web than simply passing an encrypted credit card number to a merchant. The number must be checked for validity, the consumer's bank must authorize the card, and the purchase must be processed. SSL is not designed to handle any of the steps beyond the transmission of the card number.

Secure Socket Layer (SSL)
Protocol that utilizes standard certificates for authentication and data encryption to ensure privacy or confidentiality.

Section 10.7 ▶ REVIEW QUESTIONS

1. What are the basic elements of an authentication system?
2. Describe the five basic components of encryption.
3. What are the key elements of PKI?
4. What are the basic differences between symmetric and asymmetric encryption?
5. What role does a certificate authority play?
6. What is the SSL protocol?

10.8 SECURING E-COMMERCE NETWORKS

Several technologies exist that ensure that an organization's network boundaries are secure from cyber attack or intrusion and that if the organization's boundaries are compromised the intrusion is detected. The selection and operation of these technologies should be based on certain design concepts:

▶ **Defense in depth.** Layers of security technologies must be applied at key points in a network (see Exhibit 10.7).

▶ **Need-to-access basis.** Access to a network ought to be based on the **policy of least privilege (POLP)**. By default, access to network resources should be blocked and permitted only when needed to conduct business.

▶ **Role-specific security.** As noted in Section 10.7, access to particular network resources should be based on a user's role within an organization.

▶ **Monitoring.** Real-time monitoring has become essential because of zero-day exploits and emerging hacker threats.

▶ **Patch management.** Vendors (such as Microsoft) are continually patching or upgrading their software, applications, and systems to plug security holes. The only way to take advantage of these fixes is to install the patches or upgrades. Newer

policy of least privilege (POLP)
Policy of blocking access to network resources unless access is required to conduct business.

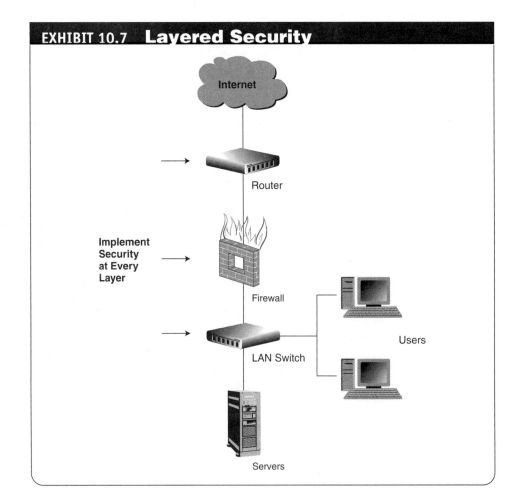

EXHIBIT 10.7 Layered Security

Internet

Router

Implement Security at Every Layer

Firewall

LAN Switch

Users

Servers

versions of software (e.g., operating systems such as Windows Vista) have automatic update functionality built in. This makes it easier for organizations and individuals to track fixes or patches.

▶ **Incident response team (IRT).** Regardless of the organization's size, its networks will be attacked. For this reason, organizations need to have a team in place that can respond to these attacks. The team needs to have well-established plans, processes, and resources and should practice responding when the pressure is off rather than learning during a crisis.

FIREWALLS

Firewalls are barriers between a trusted network or PC and the untrustworthy Internet. Technically, it is a network node consisting of hardware and software that isolates a private network from a public network. On the Internet, the data and requests sent from one computer to another are broken into segments called **packets.** Each packet contains the Internet protocol (IP) address of the computer sending the data, as well as the IP address of the computer receiving the data. A firewall examines all data packets that pass through it and then takes appropriate action—to allow or not to allow the packet to pass.

Some firewalls filter data and requests from the Internet to a private network based on the network IP addresses of the computer sending or receiving the request. These firewalls are called **packet-filtering routers**. **Packet filters** are rules that can accept or reject incoming packets based on source and destination addresses and the other identifying information. Some simple examples of packet filters include the following:

▶ **Block all packets sent from a given Internet address.** Companies sometimes use this to block requests from computers owned by competitors.

▶ **Block any packet coming from the outside that has the address of a computer on the inside.** Companies use this type of rule to block requests where an intruder is using his or her computer to impersonate a computer that belongs to the company.

Packet filters have their disadvantages. In setting up the rules, an administrator might miss some important rules or incorrectly specify a rule, thus leaving a hole in the firewall. Additionally, because the content of a packet is irrelevant to a packet filter, once a packet is let through the firewall, the inside network is open to data-driven attacks. That is, the data may contain hidden instructions that cause the receiving computer to modify access control or files.

Packet-filtering routers often are the first layer of network defense. Other firewalls form the second layer. These later firewalls block data and requests depending on the type of application being accessed. For instance, a firewall may permit requests for Web pages to move from the public Internet to the private network. This type of firewall is called an **application-level proxy**. In an application-level proxy, there is often a special server called a **bastion gateway**. The bastion gateway server has two network cards so that data packets reaching one card are not relayed to the other card (see Exhibit 10.8). Instead, special software programs called **proxies** run on the bastion gateway server and pass repackaged packets from one network to the other. Each Internet service that an organization wishes to support has a proxy. For instance, there is a Web (i.e., HTTP) proxy, a file transfer (FTP) proxy, and so on. Special proxies also can be established to allow business partners, for example, to access particular applications running inside the firewall. If a request is made for an unsupported proxy service, then it is blocked by the firewall.

---

firewall
A single point between two or more networks where all traffic must pass (choke point); the device authenticates, controls, and logs all traffic.

packet
Segment of data sent from one computer to another on a network.

packet-filtering routers
Firewalls that filter data and requests moving from the public Internet to a private network based on the network addresses of the computer sending or receiving the request.

packet filters
Rules that can accept or reject incoming packets based on source and destination addresses and the other identifying information.

application-level proxy
A firewall that permits requests for Web pages to move from the public Internet to the private network.

bastion gateway
A special hardware server that utilizes application-level proxy software to limit the types of requests that can be passed to an organization's internal networks from the public Internet.

proxies
Special software programs that run on the gateway server and pass repackaged packets from one network to the other.

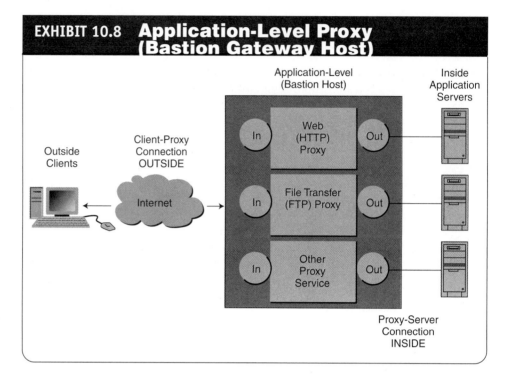

EXHIBIT 10.8   Application-Level Proxy (Bastion Gateway Host)

VIRTUAL PRIVATE NETWORKS (VPNS)

Suppose a company wants to establish a B2B application, providing suppliers, partners, and others access not only to data residing on its internal Web site, but also to data contained in other files (e.g., Word documents) or in legacy systems (e.g., large relational databases). Traditionally, communications with the company would have taken place over a private leased line or through a dial-up line to a bank of modems or a remote access server (RAS) that provided direct connections to the company's LAN. With a private line, the chances of a hacker eavesdropping on the communications between the companies would be nil, but it is an expensive way to do business.

A less expensive alternative would be to use a *virtual private network*. A **virtual private network (VPN)** uses the public Internet to carry information but remains private by using encryption, authentication, and access control to verify the identity of anyone using the network. In addition, a VPN can also support site-to-site communications between branch offices and corporate headquarters and the communications between mobile workers and their workplace.

VPNs can reduce communication costs dramatically. The costs are lower because VPN equipment is cheaper than other remote solutions; private leased lines are not needed to support remote access; remote users can use broadband connections rather than make long-distance calls to access an organization's private network; and a single access line can be used to support multiple purposes.

INTRUSION DETECTION SYSTEMS (IDS)

An **intrusion detection systems (IDS)** is software that can monitor activity across a network or on a host computer, watch for suspicious activity, and take action based on what it sees. IDSs are either host based or network based. A *host-based IDS* is positioned on the server or other host. Host-based systems are good at detecting whether critical or security-related files have been tampered with or whether a user has attempted to access files without authorization.

---

virtual private network (VPN)
A network that uses the public Internet to carry information but remains private by using encryption to scramble the communications, authentication to ensure that information has not been tampered with, and access control to verify the identity of anyone using the network.

intrusion detection systems (IDS)
A special category of software that can monitor activity across a network or on a host computer, watch for suspicious activity, and take automated action based on what it sees.

A *network-based IDS* uses rules to analyze suspicious activity at the perimeter of a network or at vulnerable network locations. It usually consists of a monitor—a software package that scans the network—and software agents that reside on various host computers and feed information back to the monitor. This type of IDS examines network traffic (i.e., packets) for known patterns of attack and automatically notifies security personnel when specific events or event thresholds occur.

HONEYNETS AND HONEYPOTS

Honeynets are another technology that can detect and analyze intrusions. A **honeynet** is a network of honeypots designed to attract hackers like honey attracts bees. **Honeypots** are information system resources—firewalls, routers, Web servers, database servers, files, and the like—that look like production systems but do no real work. The main difference between a honeypot and the real thing is that the activities on a honeypot come from intruders attempting to compromise the system. In this way, researchers watching the honeynet can gather information about why hackers attack, when they attack, how they attack, what they do after the system is compromised, and how they communicate with one another during and after the attack.

honeynet
A network of honeypots.

honeypots
Production system (e.g., firewalls, routers, Web servers, database servers) that looks like it does real work, but which acts as a decoy and is watched to study how network intrusions occur.

Section 10.8 ▶ REVIEW QUESTIONS

1. List the basic types of firewalls and briefly describe each.
2. How does a VPN work?
3. Briefly describe the two types of IDSs.
4. What is a honeynet? What is a honeypot?

10.9 FRAUD AND CONSUMER AND SELLER PROTECTION

Fraud is still a problem for online retailers. Even though actual losses are rising, the rate of those losses is flattening out. In other words, the threat actually may be lessening—somewhat. According to the Ninth Annual Online Fraud Report, released by CyberSource (2008) (cybersource.com), losses from online fraud in the United States and Canada totaled $3.6 billion in 2007, $3.0 billion in 2006, and $2.8 billion in 2005. The percentage of revenues lost to fraud was 1.4 percent in both 2007 and 2006, down from 1.6 percent in 2004.

Online merchants can use tools to estimate the risk of an order based on information gathered during the order-taking process. For example, CyberSource's Internet Fraud Screen (IFS) enables merchants to set the level of risk (threshold) that they are willing to accept in an order. IFS assigns a risk score to each transaction. Transactions with scores that fall below the risk threshold are declined.

During the first few years of EC, many types of crime came to light, ranging from the online manipulation of stock prices to the creation of a virtual bank that disappeared, together with the investors' deposits. This section is divided into the following parts: Internet fraud, consumer protection (including automatic authentication), and seller protection.

FRAUD ON THE INTERNET

Internet fraud has grown even faster than the Internet itself. The examples in Insights and Additions 10.1 demonstrate the scope of the problem.

Insights and Additions 10.1 Typical Fraud Schemes

The following are typical online fraud attempts:

▶ When one of the authors advertised online that he had a house to rent, several "doctors" and "nurses" from the United Kingdom and South America applied. They agreed to pay a premium for a short-term lease and said they would pay with a cashier's check. They asked if the author would accept checks for $6,000 to $10,000 and send them back the balance of $4,000 to $8,000. When advised that this would be fine, but that the difference would be returned only after the checks had cleared, none of the would-be renters followed up.

▶ Phishing uses spam e-mails or pop-up messages to deceive victims into disclosing credit card numbers, bank account information, Social Security numbers, passwords, or other sensitive information. Typically, the e-mail or pop-up message claims to be from a business or organization that the recipient may deal with, such as an ISP, a bank, an online payment service, or even a government agency.

▶ Extortion rings in the United Kingdom and Russia pried hundreds of thousands of dollars from online sports betting Web sites. Any site refusing to pay protection fees was threatened with zombie computers using DoS attacks.

▶ Fake escrow sites take advantage of consumers' inherent trust of escrow sites, stealing buyers' deposits. Dozens of fake escrow sites on the Internet have convincing names like Honest-Escrow.net and use ads such as: "Worried about getting scammed in an Internet auction? Just use an escrow service like us."

▶ Click fraud is a common concern for advertisers and search vendors alike. Click fraud scams and deceptions inflate advertising bills for thousands of companies of all sizes. The spreading scourge poses the single biggest threat to online advertising. It is perpetrated in both automated and human ways. The most common method is the use of online robots, or bots, programmed to click on advertisers' links that are displayed on Web sites or listed in search queries. Because advertisers pay fees based on number of clicks, bogus clicks inflate those fees. Google claims to be well-equipped to handle the dilemma. They state, "Our Click Quality team investigates every inquiry we receive from advertisers who believe they may have been affected by undetected click fraud. Many of these cases are misunderstandings, but in most cases where malicious activity is found, the clicks have already been filtered out (and not charged for) by our real-time filters" (Reprise Media 2007).

Stock fraud, as discussed in Case 10.3, is only one of many areas where swindlers are active. Other areas include the sale of bogus investments, phantom business opportunities, and other schemes. In addition, foreign-currency-trading scams are increasing on the Internet because most online currency-exchange shops are not licensed.

Many nonfinancial types of fraud also exist on the Internet. For example, customers may receive poor-quality products and services, they may not get products in time, they may be asked to pay for things they assume sellers will pay for, and much more. For typical schemes, see ftc.gov. Buyers can protect against EC fraud in several ways. We describe the major methods next.

CONSUMER PROTECTION

Consumer protection is critical to the success of any commerce, especially electronic, where buyers do not see sellers. The FTC enforces consumer protection laws in the United States (see ftc.gov). The FTC (2007) provides a list of 10 scams that are most likely to arrive by bulk e-mail (see onguardonline.gov/spam.html). In addition, the European Union and the United States are attempting to develop joint consumer protection policies. For details, see the TransAtlantic Consumer Dialogue Web site at tacd.org/about/about.htm.

CASE 10.3
EC Application

INTERNET STOCK FRAUD

Spam will not go away for two reasons: (1) It works, and (2) it is profitable. A 2006 study by Purdue University assistant professor of finance Laura Frieder and law professor Jonathan Zittrain from Oxford University's Internet Institute concluded that stock spam moves markets. The researchers found that the average investor who buys a stock during a spam promotion (campaign) and then sells after the campaign ends loses about 5.5 percent of his or her investment. In contrast, the spammer who buys stock before the spam campaign and sells during the campaign makes a 5.79 percent return.

The federal government made headlines on March 8, 2007, by cracking down on dozens of penny stocks whose prices spam e-mailers had manipulated. The success of the SEC's Operation Spamalot still will not end spam. Despite increased enforcement, warnings, and federal laws, spam is not only continuing, but flourishing. And there's no reason to think the SEC will be able to do anything to stop it.

Stock spam has gotten much worse in the last few years. Stock spam messages rose 120 percent during the 6-month period ending March 2007 (Lerer 2007). In total, stock-related messages make up about 20 percent of all e-mail spam. The SEC estimates that 100 million stock spam messages are sent each week.

Technology has increased spammers' ability to send junk e-mail. Spammers used to have to send all their messages from one computer, making them easily blocked by spam filters. Today, spammers send their messages through botnets (linked networks of computers) that they control. With the extra bandwidth, they are sending billions of messages with promotional text embedded in image files—called image spam. Image spam looks identical to normal spam but sneaks by antispam programs that look only at text, not pictures or photos.

During 2006, global spam volume tripled. During a 6-week period, Secure Computing Research saw a 50-percent increase in spam. Spam now accounts for nearly 90 percent of all e-mail. In that same time, the amount of image spam has tripled, and it now accounts for 30 percent of all spam.

Sources: Compiled from Lerer (2007) and *SecureComputing.com* (2007).

Questions

1. Why might people buy the penny stocks promoted in an e-mail message from an unknown source?

2. Use the Internet to find what can be done to filter image spam.

Tips for safe electronic shopping include the following:

▶ Users should make sure that they enter the real Web site of well-known companies, such as Wal-Mart, Disney, and Amazon.com, by going directly to the site, rather than through a link, and should shop for reliable brand names at those sites.

▶ Check any unfamiliar site for an address and telephone and fax numbers. Call and quiz a salesperson about the seller.

▶ Check out the seller with the local chamber of commerce, Better Business Bureau (bbbonline.org), or TRUSTe.

▶ Investigate how secure the seller's site is and how well it is organized.

▶ Examine the money-back guarantees, warranties, and service agreements before making a purchase.

▶ Compare prices online with those in regular stores—too-low prices may be too good to be true.

▶ Ask friends what they know. Find testimonials and endorsements.

▶ Find out what redress is available in case of a dispute.

▶ Consult the National Fraud Information Center (fraud.org).

▶ Check the resources available at consumerworld.org.

Insights and Additions 10.2 Internet Shoppers' Rights

The following are useful sources of information on the rights of Internet shoppers:

▶ The FTC (*ftc.gov*)
▶ National Fraud Information Center (*fraud.org*)
▶ Federal Citizen Information Center (*pueblo.gsa.gov*)
▶ U.S. Department of Justice (*usdoj.gov*)

▶ The FBI's Internet Fraud Complaint Center (*ic3.gov*)
▶ The American Bar Association provides online shopping tips at *safeshopping.org*.
▶ The Better Business Bureau (*bbbonline.org*)
▶ The Direct Marketing Association (*the-dma.org*)

In addition to these tips, consumers also have shopper's rights on the Internet, as described in Insights and Additions 10.2.

Third-Party Assurance Services

Several public organizations and private companies attempt to protect consumers. The following are just a few examples.

TRUSTe's "Trustmark." TRUSTe (truste.org) is a nonprofit group whose mission is to build users' trust and confidence in the Internet by promoting the policies of disclosure and informed consent. TRUSTe certifies and monitors Web site privacy, e-mail policies and practices, and resolves thousands of consumer privacy problems every year (TRUSTe 2007). Sellers who become members of TRUSTe can add value and increase consumer confidence in online transactions by displaying the TRUSTe Advertising Affiliate "Trustmark" (a seal of quality). This mark identifies sites that have agreed to comply with responsible information-gathering guidelines.

Better Business Bureau. The Better Business Bureau (BBB), a private nonprofit organization supported largely by membership, provides reports on businesses that consumers can review before making a purchase. The BBB responds to millions of inquiries each year. Its BBBOnLine program is similar to TRUSTe's Trustmark. The goal of the program is to promote confidence on the Internet through BBB seals.

Which? Supported by the European Union, WHICH? (which.co.uk) gives consumers protection by ensuring that online traders under its Which?Web Trader Scheme abide by a code of proactive guidelines. These guidelines encompass product information, advertising, ordering methods, prices, delivery of goods, consumer privacy, receipting, dispute resolution, and security.

Online Privacy Alliance. The Online Privacy Alliance privacyalliance.org is a diverse group of corporations and associations that lead and support self-regulatory initiatives that create an environment of trust and foster the protection of individuals' privacy online. They have guidelines for privacy policies, enforcement of self-regulation, and children's online activities.

SELLER PROTECTION

The Internet makes fraud by customers or others easier because of the ease of anonymity. Sellers must guard against the following:

▶ Customers who deny that they placed an order
▶ Customers who download copyrighted software and/or knowledge and sell it to others

- Customers who give false payment (credit card or bad checks) information in payment for products and services provided
- Use of their name by others (e.g., imposter sellers)
- Use of their unique words and phrases, names, and slogans and their Web addresses by others (trademark protection)

What Can Sellers Do?

Card Cops (cardcops.com) provides a database of credit card numbers that have had chargeback orders recorded against them. Sellers who have access to the database can use this information to decide whether to proceed with a sale.

Other possible solutions include the following:

- Implement intelligent software to identify possibly questionable customers.
- Identify warning signals—that is, red flags—for possible fraudulent transactions.
- Ask customers whose billing address is different from the shipping address to call their bank and have the alternate address added to their bank account.

For further discussion of what merchants can do to protect themselves from fraud, see OnGuard Online at onguardonline.gov/spam.html.

Section 10.9 ▶ REVIEW QUESTIONS

1. Why is there so much fraud on the Internet?
2. What types of fraud are most common?
3. Describe electronic signatures.
4. Describe consumer protection measures.
5. Describe assurance services.
6. What must a company do to protect itself against fraud? How can a company accomplish this?

MANAGERIAL ISSUES

Some managerial issues related to this chapter are as follows.

1. **Why should managers learn about EC security?** Debilitating and devastating EC crimes cannot be stopped, but companies can reduce the risk of a successful attack. Because the consequences of poor network security can be severe, it is imperative that senior management have a basic understanding of best practices in network risk management.

2. **Why is an EC security strategy and life cycle approach needed?** Without an EC security strategy to guide investments and defenses, security efforts tend to be reactive and more expensive to manage. Ineffective security opens the door to computer and network attacks that can result in damage to technical and information assets; theft of information and

information services; temporary loss of a Web site and Internet access; loss of income; litigation brought on by dissatisfied organizational stakeholders; loss of customer confidence; and damaged reputation and credibility. In some cases, attacks literally can put a company out of business, especially if EC is its sole source of revenue.

3. **How should managers view EC security issues?** Suppose you decide to set up a B2B site in order to service your suppliers and partners. Because it is not a public site, the only ones who are likely to know of its existence are you, your suppliers, and your partners. You assume that there is no need to institute strong security measures. Wrong!

Because of the prevalence of automated scanning tools, it will be only a matter of time before the site will be breached. Companies must thoroughly review their security requirements and institute stringent measures to guard against high-priority threats.

4. **What is the key to establishing strong e-commerce security?** Most discussions about security focus on technology, with statements like "firewalls are mandatory" or "all transmissions should be encrypted." Although firewalls and encryption can be important technologies, no security solution is useful unless it solves a business problem. Determining your business requirements is the most important step in creating a security solution. Business requirements, in turn, determine your information requirements. Once you know your information requirements, you can begin to understand the value of those assets and the steps that you should take to secure those that are most valuable and vulnerable.

5. **What steps should businesses follow in establishing a security plan?** Security risk management is an ongoing process involving three phases: asset identification, risk assessment, and implementation. By actively monitoring existing security policies and measures, companies can determine which are successful or unsuccessful and, in turn, which should be modified or eliminated. However, it also is important to monitor changes in business requirements, changes in technology and the way it is used, and changes in the way people can attack the systems and networks. In this way, an organization can evolve its security policies and measures, ensuring that they continue to support the critical needs of the business.

6. **Should organizations be concerned with internal security threats?** Except for malware, breaches perpetrated by insiders are much more frequent than those perpetrated by outsiders. This is true for both B2C and B2B sites. Security policies and measures for EC sites need to address these insider threats.

SUMMARY

In this chapter, you learned about the following EC issues as they relate to the learning objectives.

1. **Stopping e-commerce crimes.** Responsibility or blame for cyber crimes can be placed on criminals and victimized industries, users, and organizations. The EC industry does not want to enforce safeguards that add friction to the profitable wheels of online commerce. Credit card issuers try to avoid sharing leads on criminal activity with each other or law enforcement. Online shoppers fail to take necessary precautions to avoid becoming a victim. IS designs and security architectures are still incredibly vulnerable. Organizations fail to exercise due care in business or hiring practices, outsourcing, and business partnerships. Every EC business knows that the threats of bogus credit card purchases, data breaches, phishing, and malware never end—and that these threats must be addressed comprehensively and strategically.

2. **EC security strategy and life cycle approach.** EC security will remain an evolving discipline because threats change, e-businesses change, and Web-based technologies change. An EC security strategy is needed to optimize EC security programs for efficiency and effectiveness. EC security costs and efforts from reacting to crises and paying for damages are greater than if organizations had an EC security strategy. The Internet is still a fundamentally insecure infrastructure. Criminals are intent on stealing information for identity theft and fraud. Without a strategy, EC security is treated as a project instead of an ongoing, never-ending process.

3. **Information assurance.** The information assurance model for EC represents the processes for protecting information by ensuring its confidentiality, integrity, and availability. Confidentiality is the assurance of data privacy. Integrity is the assurance that data is accurate or that a message has not been altered. Availability is the assurance that access to data, the Web site, or other EC data service is timely, available, reliable, and restricted to authorized users.

4. **Enterprisewide EC security and privacy model.** EC and network security are inconvenient, expensive, tedious, and never ending. A defense-in-depth model that views EC security as a combination of

commitment, people, processes, and technology is essential. An effective program starts with senior management's commitment and budgeting support. This sets the tone that EC security is important to the organization. Other components are security policies and training. Security procedures must be defined with positive incentives for compliance and negative consequences for violations. The last stage is the deployment of hardware and software tools based on the policies and procedures defined by the management team.

5. **Basic EC security issues and perspectives.** Owners of EC sites need to be concerned with multiple security issues: authentication, verifying the identity of the participants in a transaction; authorization, ensuring that a person or process has access rights to particular systems or data; auditing, being able to determine whether particular actions have been taken and by whom; confidentiality, ensuring that information is not disclosed to unauthorized individuals, systems, or processes; integrity, protecting data from being altered or destroyed; availability, ensuring that data and services are available when needed; and nonrepudiation, the ability to limit parties from refuting that a legitimate transaction took place.

6. **Threats and attacks.** EC sites are exposed to a wide range of attacks. Attacks may be nontechnical (social engineering), in which a perpetrator tricks people into revealing information or performing actions that compromise network security. Or they may be technical, whereby software and systems expertise are used to attack the network. DoS attacks bring operations to a halt by sending floods of data to target computers or to as many computers on the Internet as possible. Malicious code attacks include viruses, worms, Trojan horses, or some combination of these. Over the past couple of years, various trends in malicious code have emerged, including an increase in the speed and volume of attacks; reduced time between the discovery of a vulnerability and the release of an attack to exploit the vulnerability; the growing use of bots to launch attacks; an increase in attacks on Web applications; and a shift to profit-motivated attacks.

7. **Securing EC communications.** In EC, issues of trust are paramount. Trust starts with the authentication of the parties involved in a transaction; that is, identifying the parties in a transaction along with the actions they can perform. Authentication can be established with something one knows (e.g., a password), something one has (e.g., a token), or something one possesses (e.g., a fingerprint). Biometric systems can confirm a person's identity. Fingerprint scanners, iris scanners, facial recognition, and voice recognition are examples of biometric systems. Public key infrastructure (PKI), which is the cornerstone of secure e-payments, also can authenticate the parties in a transaction. PKI uses encryption (private and public) to ensure privacy and integrity and digital signatures to ensure authenticity and nonrepudiation. Digital signatures are themselves authenticated through a system of digital certificates issued by certificate authorities (CAs). For the average consumer and merchant, PKI is simplified because it is built into Web browsers and services. Such tools are secure because security is based on SSL communications.

8. **Technologies for securing networks.** At EC sites, firewalls, VPNs, and IDSs have proven extremely useful. A firewall is a combination of hardware and software that isolates a private network from a public network. Firewalls are of two general types—packet-filtering routers or application-level proxies. A packet-filtering router uses a set of rules to determine which communication packets can move from the outside network to the inside network. An application-level proxy is a firewall that accepts requests from the outside and repackages a request before sending it to the inside network, thus, ensuring the security of the request. VPNs are used generally to support secure site-to-site transmissions across the Internet between B2B partners or communications between a mobile and remote worker and a LAN at a central office. IDSs monitor activity across a network or on a host. The systems watch for suspicious activity and take automated actions whenever a security breach or attack occurs. In the same vein, some companies are installing honeynets and honeypots in an effort to gather information on intrusions and to analyze the types and methods of attacks being perpetrated.

9. **Fraud on the Internet and how to protect against it.** Protection is needed because there is no face-to-face contact, there is a great possibility for fraud, there are insufficient legal constraints, and new issues and scams appear constantly. Several organizations, private and public, attempt to provide the protection needed to build the trust that is essential for the success of widespread EC.

KEY TERMS

QUESTIONS FOR DISCUSSION

1. Survey results on the incidence of cyber attacks paint a mixed picture: Some surveys show increases, others show decreases. What factors could account for the differences in the results?

2. How can hackers trick people into giving them their user IDs and passwords to their Amazon.com accounts? What are some of the ways that they might accomplish this?

3. B2C EC sites continue to experience DoS attacks. How are these attacks perpetrated? Why is it so difficult to safeguard against them? What are some of the things a site can do to mitigate such attacks?

4. All EC sites share common security threats and vulnerabilities. Discuss these threats and vulnerabilities and some of the security policies that can be implemented to mitigate them. Do you think that B2C Web sites face different threats and vulnerabilities than B2B sites? Explain.

5. How are botnet identity theft attacks and Web site hijacks perpetrated? Why are they so dangerous to e-commerce?

6. A business wants to share its customer account database with its trading partners and customers, while at the same time providing prospective buyers with access to marketing materials on its Web site. Assuming that the business is responsible for running all these network components, what types of security components (e.g., firewalls, VPNs, etc.) could be used to ensure that the partners and customers have access to the account information and others do not? What type of network configuration will provide the appropriate security?

7. A company is having problems with its password security systems and decides to implement two-factor authentication. What biometric alternatives could the company employ? What are some of the factors it should consider when deciding among the alternatives?

8. Some say that it is much easier to commit fraud online than offline. Do you agree?

INTERNET EXERCISES

1. The Attrition Organization provides an open source database of its data breach records, called the Data Loss Database–Open Source, or DLDOS. It is a flat comma-separated value (csv) file that can be imported into a database or spreadsheet program for data analysis. Visit **attrition.org/dataloss/dataloss.csv** to access the spreadsheet. Using cases that were reported in the prior year, create a table that summarizes each type of breach. For each breach type, show the frequency for each of the following factors: whether the breach was outside or inside, the total affected, and whether there was an arrest or prosecution. Discuss your results.

2. The National Vulnerability Database (NVD) is a comprehensive cyber security vulnerability database that integrates all publicly available U.S. government vulnerability resources and provides references to industry resources. Visit **nvd.nist.gov** and review 10 recent common vulnerabilities and exposures(CVE). For each vulnerability, list the publish date, severity, impact type, and the operating system or software with the vulnerability.

3. The Computer Vulnerabilities and Exposures Board (**cve.mitre.org**) maintains a list of common security vulnerabilities. Review the list. How many vulnerabilities are there? Based on the list, which system components appear to be most vulnerable to attack? What impact do these vulnerable components have on EC?

4. Your B2C site has been hacked. List two organizations where you would report this incident so that they can alert other sites. How do you do this, and what type of information do you have to provide?

5. The McAfee Avert Labs Threat Library has detailed information on viruses, Trojans, hoaxes, vulnerabilities and potentially unwanted programs (PUPs), where they come from, how they infect your system, and how to mitigate or remediate them. Enter **vil.nai.com** and select one Newly Discovered Malware and one Newly Discovered PUP. Using other online resources, describe these threats and the steps needed to combat them. Why is adware listed as a PUP?

6. Determine the IP address of your computer by visiting at least two Web sites that provide that feature. You can use a search engine to locate such Web sites or visit **ip-adress.com** or **whatismyipaddress.com**. What other information does the search reveal about your connection? Based on this information, how could a company or hacker use that information?

7. ICSA Labs (**icsalabs.com**) provides a detailed list of firewall products for corporate, small business, and residential use. Select three corporate firewall products from the list. Research and compare the benefits of each product. Based on the comparison, which product would you choose and why?

8. Select a single type of biometric system. Go online and identify at least two commercial vendors that offer biometric systems. What are the major features of each system? Which of the systems would you select and why?

9. The National Strategy to Secure Cyberspace (**whitehouse.gov/pcipb**) provides a series of actions and recommendations for each of its five national priorities. Download a copy of the strategy online. Select one of the priorities and discuss in detail the actions and recommendations for that priority.

10. The Symantec Internet Security Threat Report provides details about the trends in attacks and vulnerabilities in Internet security. Obtain a copy of the report and summarize the major findings of the report for both attacks and vulnerabilities.

11. Enter **ftc.gov** and identify some of the typical types of fraud and scams on the Internet.

12. Enter **scambusters.com** and identify and list its antifraud and antiscam activities.

13. Visit the Privacy and Technology Client Bulletin at **winston.com/siteFiles/publications/Winston_ Privacy_and_Technology_Bulletin_10_01_V1. html** and review issues posted under "ONLINE COMMERCE." Select and briefly explain one issue, and describe its implications.

TEAM ASSIGNMENTS AND ROLE PLAYING

1. Hackers' motives include money, entertainment, ego, personal cause, entrance to social groups, and status. Using the Web as your primary data source, have each team member explore one or more of these motives. Each member should describe the motive in detail, how widespread the motive is, the types of attacks that the motive encourages, and the types of actions that can combat the associated attacks.

2. Several personal firewall products are available. A list of these products can be found at **firewallguide.com/software.htm**. Assign each team three products from the list. Each team should prepare a detailed review and comparison of each of the products they have been assigned.

3. Assign each team member a different B2C or B2B Web site. Have each team prepare a report summarizing the site's security assets, threats, and vulnerabilities. Prepare a brief EC security strategy for the site.

Real-World Case

UBS PAINEWEBBER'S BUSINESS OPERATIONS DEBILITATED BY MALICIOUS CODE

Employee (Allegedly) Planned to Crash All Computer Networks

In June 2006, former systems administrator at UBS PaineWebber, Roger Duronio, 63, was charged with building, planting, and setting off a software logic bomb designed to crash the network. His alleged motive was to get revenge for not being paid what he thought he was worth. He designed the logic bomb to delete all the files in the host server in the central data center and in every server in every U.S. branch office. Duronio was looking to make up for some of the cash he felt he had been denied. He wanted to take home $175,000 a year. He had a base salary of $125,000 and a potential annual bonus of $50,000, but the actual bonus was $32,000.

Duronio quit his job, within hours went to a broker, and bought stock options that would only pay out if the company's stock plunged within 11 days. By setting a short expiration date of 11 days instead of a year, the gain from any payout would be much greater. He tried to ensure a stock price crash by crippling the company's network to rock their financial stability. His "put" options expired worthless, because the bank's national network did go down, but not UBS stock.

Discovering the Attack

In a federal court, UBS PaineWebber's IT manager Elvira Maria Rodriguez testified that on March 4, 2002, at 9:30 A.M. when the stock market opened for the day, she saw the words "cannot find" on her screen at the company's Escalation Center in Weehawken, New Jersey. She hit the enter key to see the message again, but her screen was frozen. Rodriguez was in charge of maintaining the stability of the servers in the company's branch offices.

When the company's servers went down that day in March 2002, about 17,000 brokers across the country were unable to make trades; the incident affected nearly 400 branch offices. Files were deleted. Backups went down within minutes of being run. Rodriguez, who had to clean up after the logic bomb, said "How on earth were we going to bring them all back up? How was this going to affect the company? If I had a scale of one to 10, this would be a 10-plus."

The prosecutor, Assistant U.S. Attorney V. Grady O'Malley, told the jury: "It took hundreds of people, thousands of man hours and millions of dollars to correct." The system was offline for more than a day, and UBS PaineWebber (renamed UBS Wealth Management USA in 2003) spent about $3.1 million in assessing and restoring the network. The company did not report how much was lost in business downtime and disruption.

Tracking Down the Hacker

A computer forensics expert testified that Duronio's password and user account information were used to gain remote access to the areas where the malicious code was built inside the UBS network. The U.S. Secret Service agent who had investigated the case found a hardcopy of the logic bomb's source code on the defendant's bedroom dresser. A computer forensics investigator found electronic copies of the code on two of his four home computers.

Defense Blames UBS Security Holes

Chris Adams, Duronio's defense attorney, offered another scenario. Adams claimed that the code was planted by someone else to be a nuisance or prank. Adam also said the UBS system had many security holes and backdoors that gave easy access to attackers. Adams told the jury:

> UBS computer security had considerable holes. There are flaws in the system that compromise the ability to determine what is and isn't true. Does the ability to walk around in the system undetected and masquerade as someone else affect your ability to say what has happened?

He also claimed that UBS and @Stake, the first computer forensic company to work on the incident, withheld some information from the government and even "destroyed" some of the evidence. As for the stock options, Adams explained that they were neither risky bets nor part of a scheme, but rather a common investment practice.

Disaster Recovery Efforts

While trying to run a backup to get a main server up and functional, Rodriguez discovered that a line of code (MRM-r) was hanging up the system every time it ran. She renamed the command to hide it from the system and rebooted the server. This action stopped the server from deleting anything else. After testing to confirm the fix, backup tapes brought up the remaining 2,000 servers, and the line of code was deleted from each one. Restoring each server took from 30 minutes to 2 hours, unless there was a complication. In those cases, restoration took up to 6 hours. UBS called in 200 IBM technicians to all the branch offices to expedite the recovery.

Many of the servers were down a day and a half, but some servers in remote locations were down for weeks. The incident impacted all the brokers who were denied access to critical applications because the servers were down.

Minimizing Residual Damages

UBS asked the judge to bar the public from Duronio's trial to avoid "serious embarrassment" and "serious injury" to the bank and its clients and possibly reveal sensitive information about the UBS network and operations. UBS argued that documents it had provided to the court could help a criminal hack into the bank's computer systems to destroy critical business information or to uncover confidential client information.

Duronio faced federal charges, including mail fraud, securities fraud, and computer sabotage, which carry sentences of up to 30 years in jail, $1 million in fines, and restitution for recovery costs.

Sources: Compiled from U.S. Department of Justice (2002), Gaudin (2006), and Whitman (2006).

Questions

1. What "red flags" might have indicated that Duronio was a disgruntled employee? Would any of those red flags also indicate that he would sabotage the network for revenge?

2. How could this disaster have been prevented? What policies, procedures, or technology could have prevented such an attack by an employee with full network access?

3. Did UBS have a disaster recovery plan in place for an enterprisewide network crash?

4. Do you agree with the defense lawyer's argument that anyone could have planted the logic bomb because UBS's computer security had considerable holes?

5. Given the breadth of known vulnerabilities, what sort of impact will any set of security standards have on the rise in cyber attacks?

ELECTRONIC COMMERCE PAYMENT SYSTEMS, ORDER FULFILLMENT, AND OTHER SUPPORT SERVICES

Learning Objectives

Upon completion of this chapter, you will be able to:

1. Understand the shifts that are occurring with regard to noncash and online payments.
2. Discuss the players and processes involved in using credit cards online.
3. Discuss the different categories and potential uses of smart cards.
4. Discuss various online alternatives to credit card payments and identify under what circumstances they are best used.
5. Describe the processes and parties involved in e-checking.
6. Describe payment methods in B2B EC, including payments for global trade.
7. Define EC order fulfillment and describe the EC order fulfillment process.
8. Describe the major problems of EC order fulfillment.
9. Describe various solutions to EC order fulfillment problems.
10. Discuss support services provided by general consulting and outsourcing firms.

Content

Pay-per-View Pages: The New iTunes

Managerial Issues

Real-World Case: Eliminating Letters of Credit: Rite Aid Deploys the TradeCard Solution

PAY-PER-VIEW PAGES: THE NEXT iTUNES

The Problem

Since 2004, the search engine companies Google, MSN, and Yahoo! have scanned and digitized the collections of some of the largest libraries in the world. MSN has been scanning the collections of the British Library, University of Toronto, and the University of California libraries. Yahoo! also is working with these same universities. However, the most comprehensive of these projects is certainly the Google Book Search Library Project (*books.google.com/googlebooks/library.html*). It is a partnership between Google and 19 major institutions, including Harvard, Oxford, the University of Michigan, the Universidad Complutense of Madrid, and the New York Public Library. In Google's words, the aim of the Library Project is to "make it easier for people to find relevant books—specifically books they wouldn't find any other way such as those that are out of print—while carefully respecting authors' and publishers' copyrights. Our ultimate goal is to work with publishers and libraries to create a comprehensive, searchable, virtual card catalog."

The Google project also is the most controversial. Unlike MSN and Yahoo!, Google is digitizing and making available for search not only books with expired copyrights, but those that have copyrights still in effect. If the copyright is still in effect, a search on Google will only produce a "snippet" of the text, rather than providing access to the whole text. If a publisher objects to Google's use of the copyrighted material, then Google wants the publisher to tell Google not to scan it, requiring the publisher to opt out rather than opt in. Because of this, the Authors Guild (*authorsguild.org*) filed suit against Google to block Google's scanning of books still under copyright.

Publishers are upset for another reason. Although Google has positioned the project as an altruistic endeavor, Google stands to make additional advertising revenues by offering these search capabilities. So far, Google has shown no interest in sharing any of the advertising royalties generated from the searches.

Unwilling to wait for the courts to determine the fate of Google's Library Project and to let Google, Yahoo!, and MSN determine the digital destiny of published works, Amazon.com and Random House announced separately in 2005 plans to allow consumers to purchase pages of books online. Neither of those announcements came to fruition. In November 2007, Amazon released Kindle, its e-book device, which offers a large collection of e-books at $9.99 a title. It also enables consumers to subscribe to selected blogs for either $.99 or $1.99 a month per blog (Levy 2007). In February 2008, Random House changed its strategy and began testing the idea of selling chapters online for $2.99.

Selling books online—either hardcopy or electronic—is straightforward. Selling pages, chapters, or any other sections of a book or journal online for under $5 is another story. In the online world, the vast majority of consumers use credit cards to make purchases. The financial institutions issuing credit cards charge a fixed percentage for each credit card purchase, as well as a fixed fee. For any purchase under $5 it is difficult for a vendor to break even. It is the same problem faced by merchants in the offline world. Fortunately, the credit card companies, as well as electronic payment companies, such as PayPal, are well aware of the issues associated with small value purchases and have begun to address the problem.

The Solution

Purchases under $5 also are called *micropayments*. In the offline world, "cash has been king of these small sales, because credit card companies charge merchants too much in fees to make the transactions profitable." Cash does not work in the online world. In the online world, virtually every attempt to "disintermediate" cash and credit cards has failed. Yet, there is ample evidence that consumers are willing to use their credit cards for micropayments.

In the online world, Apple iTunes has clearly been a success. The iTunes store sells songs for $0.99 a piece. By 2007, iTunes had sold over 4 billion songs (Ikram 2008). The way in which Apple has overcome the costs associated with credit and debit card fees is by having consumers set up accounts. The purchases of single items are then summed or aggregated until the total amount makes it cost-effective to submit to the credit or debit card issuer. Systems that aggregate purchases also are called *closed-loop systems*. The credit card companies are not enamored with these systems and prohibit merchants from aggregating purchases directly. However, they are currently reconsidering their stance because, as Pam Zuercher, Visa's vice president for product innovation, noted, "there is an undeniable trend—users want to use their cards for very small purchases" (Mitchell 2007).

The credit and debit card companies, as well as e-payment vendors such as PayPal, are well aware of the difficulties associated with using cards for online micropayments. In response, they have lowered their fees in an effort to entice online (and offline) vendors to permit credit and debit card micropayments. Even with these newer fees, purchases under $2 are still very cost prohibitive for the average merchant. They are much less prohibitive for larger vendors whose volume of card purchases enable them to negotiate with the card issuers for even smaller fees.

The Results

To date, companies such as Amazon.com and Random House have been unsuccessful with their pay-per-view plans. Clearly, Amazon.com is in a position to negotiate for smaller credit card fees. Like iTunes, it also has the ability to aggregate purchases for individual buyers. On the other hand, Random House will not sell directly to the public. Instead, it will rely on other vendors, such as Amazon.com, to do the selling. Even with a viable micropayment system, there is no guarantee that pay-per-page or pay-per-chapter will interest consumers, especially given the usual restrictions placed on purchases of this sort.

Consider, for a moment, a few of the restrictions Random House has placed on its viewing program:

- Books will be available for full indexing, search, and display.
- Downloading, printing, or copying will not be permitted.
- Encryption and security measures must be applied to ensure protection of the digital content and compliance with the prescribed usage rules and territorial limitations.

In essence, the only thing the purchaser can do is view the page or chapter online. This is much more onerous than the restrictions placed on music or video downloads, which at least permit the purchaser to copy the content to their PCs or multimedia players. Unless these restrictions are loosened or eliminated, they will likely lead to the long-run failure of the Random House project and similar efforts.

Sources: D'Agostino (2006), Ikram (2008), Kelly (2006), Levy (2007), and Mitchell (2007).

WHAT WE CAN LEARN . . .

The overwhelming majority of B2C purchases are paid for by credit card. For merchants, the costs of servicing card payments are high. Transaction costs, potential chargeback fees for fraudulent transactions, and the costs of creating and administering a secure EC site for handling card payments are steep. Over the years, a number of less costly e-payment alternatives to credit cards have been proposed. Digital Cash, PayMe.com, Bank One's eMoneyMail, Flooz, Beenz, Wells Fargo's and eBay's Billpoint, and Yahoo!'s PayDirect are examples of alternatives that failed to gain a critical mass of users and subsequently folded. For a variety of reasons, PayPal is one of the few alternatives to credit cards that has succeeded against significant odds. The same can be said for the world of B2B e-payments. Although a number of diverse payment methods have been proposed, few have survived. This chapter discusses various e-payment methods for B2C and B2B and the underlying reasons why some have been adopted and others have not. Once an order has been purchased, it needs to be fulfilled. In addition to discussing payment methods, this chapter also considers the processes required to fulfill the purchase as well as various customer services that are required to support fulfillment.

11.1 THE PAYMENT REVOLUTION

Today, we are in the midst of a payment revolution, with cards and electronic payments taking the place of cash and checks. In 2003, the combined use of credit and debit cards for in-store payments for the first time exceeded the combined use of cash and checks. By 2005, debit and credit cards accounted for 55 percent of in-store payments, with cash and checks making up the rest (Simon 2007). The growth in the use of plastic is attributable to the substantial growth in the use of debit cards and the decline in the use of cash.

Similar trends are occurring in noncash payments of recurring bills. In 2001, 78 percent of all recurring bills were paid by paper-based methods (e.g., paper checks), and 22 percent of these payments were made electronically. By 2005, the percent of electronic payments of recurring bills had grown to 45 percent (Dove Consulting 2006). This change in the mix of payment methods is likely to continue.

For decades people have been talking about the cashless society. Although the demise of cash and checks is certainly not imminent, many individuals can live without checks and nearly without cash. In the online B2C world, they already do. In North America, for example, 90 percent of all online consumer purchases are made with general-purpose credit cards (Dove Consulting 2006). The same is true for the overwhelming majority of online purchases in the United Kingdom, France, and Spain. Although Visa and MasterCard are certainly worldwide brands, many consumers outside these countries prefer other online payment methods. For instance, consumers in Germany, the Netherlands, and Japan prefer to pay with either direct debit or bank cards.

For online B2C merchants, the implications of these trends are straightforward. In the United States and Western Europe, it is hard to run an online business without supporting credit card payments, despite the costs. It also is becoming increasingly important to support payments by debit card. Under current growth patterns, the volume of debit card payments will soon surpass credit card payments, both online and offline. Merchants that are interested in international markets need to support a variety of e-payment mechanisms, including bank transfers, COD, electronic checks, private-label cards, gift cards, instant credit, and other noncard payment types, such as PayPal. Merchants that offer multiple payment types have lower shopping cart abandonment rates and up to 20 percent higher order conversion on average, resulting in increased revenues (CyberSource 2005).

As the opening case suggests, the short history of e-payments is littered with the remains of companies that have attempted to introduce nontraditional payment systems. It takes years for any payment system to gain widespread acceptance. For example, credit cards were introduced in the 1950s but did not reach widespread use until the 1980s. A crucial element in the success of any e-payment method is the "chicken-and-egg" problem: How do you get sellers to adopt a method when there are few buyers using it? And, how do you get buyers to adopt a method when there are few sellers using it? A number of factors come into play in determining whether a particular method of e-payment achieves critical mass. Some of the crucial factors include the following (Evans and Schmalensee 2005).

Independence. Some forms of e-payment require specialized software or hardware to make the payment. Almost all forms of e-payment require the seller or merchant to install specialized software to receive and authorize a payment. Those e-payment methods that require the payer to install specialized components are less likely to succeed.

Interoperability and Portability. All forms of EC run on specialized systems that are interlinked with other enterprise systems and applications. An e-payment method must mesh with these existing systems and applications and be supported by standard computing platforms.

Security. How safe is the transfer? What are the consequences of the transfer's being compromised? Again, if the risk for the payer is higher than the risk for the payee, then the payer is not likely to accept the method.

Anonymity. Unlike credit cards and checks, if a buyer uses cash, there is no way to trace the cash back to the buyer. Some buyers want their identities and purchase patterns to remain anonymous. To succeed, special payment methods, such as e-cash, have to maintain anonymity.

Divisibility. Most sellers accept credit cards only for purchases within a minimum and maximum range. If the cost of the item is too small—only a few dollars—a credit card will not do. In addition, a credit card will not work if an item or set of items costs too much (e.g., an airline company purchasing a new airplane). Any method that can address the lower or higher end of the price continuum or that can span one of the extremes and the middle has a chance of being widely accepted.

Ease of Use. For B2C e-payments, credit cards are the standard due to their ease of use. For B2B payments, the question is whether the online e-payment methods can supplant the existing offline methods of procurement.

Transaction Fees. When a credit card is used for payment, the merchant pays a transaction fee of up to 3 percent of the item's purchase price (above a minimum fixed fee). These fees make it prohibitive to support smaller purchases with credit cards, which leaves room for alternative forms of payment.

Regulations. A number of international, federal, and state regulations govern all payment methods. Even when an existing institution or association (e.g., Visa) introduces a new payment method, it faces a number of stringent regulatory hurdles. PayPal, for instance, had to contend with a number of lawsuits brought by state attorneys general that claimed that PayPal was violating state banking regulations.

Section 11.1 ▶ REVIEW QUESTIONS

1. Describe the trends that are occurring in cash and noncash payments in the United States.
2. What types of e-payments should B2C merchants support?
3. What is the "chicken-and-egg" problem in e-payments?
4. Describe the factors that are critical for an e-payment method to achieve critical mass.

11.2 USING PAYMENT CARDS ONLINE

payment card
Electronic card that contains information that can be used for payment purposes.

Payment cards are electronic cards that contain information that can be used for payment purposes. They come in three forms:

▶ **Credit cards.** A credit card provides the holder with credit to make purchases up to a limit fixed by the card issuer. Credit cards rarely have an annual fee. Instead, holders are charged high interest—the annual percentage rate—on their average daily unpaid balances. Visa, MasterCard, and EuroPay are the predominant credit cards.

▶ **Charge cards.** The balance on a charge card is supposed to be paid in full upon receipt of the monthly statement. Technically, holders of a charge card receive a loan for 30 to 45 days equal to the balance of their statement. Such cards usually have annual fees. American Express's Green Card is the leading charge card, followed by the Diner's Club card.

▶ **Debit cards.** With a debit card, the money for a purchased item comes directly out of the holder's checking account (called a demand-deposit account). The actual transfer of funds from the holder's account to the merchant's takes place within one to two days. MasterCard, Visa, and EuroPay are the predominant debit cards.

PROCESSING CARDS ONLINE

authorization
Determines whether a buyer's card is active and whether the customer has sufficient funds.

settlement
Transferring money from the buyer's to the merchant's account.

The processing of card payments has two major phases: authorization and settlement. **Authorization** determines whether a buyer's card is active and whether the customer has sufficient available credit line or funds. **Settlement** involves the transfer of money from the buyer's to the merchant's account. The way in which these phases actually are performed varies somewhat depending on the type of payment card. It also varies by the configuration of the system used by the merchant to process payments.

There are three basic configurations for processing online payments. The EC merchant may:

▶ **Own the payment software.** A merchant can purchase a payment-processing module and integrate it with its other EC software. This module communicates with a payment gateway run by an acquiring bank or another third party.

▶ **Use a point of sale system (POS) operated by an acquirer.** Merchants can redirect cardholders to a POS run by an acquirer. The POS handles the complete payment process and directs the cardholder back to the merchant site once payment is complete. In this case, the merchant system only deals with order information. In this configuration, it is important to find an acquirer that handles multiple cards and payment instruments. If not, the merchant will need to connect with a multitude of acquirers.

▶ **Use a POS operated by a payment service provider.** Merchants can rely on servers operated by third parties known as **payment service providers (PSPs)**. In this case, the PSP connects with the appropriate acquirers. PSPs must be registered with the various card associations they support.

For a given type of payment card and processing system, the processes and participants are essentially the same for offline (card-present) and online (card-not-present) purchases. Exhibit 11.1 compares, for instance, the steps involved in making a credit card purchase both online and offline. As the exhibit demonstrates, there is very little difference between the two.

payment service provider (PSP)
A third-party service connecting a merchant's EC systems to the appropriate acquirers; PSPs must be registered with the various card associations they support.

EXHIBIT 11.1 Credit Card Purchases: Online Versus Offline

Online Purchase	Offline Purchase
1. The *customer* decides to purchase a CD on the Web, adding it to the electronic shopping cart and going to the checkout page to enter his or her credit card information.	1. The *customer* selects a CD to purchase, takes it to the checkout counter, and hands his or her credit card to the sales clerk.
2. The *merchant* site receives the customer's information and sends the transaction information to its *payment processing service (PPS)*.	2. The *merchant* runs the credit card through the point of sale (POS) unit.
3. The PPS routes information to the *processor* (a large data center for processing transactions and settling funds to the merchant).	3. The POS terminal routes information to the *processor* via a dial-up connection.
4. The processor sends information to the *issuing bank* of the customer's credit card.	4. The processor transmits the credit card data and sales amount with a request for authorization of the sale to the *issuing bank* of the customer's credit card.
5. The issuing bank sends the transaction to the processor, either authorizing the payment or not.	5. If the cardholder has enough credit in their account to cover the sale, the issuing bank authorizes the transaction and generates an authorization code; if not the sale is declined.
6. The processor routes the transaction result to the PPS.	6. The processor sends the transaction code back through the processor to the POS.
7. The PPS passes the results to the merchant.	7. The POS unit shows the outcome to the merchant.
8. The merchant accepts or rejects the transaction.	8. The merchant tells the customer the outcome of the transaction.

Sources: Compiled from PayPal (2004) and Lamond and Whitman (1996).

Based on the processes outlined in Exhibit 11.1, the key participants in processing card payments online include the following:

▶ **Acquiring bank.** Offers a special account called an *Internet Merchant Account* that enables card authorization and payment processing.

▶ **Credit card association.** The financial institution providing card services to banks (e.g., Visa and MasterCard).

▶ **Customer.** The individual possessing the card.

▶ **Issuing bank.** The financial institution that provides the customer with a card.

▶ **Merchant.** A company that sells products or services.

▶ **Payment processing service.** The service provides connectivity among merchants, customers, and financial networks that enables authorization and payments. Usually operated by companies such as CyberSource (cybersource.com) and VeriSign (verisign.com).

▶ **Processor.** The data center that processes card transactions and settles funds to merchants.

FRAUDULENT CARD TRANSACTIONS

Although the processes used for authorizing and settling card payments offline and online are very similar, there is one substantial difference between the two. In the online world, merchants are held liable for fraudulent transactions. In addition to the lost merchandise and shipping charges, merchants who accept fraudulent transactions can incur additional fees and penalties imposed by the card associations. However, these are not the only costs. There also are the costs associated with combating fraudulent transactions. These include the costs of tools and systems to review orders, the costs of manually reviewing orders, and the revenue that is lost from rejecting orders that are valid. Recent surveys by CyberSource indicate that fraudulent card transactions are a growing problem for online merchants despite their increasing efforts to combat fraud.

For the past 8 years, CyberSource has sponsored a survey to address the detection, prevention, and management of fraud perpetrated against online merchants. CyberSource's 2007 survey of 318 merchants documented the following trends (CyberSource 2008):

▶ Although the percentage of revenue loss per merchant was relatively flat, the total dollars lost to fraud increased substantially, from $1.9 billion in 2003 to $3.6 billion in 2007. The rise was attributable to the increase in the amount of business that was being done online, which grew by 20 percent or more annually over the same time period.

▶ In 2007, merchants estimated that an average of 1.3 percent of their orders were fraudulent. This represented a slight decline from the previous year. The fraudulent orders resulted in merchants' crediting the real cardholder's account. The median value of these fraudulent orders was $200, or 67 percent above the average value of valid orders.

▶ Fifty-nine percent of the merchants surveyed accepted international orders outside the United States and Canada. These orders represented 16 percent of the sales for these merchants. The fraud rate for these orders was approximately 3.6 percent, or more than 2.7 times higher than the fraud rate for domestic orders.

▶ Certain merchants were more susceptible to fraud than others. This was due to a number of factors: the merchant's visibility on the Web, the steps the merchant had taken to combat fraud, the ease with which the merchant's products could be sold on the open market, and the merchant's size. Larger firms were less susceptible to fraud than smaller firms.

▶ Although overall security expenditures for online fraud detection remained the same from 2006 to 2007, the amount spent on manual review of orders increased over 30 percent, or about $100 million. As the volume of online orders continues to grow, this is not a viable long-term strategy for merchants.

In addition to tracking trends in online fraud, the CyberSource surveys also monitor the steps taken by merchants to combat fraud (CyberSource 2008). In 2007, merchants used more tools than in the past to combat fraud. The median number of tools was 5.4 in 2007 compared with 3 in 2003. Merchants also were spending more to combat fraud. The median amount was 0.3 percent of online revenues. Most of the money was spent on review staff (52 percent), followed by third-party tools and services (23 percent) and internally developed tools (25 percent). The keytools used in combating fraud were:

▶ **Address Verification System (AVS).** Eighty percent of all merchants use this method, which compares the address entered on a Web page with the address information on file with the cardholder's issuing bank. This method results in a number of false positives, meaning that the merchant rejects a valid order. Cardholders often have new addresses or simply make mistakes in inputting numeric street addresses or zip codes. AVS is only available in the United States and Canada.

▶ **Manual review.** Eighty-two percent of all merchants use this method, which relies on staff to manually review suspicious orders. For small merchants with a small volume of orders, this is a reasonable method. For larger merchants, this method does not scale well, is expensive, and impacts customer satisfaction. In spite of these limitations, the percentage of merchants using this method is increasing, along with the percentage of items being reviewed. In 2007, the number of orders being reviewed was one in three versus one in four in 2003.

▶ **Fraud screens and automated decision models.** Over 70 percent of all merchants use these methods, which are based on various automated rules that determine whether a transaction should be accepted, rejected, or suspended. A key element of this method is the ability of the merchant to easily change the rules to reflect changing trends in the fraud being perpetrated against the company.

▶ **Card verification number.** Seventy-four percent of all merchants use the **card verification number (CVN)**, whereby the merchant compares the verification number printed on the signature strip on the back of the card with the information on file with the cardholder's issuing bank. However, if a fraudster possesses a stolen card, the number is in plain view.

▶ **Card association payer authentication services.** In the last couple of years, the card associations have developed a new set of payer identification services (e.g., Verified by Visa and MasterCard SecureCode). These services require cardholders to register with the systems and merchants to adopt and support both the existing systems and the new systems. In 2004, it was estimated that over 55 percent of merchants would be using this method by 2005. In reality, only 25 percent of the merchants in the 2007 survey indicated that they had adopted this method.

▶ **Negative lists.** Thirty-six percent of all merchants use this method, which is a file of the customer's information (IP address, name, shipping/billing address, contact numbers, etc.) and the status of that customer. A customer's transaction is matched against this file and flagged if the customer is a known problem.

The overall impact of these tools is that merchants are rejecting a significant number of orders due to suspicion of fraud. In 2007, the average number of rejected

Address Verification System (AVS)
Detects fraud by comparing the address entered on a Web page with the address information on file with the cardholder's issuing bank.

card verification number (CVN)
Detects fraud by comparing the verification number printed on the signature strip on the back of the card with the information on file with the cardholder's issuing bank.

orders was over three for every fraudulent order accepted. This represented a rejection rate of 4 percent of all orders. The problem with these rejection rates is that a number of the rejected orders are valid, resulting in lost revenue.

smart card
An electronic card containing an embedded microchip that enables predefined operations or the addition, deletion, or manipulation of information on the card.

contact card
A smart card containing a small gold plate on the face that when inserted in a smart card reader makes contact and passes data to and from the embedded microchip.

contactless (proximity) card
A smart card with an embedded antenna, by means of which data and applications are passed to and from a card reader unit or other device without contact between the card and the card reader.

Section 11.2 ▶ REVIEW QUESTIONS

1. Describe the three types of payment cards.
2. What options does a merchant have in setting up an e-payment system?
3. List the major participants in processing cards online.
4. What costs does an online merchant incur if it submits a fraudulent card transaction?
5. Describe the major trends in fraudulent orders perpetrated against online merchants.
6. What steps are often taken by online merchants to combat fraudulent orders?

11.3 SMART CARDS

Outside North America, smart cards often are used in place of or in addition to traditional credit and debit cards. They also are used widely to support nonretail and nonfinancial applications. A **smart card** looks like a plastic payment card, but it is distinguished by the presence of an embedded microchip (see Exhibit 11.2). The embedded chip may be a microprocessor combined with a memory chip or just a memory chip with nonprogrammable logic. Information on a microprocessor card can be added, deleted, or otherwise manipulated; a memory-chip card is usually a "read-only" card, similar to a credit card. Although the microprocessor is capable of running programs like a computer does, it is not a stand-alone computer. The programs and data must be downloaded from and activated by some other device (such as an ATM machine).

TYPES OF SMART CARDS

There are two distinct types of smart cards. The first type is a **contact card**, which is activated when it is inserted into a smart card reader. The second type of card is a **contactless (proximity) card**, meaning that the card only has to be within a certain proximity of a smart card reader to process a transaction. *Hybrid cards* combine both types of cards into one.

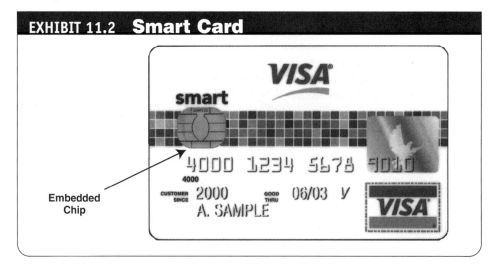

EXHIBIT 11.2 **Smart Card**

Source: Courtesy of Visa International Service Association.

Contact smart cards have a small gold plate about one-half inch in diameter on the front. When the card is inserted into the smart card reader, the plate makes electronic contact and data are passed to and from the chip. Contact cards can have electronically programmable, read-only memory (EPROM) or electronically erasable, programmable, read-only memory (EEPROM). EPROM cards can never be erased. Instead, data are written to the available space on the card. When the card is full, it is discarded. EEPROM cards are erasable and modifiable. They can be used until they wear out or malfunction. Most contact cards are EEPROM.

In addition to the chip, a contactless card has an embedded antenna. Data and applications are passed to and from the card through the card's antenna to another antenna attached to a smart card reader or other device. Contactless cards are used for those applications in which the data must be processed very quickly (e.g., mass-transit applications, such as paying bus or train fares) or when contact is difficult (e.g., security-entering mechanisms to buildings). Proximity cards usually work at short range, just a few inches. For some applications, such as payments at highway toll booths, the cards can operate at considerable distances.

With *hybrid* and *dual-interface* smart cards, the two types of card interfaces are merged into one. A hybrid smart card has two separate chips embedded in the card: contact and contactless. In contrast, a dual-interface, or combi, smart card has a single chip that supports both types of interfaces. The benefit of either card is that it eliminates the need to carry multiple cards to support the various smart card readers and applications.

With both contact and proximity cards, smart card readers are crucial to the operation of the system. Technically speaking, a smart card reader is actually a read/write device. The primary purpose of the **smart card reader** is to act as a mediator between the card and the host system that stores application data and processes transactions. Just as there are two basic types of cards, there are two types of smart card readers—*contact* and *proximity*—which match the particular type of card. Smart card readers can be transparent, requiring a host device to operate, or stand alone, functioning independently. Smart card readers are a key element in determining the overall cost of a smart card application. Although the cost of a single reader is usually low, the cost can be quite high when hundreds or thousands are needed to service a large population of users (e.g., all the passengers traveling on a metropolitan mass transit system).

Like computers, smart cards have an underlying operating system. A **smart card operating system** handles file management, security, input/output (I/O), and command execution and provides an application programming interface (API). Originally, smart card operating systems were designed to run on the specific chip embedded in the card. Today, smart cards are moving toward multiple and open application operating systems such as MULTOS (multos.com) and Java Card (java.sun.com/products/javacard). These operating systems enable new applications to be added during the life of the card.

smart card reader
Activates and reads the contents of the chip on a smart card, usually passing the information on to a host system.

smart card operating system
Special system that handles file management, security, input/output (I/O), and command execution and provides an application programming interface (API) for a smart card.

APPLICATIONS OF SMART CARDS

The use of smart cards is growing rapidly both outside and inside the United States. Globally, an estimated 3.6 billion smart cards were shipped in 2006. In North America, the number of shipments was estimated to be over 200 million, and the number of shipments is growing 27 percent annually (Frost and Sullivan 2005). The growth in smart card usage is being driven by its applications. A general discussion of these applications can be found at the GlobalPlatform Web site (globalplatform.org/showpage.asp?code=implementations). Within EC, smart cards are used in the place of standard credit cards for general retail purchases and for transit fares.

Retail Purchases

The credit card associations and financial institutions are transitioning their traditional credit and debit cards to multi-application smart cards. For example, MasterCard announced in November 2004 that it had issued more than 200 million MasterCard, Maestro, and Cirrus smart cards worldwide (MasterCard International 2004). Close to half of these support the Europay, MasterCard, and Visa (EMV) card standard. These cards are accepted at over 1.5 million EMV terminals worldwide. From MasterCard's perspective, as well as that of the other card associations and card companies, smart cards have reached mass-market adoption rates in Europe, Latin America, and APMEA (Asia/Pacific, the Middle East, and Africa). Compared to 2005, MasterCard experienced more than a 470 percent increase in the number of contactless payment cards and other payment devices issued in the APMEA region in the third quarter of 2006 (Smart Card Alliance 2006).

In most cases smart cards are more secure than credit cards and can be extended with other payment services. In the retail arena, many of these services are aimed at those establishments where payments are usually made in cash and speed and convenience are important. This includes convenience stores, gas stations, fast-food or quick-service restaurants, and cinemas. Contactless payments exemplify this sort of value-added service.

Over the past few years, the card associations have been piloting a number of contactless payment systems that are aimed at retail operations where speed and convenience are crucial. MasterCard's PayPass (mastercard.com/aboutourcards/paypass.html), American Express's ExpressPay (americanexpress.com/expresspay), and Visa's Wave fit into this category. All these systems utilize the existing POS and magnetic strip payment infrastructure used with traditional credit and debit cards. The only difference is that a special contactless smart card reader is required. To make a purchase, a cardholder simply waves his or her card near the terminal, and the terminal reads the financial information on the card.

In 2003, MasterCard introduced PayPass in a market trial conducted in Orlando, Florida, with JPMorgan Chase & Co., Citibank, and MBNA. The trial involved more than 16,000 cardholders and more than 60 retailers. The introduction of PayPass served as a catalyst to increase card usage and loyalty in the Orlando area. During the trial, MasterCard experienced an 18 percent active rate for previously inactive accounts. MasterCard also saw a 23 percent increase in transaction value, a 28 percent increase in total weekly spending, and a 12 percent month-over-month increase in transaction volumes at participating merchants.

Two years later in 2005, MasterCard began rolling out PayPass to selected markets in the United States, United Kingdom, Turkey, and the Philippines. That same year, American Express introduced ExpressPay. ExpressPay replaced the smart chip on the American Express Blue card. Currently, ExpressPay is accepted at a number of merchants and fast-food restaurants including 7-Eleven, CVS pharmacy, Walgreen's pharmacy, AMC theaters, United Artists theaters, Arby's, McDonald's, Jack in the Box, and Meijer's supermarkets. Following a pilot study in 2004, Visa began rolling out its Visa Wave card in Malaysia in February 2005. The card, which is based on the global EMV standard, was offered to 500,000 cardholders in Malaysia and accepted at 4,000 Malaysian merchants, including convenience stores, fast-food restaurants, theaters, gas stations, and supermarkets. In 2005, Visa also launched with Chinatrust Commercial Bank a second pilot program in Taiwan. The card was offered to 25,000 cardholders and was accepted at more than 150 merchants, including gas stations, DVD shops, Taiwan Railways, bus services, parking lots, laundries, cafés, and restaurants.

Transit Fares

In major U.S. cities, commuters often have to drive to a parking lot, board a train, and then change to one or more subways or buses to arrive at work. If the whole trip requires a combination of cash and multiple types of tickets, this can be a major hassle. For those commuters who have a choice, the inconvenience plays a role in discouraging the use of public transportation. To eliminate the inconvenience, most major transit operators in the United States are implementing smart card fare-ticketing systems. The U.S. federal government also is providing incentives to employers to subsidize the use of public transportation by their employees. The transit systems in Washington, D.C., San Francisco, Los Angeles, Boston, Minneapolis, Atlanta, San Diego, Orlando, and Chicago have all either instituted smart card payment systems or are currently running pilot systems (American Public Transportation Association 2006).

Metropolitan transit operators are moving away from multiple, nonintegrated fare systems to systems that require only a single contactless card regardless of how many modes of transportation or how many transportation agencies or companies are involved. The SmarTrip program run by the Washington Metropolitan Area Transit Authority (WMATA) in the District of Columbia exemplifies this movement (wmata.com /riding/smartrip.cfm). WMATA was the first transportation system in the United States to employ smart cards. The program started in 1999. SmarTrip is a permanent, contactless, rechargeable fare card that can hold up to $300 in fare value. The card can be used with 17 different transit systems, including Metro-operated parking lots, the Metrorail, Metrobuses, and other regional rail services. SmarTrip handles the complexities associated with the various systems, including zone-based and time-based fares, volume discounts, and bus-to-train and bus-to-bus transfers. To date, close to a half million SmarTrip cards have been issued and well over one-third of Metrorail riders use the cards regularly.

The U.S. smart card transit programs are modeled after the transit systems in Asia. Case 11.1 describes one of these—the TaiwanMoney Card. Online File W11.1 discusses another Asian project. Like their Asian counterparts, some U.S. transit operators are looking to partner with retailers and financial institutions to combine their transit cards with payment cards to purchase goods and services, such as snacks, bridge tolls, parking fees, or food in restaurants or grocery stores located near the transit stations.

In addition to handling transit fares, smart cards and other e-payment systems are being used for other transportation applications. For instance, Philadelphia has retooled all its 14,500 parking meters to accept payment from prepaid smart cards issued by the Philadelphia Parking Authority (philapark.org). Similarly, many of the major toll roads in the United States and elsewhere accept electronic payments rendered by devices called transponders that operate much like contactless smart cards.

CASE 11.1
EC Application
TAIWANMONEY CARD

In October 2005, the Kaohsiung City Government (KCG) in Taiwan began, as part of its e-City initiative, the Smart Transport Card Project. Similar to other municipalities in Asia, KCG was interested in utilizing smart card technology to enable contactless payments throughout its transport system. Unlike other municipalities, however, KCG was not interested in introducing a specialized transport card. Typically, transport cards are purchased from a transport authority, and their primary function is to pay transport fares. Occasionally, they can be used at other venues.

(continued)

CASE 11.1   (continued)

For example, the Hong Kong metro card, known as the Octopus Card, can be used at fast-food restaurants and convenience stores. Instead, KCG decided to partner with MasterCard to produce a single money card that could be used for both retail and transport payments. In this way, KCG could avoid many of the problems associated with issuing the cards, managing the overall payment systems, and instituting specialized legislation dictating how the cards could be used.

The card, produced by MasterCard for KCG, is called the TaiwanMoney Card. Technically the card was MasterCard's first OneSMART PayPass Chip Combi Card. The card complies with the EMV standard, making it the first EMV-based card to support transport payments. Although KCG is the owner of the Smart Transport Card Project, the cards are marketed, issued, and serviced by Cathay United Bank, E. Sun Bank, and the Bank of Kaohsiung.

The KCG system, which is operated by Mondex Taiwan, supports two types of cards: stand-alone and Payment Plus. The stand-alone cards are used for single trips; they are primarily for children, for people who do not have a bank account, and for those visiting from out of town. The Payment Plus card is for existing MasterCard holders and new account customers. It is a dual-branded MasterCard credit card or debit card that can be used for both transportation and shopping.

In order for the transportation system to support the cards, contactless TaiwanMoney Card readers had to be installed on all buses. In order for retailers to support the

cards, their POS terminals had to be upgraded to accept the TaiwanMoney or MasterCard PayPass contactless cards.

By the end of 2005, approximately 100,000 cardholders were using the TaiwanMoney Cards to pay fares on buses running in Kaohsiung and six other cities in southern Taiwan. They were also using the cards to make purchases at 5,000 convenience stores, supermarkets, and other retail outlets in the region.

Although the cards enjoy widespread use throughout southern Taiwan, they still have a major drawback. It takes about 0.6 to 0.7 seconds to complete a transaction. This is fine for retail outlets and buses, but it will not work with the metro (subway) system. The metro system requires a transaction speed of 0.4 seconds or faster. The project's systems integrator, Acer of Taiwan, is working with the chip and card manufacturers to meet this service-level requirement. Once this is accomplished, MasterCard plans to expand the program to Taipei and to the Chinese market.

Sources: Card Technology (2006), Hendry (2007), and Multos (2006).

Questions

1. What is the TaiwanMoney Card?

2. Why did KCG decide to use a smart money card for their transportation system rather than a specialized transportation card?

3. What prohibits the use of the TaiwanMoney Card with KCG's metro system?

SECURING SMART CARDS

Smart cards store or provide access to either valuable assets (e.g., e-cash) or to sensitive information (e.g., medical records). Because of this, they must be secured against theft, fraud, or misuse. In general, smart cards are more secure than conventional payment cards. If someone steals a payment card, the number on the card is clearly visible, as is the owner's signature. Although it may be hard to forge the signature, in many situations only the number is required to make a purchase. The only protection cardholders have is that there usually are limits on how much they will be held liable for (e.g., in the United States it is $50). If someone steals a stored-value card (or the owner loses it), the original owner is out of luck.

However, if someone steals a smart card, the thief is usually out of luck. The major exception is a "wave and go" card such as the Visa Wave card used for retail purchases. Some smart cards show account numbers, but others do not. Before the card can be used, the holder may be required to enter a PIN that is matched with the card. Theoretically, it is possible to "hack" into a smart card. Most cards, however, now store information in encrypted form. The smart cards can also encrypt and decrypt data that is downloaded or read from the card. Because of these factors, the possibility of hacking into a smart card is classified as a "class 3" attack, which means that the cost of compromising the card far exceeds the benefits.

Because of the highly confidential nature of medical information, PKI and other cryptographic techniques are being used to secure access to health-care data. In this instance, smart cards contain not only the encrypted keys that are required by health-care practitioners to access patient data but also pointers to data that may be housed in different databases on different networks. In France, the next generation of electronic social security cards (i.e., the *Vitale* card), which is used for health-care reimbursements, is incorporating cryptographic mechanisms based on PKI. Since 2001, Vitale cards have been issued to all individuals over the age of 16 who are entitled to social security coverage (Smart Card Alliance 2006). To date, approximately 50 million cards have been issued. In 2006, the Vitale cards were upgraded to include the enhanced security feature. This was done to ensure that the cards were in compliance with France's new identification, authentication, and signature standards for the fields of health and welfare.

Section 11.3 ▶ REVIEW QUESTIONS

1. Define each of the following: smart card, contact card, and contactless card.
2. What is a smart card operating system?
3. Describe the use of smart cards in metropolitan transportation systems.

11.4 STORED-VALUE CARDS

What looks like a credit or debit card, acts like a credit or debit card, but isn't a credit or debit card? The answer is a **stored-value card**. As the name implies, the monetary value of a stored-value card is preloaded on the card. From a physical and technical standpoint, a stored-value card is indistinguishable from a regular credit or debit card. It is plastic and has a magnetic strip on the back, although it might not have the cardholder's name printed on it. The magnetic strip stores the monetary value of the card. This distinguishes a stored-value card from a smart card. With smart cards, the chip stores the value. Consumers can use stored-value cards to make purchases, offline or online, in the same way that they use credit and debit cards—relying on the same networks, encrypted communications, and electronic banking protocols. What is different about a stored-value card is that anyone can obtain one without regard to prior financial standing or having an existing bank account as collateral.

stored-value card
A card that has monetary value loaded onto it and that usually is rechargeable.

Stored-value cards come in two varieties: *closed loop* and *open loop*. Closed-loop, or single-purpose, cards are issued by a specific merchant or merchant group (e.g., a shopping mall) and can only be used to make purchases from that merchant or merchant group. Mall cards, store cards, gift cards, and prepaid telephone cards are all examples of closed-loop cards. Gift cards represent a strong growth area, especially in the United States. According to the National Retail Federation, in 2006 spending on gift cards in the United States reached approximately $30 billion, with the average amount spent per card around $40 (cited by Block 2007).

In contrast, an open-loop, or multipurpose, card can be used to make debit transactions at a variety of retailers. Open-loop cards also can be used for other purposes, such as receiving direct deposits or withdrawing cash from ATM machines. Financial institutions with card association branding, such as Visa or MasterCard, issue some open-loop cards. They can be used anywhere that the branded cards are accepted. Payroll cards, government benefit cards, and prepaid debit cards are all examples of open-loop cards.

Stored-value cards may be acquired in a variety of ways. Employers or government agencies may issue them as payroll cards or benefit cards in lieu of checks or direct deposits. Merchants or merchant groups sell and load gift cards. Various financial institutions and nonfinancial outlets sell preloaded cards by telephone, online, or in person. Cash, bank wire transfers, money orders, cashiers' checks, other credit cards, or direct payroll or government deposits fund preloaded cards.

The stored-value card market is growing rapidly. Market analysts estimate that there are over 2,000 stored value programs with over 7 million Visa and MasterCard branded cards in use today (Mercator 2006). In 2005, the total spent on both closed- and open-loop cards was $165 billion. By 2009, the total spent is expected to reach $236 billion, a compound annual growth rate (CAGR) of over 9 percent. Although the spending on closed-loop cards in 2009 will far exceed the spending on open-loop cards ($192 billion versus $43 billion), the spending on open-loop cards is growing much more rapidly than the spending on closed-loop cards (32 percent versus 9 percent). Gift cards are the fastest-growing market, followed by employer and consumer incentives, open campus, and state unemployment cards.

Stored-value cards are being marketed heavily to the "unbanked" and "overextended." Approximately 50 million adults in the United States do not have credit cards, and 20 million do not have bank accounts—people with low incomes, young adults, seniors, immigrants, minorities, and others (Milligan 2004). Among those with credit cards, 40 percent are running close to their credit limits. The expectation is that these groups will be major users of prepaid cards in the future. For example, individuals in the United States transferred over $12 billion to individuals in Mexico. Instead of sending money orders or cash, programs such as the EasySend card from Branch Banking and Trust (BB&T) provide a secure alternative to transferring money to relatives and friends. With the EasySend program, an individual establishes a banking account, deposits money in the account, and mails the EasySend card to a relative or friend, who can then withdraw the cash from an ATM machine. When it was introduced in 2004, EasySend was focused primarily on the Hispanic community. Today, it is used by immigrant populations all over the world (Branch Banking and Trust 2006).

In a slightly different vein, the MasterCard MYPlash and Visa Buxx cards, which are described in detail in Online File W11.2, provide younger populations with a prepaid, preloaded card alternative to credit cards or cash. Among other things, these alternatives provide a relatively risk-free way to teach kids fiscal responsibility. In addition, employers who are using payroll cards as an extension of their direct deposit programs are driving the growth of the prepaid, preloaded card market. Like direct deposit, payroll cards can reduce administrative overhead substantially. Payroll cards are especially useful to companies in the health-care, retail, and other industries where the workforce is part time or transient and less likely to have bank accounts.

Section 11.4 ▶ REVIEW QUESTIONS

1. What is a closed-loop stored-value card? What is an open-loop card?
2. What are the major markets for stored-value cards?

11.5 E-MICROPAYMENTS

Consider the following online shopping scenarios:

▶ A customer goes to an online music store and purchases a single song that costs $0.99.

▶ A person goes online to a leading newspaper or news journal (such as *Forbes* or *BusinessWeek*) and purchases (downloads) a copy of an archived news article for $1.50.

▶ A person goes to an online gaming company, selects a game, and plays it for 30 minutes. The person owes the company $3 for the playing time.

▶ A person goes to a Web site selling digital images and clip art. The person purchases a couple of images at a cost of $0.80.

These are all examples of **e-micropayments**, which are small online payments, usually under $5. From the viewpoint of many vendors, credit and debit cards do not work well for such small payments. Vendors who accept credit cards typically must pay a minimum transaction fee that ranges from $0.25 to $0.35, plus 2 to 3 percent of the purchase price. The same is true for debit cards, where the fixed transaction fees are higher even though there are no percentage charges. These fees are relatively insignificant for card purchases over $5, but can be cost-prohibitive for smaller transactions. Even if the transaction costs were less onerous, a substantial percentage of micropayment purchases are made by individuals younger than 18, many of whom do not have credit or debit cards.

e-micropayments
Small online payments, typically under $5.

Regardless of the vendor's point of view, there is substantial evidence, at least in the offline world, that consumers are willing to use their credit or debit cards for purchases under $5. A random sample telephone survey conducted in 2006 by Ipsos Insight and Peppercoin, an e-micropayment company that recently folded, examined consumers' spending habits for low-priced items (Ipsos Insight 2006). Based on the survey, more than 67 million Americans had used their credit cards in the 30 days prior to the survey to purchase items priced at $5 or less. For the most part, these purchases were made at convenience stores, at quick-service restaurants, to buy coffee, or for subway or other transportation tolls.

In the online world, evidence suggests that consumers are interested in making small-value purchases, but the tie to credit or debit card payments is less direct. For example, in February of 2006 Apple's iTunes music store celebrated its billionth download. A substantial percentage of these were downloads of single songs at $0.99 a piece. Although most of iTunes' customers paid for these downloads with a credit or debit card, the payments were not on a per-transaction basis. Instead, iTunes customers set up accounts. iTunes bundles each customer's purchases, which are then paid through the account. Other areas where consumers have shown a willingness to purchase items under $5 are cellular ringtones and online games. Figures from Jupiter Research indicate that in the United States alone the cellular ringtone market eclipsed $217 million in 2004 and will grow to $724 million by 2009 (CNET 2005). Ringtone downloads are charged to the consumer's cell phone bill. Similarly, Jupiter estimated that the mobile game market in the United States will grow to $430 million by 2009. Like the download of songs, the download of a game is usually charged to the consumer's account, which is, in turn, paid by credit or debit card.

As far back as 2000, a number of companies have attempted to address the perceived market opportunity by providing e-micropayment solutions that circumvent the fees associated with credit and debit cards. For the most part, the history of these companies is one of unfulfilled promises and outright failure. Digicash, First Virtual, Cybercoin, Millicent, and Internet Dollar are just a few of the e-micropayment companies that went bankrupt during the dot-com crash. A number of factors played a role in their demise, including the fact that early users of the Internet thought that digital content should be free. More recently, Bitpass declared on January 2007 that they were going out of business. As late as fall 2006, Bitpass launched a digital wallet service that enabled consumers to store online downloads of digital content and the payment method used to fund their accounts (i.e., credit cards, PayPal, or automated clearing house debits). Bitpass succeeded in partnering with a large number of smaller vendors, as well as a number of larger companies, such as Disney Online and ABC, Inc. However, it purposely focused on the sale of digital content rather than branching out into other markets. This narrow focus was probably a major factor in its demise.

Currently, there are five basic micropayment models that do not depend solely or directly on credit or debit cards and that have enjoyed some amount of success. Some of them are better suited for offline payments than online payments, although there is nothing that precludes the application of any of the models to the online world. The models include (D'Agostino 2006):

▶ **Aggregation.** Payments from a single consumer are batched together and processed only after a certain time period has expired (20 business days) or a certain monetary threshold (e.g., $10) is reached. This is the model used by Apple's iTunes. This model is well suited for vendors with a lot of repeat business.

▶ **Direct payment.** Micropayments are added to a monthly bill for existing services, such as a cell phone bill. This is the model used by the cell phone companies for ringtone downloads. The payment service provider PaymentOne (paymentone.com) provides a network and e-commerce platform that enables consumers to add purchases of any size to their phone bills.

▶ **Stored value.** Upfront payments are made to a debit account from which purchases are deducted as they are made. Offline vendors (e.g., Starbucks) often use this model, and music download services use variants of this model.

▶ **Subscriptions.** Single payment covers access to content for a defined period of time. Online gaming companies often use this model, and a number of online newspapers and journals (e.g., *Wall Street Journal*) also use it.

▶ **Á la carte.** Vendors process purchases as they occur and rely on the volume of purchases to negotiate lower credit and debit card processing fees. GoldenTee Golf video game uses this model, and quick-service restaurants (QSRs), such as McDonald's and Wendy's, also use it.

In the past few years, micropayments have come to represent a growth opportunity for the credit card companies because credit cards are increasingly being used as a substitute for cash. In response, both Visa and MasterCard have lowered their fees, especially for vendors with high transaction volumes, such as McDonald's. In August 2005, PayPal also entered the micropayment market when it announced a new alternative fee structure of 5 percent plus $0.05 per transaction. This is in contrast to its standard fees of 1.9 to 2.9 percent plus $0.30 per transaction. If a PayPal vendor is being charged at a rate of 1.9 percent plus $0.30, then the alternative fee of 5 percent plus $0.05 will be cheaper for any item that costs $7 or less (you can do the math). It is $12 or less for 2.9 percent, plus the $0.30 rate. Overall, the movement of the credit card companies and PayPal into the micropayment market does not bode well for those companies that provide specialized software and services for e-micropayments. In the long run, the credit card companies and PayPal will dominate this market.

Section 11.5 ▶ REVIEW QUESTIONS

1. What is a micropayment?
2. List some of the situations where e-micropayments can be used.
3. Outside of using credit or debit cards, what are some of the alternative ways that an online merchant can handle micropayments?

11.6 E-CHECKING

As noted in Section 11.1, in the United States paper checks are the only payment instrument that is being used less frequently now than 5 years ago (Simon 2007). In 2003, checks represented 45 percent of all non-cash payments, down from 57 percent in 2000. In contrast, e-check usage is growing rapidly. In 2004, the use of online e-checks grew by 40 percent over the previous year, reaching 968 million transactions. Based on a CyberSource survey (2005) of Web merchants, this percentage will continue to grow. Web merchants hope that e-checks will raise sales by reaching consumers who do not have credit cards or who are unwilling to provide credit card numbers online. According to CyberSource, online merchants that implement e-checks experience a 3 percent to 8 percent increase in sales on the average.

An **e-check** is the electronic version or representation of a paper check. E-checks contain the same information as a paper check, can be used wherever paper checks are used, and are based on the same legal framework. E-checks work essentially the same way a paper check works, but in pure electronic form with fewer manual steps. With an online e-check purchase, the buyer simply provides the merchant with his or her account number, the nine-digit bank ABA routing number, the bank account type, the name on the bank account, and the transaction amount. The account number and routing number are found at the bottom of the check in the *magnetic ink character recognition (MICR)* numbers and characters.

E-checks rely on current business and banking practices and can be used by any business that has a checking account, including small and midsize businesses that may not be able to afford other forms of electronic payments (e.g., credit and debit cards). E-checks or their equivalents also can be used with in-person purchases. In this case, the merchant takes a paper check from the buyer at the point of purchase, uses the MICR information and the check number to complete the transaction, and then voids and returns the check to the buyer (see Case 11.2 for a complete description of the process).

e-check
A legally valid electronic version or representation of a paper check.

CASE 11.2
EC Application

TO POP OR BOC: DIGITAL CHECKS IN THE OFFLINE WORLD

The use of e-checks is growing in the online world. Paradoxically, the same is true in the offline world, although it is occurring at a slower rate. In the near future, the rate of adoption in the offline world is likely to hasten. First, evidence suggests that the use of a special NACHA system known as Purchase Order Processing (POP) is on the uptake. Second, another NACHA system called Back-Office Order Conversion (BOC) will become effective March 2007. With both systems, merchants convert checks written by consumers into the equivalent of e-checks and process them as ACH debits. The difference between the two systems is whether the check is converted at the POS by a cashier or converted after the sale by other staff in the back office.

The traditional processes used in handling paper checks written by consumers to make purchases in a store involve a number of steps and intermediaries (as many as 28). At a minimum, the checks taken by cashiers are collected periodically throughout the day. After collection, back-office personnel process them. Once this is done, an armored car usually takes them from the store and delivers them to the store's bank. The store's bank processes them and sends them to a clearing house. From the clearing house, they

(continued)

CASE 11.2 (continued)

move to the customer's bank. Not only is this time consuming, but it is also costly. Statistics show that it costs companies $1.25 to $1.55 to handle a paper check. This is in comparison to the administrative costs for an e-check, which can be as low as $0.10 per transaction. Based on these figures, every company stands to save a substantial amount of money by streamlining these traditional processes. This is where POP and BOC come into play.

The Gap, Wal-Mart, Old Navy, and KB Toys are some of the companies that have instituted POP. With POP, consumer checks are converted to ACH transactions at the time of the sale. When a customer writes a check for a purchase at a POS device, an MICR reader scans the check to capture the check details. The reader either keys or inserts the payment amount and the payee name at the time of purchase. At this point, the customer signs a written authorization. The cashier then voids the check and returns it to the customer with a signed receipt. Eligible transactions pass through the ACH system, and a record of payment appears on the customer's bank statement.

POP has a number of benefits:

▶ Back-office and check-handling costs are substantially reduced.
▶ Consumer payments are received more quickly.
▶ Availability of funds is improved.
▶ Notification of insufficient funds happens sooner.

Although POP saves money, it also has a number of costs. According to Hughes and Edwards (2006), critics of POP raise the following objections:

▶ It requires specialized readers for each checkout counter.
▶ Cashiers need special training to convert the checks to ACH transactions at the POS.
▶ The authorization process can be cumbersome and confusing to consumers.
▶ It slows the purchase process.

For these reasons, critics state that BOC is a better alternative for the average merchant.

With BOC, the customer experience is similar to the traditional process (Daly 2006). The customer writes a check for a purchase. The clerk either accepts or rejects the check after the merchant's verification service or guarantee provider verifies it.

This does not require explicit customer authorization to convert the check to an electronic form. Once the checks are collected and moved to the back office, they are scanned into an ACH file and processed electronically. In this way, a merchant only needs one or two scanners and a few personnel to handle the process.

Best Buy is one of the better known retailers piloting BOC. The pilot is based on a "digital payment processing" solution called PayBack from FIS Risk Management and Analytics (*Chain Store Age* 2006). The solution eliminates all manual check deposits. PayBack provides the facilities required to convert a check to a form of electronic settlement, to create and maintain images of the check, to generate an electronic deposit file, and to submit it to a financial institution. None of these processes require specialized equipment at the POS. Best Buy probably will move the pilot to production when BOC becomes official in 2007, because the project is part of a larger risk management process, which FIS has handled for Best Buy for the past 18 years.

Sources: *Chain Store Age* (2006), Hughes and Edwards (2006), and Daly (2006).

Questions

1. What does POP stand for and how does it work?
2. What does BOC stand for and how does it work?
3. What are the advantages and disadvantages of POP?

Most businesses rely on third-party software to handle e-check payments. CheckFree (checkfreecorp.com), Telecheck (telecheck.com), AmeriNet (debit-it.com), Chase Paymentech (paymentech.com), and Authorize.Net (authorize.net) are some of the major vendors of software and systems that enable an online merchant to accept and process electronic checks directly from a Web site. For the most part, these software offerings work in the same way regardless of the vendor.

The system shown in Exhibit 11.3 is based on Authorize.Net and is typical of the underlying processes used to support e-checks. Basically, it is a seven-step process. First, the merchant receives written or electronic authorization from a customer to charge his or her bank account (step 1). Next, the merchant securely transmits the transaction information to the Authorize.Net Payment Gateway server (step 2). The transaction is accepted or rejected based on criteria defined by the Payment Gateway. If accepted, Authorize.Net formats the transaction information and sends it as an Automated Clearing House (ACH) transaction

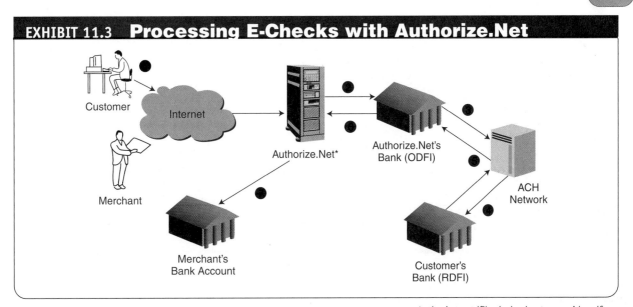

EXHIBIT 11.3   Processing E-Checks with Authorize.Net

Source: Authorize.Net.® "eCheck.Net® Operating Procedures and Users Guide," October 28, 2004. *Authorize.net/files/echecknetuserguide.pdf.* Copyright 2004. Authorize.Net and eCheck.Net are registered trademarks of Lightbridge, Inc.

to its bank (called the Originating Depository Financial Institution, or ODFI) with the rest of the transactions received that day (step 3). The ODFI receives transaction information and passes it to the ACH Network for settlement. The ACH Network uses the bank account information provided with the transaction to determine the bank that holds the customer's account (which is known as the Receiving Depository Financial Institution, or RDFI) (step 4). The ACH Network instructs the RDFI to charge or refund the customer's account (the customer is the receiver). The RDFI passes funds from the customer's account to the ACH Network (step 5). The ACH Network relays the funds to the ODFI (Authorize.Net's bank). The ODFI passes any returns to Authorize.Net (step 6). After the funds' holding period, Authorize.Net initiates a separate ACH transaction to deposit the e-check proceeds into the merchant's bank account (step 7).

As Exhibit 11.3 illustrates, the processing of e-checks in the United States relies quite heavily on the **Automated Clearing House (ACH) Network**. The ACH Network is a nationwide batch-oriented electronic funds transfer (EFT) system that provides for the interbank clearing of electronic payments for participating financial institutions. The Federal Reserve and Electronic Payments Network act as ACH operators, which transmit and receive ACH payment entries. ACH entries are of two sorts: credit and debit. An ACH credit entry credits a receiver's account. For example, when a consumer pays a bill sent by a company, the company is the receiver whose account is credited. In contrast, a debit entry debits a receiver's account. For instance, if a consumer preauthorizes a payment to a company, then the consumer is the receiver whose account is debited. In 2006, the ACH Network handled an estimated 15 billion transactions worth $30 trillion (Herd 2007). The vast majority of these were direct payment and deposit entries (e.g., direct deposit payroll). Only 1.8 billion of these entries were Web based, although this represented a 30 percent increase from 2005 to 2006.

E-check processing provides a number of benefits:

▶ It reduces the merchant's administrative costs by providing faster and less paper-intensive collection of funds.

▶ It improves the efficiency of the deposit process for merchants and financial institutions.

Automated Clearing House (ACH) Network
A nationwide batch-oriented electronic funds transfer system that provides for the interbank clearing of electronic payments for participating financial institutions.

▶ It speeds the checkout process for consumers.

▶ It provides consumers with more information about their purchases on their account statements.

▶ It reduces the float period and the number of checks that bounce because of insufficient funds (NSFs).

Section 11.6 ▶ REVIEW QUESTIONS

1. What is an e-check?

2. Briefly describe how third-party e-check payment systems work.

3. What is the ACH?

4. List the benefits of e-checking.

11.7 B2B ELECTRONIC PAYMENTS

B2B payments usually are much larger and significantly more complex than the payments made by individual consumers. The dollar values often are in the hundreds of thousands, the purchases and payments involve multiple items and shipments, and the exchanges are much more likely to engender disputes that require significant work to resolve. Simple e-billing or electronic bill presentment and payment EBPP systems lack the rigor and security to handle these B2B situations. This section examines the processes by which companies present invoices and make payments to one another over the Internet.

CURRENT B2B PAYMENT PRACTICES

B2B payments are part of a much larger financial supply chain that includes procurement, contract administration, fulfillment, financing, insurance, credit ratings, shipment validation, order matching, payment authorization, remittance matching, and general ledger accounting. From a buyer's perspective, the chain encompasses the procurement-to-payment process. From the seller's perspective, the chain involves the order-to-cash cycle. Regardless of the perspective, in financial supply chain management the goal is to optimize accounts payable (A/P) and accounts receivable (A/R), cash management, working capital, transaction costs, financial risks, and financial administration.

Unlike the larger (physical) supply chain, inefficiencies still characterize the financial supply chains of most companies. A number of factors create these inefficiencies, including (Barnhart 2004):

▶ The time required to create, transfer, and process paper documentation

▶ The cost and errors associated with manual creation and reconciliation of documentation

▶ The lack of transparency in inventory and cash positions when goods are in the supply chain

▶ Disputes arising from inaccurate or missing data

▶ Fragmented point solutions that do not address the complete end-to-end processes of the trade cycle

These inefficiencies are evident especially with A/P and A/R processes where payments are still made with paper.

Based on a survey of 375 members of the Association for Financial Professionals (2007) and a comparison of the 2007 results with those from 2004, it appears that B2B payment mechanisms have been slow to change. Approximately 80 percent of B2B payments are still made by check, and the barriers to electronic payments remain essentially the same—IT and constraints posed by the difficulty of integrating various systems, the inability of trading partners to send and receive automated remittance information, and the difficulty in convincing customers and suppliers to adopt electronic payments. However, some evidence suggests that companies are beginning to move to B2B e-payments. As the survey results noted, over 40 percent of the members expect to convert the majority of their B2B payments from checks to e-payments in the next 3 years.

ENTERPRISE INVOICE PRESENTMENT AND PAYMENT

The process by which companies present invoices and make payments to one another through the Internet is known as **enterprise invoice presentment and payment (EIPP)**. For many firms, presentment and payment are costly and time consuming. It can cost up to $15 to generate a paper invoice and between $25 and $50 to resolve a disputed invoice. On the payment side, it takes 3 to 5 days for a check to arrive by mail. This means that millions of dollars of B2B payments are tied up in floats. This reduces the recipients' cash flow and increases the amount they must borrow to cover the float. In the same vein, manual billing and remittance can result in errors, which in turn can result in disputes that hold up payments. Given that most firms handle thousands of invoices and payments yearly, any reduction in time, cost, or errors can result in millions of dollars of savings. According to a survey by Credit Research Foundation, the major reasons companies turn to EIPP solutions are improved cash flow, better customer service for billing and remittance, and cleaner data, which can lower invoice-processing costs (Lucas 2005).

enterprise invoice presentment and payment (EIPP)
Presenting and paying B2B invoices online.

EIPP Models

EIPP automates the workflow surrounding presentment and payment. Like EBPP, there are three EIPP models: seller direct, buyer direct, and consolidator.

Seller Direct. This solution links one seller to many buyers for invoice presentment. Buyers navigate to the seller's Web site to enroll in the seller's EIPP program. The seller generates invoices on the system and informs the appropriate buyers that they are ready for viewing. The buyers log into the seller's Web site to review and analyze the invoices. The buyers may authorize invoice payment or communicate any disputes. Based on predetermined rules, disputes may be accepted, rejected, or reviewed automatically. Once payment is authorized and made, the seller's financial institution processes the payment transaction.

This model typically is used when there are preestablished relationships between the seller and its buyers. If a seller issues a large number of invoices or the invoices have a high value, then there can be a substantial payoff from implementing an EIPP. For this reason, firms in the manufacturing, telecommunication, utilities, health-care, and financial services industries often use this model.

Buyer Direct. In this model, there is one buyer for many sellers. Sellers enroll in the buyer's EIPP system at the buyer's Web site. Sellers post invoices to the buyer's EIPP, using the buyer's format. Once an invoice is posted, the buyer's staff will be notified. The buyer reviews and analyzes the invoices on the system. The buyer communicates any disputes to the appropriate seller. Based on predetermined rules, disputes may be accepted, rejected, or reviewed automatically. Once an invoice is approved, the buyer will authorize payment, which the buyer's financial institution will process. This is an emerging model based on the buyer's dominant position in B2B transactions. Again, it is used when the buyer's purchases result in a high volume of invoices. Companies such as Wal-Mart are in a strong position to institute buyer-direct EIPPs.

Consolidator. This is a many-to-many model with the consolidator acting as an intermediary, collecting or aggregating invoices from multiple sellers and payments from multiple buyers. Consolidators are generally third parties who not only provide EIPP services, but also offer other financial services (e.g., insurance, escrow). In this model, the sellers and buyers register with the consolidator's EIPP system. The sellers generate and transfer invoice information to the EIPP system. The consolidator notifies the appropriate buyer organization that the invoice is ready. The buyer reviews and analyzes the invoice. Disputes are communicated through the consolidator EIPP. Based on predetermined rules, disputes may be accepted, rejected, or reviewed automatically. Once the buyer authorizes the invoice payment, the consolidator initiates the payment. Either the buyer's or the seller's financial institution processes the payment.

The consolidator model eliminates the hassles associated with implementing and running an EIPP. The model has gained ground in those industries where multiple buyers rely on the same suppliers. The Xign Payment Services Network (XPSN; xign.com) and the Global eXchange Services (GXS) Trading Grid (gxs.com) are both third-party consolidators, linking thousands of suppliers and buyers. XPSN had more than 42,000 active suppliers in its network, generating over $35 billion in transactions. GSX's Trading Grid supports online trading among 40,000 customers in over 60 countries, exchanging over 1 billion electronic transactions representing $1 trillion in goods and services. Each of these networks eliminates the need for point-to-point connections between suppliers and buyers; automates core functions of the A/P process, including invoice receipt, validation, routing, dispute management, approval, and payment; and complements and integrates with the suppliers' and buyers' existing purchasing and procurement systems.

EIPP Options

A variety of online options are available for making payments in an EIPP system. They differ in terms of cost, speed, auditability, accessibility, and control. The selection of a particular mechanism depends on the requirements of the buyers and sellers. Some frequently used B2B payment options follow.

ACH Network. The ACH Network is the same network that underlies the processing of e-checks (described in Section 11.6). The difference is that there are three types of B2B payments, which vary by the amount of remittance information that accompanies the payments. The remittance information enables a buyer or seller to examine the details of a particular invoice or payment. The three types of ACH entries for B2B transactions are: Cash Concentration or Disbursement (CCD), which is a simple payment, usually for a single invoice, that has no accompanying remittance data and is typically initiated by the buyer who credits the seller's account; Cash Concentration or Disbursement with Addenda (CCD +), which is the same as a CCD payment except that it has a small amount of remittance data (up to 80 characters); and Corporate Trade Exchange (CTX), which generally is used to pay multiple invoices and has a large amount of accompanying remittance data (up to a maximum of 9,999 records of 80 characters each).

The ACH Network does not require any special hardware. The cost of the software needed to initiate ACH transactions depends on the volume of CTX transactions. High volumes of CTX transactions require a much larger investment. In addition to hardware and software costs, the buyer's and the seller's financial institutions also charge file, maintenance, transaction, and exception-handling fees for ACH transactions.

Purchasing Cards. Although credit cards are the instrument of choice for B2C payments, this is not the case in the B2B marketplace. In the B2B marketplace, the major credit card companies and associations have encouraged businesses and government agencies to rely on *purchasing cards* instead of checks for repetitive, low-value transactions. **Purchasing cards (p-cards)** are special-purpose payment cards issued to a company's employees. They are used solely for the purpose of paying for nonstrategic materials and services (e.g., stationery, office supplies, computer supplies, repair and maintenance services, courier services, and temporary labor services) up to a limit (usually $1,000 to $2,000). These purchases often represent the majority of a company's payments but only a small percentage of the dollars spent. Purchasing cards operate essentially the same as any other charge card and are used for both offline and online purchases. The major difference between a credit card and a purchase card is that the latter is a nonrevolving account, meaning that it needs to be paid in full each month, usually within 5 days of the end of the billing period.

> **purchasing cards (p-cards)**
> Special-purpose payment cards issued to a company's employees to be used solely for purchasing nonstrategic materials and services up to a preset dollar limit.

Purchasing cards enable a company or government agency to consolidate the purchases of multiple cardholders into a single account and, thus, issue a single invoice that can be paid through EDI, EFT, or an e-check. This has the benefit of freeing the purchasing department from day-to-day procurement activities and from the need to deal with the reconciliation of individual invoices. With a single invoice, accounts can be settled more quickly, enabling a company or agency to take advantage of discounts associated with faster payment. A single invoice also enables a company or agency to more easily analyze the spending behavior of the cardholders. Finally, the spending limits make it easier to control unplanned purchases. Some estimates suggest that efficiencies resulting from the use of purchasing cards can reduce transaction costs from 50 percent to 90 percent. To learn more about purchasing cards, see the National Association of Purchasing Card Professionals (napcp.org).

Fedwire. Among the forms of online B2B payments, Fedwire is second only to ACH in terms of frequency of use. Fedwire, also known as *wire transfer*, is a funds transfer system developed and maintained by the U.S. Federal Reserve system. It typically is used with larger dollar payments where time is the critical element. The settlement of real estate transactions, the purchase of securities, and the repayment of loans are all examples of situations where Fedwire is likely to be used. When Fedwire is used, a designated Federal Reserve Bank debits the buyer's bank account and sends a transfer order to the seller's Federal Reserve Bank, which credits the seller's account. All Fedwire payments are immediate and irrevocable.

Letters of Credit for Global Payments. Letters of credit often are used when global B2B payments need to be made, especially when there is substantial risk associated with the payment. A **letter of credit (L/C)**, also called a *documentary credit*, is issued by a bank on behalf of a buyer (importer). It guarantees a seller (exporter) that payment for goods or services will be made, provided the terms of the L/C are met. Before the credit is issued, the buyer and seller agree on all terms and conditions in a purchase and sale contract. The buying company then instructs its bank to issue a documentary credit in

> **letter of credit (L/C)**
> A written agreement by a bank to pay the seller, on account of the buyer, a sum of money upon presentation of certain documents.

accordance with the contract. A credit can be payable at sight or at term. *At sight* means that payment is due upon presentation of documents after shipment of the goods or after a service is provided. Alternatively, if the seller allows the buyer an additional period, after presentation of documents, to pay the credit (30, 60, 90 days, etc.), then the credit is payable *at term*. L/C arrangements usually involve a series of steps that can be conducted much faster online than offline. The Real-World Case at the end of the chapter and Online File W11.3 describe the benefits of replacing L/Cs with online payments.

For sellers the main benefit of an L/C is reduced risk—the bank assures the creditworthiness of the buyer. For those global situations where the buyer is a resident in a country with political or financial instability, the risk can be reduced if the L/C is confirmed by a bank in the seller's country. Reduced risk also is of benefit to buyers who may use this fact to negotiate lower prices.

Section 11.7 ▶ REVIEW QUESTIONS

1. Describe the financial supply chain.
2. Describe the current state of B2B e-payments.
3. What is electronic invoice presentment and payment (EIPP)?
4. Describe the three models of EIPP.
5. Describe the basic EIPP options.
6. What is a purchasing card?

11.8 ORDER FULFILLMENT AND LOGISTICS—AN OVERVIEW

Taking orders over the Internet could well be the easy part of B2C. Fulfillment and delivery to customers' doors are the tricky parts (e.g., see Vitasek and Manrodt 2006). Many e-tailers have experienced fulfillment problems, especially during the 1990s. Amazon.com, for example, which initially operated as a totally virtual company, added physical warehouses with thousands of employees in order to expedite deliveries and reduce order fulfillment costs.

Deliveries may be delayed for several reasons. These range from an inability to accurately forecast demand to ineffective e-tailing supply chains. Many of the same problems affect offline businesses. One issue typical to EC is that EC is based on the concept of "pull" operations that begin with an order, frequently a customized one. This is in contrast with traditional retailing, which usually begins with a production to inventory that is then "pushed" to customers. In the EC pull case, it is more difficult to forecast demand because of lack of experience and changing consumer tastes. Another reason for delays is that in a B2C pull model, many small orders need to be delivered to the customers' doors, whereas in brick-and-mortar retailing, the goods are shipped in large quantities to retail stores where customers pick them up.

Before we analyze the order fulfillment problems and describe some solutions, we need to introduce some basic order fulfillment and logistics concepts.

OVERVIEW OF ORDER FULFILLMENT

order fulfillment
All the activities needed to provide customers with their ordered goods and services, including related customer services.

Order fulfillment refers not only to providing customers with what they have ordered and doing so on time but also to providing all related customer services. For example, a customer must receive assembly and operation instructions with a new appliance. This can be done by including a paper document with the product or by providing the instructions on the Web. In addition, if the customer is dissatisfied with a product, an exchange or return must be arranged.

Order fulfillment involves **back-office operations**, which are the activities that support the fulfillment of orders, such as packing, delivery, accounting, and logistics not limited to inventory management and shipping. It also is strongly related to the **front-office operations**, or *customer-facing activities*, such as advertising and order taking, that are visible to customers.

OVERVIEW OF LOGISTICS

The Council of Supply Chain Management Professionals defines **logistics** as "the process of planning, implementing, and controlling the efficient and effective flow and storage of goods, services, and related information from point of origin to point of consumption for the purpose of conforming to customer requirements" (Council of Supply Chain Management Professionals 2008). Note that this definition includes inbound, outbound, internal, and external movement and the return of materials and goods. It also includes *order fulfillment*. However, the distinction between logistics and order fulfillment is not always clear, and the terms are sometimes used interchangeably, as we do in this text.

The key aspects of order fulfillment are delivery of materials or services at the right time, to the right place, and at the right cost.

THE EC ORDER FULFILLMENT PROCESS

In order to understand why there are problems in order fulfillment, it is beneficial to look at a typical EC fulfillment process, as shown in Exhibit 11.4. The process starts on the left, when an order is received and after verification that it is a real order. Several activities take place, some of which can be done simultaneously; others must be done in sequence. These activities include the following steps:

▶ **Step 1: Making sure the customer will pay.** Depending on the payment method and prior arrangements, the validity of each payment must be determined. In B2B, the company's finance department or financial institution (i.e., a bank or a credit card issuer, such as Visa) may do this. Any holdup may cause a shipment to be delayed, resulting in a loss of goodwill or a customer. In B2C, the customers usually prepay, frequently by credit card.

▶ **Step 2: Checking for in-stock availability.** Regardless of whether the seller is a manufacturer or a retailer, as soon as an order is received an inquiry needs to be made regarding stock availability. Several scenarios are possible here that may involve the material management and production departments, as well as outside suppliers and warehouse facilities. In this step, the order information needs to be connected to the information about in-stock inventory availability.

▶ **Step 3: Arranging shipments.** If the product is available, it can be shipped to the customer right away (otherwise, go to step 5). Products can be digital or physical. If the item is physical and it is readily available, packaging and shipment arrangements need to be made. It may involve both the packaging and shipping department and internal shippers or outside transporters. Digital items are usually available because their "inventory" is not depleted. However, a digital product, such as software, may be under revision and unavailable for delivery at certain times. In either case, information needs to flow among several partners.

back-office operations
The activities that support fulfillment of orders, such as packing, delivery, accounting, inventory management, and shipping.

front-office operations
The business processes, such as sales and advertising, that are visible to customers.

logistics
The operations involved in the efficient and effective flow and storage of goods, services, and related information from point of origin to point of consumption.

EXHIBIT 11.4   Order Fulfillment and the Logistics System

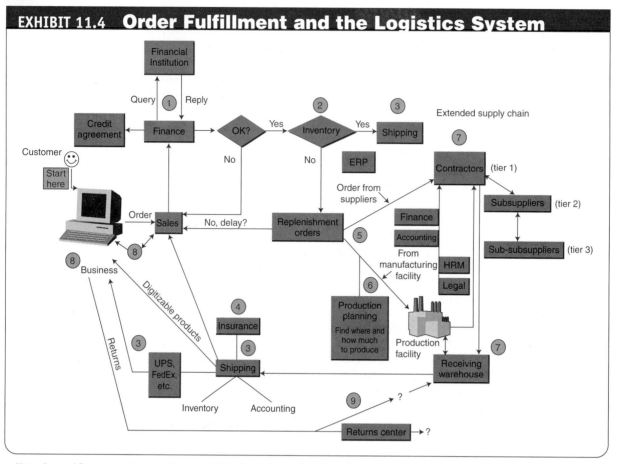

Note: Demand forecasts and accounting are conducted at various points throughout the process.

▶ **Step 4: Insurance.** Sometimes the contents of a shipment need to be insured. This could involve both the finance department and an insurance company. Again, information needs to flow, not only inside the company, but also to and from the customer and insurance agent.

▶ **Step 5: Replenishment.** Customized orders will always trigger a need for some manufacturing or assembly operation. Similarly, if standard items are out of stock, they need to be produced or procured. Production can be done in-house or by contractors. The suppliers involved may have their own suppliers (subsuppliers or tier-2 suppliers).

▶ **Step 6: In-house production.** In-house production needs to be planned. Production planning involves people, materials, components, machines, financial resources, and possibly suppliers and subcontractors. In the case of assembly, manufacturing, or both, several plant services may be needed, including possible collaboration with business partners. Services may include scheduling of people and equipment, shifting other products' plans, working with engineering on modifications, getting equipment, and preparing content. The actual production facilities may be in a different country than the company's headquarters or retailers. This can further complicate the flow of information and communication.

▶ **Step 7: Use contractors.** A manufacturer may opt to buy products or subassemblies from contractors. Similarly, if the seller is a retailer, such as in the case of amazon.com or walmart.com, the retailer must purchase products from its manufacturers. Several scenarios are possible. Warehouses can stock purchased items, which is what Amazon.com does with its best-selling books, toys, and other commodity items. However, Amazon.com does not stock books for which it receives only a few orders. In such cases, the publishers or intermediaries must make the special deliveries. In either case, appropriate receiving and quality assurance of incoming materials and products must take place.

Once production (step 6) or purchasing from suppliers (step 7) is completed, shipments to the customers (step 3) are arranged.

▶ **Step 8: Contacts with customers.** Sales representatives need to keep in constant contact with customers, especially in B2B, starting with notification of orders received and ending with notification of a shipment or a change in delivery date. These contacts are usually done via e-mail and are frequently generated automatically.

▶ **Step 9: Returns.** In some cases, customers want to exchange or return items. Such returns can be a major problem; more than $100 billion in North American goods are returned each year (Kuzeljevich 2004). Returns cost UK retailers approximately $1.4 billion a year (Boles 2004). The movement of returns from customers back to vendors is called **reverse logistics**.

reverse logistics
The movement of returns from customers to vendors.

Order fulfillment processes may vary, depending on the product and the vendor. The order fulfillment process also differs between B2B and B2C activities, between the delivery of goods and of services, and between small and large products. Furthermore, certain circumstances, such as in the case of perishable materials or foods, require additional steps.

Such a complex process may have problems (Section 11.9); automating the various steps can minimize or eliminate several of these problems.

Order Fulfillment and the Supply Chain

The nine-step order fulfillment process previously described, as well as order taking, are integral parts of the *supply chain*. The flows of orders, payments, information, materials, and parts need to be coordinated among all the company's internal participants, as well as with and among external partners (see Kelsall 2006). The principles of supply chain management must be considered when planning and managing the order fulfillment process.

Traditional Versus EC Logistics

EC logistics, or **e-logistics**, refers to the logistics of EC systems mainly in B2C. The major difference between e-logistics and traditional logistics is that the latter deals with the movement of large amounts of materials to a few destinations (e.g., to retail stores). E-logistics shipments typically are small parcels sent to many customers' homes. Other differences are shown in Exhibit 11.5.

e-logistics
The logistics of EC systems, typically involving small parcels sent to many customers' homes (in B2C).

Section 11.8 ▶ REVIEW QUESTIONS

1. Define order fulfillment and logistics.
2. List the nine steps of the order fulfillment process.
3. Compare logistics with reverse logistics.
4. Compare traditional logistics with e-logistics.

EXHIBIT 11.5   How E-Logistics Differs from Traditional Logistics

Characteristic	Traditional Logistics	EC Logistics
Type, quantity	Bulk, large volume	Small, parcels
Destinations	Few	Large number, highly dispersed
Demand type	Push	Pull
Value of shipment	Very large, usually more than $1,000	Very small, frequently less than $50
Nature of demand	Stable, consistent	Seasonal (holiday season), fragmented
Customers	Business partners (in B2B), usually repeat customers (B2C), not many	Usually unknown in B2C, many
Inventory order flow	Usually unidirectional, from manufacturers	Usually bidirectional
Accountability	One link	Through the entire supply chain
Transporter	Frequently the company, sometimes outsourced	Usually outsourced, sometimes the company
Warehouse	Common	Only very large shippers (e.g., *amazon.com*) operate their own

11.9   ADDRESSING PROBLEMS IN ORDER FULFILLMENT

Even supply chain experts such as Amazon.com can experience problems with order fulfillment. As the opening EC application noted, Amazon.com introduced its Kindle e-book reader during the 2007 holiday season. Within a short period of time, demand for the $399 reader far outpaced forecasts and the device quickly sold out. Well after the season was over, the device remained backordered. Part of the problem was due to the inability of one of Amazon's key parts suppliers, Prime View International (pvi.com.tw/index_en.php), to manufacture displays fast enough to meet consumer demand (Kuo 2008). Obviously, the overall result for Amazon.com was lost sales.

TYPICAL SUPPLY CHAIN PROBLEMS

Amazon.com's fulfillment problems are typical of those experienced in both offline and online commerce. First, *demand forecasting* is difficult. In the case of standard or commodity items, such as toys, a demand forecast must be done in order to determine appropriate inventories of finished goods at various points in the supply chain. In the case of customized products, it is necessary to forecast the demand for the components and materials required for fulfilling customized orders. Difficulties arise from a number of factors. Factors such as consumer behavior, economic conditions, competition, prices, weather conditions, technological developments, and consumer taste and confidence influence demand. Any one of these factors can change quickly. This means that the demand forecast needs to be adjusted frequently based on inputs from all the manufacturers and suppliers along the supply chain in order to correctly gauge and meet the real demand.

Second, many of the problems along the EC supply chain stem from the need to *coordinate* several activities, internal units, and business partners in the face of uncertainties. Some of these uncertainties include variable delivery times created by factors ranging from machine failures, to poor road conditions, to quality problems of materials and parts, all of which add up to production or delivery delays.

The chance that such problems will occur in EC is even higher due to the lack of appropriate infrastructure and e-tailing experience, as well as the special characteristics of EC. For example, most manufacturers' and distributors' warehouses are designed to ship large quantities to several stores; they cannot optimally pack and ship many small packages to many customers' doors. Improper inventory levels are typical in EC, as are poor delivery scheduling and mixed-up shipments. Pure EC companies are likely to have more problems because they do not have a logistics infrastructure already in place and are forced to use external logistics services rather than in-house departments for these functions. These external logistics services are called **third-party logistics suppliers (3PL)**, or *logistics service providers*. Outsourcing such services can be expensive, and it requires more coordination and dependence on outsiders who may not be reliable. For this reason, many large virtual retailers are following Amazon.com's lead and have or are developing their own physical warehouses and logistics systems. Other virtual retailers are creating strategic alliances with logistics companies or with experienced mail-order companies that have their own logistics systems.

third-party logistics suppliers (3PL)
External, rather than in-house, providers of logistics services.

SOLUTIONS TO ORDER FULFILLMENT PROBLEMS

Many EC logistics problems are generic; they can be found in the non-Internet world as well. Therefore, many of the solutions that have been developed for these problems in brick-and-mortar companies also work for e-tailers. This section describes some of the specific solutions to the EC order fulfillment problems (Hett and Davis, 2006).

IMPROVEMENTS IN THE ORDER-TAKING PROCESS

One way to improve order fulfillment is to improve the order-taking process and its links to fulfillment and logistics. Order taking can be done via EDI, EDI/Internet, the Internet, or an extranet, and it may be fully automated. For example, in B2B, orders can be generated and transmitted automatically to suppliers when inventory levels fall below a certain threshold. The result is a fast, inexpensive, and more accurate (no need to rekey data) order-taking process. In B2C, Web-based ordering using electronic forms expedites the process, makes the process more accurate (e.g., intelligent agents can check the input data and provide instant feedback), and reduces processing costs for sellers. When EC order taking can interface or integrate with a company's back-office system, it shortens cycle times and eliminates errors.

Order-taking improvements also can take place *within* an organization, for example, when a manufacturer orders parts from its own warehouse. Whenever delivery of such parts runs smoothly, it minimizes disruptions to the manufacturing process, reducing losses from downtime. For example, as detailed in the Online File W11.4, Dell has improved the flow of parts in its PC repair operations, resulting in greater efficiency and cost savings.

Implementing linkages between order-taking and payment systems also can be helpful in improving order fulfillment. Electronic payments can expedite both the order fulfillment cycle and the payment delivery period. With such systems, payment processing can be significantly less expensive and fraud can be better controlled.

WAREHOUSING AND INVENTORY MANAGEMENT IMPROVEMENTS

A popular EC inventory management solution is a **warehouse management system (WMS)**. WMS refers to a software system that helps in managing warehouses. It has several components. For example, in the case of Amazon.com the system supports item

warehouse management system (WMS)
A software system that helps in managing warehouses.

pickers as well as packaging. Amazon.com's B2C WMS can handle hundreds of millions of packages. Manhattan (manhattan.com), RedPrairie (redprairie.com), and High Jump (highjumpsoftware.com) are leaders in the WMS market space. Case 11.3 illustrates how one company, Schurman Fine Paper, has utilized its WMS to improve demand forecasting and inventory management.

Other Inventory Management Improvements

WMS is useful in reducing inventory and decreasing the incidence of out-of-stocks. Such systems also are useful in maintaining an inventory of repair items so repairs can be expedited (e.g., Dell, see Online File W11.4); picking items out of inventory in the warehouse; communicating; managing product inventory; receiving items at the warehouse; and automating the warehouse (e.g., Amazon.com). For example, introducing a make-to-order (pull) production process and providing fast and accurate demand information to suppliers can minimize inventories. Allowing business partners to electronically

---

CASE 11.3
EC Application

HOW WMS HELPS SCHURMAN IMPROVE ITS INTERNAL AND EXTERNAL ORDER FULFILLMENT SYSTEM

Schurman Fine Paper (now *papyrusonline.com*) is a manufacturer and retailer of greeting cards and related products. It sells through its own 170 specialty stores (Papyrus), as well as through 30,000 independent retail outlets.

Using integrated logistics software solutions from RedPrairie (*redprairie.com*), Schurman improved its demand forecast and minimized both out-of-stocks and overstocking. The system also allows physical inventory counts to be conducted without the need to shut down the two central warehouses for a week three times a year.

The central warehouses receive shipments from about 200 suppliers worldwide (500 to 1,000 orders per day). Until 2003, all inventory and logistics management was done manually. One problem solved by the software is picking products from multiple stock-keeping-unit (SKU) locations. Picking is faster now, with a minimum of errors.

Customers' orders go directly from the EDI to shipping, which ignites the fulfillment and shipment process. This system automatically generates an advanced shipping notice (replacing the lengthy process of manual scanning). The new system also automates the task of assessing the length, width, height, and weight of each item before it goes into a box (to determine which item goes into what box). The system also improved inventory replenishment allocations. In the past, the list of items to be picked up included items not available in the primary location. Pickers wasted time looking for these items, and

unfound items had to be picked up later from the reserve storage center, resulting in delays. The WMS simultaneously created two lists, expediting fulfillment. This tripled the number of orders fulfilled per picker per day. The system also generates automatic replenishment orders for items falling below a minimum level at any storage location.

In addition, special software provides Schurman's customer service department with real-time access to inventory and distribution processes, allowing the department to track the status of all orders. The WMS also tracks the status of all orders and sends alerts when an order problem occurs (e.g., delay in downloading). An e-mail goes to all necessary parties in the company so they can fix the problem. Finally, information collected about problems can be analyzed so remedies can be made quickly. All of this helps to reduce both overstocks and out-of-stocks.

Sources: Compiled from Parks (2004), *papyrusonline.com* (accessed February 2008), Maloney (2006), and *redprairie.com* (accessed February 2008).

Questions

1. Identify what the WMS automates, both in receiving and shipping.

2. How has inventory management been improved?

track and monitor inventory levels and production activities can improve inventory management and inventory levels, as well as minimize the administrative expenses of inventory management. In some instances, the ultimate inventory improvement is to have no inventory at all; for products that can be digitized (e.g., software), order fulfillment can be instantaneous, eliminating the need for inventory.

Automated Warehouses

Large-volume EC fulfillment requires automated warehouses. Regular warehouses are built to deliver large quantities to a small number of stores and plants. In B2C, however, businesses need to send small quantities to a very large number of individuals. Automated warehouses can minimize the order fulfillment problems that arise from this need.

Automated warehouses may include robots and other devices that expedite the pick-up of products. An example of a company that uses such warehouses is Amazon.com.

The largest EC/mail-order warehouse in the United States is operated by a mail-order company, Fingerhut. This company handles its own order fulfillment process for mail orders and online orders, as well as orders for Wal-Mart, Macy's, and many others. Other companies (e.g., fosdickfulfillment.com) provide similar order fulfillment services. The keys to successful inventory management, in terms of order fulfillment, are efficiency and speed, which can be facilitated by wireless devices.

PARTNERING EFFORTS AND OUTSOURCING LOGISTICS

An effective way to solve order fulfillment problems is for an organization to partner with other companies. For example, several EC companies partner with UPS or FedEx. Logistics-related partnerships can take many forms. Another partnering example is marketplaces managed by forwarders.com and aacb.com, which help companies with goods find "forwarders"—the intermediaries that prepare goods for shipping. They also help forwarders find the best prices on air carriers, and the carriers bid to fill the space with forwarders' goods that need to be shipped.

SkyMall (skymall.com), now a subsidiary of Gem-Star TV Guide International, is a retailer that sells from catalogs on airplanes, over the Internet, and by mail order. It relies on its catalog partners to fill the orders. For small vendors that do not handle their own shipments and for international shipments, SkyMall contracts distribution centers owned by fulfillment outsourcer Sykes Enterprise. As orders come in, SkyMall conveys the data to the appropriate vendor or to a Sykes distribution center. A report is then sent to SkyMall.

Comprehensive Logistics Services

Major shippers, notably UPS and FedEx, offer comprehensive logistic services. These services are for B2C, B2B, G2B, and other types of EC. See Case 11.4 for a description of the broad EC services UPS offers.

SPEEDING DELIVERIES

In the digital age, the standard delivery services provided by companies such as FedEx and UPS may not be fast enough. Today, we talk about *same-day delivery*, and even delivery within an hour. Deliveries of urgent materials to and from hospitals are an example of such a service. eFullfillment Service (efulfillmentservice.com) and One World (owd.com) are two companies that have created networks for the rapid distribution of products, mostly EC-related ones. They offer national distribution systems across the United States in collaboration with shipping companies, such as FedEx and UPS.

CASE 11.4
EC Application

UPS PROVIDES BROAD EC SERVICES

UPS is not only a leading transporter of goods sold on the Internet, but it also is a provider of expertise, infrastructure, and technology for managing global commerce—synchronizing the flow of goods, information, and funds for its customers.

UPS has a massive infrastructure to support these efforts. For example, it has an over 120-terabyte (1012-byte) database (in 2003) that contains customer information and shipping records. More than 100,000 UPS customers have incorporated UPS Online Tools into their own Web sites to strengthen their customer services. In addition, UPS offers the following EC applications:

▶ Electronic supply chain services for corporate customers, by industry. This includes a portal page with industry-related information and statistics.
▶ Calculators for computing shipping fees.
▶ Helping customers manage their electronic supply chains (e.g., expediting billing and speeding up accounts receivable).
▶ Improved inventory management, warehousing, and delivery.
▶ A shipping management system that integrates tracking systems, address validation, service selection, and time-in-transit tools with Oracle's ERP application suite (similar integration with SAP exists).
▶ Notification of customers by e-mail about the status and expected arrival time of incoming packages.

Representative Tools

UPS's online tools—a set of seven transportation and logistics applications—lets customers do everything from tracking packages to analyzing their shipping history using customized criteria to calculating exact time-in-transit for shipments between any two postal codes in the continental United States.

The tools, which customers can download to their Web sites, let customers query UPS's system to get proof that specific packages were delivered on schedule. For example, if a company is buying supplies online and wants them delivered on a certain day, a UPS customer can use

an optimal-routing feature to ensure delivery on that day, as well as to automatically record proof of the delivery in its accounting system.

UPS offers logistics services tailored for certain industries. For example, UPS Logistics Group provides supply chain reengineering, transportation network management, and service parts logistics to vehicle manufacturers, suppliers, and parts distributors in the auto industry worldwide. UPS Autogistics improves automakers' vehicle delivery networks. For example, Ford reduced the time to deliver vehicles from plants to dealers in North America from an average of 14 days to about 6. UPS Logistics Group offers similar supply chain and delivery tracking services to other kinds of manufacturers.

UPS also is expanding into another area important to e-business—delivery of digital documents. The company was the first conventional package shipper to enter this market in 1998 when it launched UPS Document Exchange. This service monitors delivery of digitally delivered documents and provides instant receipt notification, encryption, and password-only access.

UPS offers many other EC-related services. These include the ability to enter the UPS system from wireless devices; helping customers configure and customize services; and providing for electronic bill presentation and payment (for B2B), EFT, and processing of COD payments.

Sources: Compiled from Violino (2006) and UPS (2008).

Questions

1. Why would a shipper, such as UPS, expand to other logistic services?
2. Why would shippers want to handle payments?
3. Why does UPS provide software tools to customers?
4. What B2B services does UPS provide? (Note: Check *ups.com* to make sure that your answers are up-to-date.)

Delivering food is an area where speed is important. Quick pizza deliveries have been available for a long time. Today, many pizza orders can be placed online, some wirelessly (see Chapter 9). Also, many restaurants deliver food to customers who order online, a service called "dine online." Examples of this service can be found at dineonline.com, and gourmetdinnerservice.com.au. Some companies even offer aggregating supply services, processing orders from several restaurants and then making deliveries (e.g., dialadinner.com.hk in Hong Kong).

Grocery and supermarket deliveries are done same day or next day. Arranging and making such deliveries may be difficult, especially when fresh food is to be transported. Buyers may need to be home at certain times to accept the deliveries. Therefore, the distribution systems for such enterprises are critical. One of the most comprehensive delivery systems was that of WoolWorths (an Australian grocery store chain). Online File W11.5 illustrates this system. Note that the delivery trucks can pick up and deliver other items (such as rented videos and dry cleaning).

HANDLING RETURNS (REVERSE LOGISTICS)

Allowing for the return of unwanted merchandise and providing for product exchanges are necessary to maintain customers' trust and loyalty. A number of years back, the "absence of a good return mechanism" was one of the major impediments to online buying. According to Ellis (2006), a good return policy is a must in EC.

Dealing with returns is a major logistics problem for EC merchants. Several options for handling returns exist:

> ▶ **Return the item to the place of purchase.** This is easy to do with a purchase from a brick-and-mortar store but not a virtual one. To return a product to a virtual store, a customer needs to get authorization, pack everything up, pay to ship it back, insure it, and wait up to two billing cycles for a credit to show up on his or her statement. The buyer is not happy and neither is the seller, who must unpack, check the paperwork, and resell the item, usually at a loss. This solution is workable only if the number of returns is small or the merchandise is expensive.
>
> ▶ **Separate the logistics of returns from the logistics of delivery.** With this option, returns are shipped to an independent returns unit and are handled separately. This solution may be more efficient from the seller's point of view, but it does not ease the returns process for the buyer.
>
> ▶ **Completely outsource returns.** Several outsourcers, including UPS and FedEx, provide logistics services for returns. The services deal not only with delivery and returns, but also with the entire logistics process. FedEx, for example, offers several options for returning goods.
>
> ▶ **Allow the customer to physically drop the returned item at a collection station.** Offer customers locations (such as a convenience store or the UPS Store) where they can drop off returns. In Asia and Australia, returns are accepted in convenience stores and at gas stations. For example, BP Australia Ltd. (gasoline service stations) teamed up with wishlist.com.au, and Caltex Australia is accepting returns at the convenience stores connected to its gasoline stations. The accepting stores may offer in-store computers for ordering and may also offer payment options, as at Japanese 7-Eleven's (7dream.com). In Taiwan, you can pay, pick up books and other item orders, and return unwanted items at a 7-Eleven store. Click-and-mortar stores usually allow customers to return merchandise that was ordered from the online outlet to their physical stores (e.g., walmart.com and eddiebauer.com).
>
> ▶ **Auction the returned items.** This option can go hand-in-hand with any of the previous solutions.

For strategy and guidelines on returns, see Parry (2006) and Ellis (2006). Reverse Logistics Executive Council (rlec.org) is a major portal on reverse logistics.

ORDER FULFILLMENT IN B2B

Most of the discussion in this section has centered on B2C order fulfillment. Some of the discussion pertains to B2B fulfillment as well. Exhibit 11.6 shows the B2B fulfillment options. The exhibit shows how the buy options (brown lines) relate to the shipping options (blue lines). For another overview of B2B fulfillment, see *Supplychainer.com* (2006). B2B fulfillment may be more complex than that of B2C because it has at least six dimensions of complexity (versus two in B2C): shipment size, multiple distribution channels, more variety of shipment frequency, uneven breadth of carrier services, fewer carrier EC offerings, and complex EC transaction paths.

Using BPM to Improve Order Fulfillment

B2B order fulfillment commonly uses business processes management (BPM) software to automate various steps in the process, as done by Daisy Brand (Case 11.5). The case also demonstrates how customers pressure suppliers to improve the order fulfillment process. Note that a video supporting this case is available at tibco.com.

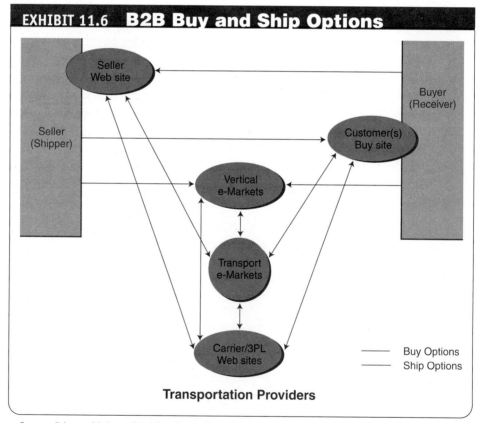

EXHIBIT 11.6 B2B Buy and Ship Options

Source: Fahrenwald, B., and D. Wise. "Logistics and Fulfillment: E-Commerce Meets the Material World." *BusinessWeek*, special advertising section, June 26, 2000. Courtesy of Norbridge Inc. © 2003.

CASE 11.5
EC Application
HOW DAISY BRAND FULFILLS B2B ORDERS

Daisy Brand is a large U.S. producer of sour cream products known for its quality products. Its major customers are supermarkets that operate in a very competitive environment. Many customers require that suppliers provide certain services that will improve the efficiency of their operations—for example, vendor-managed inventory (VMI; see Chapter 7), collaborative planning, and forecasting (Chapter 7). Most of Daisy Brand's large customers did the same. The customers pressured Daisy Brand to improve its services along the supply chain, and order processing became a prime target for improvement.

The Daisy Brand IS team sought technology that would improve the efficiency of its existing order fulfillment process. Customers submit orders electronically. Every order that Daisy Brand handles travels through three applications: Customers submit orders through an EDI transaction. From there, orders flow to an Invensys Protean ERP system and various other systems for fulfillment and ultimately to shipping. The company sought to implement a workflow solution that could integrate and automate this order-to-delivery process.

Using TIBCO's business integration and business process management solution (see *tibco.com*), the IS team designed, developed, tested, and deployed a workflow in only 3 weeks. The workflow manages the order process from inception all the way to the point of delivery to ensure that orders move forward within the set time frame. The company can also send notifications about shipping activity back to the customer.

If an order is to ship out within a certain number of hours and has not shipped, TIBCO's solution can trace that order and get it moving faster. TIBCO's solution also helps stop problems before they start by auditing customer order information before it enters the ERP system.

In addition to improving the efficiency of order processing at Daisy Brand, TIBCO's solution also enables the company to more flexibly accommodate customer needs. For example, a retail customer might change an order after the order is sent to the warehouse—perhaps to request that the order ship on a different day or with a different amount. In these cases, the system sends an alert to the logistics management workbench to immediately notify the warehouse that the order has been modified. Thus, the logistics team can quickly implement the change, ensuring minimum impact on the order cycle time.

The workflow software is part of TIBCO's BPM software suite, which includes other applications for control of business processes and to improve agility. Future projects include automation of new customer entry; integration of plant control systems; support for collaborative planning, forecasting, and replenishment (CPFR) and VMI; and implementation of a real-time order-arrival board.

Sources: Compiled from *Tibco.com* (2006) and *Staffware.com* (2006).

Questions

1. Describe the steps in order fulfillment at Daisy Brand.
2. How is the automation of order fulfillment done?
3. How can supermarkets benefit from introducing electronic processing by Daisy Brand?
4. Enter *tibco.com* and find information about its BPM and workflow products. How can they support order fulfillment?
5. How can Daisy Brand improve its agility?

Section 11.9 ▶ REVIEW QUESTIONS

1. Describe some of the typical EC supply chain problems.
2. Discuss some of the ways of addressing the fulfillment problem in EC.
3. Describe some EC businesses where speed of delivery is crucial.
4. Describe some of the ways for handling returns in EC.
5. Describe how to effectively manage the return of items.
6. Describe issues in B2B fulfillment.

11.10 OTHER EC SUPPORT SERVICES

Both B2C and B2B involve a number of complex processes. A number of businesses do not possess the staff or the expertise to deal with these processes, especially for large-scale initiatives. For this reason, companies often require outside support. This may come in the form of specialized services (e.g. handling online payments) or in the form of more generalized consulting and outsourcing services.

CONSULTING SERVICES

How does a firm learn how to do something that it has never done before? Many firms, both startups and established companies, are turning to consultants that have established themselves as experts in guiding their clients through the maze of legal, technical, strategic, and operational problems and decisions that must be addressed in order to ensure success in this new business environment. Some of these firms have established a reputation in one area of expertise, whereas others are generalists. Some consultants even take equity (ownership) positions in the firms they advise. Some consultants will build, test, and deliver a working Web site and may even host it and maintain it for their clients. There are three broad categories of consulting firms:

- **EC consultants.** The first type of consulting firm includes those that provide expertise in the area of EC but not in traditional business. Some of the consultants that provide general EC expertise are Agency.com, Virtusa, Inforte, Sapient, Autonomy, and WebTrends.
- **Traditional consulting firms.** The second type of consulting firm is a traditional consulting company that maintains divisions that focus on EC. These include the so-called Big Four U.S. accounting firms and the large established U.S. national consulting firms. These firms leverage their existing relationships with their corporate clients and offer EC value-added services. Representative companies are Accenture, Computer Service Corp., Cambridge Technology Partners, Boston Consulting Group, Booz-Allen & Hamilton, Deloitte & Touche, Ernst and Young, EDS, KPMG, McKinsey, and PricewaterhouseCoopers. Also, most large technology companies have extensive management-oriented consulting services (e.g., IBM, Microsoft, Sun Microsystems, Oracle, SAP, and Intel).
- **EC hardware and software vendors.** The third category of consulting firms is EC hardware and software vendors that provide technology-consulting services. These include SAP, IBM, Oracle, Sun Microsystems, and many more.

It is imperative that any firm seeking help in devising a successful online strategy select not only an experienced and competent consulting firm, but also one with sufficient synergies with the client firm.

EC OUTSOURCING SERVICES

Most companies do not maintain in-house support services. Instead, they outsource many of these services. Why is outsourcing used? Historically, early businesses were vertically integrated—they owned or controlled their own sources of materials, manufactured components, performed final assembly, and managed the distribution and sale of their products to consumers. Later, nearly all firms began to contract with other firms to execute various activities along the supply chain, from manufacturing to distribution and sale, in order to concentrate their activities in their core competency. This contracting practice is known as *outsourcing*. When EC emerged, it became obvious that it would be necessary to outsource some of the support services involved in its deployment. The major reasons why many companies prefer to do this include the following:

▶ A desire to concentrate on the core business
▶ The need to have services up and running rapidly
▶ Lack of expertise (experience and resources) for many of the required support services
▶ The inability to have the economy of scale enjoyed by outsourcers, which often results in high costs for in-house options
▶ Inability to keep up with rapidly fluctuating demands if an in-house option is used
▶ The number of required services, which usually are simply too many for one company to handle

To understand the importance of outsourcing, consider the typical process of developing and managing EC applications (the e-infrastructure). The process includes the following major steps:

1. EC strategy formulation
2. Application design
3. Building (or buying) the systems
4. Hosting, operating, and maintaining the EC site

Each of these steps may include several activities, as shown in Exhibit 11.7. A firm may execute all the activities of this process internally, or it may outsource some or all of them. In addition to design and maintenance of technical systems, many other system design issues and business functions related to using a Web site also must be addressed. For example, a firm doing EC must design and operate its order fulfillment system and

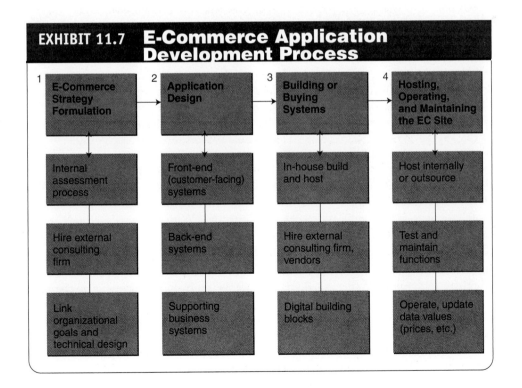

EXHIBIT 11.7 E-Commerce Application Development Process

1 E-Commerce Strategy Formulation	2 Application Design	3 Building or Buying Systems	4 Hosting, Operating, and Maintaining the EC Site
Internal assessment process	Front-end (customer-facing) systems	In-house build and host	Host internally or outsource
Hire external consulting firm	Back-end systems	Hire external consulting firm, vendors	Test and maintain functions
Link organizational goals and technical design	Supporting business systems	Digital building blocks	Operate, update data values (prices, etc.)

outbound logistics (delivery) functions; it must provide dynamic content on the site; and it must also provide services to its customers and partners.

IT OUTSOURCING AND APPLICATION SERVICE PROVIDERS

Most enterprises engaged in EC rely on IT outsourcing. While concentrating on core competencies, they develop strategic alliances with partner firms in order to provide activities such as payment processing, order fulfillment, outbound logistics, Web site hosting, and customer service.

Outside contractors are the best option for SMEs with few IT staff and smaller budgets. Outside contractors also have proven to be a good choice for large companies who want to control their EC investments and expenses. In addition, outsourcing allows them to protect their own internal networks or to rely on experts to establish sites over which they will later assume control. Some of the best-known B2C sites on the Web are run by third-party vendors. For example, a number of companies, such as Sony, rely on Amazon.com to run their EC operations.

One of the most interesting types of EC outsourcing is the use of **application service providers (ASPs)**. An ASP is an agent or vendor who assembles the functions needed by enterprises and packages them with outsourced development, operation, maintenance, and other services.

application service provider (ASP)
An agent or vendor who assembles the functions needed by enterprises and packages them with outsourced development, operation, maintenance, and other services.

Section 11.10 ▶ REVIEW QUESTIONS

1. Describe the major types of EC consulting.
2. Describe the benefits of outsourcing EC services.
3. Detail some of the key areas where EC outsourcing services may be used.

MANAGERIAL ISSUES

Some managerial issues related to this chapter are as follows.

1. **What B2C payment methods should we use?** Companies that only accept credit cards rule out a number of potential segments of buyers. Teenagers, non–U.S. customers, and customers who cannot or do not want to use credit cards online are examples of market segments that are unable or unwilling to use credit cards to make online purchases. E-checks, virtual credit cards, stored-value cards, and PayPal are some possible alternatives to credit cards. Also, when the purchase price is less than $5, credit cards are not a viable solution. In this case, various e-micropayment systems can be used. Online merchants and other sellers need to be aware of the volatility and true costs of many of these alternatives. Because many of the various alternatives do not yet enjoy widespread use, it is always possible that they will not exist tomorrow.

2. **What B2B payment methods should we use?** Keep an open mind about online alternatives.

When it comes to paying suppliers or accepting payments from partners, most large businesses have opted to stick with the tried-and-true methods of EFT or checks over other methods of electronic payment. For MROs, consider using purchasing cards. For global trade, electronic letters of credit are popular. The use of e-checks is another area where cost savings can accrue. Finally, innovative methods such as TradeCard can be very effective. With all these methods, a key factor is determining how well they work with existing accounting and ordering systems and with business partners.

3. **Should we use an in-house payment mechanism or outsource it?** It takes time, skill, money, software, and hardware to integrate the payment systems of all the parties involved in processing any sort of e-payment. For this reason, even a business that runs its own EC site should consider

outsourcing the e-payment component. Many third-party vendors provide payment gateways designed to handle the interactions among the various financial institutions that operate in the background of an e-payment system. Also, if a Web site is hosted by a third party (e.g., Yahoo! Store), an e-payment service will be provided.

4. **How secure are e-payments?** Security and fraud continue to be a major issue in making and accepting e-payments of all kinds. This is especially true for online credit cards. B2C merchants are employing a wide variety of tools (e.g., address verification and other authentication services) to combat fraudulent orders. These and other measures that are employed to ensure the security of e-payments have to be part of a broader security scheme that weighs risks against issues such as the ease of use and the fit within the overall business context.

5. **Have we planned for order fulfillment?** Order fulfillment is a critical task, especially for virtual EC vendors. Even for brick-and-mortar retailers with physical warehouses, delivery to customers' doors is not always easy. The problem is not just the physical shipment, but also the efficient execution of the entire order fulfillment process, which may be complex along a long supply chain. A number of companies rely on packaged software solutions such as warehouse management systems (WMS) to manage major segments of their fulfillment processes.

6. **How should we handle returns?** Dealing with returns can be a complex issue. A company should estimate its percentage of returns and design and plan a process for receiving and handling them. Some companies completely separate the logistics of returns from that of order fulfillment and outsource its execution.

7. **Do we want alliances in order fulfillment?** A number of complex supply chain issues arise in forecasting and meeting demand and in fulfilling orders. A number of third-party companies, including companies such as FedEx and UPS, have the capabilities to address many of the issues arising with fulfillment and alleviate a number of supply chain problems. The key is to determine which activities are core to a company's competitiveness and which can be more readily outsourced.

8. **Should we employ outside consulting or outsourcing for our EC initiatives?** Even for those companies with substantial EC experience, it may make sense to consider using generalized consulting and outsourcing services to manage many, if not most, of the major EC processes. Because of the costs associated with EC, a number of firms have relied on outside support provided by companies such as Amazon.com.

SUMMARY

In this chapter, you learned about the following EC issues as they relate to the learning objectives.

1. **Payment revolution.** Cash and checks are no longer kings. Debit and credit cards now rule—both online and offline. This means that online B2C businesses need to support debit and credit card purchases. In international markets outside of Western Europe, buyers often favor other forms of e-payment (e.g., bank transfers). With the exception of PayPal, virtually all the alternatives to charge cards have failed. None have gained enough traction to overcome the "chicken-and-egg" problem. Their failure to gain critical mass has resulted from the confluence of a variety of factors. (e.g., they required specialized hardware or setup or they failed to mesh with existing systems).

2. **Using payment cards online.** The processing of online card payments is essentially the same as it is for brick-and-mortar stores and involves essentially the same players and the same systems—banks, card associations, payment processing services, and the like. This is one of the reasons why payment cards predominate in the online world. The major difference is that the rate of fraudulent orders is much higher online. Surveys, such as those conducted annually by CyberSource, indicate that merchants have adopted over the past few years a wide variety of methods to combat fraudulent orders, including address verification, manual review, fraud screens and decision models, card verification numbers,

card association authentication services, and negative files. In the same vein, some consumers have turned to virtual or single-use credit cards to avoid using their actual credit card numbers online.

3. **Smart cards.** Smart cards look like credit cards but contain embedded chips for manipulating data and have large memory capacity. Cards that contain microprocessor chips can be programmed to handle a wide variety of tasks. Other cards have memory chips to which data can be written and from which data can be read. Most memory cards are disposable, but others—smart cards—can hold large amounts of data and are rechargeable. Smart cards have been and will be used for a number of purposes, including contactless retail payments, paying for mass transit services, identifying cardholders for government services, securing physical and network access, storing health-care data, and verifying eligibility for health-care and other government services. Given the sensitive nature of much of the data on smart cards, PKI and other cryptographic techniques are used to secure their contents.

4. **Stored-value cards.** A stored-value card is similar in appearance to a credit or debit card. The monetary value of a stored value card is housed in a magnetic strip on the back of the card. Closed-loop stored-value cards are issued for a single purpose by a specific merchant (e.g., a Starbucks gift card). In contrast, open-loop stored-value cards are more like standard credit or debit cards and can be used for multiple purposes (e.g., a payroll card). Those segments of the population without credit cards or bank accounts—people with low incomes, young adults, seniors, and immigrants—are spurring the substantial growth of stored-value cards. Specialized cards, such as EasySend, make it simple for immigrant populations to transfer funds to family members in other countries. Similarly, specialized cards, such as MasterCard's MYPlash, provide teens and preteens with prepaid debit cards that function like standard credit or debit cards while helping parents monitor and maintain control over spending patterns.

5. **E-micropayments.** When an item or service being sold online costs less than $5, credit cards are too costly for sellers. A number of other e-payment systems have been introduced to handle these micropayment situations. For the most part, they have failed. Yet, there is ample evidence indicating that consumers are interested in using their credit and debit cards for small-value online purchases (e.g., iTunes, online games, and ringtone sales). In response, a number of newer micropayment models, such as aggregated purchases, have been developed to reduce the fees associated with credit and debit cards.

6. **E-checking.** E-checks are the electronic equivalent of paper checks. They are handled in much the same way as paper checks and rely quite heavily on the Automated Clearing House (ACH) Network. E-checks offer a number of benefits, including speedier processing, reduced administrative costs, more efficient deposits, reduced float period, and fewer "bounced" checks. These factors have resulted in the rapid growth of e-check usage. The rapid growth is also being spurred by the use of e-checks for in-store purchases. Purchase Order Processing (POP) and Back-Office Order Conversion (BOC) are two systems, established by NACHA, that enable retailers to convert paper checks used for in-store purchases to ACH debits (i.e., e-checks) without the need to process the checks using traditional procedures.

7. **B2B electronic payments.** B2B payments are part of a much larger financial supply chain that encompasses the range of processes from procurement to payment and order to cash. Today, the vast majority of B2B payments are still made by check, although many organizations are moving to enterprise invoice presentment and payment (EIPP). There are three models of EIPP: seller direct (buyers go to the seller's Web site), buyer direct (sellers post invoices at the buyer's Web site), and consolidator (many buyers and many sellers are linked through the consolidator's Web site). Two of the largest consolidators are Xign Payment Services and GSX Trading Grid. In addition to these models, there are several EIPP payment options, including the ACH Network, purchasing cards, wire transfers, and letters of credit (L/C). The move to EIPP is being inhibited by the shortage of IT staff, the lack of integration of payment and account systems, the lack of standard formats for remittance information, and the inability of trading partners to send or receive electronic payments with sufficient remittance information.

8. **Order fulfillment and logistics.** Large numbers of support services are needed for EC implementation. Most important are payment mechanisms and

order fulfillment. On-time delivery of products to customers may be a difficult task, especially in B2C. Fulfilling an order requires several activities ranging from credit and inventory checks to shipments. Most of these activities are part of back-office operations and are related to logistics. The order fulfillment process varies from business to business and also depends on the product. Generally speaking, however, the following steps are recognized: payment verification, inventory checking, shipping arrangement, insurance, production (or assembly), plant services, purchasing, customer contacts, and return of products.

9. **Addressing problems in order fulfillment.** It is difficult to fulfill B2C orders due to uncertainties in demand and potential delays in supply and deliveries. Problems also result from lack of coordination and information sharing among business partners. Automating order taking (e.g., by using forms over the Internet) and smoothing the supply chain are two ways to solve order fulfillment problems. Several other innovative solutions exist, most of which are supported by software that facilitates correct inventories, coordination along the supply chain, and appropriate planning and decision making.

10. **Other EC support services.** EC involves a number of complex processes. Both large and small firms, as well as experienced and inexperienced firms, often rely on outside support to help with these processes. This outside support comes in the form of both EC-focused and traditional consulting firms, as well as various outsourcing firms. Companies use these firms for various reasons, ranging from the need to focus on core competencies to the inability to keep up with the dynamic nature of EC and its requirements. Among the various support services, IT outsourcing is the one that is most frequently used.

KEY TERMS

Address Verification System (AVS)	435	E-check	445	Purchasing cards (p-cards)	451
		E-logistics	455	Reverse logistics	455
Application service provider (ASP)	466	E-micropayments	443	Settlement	432
		Enterprise invoice presentment and payment (EIPP)	449	Smart card	436
Authorization	432			Smart card operating system	437
Automated Clearing House (ACH) Network	447	Front-office operations	453	Smart card reader	437
		Letter of credit (L/C)	451	Stored-value card	441
Back-office operations	453	Logistics	453	Third-party logistics suppliers (3PL)	457
Card verification number (CVN)	435	Order fulfillment	452		
Contact card	436	Payment cards	432	Warehouse management system (WMS)	457
Contactless (proximity) card	436	Payment service provider (PSP)	433		

QUESTIONS FOR DISCUSSION

1. Suppose a company wanted to introduce a new e-micropayment method on the Web. What factors should it consider to increase the chance of success?

2. A textbook publisher is interested in selling individual book chapters on the Web. Should it let students use credit or debit cards to purchase individual chapters? Why or why not? If credit or debit cards are not permitted, what other e-payment methods would you recommend to the publisher?

3. Recently, a merchant who accepts online credit card payments has experienced a wave of fraudulent orders. What steps should the merchant take to combat the fraud?

4. A retail clothing manufacturer is considering e-payments for both its suppliers and its buyers.

What sort of e-payment method should it use to pay for office supplies? How should it pay suppliers of raw materials? How should its customers—both domestic and international clothing retailers—pay?

5. A metropolitan area wants to provide riders of its public transportation system with the ability to pay transit fares, as well as make retail purchases, using a single contactless smart card. What sorts of problems will it encounter in setting up the system, and what types of problems will the riders encounter in using the cards?

6. Discuss the problem of reverse logistics in EC. What types of companies may suffer the most?

7. Explain why UPS defines itself as a "technology company with trucks" rather than as a "trucking company with technology."

8. Under what situations might the outsourcing of EC services not be desirable?

9. Why does it make sense to use a consultant to develop an e-strategy?

10. Differentiate order fulfillment in B2C from that of B2B.

11. Discuss the motivation of suppliers to improve the supply chain to customers.

INTERNET EXERCISES

1. This chapter listed the names of e-payment companies that failed to gain critical mass (e.g., Digital Cash, Flooz, etc.). Select two of these companies. Using information gathered from the Web, explain why you think they failed.

2. Select a major B2C merchant and detail the e-payment options offered. Based on CyberSource's "The Insider's Guide to E-Commerce Payment, Second Edition," (**cybersource.com/resources/collateral/Resource_Center/whitepapers_and_reports/insiders_guide.pdf**), what other types of e-payment systems should it offer?

3. Enter **tradecard.com**. Run the procure-to-pay demo. Summarize the processes and benefits of the service to a small exporter.

4. Go to **cybersource.com**. Identify the services it provides for B2B e-payments. Describe the features of CyberSource's major products that provide these merchant services.

5. Download "Transit and Contactless Financial Payments" (October 2006) from **smartcard alliance.org/pages/publications-transit-financial**. Based on the report, what type of payment system is New York City Transit (NYCT) piloting? Who are NYCT's partners in the pilot? What factors helped determine the type of system to be piloted? How does the pilot work?

6. Enter **xign.com**. What types of companies are serviced by Xign Payment Services Network? What types of products and services does Xign provide?

7. Go to **nacha.org**. What is NACHA? What is its role? What is the ACH? Who are the key participants in an ACH e-payment? Describe the "pilot" projects currently underway at ACH.

8. The U.S. Postal Service also is in the EC logistics field. Examine its services and tracking systems at **usps.com/shipping**. What are the potential advantages of these systems for EC shippers?

9. Enter **redprairie.com** and find their order-fulfillment-related products and services. Prepare a list. Also, review the RFID products that can be used for order fulfillment.

10. Enter **b2byellowpages.com** and **a2zofb2b.com**. Compare the information provided on each site. What features do both sites share? How do the sites differ?

11. Enter **ahls.com** and find out what services it offers. Comment on the uniqueness of the services.

12. Enter **rlec.org** and summarize the differences between reverse and forward logistics. Also discuss returns management.

TEAM ASSIGNMENTS AND ROLE PLAYING

1. Select some B2C sites that cater to teens and some that cater to older consumers. Have team members visit these sites. What types of e-payment methods do they provide? Are there any differences among the methods used on different types of sites? What other types of e-payment would you recommend for the various sites and why?

2. Write a report comparing smart card applications in two or more European and/or Asian countries. In the report, discuss whether those applications would succeed in North America.

3. Have one team represent MasterCard's PayPass and another represent American Express's ExpressPay. The task of each team is to convince a company that its product is superior.

4. Have each team member interview three to five people who have made a purchase or sold an item at auction over the Internet. Find out how they paid. What security and privacy concerns did they have regarding the payment? Is there an ideal payment method?

5. Each team should investigate the order fulfillment process offered at an e-tailer's site, such as **amazon.com**, **staples.com**, or **landsend.com**.

Contact the company, if necessary, and examine any related business partnerships. Based on the content of this chapter, prepare a report with suggestions for how the company can improve its order fulfillment process. Each group's findings will be discussed in class. Based on the class's findings, draw some conclusions about how companies can improve order fulfillment.

6. FedEx, UPS, the U.S. Postal Service, DHL, and others are competing in the EC logistics market. Each team should examine one such company and investigate the services it provides. Contact the company, if necessary, and aggregate the team's findings into a report that will convince classmates or readers that the company in question is the best. (What are its best features? What are its weaknesses?)

7. Each team should select an overnight delivery service company (FedEx, DHL, UPS, U.S. Postal Service, and so on). The team will then identify all the online customer service features offered by the company. Each team then will try to convince the class that its company provides the best customer service.

Real-World Case

ELIMINATING LETTERS OF CREDIT: RITE AID DEPLOYS THE TRADECARD SOLUTION

Rite Aid Corporation (*riteaid.com*) is one of the leading drugstore chains in the United States. The company began in 1962 as Thrift D Discount Center in Scranton, Pennsylvania. Over the years it has grown by acquisition. Today, Rite Aid has over 3,300 stores in 27 states and employs approximately 70,000 full- and part-time associates. At the end of 2006, it had total sales of over $17 billion. The typical Rite Aid store handles a large number of items, although pharmaceuticals account for the majority of the sales. Like other major drugstore chains, Rite Aid's import supplier base, which includes over 300 vendors located throughout the world, provides a number of the items carried in its stores.

As far back as 2002, Rite Aid established a fairly strict set of supply chain guidelines and policies for its warehouse vendors. The guidelines cover the following areas:

▶ **Merchandise information and technology:** Provides requirements for accurate item information, source tagging guidelines, purchase orders, unsaleable merchandise, and EDI.

▶ **Shipment and routing:** Outlines requirements for distribution and transportation of merchandise.

▶ **Accounts payable:** Provides requirements for accurate vendor information and invoice processing.

▶ **Key performance indicators (KPIs):** Details the KPIs that have been selected to monitor the compliance or performance of warehouse vendors.

▶ **Expense offsets:** Identifies noncompliance areas and penalties.

▶ **Import information:** Outlines requirements for import vendors.

Prior to 2004, Rite Aid encountered substantial difficulties in dealing with its import vendors, even with the detailed guidelines. One area of major concern revolved around the use of letters of credit (L/C). In the past, virtually all Rite Aid's orders to its import vendors required an L/C. This is general practice in the world of global procurement. An L/C requires the retailer to commit its money early in the purchase process. The money lies in wait until all the required documents have been filed. Not only does this leave the money in a nonproductive state for the retailer and vendor, but it can also result in cash-flow issues. The only one that benefits from this impasse is the financial institution that holds the money and collects fees from both the retailer and the vendor.

In 2004, Rite Aid decided to implement a Web-based financial platform for payments to its import vendors. The platform was based on a solution from TradeCard (*tradecard.com*). TradeCard is a New York City–based provider of technology and services designed to automate the financial processes of a global supply chain. TradeCard's solution handles the major areas of trading partner management (e.g., purchase order management), accounts payable management (e.g., electronic invoicing), and financial management (e.g., L/C replacement). TradeCard has an open network of partners—suppliers and buyers—that facilitate services, such as credit protection and trade finance, in many countries.

The solution provided by TradeCard handles all the steps from purchase order to settlement and receipt of goods:

1. Rite Aid initiates purchase orders and sends them electronically to TradeCard.
2. TradeCard notifies sellers of all new purchase orders and asks the sellers to approve them online.
3. Sellers create and approve invoices on TradeCard as goods are readied for shipment.
4. Sellers send the goods and documents to the logistics service provider (LSP).
5. The LSP issues a hard-copy forwarder's cargo receipt to sellers once goods have been received and all document requirements have been met. The LSP then transmits proof of delivery (POD) data to TradeCard.
6. TradeCard's automated compliance check will compare the shipment documents (invoice and POD) to the procurement documents (purchase order, including any amendments).
7. After TradeCard completes the compliance check, it will alert Rite Aid to review any discrepancies and approve or negotiate the payment authorization documents. Once finalized, TradeCard determines payments based on the terms of the transactions.
8. Rite Aid wires payment to TradeCard's payment service provider, JPMorgan Chase, who then remits payment to the sellers' bank accounts.

Because the new workflow provided by the TradeCard solution eliminated L/Cs, Rite Aid and TradeCard were concerned about the response from its import vendors. Rite Aid and TradeCard held a face-to-face meeting with the vendors to describe and discuss the new system. Based on the meeting, Rite Aid decided to roll out the system in two phases corresponding to the Christmas holiday and back-to-school seasons. In January 2005, Rite Aid started using the system for online transactions. The processes and workflow have become part of its written supply chain guidelines and policies. Today, the system handles virtually all global payments.

In addition to eliminating the fees and cash-flow problems associated with L/Cs, Rite Aid has documented a variety of benefits provided by their system. These include:

▶ Electronic delivery of purchase orders
▶ Automated creation of a commercial invoice based on purchase order information
▶ Automated document-compliance checking
▶ Real-time visibility and reporting to all parties
▶ Improved communication among all parties
▶ Improved data quality across shipping documents
▶ Improved planning and reporting capabilities
▶ Payment assurance, if desired, for 100 percent of the value of an order
▶ Access to a variety of export financing options

Sources: Gentry (2006) and Rite Aid (2006).

Questions

1. Enter Rite Aid's portal (*extsupplier.riteaid.com/browvererr.htm*). Click "Vendor Management Section" and download the "Vendor Supplier Guide." In the guide, go to the "Imports" section. Based on this section, what policies must

an import vendor follow in order to do business with Rite Aid? Which of the major tasks in the order-settlement process are handled by Rite Aid, by TradeCard, and by the vendor?

2. One of the key benefits of the TradeCard system is that it provides a merchant with real-time visibility into the complete financial supply chain. Based on the Rite Aid–TradeCard workflow diagram displayed in the Guide, which steps of the order-settlement supply chain can Rite Aid and its vendors track with the system?

3. Do a Google search for electronic letters of credit. Based on the results of this search, what other companies might Rite Aid have used to implement its order-settlement system? Describe some of the functions provided by these vendors. Do the capabilities of these companies match those provided by TradeCard?

E-COMMERCE STRATEGY, JUSTIFICATION, AND GLOBAL IMPLEMENTATION

Learning Objectives

Upon completion of this chapter, you will be able to:

1. Describe the strategic planning process.
2. Describe the purpose and content of a business plan in e-commerce.
3. Describe EC strategy implementation including the use of metrics.
4. Describe the need for justifying EC investments, how it is done, and how metrics are used to determine justification.
5. Understand the difficulties in measuring and justifying EC investments.
6. Evaluate the issues involved in global EC.
7. Analyze the impact of EC on SMEs.
8. Understand the foundations for legal and ethical issues in EC.
9. Explain privacy, free speech, and defamation and their challenges.
10. Discuss the challenges caused by spam, splogs, and pop-ups.
11. Describe the anticipated future of EC.

Content

Travelocity's Successful E-Strategy

TRAVELOCITY'S SUCCESSFUL E-STRATEGY

The Problem

Travelocity (*travelocity.com*) was the first online travel company (owned by American Airlines and Sabre). Its initial strategy was to concentrate on airline ticketing and some hotel booking and to sell advertisements on its Web site. This business model worked very well initially, making the company the leading online travel service. However, this business model became ineffective when the airlines reduced, and then eliminated, travel agents' commissions and when competitors entered the market.

Expedia became the market leader, and by 2002 it pulled in nearly five times more revenue than Travelocity. The losses in market share resulted in mounting financial losses.

The Solution

Guided by rigorous study of customer behavior, the company developed a new strategy. Specifically, instead of focusing on airline tickets, Travelocity moved to selling customized packages, including more hotel rooms and car rentals. Instead of being a commission-based intermediary, it started to buy blocks of airline tickets and hotel rooms (discounted wholesale) and sold them to individual customers in customized "merchant travel" packages. Another strategy was to create a fast and effective search engine for finding the lowest prices for its customers.

To better understand customer behavior and to set performance standards for its e-strategy, the company used business analysis done by the operations research department of Sabre Holding, Travelocity's parent company. The study identified a need for better customer service. This became a top priority.

Improving the performance of the overall system meant setting performance goals for each of the subsystems and then improving them by using several software packages. Quantitative targets and goals formed the basis for the whole system. Once these were set, the planning focused on how to achieve them. The performance standards were related to a mathematical model of how customers choose between travel options, based on the perceived value of each option. Different customers prioritize criteria such as price or departure time differently, and Travelocity is trying to provide their needs. For example, cost-conscious travelers receive e-mails about price drops of more than 20 percent (from or to their favorite destinations). This program, known as "Good Day to Buy," is a major CRM activity.

The Results

By the first quarter of 2006, revenue grew to almost half of Expedia's (versus 20 percent in 2002), about 300 percent above its performance in 2002. The acquisition of Lastminute.com, a strategic acquisition completed in 2005, contributed to part of this growth.

Travelocity made the following progress on three performance metrics:

- **Brand impact index.** This gauges the image people have of the company. Travelocity moved from sixth place in 2004 to third in 2005.

- **Conversion impact index.** This measures the conversion from browsing to shopper. Travelocity showed a 55-percent improvement, placing it in first place in the industry in 2005 versus second place in 2004.

- **Customer satisfaction from the Web site.** Travelocity was second place in 2005 versus fourth in 2004. (Only 6 percent of customers said they could not find the lowest fares on the site in 2005 versus 18 percent in 2004.)

Overall, Travelocity is turning itself around from a loser to a winner. It trimmed losses from $100 million in 2003 to $2.8 million in 2005.

Sources: Compiled from Carr (2006) and Gagnon et al. (2002).

WHAT WE CAN LEARN . . .

Proper strategy can help companies survive and excel. For pure-play companies, it may be even more important to be able to change strategies quickly. Strategies are based on *performance indexes*, which are used as targets as well as measures of success. Once performance targets are set, including quantitative measures, improvement plans can be initiated; then the strategy can be implemented. Later progress can be assessed. These are the basic steps in EC strategy, which is the first subject of this chapter. The chapter also presents the related topics of EC investment justification, global EC, and EC in SMEs. Then success factors are presented. Finally regulatory and ethical issues are discussed.

12.1 STRATEGY, PLANNING, AND IMPLEMENTATION OF ELECTRONIC COMMERCE

strategy

A broad-based formula for how a business is going to accomplish its mission, what its goals should be, and what plans and policies will be needed to carry out those goals.

An organizational **strategy** is a broad-based formula for how a business is going to accomplish its mission, what its goals should be, and what plans and policies it will need to accomplish these goals. An EC strategy addresses fundamental questions about the current position of a company and its future directions, such as (Jelassi and Enders 2005):

▶ What is the long-term direction of our organization?

▶ What is the overall plan for deploying our organization's resources?

▶ What trade-offs are necessary? What resources will we need to share?

▶ What is our unique positioning vis-à-vis competitors?

▶ How do we achieve sustainable competitive advantage over rivals in order to ensure lasting profitability?

STRATEGY AND THE WEB ENVIRONMENT

Strategic positioning is about making decisions about trade-offs, recognizing that a company must abandon or not pursue some products, services, and activities in order to excel at others. How are these trade-offs determined? Not merely with a focus on growth and increases in revenue, but also on profitability and increases in shareholder value over the long run. How is this profitability and economic value determined? By establishing a unique *value proposition* and the configuration of a tailored *value chain* that enables a company to offer unique value to its customers. Therefore, strategy has been, and remains, focused on questions about organizational fit, trade-offs, profitability, and value (Porter 2001).

Any contemporary strategy-setting process must include the Internet. Strategy guru Michael Porter (2001) argues that a coherent organizational strategy that includes the Internet is more important than ever before: "Many have argued that the Internet renders strategy obsolete. In reality, the opposite is true . . . it is more important than ever for companies to distinguish themselves through strategy. The winners will be those that view the Internet as a complement to, not a cannibal of, traditional ways of competing" (p. 63).

To illustrate this point, Porter (2001) has identified several ways that the Internet impacts each of the five forces of competitiveness—bargaining power of consumers and suppliers, threats from substitutes and new entrants, and rivalry among existing competitors—that were originally described in one of his seminal works on strategy (Porter 1980). These five forces and associated Internet impacts are shown in Exhibit 12.1. The majority of impacts are negative, reflecting Porter's view that "The great paradox of the Internet is that its very benefits—making information widely available; reducing the difficulty of purchasing, marketing, and distribution; allowing buyers and sellers to find and transact business with one another more easily—also make it more difficult for companies to capture those benefits as profits" (Porter 2001, p. 70).

e-commerce strategy (e-strategy)

The formulation and execution of a vision of how a new or existing company intends to do business electronically.

Exhibit 12.1 is a generalization, and the impact of the Internet on strategic competitiveness and long-term profitability will differ from industry to industry. Accordingly, many businesses are taking a focused look at the impact of the Internet and EC on their future. For these firms, an **e-commerce strategy**, or **e-strategy**, is the formulation and execution of a vision of how a new or existing company intends to do business electronically. (See Wang and Forgionne 2006.)

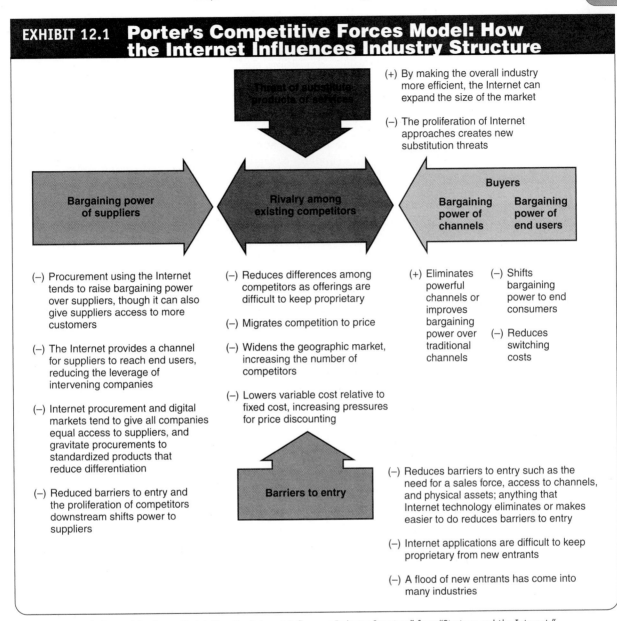

EXHIBIT 12.1 **Porter's Competitive Forces Model: How the Internet Influences Industry Structure**

Threat of substitute products or services

(+) By making the overall industry more efficient, the Internet can expand the size of the market

(–) The proliferation of Internet approaches creates new substitution threats

Bargaining power of suppliers

Rivalry among existing competitors

Buyers

Bargaining power of channels   **Bargaining power of end users**

(–) Procurement using the Internet tends to raise bargaining power over suppliers, though it can also give suppliers access to more customers

(–) The Internet provides a channel for suppliers to reach end users, reducing the leverage of intervening companies

(–) Internet procurement and digital markets tend to give all companies equal access to suppliers, and gravitate procurements to standardized products that reduce differentiation

(–) Reduced barriers to entry and the proliferation of competitors downstream shifts power to suppliers

(–) Reduces differences among competitors as offerings are difficult to keep proprietary

(–) Migrates competition to price

(–) Widens the geographic market, increasing the number of competitors

(–) Lowers variable cost relative to fixed cost, increasing pressures for price discounting

Barriers to entry

(+) Eliminates powerful channels or improves bargaining power over traditional channels

(–) Shifts bargaining power to end consumers

(–) Reduces switching costs

(–) Reduces barriers to entry such as the need for a sales force, access to channels, and physical assets; anything that Internet technology eliminates or makes easier to do reduces barriers to entry

(–) Internet applications are difficult to keep proprietary from new entrants

(–) A flood of new entrants has come into many industries

Source: "Porter's Competitive Forces Model: How the Internet Influences Industry Structure" from "Strategy and the Internet," by M. E. Porter, March 2001 © 2001 by the Harvard Business School Publishing Corp. *Harvard Business Review.* Reprinted by permission.

Strategy Initiation

In the **strategy initiation** phase, the organization examines itself and its environment. The principal activities include setting the organization's mission and goals, examining organizational strengths and weaknesses, assessing environmental factors impacting the business, and conducting a competitor analysis. As emphasized throughout this chapter, this includes an examination of the potential contribution that the Internet and other emerging technologies can make to the business.

strategy initiation
The initial phase of strategic planning in which the organization examines itself and its environment.

Specific outcomes from this phase include:

▶ **Company analysis and value proposition.** The company analysis includes the vision, mission, value proposition, goals, capabilities, constraints, strengths, and weaknesses of the company. Questions typically asked in a company analysis are: What business are we really in? Who are our future customers? Do our mission statement and our goals adequately describe our intended future? What opportunities and threats do our business and our industry face? One key outcome from this analysis should be a clear statement of the company's **value proposition**—the benefit that a company's products or services provide to a company and its customers. Value proposition is actually a statement that summarizes the customer segment, competitor target, and the core differentiation of one's product from the offering of competitors. It describes the value added by the company (or the e-commerce projects), and usually is included in the business plan. It is only by knowing what benefits a business is providing to customers that chief-level executives can truly understand "what business they are in" and who their potential competitors are (Clegg and Tan 2006).

▶ **Core competencies.** A core competency refers to the unique combination of the resources and experiences of a particular firm. It takes time to build these core competencies, and they can be difficult to imitate. For example, Google's core competency is its expertise in information search technology, and eBay's core competency is in conducting online auctions. A company is using its core competency to deliver a product or service. Google's products are AdWords and AdSense, and Intel produces chips.

▶ **Forecasts.** Forecasting means identifying business, technological, political, economic, and other relevant trends that are currently affecting the business or that have the potential to do so in the future.

▶ **Competitor (industry) analysis.** Competitor analysis involves scanning the business environment to collect and interpret relevant information about direct competitors, indirect competitors, and potential competitors. Several methodologies are available to conduct such an analysis, including a strengths, weaknesses, opportunities, and threats (SWOT) analysis, and competitor analysis grid.

Existing firms with a weak brand or a brand that does not reflect the intent of the online effort may decide to create a new brand. Axon Computertime's analysis from an e-commerce strategic planning effort identified an opportunity to deliver an integrated e-commerce solution in the marketplace (see Case 12.1, p. 480). To capitalize on this opportunity and retain its reputation, the company created a new division and launched a new brand, Quality Direct, to distinguish this effort within the parent company.

Strategy Formulation

Strategy formulation is the development of strategies to exploit opportunities and manage threats in the business environment in light of corporate strengths and weaknesses. In an EC strategy, the end result is likely to be a list of EC applications or projects to be implemented.

Specific activities and outcomes from this phase include:

▶ **Business opportunities.** If the strategy initiation has been done well, a number of scenarios for future development of the business will be obvious. How well these scenarios fit with the future direction of the company are assessed. Similarly, the first phase may also have identified some current activities that are no longer relevant to the company's future and are candidates for divestiture, outsourcing, or elimination.

value proposition
The benefit that a company's products or services provide to a company and its customers.

strategy formulation
The development of strategies to exploit opportunities and manage threats in the business environment in light of corporate strengths and weaknesses.

- **Cost-benefit analysis.** Each proposed opportunity must be assessed in terms of the potential costs and benefits to the company in light of its mission and goals. These costs and benefits may be financial or nonfinancial, tangible or intangible, or short-term or long-term. More information about conducting a cost-benefit analysis is included in Section 12.2. A major part of such analysis is measuring profits on the Web (see Case 12.1).

- **Risk analysis, assessment, and management.** The risks of each proposed EC initiative (project) must be analyzed and assessed. If a significant risk is evident, then a risk management plan is required. Of particular importance in an EC strategy are business risk factors such as transition risk and partner risk.

- **Business plan.** Many of the outcomes from these first two phases—goals, competitor analysis, strategic opportunities, risk analysis, and more—come together in a business plan. Every business—large or small, new or old, successful or not—needs a business plan to acquire funding and to ensure that a realistic approach is being taken to implement the business strategy. According to *Access eCommerce* (2006), a business plan for EC is likely to include the following activities: introduction, technology audit, check out the competition, set goals, identify the audience, build a team, create a budget, locate resources, use a Web site planning checklist, try a Web site promotion checklist, send a press release, evaluate the plan, prepare appendices to the plan, and identify related resources. The value-proposition part of a business plan includes four phases: (1) value definition, (2) value development, (3) value measurement, and (4) value communication (see en.wikipedia.org/wiki/Value_proposition for details). For a comprehensive treatment see Online Tutorial T1. The major strategic planning tools are described in Online File W12.1.

Strategy Implementation

In this phase, the emphasis shifts from "what do we do?" to "how do we do it?" In the **strategy implementation** phase, detailed, short-term plans are developed for carrying out the projects agreed on in strategy formulation. Specifically, decision makers evaluate options, establish specific milestones, allocate resources, and manage the projects.

Specific activities and outcomes from this phase include:

- **Project planning.** Inevitably, strategy implementation is executed through an EC project or a series of projects. Project planning includes setting specific project objectives, creating a project schedule with milestones, and setting measurable performance targets. Normally, a project plan would be set for each project and application.

- **Resource allocation.** Organizational resources are those owned, available to, or controlled by a company. They can be human, financial, technological, managerial, or knowledge based. This phase includes business process outsourcing (BPO) consideration and use.

- **Project management.** This is the process of making the selected applications and projects a reality—hiring staff; purchasing equipment; licensing, purchasing, or writing software; contracting vendors; and so on.

Strategy Assessment

Just as soon as implementation is complete, assessment begins. **Strategy assessment** is the continuous evaluation of progress toward the organization's strategic goals, resulting in corrective action and, if necessary, strategy reformulation. In strategy assessment, specific measures called *metrics* assess the progress of the strategy. In some cases, data gathered in

strategy implementation
The development of detailed, short-term plans for carrying out the projects agreed on in strategy formulation.

strategy assessment
The continuous evaluation of progress toward the organization's strategic goals, resulting in corrective action and, if necessary, strategy reformulation.

CASE 12.1
EC Application

MEASURING PROFIT ON THE WEB

Axon Computertime (*axon.co.nz*) is an IT solutions company with locations in New Zealand's four largest cities. Axon's goal is "to be New Zealand's most recommended IT Services Company."

In 2002, as part of an examination of the success of its Quality Direct service, Axon issued a white paper that examined business profitability on the Web. Specifically the white paper listed four areas of potential profits from Web activities and metrics that Axon used to assess the impact of the Web on business profit. This case provides a real example of a small business that is profiting from its Web-based delivery of services and has collected some quantitative data to demonstrate its EC success.

Metrics were applied in four areas. Each of the four areas are described briefly next, followed by some of the metrics (a partial list) Axon used to assess goal achievement.

Cost Avoidance and Reduction

Web technologies can enhance profitability by reducing or eliminating transaction costs (e.g., product purchase) or interaction costs (e.g., a meeting, a phone call). Cost avoidance and reduction happens through activities such as improved access to information, customer self-help, and error reduction.

The following metrics demonstrated cost avoidance and reduction by Axon:

▶ Selling costs were reduced by 40 percent for each dollar of margin generated.
▶ Call volume to sales support increased at less than 50 percent of the traditional rate.
▶ Warehouse space was reduced by 40 percent, while volume increased by 40 percent.
▶ Obsolete stock write-offs as percentage of revenue were reduced by 93 percent.

Customer Service Enhancements

Delivering information to customers on all aspects of their transactions helps make the product or service more visible. Increased visibility generates increased value from a customer's perspective.

The following metrics demonstrated customer service enhancements by Axon:

▶ Average days to delivery were reduced by 20 percent over 2 years.
▶ Satisfaction with the delivery process is consistently greater than 80 percent.

New Market Opportunities

New market opportunities include new services to existing clients, changing the value proposition for existing clients, and targeting new markets.

The following metrics demonstrated new market opportunities by Axon:

▶ Product revenue increased over 40 percent in the first 12 months of full operation.
▶ New customers were added at twice the rate that previously was being achieved.

New Media Options

"New media" includes improved communication, advertising, and marketing efforts through lower collateral costs, improved target marketing, subscriber lists, and sold advertising space.

The following metrics demonstrated the use of new media options by Axon:

▶ Cost per item for e-mail is less than 1 percent of the cost per item for postal mail.
▶ Response rate to e-mail is five times the response rate to postal mail.
▶ Expenditures on brochure design and production were reduced by 45 percent.

IT Best Investment Opportunities for 2005 and Beyond

The following are leading investment opportunities related to e-commerce:

▶ Application management and access to applications
▶ Desktop and server management
▶ Information collaboration
▶ Mobile and convergence technologies
▶ Server and storage consolidation
▶ Service optimization

Sources: Compiled from Green (2002) and from *axon.co.nz* (accessed February 2008).

Questions

1. List four areas in which Axon is demonstrating increased profitability through the use of the Web.

2. Describe the characteristics of the metrics listed here (e.g., financial, customer service, quantitative, time based).

3. What other metrics might apply?

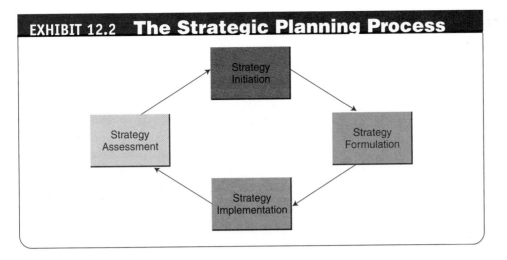

EXHIBIT 12.2   The Strategic Planning Process

the first phase can be used as baseline data to assess the strategy's effectiveness. If not, this information will have to be gathered. For large EC projects, business performance management tools can be employed (see hyperion.com).

What happens with the results from strategy assessment? As shown in Exhibit 12.2 the strategic planning process starts over again, immediately. Note that a cyclical approach is required—a strategic planning process that requires constant reassessment of today's strategy while preparing a new strategy for tomorrow.

A major organizational restructuring and transformation was the reason for the development of a new strategic plan for InternetNZ, as Case 12.2 describes.

BUSINESS PLANNING IN E-COMMERCE

One almost inevitable outcome of strategy setting is a business plan. A **business plan** is a written document that identifies the company's goals and outlines how the company intends to achieve the goals. Exhibit 12.3 shows a typical, nondetailed outline of a business plan. This outline follows Online Tutorial T1.

BUSINESS CASE

A distinctive type of business plan is the *business case*. As described in the previous section, a business plan usually is used when launching a new business. A **business case** is a business plan for a new initiative or large, new project *inside an existing organization*. Its purpose is the same as with a business plan—to justify a specific investment of funds—but the audience is the company's board of directors and senior management, not an external funding agency. The business case helps clarify how the organization will use its resources by identifying the strategic justification ("Where are we going?"), technical justification ("How will we get there?"), operational justification ("When will we get there?"), and financial justification ("Why will we win?") (Dell Public 2005). Examples of EC initiatives that may require a business case include the launch or major revision of a Web site, implementation of an e-procurement project, or deploying a CRM system.

The content of a business case is similar to that of a business plan. One difference is that the business plan concentrates on the viability of a company, whereas a business case assesses both viability of the project and the fit of the initiative with the firm's

business plan
A written document that identifies a company's goals and outlines how the company intends to achieve the goals and at what cost.

business case
A business plan for a new initiative or large, new project inside an existing organization.

CASE 12.2
EC Application

STRATEGIC PLANNING AT INTERNETNZ

InternetNZ is not only an Internet-based business; its business is the Internet. An incorporated, nonprofit organization, InternetNZ describes itself as "the guardian of the Internet for New Zealand," and its primary business activity is management of the .nz ccTLD (Country Code Top-Level Domain).

After a somewhat turbulent transition from its predecessor organization, the Internet Society of New Zealand, in early 2004 InternetNZ embarked on a comprehensive strategic-planning exercise. The result of that exercise, *InternetNZ Strategic Plan: 2004–2007*, is a model of content that should be in every strategic plan.

▶ **Environment analysis.** In addition to describing trends that affect the global Internet and the Internet in New Zealand, a PEST analysis (political, economic, social, and technological) lists factors in the political, economic, and social environment that affect the conduct of InternetNZ's business. For example: "No large pro-censorship lobby in NZ" (political), "Increasing dependence on the Internet for information" (social), and "The Internet bridges NZ's geographical disadvantage" (economic).

▶ **Vision statement.** Sixteen visionary goals (e.g., "Benefits of the Internet have been extended to all New Zealanders") follow a vision statement for 2007 ("The Internet, open and uncapturable, offering high performance and unfettered access for all").

▶ **Mission statement.** "To protect and promote the Internet in New Zealand" captures many of the characteristics— visionary, realistic, easily understood, short and concise— of a good mission statement.

▶ **SWOT analysis.** A SWOT analysis lists 13 strengths (e.g., "Committed, involved, clever volunteers," "Has created a best practice model for .nz ccTLD"), 13 weaknesses (e.g., "Perception of InternetNZ as mainly 'geeks' or 'techies,'" "Lack of internal resources to respond to rapidly changing environment"), 14 opportunities (e.g., "A leader in the fight against spam," "Help insure widespread broadband access"), and 11 threats (e.g., "Unnecessary government intervention or regulation," "Low level of membership, hence, providing little funding and vulnerable to take over").

▶ **Core values.** Six core values—openness, transparency, ethical behavior, neutrality, supportive, commitment— are identified and described briefly.

▶ **Goal statements.** Eight strategies (e.g., management of .nz ccTLD, advocacy and representation to government, promote the Internet, support Internet innovation and technical leadership) are listed. For each strategy, one to eight goals are listed, and it clearly identifies the InternetNZ committee held accountable for achievement of the strategy. The 2004–2007 InternetNZ business plan identifies a goal statement of purpose, projected outcomes, and specific examples for execution of the goal for each goal.

▶ **Business plan.** Separate from, but an integral part of the *InternetNZ Strategic Plan: 2004–2007*, is the *InternetNZ Business Plan: 2004–2007*. This document lists, describes, and prioritizes the specific activities that are necessary to achieve the goals, with associated income and expenses, also available in both the *InternetNZ Strategic Plan: 2008–2009* and the *InternetNZ Business Plan: 2007–2009*.

The InternetNZ Council adopted the strategic plan and the business plan at its April 2004 meeting, and both plans are in the process of being implemented.

Finally, Davidson, who was appointed as executive director of the company in 2005 said that the continued fulfillment of InternetNZ's Strategic Plan is his major focus in his new role. This plan outlines steps for InternetNZ's management of the .nz ccTLD advocacy to the government, support for industry best practice and self-regulation, protection and promotion of the Internet, as well as NZ representation globally.

Sources: Compiled from *InternetNZ* (2004), *InternetNZ* (2006), and Auckland (2005).

Questions

1. Why would a nonprofit organization, such as InternetNZ, need a strategic plan or a business plan?

2. What is the difference between a vision statement and a mission statement?

mission and goals. A business case also will almost certainly have more operational detail and a justification that it is the best way for the organization to use its resources to accomplish the desired strategy. Online Tutorial T1 highlights other differences between a business plan and a business case.

EXHIBIT 12.3   Outline of a Business Plan

Executive Summary: The executive summary is a synopsis of the key points of the entire business plan. Its purpose is to explain the fundamentals of the business in a way that both informs and excites the reader.

Business Description: The business description describes the nature and purpose of the business and includes the firm's mission statement, goals, value proposition, and a description of the products and services it provides. The purpose of the business description is to objectively explain and justify the business idea in a positive and enthusiastic manner.

Operations Plan: The operations section of the business plan describes the inputs, processes, procedures, and activities required to create what products the business will sell or what services it will deliver.

Financial Plan: The financial plan estimates the monetary resources and flows that will be required to carry out the business plan. The financial plan also indicates when and by how much the business intends to be profitable. Finally, the financial statements (e.g., balance sheet, cash flow statement) tell a lot about the entrepreneur in terms of business commitment and financial wherewithal to make the business a profitable success.

Marketing Plan: The central part of the marketing plan is the market analysis, which defines the firm's target markets and analyzes how the organization will position its products or services to arouse and fulfill the needs of the target markets in order to maximize sales. Other aspects of the marketing plan include pricing strategy, promotion plan, distribution plan, and a demand forecast.

Competitor Analysis: The competitor analysis (a) outlines the competitive strengths and weaknesses of rivals in the industry and (b) reveals the firm's competitive position in the market space.

With a firm foundation of organizational strategy and business planning in place, we now turn our attention to e-commerce strategy.

E-COMMERCE STRATEGY: CONCEPTS AND OVERVIEW

What is the role of the Internet in organizational strategy? According to Ward and Peppard (2002), strategy setting begins with the business strategy—determining an organization's vision, mission statement, and overall goals (see Exhibit 12.4). Then the information systems (IS) strategy is set, primarily by determining *what* information and associated information systems are required to carry out the business strategy. The information and communications technology (ICT) strategy is decided based on *how* to deliver the information and information systems via technology. The EC strategy is a derivative of both the IS strategy and the ICT strategy. The solid downward pointing arrows in Exhibit 12.4 depict the top-down portion of the process. The broken line indicates possible bottom-up activities, which means that lower-level strategies cause adjustments in higher-level strategies.

The Internet impacts all levels of organizational strategy setting, and it is shown by the shaded boxes in Exhibit 12.4. Business strategists need to consider the Internet's role in creating or innovating products, in product and service delivery, in supplier and customer relationships, and in assessing the impact on competition in the marketplace. Generally, strategic planners need to view the Internet as a complement to traditional ways of marketing and competing, not as a source of competitive advantage in and of itself (Porter 2001). IS strategists need to consider the Internet as a tool for collecting information and distributing it to where it is required. ICT planners will need to plan the integration of the Internet-based technologies into the existing and future ICT infrastructure. Thinking about and planning for the Internet should be subsumed into each of the four strategy levels (McKay and Marshall 2004).

Using the above process, businesses continue to evolve their own e-commerce strategies, defined as the formulation and execution of a vision of how a new or existing

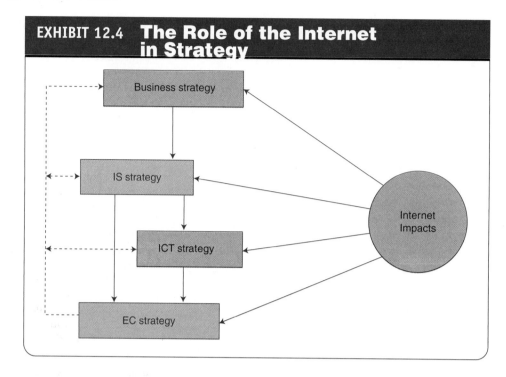

EXHIBIT 12.4   The Role of the Internet in Strategy

company intends to do business electronically. The following section explains in detail one of the most important aspects of e-strategy: The justification of EC start up and EC projects.

Section 12.1 ▶ REVIEW QUESTIONS

1. What is strategy?
2. Describe the strategic planning process.
3. Describe the four phases of strategic planning.
4. What is a business plan?
5. What is a business case? How is it different from a business plan?
6. Describe the process of deriving an EC strategy.
7. Describe the role of the Internet in setting EC strategy.

12.2 JUSTIFICATION AND COST-BENEFIT ANALYSIS

Companies need to justify their EC investments as part of strategy formulation for a number of different reasons, but most face an uphill battle to address this new accountability, as demonstrated by the following statistics from Peppard and Ward (2005):

- ▶ Sixty-five percent of companies lack the knowledge or tools to do ROI calculations.
- ▶ Seventy-five percent have no formal processes or budgets in place for measuring ROI.
- ▶ Sixty-eight percent do not measure how projects coincide with promised benefits 6 months after completion.

At the same time, demand for expanding or initiating e-business projects remains strong. In order to achieve the optimal level of investment, CIOs will need to effectively communicate the value of proposed EC projects in order to gain approval.

OTHER REASONS WHY EC JUSTIFICATION IS NEEDED

The following are some additional reasons for conducting EC justification:

- Companies now realize that EC is not necessarily the solution to all problems. Therefore, EC projects must *compete for funding and resources* with other internal and external projects. Analysis is needed to determine when funding of an EC project is appropriate.
- Some large companies, and many public organizations, mandate a formal evaluation of requests for funding.
- Companies need to assess the success of EC projects after completion and later on a periodic basis.
- The success of EC projects may be assessed in order to pay bonuses to those involved with the project.

CIO Insight (2004) reports the following reasons for IT and EC justification: pressure from top management, internal competition for funding, the large amount of money involved, and weak business conditions. The same study found that justification forces EC and IT into better alignment with the corporate business strategy. Finally, justification increases the credibility of EC projects. Similar reasons exist for justifying new EC startups.

EC INVESTMENT CATEGORIES AND BENEFITS

Before we look at how to justify EC investments, let's examine the nature of such investments. One basic way to categorize different EC investments is to distinguish between investment in infrastructure and investment in specific EC applications.

The IT *infrastructure* provides the foundation for EC applications in the enterprise. The IT infrastructure includes intranets, extranets, data centers, data warehouses, and knowledge bases, and many applications throughout the enterprise share the infrastructure. Infrastructure investments are made for the long term.

EC applications are specific systems and programs for achieving certain objectives; for example, taking a customer order online or providing e-CRM. The number of EC applications can be large. They may be in one functional department or several departments may share them, which makes evaluation of their costs and benefits more complex.

Ross and Beath (2002) propose another way to look at EC and investment categories. They base their categories on the *purpose of the investment*. They also suggest a cost-justification (funding) approach as well as the probable owner of each application (e.g., specific department or corporate ownership). The variety of EC investment categories demonstrates the complex nature of EC investments.

The basic reasons that companies invest in IT and EC are to improve business processes, lower costs, increase productivity, increase customer satisfaction and retention, increase revenue, reduce time-to-market, and increase market share.

According to a *CIO Insight* (2004) survey, companies want to get the following benefits from an IT (including EC) investment: cost reduction (84 percent); productivity improvement (77 percent); improved customer satisfaction (66 percent); improved staffing (57 percent); higher revenues (45 percent); higher earnings (43 percent); better customer retention (42 percent); more return of equity (33 percent); and faster time-to-market (31 percent). (Note that separate data for EC are not available.)

HOW IS AN EC INVESTMENT JUSTIFIED?

cost-benefit analysis
A comparison of the costs of a project against the benefits.

Justifying an EC investment means comparing the costs of each project against its benefits in what is known as a **cost-benefit analysis**. To conduct such an analysis, it is necessary to define and measure the relevant EC benefits and costs. Cost-benefit analysis is frequently assessed by *return on investment (ROI)*, which is also the name of a specific method for evaluating investments (see Paton and Troppito 2004).

A number of different methods measure the *business value* of EC and IT investments. Traditional methods that support such analyses are net present value (NPV) and ROI (see Online File W12.2).

The cost-benefit analysis and the business value are part of the business case (Section 12.1).

Several vendors provide templates, tools, guidelines, and more for preparing the business case for specific areas. For example, IT Business Edge (itbusinessedge.com) provides an SOA Business Case Resource Kit (The templates are in Microsoft Word). ROI is calculated with Excel templates.

WHAT NEEDS TO BE JUSTIFIED? WHEN SHOULD JUSTIFICATION TAKE PLACE?

Not all EC investments need to be formally justified. In some cases, a simple one-page qualitative justification will do. The following are cases where formal evaluation may not be needed:

 ▶ When the value of the investment is relatively small for the organization
 ▶ When the relevant data are not available, are inaccurate, or are too volatile
 ▶ When the EC project is mandated—it must be done regardless of the costs and benefits involved

However, even when formal analysis is not required, an organization should have at least some qualitative analysis to explain the logic of investing in the EC project. For more details, see Martin (2006).

USING METRICS IN EC JUSTIFICATION

metric
A specific, measurable standard against which actual performance is compared.

A **metric** is a specific, measurable standard against which actual performance is compared. Metrics are used to describe costs, benefits, or the ratio between them. They are used not only for justification, but also for other economic activities (e.g., to compare employee performance in order to reward specific employees). Metrics can produce very positive results in organizations by driving behavior in a number of ways. According to Rayport and Jaworski (2004), metrics can:

 ▶ Define the value proposition of business models
 ▶ Communicate a business strategy to the workforce through performance targets
 ▶ Increase accountability when metrics are linked with performance-appraisal programs
 ▶ Align the objectives of individuals, departments, and divisions to the enterprise's strategic objectives
 ▶ Track the performance of EC systems, including usage, types of visitors, page visits, conversion rate, and so on
 ▶ Assess the health of companies by using tools such as balanced scorecards and performance dashboards

EC metrics can be tangible or intangible, see Exhibit 12.5 for examples.

EXHIBIT 12.5 Sample EC Metrics for Various Entities of Users

EC User	Tangible Metrics	Intangible Metrics
Buyer (B2C)	• Cost/price of the product • Time in executing the transaction • Number of available alternatives	• Ease of use of EC • Convenience in purchasing • Information availability • Reliability of the transaction • Privacy of personal data
Seller (B2C)	• Profit per customer • Conversion rate of visitors • Customer retention rate • Inventory costs • Profit per item sold • Market share	• Customer satisfaction • Customer loyalty • Transaction security
Net-enhanced organization (B2B)	• From design to market (time) • Cash-to-cash cycle • Percentage of orders delivered on time or early • Profit per item sold	• Flexibility in changing purchase orders • Ability to sustain unplanned production increase • Risk reduction • Improved quality of products/services
Government (G2C)	• Reduction in cost of transactions • Reduction in licensing fees • Increase in participation in government programs • Lower tax rates	• Citizen satisfaction • Reelection of candidates • Choice of interacting with elected officials • Promoting democratic principles • Disseminating more information quickly

Additional Examples of Metrics

• More than one-third of consumers use the same password for online banking as they do for other online activities.
• More than 50 brands were targeted by phishing scams in November 2004.
• More than half of consumers say they are less likely to respond to an e-mail from their bank because of phishing threats.
• Experts say that 80 percent of the infrastructures of large industries are likely to be hit by cyber attacks.
• Some consumers of financial products say phishing has turned them away from Web transactions.
• Consumers are slightly more likely to receive permission-based e-mails from online merchants than other retail businesses.
• Two-thirds of computers have spyware on them.
• Spam messages are considerably shorter than legitimate e-mails.
• eBay tops the list of online destinations on Black Friday (the day after Thanksgiving).
• Spam takes up volume, but not bandwidth.

Sources: Compiled from *www2.cio.com/metrics* (accessed March 2007), Borenstein et al. (2005), and from Sardar et al. (2006).

Metrics, Measurements, and Key Performance Indicators

Metrics need to be defined properly with a clear way to measure them. For example, *revenue growth* can be measured in total dollars, in percentage change over time, or in percentage growth as compared to the entire industry. *Cost avoidance*, for example, can be achieved in many ways, one of which may be "decrease obsolete stock write-offs as

indicators (KPIs)
The quantitative
expression of critically
important metrics.

percentage of revenue." Defining the specific measures is critical; otherwise, what the metrics actually measure may be open to interpretation.

The *balanced scorecard method* (Niven 2005) uses customer metrics, financial metrics, internal business processes metrics, and learning and growth metrics. Metrics are related to the organization's goals, objectives, vision, and plans. **Key performance indicators (KPIs)**, which are the quantitative expression of critically important metrics (known as *critical success factors*), frequently measure metrics that deal directly with performance (e.g., sales, profits). Frequently, one metric has several KPIs. Examples of metrics were provided in Case 12.1 (p. 480).

Any organization, private or public, can use metrics. Let's look at an example. In Australia, the government of Victoria (vic.gov.au) is one of the leaders in exploiting the Internet to provide a one-stop service center called "Do It Online." In the United States, MyCalifornia (my.ca.gov) offers many services for the citizens of California. In either case, the metric of "travel and wait time" for the citizens who would otherwise have to visit a physical office justifies offering the service of renewing driver's licenses.

We limit our discussion here mostly to individual EC projects or initiatives. EC projects deal mostly with the automation of business processes, and, as such, they can be viewed as *capital investment* decisions. Online Chapter 13 discusses investment in a startup company.

Now that we understand the need for conducting EC justification and the use of metrics, let's see why EC justification is so difficult to accomplish.

Section 12.2 ▶ REVIEW QUESTIONS

1. List some of the reasons for justifying an EC investment.
2. Describe the risks of not conducting an EC justification study.
3. Describe how an EC investment is justified.
4. List the major EC investment categories.
5. When is justification of EC investments unnecessary?
6. What are metrics? What benefits do they offer?

12.3 DIFFICULTIES IN MEASURING AND JUSTIFYING E-COMMERCE INVESTMENTS AND SUCCESS

Justifying EC (and IT) projects can be a complex and, therefore, difficult process. Let's see why.

THE EC JUSTIFICATION PROCESS

The EC justification process varies depending on the situation and the methods used. However, in its extreme, it can be very complex, as shown by Misra (2006) who identified five areas that must be considered in the justification of IT projects, as shown in Exhibit 12.6. In this section, we also discuss intangibles and tangibles.

We will see later in this section that one major difficulty with EC justification is measuring intangible benefits and costs. Next, we provide other difficulties in conducting justifications.

DIFFICULTIES IN MEASURING PRODUCTIVITY AND PERFORMANCE GAINS

One of the major benefits of using EC is increased productivity. However, productivity increases may be difficult to measure for a number of different reasons.

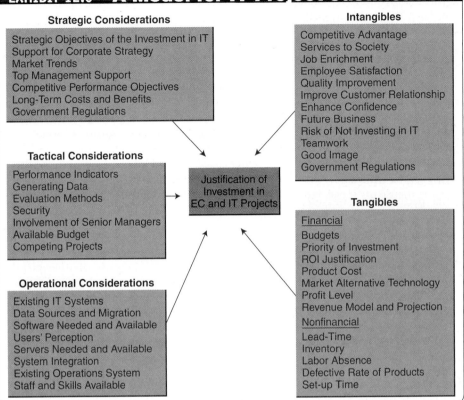

EXHIBIT 12.6 A Model for IT Project Justification

Strategic Considerations

Strategic Objectives of the Investment in IT
Support for Corporate Strategy
Market Trends
Top Management Support
Competitive Performance Objectives
Long-Term Costs and Benefits
Government Regulations

Tactical Considerations

Performance Indicators
Generating Data
Evaluation Methods
Security
Involvement of Senior Managers
Available Budget
Competing Projects

Operational Considerations

Existing IT Systems
Data Sources and Migration
Software Needed and Available
Users' Perception
Servers Needed and Available
System Integration
Existing Operations System
Staff and Skills Available

Justification of Investment in EC and IT Projects

Intangibles

Competitive Advantage
Services to Society
Job Enrichment
Employee Satisfaction
Quality Improvement
Improve Customer Relationship
Enhance Confidence
Future Business
Risk of Not Investing in IT
Teamwork
Good Image
Government Regulations

Tangibles

Financial
Budgets
Priority of Investment
ROI Justification
Product Cost
Market Alternative Technology
Profit Level
Revenue Model and Projection

Nonfinancial
Lead-Time
Inventory
Labor Absence
Defective Rate of Products
Set-up Time

Sources: Complied from *International Journal of Information Management*, March 2001, Gunasekaran A., P. Love, F. Rahimi, and R. Miele. "A Model for Investment Justification in Information Technology Projects," with permission from Elsevier; and R. Misra, "Evolution of the Philosophy of Investments in IT Projects," *Issues in Informing Sciences and Information Technology*, Vol 3, 2006.

Data and Analysis Issues

Data, or the analysis of the data, may hide productivity gains. Why is this so? For manufacturing, it is fairly easy to measure outputs and inputs. For example, General Motors produces motor vehicles—a relatively well-defined product—that show gradual quality changes over time. It is not difficult to identify the inputs used to produce these vehicles with reasonable accuracy. However, in service industries, such as finance or health-care delivery, it is more difficult to define what the products are, how they change in quality, and how they may be related to corresponding benefits and costs.

For example, banks now use EC to handle a large portion of deposits and withdrawal transactions through ATMs. The ability to withdraw cash from ATMs 24/7 is a substantial benefit for customers compared with the limited hours of the physical branch. But, what is the value of this to the bank in comparison with the associated costs? If the incremental value exceeds the incremental costs, then it represents a productivity gain; otherwise the productivity impact is negative.

EC Productivity Gains May Be Offset by Losses in Other Areas

Another possible difficulty is that EC gains in certain areas of the company may be offset by losses in other areas. For example, increased online sales may decrease offline sales, a situation known as *cannibalism*. Or, consider the situation where an organization installs a new EC system that makes it possible to increase output per employee; if the organization reduces its production staff but has to increase its IT staff, the productivity gains from EC could be small, or even negative.

Incorrectly Defining What Is Measured

The results of any investment justification depend on what is actually measured. For example, to assess the benefits of EC investment, one should usually look at productivity improvement in the area where the EC project was installed. However, productivity increase may not necessarily be a profitable improvement (e.g., due to losses in other areas). The problem of definitions can be overcome by using appropriate metrics and key performance indicators.

Other Difficulties

Other performance measurement difficulties also have been noted. A number of researchers have pointed out, for example, that time lags may throw off productivity measurements (Misra 2006). Many EC investments, especially those in e-CRM, take 5 to 6 years to show significant positive results, but many studies do not wait that long to measure productivity changes. Devaraj and Kohli (2003) suggested another possible problem when they tried to relate the actual rather than the potential uses of a system with IT expenditures. For a list of other factors that impact performance, see Devaraj and Kohli (2002).

Furthermore, changes in organizational performance may occur years after installing an EC application. Thus, proper evaluation must be done over the entire life cycle of the system. This requires forecasting, which may be difficult. In EC, it is even more difficult, because investors often require that risky and fast-changing EC systems pay for themselves within 3 years. For further discussion, see Keystone Strategy, Inc. (2006). For difficulties in measuring intangible costs and benefits, see Online File W12.3.

DETERMINING E-COMMERCE SUCCESS

The success factors of EC depend on the industry, the sellers and buyers, and the products sold. Furthermore, the ability of sellers to create economic value for consumers will determine the EC success. When deciding to sell online, looking at the major factors that determine the impact of EC can evaluate the potential for success.

Strader and Shaw (1997) have identified four categories of e-market success factors: product, industry, seller, and consumer characteristics.

Product Characteristics

Digitized products, such as software, documents, music, and videos, are particularly well suited for e-markets because they can be distributed to customers electronically, resulting in instant delivery and very low distribution costs. Digitization also decreases the amount of time involved in the order-taking cycle because automation can be introduced to help customers search for, select, and pay for a product, anyplace and anytime, without the intervention of a sales or technical person. Finally, product updates can be communicated to customers rapidly.

A product's *price* may also be an important determinant of its success. The higher the product price, the greater the level of risk involved in the market transaction between buyers and sellers who are geographically separated and who may have never dealt with each other before.

Another product characteristic is the cost and speed of *product customization*. Millions of consumers configure computers, cars, toys, clothes, and services to their liking, and if sellers can fulfill such requests at a reasonable cost and in a short amount of time, they can assure success (e.g., Dell). Finally, computers, electronic products, consumer products, and even cars can be sold online because consumers know exactly what they are buying. The more product information that is available, the easier it is to sell. The use of multimedia and product tutorials (e.g., see bluenile.com) can dramatically facilitate product description.

Another aspect of a product's characteristics is *cross-selling* and *up-selling*. EC enables efficient and effective cross-selling and up-selling of many (but not all) products and services.

Industry Characteristics

Electronic markets are most useful when they are able to match buyers and sellers directly. However, some industries require transaction brokers. E-markets affect these industries less than those that do not require brokers. Stockbrokers, insurance agents, and travel agents may provide needed services, but in some cases software may reduce the need for these brokers. This is particularly true as intelligent systems become more available to assist consumers.

Other important industry characteristics include the following: Who are the major players (corporations) in the industry? How many companies in the industry are well managed? How strong is the competition, including foreign companies?

Seller Characteristics

Electronic markets reduce *search costs*, allowing consumers to find sellers that offer lower prices, better service, or both. As in the case of the motion picture industry, this may reduce profit margins for sellers that compete in e-markets, but it may increase the number of transactions that take place (i.e., people watching more movies). However, if sellers are unwilling to participate in this environment, it may reduce the impact of e-markets. In highly competitive industries with low barriers to entry, sellers may not have a choice but to join in; if they do not, online customers' searches will lead them to an online competitor's distribution channel.

Consumer Characteristics

Consumers can be classified as impulse, patient, or analytical. Electronic markets may have little impact on industries in which impulse buyers make a sizable percentage of purchases. Because e-markets require a certain degree of effort and preparation on the part of the consumer, e-markets are more conducive to consumers who do some comparisons before buying (i.e., the patient and analytical buyers). Mobile devices are changing this situation because real-time information is available now while shoppers are in physical stores.

Analytical buyers can use the Internet to evaluate a wide range of information before deciding on what and where to buy. In contrast, *m-commerce*, and especially *l-commerce*, which provides and even customizes services based on a customer's location, are banking on impulse buyers—on the customer's being in the right place at the right time. However, m-commerce also offers indirect benefits to consumers through improved location services.

Section 12.3 ▶ REVIEW QUESTIONS

1. List the major difficulties in measuring costs, benefits, and success of EC.
2. Describe product characteristics in EC.

3. What are industry characteristics in EC?

4. What are seller characteristics in EC?

5. What are consumer characteristics in EC?

12.4 GLOBAL E-COMMERCE

Global electronic activities have existed for more than 25 years, mainly EFT and EDI in support of B2B and other repetitive, standardized financial transactions. However, these activities required expensive and inflexible private telecommunications lines and, therefore, were limited mostly to large corporations. The emergence of the Internet and technologies such as extranets and XML has resulted in an inexpensive and flexible infrastructure that can greatly facilitate global trade. For global marketing considerations, see Egea and Mendez (2006).

A global electronic marketplace is an attractive thrust for an EC strategy. "Going global" means access to larger markets, mobility (e.g., to minimize taxes), and flexibility to employ workers anywhere. However, going global is a complex and strategic decision process due to a multiplicity of issues. Geographic distance is one of the most obvious dimensions of conducting business globally, but frequently it is not the most important dimension. Instead cultural, political, legal, administrative, and economic dimensions are equally likely to threaten a firm's international ambitions (Kraemer 2006). This section briefly examines the opportunities, problems, and solutions for companies using e-commerce to go global.

BENEFITS AND EXTENT OF OPERATIONS

The major advantage of EC is the ability to do business at any time, from anywhere, and at a reasonable cost. These also are the drivers behind global EC, and there have been some incredible success stories in this area. For example:

- eBay conducts auctions in hundreds of countries worldwide.
- Alibaba.com (Chapter 5) provides B2B trading services to hundreds of thousands of companies in hundreds of countries.
- Amazon.com sells books and hundreds of other items to individuals and organizations in over 190 countries.
- Small companies, such as ZD Wines (zdwines.com), sell to hundreds of customers worldwide. Hothothot (hothothot.com) reported its first international trade only after it went online; within 3 years global sales accounted for 25 percent of its total sales. By 2007, the company had over 10,000 hits per day (up from 500 in 1997), and its annual growth rate was over 125 percent, selling to customers in 45 countries.
- Major corporations, such as GE and Boeing, have reported an increasing number of out-of-the-country vendors participating in their electronic RFQs. These electronic bids have resulted in a 10 to 15 percent cost reduction and an over 50 percent reduction in cycle time.
- Many international corporations considerably increased their success in recruiting employees for foreign locations when they used online recruiting (see xing.com and linkedin.com).

BARRIERS TO GLOBAL EC

Despite the benefits and opportunities offered by globalization, there are many barriers to global EC. Some of these barriers face any EC venture but become more difficult when international impacts are considered. These barriers include authentication of buyers and sellers (Chapter 10), generating and retaining trust (Chapter 4), order fulfill-ment and delivery (Chapter 11), security (Chapter 10), and domain names. Others are unique to global EC. We will use the culture, administration, geography, economics (CAGE) distance framework proposed by Ghemawat (2001) to identify areas in which natural or human-made barriers hinder global EC. Each of the four factors represents a different type of distance (difference) between two companies.

Cultural Issues

The Internet is a multifaceted marketplace made up of users from many cultures. The multicultural nature of global EC is important because cultural attributes determine how people interact with companies, agencies, and each other based on social norms, local standards, religious beliefs, and language. Doing business globally requires *cultural marketing*, a strategy for meeting the needs of a culturally diverse population.

Cultural and related differences include language, spelling differences (e.g., American versus British spelling), information formatting (e.g., dates can be mm/dd/yy or dd/mm/yy), graphics and icons (e.g., mailbox shapes differ from country to country), measurement standards (e.g., metric versus imperial system), the use of color (e.g., white is a funeral color in some countries), protection of intellectual property (e.g., Chinese toler-ance of copyright infringement has Confucian roots), time standards (e.g., local time zones versus Greenwich Mean Time), and information requests (e.g., requiring a zip code in an order form can lead to abandoned shopping carts in countries without postal codes). One solution involves language translation.

Solutions for overcoming cultural barriers begin with an awareness of the cultural identities and differences in the target markets. Different sites may need to be created for different cultural groups, taking into account site design elements, pricing and payment infrastructures, currency conversion, customer support, and language translation.

Language translation is one of the most obvious and most important aspects of maintaining global Web sites. The primary problems with language translation are speed and cost. It may take a human translator a week to translate a medium-sized Web site into another language. For large sites, the cost can be up to $500,000, depending on the complexity of the site and languages of translation, and it may take a long time. A good translator needs to pay attention to cultural issues. Some companies address the cost and time problems by translating their Web pages into different languages through so-called *machine translators* (a list of these translator programs is available in Online File W12.4). However, machine translation is only about 75 percent accurate (CNN.com 2006), which is why many companies use native-language, in-country translators to review and revise the results from machine translation software (see He 2006). For an organization that is successfully using machine translation, see Online File W12.4.

Transclick (transclick.com) provides real-time machine translation of e-mails, SMS, text messages, and instant messaging over computers, smart phones, and mobile PDAs in 16 different languages. For more on machine translation, see en.wikipedia.org/wiki/Machine_Translation.

Nutralogic Laboratories Inc. provides its global customers with an advanced multi-language e-commerce site (nutralogixlabs.com). Revenues from Europe and Asia increased significantly since the introduction of the native languages.

Administrative and Legal Issues

One of the most contentious areas of global EC is the resolution of international legal issues. A number of national governments and international organizations are working together to find ways to avoid uncoordinated actions and encourage uniform legal standards.

An ambitious effort to reduce differences in international law governing EC is the United Nations Commission on International Trade Law (UNCITRAL) Model Law on Electronic Commerce. Its purpose is to "offer national legislators a set of internationally acceptable rules which detail how a number of legal obstacles to the development of e-commerce may be removed, and how a more secure legal environment may be created" (*e-Business World* 2000).

International trade organizations, such as the World Trade Organization (WTO) and the Asia-Pacific Economic Cooperation (APEC) forum, have working groups that are attempting to reduce EC trade barriers in areas such as pricing regulations, customs, import/export restrictions, tax issues, and product specification regulations.

Geographic Issues and Localization

The geographic issues of shipping goods and services across international borders are well known. Barriers posed by geography differ based on the transportation infrastructure between and within countries and the type of product or service being delivered. For example, geographic distance is almost irrelevant with online software sales.

Many companies use different names, colors, sizes, and packaging for their overseas products and services. This practice is referred to as *localization*. In order to maximize the benefits of global information systems, the localization approach should also be used in the design and operation of the supporting information systems. For example, many Web sites offer different language or currency options, as well as special content. Europcar (europcar.com), for example, offers portals in 118 countries, each with an option for 1 of 10 languages. For more on localization, see Rigby and Vishwanath (2006).

Economic and Financial Issues

Economic and financial issues encompassing global EC include government tariffs, customs, and taxation. In areas subject to government regulation, tax and regulatory agencies have attempted to apply the rules used in traditional commerce to electronic commerce, with considerable success. Exceptions include areas such as international tariff duties and taxation. Software shipped in a box would be taxed for duties and tariffs when it arrives in the country. However, software downloaded online relies on self-reporting and voluntary payment of tax by the purchaser, something that does not happen very often.

The key financial barrier to global EC is electronic payment systems. To sell effectively online, EC firms must have flexible payment methods that match the ways different groups of people pay for their online purchases. Although credit cards are used widely in the United States, many European and Asian customers prefer to complete online transactions with offline payments. Even within the category of offline payments, companies must offer different options depending on the country. For example, French consumers prefer to pay with a check, Swiss consumers expect an invoice by mail, Germans commonly pay for products only upon delivery, and Swedes are accustomed to paying online with debit cards.

Pricing is another economic issue. A vendor may want to price the same product at different prices in different countries in consideration of local prices and competition. However, if a company has one Web site, differential pricing will be difficult or impossible. Similarly, what currency will be used for pricing? What currency will be used for payment?

BREAKING DOWN THE BARRIERS TO GLOBAL EC

A number of international organizations (e.g., OECD 2001) and experts (e.g., Stone 2005) have offered suggestions on how to break down the barriers to global EC. Some of these suggestions include the following:

▶ **Be strategic.** Identify a starting point and lay out a globalization strategy. Remember that Web globalization is a business-building process. Consider what languages and countries it makes sense for the company to target and how the company will support the site for each target audience.

▶ **Know your audience.** Carefully consider the target audience. Be fully informed of the cultural preferences and legal issues that matter to customers in a particular part of the world.

▶ **Localize.** As much as practical and necessary, offer Web sites in national languages; offer different sites in different countries (e.g., "Yahoo! Japan" is at yahoo.co.jp); price products in local currencies; and base terms, conditions, and business practices on local laws and cultural practices.

▶ **Think globally, act consistently.** An international company with country Web sites managed by local offices must make sure that areas such as brand management, pricing, corporate information, and content management are consistent with company strategy (Cagni 2004).

▶ **Value the human touch.** Trust the translation of the Web site content only to human translators, not machine translation programs (Dubie 2003). Involve language and technical editors in the quality assurance process. One slight mistranslation or one out-of-place graphic may turn off customers forever.

▶ **Clarify, document, explain.** Pricing, privacy policies, shipping restrictions, contact information, and business practices should be well documented and located on the Web site and visible to the customer. To help protect against foreign litigation, identify the company's location and the jurisdiction for all contract or sales disputes.

▶ **Offer services that reduce barriers.** It is not feasible to offer prices and payments in all currencies, so link to a currency exchange service (e.g., xe.com) for the customer's convenience (see Yunker 2006). In B2B e-commerce, be prepared to integrate the EC transaction with the buyer's accounting/finance internal information systems.

We close our discussion of global e-commerce with an example of a company's expansion into the international market in Case 12.3.

Section 12.4 ▶ REVIEW QUESTIONS

1. Describe globalization in EC and the advantages it presents.
2. Describe the major barriers to global EC.
3. What can companies do to overcome the barriers to global EC?

12.5 E-COMMERCE IN SMALL AND MEDIUM-SIZED ENTERPRISES

Some of the first companies to take advantage of Web-based electronic commerce were SMEs. Whereas larger, established, tradition-bound companies hesitated, SMEs moved onto the Web because they realized there were opportunities in marketing, business

CASE 12.3

PIERRE LANG EXPANDS INTO EASTERN EUROPE

Pierre Lang Europe (*pierrelang.com*) sells designer jewelry throughout Western Europe. Its traditional business model was to sell earrings, pendants, necklaces, and other jewelry through the firm's 5,500 sales representatives. When Pierre Lang decided to expand into Eastern Europe, the firm decided it needed to change this business model and the underlying information systems and business processes.

The company knew it was losing business because it was unable to keep track of customers and it did not have direct contact with them. If sales representatives left the company for any reason, they would take their customers with them. Pierre Lang Europe wanted more than sales from its customers, it wanted customer relationships for follow-on sales and customer support.

Like many companies expanding globally, Pierre Lang also anticipated that this expansion could double its revenues and order volume. The company needed better information about its finances, improved control of its order process, and a system that could handle the multiple legal and language requirements of doing business in many different countries.

Lang selected mySAP after evaluating several competing solutions. Installation began in July 2003; early rollout projects were in place by November; and financial and controlling capabilities went live in all company locations in January 2004.

Today, Pierre Lang uses country-specific versions of mySAP to handle invoicing, tax, language, and fiscal issues. France, for example, has unique requirements for tracking the import and export of gold and silver. "Lots of small things like that have to be considered because they're vital for Pierre Lang. It has to work perfectly in every country, so they have to know whom they will charge what, and do that automatically," says Rudolf Windisch, one of Pierre Lang's consulting partners on this project. "They also have to deal with all the tax issues, which vary considerably from one country to another. There are no homogeneous tax systems in Europe."

Pierre Lang expects to increase the accuracy of its information and eliminate the need for manual transfers of tax data to develop reports. Executives also anticipate decreased inventory costs through improved material disposition as well as better information about sales efforts and costs that will lead to improved forecasting and planning.

As noted in this chapter, expanding regionally or globally can have a dramatic impact on a company's bottom line but only if it is prepared to deal with the heterogeneous legal and financial systems in different countries. Pierre Lang knew this and met the challenge.

To safeguard its multinational enterprise network, the company uses an integrated network security platform (from *fortinet.com*). The system protects both the headquarters in Vienna and 65 sales offices throughout Europe. The centrally managed system protects every remote user. The system is updated in real time.

Sources: SAP AG (2004), *sap.com* (accessed February 2008), and *Fortinet.com* (2005).

Questions

1. Why was it necessary for Pierre Lang to look at fundamental changes in its business model and information systems?

2. What have been the results of implementing mySAP at Pierre Lang?

3. Why is security so important to the company and how is it protected?

4. Enter *fortinet.com* and examine the capabilities of its FortiGate products.

---

expansion, business launches, cost cutting, and tighter partner alliances. Some examples of small companies that have embraced EC are virtualvine.com, hothothot.com, and philaprintshop.com.

SMEs consider the Internet to be a valuable business tool. According to a 2004 survey by Interland (*eMarketer* 2004), 28 percent of small businesses expect more than three-quarters of their annual sales to come from the Internet. And it isn't only online sales that are being used to measure success. Although one-third of respondents measure site success by sales, almost half (47 percent) measure site success based on measures such as customer comments about the site and the volume of site traffic. For further discussion, see Tatnall and Burgess (2006).

However, many SMEs have found it difficult to formulate or implement an EC strategy, mainly because of low use of EC and IT by customers and suppliers, lack of knowledge or IT expertise in the SME, and limited awareness of the opportunities and risks (OECD 2001). Exhibit 12.7 provides a more complete list of major advantages and disadvantages of EC for SMEs. For critical success factors for SMEs, see Online File W12.5.

When analyzing e-commerce for SMEs, one should distinguish between B2C, which may be simple, and B2B, which may be complex when the SME is a supplier to a large company (e.g., see Lawson-Body and Illia 2006).

For the successful implementation of an EC strategy by an SME, see Case 12.4. For another success story, see Case 13.3 in Online Chapter 13.

SUPPORTING SMEs

SMEs have a variety of support options. Almost every developed country in the world has a government agency devoted to helping SMEs become more aware of and able to participate in electronic commerce (e.g., sba.gov, business.gov.au).

EXHIBIT 12.7 Advantages and Disadvantages of EC for Small and Medium-Sized Businesses	
Advantages/Benefits	**Disadvantages/Risks**
• Inexpensive sources of information. A Scandinavian study found that over 90 percent of SMEs use the Internet for information search (OECD 2001). • Inexpensive ways of advertising and conducting market research. Banner exchanges, newsletters, chat rooms, and so on are nearly zero-cost ways to reach customers. • Competitor analysis is easier. The Scandinavian study found that Finnish firms rated competitor analysis third in their use of the Internet, after information search and marketing. • Inexpensive ways to build (or rent) a storefront. Creating and maintaining a Web site is relatively easy and cheap (see Online Chapter 13). • SMEs are less locked into legacy technologies and existing relationships with traditional retail channels. • Image and public recognition can be generated quickly. A Web presence makes it easier for a small business to compete against larger firms. • An opportunity to reach worldwide customers. No other medium is as efficient at global marketing, sales, and customer support. • Other advantages for SMEs include increased speed of customer payments, closer ties with business partners, reduced errors in information transfer, lower operating costs, and other benefits that apply to all businesses.	• Lack of financial resources to fully exploit the Web. A transactional Web site may entail relatively high up-front, fixed costs in terms of cash flow for an SME. • Lack of technical staff or insufficient expertise in legal issues, advertising, etc. These human resources may be unavailable or prohibitively expensive to an SME. • Less risk tolerance than a large company. If initial sales are low or the unexpected happens, the typical SME does not have a large reserve of resources to fall back on. • When the product is not suitable or difficult for online sales (e.g., experiential products such as clothes or beauty products; perishable products, such as certain foods), the Web opportunity is not as great. • Reduced personal contact with customers represents the dilution of what is normally a strong point for a small business. • Inability to afford entry to or purchase enough volume to take advantage of digital exchanges.

CASE 12.4
EC Application

NETWORX EVENTS USES E-COMMERCE

Networx Events (*networxevents.com.au*) is a relatively new, small business (two full-time and one part-time staff members) that arranges professional events in Melbourne and Sydney, Australia. Networx's founder, Kimberly Palmer, started the business by sending e-mail invitations to 20 of her friends and colleagues. The mailing list grew rapidly, and orders for tickets exploded. This required a sophisticated and secure transaction-enabled ticketing system. By 2004, sales over the Internet reached AU$140,850, for a gross profit of $100,350. The system also saved $3,240 on reduced postage, telephone calls, etc. The initial investment was only $13,100 and the operating expenses $4,040. Thus, the system net profit was $86,450, an amazing return on the investment. The system also provides CRM and payment arrangement.

Here is how the ticket-purchasing process works:

1. A prospect "opts-in" to receive e-mail invitations to future events (permission e-mail, see Chapter 4).
2. A personalized invitation is e-mailed to the opt-in database of recipients.
3. To accept, the recipient fills out an online form to register for the event.
4. Once booking details are confirmed, the recipient fills in credit card details (if they are not stored already).
5. The recipient pays using credit card and Secure Socket Layer payment system (Chapter 10).
6. Upon successful transmission, the e-ticket and receipt are automatically returned to the recipient via e-mail.

For a small business, it made sense to get the required technology via outsourcing. Invitee and member contact details are stored in a third-party database. E-mails are delivered via an ASP on a cost-per-e-mail basis. The Eventix (*eventix.com.au*) ticketing system provides the ticketing, e-mail, and payment component. In addition to the

implementation cost, Networx pays a percentage of its ticket price to the operator.

The ASP model reduces up-front costs. Networx has avoided much of the negative publicity surrounding spam due to careful adherence to its privacy policy. Networx has always sought permission to send e-mails and, therefore, was not obligated to make any major change once the Australian Government's Spam Act was introduced in April 2004.

However, Networx has always promoted the notion of "forwarding" invitations to other friends and colleagues (viral marketing, Chapter 4), which does not contravene the current Spam Act requirements.

Networx Events plans to expand in both territory and range. It is about to launch its first franchise in Queensland—a move set to be replicated in other territories while expanding from marketing into entrepreneurship and other vertical professions. Both of these plans will continue to be underpinned by opt-in e-mail, electronic CRM, and online ticketing infrastructures.

Sources: Compiled from *networxevents.com.au* (accessed February 2008), *Vic.gov.au* (2007), and *Aptstrategies.com* (2007).

Questions

1. What were the drivers of e-commerce in this case?
2. Discuss the strategy of dealing with technological issues.
3. Discuss the strategies of permission and viral marketing.
4. Would you recommend a Web site for order fulfillment (Chapter 11)? Why or why not?
5. Does the planned expansion make sense?

Vendors realized the opportunity represented by thousands of businesses going online, and many have set up a variety of service centers that typically offer a combination of free information and fee-based support. Examples are IBM's Small Business Center (ibm.com/businesscenter) and Microsoft's Small Business Center (microsoft.com/smallbusiness/hub.mspx). Professional associations, Web resource services (e.g., smallbusiness.yahoo.com, workz.com), and small businesses that are in the business of helping other small businesses go online sponsor other small business support centers. For information on e-commerce barriers for SMEs, see Sharma (2006).

Section 12.5 ▶ REVIEW QUESTIONS

1. What are the advantages or benefits of EC for small businesses?
2. What are the disadvantages or risks of EC for small businesses?
3. What are the CSFs for small businesses online? (Hint: see Online File W12.5.)
4. How can one support EC in a small company?

12.6 FUNDAMENTAL LEGAL, ETHICAL, AND REGULATORY ISSUES

A large number of ethical legal and regulatory issues may be involved in EC implementation.

ETHICS, LEGAL, AND REGULATORY CONCEPTS

Ethics characterize how individuals choose to interact with one another. In philosophy, ethics define what is good for the individual and society and the nature of duties that people owe themselves and one another. One duty is to not intrude on a person's **privacy**, which stems from the right to be left alone and free of unreasonable personal intrusions.

A common agreement in a society as to what is right and wrong determines ethics, but they are not subject to legal sanctions except when they overlap with activities that also are illegal. Online File W12.6 shows a framework for ethical issues.

Law (i.e., public law) embodies ethical principals, but they are not the same. Acts that are generally considered unethical may not be illegal. Lying to a friend may be unethical, but it is not illegal. Conversely, the law is not simply the coding of ethical norms, nor are all ethical codes incorporated into public law.

Regulation in cyberspace does not consist only of laws that government issues and enforces. Private parties (e.g., individuals, special interest groups, a cluster of consumer groups, organizations), use online interactive technology to regulate—or attempt to regulate—what is communicated or done on the Internet. Private regulation may have positive impacts (Google filtering out search engine spam) or it might potentially lead to abusive behavior or illegal acts and interfere with free speech, privacy, or intellectual property. **Intellectual property** is a creation of the mind, such as inventions, literary and artistic works, and symbols, names, images, and designs, used in commerce.

LAWS ARE SUBJECT TO INTERPRETATION

Keep in mind that *many* laws and regulations are broadly and sometimes vaguely written and, therefore, only provide outlines to guide public policy. Even physical crime laws that sound specific (e.g., killing a human being is illegal) do not apply in all situations, such as in self-defense.

Specific disputes (such as the legality of spam) cannot be resolved by simply referring to relevant laws for two reasons. First, the scope of a law (i.e., whether it applies to a specific situation) needs to be interpreted by looking at lawmakers' intent. Second, laws may conflict with each other. For example, how companies use information collected from customers via their Web sites are subject to privacy laws. One privacy law may prohibit a company from sharing customers' social security numbers with business partners, whereas a homeland security law may require revealing the identity of customers. (Banks with CRM programs often encounter these legal conflicts). Another example of legal conflict is the debate between free speech and protection of children from offensive content.

ethics
The branch of philosophy that deals with what is considered to be right and wrong.

privacy
The right to be left alone and free of unreasonable personal intrusions.

intellectual property
Creations of the mind, such as inventions, literary and artistic works, and symbols, names, images, and designs, used in commerce.

Free Speech Online Versus Child Protection

Children's Internet Protection Act (CIPA)
U.S. law that mandates the use of filtering technologies in schools and libraries that receive certain types of federal funding.

legal precedent
A judicial decision that may be used as a standard in subsequent similar cases.

A fierce debate occurred over whether it was legal for public libraries to filter out offensive online content. The conflict over free speech versus child protection erupted after the **Children's Internet Protection Act (CIPA)** was signed into law in December 2000. CIPA mandated the use of filtering technologies in schools and libraries that received certain types of federal funding. CIPA was immediately challenged in court, so it did not go into effect at that time.

Opponents of the law relied on earlier court cases (i.e., a legal precedent) saying that government-imposed limitations on the public's right to freely read and learn at public libraries violated the free speech protections of the First Amendment. A **legal precedent** is a judicial decision that may be used as a standard in subsequent similar cases. For details of the debate, see ACLU (2006). It was a major victory for proponents of free speech online in May 2002 when a district court declared the CIPA to be unconstitutional. The district court judges ruled that CIPA was overbroad and would violate the First Amendment rights of library patrons, both adults and minors. That court ordered that CIPA not be enforced. The conflict did not end there. The district court's decision was appealed to the U.S. Supreme Court. In June 2003, the Supreme Court declared that the CIPA was constitutional. Their review represented the third time justices had heard arguments pitting free speech against attempts to protect children from offensive online content. CIPA went into effect in 2004, and efforts to defeat it have continued.

For another example of the courts resolving novel conflicts, such as whether a company can link to a Web site without permission, see the story of *Ticketmaster v. Microsoft* provided in Online File W12.7.

Political Spam Versus Political Fund-Raising

Another legal complication arises when determining the scope of a law, particularly when it involves ethical issues. Consider the use of unsolicited bulk e-mails to reach voters by candidates for political office—and the difficulty in determining its legality and possible ethical impacts. Commonly known as *political spam*, this campaign tactic offers an inexpensive alternative to television, radio, and print ads. Those who favor the use of political spam believe that campaigning via the Internet reduces candidates' dependence on wealthy fund-raisers, which reduces political favoritism and other paybacks that are not in the public's best interest. Critics believe that political spam is no different from other types of spam. All spam is a nuisance, clogs mail servers, and creates security risks. See Exhibit 12.8 for a list of the fiercely debated questions that this situation has triggered.

In March 2007, a 74-second video of political satire was posted anonymously on YouTube. The video, called "Hillary 1984," raised ethical questions about the power of the Internet in the political process—and the opportunities for subterfuge (Helmore 2007).

EXHIBIT 12.8   Controversial Issues Regarding Political Spam

- Is political spam legal given that communication over the Internet (including e-mail) is a form of speech protected by the Constitution?
- What distinguishes political spam from other forms of speech, from regulated political speech, and from advertising spam?
- Does it diminish candidates' dependence on wealthy special interest groups (SIG)?
- If political spam does diminish candidates' dependence on wealthty SIGs, can it actually improve the integrity of elected officials? To what extent?

The video depicted Hillary Clinton, a candidate for the Democratic nomination for U.S. president, as a politically correct and totalitarian Big Sister, and her supporters as compliant automatons. The "Hillary 1984" video had been created by Phil de Vellis, a technician who worked for the firm that designed Barack Obama's Web site, a rival presidential candidate, but it was released without Obama's endorsement. Within 2 weeks after being posted on YouTube, the video had been viewed several million times. This attack highlights how the author of a viral political video can damage the person being ridiculed as well as his unwitting sponsor, in this case Barack Obama.

PERSONAL AND PROPERTY RIGHTS

In a legal system, the government produces a set of rules and regulations and has the power to enforce them, as shown in the legal framework in Exhibit 12.9.

Rights are divided into two categories: personal rights and property rights. Generally, the interests of *life* and *liberty* fall into the personal rights category. *Property* interests are in the category of property rights. Internet business Web sites, proprietary systems, and customer lists are examples of property. Exhibit 12.10 lists property rights relevant to EC and Web sites.

Referring to both Exhibits 12.9 and 12.10, it is clear that an online business has the legal right to prevent spammers or other businesses from interfering with or harming the benefits (profits) from its EC site—and can file lawsuits against them. Lawsuits are one type of **civil litigation**, which is an adversarial proceeding in which a party (the plaintiff) sues another party (the defendant) to get compensation for a wrong committed by the defendant. For example, the entertainment industry has the right to its intellectual property (IP) and can file lawsuits (civil charges) against online businesses,

civil litigation
An adversarial proceeding in which a party (the plaintiff) sues another party (the defendant) to get compensation for a wrong committed by the defendant.

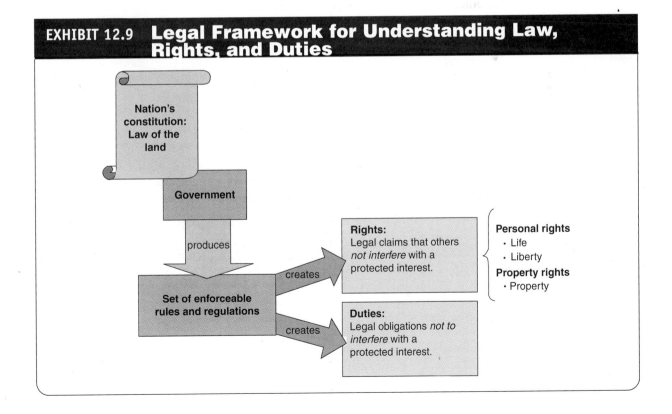

EXHIBIT 12.9   Legal Framework for Understanding Law, Rights, and Duties

EXHIBIT 12.10 Property Rights Relevant to Electronic Commerce

Owners of property, including intellectual property, are entitled to:
- Control of the use of the property.
- The right to any benefit from the property.
- The right to transfer or sell the property.
- The right to exclude others from the property.

such as YouTube and MySpace, for any interference with the ability to profit from its IP or for profiting from the recording industry's property without authorization and compensation. In contrast, law enforcement or a public official brings criminal litigation. The next section discusses criminal and civil laws further. You will also learn the terminology needed to understand legal issues.

INTELLECTUAL PROPERTY LAW (A CIVIL LAW)

Intellectual property law is the area of the law that includes patent law, copyright law, trademark law, trade secret law, and other branches of the law, such as licensing and unfair competition.

Another perspective is that intellectual property law is concerned with the legal regulation of mental products, including creativity. It affects such diverse subjects as the visual and performing arts, electronic databases, advertising, and video games. Creativity is an integral part of the entire business world, as is the protection of innovation. See Online File W12.8 for intellectual property Web sites.

Copyright

Numerous high-profile lawsuits have been filed for EC copyright infringement. A **copyright** is an exclusive right of the author or creator of a book, movie, musical composition, or other artistic property to print, copy, sell, license, distribute, transform to another medium, translate, record, perform, or otherwise use. In the United States, as soon as a work is created and in a tangible form such as through writing or recording, the work automatically has federal copyright protection. A copyright does not last forever; it is good for a fixed number of years after the death of the author or creator (e.g., 50 in the United Kingdom). In the United States, copyright was extended to 70 years after the death of the author by the *1998 Sonny Bono Copyright Extension Act*. After the copyright expires, the work reverts to the public domain. The legal term for the use of the work without permission or contracting for payment of a royalty is **infringement**. For more on copyrights, see en.wikipedia.org/wiki/Wikipedia:Copyrights.

To protect its interests, the Recording Industry Association of America (RIAA), the recording industry's trade group, uses lawsuits to stamp out rampant music piracy on university campuses. RIAA launched a lawsuit-settlement Web site, p2plawsuits.com and sent a mass mailing to college and university presidents across the United States asking for their cooperation in its ongoing war against file sharing. RIAA sought compensation from university students for losses that it alleged were caused by copyright infringement. In February 2007, RIAA announced that it would give 400 college students at 13 universities suspected of illegally pirating music online the option to reach discounted settlements before being sued for greater damages for copyright infringement. According to Mitch Bainwol, RIAA chairman and CEO, "theft of music remains unacceptably high and undermines the industry's ability to invest in new music"

---

copyright
An exclusive right of the author or creator of a book, movie, musical composition, or other artistic property to print, copy, sell, license, distribute, transform to another medium, translate, record, perform, or otherwise use.

infringement
Use of the work without permission or contracting for payment of a royalty.

(Veiga 2007). Judges' decisions on legal cases, such as this one, can have an immediate and long-lasting impact because they become common law.

Universal Music Group, the world's largest music company, filed a lawsuit against MySpace for copyright infringement of thousands of artists' work (Reuters 2007). French media giant Vivendi owns Universal. It filed the lawsuit at the U.S. District Court of California. Universal estimated maximum damages for each copyrighted work at $150,000. YouTube avoided a similar lawsuit by reaching a licensing agreement with Universal Music.

The entertainment industry, led primarily by the Motion Picture Association of America (MPAA) and the RIAA, also is attempting technical solutions via the legal system to protect its interests. It is actively pursuing digital rights management policy initiatives through federal legislation and the courts.

Digital Rights Management (DRM)

Digital rights management (DRM) is an umbrella term for any of several arrangements that allow a vendor of content in electronic form to control the material and restrict its usage. These arrangements are really technology-based protection measures. Typically, the content is a copyrighted digital work to which the vendor holds rights.

In the past, when content was analog in nature, it was easier to buy a new copy of a copyrighted work on a physical medium (e.g., paper, film, tape) than to produce such a copy independently. The quality of most copies often was inferior. Digital technologies make it possible to produce a high-quality duplicate of any digital recording with minimal effort. The Internet virtually has eliminated the need for a physical medium to transfer a work, which has led to the use of DRM systems for protection.

However, DRM systems may restrict the *fair use* of material by individuals. In law, **fair use** refers to the use of copyrighted material for noncommercial purposes. Several DRM technologies were developed without regard for privacy protection. Many systems require the user to reveal his or her identity and rights to access protected content. Upon authentication of identity and rights to the content, the user can access the content (see epic.org/privacy/drm).

Patents

A **patent** is a document that grants the holder exclusive rights to an invention for a fixed number of years (e.g., 17 years in the United States and 20 years in the United Kingdom). Patents serve to protect tangible technological inventions, especially in traditional industrial areas. They are not designed to protect artistic or literary creativity. Patents confer monopoly rights to an idea or an invention, regardless of how it may be expressed. An invention may be in the form of a physical device or a method or process for making a physical device. Similar to a patent is a **trademark,** which is a symbol businesses use to identify their goods and services; government registration of the trademark confers exclusive legal right to its use.

Certain patents granted in the United States deviate from established practices in Europe. For example, Amazon.com successfully obtained a U.S. patent on its *1-Click* ordering procedure. Using this patent, Amazon.com sued Barnes & Noble in 1999 and in 2000, alleging that its rival had copied its patented technology. Barnes & Noble was enjoined by the courts from using the procedure. Similarly, in 1999 Priceline.com filed a suit against Expedia.com alleging that Expedia was using Priceline's patented reverse-auction business model. The suit was settled in 2001 when Expedia.com agreed to pay Priceline.com royalties for use of the model. However, in Europe and many Asian, African, and South American countries, it is almost impossible to obtain patents on business methods or computer processes.

digital rights management (DRM)
An umbrella term for any of several arrangements that allow a vendor of content in electronic form to control the material and restrict its usage.

fair use
The legal use of copyrighted material for noncommercial purposes without paying royalties or getting permission.

patent
A document that grants the holder exclusive rights to an invention for a fixed number of years.

trademark
A symbol used by businesses to identify their goods and services; government registration of the trademark confers exclusive legal right to its use.

1. Define ethics and relate it to legality.
2. Define intellectual property.
3. Define copyright.
4. Define civil law.
5. Define DRM. Describe one potential impact on privacy.
6. Define patents and relate them to EC.

12.7 PRIVACY, FREE SPEECH, AND DEFAMATION

The explosion in communications technologies has created complex new ethical dilemmas for businesses. As transaction costs for processing, storing, and transmitting data have dropped dramatically and sophisticated tracking and monitoring software have become widespread, concerns have arisen regarding online consumer privacy, free speech, and defamation. There is increasing risk of personal privacy invasion from compromising photos that digital cameras or cell phones capture, particularly when they are posted on the Internet (Puente 2007).

Privacy means different things to different people. In general, *privacy* is the right to be left alone and the right to be free of unreasonable personal intrusions. (For other definitions of privacy, see the Privacy Rights Clearinghouse [privacyrights.org].) Privacy has long been a legal, ethical, and social issue in most countries.

Section 5 of the FTC Act gives the U.S. Federal Trade Commission the authority to take action against companies whose lax security practices could expose customers' personal financial information to theft or loss. For explanation of the Act, see ftc.gov/privacy/privacyinitiatives/promises.html. Those practices extend to privacy, free speech, and defamation if the company does not fulfill its duty to protect the rights of others.

Today, virtually all U.S. states and the federal government, either by statute or by common law, recognize the right to privacy. The definition of privacy can be interpreted quite broadly. However, the following two rules have been followed fairly closely in past U.S. court decisions: (1) The right of privacy is not absolute. Privacy must be balanced against the needs of society. (2) The public's right to know is superior to the individual's right of privacy. These two rules show why it is sometimes difficult to determine and enforce privacy regulations.

To some extent privacy concerns have been overshadowed by post–September 11 terrorism efforts, but consumers still expect and demand that companies behave as responsible custodians of their personal data. One way to manage this issue is opt-in and opt-out information practices. **Opt out** is a businesses practice that gives consumers the opportunity to refuse to share information about themselves. Offering opt out is good customer service, but it is difficult to opt out in some industries, either because consumer demand for opt out is low or the value of the customer information is high. In contrast, **opt in** is based on the principle that information sharing should not occur unless customers specifically allow it or request it.

opt out
Business practice that gives consumers the opportunity to refuse sharing information about themselves.

opt in
Agreement that requires computer users to take specific steps to allow the collection of personal information.

FREE SPEECH

Rights to privacy and free speech have an increasingly important role in an information society and to EC. As with all rights, the right of free speech is not unlimited. Free speech does not mean any speech. Some of the traditional restrictions on what may be freely said or published are defamation laws, contempt of court, and national security. For example, it is illegal to scream "fire" in a crowded theatre or make bomb threats in an airport. Laws against libel (making defamatory statements in a fixed medium, such as blogs or Web sites) may be out-of-date now that victims of defamation have the ability to respond via the Internet.

The Internet offers a number of opportunities to collect private information about individuals. Exhibit 12.11 lists several ways that the Internet can be used to find information about an individual.

Of those methods listed in Exhibit 12.11, the last three are the most common ways of gathering personal information on the Internet.

Web Site Registration

A joint study by TNS and TRUSTe (2004) found that Internet users were skeptical of the necessity of giving personal information to online businesses. Among the 1,068 participants, 71 percent dislike registering at Web sites they visit, 15 percent refuse to register at all, and 43 percent do not trust companies not to share their personal information.

Virtually all B2C, marketing Web sites, and social networks ask visitors to fill out registration forms. During the process, individuals voluntarily provide their names, addresses, phone numbers, e-mail addresses, hobbies and likes or dislikes, and other personal information to participate, win a lottery, or for some other item of exchange. There are few restraints on the ways in which the site can use this information. The site might use it to improve customer service. Or the site could just as easily sell the information to another company, which could use it in an inappropriate or intrusive manner.

Cookies

Another way that a Web site can gather information about an individual is by using cookies. As described in Chapter 4, a cookie contains data that are passed back and forth between a Web site and an end user's browser as the user navigates the site. Cookies enable sites to keep track of users without having to constantly ask the users to identify themselves. Web bugs and spyware, described in Section 4.2, are similar to cookies.

Originally, cookies were designed to help with personalization and market research, as described in Chapter 4. However, cookies also can invade an individual's privacy. Cookies allow Web sites to collect detailed information about a user's preferences, interests, and surfing patterns. The personal profiles created by cookies often are more accurate than self-registration, because users have a tendency to falsify information in a registration form.

EXHIBIT 12.11 How the Internet Can Be Used to Find Information on an Individual

- Reading an individual's blogs or newsgroup postings
- Looking up an individual's name and identity in an Internet directory
- Reading an individual's e-mail, IM, or text messages
- Monitoring and conducting surveillance on employees
- Wiretapping wireline and wireless communication lines
- Asking an individual to complete a registration form on a Web site
- Recording an individual's actions as they navigate the Web with a browser, usually with cookies
- Using spyware, keystroke loggers, and similar methods

Although the ethics of the use of cookies are still being debated, concerns about cookies reached a pinnacle in 1997 at the U.S. FTC hearings on online privacy. Following those hearings, Netscape and Microsoft introduced options enabling users to block cookies. Since that time, the uproar has subsided because most users accept cookies rather than fight them. The problem with deleting or disabling cookies is that the user will have to keep reentering information and, in some instances, may be blocked from viewing particular pages.

Spyware and Similar Methods

Spyware can be used as a tool that some merchants use to spy on users without their knowledge. Sixty-two person of corporate IT security professionals identified spyware infections as the number one threat to intellectual property, according to the "Survey on the Corporate Response to Spyware," a study conducted by the Ponemon Institute (ponemon.org) and sponsored by Mi5 Networks (mi5networks.com) (Burns 2006). Spyware, also referred to as *crimeware*, is defined in the study as "all unwanted software programs designed to steal proprietary information or that target data stores housing confidential information."

Spyware may enter the user's computer as a virus or as a result of the user's clicking an option in a deceptive pop-up window. Sometimes when users download and install legitimate programs they get spyware as well. Spyware is very effective in tracking users' Web surfing habits. It can scan computer hard drives for sensitive files and send the results to hackers or spammers. Spyware is clearly a violation of the computer user's privacy. It can also slow computer performance. Spyware writers are getting more innovative and are trying to avoid detection. For example, a keystroke logger runs in the background of the user's computer and records every keystroke the user makes. A hacker can then steal the user's social security number, bank account number, and password!

Antivirus software and Internet firewalls cannot "see" spyware; special protection is needed. Many free and low-cost antispyware software packages are on the market. Representative free programs are Ad-Aware, Spybot, SpyKiller, and PestPatrol. For-fee programs include SpySubtract, Spy Sweeper, Ad-Aware Plus, and SpyWasher.

RFID's Threat to Privacy

As mentioned in earlier chapters, privacy advocates fear that the information stored on RFID tags or collected with them may be used to violate an individual's privacy. To protect the individual, RSA Security and others are developing locking technologies that will protect consumers from being tracked after buying products with RFID tags. Several states (e.g., California) are considering legislation to protect customers from a loss of privacy due to the tags.

Privacy of Employees

In addition to customers' privacy, there is the issue of employees' privacy. Many employers monitor their employees' e-mail and Web activities. In addition to wasting time online, employees may disclose trade secrets and possibly make employers liable for defamation based on what they do on the corporate Web site. In response to these concerns, most companies monitor their employees' communications.

darknets
Private online community that is only open to those who belong to it.

Another privacy concern stems from the "underground Internet" of private online communities called **darknets** that are only open to those who belong to the private network.

PRIVACY PROTECTION

The ethical principles commonly applied to the collection and use of personal information also apply to information collected in e-commerce. These principles include the following:

- **Notice or awareness.** Consumers must be given notice of an entity's information practices prior to the collection of personal information. Consumers must be able to make informed decisions about the type and extent of their disclosures based on the intentions of the party collecting the information.
- **Choice or consent.** Consumers must be made aware of their options as to how their personal information may be used, as well as any potential secondary uses of the information. Consent may be granted through opt-in clauses.
- **Access or participation.** Consumers must be able to access their personal information and challenge the validity of the data.
- **Integrity or security.** Consumers must be assured that their personal data are secure and accurate. It is necessary for those collecting the data to take whatever precautions are required to ensure that they protect data from loss, unauthorized access or alteration, destruction, and fraudulent use, and to take reasonable steps to gain information from reputable and reliable sources. This principle has been extended to digital property.
- **Enforcement or redress.** A method of enforcement and remedy must be available. Otherwise, there is no real deterrent or enforceability for privacy issues.

THE USA PATRIOT ACT

The **USA PATRIOT Act** (officially, Uniting and Strengthening America by Providing Appropriate Tools to Intercept and Obstruct Terrorism) was passed in October 2001, in the aftermath of the September 11 terrorist attacks. Its intent is to give law enforcement agencies broader range in their efforts to protect the public. The American Civil Liberties Union (ACLU), the Electronic Freedom Foundation (EFF), and other organizations have grave concerns, including (1) expanded surveillance with reduced checks and balances, (2) overbreadth with a lack of focus on terrorism, and (3) rules that would allow U.S. foreign intelligence agencies to more easily spy on Americans.

On March 9, 2007, the U.S. Department of Justice (DOJ) said that the FBI had improperly used provisions of the USA PATRIOT Act to obtain thousands of telephone, business, and financial records without prior judicial approval (Johnson and Lipton 2007). The report is available on the DOJ's Web site at justice.gov/oig/new.htm. The result of this report may restrain some of the parts of the Act that allowed expanded surveillance in the following areas:

USA PATRIOT Act
Uniting and Strengthening America by Providing Appropriate Tools to Intercept and Obstruct Terrorism Act passed in October 2001, in the aftermath of the September 11 terrorist attacks. Its intent is to give law enforcement agencies broader range in their efforts to protect the public.

- E-mail and Internet searches
- Nationwide roving wiretaps
- Requirement that ISPs hand over more user information
- Expanded scope of surveillance based on new definitions of terrorism
- Government spying on suspected computer trespassers with no need for a court order
- Wiretaps for suspected violations of the Computer Fraud and Abuse Act
- Dramatic increases in the scope and penalties of the Computer Fraud and Abuse Act
- General expansion of Foreign Intelligence Surveillance Act (FISA) authority
- Increased information sharing between domestic law enforcement and intelligence
- FISA detours around federal domestic surveillance limitations; domestic surveillance detours around FISA limitations

Section 12.7 ▶ REVIEW QUESTIONS

1. Define privacy.
2. List some of the ways that the Internet can collect information about individuals.
3. What are cookies and what do they have to do with online privacy?
4. List four common ethical principles related to the gathering of personal information.
5. How has the USA PATRIOT Act expanded the government's reach?

12.8 SPAM, SPLOGS, AND POP-UPS

A blog—a Web site or Web page that displays journal-like entries—often contains genuine (nondeceitful) links to other pages, images, music, or videos. Hosted on Web sites such as MySpace, blogs offer a way for users to keep in touch with each other and share and watch music and videos. In contrast, a splog is a blog-style site consisting of nonsense words or nonsensical content.

Spam, splogs, and other scams damage online businesses. Dubious businesses promote their Web sites by using tactics to improve their search engine rankings. Referring to these problems, David Sifry, chief executive of Technorati, a search engine that indexes blogs, warned: "The first thing to recognize is that every healthy ecosystem has its parasites" (Rigby 2006).

SPAM AND SPLOGS

Just as with e-mail spam, unsolicited advertising in blogs (*splogs*) affects blogs. The growth of splogs parallels the growth of blogs—both are now too numerous to count. These bogus blog sites contain nothing but gibberish and advertisements. However, that gibberish is full of keywords carefully selected to capture users of search engines. In effect, it is an unethical (possibly illegal) application of **search engine marketing (SEM)**, which are marketing methods used to increase the ranking of a Web site in the search results. (See en.wikipedia.org/wiki/Spam_blog.) **Comment spam** is sent to all types of messaging media to promote prescription drugs, gambling sites, and the like. **Search engine spam** are pages created deliberately to trick the search engine into offering inappropriate, redundant, or poor quality search results. **Search engine spamming** refers to deceptive online advertising practices. **Spam sites** artificially inflate the sites' rankings by deliberately subverting a search engine's algorithms.

A **splog**, short for "spam blog," is a site created solely for marketing purposes (see the Real-World Case at the end of this chapter). Sploggers work on the principle that once Web surfers arrive at their site, a few will click on one of the linked advertisements. Each of these clicks earns the splogger a few cents. And because any one splogger can run thousands of splogs, the scam can be very profitable. One splog partnership claimed $71,136.89 in earnings in the 3 months from August to October 2005 (World Intellectual Property Organization 2006).

Trackback

Abusive tactics also include the misuse of trackbacks. A **trackback** is an acknowledgment or signal from an originating site to a receiving site. For example, when an advertisement link is clicked on another's Web page, the advertiser receives a signal of that click. The trackback feature is abused when spammers insert their links without authority on legitimate blogs. Spammers do this to make money when visitors to the blog unwittingly click the link. This is similar to comment spam (a type of blog spam), except that it avoids some of the safeguards designed to stop that practice. For an illustration of how trackback

---

search engine marketing (SEM)
Marketing methods used to increase the ranking of a Web site in the search results.

comment spam
Spam sent to all types of messaging media, including blogs, IM, and cellular telephones to promote products or services.

search engine spam
Pages created deliberately to trick the search engine into offering inappropriate, redundant, or poor-quality search results.

search engine spamming
Collective term referring to deceptive online advertising practices.

spam site
Page that uses techniques that deliberately subvert a search engine's algorithms to artificially inflate the page's rankings.

splogs
Short for (spam blog) are sites that are created solely for marketing purposes.

trackback
An acknowledgment or signal from an originating site to a receiving site.

works, see cruftbox.com/cruft/docs/trackback.html. Although many blogs allow readers to post comments, unscrupulous individuals can use software to generate comments automatically.

As a defense against abusive trackback tactics, trackback spam filters (similar to those fighting against comment spam) have been implemented in blog publishing systems. Because filtering can be ineffective, many blogs have stopped using trackbacks, because dealing with the spam is too burdensome. The persistent problem with spam-blocking software is that spammers find ways to circumvent the programs.

Automated Spam

Bloggers may encounter hundreds of automatically generated comments with links to herbal Viagra and gambling vendors on their pages. Software bots that trawl the Internet looking for suitable forms to fill in automatically generate the majority of blog spam. Blog owners can use tools to ensure that humans—and not an automated system—enter comments on their blogs. Blog owners can also use a **Captcha tool** (short for "completely automated public Turing test to tell computers and humans apart"), which uses a verification test on comment pages to stop scripts from posting automatically. These tests may require the person to enter sequences of random characters, which automated systems (software scripts) cannot read.

Another potential effective measure against blog spam and other undesirable content is to only allow comments posted on the blog to be made public after they have been checked. But like the fight against e-mail spam, it is a constant battle in which the spammers seem to have the advantage. Sometimes the only solution to comment spam is for users to turn off their comments function. For more information, see the CAUCE Web site (cauce.org). Exhibit 12.12 shows an example of how a spam blocker works.

Even with tools such as Captcha turned on, it is risky to simply allow comments to go unchecked. Blog owners may be held responsible for anything illegal or defamatory

Captcha tool
Short for "completely automated public Turing test to tell computers and humans apart," this tool uses a verification test on comment pages to stop scripts from posting automatically.

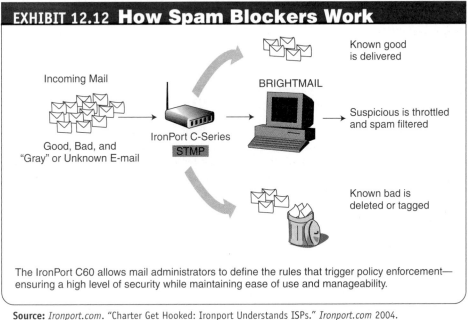

EXHIBIT 12.12 How Spam Blockers Work

Incoming Mail

Good, Bad, and "Gray" or Unknown E-mail

IronPort C-Series
STMP

BRIGHTMAIL

Known good is delivered

Suspicious is throttled and spam filtered

Known bad is deleted or tagged

The IronPort C60 allows mail administrators to define the rules that trigger policy enforcement—ensuring a high level of security while maintaining ease of use and manageability.

Source: *Ironport.com*. "Charter Get Hooked: Ironport Understands ISPs." *Ironport.com* 2004. *ironport.com/pdf/ironport_charter_communications_case_study.pdf* (accessed January 2005). Used by permission of IronPort Systems, Inc.

posted on their blogs. Blog owners can be sued for damages or face criminal charges in court for libel.

PROTECTING AGAINST POP-UP ADS

As discussed in Chapter 4, use of pop-ups and similar advertising programs is exploding. Sometimes it is even difficult to close these ads when they appear on the screen. Some of these ads may be part of a consumer's permission marketing agreement, but most are unsolicited. What can a user do about unsolicited pop-up ads? The following tools help stop pop-ups.

Tools for Stopping Pop-Ups

One way to avoid the potential danger lurking behind pop-up ads is to install software that will block pop-up ads and prevent them from appearing in the first place. Several software packages offer pop-up stoppers. Some are free (e.g., panicware.com and adscleaner.com); others are available for a fee. For a list of pop-up blocking software, visit snapfiles.com/Freeware/misctools/fwpopblock.html and netsecurity.about.com/od/popupadblocking/a/aafreepopup.htm.

Many ISPs offer tools to stop pop-ups from appearing. The Mozilla's Firefox Web browser does not allow pop-ups. Even the Google Toolbar will block pop-up ads. Microsoft added pop-up blocking to its Internet Explorer browser with Windows XP Service Pack 2.

However, adware or software that gets bundled with popular applications, such as KaZaa, is able to deliver the pop-up ads because they originate from the desktop, not the browser, and blocking tools do not govern them.

Section 12.8 ▶ REVIEW QUESTIONS

1. Why is it difficult to control spamming?
2. Why is it difficult to control splogs?
3. How can blog owners protect themselves against automatically generated comments?
4. Explain how sploggers make money.
5. Identify which types of pop-ups you can block and which types you cannot. Explain why.

12.9 THE FUTURE OF ELECTRONIC COMMERCE

Generally speaking, the consensus is that the future of EC is bright. EC will become an increasingly important method of reaching customers, providing services, and improving operations of organizations. Also, EC facilitates collaboration and people-to-people interactions. Analysts differ in their predictions about the anticipated growth rate of EC and how long it will take for it to become a substantial portion of the economy, as well as in the identification of industry segments that will grow the fastest. However, based on nontechnological success factors (see Online File W8.7) and technological factors and trends (see Online File W8.8), there is general optimism about the future of EC. For a discussion, see Stafford (2006).

INTEGRATING THE MARKETPLACE WITH THE MARKETSPACE

Throughout this book, we have commented on the relationship between the physical marketplace and the marketspace. We have pointed out conflicts in certain areas, as well as successful applications and cooperation. The fact is that from the point of view of the consumer, as well as of most organizations, these two entities exist, and will continue to exist, together.

Probably the most noticeable integration of the two concepts is in the click-and-mortar organization. For the foreseeable future, the click-and-mortar organization will be the most prevalent model (e.g., see Wal-Mart and Walmart.com), although it may take different shapes and formats. Some organizations will use EC as just another selling channel, as most large retailers do today. Others will use EC for only some products and services, selling other products and services the conventional way (e.g., LEGO and GM). As experience is gained on how to excel at such a strategy, more organizations, private and public, will move to this dual mode of operation.

A major problem with the click-and-mortar approach is how the two outlets can cooperate in planning, advertising, logistics, resource allocation, and so on, and how the strategic plans of the marketspace and marketplace can align. Another major issue is the potential conflict with existing distribution channels (i.e., wholesalers, retailers).

Another area of coexistence is in many B2C ordering systems, where customers have the option to order the new way or the old way. For example, consumers can bank both online and offline. People can trade stocks via the computer, by placing a call to their broker, or just by walking into a brokerage firm and talking to a trader. In the areas of B2B and G2B, the option to choose the old way or the new way may not be available much longer; some organizations may discontinue the old-economy option as the number of offline users declines below a certain threshold. However, in most B2C activities, the option will remain, at least for the foreseeable future.

In conclusion, many people believe that the impact of EC on our lives will be as much as, and possibly more profound than, that of the Industrial Revolution. No other phenomenon since the Industrial Revolution has been classified in this category. It is our hope that this book will help you move successfully into this exciting and challenging digital revolution.

MOBILE SOCIAL NETWORKS

An explosive growth of mobile social networks is predicted by ABI Research (see Mello 2006), tripling the 50 million members in 2006 to 174 million in 2011. The explosion of wireless Web 2.0 services and companies (see Longino 2006) enables many social communities to be based on the mobile phone and other portable wireless devices. This extends the reach of social interaction to millions of people who don't have regular or easy access to computers. For example, MySpace can be accessed via Cingular's mobile system. At minimum, existing members who use PCs will supplement their activities with wireless devices.

FUTURE THREATS

According to Stafford (2006) the following four trends may slow EC and Web 2.0, and even cripple the Internet:

- ▶ **Security concern.** Both shoppers and users of e-banking and other services worry about online security. The Web needs to be made safer.
- ▶ **Lack of Net neutrality.** If the big telecom companies are allowed to charge companies for a guarantee of faster access, critics fear that small innovative Web companies could be crowded out by the Microsofts and Googles that can afford to pay more.
- ▶ **Copyright complaints.** The legal problems of YouTube, Wikipedia, and others may result in a loss of vital outlets of public opinion, creativity, and discourse.

▶ **Choppy connectivity.** Upstream bandwidths are still constricted, making uploading of video files a time-consuming task. Usable mobile bandwidth still costs a lot, and some carriers impose limitations on how Web access can be employed.

Section 12.9 ▶ REVIEW QUESTIONS

1. Describe nontechnological EC trends. (See Online File W12.9.)
2. Describe technological trends for EC. (See Online File W12.10.)
3. Discuss the integration of marketplaces and market spaces.
4. Describe mobile social networks.
5. List the major potential inhibitors of e-commerce.

MANAGERIAL ISSUES

Some managerial issues related to this chapter are as follows

1. **What is the strategic value of EC to the organization?** Management needs to understand how EC can improve marketing and promotions, customer service, and sales. More significant, the greatest potential of EC is realized when management views EC from a strategic perspective, not merely as a technological advancement.

2. **Who determines EC strategy?** Strategy is ultimately the responsibility of senior management. But participation in setting an e-commerce strategy is something that should happen at all levels and in all areas of the organization. It frequently is said that "soon all business will be e-business." If this is true, then planning this evolutionary process must include marketing, operations, information technology, and all other areas of the business.

3. **What are the benefits and risks of EC?** Strategic moves have to be carefully weighed against potential risks. Identifying CSFs for EC and doing a cost-benefit analysis should not be neglected. Benefits often are hard to quantify, especially because gains tend to be strategic. In such an analysis, risks should be addressed with contingency planning (deciding what to do if problems arise).

4. **What metrics should we use?** The use of metrics is very popular, but the problem is that one must compare "apples with apples." Companies first must choose appropriate metrics for the situation and then exercise caution in deriving conclusions whenever gaps between the metrics and actual performance exist.

5. **How do we measure the value of EC investment?** EC investments must be measured against their contribution to business objectives. Such investments will involve direct and indirect costs as well as benefits. The impact of EC on integrating existing processes and systems must not be ignored. Furthermore, EC must create value for all participants, support or improve existing processes, and supplement rather than replace the human element of transactions. The measurement of EC value should occur against the backdrop of metrics that define business performance and success.

6. **How can we go global?** Going global is a very appealing proposition, but it may be difficult to do, especially on a large scale. In B2B, one may create collaborative projects with partners in other countries.

7. **Can we learn to love smallness?** Small can be beautiful to some; to others it may be ugly. Competing on commodity-type products with the big guys is very difficult, and even more so in cyberspace. Finding a niche market is advisable, but it will usually be limited in scope. More opportunity exists in providing specialized support services than in selling goods and services.

8. **What legal and ethical issues should be of major concern to an EC enterprise?** Key issues to consider include the following: (1) What type of proprietary information should we allow and disallow on our site? (2) Who will have access to information that visitors post to our site? (3) Do the content and

activities on our site comply with laws in other countries? (4) What disclaimers do we need to post on our Web site? (5) Are we using trademarked or copyrighted materials without permission? Regardless of the specific issues, an attorney should periodically review the content on the site, and someone should be responsible for monitoring legal and liability issues.

9. **What are the most critical ethical issues?** Negative or defamatory articles published about

people, companies, or products on Web sites or blogs can lead to charges of libel—and libel can stretch across countries. Issues of privacy, ethics, and legal exposure may seem tangential to running a business, but ignoring them puts the company at risk of fines, customer anger, and disruption of the operation of an organization. Privacy protection is a necessary investment.

SUMMARY

In this chapter, you learned about the following EC issues as they relate to the learning objectives.

1. **The strategic planning process.** Four major phases compose this cyclical process: initiation, formulation, implementation, and assessment. A variety of tools are available to carry out this process.

2. **Writing a business plan.** A business plan is an essential outcome of a strategic planning process. Writing the business plan may produce more significant outcomes than the plan itself. The purpose of the plan is to describe the operation of the business, and its content includes revenue sources, business partners, and trading procedures.

3. **The EC strategic process.** Considering e-commerce in strategy development does not radically change the process, but it does impact the outcome. Move-to-the-Net firms must approach the process differently than born-on-the-Net firms, but both types of firms must recognize the way electronic technologies, such as the Internet, make an e-difference. Because of the comprehensiveness of EC, formal strategic planning is a must.

4. **The need for EC justification.** Like any other investment, EC investment (unless it is small) needs to be justified. Many startup EC companies have crashed because of no or incorrect justification. In its simplest form, justification looks at revenue minus all relevant costs. Analysis is done by defining metrics related to organizational goals.

5. **The difficulties in justifying EC investment.** The nature of EC makes it difficult to justify due to the presence of many intangible costs and benefits. In addition, the relationship between investment and

results may be complex, extending over several years. Also, several projects may share both costs and benefits, several areas may feel the impacts (sometimes negative).

6. **Issues in global EC.** Going global with EC can be done quickly and with a relatively small investment. However, businesses must deal with a number of different issues in the cultural, administrative, geographic, legal, and economic dimensions of global trading.

7. **Small businesses and EC.** Depending on the circumstances, innovative small companies have a tremendous opportunity to adopt EC with little cost and to expand rapidly. Being in a niche market provides the best chance for small business success, and a variety of Web-based resources are available that small business owners can use to help ensure success.

8. **Understanding the foundation for legal and ethical issues.** Laws and regulations are broadly written and can only provide outlines to guide public policy. Ethics also are generally defined. Simply referring to relevant laws or philosophical principles cannot resolve specific legal disputes or ethical dilemmas. Law and ethics provide systems for social control and achieving the greater good. As with all systems, the formation of laws is a dynamic process that responds to ever-changing conditions. The nature of law is dynamic so that it can be responsive to new threats to individual rights or failures to perform one's duties. The Net not only

offers freedom of speech, but also widens opportunities for irresponsible activity.

9. **Privacy, free speech, and defamation and their challenges.** B2C companies depend on customer information to improve products and services and use CRM. Registration and cookies are two of the ways used to collect this information. The key privacy issues are who controls this information and how private it should remain. Strict privacy laws have been passed recently that carry harsh penalties for any negligence that exposes personal or confidential data. Debate continues about censorship on the Internet. Proponents of censorship feel that it is up to the government and various ISPs and Web sites to control inappropriate or offensive content. Others oppose any form of censorship; they believe that control is up to the individual. In the United States, most legal attempts to censor content on the Internet have been found unconstitutional. The debate is not likely to be resolved.

10. **Challenges caused by spam, splogs, and pop-ups.** Spam, splogs, and other scams damage online businesses. They are easy to deploy and can be quite profitable, thus they continue to mutate for survival, making it impossible to control them legally or with technological tools. A dangerous development is the use of deceptive marketing practices by legitimate companies trying to gain a competitive advantage.

11. **The future of EC.** EC will continue to expand fairly rapidly for a number of reasons. To begin with, its infrastructure is becoming better and less expensive with time. Consumers will become more experienced and will try different products and services and tell their friends about them. Security, privacy protection, and trust will be much higher, and more support services will simplify the transaction process. Legal issues will be formally legislated and clarified, and more products and services will be online at reduced prices. The fastest growing area is B2B EC. Company-centric systems (especially e-procurement) and auctions will also continue to spread rapidly. The development of exchanges and other many-to-many e-marketplaces will be much slower. Wireless technologies (especially Wi-Fi) will facilitate EC. Finally, and most important, is the increased rate of innovation with new business models and applications appearing constantly. Finally, Web 2.0 and social networks will play a major role in EC.

KEY TERMS

Business case	481	Ethics	499	Search engine spam	508
Business plan	481	Fair use	503	Search engine spamming	508
Captcha tool	509	Infringement	502	Spam sites	508
Children's Internet Protection Act (CIPA)	500	Intellectual property	499	Splogs	508
		Key performance indicators (KPIs)	488	Strategy	476
Civil litigation	501			Strategy assessment	479
Comment spam	508	Legal precedent	500	Strategy formulation	478
Copyright	502	Metric	486	Strategy implementation	479
Cost-benefit analysis	486	Opt in	504	Strategy initiation	477
Darknets	506	Opt out	504	Trackback	508
Dashboards		Patent	503	Trademark	503
Digital rights management (DRM)	503	Privacy	499	USA PATRIOT Act	507
E-commerce strategy (e-strategy)	476	Search engine marketing (SEM)	508	Value proposition	478

QUESTIONS FOR DISCUSSION

1. How would you identify competitors for a small business that wants to launch an EC project?

2. How would you apply Porter's five forces and Internet impacts in Exhibit 12.1 to the Internet search engine industry?

3. Why must e-businesses consider strategic planning to be a cyclical process?

4. How would you apply the SWOT approach to a small, local bank that is evaluating its e-banking services? (See Online File W12.1.)

5. Discuss how writing an e-business plan differs from writing a traditional business plan. (See Online Tutorial T.1.)

6. Amazon.com decided not to open physical stores, whereas First Network Security Bank (FNSB), which was the first online bank, opened its first physical bank in 1999. Compare and discuss the two strategies.

7. Discuss the pros and cons of going global with a physical product.

8. Find some SME EC success stories and identify the common elements in them.

9. Enter **businesscase.com** and find material on ROI analysis. Discuss how ROI is related to a business case.

10. A company is planning a wireless-based CRM system. Almost all the benefits are intangible. How can you justify the project to top management?

11. What are some of the things that EC Web sites can do to ensure the safeguarding of personal information?

12. Privacy is the right to be left alone and free of unreasonable personal intrusions. What are some intrusions that you consider to be "unreasonable"?

13. Discuss what the RIAA hopes to achieve by using lawsuits (civil law) against college students for copyright infringement.

14. Discuss the insufficient protection of opt-in and opt-out options. Which method do you prefer?

15. Many hospitals, health maintenance organizations, and federal agencies are converting, or plan to convert, all patient medical records from paper to electronic storage (using imaging technology). Once completed, electronic storage will enable quick access to most records. However, the availability of these records in a database and on networks or smart cards may allow people, some of whom are unauthorized, to view another person's private medical data. To protect privacy fully may cost too much money or may considerably slow the speed of access to the records. What policies could health-care administrators use to prevent unauthorized access? Discuss.

INTERNET EXERCISES

1. Survey several online travel agencies (e.g., **travelocity. com, orbitz.com, cheaptickets.com, priceline.com, expedia.com, bestfares.com**, and so on) and compare their business strategies. How do they compete against physical travel agencies?

2. Enter **digitalenterprise.org** and go to Web analytics. Read the material on Web analytics and prepare a report on the use of Web analytics for measuring advertising success. Also see **en.wikipedia.org/ wiki/Web_analytics**.

3. Check the music CD companies on the Internet (e.g., **cduniverse. com, musica.co.uk**). Do any companies focus on specialized niche markets as a strategy? What is the uniqueness of **venusrecords.com**?

4. One of the most global companies is Amazon.com (**amazon.com**). Find stories about its global strategies and activities (perform a Google search and

check **forbes.com**). What are the most important lessons you learned?

5. Visit **abcsmallbiz.com** and find some of the EC opportunities available to small businesses. Also, visit the Web site of the Small Business Administration (SBA) office in your area. Summarize some EC-related topics for SMEs.

6. Find out how Web sites such as **tradecard. com** facilitate the conduct of international trade over the Internet. Prepare a report based on your findings.

7. Use a currency conversion table (e.g., **xe.com/ucc**) to find out the exchange rate of US$100 with the currencies of Brazil, Canada, China, India, Sweden, the European Union, and South Africa.

8. Conduct research on small businesses and their use of the Internet for EC. Visit sites such as **microsoft. com/smallbusiness/hub.mspx** and **uschamber.org**. Also, enter **google.com** or **yahoo.com** and type "small businesses + electronic commerce." Use your findings to write a report on current small business EC issues.

9. Enter **businesscase.com** and review its products.

10. Enter **advisorzones.com/adv/e-commerceAdvisor**. Find the services provided for areas related to this chapter. Write a summary.

11. Enter **languageweaver.com** and find its language translation product. Write a report.

12. Enter **alinean.com/PDFs/IDC%20-%20Alinean %20The%20Power%20of%20ROI.pdf** and other sources in the site and find information that explains Alinean's approach to measuring return on IT. You can download two free e-books from the site that relate to this chapter. Summarize your findings in a report.

13. Enter **nucleusresearch.com**. Go to "Research," "Latest Research," and then click "View ROI Scorecards." Open the PDF file titled "Market Scorecard: Hosted CRM" for a review of hosted CRM vendors. Summarize your findings in a report. (Note: Use Google to find this information.)

14. Go to **google.com** and search for articles dealing with the ROI of RFID. List the key issues in measuring the ROI of RFID.

15. Enter **citrix.com**, **sharkfinesse.com**, and **search-marketing.yahoo.com/calculator/roi.php**. Review their calculators. Write a report.

16. You want to set up an ethical blog. Review "A Bloggers' Code of Ethics" at **cyberjournalist.net/news/000215.php**. Make a list of the top 10 ethical issues for blogging.

17. Use **google.com** to prepare a list of industry and trade organizations involved in various computer privacy initiatives. One of these groups is the World Wide Web Consortium (W3C). Describe its Privacy Preferences Project (**w3.org/tr/2001/wd-p3p-20010928**).

18. Download freeware from **junkbuster.com** and learn how to prohibit unsolicited e-mail. Describe how your privacy is protected.

TEAM ASSIGNMENTS AND ROLE PLAYING

1. Have three teams represent the following units of one click-and-mortar company: (1) an offline division, (2) an online division, and (3) top management. Each team member represents a different functional area within the division. The teams will develop a strategy in a specific industry (a group of three teams will represent a company in one industry). Teams will present their strategies to the class.

2. The relationship between manufacturers and their distributors regarding sales on the Web can be very strained. Direct sales may cut into the distributors' business. Review some of the strategies available to handle such channel conflicts. Each team member should be assigned to a company in a different industry. Study the strategies, compare and contrast them, and derive a proposed generic strategy.

3. Each team must find the latest information on one global EC issue (e.g., cultural, administrative, geographic, economic). Each team will offer a report based on its findings.

4. Survey **google.com** and **isworld.org** to find out about EC efforts in different countries. Assign a

country or two to each team. Relate the developments to each country's level of economic development and to its culture.

5. Compare the services provided by Yahoo!, Microsoft, and Website Pros Inc. to SMEs in the e-commerce area. Each team member should take one company and make a presentation.

6. Download the ROI case study "Venda Xerox Document Supplies (Case Study E11)" from Nucleus Research (**nucleusresearch.com/research/ roi-case-studies/roi-case-study-venda-xerox-document-supplies**). Read the Venda Xerox case study. While you are connected to the Internet, click "ROI Help Tutorial" in the NR_Standard_ROI_ Tool.xls file and read modules 1 through 4. Enter your assumptions of costs and benefits into the calculator and examine how they impact the overall

ROI, payback period, NPV, and average yearly cost of ownership (under the Summary tab).

Answer the following questions based on the Venda Xerox Document Supplies ROI case study.

a. What were the key reasons why Xerox developed an EC system?

b. What were the areas in which Xerox could benefit from EC?

c. How did Xerox calculate the ROI of the EC system?

7. Enter **whatis.techtarget.com** or similar resource sites. Read about spam and splogs. Find how spam and splog filters work (also see **ironport.com** and other vendors). Finally, take the self-assessment quiz at **searchcrm.techtarget.com** or **networkcomputing. com**. Prepare a report and class presentation.

Real-World Case

SPLOGS AND SEARCH ENGINE SPAM TO CAPTURE CUSTOMER TRAFFIC

The Problem

For many online businesses, a majority of their customer traffic comes from search engines. Various surveys indicate that up to 75 percent of Internet shoppers use search engines to find products and services. "Getting found" among the millions of competing Web sites is what businesses want. Several ethical marketing methods are available. One of these methods is using *search engine marketing (SEM)* to increase the ranking of a Web site in the search results. One SEM method, *search engine optimization (SEO)*, takes into consideration how search engines work (e.g., logical deep-linking or strategic keyword) to maximize the number of qualified visitors to a site. Because SEO improves sales, (see success cases at *reprisemedia.com/clients.aspx* as well as in Chapter 4 and Online Chapter 13), a dark side quickly emerged—one that uses spam-based practices to get a high ranking or to divert traffic away from intended Web sites.

With antispam software and ISP spam filters defeating traditional e-mail spam, spamming tactics have mutated. Those mutations seek to ensure—*by any means*—a good shopper delivery rate. To capture

customers, unsolicited junk advertisements are sent to all types of messaging media, including blogs, instant messages (IM), and cellular telephones. Spammers flood these media with so-called *comment spam* promoting their gambling sites, prescription drugs, get-rich schemes, and the like.

Whereas content spam impacts media users, the greater concern to ethical e-commerce sites is *search engine spam*, which Yahoo! defines as "pages created deliberately to trick the search engine into offering inappropriate, redundant, or poor-quality search results" (Hunt 2005). Those pages, called *spam sites,* use techniques that deliberately subvert a search engine's algorithms to artificially inflate the page's rankings. A similar tactic involves the use of *splogs.* Spammers create hundreds of splogs that they link to the spammer's site to increase that site's search engine ranking. This method makes use of the fact that links can influence a page's search engine ranking. For example, Google's PageRank system calculates a page's position in search results by weighing the links to that page. These deceptive practices are collectively referred to as *search engine spamming.* For information on search engine algorithms and page rankings, see *google.com/technology* and Slegg (2006).

The Solution

Both legal and technological defenses are used to prevent or punish search engine spamming and other forms of commercial spam. In one case, Verizon Wireless filed a lawsuit against the Florida-based travel agency Passport Holidays for violating federal and state laws by sending 98,000 unsolicited text messages to Verizon Wireless customers. Passport's messages encouraged recipients to call a toll-free number to claim a cruise to the Bahamas. In February 2006, a federal court judge granted Verizon Wireless's request for an injunction barring Passport Holidays from sending text message spam. Passport Holidays agreed to pay $10,000 to compensate Verizon Wireless.

Sending spam that disguises a sales pitch to look like a personal e-mail to bypass filters violates the U.S. Controlling the Assault of NonSolicited Pornography and Marketing (CAN-SPAM) Act of 2003. However, many spammers hide their identity to escape detection by using hijacked PCs, or spam zombies, to send spam, as discussed in Chapter 10.

Filtering achieves more immediate solutions. Bloggers plagued by comment spam can get help from sites such as SplogSpot *splogspot.com* or Splog Reporter *splogreporter.com*, which collect information on such content to help network administrators filter it out. Search engines constantly test and implement new algorithms with stronger filters to keep Web site rankings honest and objective.

The Results

The motivation for splogs, fraud, and other online scams is quick profit. Online scams create millionaires—even in remote areas like Lagos (Lawal 2006). Not only are they the fastest path to wealth for criminals of any age, they are near-instant businesses with no deterrent factor. Sploggers and spammers know the risk of detection, and prosecution is low.

Evidence shows that unethical and illegal business tactics that exploit or mimic e-commerce operations will not stop. To defend themselves, Google (*google.com/contact/spamreport.html*), MSN Search (*feedback.search.msn.com/default.aspx*) and Yahoo! (*add.yahoo.com/fast/help/us/ysearch/cgi_reportsearchspam*) have turned to aggressive measures. They have implemented spam site reporting systems, built algorithms that check for and penalize deceptive rank-boosting practices, and banned violators' sites outright. In 2006, Google temporarily banned BMW and Ricoh's German Web sites from its search index for using JavaScript redirect, or doorway pages that presented visitors with different content than they had displayed to the search engine.

Google has warned that it is expanding its efforts to clamp down on unethical tricks and tactics. As abuses become known or intolerable, additional laws will be passed with varying degrees of effectiveness.

Sources: Compiled from Harwood (2006), Hunt (2005), Spring (2006), MSNBC (2006), and Verizon Wireless News Center (2005).

Questions

1. Identify ethical issues in this case.
2. Why is SEM so popular with marketers? What are its strategic advantages?
3. Compare spammers to sploggers.
4. What are the benefits of SEO?

CHAPTER 13

LAUNCHING A SUCCESSFUL ONLINE BUSINESS AND EC PROJECTS

Content

Learning Objectives

Upon completion of this chapter, you will be able to:

1. Understand the fundamental requirements for initiating an online business.
2. Describe the process of initiating and funding a start-up e-business or large e-project.
3. Understand the process of adding EC initiatives to an existing business.
4. Describe the issues and methods of transforming an organization into an e-business.
5. Describe the process of acquiring Web sites and evaluating building versus hosting options.
6. Understand the importance of providing and managing content and describe how to accomplish this.
7. Evaluate Web sites on design criteria, such as appearance, navigation, consistency, and performance.
8. Understand how search engine optimization can help a Web site obtain high placement in search engines.
9. Understand how to provide some major support e-services.
10. Understand the process of building an online storefront.
11. Be able to build an online storefront with templates.

A complete version of this chapter is available on the textbook's Web site.

CHAPTER 14

BUILDING E-COMMERCE APPLICATIONS AND INFRASTRUCTURE

Learning Objectives

Upon completion of this chapter, you will be able to:

1. Discuss the major steps in developing an EC application.
2. Describe the major EC applications and list their major functionalities.
3. List the major EC application development options along with their benefits and limitations.
4. Discuss various EC application outsourcing options, including application service providers (ASPs), software as a service (SaaS), and utility computing.
5. Discuss the major EC software packages and EC application suites.
6. Describe various methods for connecting an EC application to back-end systems and databases.
7. Discuss the value and technical foundation of Web Services and their evolution into second-generation tools in EC applications.
8. Understand service-oriented architecture (SOA) and virtualization and their relationship to EC application development.
9. Describe the criteria used in selecting an outsourcing vendor and package.
10. Understand the value and uses of EC application log files.
11. Discuss the importance of usage analysis and site management.

Content

Helping Customers Navigate the Web Site and Increase Sales at Campmor

A complete version of this chapter is available on the textbook's Web site.

CHAPTER 1

Afuah, A., and C. L. Tucci. *Internet Business Models and Strategies*, 2d ed. New York: McGraw-Hill, 2003.

Ames, B. "HP Tops Dell as PC Sales Continue to Slow." IDG News Service, January 18, 2007. **infoworld.com/article/07/01/18/HNhptopsdell_1.html** (accessed October 2007).

Amit, R., and C. Zott. "Value Creation in E-Business." *Strategic Management Journal*, 22, no. 6 (2001).

Angermeier, M. "The Huge Cloud Lens Web 2.0." *Kosmar.de*, November 11, 2005. **kosmar.de/archives/2005/11/11/the-huge-cloud-lens-bubble-map-web20** (accessed March 2007).

Ariguzo, G. C., E. G. Mallach, and D. S. White. "The First Decade of E-Commerce." *International Journal of Business Information Systems*, 2, no. 3 (2006).

Bandyopadhyay, S. "A Critical Review of Pricing Strategies for Online Business Model." *Quarterly Journal of Electronic Commerce*, 2, no. 1 (2001).

Berstein, M. "Boeing Shrinks Supply Chain to Facilitate Risk Sharing." *World Trade*, April 1, 2006.

Brown, M. C. "Hacking Google Maps: A Conceptual Approach." *ExtremeTech.com*, August 31, 2006. **extremetech.com/article2/0,1558,2011239,00.asp** (accessed October 2007).

Carr, D. F. "How Google Works." *Baseline*, July 2006.

Carr, D. F. "Tapping into Virtual Markets." *Baseline*, March 1, 2007. **baselinemag.com/article2/0,1540,2098846,00.asp** (accessed January 2008).

Cashmore, P. "MySpace Hits 100 Million Accounts." *Mashable.com*, August 9, 2006. **mashable.com/2006/08/09/myspace-hits-100-million-accounts** (accessed January 2008).

Cassidy, J. *Dot.com: The Greatest Story Ever Sold*. New York: HarperCollins, 2002.

Chesbrough, H., and R. Rosenbloom. "The Role of the Business Model: Evidence from Xerox Corp." *Industrial and Corporate Change*, 11, no. 3 (2002).

Choi, S. Y., and A. B. Whinston. *The Internet Economy, Technology, and Practice*. Austin, TX: Smartecon.com, 2000.

Cone, E. "Flying in Formation." *CIO Insights*, March 2006.

Copeland, V. M., and K. Kelleher. "The New New Careers." *Business 2.0*, May 2007.

Currie, W. *Value Creation from E-Business Models*. Burlington, MA: Butterworth-Heinemann, 2004.

Davis, J. E. "Toward the Digital Enterprise." White paper, Intel Corporation, 2005. **intel.com/it/digitalenterprise** (no longer available online).

Drucker, P. *Managing in the Next Society*. New York: Truman Talley Books, 2002.

Emarketer.com. "Online Purchases in the U.S., by Category, 2002." *Emarketer.com,* June 26, 2002.

Farivar, C. "New Ways to Pay." *Business 2.0,* July 1, 2004.

Fass, A. "TheirSpace.com." *RedOrbit.com,* April 25, 2006. **redorbit.com/news/technology/481499/theirspacecom** (accessed January 2008).

FastPitch. "Top Internet Security Website Finds Suitable Partner to Fight Online Crime." December 8, 2007. **fastpitchnetworking.com/pressrelease.cfm?PRID=19752** (accessed December 2007).

Ferguson, S., and J. Davis. "A New Dell Direction." *eWeek,* May 14, 2007.

Foley, J. "Data Debate." *InformationWeek,* May 19, 2003.

Forrester Research. "Retail First Look," *Forrester.com,* June 1, 2006. **forrester.com/FirstLook/Vertical/Issue/ 0,6454,600,00.html** (accessed October 2007).

Goldberg, M. "Market Wrap Up." *Financial Sense Online,* December 13, 2006. **financialsense.com/Market/goldberg/ 2006/1214.html** (accessed January 2008).

Greenberg, P. *CRM at the Speed of Light: Capturing and Keeping Customers in Internet Real Time,* 3d ed. New York: McGraw-Hill, 2004.

Harmonyhollow.net, "What Are the Barriers of Implementing E-Commerce Solutions?" 2006. **harmonyhollow.net/ webmaster-resources/ecommerce/15604.php** (accessed January 2008).

Harrington, R. "The Transformer" (an e-mail interview with *Baseline's* editor-in-chief, J. McCormic). *Baseline,* April 2006.

Hicks, M. "Google's Next Step: Banner Ads," *eWeek.com,* May 13, 2004. **eweek.com/article2/0,1895,1592027,00.asp** (accessed January 2008).

Hoffman, K. L., and T. P. Novak. "How to Acquire Customers on the Web." *Harvard Business Review* (May–June 2000).

Hwang, H. S., and C. Stewart. "Lessons from Dot-Com Boom and Bust," in Khosrow-Pour (2006).

Jana, R. "American Apparel's Virtual Clothes." *BusinessWeek,* June 27, 2006. **businessweek.com/innovate/content/ jun2006/id20060627_217800.htm** (accessed January 2008).

Jelassi, T., and A. Enders. *Strategies for e-Business.* Harlow, England: FT, Prentice Hall, 2005.

Jupiter Media. "Jupiter Research Forecasts Online Retail Spending Will Reach $144 Billion in 2010, a CAGR of 12% from 2005." February 6, 2006. **jupitermedia.com/corporate/ releases/06.02.06-newjupresearch.html** (accessed January 2008).

Kaplan, P. J. *F'd Companies: Spectacular Dot.com Flameouts.* New York: Simon and Schuster, 2002.

Khosrow-Pour, M. (ed.). *Encyclopedia of E-Commerce, E-Government, and Mobile Commerce.* Hershey, PA: Idea Group Reference, 2006.

Kraemer, K., and J. Dedrick. "Dell Computer: Using E-Commerce to Support a Virtual Company," a special report, June 2001, available in M. Rappa, "Case Study: Dell Computer." **digitalenterprise.org/cases/dell.html** (accessed January 2008).

Krishnan, S. A., and A. Ravi. "Group Buying on the Web: A Comparison of Price-Discovery Mechanisms." *INFORMS,* November 2003.

Lashinsky, A. "The Boom Is Back." *Fortune,* May 1, 2006.

Loebbecke, C. "RFID in the Retail Supply Chain," in Khosrow-Pour (2006).

Lee, C. S., Y. G. Chen, and Y.-H. Fan. "Structure and Components of E-Commerce Business Model," in Khosrow-Pour 2006.

Li, E. Y., and T. C. Du. *Advances in Electronic Business,* Volume 1. Hershey, PA: Idea Group Publishing, 2004.

Mann, J. "700 Million Internet Users Says ComScore Network." *TechSpot.com,* May 5, 2006. **techspot.com/news/ 21504–700-million-internet-users-says-comscore-net- works.html** (accessed January 2008).

Marketingcharts.com. "Online Shoppers, Going Forth and Multiplying." May 18, 2007. **marketingcharts.com/inter- active/online-shoppers-going-forth-multiplying-417** (accessed January 2008).

McGee, M. K. "Chiefs of the Year: Internet Call to Arms." *InformationWeek,* November 27, 2000.

McKay, J., and P. Marshall. *Strategic Management of E-Business.* Milton, Qld., Australia: John Wiley and Sons, 2004.

McNichol, T. "Building a Wiki World (Wikia vs. Wikipedia)." *Business 2.0,* March 2007.

Mendelsohn, T., C. Johnson, and B. Tesch. "The Web's Impact on In-Store Sales: U.S. Cross-Channel Sales Forecast, 2006 to 2012." Forrester Research, June 1, 2007. **forrester.com/Research/Document/Excerpt/0,7211,420 84,00.html** (accessed January 2008).

Miller, J. L. "No Place Like MySpace," *Webpronews.com,* October 11, 2005. **webpronews.com/insiderreports/2005/ 10/11/ no-place-like-myspace** (accessed January 2008).

Mockler, R. J., D. G. Dologite, and M. E. Gartenfeld. "B2B E-Business," in Khosrow-Pour (2006).

Mullaney, T. J. "E-Biz Strikes Again!" *BusinessWeek,* May 10, 2004.

National Cristina Foundation. "Dell Recycling." *Cristina.org.* **cristina.org/dell.html** (accessed January 2008).

O'Reilly, T. "What Is Web 2.0?" *OReillynet.com,* September 30, 2005. **oreillynet.com/pub/a/oreilly/tim/news/2005/09/30/ what-is-web-20.html** (accessed January 2008).

Papazoglou, M. P., and P. M. A. Ribbers. *e-Business: Organizational and Technical Foundations.* West Sussex, England: Wiley 2006.

People's Daily Online (China). "Distressed Parents Create Blog to Track Down Missing Son." **english.peopledaily. com.cn/200608/01/eng20060801_288726.html** (accessed January 2008).

Peters, K. M. "Homeland Security Hurdles." *Government Executive,* February 2003.

Plunkett, J. W. *Plunkett's E-Commerce and Internet Business Almanac 2006.* Houston, TX: Plunkett Research, Ltd., February 2006.

Rappa, M. "Business Models on the Web," *Digitalenterprise.org*, 2007. **digitalenterprise.org/models/models.html** (accessed October 2007).

Reda, S. "Godiva.com's Story Parallels Dynamic Growth of E-Commerce." *Stores*, February 2004.

Reuters, A. "IBM Eyes Move into Second Life 'V-Business.'" *Second Life News Center*, October 24, 2006. **secondlife. reuters.com/stories/2006/10/24/ibm-eyes-move-into-second-life-v-business** (accessed January 2008).

Rosedale, P. "Alter Egos." *Forbes*, May 7, 2007.

Roush, W. "Second Earth." *Technology Review*, July–August 2007.

Schonfeld, E. "Web 2.0 Around the World." *Business 2.0*, August 2006a.

Schonfeld, E. "Cyworld Attacks!" *Business 2.0*, August 2006b.

SecondLife.com. "The World." 2007. **secondlife.com/whatis/world.php** (accessed January 2008).

Sellers, P. "MySpace Cowboys." *Fortune*, September 4, 2006.

Seoul Digital City. "E-Commerce in Korea: Myths, Facts." April 28, 2004. **urban.blogs.com/seoul/2004/04/ecommerce_in_ko.html** (accessed January 2008).

Sharma, S. K. "E-Commerce in the Digital Economy," in Khosrow-Pour (2006).

Sloan, P. "The Quest for the Perfect Online Ad." *Business 2.0*, March 2007.

Strategic Direction. "DotCom Boom and Bust: The Secrets of E-Commerce Failure and Success." *Strategic Direction*, February 2005.

Tatnall, A. "Web Portal Gateways," in Khosrow-Pour (2006).

Tian, Y., and C. Stewart. "History of E-Commerce," in Khosrow-Pour (2006).

Totty, M. "New Tools Emerge for Frazzled Recruiters." *Wall Street Journal*, October 23, 2006.

Turban, E., et al. *Information Technology for Management*, 6th ed. New York: John Wiley & Sons, 2007.

U.S. Department of Commerce. "The Emerging Digital Economy II." June 1999. **esa.doc.gov/reports/EDE2 report.pdf** (January 2008).

Van Toorn, C., D. Bunker, K. Yee, and S. Smith. "The Barriers to the Adoption of E-Commerce by Micro Businesses, Small Businesses and Medium Enterprises," *Sixth International Conference on Knowledge, Culture, and Change in Organisations*, Prato, Tuscany, Italy, July 11–14, 2006.

Weill, P., and M. R. Vitale. *Place to Space: Migrating to eBusiness Models*. Boston: Harvard Business School Press, 2001.

Workforce-Performance. "Boeing 787 Global Design Team Benefits from Collaboration Solution Incorporating Simulation," *Tech Horizon*, May 22, 2006, **techlearn newsline.com/News/05–22–06a.html** (accessed January 2008).

Zhengzhou Evening News (in Chinese), September 27, 2004.

CHAPTER 2

123jump.com. "Bidz.com." March 17, 2006. **123jump.com/ipo/ipo_view/BIDZ/Bidz.com?PHPSESSID=5a408d8 210836e2ca9569498a39682b5** (accessed January 2008).

Anonymous. "How to Turn a Paper Clip into a House." *ABC News*, July 14, 2006.

Bakos, Y. "The Emerging Role of Electronic Marketplaces on the Internet." *Communications of the ACM* (August 1998).

Beckmann, H., P. van der Eijk, V. Schmitz, and N. Ondracek. "Multilingual Catalogue Strategies for eCommerce and eBusiness." *CEN/ISSS WS/eCat Report*, July 2004. **domino.cni.cz/NP/NotesPortalCNI.nsf/key/62F699B A499EA8A2C1256FAB00319E30/$File/CWA15045– 00.pdf** (accessed January 2008).

Bennett, E. "Winery Blogs to Turn Browsers into Buyers." *Baseline*, June 2007.

Beynon-Davies, P. *@-business*. New York: Palgrave-Macmillan, 2004.

Bichler, M., G. Kersten, and C. Weinhardt. "Electronic Negotiations: Foundations, Systems, and Experiments." Introduction to the Special Issue of *Group Decision and Negotiation*, 12 (May–December 2003).

Blecker, T. "Product Configuration Systems," in Khosrow-Pour (2006).

Bluenile.com. "Blue Nile Launches New Interactive Diamond Search." March 27, 2006. **investor.bluenile.com/phoenix. zhtml?c=177247&p=irol-newsArticle&ID=835771& highlight=** (accessed January 2008).

Brandon, E. "Finding an Apartment on Craigslist: Five Tips." *U.S. News and World Report*, July 10, 2006.

BusinessWeek Online. "*BusinessWeek's* Hot Growth Companies: Blue Nile," 2006a. **businessweek.com/hot_growth/2006/ company/10.htm** (accessed January 2008).

BusinessWeek Online. "The Organic Myth." 2006b. **businessweek. com/magazine/content/06_42/b4005001.htm** (accessed January 2008).

Carbone, J. "Reverse Auctions Become More Strategic for Buyers." *Purchasing Magazine Online*, December 8, 2005.

CBC News. "From Paper-Clip to House, in 14 Trades." July 7, 2006. **cbc.ca/canada/story/2006/07/07/paperclip-house.html** (accessed January 2008).

Coffin, A. M. *eBay for Dummies*, 4th ed. Hoboken, NJ: John Wiley & Sons, 2004.

Cook, T. "Success with Internet Auctions: Tips and Techniques." *PowerHomeBiz.com*, 2006. **powerhomebiz.com/column/ terri/tips.htm** (accessed January 2008).

Copeland, M. V. "The Big Guns' Next Target: eBay." *CNNMoney.com*, January 31, 2006a. **money.cnn.com/ magazines/business2/business2_archive/2006/01/01/83 68106/index.htm** (accessed January 2008).

Copeland, M. V. "Swaptree: The eBay of Swap." *CNNMoney.com*, May 11, 2006b. **money.cnn.com/magazines/business2/**

business2_archive/2006/05/01/8375930/index.htm (accessed January 2008).

Cox, B. G., and W. Koelzer. *Internet Marketing: Strategy, Implementation, and Practice*, 3d ed. Upper Saddle River, NJ: Prentice Hall, 2006.

Craigslist.org. "Craigslist Fact Sheet." 2006. **craigslist.org/about/pr/factsheet.html** (accessed January 2008).

Datta, S. "The 7 Habits of Highly Effective Bloggers." *Business 2.0*, September 2006.

eBay. "eBay Express." 2006a. **pages.ebay.com/sell/announcement/overview/express.html** (accessed January 2008).

eMarketer. "Top Ten E-Business Trends for 2005." *eMarketer.com*, January 5, 2005. **emarketer.com/article.aspx?1003202** (no longer available online).

E-Market Services. "Why Use E-Markets?" *E-MarketServices.com*. **emarketservices.com/templates/Page_434/aspx** (accessed January 2008).

Flynn, N. *Blog Rules A Business Guide to Managing Policy, Public Relations, and Legal Issues*. New York: AMACOM/American Management Association, 2006.

Gallaugher, J. M. "E-Commerce and the Undulating Distribution Channel." *Communications of the ACM* (July 2002).

Gibson, S. "RSS in the Enterprise." *eWeek*, January 15, 2007.

Grossman, L. "Time's Person of the Year: You." *Time*, December 13, 2006. **time.com/time/magazine/article/0,9171,1569514,00.html** (accessed May 2008).

Guan, S. U. "E-Commerce Agents and Payment Systems," in Khosrow-Pour (2006).

Holden, G. "Fast Forward." *Entrepreneur*, May 2006.

Khosrow-Pour, M. (ed.). *Encyclopedia of E-Commerce, E-Government, and Mobile Commerce*. Hershey, PA: Idea Group Reference, 2006.

Lepouras, G., and C. Vassilakis. "Adaptive Virtual Reality Shopping Malls," in Khosrow-Pour (2006).

Lewin, J. "Blog Risk." *E-Commerce in Action*, September 29, 2004. **66.51.97.137/2367202.txt** (no longer available online).

Li, E. Y., and T. C. Du. *Advances in Electronic Business*, Volume 1. Hershey, PA: Idea Group Publishing, 2005.

McGillicuddy, S. "Firms Mull Over Blogs, but Doubt Business Value." *SearchCIO.com*, July 18, 2007. **searchcio.techtarget.com/originalContent/0,289142,sid19_gci1264590,00.html** (accessed January 2008).

McNichol, T. "How a Small Winery Found Internet Fame." *Business 2.0*, August 8, 2007.

Mullaney, T. J. "E-Biz Strikes Again!" *BusinessWeek*, May 10, 2004. **businessweek.com/magazine/content/04_19/b3882001_mz001.htm** (accessed January 2008).

Naughton, J. "Web Sites That Changed the World." *The Guardian*, August 14, 2006. **guardian.co.uk/technology/2006/aug/13/observerreview.onlinesupplement** (accessed January 2008).

Needleman, S. "Blogging Becomes a Corporate Job: Digital 'Handshake'?" *Wall Street Journal*, May 2005.

Nissanoff, D. *Future Shop: How the New Auction Culture Will Revolutionize the Way We Buy, Sell, and Get Things We Really Want*. New York: The Penguin Press, 2006.

O'Buyonge, A. A., and L. Chen. "E-Health Dot-Coms' Critical Success Factors," in Khosrow-Pour (2006).

Ozzie, R. CEO of Groove Networks personal blog, August 24, 2002. **ozzie.net/blog/2002/08/24.html** (accessed January 2007).

Park, S. "eBay's Dominance in Internet Auctions," in Khosrow-Pour (2006).

Prince, D. L. *How to Sell Anything on eBay . . . and Make a Fortune*. New York: McGraw-Hill, 2004.

Rapoza, J. "How to Spot Fake Blogs." *eWeek*, October 2006.

Saarinen, T., M. Tinnild, and A. Tseng (eds.). *Managing Business in a Multi-Channel World*. Hershey, PA: Idea Group, Inc., 2006.

Schmitz, V., J. Leukel, and F. D. Dorloff. "Do E-Catalog Standards Support Advanced Processes in B2B ECommerce?" *Proceedings of the 38th Hawaii International Conference on System Sciences*, Big Island, Hawaii, January 3–6, 2005.

Schonfeld, E. "The World According to eBay." *CNNMoney.com*, January 1, 2005. **money.cnn.com/magazines/business2/business2_archive/2005/01/01/8250238/index.htm** (accessed January 2008).

Search Engine Roundtable. "eBay AdContext—eBay's Contextual Ad System." June 12, 2006. **seroundtable.com/archives/003926.html** (accessed January 2008).

Sifry, D. "State of the Blogosphere." *Sifry.com*, August 7, 2006. **sifry.com/alerts/archives/000436.html** (accessed January 2008).

Sloan, P., and P. Kaihla. "Blogging for Dollars." *Business 2.0*, September 2006.

Southwick, K. "Diagnosing WebMD: Ultimate Dot-Com Survivor Faces New Challenges." *CNetNews.com*, May 11, 2004. **news.com/Diagnosing+WebMD/2009–1017_3–5208510.html** (accessed January 2008).

Stroebel, M. *Engineering Electronic Negotiations*. Boston: Kluwer Academics, 2003.

Tapscott, D., and A. D. Williams. *Wikinomics: How Mass Communications Changes Everything*. New York: Portfolio/Penguin Group, 2007.

Time. "50 Coolest Web Sites 2006." *Time*, August 23, 2006.

Turban, E., et al. *Information Technology for Management*, 6th ed. Hoboken, NJ: Wiley, 2007.

Wagner, B. "Best Seats." *The New Yorker*, August 6, 2007.

Weber, S. *Plug Your Business*. Falls Church, VA: Weber Books, 2007.

Webopedia. "Infomediary." 2006. **webopedia.com/TERM/I/infomediary.html** (accessed January 2008).

Woolard, D. "Jay Leno Harley Davidson Up on eBay." *Luxist.com*, September 20, 2006. **luxist.com/2005/09/20/jay-leno-harley-davidson-up-on-ebay** (accessed January 2008).

Yap, A. "Secrets to Successful Blogging." *Searchwarp.com*, May 3, 2006. **searchwarp.com/swa60483.htm** (accessed January 2007).

Zwass, V. "Electronic Commerce and Organizational Innovation: Aspects and Opportunities." *International Journal of Electronic Commerce*, 7, no. 3 (2003).

APPENDIX 2A

Anke, J., and D. Sundaram. "Personalization Techniques and Their Application," in Khosrow-Pour (2006).

Blecker, T. "Product Configuration Systems," in Khosrow-Pour (2006).

Chandra, C., and A. K. Kamrani (eds.). *Mass Customization: Supply Chain Approach.* New York: Kluwer Academic, 2005.

Khosrow-Pour, M. (ed.). *Encyclopedia of E-Commerce, E-Government, and Mobile Commerce.* Hershey, PA: Idea Group Reference, 2006.

Warschat, J., M. Kurumluoglu, and R. Nostdal. "Enabling IT for Mass Customization." *International Journal of Mass Customization*, 1, nos. 2–3 (2005).

Zipkin, P. "The Limits of Mass Customization." *MIT Sloan Management Review* (Spring 2001).

CHAPTER 3

Aquino, G. "Deal Finders." *PCWorld.com*, October 28, 2005. **pcworld.com/reviews/article/0,aid,122931,00.asp** (accessed January 2008).

Atkinson, W. "Internet Impacts Potential, Current Owners." *Hotel and Motel Management*, June 6, 2005. **hotelmotel.com/hotelmotel/article/articleDetail.jsp?id=164387** (accessed January 2008).

Bhatnagar, P. "Walmart.com's Going Upscale." *CNNMoney*, November 18, 2004. **money.cnn.com/2004/11/18/news/fortune500/walmart_online** (accessed January 2008).

Biz Report. "Toys Made in China off Christmas Shopping Lists." *BizReport.com*, November 14, 2007. **bizreport.com/2007/11/toys_made_in_china_off_christmas_shopping_lists.html** (accessed January 2008).

Bloch, M., and A. Segev. "The Impact of Electronic Commerce on the Travel Industry." *Proceedings of the 30th Annual HICSS*, Maui, Hawaii, January 1997.

Borrell Associates. "2006 Update: Online Real Estate Advertising." *Borrellassociates.com*, July 2006. **borrellassociates.com/report.aspx** (accessed January 2008).

Burns, E. "Online Retail Revenues to Reach $200 Billion." *Clickz.com*, June 5, 2006. **clickz.com/showPage.html?page=3611181** (accessed January 2008).

BusinessWire. "Amazon.com Announces 22% Sales Growth Fueled by Lower Prices, Free Shipping." July 25, 2006. **goliath.ecnext.com/coms2/gi_0199–5603645/Amazon-com-Announces-22-Sales.html** (accessed January 2008).

Careerbuilder.com. "CareerBuilder.com's Job Forecast: Q3 2006." March 2006. **img.icbdr.com/images/aboutus/pressroom/CB-JobForecast-Q3–2006.pdf** (accessed January 2008).

Carter, M. "Subprime Origination Migrates to the Net." *InmanNews*, December 20, 2007. **blog.inman.com/inmanblog/2007/12/subprime-origin.html** (accessed January 2008).

Cashedge.com. "Cash Edge Survey Confirms Consumer Demand for Value Added Online Banking Services." October 12, 2006. **cashedge.com/pressRoom/press_20061012_1_cashedge.html** (accessed January 2008).

Castex, S. "Trends and News." *Promotional Products Business*, July 2003. **ppbmag.com/Article.aspx?id=1704** (accessed January 2008).

Celent. "Banks Increase Their Focus on Small Businesses." *Celent.com*, November 3, 2004. **celent.com/PressReleases/20041103/SmallBusVendors.htm** (accessed January 2008).

Cooperativebank.co.uk. "Important Information." 2006. **co-operativebank.co.uk/servlet/Satellite?pagename=CB/Page/tplStandard&cid=1179298984499** (accessed January 2008).

Cox, J. "Online Recruitment Increases Exponentially." March 31, 2006. **wiliam.com.au/wiliam-blog/business** (accessed January 2008).

Cropper, C. M. "Choosing an Online Broker; Most—But Not All—Brokerage Web Sites Now Slap on a Slew of Fees." *BusinessWeek*, May 17, 2004.

Dandapani, K. "Success and Failures in Web-Based Financial Services." *Communications of the ACM* (May 2004).

Dernovsek, D. "The Move to E-payments." *Credit Union Magazine*, August 2004.

DiamondView.com. "2006 Internet Sales Top $100 Billion!" January 2, 2007. **diamondvues.com/2007/01/2006_internet_sales_top_100_bi_1.html** (accessed January 2008).

Direct Marketing Association. "Toy Sales Fell in 2005, Reports NPD Group; Sales Hit $21.3 Billion Last Year." 2006. **the-dma.org/cgi/newsstandarchive** (accessed January 2008).

Ebcenter.org. "Dell Invests in Physical Stores to Reach Customers." *Newsletter*, June 1–15, 2006. **iese.edu/en/ad/eb-center.junio20061/newsletter/asp#22797** (no longer available online).

Ericson, J. "Name Your Price." *Line56*, January 19, 2004.

Fox, S., and J. Beier. "Online Banking 2006: Surfing to the Bank" *PewInternet.org* June 14, 2006. **pewinternet.org/PPF/r/185/report_display.asp** (accessed January 2008).

Global Finance. "World's Best Foreign Exchange Banks 2004." *Global Finance*, March 2004.

Hanks, J. "Internet Retailer 2007." *JeremyHanks.com*, June 6, 2007. **jeremyhanks.com/2007/06/06/internet-retailer-2007** (accessed January 2008).

Harteveldt, H. H. "Travelers Embrace Social Computing Technologies." *Forrester Research Report*, October 23, 2006. **forrester.com/Research/Document/Excerpt/0,7211,399 28,00.html** (accessed February 2007).

Hedna.org. "Travel Search Engines Redefine Distribution." 2005, Executive White Paper Series. **hedna.org/pdf/Executive_Summary_Travel_Search_Engines_Redefine_Distribution.pdf** (accessed January 2008).

Internetretailer.com. "45% of U.S. Adults Shop Online, but Security Concerns Hold Others Back." November 16, 2007a. **internetretailer.com/internet/marketing-conference/72196–45-us-adults-shop-online-but-security-concerns-hold-others-back.html** (accessed January 2008).

Internetretailer.com. "Amazon Grows 23% in 2005, but Profits Slide." February 3, 2006a. **internetretailer.com/dailyNews.asp?id=17513** (accessed January 2008).

Internetretailer.com. "First-Half Online Retail Spending Rises 25% to 46 Billion." August 3, 2006b. **internetretailer.com/printArticle.asp?id=19450** (accessed January 2008).

Internetretailer.com. "Target Posts Largest July Traffic Gain Among Top 10 Shopping Sites." September 1, 2006c. **internetretailer.com/dailyNews.asp?id=19761** (accessed January 2008).

Internetretailer.com. "Wal-Mart Moves Up in the Ranks of Shopping Destinations." February 23, 2007b. **interne tretailer .com/dailyNews.asp?id=21528** (accessed January 2008).

Internetretailer.com. "Wal-Mart's New In-Store Pick-Up Service Might Not Be Fast, But It's Free." March 6, 2007c. **internetretailer.com/dailyNews.asp?id=2164** (accessed January 2008).

JobCentral.com. "Welcome to JobCentral." 2006. **jobcentral.com/aboutus.asp** (accessed January 2008).

Jobsearch.gov.au. "Australian JobSearch Overview." 2006. **jobsearch.gov.au** (accessed January 2008).

Khosrow-Pour, M. (ed.). *Encyclopedia of E-Commerce, E-Government, and Mobile Commerce.* Hershey, PA: Idea Group Reference, 2006.

Knowledge@Wharton. "Car Trouble: Should We Recall the U.S. Auto Industry?" May 4, 2005. **knowledge.wharton.upenn.edu/article.cfm?articleid=1183,2005** (accessed January 2008).

Knox, N. "It's Always 'OPEN HOUSE' as Real Estate Goes Online." *USA Today*, May 16, 2006.

Lee, S. C., and A. A. Brandyberry. "The E-tailer's Dilemma." *ACM SIGMIS Database*, June 2003.

Leggatt, H. "Half of Leisure Travelers Book Online." *BizReport*, October 17, 2007. **bizreport.com/2007/10/half_of_leisure_travelers_book_online.html** (accessed January 2008).

Linn, A. "Online Shopping Growth to Slow in Next Decade." *MSNBC.com*, September 4, 2007. **msnbc.msn.com/id/20321999** (accessed January 2008).

Mallat, N., M. Rossi, and V. K. Tuunainen. "Mobile Banking Services." *Communications of the ACM* (May 2004).

McKay, J., and P. Marshall. *Strategic Management of eBusiness.* New York: John Wiley and Sons, 2004.

McTaggart, J. "Online Retailing: E-Grocery's Reality Check." *Progressive Grocer*, August 2006.

Moules, J. "Online Banking Gains Popularity." *Financial Times*, October 14, 2006.

Mullaney, T. J. "E-Biz Strikes Again." *BusinessWeek*, May 10, 2004.

Mulpuru, S. "2005 U.S. eCommerce: The Year in Review." *Forrester Research.* **forrester.com/Research/Document/Excerpt/0,7211,38809,00.html** (accessed January 2008).

New York Times News. "Real Estate Sales and Advertising Enter Cyberspace." *New York Times*, December 17, 2007.

NPD.com. Press release, July 17, 2001. (No longer available online.)

Omniture.com. "Industry Guide: Travel and Hospitality Sites." 2006. **omniture.com/static/378** (accessed January 2008).

Oo, P. "Grocery Stores: Trends and Tips." *UM News*, May 5, 2006. **umn.edu/umnnews/Feature_Stories/Grocery_stores3A_trends_and_tips.html** (accessed January 2008).

Parker, P. "Amazon to Develop Online Talk Show." *Clickz.com*, January 19, 2006. **clickz.com/showPage.html?page=3578551** (accessed January 2008).

Parks, L. "Making Sure the Price Is Right." *Stores*, August 2004.

PRWeb.com. "A New Way of Keeping in Touch." 2003. **prweb.com/releases/2003/8/prweb77491.htm** (accessed January 2008).

Qantas.com.au. "Qantas to Conduct an Evaluation of New Technology Allowing Customers to Stay Connected Inflight." August 28, 2006. **qantas.com.au/regions/dyn/au/publicaffairs/details?ArticleID=2006/aug06/Q3469** (accessed January 2008).

Reda, S. "Online Retail Grows Up." *Stores*, February 2002.

Regan, K. "E*TRADE Buys Harrisdirect as Online Brokers Consolidate." *E-Commerce Times*, August 8, 2005. **ecommerce-times.com/story/45304.html** (accessed January 2008).

Rickards, G. "What's All This about Online Banking?" *MsMoney.com*. **msmoney.com/mm/banking/articles/about_online_banking.htm** (accessed November 2006).

Riseley, M. J. "Findings: Amazon Moves into Online Grocery Shopping Niche." *Gartner Industry Research*, July 3, 2006.

Rose, B. "More Employers Use Personality Tests to Screen Job Candidates." *Chicago Tribune*, January 14, 2008. **chicagotribune.com/business/chi-mon_space_0114jan14,0,7887354.story** (accessed January 2008).

Schonfeld, E., and J. Borzo, "Social Networking for Dollars." *CNNMoney.com*, September 20, 2006. **money.cnn.com/2006/09/15/technology/disruptors_zopa.biz2/index.htm** (accessed January 2008).

Shoniregun, C. A. "Is Cybermediation Really the Future or Risk?" *International Journal of Electronic Business* 2, no. 6 (2004).

Soopramanien, D. G. R., and A. Robertson. "Adoption and Usage of Online Shopping: An Empirical Analysis of the Characteristics of 'Buyers,' 'Browsers,' and 'Non-Internet' Shoppers." *Journal of Retailing and Consumer Services* (January 2007).

Southard, P., and K. Siau. "A Survey of Online E-Banking Retail Initiatives." *Communications of the ACM* (October 2004).

Tessler, F. N. "Online Banking Made Easy." *Macworld* 21, no. 8 (August 2004).

Thestatebank.com. "Security Information." 2006. **thestatebank. com/security.htm** (accessed January 2008).

Tia.org. "Executive Summaries—E-Travel Consumers: How They Plan and Buy Leisure Travel Online." 2005. **tia.org/researchpubs/executive_summaries_e_travel. html** (accessed January 2008).

TravelBizMonitor, "Industry Trends 2008." January 7, 2008. **travelbizmonitor.com/ArticleDetails.aspx?aid=1909& sid=18&sname=Coverstory** (accessed May 2008).

U.S. Census Bureau. "E-Stats." May 25, 2006. **census.gov/eos/ www/ebusiness614.htm** (accessed January 2008).

U.S. Census Bureau. "Quarterly Retail E-Commerce Sales 3rd Quarter 2007." November 19, 2007. **census.gov/mrts/ www/data/html/07Q3.html** (accessed January 2008).

Van der Heijden, J. G. M. "The Changing Value of Travel Agents in Tourism Networks: Towards a Network Design Perspective." In Stefan Klein, et al. (eds.), *Information and Communication Technologies in Tourism*, pages 151–159. New York: Springer-Verlag, 1996.

Walsh, M. "Online Job Ad Revenues Surpass Print." *MediaPost.com*, December 20, 2006. **publications. mediapost.com/index.cfm?fuseaction=Articles.show-Article&art_aid=52814** (accessed January 2008).

Wang, F. "E-Shoppers' Perception of Web-Based Decision Aid," in Khosrow-Pour (2006).

Weiner, M. (2006) "The 5-Day Car: Ordered on Monday—Delivered on Friday." *Ilipt.org*, February 28, 2006. **fraunhofer.de/fhg/Images/magazine_2–2006_28_tcm6–64704.pdf** (accessed January 2008).

Xu, M. X., S. Wilkes, and M. H. Shah. "E-Banking Application and Issues in Abbey National PLC," in Khosrow-Pour (2006).

Yao, J. T. "Ecommerce Adoption of Insurance Companies in New Zealand." *Journal of Electronic Commerce Research* 5, no. 1 (2004).

CHAPTER 4

Akamai Technologies, Inc. "Best Practices for Successful Live Web Event." 2000a. Akamai Technologies, Inc., report.

Akamai Technologies, Inc. "Delivering the Profits: How the Right Content Delivery Provider Can Drive Traffic, Sales, and Profits through Your Web Site." 2000b. Akamai Technologies, Inc., white paper.

Angel, G. "The Art and Science of Choosing Net Marketing Channels." *E-Commerce Times*, September 21, 2006. **ecommercetimes.com/story/53141.html** (accessed November 2007).

Anke, J., and D. Sundaram. "Personalization Techniques and Their Application," in Khosrow-Pour (2006).

Anywhere You Go. "2006 Will Be Year of Mobile Advertising Experimentation." March 20, 2006. **anywhereyougo. com/2006/03/2006-year-of-mobile-advertising.html** (accessed November 2007).

Armstrong, G., and P. Kotler. *Marketing: An Introduction*, 7th ed. Upper Saddle River, NJ: Prentice Hall, 2007.

Atlantic Media Company. "American Advertising Federation's Survey on Digital Media Trends." 2006. **aaf.org/news/ pdf/execsummarysurvey0606.doc** (no longer available online).

Balabanis, G., N. Reynolds, and A. Simintiras. "Bases of E-Store Loyalty: Perceived Switching Barriers and Satisfaction." *Journal of Business Research* 59 (2006).

Bosman, J. "Hey, Kid, You Want to Buy a Toyota Scion?" *New York Times*, June 14, 2006. **nytimes.com/2006/06/ 14/business/media/14adco.html?r=2&oref=slogin& oref=slogin** (accessed April 2008).

Boswell, K. "Digital Marketing vs. Online Advertising Breaking Waves for Marketers to Catch." *The Marketleap Report* 2, no. 5 (2002). **marketleap.com/report/ml_ report_24.htm** (accessed November 2007).

Bridges, E., R. E. Goldsmith, and C. F. Hofacker. "Businesses and Consumers as Online Customers," in Khosrow-Pour (2006).

Buckley, N. "E-Route to Whiter Smile." *Financial Times*, August 26, 2002.

Chan, S. *Strategic Management of e-Business*, 2d ed. Chichester, UK: John Wiley & Sons, 2005.

Chase, L. "Advertisement Methods." *Web Digest for Marketing*, October 2, 2006.

Chellappa, R., and R. G. Sin. "Personalization versus Privacy: An Empirical Examination of the Online Consumer's Dilemma." *Information Technology and Management* 4 (2005).

Chen, A. Y. A., and D. McLeod. "Collaborative Filtering for Information Recommendation Systems," in Khosrow-Pour (2006).

Cheung, C. M. K., and M. K. O. Lee. "The Asymmetric Impact of Website Attribute Performance on User Satisfaction: An Empirical Study." *Proceedings of Hawaii International Conference on System Sciences*, Big Island, Hawaii, January 2005a.

Cheung, C. M. K., and M. K. O. Lee. "The Asymmetric Impact of Website Attribute Performance on User Satisfaction: An Empirical Study." *e-Service Journal* 3, no. 3 (2005b).

Cheung, C. M. K., L. Zhu, T. C. H. Kwong, G. W. W. Chan, and M. Limayem. "Online Consumer Behavior: A Review and Agenda for Future Research." *Proceedings of Bled eCommerce Conference*, Bled, Slovenia, June 2003.

Clow, K., and D. Baack. *Integrated Advertising, Promotion, and Marketing Communication.* Upper Saddle River, NJ: Prentice Hall, 2004.

Collier, J. E., and C. C. Bienstock. "How Do Customers Judge Quality in an E-Tailer?" *MIT Sloan Management Review* 48, no. 1 (2006).

Computer Industry Almanac. "Worldwide Internet Users Top 1 Billion in 2005. USA Reach Nearly 200M Internet Users." January 4, 2006. **c-i-a.com/pr0106.htm** (accessed January 2008).

Covel, S. "Paying Bloggers for Online Reviews Can Fan Fame." *Wall Street Journal,* August 27, 2007. **online.wsj. com/public/article/SB118729653805300071.html** (accessed January 2008).

Cox, B., and W. Koelzer. *Internet Marketing.* Upper Saddle River, NJ: Prentice Hall, 2004.

Delaney, K. J. "Once-Wary Industry Giants Embrace Internet Advertising," *Wall Street Journal*, April 17, 2006.

Doyle, K., A. Minor, and C. Weyrich. "Banner Ad Location Effectiveness Study." University of Michigan, 1997. **webreference.com/dev/banners** (accessed November 2007).

Evans, G. "The Big Payoff." *Teradata Magazine*, June 2006.

Faught, K. S., K. W. Green Jr., and D. Whitten. "Doing Survey Research on the Internet." *Journal of Computer Information Systems* 44, no. 3 (2004).

Firstfold.com. "The Big E-Mail Opportunity Lies Ahead." September 29, 2006. **firstfold.com/the-big-email-opportunity-lies-ahead** (accessed November 2007).

Fleita, A. "The Top Nine E-Mail Hoaxes." *MSN Money*, news item, November 15, 2003. **moneycentral.msn.com** (no longer available online).

Floh, A., and H. Treiblmaier. "What Keeps the E-Banking Customer Loyal? A Multigroup Analysis of the Moderating Role of Consumer Characteristics on E-Loyalty in the Financial Service Industry." *Journal of Electronic Commerce Research* 7, no. 2 (2006).

Flynn, L. J. "Like This? You'll Hate That. (Not All Web Recommendations Are Welcome)." *New York Times*, January 23, 2006.

Gao, Y., M. Koufaris, and R. H. Ducoffe. "Negative Effects of Advertising Techniques in Electronic Commerce," in Khosrow-Pour, 2006.

Gelb, B. D., and S. Sundaram. "Adapting to 'Word of Mouse.'" *Business Horizons*, July–August 2002.

Goldsmith, R. E. "Electronic Word-of-Mouth," in Khosrow-Pour (2006).

Goodman, A. E. *Winning Results with Google AdWords.* New York: McGraw-Hill, 2005.

Gopal, R. D., A. K. Tripathi, and Z. D. Walter. "Economic Issues in Advertising via Email: A Role for A Trusted Third Party?" in *Contemporary Research in EMarketing*, Volume 1, S. Krishnamurthy (ed.). Hershey, PA: The Idea Group Inc., 2005.

Graham, R. "Advergaming Goes Mainstream." *iMedia-Connection*, December 5, 2005. **imediaconnection. com/content/7362.asp** (accessed November 2007).

Gregg, D. G., and S. Walczak. "Adaptive Web Information Extraction." *Communications of the ACM* (2006).

Guan, S.-U. "Intelligent Product Brokering and Preference Tracking Services," in Khosrow-Pour (2006).

Gurau, C. "Managing Advergames," in Khosrow-Pour (2006).

Hallerman, D. "The Death of Mass Marketing," *iMediaConnection*, June 16, 2006. **imediaconnection. com/content/10063.asp** (accessed November 2007).

Harris, L. C., and M. M. H. Goode. "The Four Levels of Loyalty and the Pivotal Role of Trust: A Study of Online Service Dynamics." *Journal of Retailing* 80, no. 2 (2004).

Harrison-Walker, L. S., and S. E. Neeley. "Customer Relationship Building on the Internet in B2B Marketing: A Proposed Typology." *Journal of Marketing Theory and Practice* 12, no. 1 (2004).

Hewson, C., et al. *Internet Research Methods.* London: Sage, 2003.

Hoffman, L. J., K. Lawson-Jenkins, and J. Blum. "An Expanded Trust Model." *Communications of the ACM* (July 2006).

Howard, T. "KFC Mines Consumers' Videos for Ads." *USA Today*, May 21, 2007.

InPage. "Internet Advertising Revenues to Reach US$147 Billion Globally by 2012." *InPageAds.com*, March 8, 2008. **blog.inpageads.com/index.php/2008/03/04/internet-advertising-revenues-to-reach-us147-billion-globally-by-2012-a-significant-increast-from-us45-billion-in-2007-representing-a-234-percent/?inpage_ad=0** (accessed May 2008).

Inmon, B. "Why Clickstream Data Counts." *e-Business Advisor*, April 2001.

Jeanson, B., and J. Ingham. "Consumer Trust in E-Commerce," in Khosrow-Pour (2006).

Jiang, Z., W. Wang, and I. Benbast, "Online Customer Decision Support," *Communications of the ACM* (2005).

Kalyanam, K., and M. Zweben. "The Perfect Message at the Perfect Moment." *Harvard Business Review* 83, no. 11 (2005).

Kent, P. *Search Engine Optimization for Dummies.* New York: Hungry Minds Inc., 2006.

Khosrow-Pour, M. (ed.). *Encyclopedia of E-Commerce, E-Government, and Mobile Commerce.* Hershey, PA: Idea Group Reference, 2006.

Lee, M., and E. Turban. "Trust in B2C Electronic Commerce: A Proposed Research Model and Its Application." *International Journal of Electronic Commerce* 6, no. 1 (2001).

Markellou, P., M. Rigou, and S. Sirmakessis. "A Closer Look to the Online Consumer Behavior," in Khosrow-Pour (2006).

Marketingsherpa.com. "How Southwest Airlines Sold $1.5 Million in Tickets by Posting Four Press Releases." October 27, 2004. **marketingsherpa.com/barrier.html? ident=23758** (accessed November 2007).

MarketingVox.com. "Automakers Look to Create Own Broadband Channels." July 10, 2007a. **marketingvox.com/ archives/2007/07/10/automakers-look-to-create-own-broadband-channels** (accessed April 2008).

MarketingVox.com "Scion Joins Fourth—Yes, Fourth—Virtual World." August 16, 2007b. **marketingvox.com/scion-joins-fourth-yes-fourth-virtual-world-032282** (accessed April 2008).

MarketingVox.com. "Scion's Online Strategy Favors Niche over Reach." July 5, 2007c. **marketingvox.com/scions-online-strategy-favors-niche-over-reach-031136** (accessed April 2008).

McDougall, P., and E. Malykhina. "Get E-Mail under Control." *InformationWeek*, August 21, 2006.

MediaBuyerPlanner.com. "Toyota Targets Kids, Hopes to Influence Parents." June 14, 2006. **mediabuyer-planner.com/2006/06/14/toyota_targets_kids_hopes_to** (accessed April 2008).

Mills, E. "How Deep Is the Online-Ad Well?" *ZDNet News*, May 9, 2006. **zdnet.com/2100–9595_22–6069983.html** (accessed November 2007).

MixedMarketArts. "Forbes launching a Business Blog Network". January 14, 2008. **mixedmarketarts.com/2008/01/14/forbes-launching-a-business-blog-network0** (accessed May 2008).

Mordkovich, B., and E. Mordkovich. *Pay-Per-Click Search Engine Marketing Handbook.* Morrisville, NC: **Lulu.com**, 2005.

MoreBusiness.com. "Viral Marketing and Brand Awareness." March 5, 2007. **morebusiness.com/running_your_business/marketing/viral-marketing.brc** (accessed November 2007).

Netflix.com. "Netflix and USA Weekend Partner on 'Netflix Movie Picks' Promotion." September 13, 2006. **netflix.com/MediaCenter?id=5363** (accessed November 2007).

Nissim, B. "Virtual Worlds: The Next Realm in Advertising?" *BrandChannel*, 2007. **brandchannel.com/papers_review.asp?sp_id=1269** (accessed November 2007).

Null, C. "How Netflix Is Fixing Hollywood by Finding a Market for Niche Titles." July 1, 2003, **money.cnn.com/magazines/business2/business2_archive/2003/07/01/345263/index.htm** (accessed November 2007).

Nucifera, A. "Online Fantasy Sports Attract Real Fans." *The Alf Report,* July–August 2004. **nucifora.com/newsletter/0704–0804/estats.html** (accessed November 2006).

O'Keefe, R. M., and T. McEachern. "Web-Based Customer Decision Support System." *Communications of the ACM* (March 1998).

Paravastu, N., and D. Gefen. "Trust as an Enabler of E-Commerce," in Khosrow-Pour (2006).

Peppers and Rogers Group. "E-mail Marketing as a Relationship Strategy: The Four Steps to High Impact E-mail Marketing." Peppers and Rogers, white paper, 2004.

Petrecca, L. "In Limbo, Bidders Asked 'How Low Can You Go?'" *USA Today*, October 25, 2006.

Pons, A. P. "Biometric Marketing: Targeting the Online Consumer." *Communications of the ACM* (August 2006).

RightNow.com. "Procter & Gamble Applies Right Now to Deliver Superior Consumer Experience." August 30, 2006. **rightnow.com/news/article.php?id=7072** (accessed November 2007).

Sackmann, S., J. Struker, and R. Accorsi. "Personalization in Privacy-Aware Highly Dynamic Systems." *Communications of the ACM* 49, no. 9 (2006).

Sanders, T. "Extortionists behind Million Dollar DoS Attack." *Computing*, January 19, 2006. **computing.co.uk/vnunet/news/2148849/cyber-criminalstarget-pixel** (accessed November 2007).

SAS.com. "Harrah's Hits Customer Loyalty Jackpot." 2006. **sas.com/success/harrahs.html** (accessed November 2007).

Schonfeld, E. "Web TV's Top Rated Acts." *Business 2.0*, March 1, 2007.

Schonfeld, E., and J. Borzo. "The Next Disruptors." *Business 2.0*, October 2006.

Shih, Y. Y., and K. Fang. "Overall Satisfaction Prediction," in Khosrow-Pour (2006).

Silverman, B. G., M. Bachann, and K. Al-Akharas. "Implications of Buyer Decision Theory for Design of E-Commerce Web Sites." *International Journal of Human Computer Studies* 55, no. 5 (2001).

Sloan, P. "Masters of Their Domains." *Business 2.0*, December 2005.

Sloan, P. "Playing the Angles: Working the Spread." *Business 2.0*, July 2007.

Sutel, S. "As Internet Ad Market Grows, Advertisers Want Better Audience Measures." *Savanna Morning News*, December 25, 2007.

Tedeschi, B. "E-Commerce Report: New Alternatives to Banner Ads." *New York Times*, February 20, 2001.

Tode, C. "Survey: E-Commerce Leads in Customer Satisfaction." *DMNews*, February 21, 2006.

Turban, E., et al. *Business Intelligence: A Managerial Approach.* Upper Saddle River, NJ: Prentice Hall, 2008.

UCLA Center for Communication Policy. "UCLA Internet Report 2004: Surveying the Digital Future, Year 4." UCLA Center for Communication Policy, 2004. **digitalcenter.org/downloads/DigitalFutureReport-Year4–2004.pdf** (accessed November 2007).

Vert.net. "Patented Geo-Targeting Technology." 2006. **vert.net/geotargeting.html** (accessed November 2007).

Wang, N. "Marketers Connect with Online Video." *B2B Online*, August 9, 2004. **btobonline.com/article.cms?articleId=13042** (no longer available online).

Wang, E. T. G., H. Y. Yeh, and J. J. Jiang. "The Relative Weights of Internet Shopping Fundamental Objectives: Effect of Lifestyle Differences." *Psychology and Marketing* 23, no. 5 (2006).

Weber, S. *Plug Your Business!* Falls Church, VA: Weber Books, 2007.

Yeo, A. Y. C., and K. M. Chiam. "E-Customer Loyalty," in Khosrow-Pour (2006).

Yoon, S. J., and J. H. Kim. "Is the Internet More Effective Than Traditional Media? Factors Affecting the Choice of Media." *Journal of Advertising Research* (November–December 2001).

CHAPTER 5

About.com. "B2B Trading Communities Evolution." 2006. **logistics.about.com/library/weekly/aa060600a.htm** (accessed January 2008).

Al Mosawi, A., L. Zhao, and L. Macaulay, "A Model Driven Architecture for Enterprise Application Integration," *Proceedings of the 39th Annual Hawaii International Conference on Systems Sciences*, January 4–7, 2006, Kauai, Hawaii.

Angwin, J. "Top Online Chemical Exchange Is an Unlikely Success Story." *Wall Street Journal Online*, January 8, 2004. **webreprints.djreprints.com/907660072246.html** (accessed January 2008).

Bandyopadhyay, S., J. M. Barron, and A. R. Chaturved. "Competition Among Sellers in Online Exchanges." *Information Systems Research* (March 2005).

Bush, D. "e-Sourcing Does Not Equal Reverse Auction." *E-Sourcing Forum*, March 24, 2006. **esourcingforum.com/index.php?s=e-Sourcing+Does+Not+Equal+Reverse+Auction** (accessed January 2008).

Chandler, C. "China's Web King." *Fortune*, November 23, 2007.

Commonwealth of Pennsylvania. "Pennsylvania's Surplus Property Programs." 2006. **portal.state.pa.us/portal/server.pt?open=512&objID=1393&mode=2** (accessed January 2008).

Dasgupta, P., L. E. Moser, and P. M. Melliar-Smith. "Dynamic Pricing for E-Commerce," in Khosrow-Pour (2006).

Emiliani, M. L. "Executive Decision-Making Traps and B2B Online Reverse Auctions." *Supply Chain Management: An International Journal* 11, no. 1 (2006).

Fortune. "E-Procurement: Unleashing Corporate Purchasing Power." 2000. **jobfunctions.bnet.com/whitepaper.aspx?docid=70133** (accessed January 2008).

Grainger.com. "Grainger at a Glance." 2006. **pressroom.grainger.com/phoenix.zhtml?c=194987&p=irol-fact-sheet** (accessed January 2008).

Hagel, J. "Offshoring Goes on the Offensive." *The McKinsey Quarterly* no. 2 (2004).

Hancock, M. Q., R. H. John, and P. J. Wojcik. "Better B2B Selling." *The McKinsey Quarterly*, June 16, 2005.

Harris, L. "B2B E-Commerce Sites Increase Profitability through Intelligent Search." *B2B Marketing Trends*. **b2bmarketingtrends.com/abstract.asp?id=198&groupid=9** (accessed January 2008).

Heilemann, J. "Jack Ma Aims to Unlock the Middle Kingdom." *Business 2.0*, July 31, 2006.

IBM. *Whirlpool's B2B Trading Portal Cuts per Order Cost Significantly*. White Plains, NY: IBM Corporation Software Group, Pub. G325–6693–00, 2000.

Jakovljevic, P. J. "Differences in Complexity between B2C and B2B E-Commerce." *TechnologyEvaluation.Com*, March 4, 2004. **facweb.cs.depaul.edu/econfer/ect455/Class%20Material/B2B%20B2C%20Distinctions.pdf** (accessed January 2008).

Khosrow-Pour, M. (ed.). *Encyclopedia of E-Commerce, E-Government, and Mobile Commerce*. Hershey, PA: Idea Group Reference, 2006.

Killeen, J. F. "The Value of Vertical Search for B2B Markets." *Ecommercetimes.com*, October 27, 2006. **ecommercetimes.com/story/53931.html** (accessed January 2008).

Langelier, P., and V. Lapierre. *Winning Strategies for B2B E-Commerce*. Montreal, Canada: IQ Collectif, 2003.

Lucas, H. C. *Information Technology: Strategic Decision Making for Managers*. Hoboken, NJ: John Wiley and Sons, 2005.

Malhotra, R., and D. K. Malhotra. "The Impact of Internet and E-Commerce on the Evolving Business Models in the Financial Services Industry." *International Journal of Electronic Business* 4, no. 1 (2006).

Markus, L. "The Golden Rule." *CIO Insight*, July 2006.

MasterCard. "MasterCard Purchasing Card Program." *Mastercard.com*, 2006. **mastercard.com/us/business/en/pdf/MC%20Sell%20Sheet%20Purchasing%20053006.pdf** (accessed September 2006).

Microsoft. "Business Review: Eastman Chemical." 2000. **download.microsoft.com/documents/customerevidence/5484_eastman_commerceone.doc** (accessed January 2008).

Mockler, R. J., D. G. Dologite, and M. E. Gartenfeld. "B2B E-Business," in Khosrow-Pour (2006).

Papazoglou, M., and P. Ribbers. *Building B2B Relationships—Technical and Tactical Implementations of E-Business Strategy*. Hoboken, NJ: Wiley & Sons, 2006.

Patton, S. "Answering the Call." *CIO.com*, June 1, 2006. **cio.com.au/index.php/id;548021184** (accessed January 2008).

Rappa, M. "Case Study: ChemConnect—Managing the Digital Enterprise." 2006. **digitalenterprise.org/cases/chemconnect_text.html** (accessed January 2008).

Ratnasingam, P., and D. D. Phan. "Trading Partner Trust in B2B E-Commerce: A Case Study." *Information Systems Management* (Summer 2003).

Richard, P. J., and T. M. Devinney. "Modular Strategies: B2B Technology and Architecture Knowledge." *California Management Review* (Summer 2005).

Rincon, A. "Gregg's Cycles Succeeds in E-Commerce by Not Selling Bikes Online." **onlinebusiness.about.com/od/casestudies/a/greggscycles.htm** (accessed November 2006).

Rudnitsky, H. "Changing the Corporate DNA." *Forbes*, July 24, 2000.

Saryeddine, R. *E-Procurement: Another Tool in the Tool Box*. Ottawa, Ontario, Canada: The Conference Board of Canada, 2004.

Small Business Administration. **sba.gov/advo/stats** (accessed January 2008).

Smeltzer, L. R., and A. Carr. "Reverse Auctions in Industrial Marketing and Buying." *Business Horizons*, March–April 2002.

Tumolo, M. "Business to Business Exchanges." *Brint. com*, February 2001. **brint.com/members/01040530/b2bexchanges** (accessed January 2008).

Ward's Auto World. "Auto Talk: GM Rings in Era of e-Commerce." March 2000. **wardsautoworld.com/ar/auto_auto_talk_gm_2/index.html** (accessed January 2008).

WWRE. "WWRE Overview." 2005. **worldwideretailexchange.org/cs/en/about_wwre/overview.htm** (accessed January 2008).

Zeng, Y. E., H. J. Wen, and D. C. Yen. "Customer Relationship Management (CRM) in Business-to-Business (B2B) E-Commerce." *Information Management and Computer Security* 11 (2003).

CHAPTER 6

Amato-McCoy, D. "Michael Foods Dishes out Superior Service with Business Integration Solution." *Stores*, February 2004.

Austin, T., N. Drakos, and J. Mann. "Web Conferencing Amplifies Dysfunctional Meeting Practices." *Gartner Research*, ID Number: G00138101, March 13, 2006.

Bacheldor, B. "Harmon Hospital Implements RFID to Track Assets." *RFID Journal*, December 22, 2006a. **rfidjournal.com/article/articleprint/2933/-1/1** (accessed January 2008).

Bacheldor, B. "CHEP RFID-Enables Reusable Containers for Auto Industry." *RFID Journal*, December 1, 2006b. **rfidjournal.com/article/articleprint/2859/-1/1** (accessed January 2008).

Bacheldor, B. "Gentag Foresees Cell Phones as Thermometers, Glucose Readers." *RFID Journal*, December 19, 2006c. **rfidjournal.com/article/articleview/2910** (accessed January 2008).

Bacheldor, B. "Nokia Uses RFID-Enabled Phones to Police Its Security Guards." *RFID Journal*, December 18, 2006d. **rfidjournal.com/article/articleprint/2904/-1/1** (accessed January 2008).

BEA Systems. "State of the Portal Market 2006: Portals and the New Wisdom of the Enterprise." 2006. **contact2.bea.com/bea/www/pswp/alsom_wp.jsp?PC=40TU2GXXWPBEm** (accessed January 2008).

Bendoly, E., A. Soni, and M. A. Venkatraman. "Value Chain Resource Planning: Adding Value with Systems Beyond the Enterprise." *Business Horizons* 49, no. 2 (2004), pp. 79–86.

Blickstein, J. "Internet Telephony: A Sound Move?" *CIO Insight*, July 2004.

Boucher-Ferguson, R. "A Healthy Dose of RFID." *eWeek*, June 18, 2007.

BusinessWeek Online. "Talking RFID with Wal-Mart's CIO." February 4, 2004. **businessweek.com/technology/content/feb2004/tc2004024_3168_tc165.htm** (accessed January 2008).

Buxmann, P., et al. *Interorganizational Cooperation with SAP Solutions*. Boston: Springer, 2004.

Cassivi, L. "Collaboration Planning in a Supply Chain." *Supply Chain Management* 11, no. 3 (2006).

Chaturvedi, R. N., and V. Gupta. "SCM and ERP Software Implementation at Nike—From Failure to Success." *ICFAI Center for Management Research*, Hyderabad, India, 2005, OPER/049.

Chopra, S., and P. Meindl. *Supply Chain Management*, 3d ed. Upper Saddle River, NJ: Prentice Hall, 2006.

Chow, W. S. "An Exploratory Study of the Success Factors for Extranet Adoption in E-supply Chain." *Journal of Global Information Management*, January–March 2004.

Clarion Group. "Clarion Group: Company Information." 2006. **clarion.com/au/en/company/index.html** (accessed January 2008).

CompMechLab. "Boeing 787 Dreamliner Program Uses DELMIA, CATIA and ENOVIA." December 13, 2006. **eng.fea.ru/FEA_news_370.html** (accessed January 2008).

Davenport, T. H., and J. D. Brooks. "Enterprise Systems and the Supply Chain." *Enterprise Information Management* 17, no. 1 (2004).

Davies, C. "Game Shows It's Professionals Who Cause the Bullwhip Effect." *Supply Chain Europe* 13, no. 4 (2004).

Divitini, M., B. A. Farshchian, and H. Samset. "Mobile Computing and Applications (MCA): Collaboration Support for Mobile Users." *Proceedings of the 2004 ACM Symposium on Applied Computing*, Nicosia, Cyprus, March 14–17, 2004.

DM Review. "Top Priorities in Deploying Portal Software: Delphi Group." *DM Direct Special Report*, July 8, 2003. **dmreview.com/article_sub.cfm?articleId=7068** (accessed January 2008).

Duvall, M. "Radio Interference (RFID at Wal-Mart)." *Baseline*, October 2007.

Ferguson, M. "Corporate and E-Business Portals." *myITadviser*, April 2001.

Ferguson, R. B. "Wal-Mart's New CIO Says He'll Back RFID." *eWeek*, August 13, 2006. **eweek.com/article2/0,1759,1949396,00.asp** (accessed January 2008).

Fiala, P. "Information Sharing in Supply Chains." *Omega* 33, no. 5 (2005), pp. 419–423.

Finin, T. "RuBee as RFID 2.0?" December 29, 2006. **ebiquity.umbc.edu/blogger/2006/06/15/rubee-as-rfid-20** (accessed January 2008).

Finley, F., and S. Srikanth. "Seven Imperatives for Successful Collaboration." *Supply Chain Management Review* 9, no. 1 (2005).

Gibson-Paul, L. "Suspicious Minds." *CIO Magazine*, January 15, 2003.

Gregory, A. "How Best to Deal with the Unexpected?" *Works Management* 57, no. 6 (2004).

Handfield, R. B., and E. L. Nichols, Jr. *Supply Chain Management Redesign.* Upper Saddle River, NJ: Prentice Hall, 2002.

Heinrich, C. *RFID and Beyond.* Indianapolis, IN: Wiley Publishing Inc., 2005.

Henrie, K. S. "All Together Now." *CIO Insight*, July 2004.

Hillman, M. "Strategies for Managing Supply Chain Risk." *Supply Chain Management Review* 10, no. 5 (2006).

IBM.com. "Product Lifecycle Management." **ibm.com/solutions/plm** (accessed January 2008).

IBM.com. "Toysolution.com Pioneers Collaborative Commerce on Lotus Domino Infrastructure." 2006a. **www-8.ibm.com/hk/software/case_studies/lotus/toysolution1.html** (accessed January 2008).

IBM.com. "Clarion Malaysia Reduces Design Time by 50 Percent with CATIA V5." 2006b. **www-01.ibm.com/software/success/cssdb.nsf/CS/JSTS-6Q2SA9?OpenDocument&Site=** (accessed October 2006).

IDTechEX. "RFID Progress at Wal-Mart." October 1, 2005. **idtechex.com/products/en/articles/00000161.asp** (accessed January 2008).

Industry Directions. "The Next Wave of Supply Chain Advantage: CPFR." White paper, April 2000. **industrydirections.com/pdf/CPFRPublicReport.pdf** (accessed January 2008).

Intel. "Enhance Communication and Collaboration through VoIP." Intel.com, 2005. **intel.com/netcomms/technologies/voice/311747.pdf** (accessed May 2008).

Ireland, R., and R. Bruce. "CPFR: Only the Beginning of Collaboration." *Supply Chain Management Review*, September–October 2000.

Ireland, R. K., and C. Crum. *Supply Chain Collaboration: How to Implement CPFR and Other Best Collaborative Processes.* Boca Raton, FL: J. Ross Publishing, 2005.

Jeston, J., and J. Nelis. *Business Process Management: Practical Guides to Successful Implementation.* Burlington, MA: Butterworth-Heinemann, 2006.

Johnson, J. R. "Coming to a Store Near You." *DC Velocity*, August 2006a.

Johnson, J. R. "The Death Knell for RFID?" *DC Velocity*, June 21, 2006b.

Kesner, R. M. "Building a Knowledge Portal: A Case Study in Web-Enabled Collaboration." *Information Strategy: The Executive Journal* (Winter 2003).

Khosrow-Pour, M. (ed.). *Encyclopedia of E-Commerce, E-Government, and Mobile Commerce.* Hershey, PA: Idea Group Reference, 2006.

Kidman, A. "Dreamliner Sets SOA in Flight for Boeing." *ZDNet News*, July 12, 2006. **zdnet.com.au/news/software/soa/Dreamliner_sets_SOA_in_flight_for_Boeing/0,130061733,139263107,00.htm** (accessed January 2008).

Koch, C. "Nike Rebounds: How (and Why) Nike Recovered from Its Supply Chain Disaster." *CIO Magazine*, June 15, 2004. **cio.com/article/32334/Nike_Rebounds_How_and_Why_Nike_Recovered_from_Its_Supply_Chain_Disaster** (accessed January 2008).

Konicki, S. "The New Desktop: Powerful Portals." *InformationWeek*, May 1, 2001. **informationweek.com/784/portal.htm** (accessed January 2008).

Kotabe, M., and M. J. Mol. *Global Supply Chain Management.* North Hampton, MA: Edward Elgar Publishing, 2006.

Kounadis, T. "How to Pick the Best Portal." *e-Business Advisor*, August 2000.

Kumar, M. V., and V. Gupta. "The Making of Boeing's 787 'Dreamliner.'" *ICFAI Center for Management Research*, Hyderabad, India, 2006, OPER/053.

Lee, H., and L. Denend. "West Marine: Driving Growth through Shipshape Supply Chain Management." *Stanford Graduate School of Business*, Case GS-34 (2005).

Lee, H., and G. Michlin. "Netafim: Migrating From Products to Solutions." *Stanford Graduate School of Business*, Case GS-46, February 2006.

LeightonsOpticians.com. "A Family Business." **leightonsopticians.com/a_family_business** (accessed January 2008).

Leonard, L. N. K., and C. C. Davis. "Supply Chain Replenishment: Before and After EDI Implementation." *Supply Chain Management* 11, no. 3 (2006).

Line56.com. "Procurement and Buy-Side." **line56.com/topics/whatis.asp?TopicID-1** (accessed January 2008).

Loebbecke, C. "RIFD in the Retail Supply Chain," in Khosrow-Pour (2006).

Mamberto, C. "Instant Messaging Invades the Office." *Enuan*, July 24, 2007. **enuan.wordpress.com/2007/07/25/instant-messaging-invades-the-office** (accessed January 2008).

Microsoft.com. "New Research Reveals Collaboration Is a Key Driver of Business Performance Around the World." 2006. **microsoft.com/presspass/press/2006/jun06/06–05VerizonBusinessCollaborationPR.mspx** (accessed January 2008).

Moody, P. "With Supply Chain Management, Technology Rules!" *Supply Chain Management Review* 10, no. 4 (2006).

NerveWire. "Collaborative Commerce: Compelling Benefits, Significant Obstacles." 2002. **xml.coverpages.org/Nervewire200210.pdf** (accessed January 2008).

Norris, G., et al. *E-Business and ERP: Transforming the Enterprise.* New York: McGraw-Hill, 2000.

Nunamaker, J., R. Briggs, D. Mittleman, D. Vogel, and P. Balthazard, "Lessons from a Dozen Years of Group Support Systems Research: A Discussion of Lab and Field Findings." *Journal of Management Information Systems*, 13, no. 3 (1997).

O'Connor, M. C. "Wal-Mart Seeks UHF for Item-Level." *RFID Journal*, March 30, 2006a. **rfidjournal.com/article/articleprint/2228/-1/1** (accessed January 2008).

O'Connor, M. C. "Visible Assets Promotes RuBee Tags for Tough-to-Track Goods." *RFID Journal*, June 19, 2006b. **rfidjournal.com/article/articleprint/2436/-1/1** (accessed January 2008).

O'Connor, M. C. "Philly Cabs Taking RFID Payments on the Road." *RFID Journal*, November 29, 2006c. **rfidjournal.com/article/articleprint/2852/-1/1** (accessed January 2008).

Plumtree. "A Framework for Assessing Return on Investment for a Corporate Portal Deployment: The Industry's First Comprehensive Overview of Corporate Portal ROI." *Plumtree.com*, April 2002. **plumtree.com/webforms/MoreInfo_FormActionTemplate.asp** (no longer available online).

Reda, S. "New Systems Foster Interaction with Store Employees." *Stores*, February 2002.

Reda, S. "The Path to RFID." *Stores*, June 2003.

Regan, K. "Redback Networks, Partner Approach." *The Manufacturer US*, October 2006. **themanufacturer.com/us/detail.html?contents_id=4600&PHPSESSID=fd527f2956c982d428b907f96674ddfe** (accessed January 2008).

RFID Gazette. "RFID Used on Boeing's 787 Dreamliner." April 4, 2006. **rfidgazette.org/2006/04/rfid_used_on_bo.html** (accessed January 2008).

RFID Journal. "Starbucks Keep Fresh with RFID." *RFID Journal*, December 13 2006. **rfidjournal.com/article/articleprint/2890/-1/1** (accessed January 2008).

RFID Solutions Online. "Active RFID Tag: AeroScout Enhances Industry's Leading Wi-Fi Based Active RFID Tag." September 6, 2006. **rfidsolutionsonline.com/IndustrySearch/SearchResults.aspx?keyword=%22RFID+Active+Tags%22&TabIndex=0&image1.x=37&image1.y=11** (accessed January 2008).

Richardson, H. L. "The Ins & Outs of VMI." *Logistics Today* 45, no. 3 (2004).

Roberti, M. "A 5-Cent Breakthrough." *RFID Journal*, May 1, 2006. **rfidjournal.com/article/articleprint/2295/-1/2** (accessed January 2008).

Scherago, D. "Wal-Smart." *Retail Technology Quarterly*, January 2006.

Schneider, M. "Samsung's Partner Portal Delivers a 30 percent Sales Increase." *CRM Magazine*, May 2004.

Schrage, M. "Now You See It, Now You Don't." *CIO*, March 15, 2004.

Schram, P. *Collaborative Commerce: Going Private to Get Results*. New York: Deloitte Consulting.

Schuman, E. "RuBee Offers Alternative to RFID." *eWeek*, June 9, 2006a. **eweek.com/article2/0,1895,1974931,00.asp** (accessed January 2008).

Schuman, E. "RuBee May Be Savior for Frustrated RFID Proponents." *eWeek*, June 10, 2006b. **eweek.com/article2/0,1895,1975003,00.asp** (accessed January 2008).

Schurman, K. "White Paper: RuBee Adding Flexibility to the RFID Market." *Computer Power User* 6, no. 9 (2006). **computerpoweruser.com/editorial/article.asp?article=articles/archive/c0609/29c09/29c09.asp&guid=668DE17F72E44FC4A135532323F722A0** (accessed January 2008).

Seideman, T. "QVC.com and Costco.com Talk to Business Partners in the Same Language." *Stores*, February 2004.

Siau, K., and Y. Tian. "Supply Chains Integration: Architecture and Enabling Technologies." *Journal of Computer Information Systems* (Spring 2004).

Singh, N., K.-H. Lai, and T. C. E. Cheng. "Intra-Organization Perspectives of IT-Enabled Supply Chains." *Communications of the ACM* (January 2007).

Smith, L. "West Marine: A CPFR Success Story." *Supply Chain Management Review* 10, no. 2 (2006).

Songini, M. L. "Wal-Mart Shifts RFID Plans." *Computerworld*, February 26, 2007.

Staff. "AS2 Is A-OK at Wal-Mart." *Chain Store Age* 80, no. 2 (2004).

Stevenson, W. *Operations Management*, 8th ed. New York: McGraw-Hill, 2004.

Sturdevant, C. "How to Make the Move to IP Telephony." *CIO Insight*, Special Report, July 2004.

Sullivan, L. "Metro Moves Tagging Up the Supply Chain." *RFID Journal*, December 6, 2006. **rfidjournal.com/article/articleprint/2873/-1/1** (accessed January 2008).

Supply and Demand Chain Executive. "Exostar Marks One Year Enabling Boeing's 787 Supply Chain." December 19, 2006. **sdcexec.com/online/article.jsp?id=9020&siteSection=29** (accessed January 2008).

SupplyChainConnect.com. "Leightons Opticians Sees the Business Case for Electronic Ordering in the UK Optical Industry." February 10, 2005. **supplychainconnect.com/pdfs/Leightons.pdf** (accessed January 2008).

SupplyChainManagement101.com. "Info Guide to Supply Chain Management Software." **supplychainmanagement101.com/?gg=us&kw=supply%20chain&gclid=CL6i5MqI3ocCFSMhYQodWX8Bog** (accessed January 2008).

Taylor, D. H., and A. Fearne. "Towards a Framework for Improvement in the Management of Demand in Agri-Food Supply Chains." *Supply Chain Management: An International Journal* 11, no. 5 (2006).

Vics.org. "CPFR Committee." 2006. **vics.org/committees/cpfr** (accessed January 2008).

Wessel, R. "Environmental Concerns Lead Deutsche Post to RFID." *RFID Journal*, December 20, 2006. **rfidjournal.com/article/articleprint/2912/-1/1** (accessed January 2008).

CHAPTER 7

Accenture. "eGovernment Leadership: Engaging the Customer." 2003. **accenture.com/xdoc/en/newsroom/epresskit/egovernment/egov_epress.pdf** (accessed February 2007).

Aldrich, C. "1996–2006 E-Learning in the Workplace." *TD*, September 2006.

Arar, Y. "New E-Book Reader Is Worth Looking At." **PCWorld.com**, November 2006.

AskMe.com. "Demonstrated ROI Prompts Department of Commerce to Expand Deployment Across Global Commercial Service Operations." **askme.com/press/docrelease.asp** (accessed February 2008).

Association for Federal Information Resources Management. "A Blueprint for Successful E-Government Implementation: Steps to Accelerate Cultural Change and Overcome

Stakeholder Resistance." *Affirm.org*, June 2002. **affirm.org/ Pubs/Affirm. pdf** (accessed January 2007).

Association of American Publishers. "Book Sales Continue to Climb in October." AAP press release, December 11, 2006. **publishers.org/press/releases.cfm?PressRelease ArticleID=360** (accessed January 2007).

Bach, S., P. Haynes, and J. L. Smith. *Online Learning and Teaching in Higher Education*. Berkshire, UK: Open University Press, 2007.

Bhattacharjee, S., R. D. Gopal, K. Lertchwara, and J. Marsden. "Impact of Legal Threats on Online Music Sharing Activity: An Analysis of Music Industry Legal Actions." *The Journal of Law and Economics* 49 (2006).

Boehle, S. "Rapid e-Learning." *Training*, July 2005.

Boxer, K. M., and B. Johnson. "How to Build an Online Center." *Training and Development*, August 2002. **findarticles.com/p/articles/mi_m0MNT/is_8_56/ai_ 90512522** (accessed February 2007).

Chao, Y., and F. Tong. "The Problems in the Implementation of E-Government Administration, the Analysis and Strategies." *Proceedings of the 7th International Conference on Electronic Commerce*, Xi'an, China, August 15–17, 2005.

Chen, Y. N., H. M. Chen, W. Huang, and R. K. H. Ching. "E-Government Strategies in Developed and Developing Countries: An Implementation Framework and Case Study." *Journal of Global Information Management* 14, no. 1 (2006).

Chu, K. C., and Q. Lam. "Using an E-Book for Learning," in Khosrow-Pour (2006).

Crawford, K. "A Degree of Respect for Online MBAs." *Business 2.0*, December 2005.

D'Agostino, D. "Expertise Management: Who Knows about This?" *CIO Insight*, July 1, 2004.

Dahl, E. "Online Music: New Hits and Misses." *PCWorld*, September 2003.

Davenport, T. H., and L. Prusak. *Working Knowledge: How Organizations Manage What They Know*. Cambridge, MA: Harvard Business School Press, 2000.

Davies, N., K. Cheverst, A. Friday, and K. Mitchell. "Future Wireless Applications for a Networked City." *IEEE Wireless Communications*, February 2002.

Dean, J. "E-Gov in the Works." *GovExec.com*, November 2000. **govexec.com/features/1100/egov/egovworks.htm** (accessed January 2007).

Delahoussaye, M., and R. Zemke. "About Learning Online." *Training*, September 2001.

Delphi Group. "Information Intelligence: Content Classification and the Enterprise Taxonomy Practice." *Delphi Group Report*, June 2004.

"Digital 21 IT Strategies." **info.gov.hk/digital21,student inter- view**, February 2001 and 2002 (accessed January 2007).

Ding, E. "Virtual Property: Treasure or Trash?" *China International Business*, September 2004.

Emarketer. "U.S. Government Web Sites Concentrate on Security, Privacy." October 2, 2002.

Epstein, J. "Electronic Voting." *Computer*, August 2007.

Ergonomics Today. "Study Links Long-Term Back Pain to Backpacks." *Ergonomics Today*, September 8, 2004. **ergoweb. com/news/detail.cfm?id=985** (accessed January 2007).

ESI International. "Case Study: ESI Helps Henkels & McCoy, Inc. Improve Bottom Line with E-Training." 2007. **esi-intl.com/Public/esiadvantage/Henkels_ McCoy.asp** (accessed January 2008).

Fastrak-Consulting.com. "Making E-Learning Work: Case Study 1—Royal Bank of Scotland." 2000. **fastrak- consulting.co.uk/tactix/features/work/work.htm#Case %20study%201:%20Royal%20Bank%20of%20Scotland** (accessed May 2008).

Financial Times. "Distance Learning MBA Programmes 2007." **media.ft.com/cms/a47575cc-d316–11db-829f- 000b5df10621,dwp_uuid=70d09d1c-b811–11da- bfc5–0000779e2340.pdf** (accessed January 2008).

Galagan, P. A. "Delta Force at Cisco." *Training and Development*, July 2002.

Gibson, R., and C. Brown. "Electronic Voting as the Key to Ballot Reform," in Khosrow-Pour (2006).

Holsapple, C. W. (ed.). *Handbook on Knowledge Management*. Heidelberg, Germany: Springer Computer Science, 2003.

Hopfner, J. "A Revolution in (Tax) Revenue." *MIS Asia*, May 2002.

Howe, J. "Your Web, Your Way." *Time*, December 13, 2007. **time.com/time/magazine/article/0,9171,1570815,00.html** (accessed January 2007).

Huang, W., et al. "E-Government Development and Implementation," in Khosrow-Pour (2006).

Hyperion.com. "Federal Government—Additional Details." 2007. **hyperion.com/solutions/federal_division/legislation_ summaries.cfm** (accessed February 2007).

Impact-information.com. "Making e-Learning Work." July 18, 2006. **impact-information.com/impactinfo/newsletter/ plwork26.htm** (accessed January 2007).

Joia, L. A. "Building Government-to-Government Enterprise," in Khosrow-Pour (2006).

Jones, N. B., D. Provost, and D. Pascale. "Developing a University Research Web-Based Knowledge Portal." *International Journal of Knowledge and Learning*, January–February 2006.

Keen, J. "Politicians' Campaigns Invade MySpace." *USA Today*, October 17, 2006.

Khosrow-Pour, M. (ed.). *Encyclopedia of E-Commerce, E-Government, and Mobile Commerce*. Hershey, PA: Idea Group Reference, 2006.

Kim, G., and S. M. Ong. "An Exploratory Study of Factors Influencing M-Learning Success." *Journal of Computer Information Systems*, Fall 2005.

Korolishin, J. "Sheetz Keeps Tabs on Training Compliance via Web Portal." *Stores*, February 2004a.

Korolishin, J. "Tweeter Gives Training a Tweak." *Stores*, August 2004b.

Kumar, N., and Q. Peng. "Strategic Alliances in E-Government Procurement." *International Journal of Electronic Business* 4, no. 2 (2006).

Lagoio, C. "Cyberclasses." *New York Times News Service*, published in *Taipei Times*, January 7, 2007.

Lai, H., and T. H. Chu. "Knowledge Management: A Review of Industrial Cases." *Journal of Computer Information Systems*, special issue 42, no. 5 (2002).

Langenbach, C., and F. Bodendorf. "The Electronic Mall: A Service Center for Distance Learning." *International Journal of Electronic Commerce*, Winter 1999–2000.

Lee, D. H. "Contextual IT Business Value and Barriers: An E-Government and E-Business Perspective." *Proceedings of the 38th HICSS*, Big Island, Hawaii, January 2005.

Lee, S. M., X. Tan, and S. Trimi. "Current Practices of Leading E-Government Countries." *Communications of the ACM* 48, no. 10 (October 2005).

Li, X. "Intelligent Agent-Supported Online Education." *Decision Sciences Journal of Innovative Education*, July 2007.

Lin, J. "Ilan County Seeks Online Buyers for Produce." *Taipei Times*, November 16, 2006.

Mack, R., Y. Ravin, and R. J. Byrd. "Knowledge Portals and the Emerging Digital Knowledge Workplace." *IBM Systems Journal* 40, no. 4 (2001).

Mahapatra, R., and V. S. Lai. "Evaluating End-User Training Programs." *Communications of the ACM*, January 2005.

Malkia, M., et al. *E-Transformation in Governance: New Directions in Government.* Hershey, PA: The Idea Group, 2004.

Marchioni, G., et al. (eds.). "Digital Government." *Communications of the ACM*, Special Issue (January 2003).

Mark, R. "Election 2.0." *eWeek*, November 12, 2007.

McKinley, E. "Multitasking Solution Ushers in New Era of Computer-Based Training at Shoney's." *Stores*, April 2003.

Metz, C. "Who Owns Print-on-Demand?" *PCMagazine*, March 2004.

Miller, R. "Ebooks Worm Their Way into the Reference Market." *EcontentMag.com*, July–August 2005. **econtentmag.com/ Archives/Issue.aspx?IssueID=219** (accessed January 2007).

Moon, J. M. *From E-Government to M-Government: Emerging Practices in the Use of Mobile Technology by State Governments.* Arlington, VA: IBM Center for the Business of Government, 2004.

Naka, I. *Knowledge Management and Risk Strategy.* Taipei, Taiwan: World Scientific Publishing Company, 2007.

Neal, L. "Predictions for 2007." *eLearn Magazine*, January 12, 2007. **elearnmag.org/subpage.cfm?section=articles& article=42–1** (accessed January 2007).

NestleUSA.com. "Working with Us: Training." 2008. **nestleusa.com/PubCareers/wwuTraining.aspx** (accessed May 2008).

Neumann, P. (ed.). "The Problems and Potentials of Electronic Voting Systems." *Communications of the ACM* (October 2004).

Ng, F. F. "E-Learning Concepts and Development," in Khosrow-Pour (2006).

OGCIO. "Success Story of Project Completed for the Government." *Info.gov.hk*, December 12, 2005. **info.gov. hk/digital21/eng/scp/success_stories/ESDServics_ Success_Story_ESD.pdf** (accessed January 2007).

Paskaleva-Shapira, K. "Transitioning from e-Government to e-Governance in the Knowledge Society: The Role of the Legal Framework for Enabling the Process in the European Union's Countries." *Proceedings of the 7th Annual International Conference on Digital Government*, San Diego, California, May 21–24, 2006.

Price, G. "Google Partners with Oxford, Harvard, and Others to Digitize Libraries." *SearchEngineWatch*, December 14, 2004. **searchenginewatch.com/searchday/article.php/ 3447411** (accessed January 2007).

Putnik, G., and M. M. Cunha (eds.). *Knowledge and Technology Management in Virtual Organizations.* Hershey, PA: Idea Group Publishing, 2007.

Rash, W., and M. Hines. "Co-Confidence Vote." *eWeek*, November 6, 2007.

Resta, P., T. Laferriere, A. Breuleux, and N. Davis. "Global Perspectives on Trends, Issues and Challenges in E-Learning for Teacher Development," in G. Richards (ed.), *Proceedings of World Conference on E-Learning in Corporate, Government, Healthcare, and Higher Education*, Quebec City, Canada, October 15–19, 2007.

Roberts-Witt, S. "A 'Eureka!' Moment at Xerox." *PC Magazine*, March 26, 2002. **pcmag.com/article2/0,4149,28792,00.asp** (accessed January 2007).

Rowe, D., and O. Bell. "Experiences in E-Government Best Practices and Solution Sharing." *Journal of E-Government* 1, no. 3 (2005).

Scholl, H. "What Can E-Commerce and E-Government Learn from Each Other?" *Proceedings of the 7th Annual International Conference on Digital Government*, San Diego, California, May 21–24, 2006.

Schuman, E. "Microsoft, Amazon and Google Tackle E-Books Their Own Way." *eWeek*, November 2005.

Siau, K., and Y. Long "Using Social Development Lenses to Understand E-Government Development." *Journal of Global Information Management* 1, no. 1 (2006).

Song, S. "An Internet Knowledge Sharing System." *Journal of Computer Information Systems* (Spring 2002).

Spanbauer, S. "Internet Tips: Self-Publish Your Books, Songs, and Movies Online." *PCWorld.com*, September 22, 2006. **pcworld.com/article/id,127053c,webauthoringsoftware/ article.html** (accessed January 2007).

Summerfield, B. "The Wings of Learning." *Clomedia.com*, August 2005. **clomedia.com/content/templates/clo_article.asp? articleid=1026&zoneid=9** (accessed May 2008).

Tarnoff, D. L. "Shifting Students' Financial Responsibilities from Textbooks to Laboratory Resources." *Journal of Computing Sciences in Colleges* 22, no. 3 (January 2007).

Thong, J. Y., L. H.Weiyin, and Y. T. Kar. "What Leads to User Acceptance of Digital Libraries." *Communications of the ACM* (November 2004).

U.S. Department of Housing and Urban Development. *FY 2006 Performance and Accountability Report.* November 2006. **hud.gov/offices/cfo/reports/2006/2006par.pdf** (accessed January 2007).

U.S. Department of the Interior. *E-Government Strategy 2007–2013.* September 2007. **doi.gov/e-government/E-Gov%20Strategy%20FY2008-FY2013.pdf** (accessed January 2008).

U.S. Government. "E-Government Strategy." *Office of the President of the United States*, Special Report, 2003. **whitehouse.gov/omb/egov/2003egov_strat.pdf** (accessed January 2008).

U.S. Office of Management and Budget. "E-Government Strategy: Delivery of Services to Citizens." *OMB Internal Report*, February 27, 2002.

Urdan, T., and C. Weggen. "Corporate E-Learning: Exploring a New Frontier." W. R. Hambrecht & Co., March 2000. **spectrainteractive.com/pdfs/CorporateELearingHamrecht.pdf** (accessed January 2007).

Wang, H., and S. Wang. "Cyber Warfare: Steganography vs. Steganalysis." *Communications of the ACM* (October 2004).

Warkentin, M., D. Gefen, P. A. Pavlou, and G. M. Rose. "Encouraging Citizen Adoption of E-Government by Building Trust." *Electronic Markets* 12, no. 3 (2002).

Watts, N. "Bringing Online Learning to a Research-Intensive University." *eLearn Magazine*, August 31, 2007.

Weaver, P. "Preventing E-Learning Failure." *Training and Development* 56, no. 8 (2002).

Weinstein, M. "On Demand Is in Demand." *Training*, October 2006.

West, D. "State and Federal E-Government in the United States, 2004." *Center for Public Policy Report*, September 2004. **insidepolitics.org/egovt04us.html** (accessed January 2007).

Wimmer, M. A. "Integrated Service Modeling for Online One-Stop Government." *Electronic Markets* 12, no. 3 (2002).

Wimmer, M. A. "Implementing a Knowledge Portal for eGovernment Based on Semantic Modeling: The E-Government Intelligent Portal." *Proceedings of the 39th Hawaiian International Conference on Systems Sciences*, Kauai, Hawaii, January 4–7, 2006.

Wong, W. Y. *At the Dawn of E-Government.* Report, Deloitte & Touche, New York, 2000.

Xerox. "Eureka." PARC Research. **parc.com/research/projects/commknowledge/eureka.html** (accessed January 2008).

Zhang, D., and J. F. Nunamaker. "Powering E-Learning in the New Millennium: An Overview of E-Learning Enabling Technology." *Information Systems Frontiers*, April 2003.

CHAPTER 8

Baage, J. "More Support for Class Action Copyright Lawsuit Against YouTube." *DigitalMediaWire*, August 6, 2007. **dmwmedia.com/news/2007/08/06/more-support-for-class-action-copyright-lawsuit-against-youtube** (accessed January 2008).

Bilsborrow-Koo, R. "Ten Video Sharing Services Compared." *Dvguru.com*, April 7, 2006. **dvguru.com/2006/04/07/ten-video-sharing-services-compared** (accessed January 2008).

Borland, J. "A Smarter Web." *Technology Review*, March–April 2007.

Business 2.0. "The Next Net 25." *Business 2.0*, February 22, 2007.

Carr, D. F. "E-Discovery." *Baseline*, November 2006.

Carr, D. F. "Inside MySpace." *Baseline*, January 2007a.

Carr, D. F. "Tapping into Virtual Markets." *Baseline*, March 1, 2007b. **baselinemag.com/article2/0,1540,2098846,00.asp** (accessed January 2008).

Cashel, J. "Top Ten Trends for Online Communities." *ProvidersEdge.com*. **providersedge.com/docs/km_articles/Top_Ten_Trends_for_Online_Communities.pdf** (accessed January 2008).

Chesbrough, H. W. *Open Business Models.* Boston, MA: Harvard Business School Press, 2006.

comScore. "MySpace Leads in Number of U.S. Video Streams Viewed Online, Capturing 20 Percent Market Share; Yahoo! Ranks #1 in Number of People Streaming." September 27, 2006. **files.shareholder.com/downloads/SCOR/0x0x102145/22a3b6dd-1795–419c-a9fd-7403d3c70fd7/245940.pdf** (accessed January 2008).

comScore. "YouTube Continues to Lead U.S. Online Video Market with 28 Percent Market Share, According to comScore Video Metrix." *comScore.com*, November 2007. **comscore.com/press/release.asp?press=1929** (accessed January 2008).

Cone, E. "Comment: Put a Fork in the Plan to Fork." *Blog.eweek.com*, January 22, 2007a.

Cone, E. "Social Networks at Work Promise Bottom-Line Results." *CIO Insight*, October 8, 2007b.

Copeland, M. V. "The Missing Link." *Business 2.0*, September 2006.

D'Agostino, D. "Security in the World of Web 2.0." *Innovations*, Winter 2006.

Dholakia, U. M., R. Bagozzi, and L. K. Pearo. "A Social Influence Model of Consumer Participation in Network- and Small-Group-Based Virtual Communities." *International Journal of Research in Marketing* 21, no. 3 (2004).

Demopoulos, T. *Blogging and Podcasting.* Chicago, IL: Kaplan Publishing, 2007.

Duffy, D. "It Takes an E-Village." *CIO Magazine*, October 25, 1999.

The Economist. "How Google Works." September 16, 2004.

The Economist. "Watching the Web Grow Up." March 10, 2007.

Farrell, N. "Microsoft Rumbled over Wikipedia Edits." *The Inquirer*, January 24, 2007. **theinquirer.net/gb/inquirer/news/2007/01/24/microsoft-rumbled-over-wikipedia-edits** (accessed January 2008).

Flynn, N. *Blog Rules: A Business Guide to Managing Policy, Public Relations, and Legal Issues.* Saranac Lake, NY: AMACOM, 2006.

Fortune Technology Staff. "The Browser: Analyzing the Tech Biz." February 7, 2007. **thebrowser.blogs. fortune.cnn.com** (accessed January 2008).

Gibson, S. "RSS in the Enterprise." *eWeek*, January 15, 2007.

Gillin, P. *The New Influencers.* Sanger, CA: Quill Driver Books, March, 2007a.

Gillin, P. "Web 2.0 Tools of the Trade." *SearchSMB.com*, March 22, 2007b.

Gogoi, P. "Retailers Take a Tip from MySpace." *BusinessWeek Online*, February 13, 2007. **businessweek.mobi/detail.jsp?key=6158&rc=sb&p=4&pv=1** (accessed March 2007).

Goldsmith, R. "Electronic Word-of-Mouth," in Khosrow-Pour, 2006.

Grossman, L. "Time Person of the Year—YOU." "Power to People." *Time*, December 25, 2006–January 1, 2007.

Hagel, J., and A. Armstrong. *Net Gain.* Boston: Harvard Business School Press, 1997.

Hammond, T., T. Hannay, B. Lund, and J. Scott. "Social Bookmarking Tools I." *D-Lib Magazine*, April 2005. **dlib.org/dlib/april05/hammond/04hammond.html** (accessed January 2008).

Heilemann, J. "Capturing the Buzz." *Business 2.0*, October 2006a.

Heilemann, J. "Digging Up News." *Business 2.0*, April 2006b.

Hinchcliffe, D. "Profitably Running an Online Business in the Web 2.0 Era." *SOA Web Services Journal*, November 29, 2006. **web2.wsj2.com** (accessed January 2008).

Hoover, N. J. "Lotus' Leap." *InformationWeek*, January 29, 2007.

Innovations. "Going Beyond Networking." (Winter 2006).

Kafka, P. "Blue Sky." *Forbes*, February 12, 2007.

Khosrow-Pour, M. (ed.). *Encyclopedia of E-Commerce, E-Government, and Mobile Commerce.* Hershey, PA: Idea Group Reference, 2006.

La Monica, P. R. "Big Media Beats Up on YouTube." *CNNMoney.com*, February 9, 2007.

Lashinsky, A. "Catching Google's YouTube Won't Be Easy." *Fortune*, March 26, 2007 **money.cnn.com/2007/03/26/magazines/fortune/lashinsky_pluggedin_nbcu.fortune/index.htm** (accessed January 2008).

Lee, M., D. Vogel, and L. Moez. "Virtual Communities Informatics: A Review and Research Agenda." *Information Technology Theory and Applications* 5, no. 1 (2003).

Leimeister, J. M., and H. Krcmar. "Success Factors of Virtual Communities from the Perspective of Members and Operators: An Empirical Study." *Proceedings of the 37th Annual HICCS Conference*, Kauai, Hawaii, January 4–7, 2004.

Longino, C. "Your Wireless Future." *Business 2.0*, May 2006.

MacManus, R. "2007 Will Be a Big Year for RSS." *ReadWriteWeb*, October 10, 2006. **readwriteweb.com/archives/2007_rss.php** (accessed January 2008).

Markoff, J. "Entrepreneurs See a Web Guided by Common Sense," *New York Times*, November 12, 2006.

Martens, C. "Wikipedia to Strive for Higher Quality Content." *PC World*, August 4, 2006.

McAfee, A. P. "Enterprise 2.0: The Dawn of Emergent Collaboration." *MIT Sloan Management Review* (Spring 2006).

McCarthy, C. "MySpace Brazil Launches, Entering Orkut Jungle." *Webware.com*, December 14, 2007. **webware.com/ 8300–1_109–2–0.html?keyword=Orkut** (accessed May 2008).

McGillicuddy, S. "IT Executives Eager to Exploit 2.0 Wave." *SMB News*, October 24, 2006a. **searchcio.techtarget.com/originalContent/0,289142,sid182_gci1226050,00.htm** (accessed January 2008).

McGillicuddy, S. "Wikis and Blogs Transforming Workflow." *CIO News*, April 25, 2006b. **searchcio.techtarget.com/originalContent/0,289142,sid19_gci1184607,00.html** (accessed January 2008).

McNichol, T. "Building a Wiki World." *Business 2.0*, March 2007a.

McNichol, T. "Vin Du Blogger." *Business 2.0*, August 2007b.

Mello, J. P. "Explosive Growth Predicted for Mobile Social Networks." *E-Commerce Times*, December 12, 2006.

Metz, C. "First Look: iPhone Truly Is a Revelation." *PCMAG.com*, January 12, 2007.

Millard, E. "Online Social Networks and the Profit Motive." *E-Commerce Times*, June 12, 2004. **ecommercetimes.com/story/34422.html** (accessed January 2008).

Mossberg, W. "Netvibes Brings Personalized Web Pages to Another Level." *Honolulu Advisor*, February 6, 2007.

Murray-Buechner, M. "25 Sites We Can't Live Without." *Time*, August 3, 2006.

Nerille, J. "X-treme Web 2.0." *Optimize Magazine*, January 2007.

New York Times. "CBS Buys Last FM Online Radio Site." May 31, 2007. **nytimes.com/2007/05/31/business/media/31radios.html** (accessed January 2008).

O'Brien, J. M. "What's Your House Really Worth?" *Fortune*, February 29, 2007.

O'Malley, G. "MySpace vs. eBay? Site Leaps into E-Commerce." *Advertising Age*, September 11, 2006.

O'Reilly, T. "What Is Web 2.0?" *OReillynet.com*, September 30, 2005. **oreillynet.com/pub/a/oreilly/tim/news/2005/09/30/what-is-web-20.html** (accessed January 2008).

Phillips, D. "Social Media Drives Retail Visits in USA." *Leverwealth.com*, September 27, 2006. **leverwealth.blogspot.com/2006/09/social-media-drives-retail-visits-in.html** (accessed May 2008).

Prescott, L. "YouTube: 50% More Traffic than Other Video Sites Combined." *Hitwise*, June 27, 2007. **weblogs.hitwise.**

com/leeann-prescott/2007/06/youtube_50_more_traffic_than_o_1.html (accessed January 2008).

Raman, M. "Wiki Technologies as 'Free' Collaborative Tools within an Organization." *Information Systems Management* (Fall 2006).

Read/WriteWeb. "Latest NSN Numbers, MySpace Streaks Ahead." January 9, 2006. **readwriteweb.com/archives/latest_sns_numb.php** (accessed January 2008).

Regan, K. "Plugging In: Can E-Commerce Leverage Social Networks?" *E-Commerce Times*, November 2, 2006.

Revenue News. "MyPickList Tackles Social Networking and Word-of-Mouth Advertising." May 25, 2006.

Rheingold, H. *The Virtual Community: Homesteading on the Electronic Frontier*, rev. ed. Boston: MIT Press, 2000.

Ricadela, A. "Under Construction." *InformationWeek*, November 6, 2006.

Riley, D. "Wikipedia Hits Mid Life Slow Down." *TechCrunch*, October 11, 2007. **techcrunch.com/2007/10/11/wikipedia-hits-mid-life-slow-down** (accessed January 2008).

Rouch, W. "Social Networking 3.0." *Technology Review from MIT's Emerging Technologies Conference*, September 27–29, 2006. **technologyreview.com/read_article.aspx?id=15908&ch=infotech** (accessed January 2008).

Rowse, D. "Blog Tools." *Problogger.net*, April 15, 2006. **problogger.net/archives/2006/04/15/blog-tools** (accessed January 2008).

Sachoff, M. "YouTube's Role in Election 2008." *WebProNews.com*, March 1, 2007. **webpronews.com/topnews/ 2007/03/01/presidential-candidates-turn-to-youtube** (accessed January 2008).

Sandoval, G. "Teen Filmmaker Attracts Logitech's Focus." *ZDNet News*, March 28, 2006. **news.zdnet.com/2100–1040_22–6054602.html** (accessed January 2008).

Scable, R., and S. Israel. *Naked Conversations: How Blogs Are Changing the Way Businesses Talk with Customers.* New York: Hungry Minds/Wiley, 2006.

Schonfeld, E. "Cyworld Attacks!" *Business 2.0*, August 2006a.

Schonfeld, E. "The Disruptors Get Rowdy." *The.Next.Net*, October 27, 2006b. **emedia.blogspot.com/2006/10/next-net-27102006-disruptors-get-rowdy.html** (accessed January 2008).

Schonfeld, E. "Make Way for Must Stream TV." *Business 2.0*, March 2007.

Schonfeld, E., and J. Borzo. "The Next Disruptors." *Business 2.0*, October 2006.

Schubert, P., and M. Ginsburg. "Virtual Communities of Transaction: The Role of Personalization in E-Commerce." *Electronic Markets* 10, no. 1 (2000).

Sharma, A. "Banner Year: Companies Compete for Ad Revenue on Mobile Internet." *Wall Street Journal*, January 18, 2007.

Sifrey, D. "The State of the Live Web, April 2007." *Sifrey.com*, April 05, 2007. **sifry.com/alerts/archives/000493.htm** (accessed January 2008).

Sloan, P. "The Next Net 25 (Web 2.0 Companies)." *Business 2.0*, March 2007.

Sloan, P., and P. Kaihla. "Blogging for Dollars." *Business 2.0*, September 2006.

Smith, D. "Discovering Where Web Evolution Is Taking Us." *The Observer* (Silicon Valley, California); reprinted in the *Taipei Times*, December 1, 2006.

Stafford, A. "The Future of the Web." *PC World*, November 2006.

Taft, D. K. "IBM Enters Social Scene." *eWeek*, January 29, 2007.

Taipei Times. "Trawling the Net for Your Innermost Desires." December 17, 2006.

Tapscott, D., and A. D. Williams. *Wikinomics: How Mass Collaboration Changes Everything.* Woodlands, TX: Portfolio (December 28, 2006).

Turban, E., et al. *Business Intelligence: A Managerial Approach.* Upper Saddle River, NJ: Prentice Hall, 2008.

Tynan, D. "Entertainment on Demand." *PC World*, November 2006.

Urlocker, M. "Urlocker on Disruption." *The Disruption Group.*" September 20, 2006. **ondisruption.com/my_weblog/2006/09/business_20_top.html** (accessed January 2008).

Wagner, M. "Can Bloggers Be Bought?" *InformationWeek*, October 16, 2006.

Wainewright, P. "What to Expect from Web 3.0." *ZDNet.com*, November 29, 2005. **blogs.zdnet.com/SAAS/?p=68** (accessed January 2008).

Watson, B. P. "Web 2.0: Business Tools That Save Time, Money." *Baseline*, February 2, 2007a.

Watson, B. "Web 2.0: The Internet Refreshed." *Baseline*, January 2007b.

Weber, S. *Plug Your Business.* Falls Church, VA: Weber Books, 2007.

Websloginc.com. "The Social Software Weblog." 2007. **socialsoftware.Weblogsinc.com** (accessed January 2008).

Weinstein, M. "On Demand Is in Demand." *Training*, October 2006.

Wikipedia. "About Wikipedia." 2008. **en.wikipedia.org/wiki/Wikipedia:About** (accessed January 2008).

Woyke, E. "The eBay Model Goes to the Movies." *BusinessWeek*, December 11, 2006.

Wright, J. *Blog Marketing.* New York: McGraw-Hill, 2006.

YouTube. "Sundance Channel Video Clips Available on YouTube in 2007." January 17, 2007. **youtube.com/press_room_entry?entry=pmcIOsL7s98** (accessed January 2008).

YouTube. "YouTube and Coca Cola Introduce Video Greeting Cards for the Holidays." December 8, 2006a. **youtube.com/press_room_entry?entry=3qfzQhQXryg** (accessed January 2008).

YouTube. "YouTube, Chevrolet and Warner Music Group Present New Year's Eve Countdown Around the World." December 29, 2006b. **youtube.com/press_room_entry?entry=JrYI-yzd3Q0** (accessed January 2008).

Zappone, C. "Help! YouTube Is Killing My Business." *CNNMoney.com*, October 12, 2006. **money.cnn.com/2006/10/12/news/companies/utube/index.htm** (accessed May 2008).

Zetlin, M., and B. Pfleging. "The Cult of Community." *Smart Business,* June 2002.

CHAPTER 9

3GNewsroom.com. "2006 Will Be Year of Mobile Advertising Experimentation." March 19, 2006. **3gnewsroom.com/3g_news/mar_06/news_6820.shtml** (accessed February 2008).

Accenture.com. "Pickberry Vineyard: Accenture Prototype Helps Improve Crop Management." 2006. **accenture.com/ xd/xd.asp?it=enweb&xd=services%5Ctechnology%5Ccase%5Cpickberry.xml** (accessed February 2008).

Anderson, N. "PDA Sales Drop by 40 Percent in a Single Year, Vendors Bolt for Exit." *Ars Technica*, August 13, 2007. **arstechnica.com/news.ars/post/20070813-pda-sales-drop-by-40-percent-in-a-single-year-vendors-bolt-for-exit.html** (accessed February 2008).

Becker, K. "Mobile Phone: The New Way to Pay?" *Federal Reserve Bank of Boston Industrial Briefing,* February 2007. **bos.frb.org/economic/eprg** (accessed February 2008).

Belew, B. "M-Commerce Is Future of Japan Retail." *Rising Sun of Nihon*, September 15, 2006.

Bial, R. G., and D. J. Mayhew. *Cost-Justifying Usability: An Update for the Internet Age*, 2d ed. San Francisco: Elsevier, 2005.

Bonkoo, T. "Grocery Stores Providing a New Way of Shopping to Customers: Handheld Device Allows Customer to Forgo Long Line." *Associated Content Media*, January 18, 2007. **associatedcontent.com/article/284899/grocery_stores_providing_a_new_way.html** (accessed February 2008).

Chen, A. "Dot Net and J2EE for Web Services," in Khosrow-Pour (2006).

Commonwealth Telecommunications Organization. "Barriers and Enablers to Sustainable Growth in Emerging Markets." CTO Forum 2006, London, England, September 4–6, 2006.

Cybit. "Cybit Announces Total Mobile Resource Management (MRM) Solution for Managing Mobile Workforce." August 30, 2006. **goliath.ecnext.com/coms2/gi_0199–5728722/Cybit-announces-total-Mobile-Resource.html** (accessed February 2008).

Downey, K. "Soon, a Better Way to Track Billboards." *Media Life Magazine*, October 23, 2007. **medialifemagazine.com/artman2/publish/Research_25/Soon_a_better_way_to_track_billboards.asp** (accessed February 2008).

Fleishman, G. "Comprehensive U.S. Airport Wi-Fi Guide." *Wifinetnews.com*, September 12, 2006. **wifinetnews.com/archives/006954.html** (accessed February 2008).

Fox News. "Municipal Wi-Fi Networks Run into Financial, Technical Trouble." May 23, 2007. **foxnews.com/story/0,2933,274728,00.html** (accessed May 2008).

Fujitsu. "Large Field Sales Operation to Boost Revenues by More Than £1 Million with Mobile Solution." 2005. **fujitsu.com/uk/casestudies/fs_hillarys.html** (accessed February 2008).

Goodman, D. N. "Used Phones Help Drive Third World Wireless Boom." MSNBC, October 29, 2006. **msnbc.msn.com/id/15434609** (accessed February 2008).

GSM Association. "GSM Association 2007 Brochure." February 2007. **gsmworld.com/documents/gsm_brochure.pdf** (accessed February 2008).

Horowitz, B. "Fast Food Chains Bank on Burgeoning Text-Ordering Business." *USA Today*, January 4, 2008. **ecommerce-times.com/story/61048.html** (accessed February 2008).

Hu, W.-C., J.-H.Yeh, H.-J.Yang, and C.-W. Lee. "Mobile Handheld Devices for Mobile Commerce," in Khosrow-Pour (2006).

Intel. "Increase Productivity: Boost Employee Productivity with High-Performance PCs." 2006a. **intel.com/cd/business/enterprise/emea/eng/bss/products/client/189384.htm** (accessed February 2008).

Intel. "Creating the Future at the Metro Group." 2006b. **intel.com/ca/business/casestudies/pdf/metro.pdf** (accessed February 2008).

Jupiter. "Gambling on Mobile: Second Edition." February 2005. **mobileeurope.co.uk/asset/8/mobilegamblingv2.pdf** (accessed February 2008).

Khosrow-Pour, M. (ed.). *Encyclopedia of E-Commerce, E-Government, and Mobile Commerce.* Hershey, PA: Idea Group Reference, 2006.

Kontzer, T. "Top Ten Uses for SMS." *InformationWeek*, June 11, 2003. **informationweek.com/techcenters/networking/wireless** (no longer available online).

Kou, W., and Y. Yesha (Eds.) *Enabling Technologies for Wireless E-Business.* Heidelberg, Germany: Springer, 2006.

Laudermilch, N. "Will Cell Phones Be Responsible for the Next Internet Worm?" *InformIT*, April 28, 2006. **informit.com/articles/article.aspx?p=465449** (accessed February 2008).

Malykhina, E. "Get Smart." *InformationWeek*, October 30, 2006a.

Malykhina, E. "Leave the Laptop Home." *InformationWeek*, October 30, 2006b.

MasterCard. "MasterCard Trials Mobile Phone Payment Service." November 2, 2006. **cbronline.com/article_news.asp?guid=BB14346F-F176-460E-8342-B649DD176A27** (accessed February 2008).

Microsoft. "Large Field Sales Operation to Boost Revenues by More Than £1 Million with Mobile Solution." 2005. **whitepapers.techrepublic.com/thankyou.aspx?&docid=268246&view=268246** (accessed February 2008).

Mullen, J. "For Those in Paris about to Park, a Service That Tells Them Where." *New York Times*, November 21, 2006. **nytimes.com/2006/11/20/business/worldbusiness/**

20garage.html?ex=1321678800&en=9e1908a053b88365 &ei=5088&partner=rssnyt& emc=rss (accessed February 2008).

Network for Online Commerce. "2006 New Year SMS Records Rocket Around the World." January 27, 2006. **newsweaver. co.uk/noc/e_article000520133.cfm?x=b11,0,w** (accessed February 2008).

Nobel, C. "Home Depot Tackles Network Challenge," *eWeek*, November 21, 2005.

Olsder, A. "The Global Mobile Game Industry, 10 Years On." *Mobile Game Blog*, January 2008. **mobilegames.blogs.com/ mobile_games_blog/2008/01/the-global-mobi.html** (accessed February 2008).

Payment News. "Mobile Banking Stages a Remarkable Comeback." *Paymentnews.com*, February 6, 2006. **paymentsnews.com/2006/02/mobile_banking_.html** (accessed February 2008).

Petrova, K. "Mobile Commerce Applications and Adoption," in Khosrow-Pour (2006).

Pierre, S. "Mobile Electronic Commerce," in Khosrow-Pour (2006).

Philadelphia Inquirer. "It's Getting There: Wi-Fi Baby Steps." December 17, 2007. **philly.com/inquirer/opinion/ 20071217_Editorial__Its_Getting_There.html?adString= inq.news/opinion;!category=opinion;&randomOrd= 020408041722** (accessed February 2008).

Pmai.org. "'Sony Electronics' ImageStation.com Joins with CVS/Pharmacy on In-Store Photo Pick-up Service." February 19, 2005. **news.sel.sony.com/en/press_room/ consumer/digital_imaging/image_station/archive/8941. html?archive=1** (accessed February 2008).

Raskin, A. "Your Ad Could Be Here! (And Now We Can Tell You Who Will See It)." *Business 2.0*, May 2003. **money.cnn.com/magazines/business2/business2_archive/ 2003/05/01/341929/index.htm** (accessed February 2008).

Reed, B. "How Four Airlines Plan to Connect Fliers to the Web." *PC World*, December 7, 2007. **pcworld.com/article/ id,140416-c,wireless/article.html** (accessed February 2008).

Salo, J., and J. Tähtinen. "Special Features of Mobile Advertising and Their Utilization," in Khosrow-Pour (2006).

Taipei Times. "New GPS Parking Hits the Spot for Paris." November 21, 2006. **taipeitimes.com/News/world/ archives/2006/11/21/2003337287** (accessed February 2008).

Telephia Research. "Telephia Research Shows Nearly 13.5 Million Wireless Subscribers Downloaded a Mobile Game, with Average Monthly Revenues Reaching $46.9 Million in Q2 2006." August 24, 2006. **telephia. com/html/insights_082406.html** (accessed February 2008).

Virki, T. "Global Cell Penetration Reaches 50 Percent." *Reuters*, November 29, 2007. **investing.reuters.co.uk/ news/articleinvesting.aspx?type=media&storyID=nL2 9172095&pageNumber=1&imageid=&cap=&sz= 13&WTModLoc=InvArt-C1-ArticlePage1** (accessed February 2008).

Ward, M. "Wi-Fi Sensor Net Aids Wine Makers." *BBC News*, July 6, 2004. **news.bbc.co.uk/1/hi/technology/ 3860863.stm** (accessed February 2008).

Wikipedia. "Bluetooth." 2008. **en.wikipedia.org/wiki/ Bluetooth** (accessed February 2008).

CHAPTER 10

Berghel, H., and J. Uecker. "WiFi Attack Vectors." *Communications of the ACM* 48, no. 8 (2005).

CompTIA. "Summary of "Information Security: A CompTIA Analysis of IT Security and the Workforce" April 2007. **comptia.org/sections/research/research%20docs/ securitysummary407.pdf** (accessed February 2008).

CyberSource. "Online Fraud Report, 9th edition." 2008. **cybersource.com** (accessed February 2008).

Ellis, S. "How to Avoid Festive Fraudsters." *The Daily Telegraph* (London), November 17, 2007.

Emigh, J. "The Eyes Have It." *Security Solutions*, March 1, 2003. **securitysolutions.com/mag/security_eyes/** (accessed February 2008).

FTC. "FTC Consumer Fraud and Identity Theft Complaint Data." February 2007. **consumer.gov/sentinel/pubs/ Top10Fraud2006.pdf** (accessed February 2008).

Gage, D. "Bank of America Seeks Anti-Fraud Anodyne." *Baseline*, May 15, 2006. **baselinemag.com/article2/ 0,1540,1962470,00.asp** (accessed February 2008).

Gaudin, S. "Nightmare on Wall Street: Prosecution Witness Describes 'Chaos' in UBS PaineWebber Attack." *InformationWeek*, June 6, 2006. **informationweek.com/ story/showArticle.jhtml?articleID=188702216** (accessed February 2008).

Grau, J. "Cyber Fraud Eats into Retailers' Revenues." *eMarketer*, December 20, 2006. **emarketer.com/ Article.aspx?id=1004390** (accessed February 2008).

Hodgkinson, T. "G2: With Friends Like These." *The Guardian*, January 14, 2008. **Honeynet.org** (accessed February 2008).

Lerer, L. "Why the SEC Can't Stop Spam." *Forbes*, March 8, 2007.

Lopez, D. "Thieves Lie in Wait for Online Shoppers." *McClatchy-Tribune Business News*. November 27, 2007.

Musthaler, L. "Facebook Fiasco Highlights Privacy Concerns." *Network World* 25, no. 1 (2008).

O'Donnell, J. "Some Retailers Tighten Return Policies." *USA Today*, February 1, 2008.

Reprise Media. "Click Fraud . . . Is Google Finally Solving the Problem?" *SearchViews*, March 1, 2007. **searchviews. com/index.php/archives/2007/03/click-fraud% e2%80%a6is-google-finally-solving-the-problem.php** (accessed February 2008).

Richtel, M. "Holiday Online Receipts Are Strong, but Reflect a Decline in Rate of Growth." *New York Times*, December 28, 2007.

Roberts, P. F. "Webroot Uncovers Thousands of Stolen Identities." *InfoWorld,* May 8, 2006. **infoworld.com/article/ 06/05/09/78139_HNTrojanrebery_1.html** (accessed February 2008).

SANS. "SANS Top-20 Internet Security Attack Targets, 2007 Annual Update." 2007. **sans.org/top20** (accessed February 2008).

SecureComputing.com. "How To Protect Your Company and Employees from Image Spam." **securecomputing.com/ image_spam_WP.cfm** (accessed February 2008).

TRUSTe. **truste.org/about/index.php** (accessed February 2008).

Tsai, J. "Facebook's About-Face." *Customer Relationship Management.* 25(1), Jan. 2008.

TSSI. "Biometrics Gains UK Approval." *IT Reseller Magazine,* December 19, 2006.

U.S. Department of Justice. "Disgruntled UBS PaineWebber Employee Charged with Allegedly Unleashing 'Logic Bomb' on Company Computers." December 17, 2002. **usdoj.gov/criminal/cybercrime/duronioIndict.htm** (accessed February 2008).

Whitman, J. "UBS Wants to Bar Public at Tech 'Bomb' Trial." *New York Post,* June 6, 2006.

CHAPTER 11

American Public Transportation Association (APTA). "Smart Cards and U.S. Public Transportation." June 2006. **apta.com/research/info/briefings/briefing_6.cfm** (accessed February 2008).

Association for Financial Professionals (AFP). "2007 Electronic Payments Survey." 2007. **afponline.org/pub/ pdf/2007_AFP_Electronic_Payments_Survey.pdf** (accessed February 2008).

Barnhart, T. "The Financial Supply Chain: Could This Be the Next Corporate Paradigm after ERP?" *Darwin Magazine,* April 1, 2004. **dso-news.info/The-Financial-Supply-Chain-Could-this-be-the-next-corporate-paradigm-after-ERP-_a1469.html** (accessed February 2008).

Block, S. "Some Holiday Gift Cards Can Come Wrapped in Fine Print." *USA Today.* November 19, 2007. **usatoday.com/ money/perfi/columnist/block/2007-11-19-gift-cards_N.htm** (accessed February 2008).

Boles, T. "Returned Goods Clog British Roads." *Knight Ridder Tribune Business News,* October 24, 2004.

Branch Banking and Trust (BB&T). "BB&T Makes EasySend Money Transfer Free." June 2006. **paymentsnews.com/2006/06/bbt_makes_easys.html** (accessed February 2008).

Business Wire. "MasterCard PayPass Continues to Build Momentum as 'The Simpler Way to Pay.'" May 13, 2003. **findarticles.com/p/articles/mi_m0EIN/is_2003_May_13/ ai_101616570** (accessed May 2008).

Card Technology. "The TaiwanMoney Card Is Still Too Slow for Subways." 2006. **cardtechnology.com/article.html? id=20060317366M1LIB** (accessed February 2008).

Chain Store Age. "Checks in a Digital World." June 2006.

CNET. "Study: Ring Tones, Mobile Games to SkyRocket." *CNET News,* March 15, 2005. **news.com.com/Study+ Ring+tones,+mobile+games+to+skyrocket/ 2100-1039_3-5618320.html** (accessed February 2008).

Council of Supply Chain Management Professionals. **cscmp.org** (accessed February 2008).

CyberSource. "The 2008 ePayment Management Project Guide." 2008. **cybersource.com/XX** (accessed February 2008).

CyberSource. "Insiders Guide to E-Commerce Payment: 20 Tools Successful Merchants Are Using to Unlock Hidden Profit: Second Edition." 2005. **cybersource.com/resources/ collateral/Resource_Center/whitepapers_and_reports/ insiders_guide.pdf** (accessed February 2005).

D'Agostino, D. "Pennies from Heaven." *CIO Insight,* January 2006.

Daly, J. "Will Those Who Won't POP Do BOC Instead?" *DigitalTransactions.net,* October 2006. **digitaltransactions. net/files/1006Networks.doc** (accessed February 2008).

Dove Consulting. "Consumer Payment Preferences: Understanding Choice." 2006. **aciworldwide.com/ pdfs/consumer_payment_preferences_trend.pdf** (accessed February 2008).

Ellis, D. "Seven Ways to Improve Returns Processing." *Multichannelmerchant.com,* January 4, 2006. **multichannel merchant.com/opsandfulfillment/returns/improve_ returns_processing_01042006** (accessed February 2008).

Evans, D., and R. Schmalensee. *Paying with Plastic: The Digital Revolution in Buying and Borrowing,* 2d ed. Cambridge, MA: MIT Press, 2005.

Frost and Sullivan. "America's Smart Card Market." *SmartCardAlliance.org,* August 2005. **smartcardalliance.org/ resources/pdf/SCA_Executive_Summary_Final_092605. pdf** (accessed February 2008).

Gentry, C. "Moving Money." *Chain Store Age.* February 2006. **tradecard.com/languages/EN/news/articles/chainStore Age_Feb2006.pdf** (accessed February 2008).

Hendry, M. *Multi-application Smart Cards: Technology and Applications.* Cambridge, UK: Cambridge University Press, 2007.

Herd, M. "NACHA Reports Nearly 16 Billion ACH Payments in 2006." *Nacha.org,* April 16, 2007. **nacha.org/ news/news/pressreleases/2007/Pr041607/pr041607.htm** (accessed February 2008).

Hett, S., and S. Davis. "System for Order Allocation Among Warehouses." *Issues in Information Systems* 7, no. 2 (2006).

Hughes, S., and N. Edwards. "Best Practices for a Successful POP Implementation." *Epson.com,* May 9, 2006. **pop.epson.com/checks/pdfs/walmartpres.ppt** (accessed February 2008).

Ikram, G. "Digital Music Downloads Flourish as Apple Grabs No 2 Spot." *Dailytech.* February 26, 2008.

dailytech.com/Digital+Music+Downloads+Flourish+as+ Apple+Grabs+No+2+Spot+/article10870.htm (accessed February 2008).

Ipsos Insight. "More than 67 Million Americans Have Used Credit or Debit Cards for Purchases of Less Than $5 in the Past 30 Days." June 2006. ipsosinsight.com/pressrelease. aspx"id=3284 (accessed February 2008).

Kelly, K. "Scan This Book!" *New York Times*, May 14, 2006. nytimes.com/2006/05/14/magazine/14publishing.html? ei=5090&en=c07443d368771bb8&ex=1305259200& adxnnl=1&adxnnlx=171852200KMPhOGBlav8LFn/ Vt95ugw (accessed February 2008).

Kelsall, A. "Matching Customer Service Agents to Your Customers' Needs." *Multichannelmerchant.com*, July 25, 2006. multichannelmerchant.com/opsandfulfillment/ contact_center_advisor/customeragents_need (accessed February 2008).

Kuo, R. "PVI enjoys growth in profits and gross margin in 4Q07." *DIGITIMES.com.* January 29, 2008. digitimes. com/displays/a20080129PD207.html (accessed May 2008).

Kuzeljevich, J. "Targeting Reverse Logistics." *Canadian Transportation Logistics* 107, no. 9 (2004).

Lamond, K., and D. Whitman, "Credit Card Transactions: Real World and Online," VirtualSchool.edu, 1996. virtual school.edu/mon/ElectronicProperty/klamond/ credit_card.htm (accessed May 2008).

Levy, S. "The Future of Reading." *Newsweek*. November 26, 2007. newsweek.com/id/70983 (accessed February 2008).

Lucas, P. "Taming the Paper Tiger." *Collectionsworld.com*, February 2005. collectionsworld.com/cgi-bin/readtory2.pl?story= 20040601CCRV263.xml (accessed February 2008).

Maloney, D. "More Than Paper Savings." *DC Velocity*, January 2006. dcvelocity.com/articles/20060101/pdfs/06_01 techreview.pdf (accessed February 2008).

MasterCard International. "MasterCard International Surpasses 200 Million Smart Card Milestone." November 4, 2004. mastercardintl.com/cgi-bin/newsroom.cgi?id=950& category=date&date=2004 (accessed February 2008).

Mercator. "Mercator Announces Survey of Prepaid Market." *Payment News*, September 2006. paymentsnews.com/ 2006/09/mercator_announ.html (accessed February 2008).

Merchant Risk Council. "Online Fraud Rates Approaching Fraud Rates at Card-Present Retail According to 5th Annual Survey by Merchant Risk Council; Fraudsters Get More Sophisticated and Merchants Must Invest to Keep Up," April 18, 2006. merchantriskcouncil.org/files/press_ pdf/24_041805.pdf (accessed February 2008).

Milligan, J. "Future Threat?" *BAI Banking Strategies*, May–June 2004. bai.org/bankingstrategies/2004-may- jun/future (accessed February 2008).

Mitchell, D. "In Online World, Pocket Change Is Not Easily Spent." *New York Times*. August 27, 2007. nytimes.com/ 2007/08/27/technology/27micro.html?scp=1&sq=In+ Online+World%2C+Pocket+Change+Is+Not+Easily+ Spent&st=nyt (accessed February 2008).

Multos. "TaiwanMoney Card." *Multos.com*, 2006. multos.com/ downloads/marketing/CaseStudy_Taiwan_Money.pdf (accessed February 2008).

Parks, L. "Schurman Fine Papers Rack Up Labor Savings." *Stores,* February 2004.

Parry, T. "Study: Simpler Online Returns Make Happier Customers." *Multichannelmerchant.com*, January 11, 2006. multichannelmerchant.com/opsandfulfillment/returns/ onlinereturn_customer (accessed March 2008).

PayPal. "Business Guide to Online Payment Processing." 2004, paypal.teamingup.net/pdf/OPPBusinessGuide.pdf (accessed January 2008).

RFIDNews. "Visa Launches Mobile Visa Wave Payment Pilot in Malaysia." April, 27, 2006. rfidnews.org/news/2006/ 04/27/ visa-launches-mobile-visa-wave-payment-pilot- in-malaysia (accessed May 2008).

Rite Aid. "Vendor Supply Chain Guide." September 2006. riteaidediservices.com/SupplyChain/RiteAid_Ven dor_Supply_Chain_Guide.pdf (accessed February 2008).

Simon, J. "Paper to Plastic: Checks and Cash Losing to Debit and Credit." October 3, 2007. creditcards.com/credit- card-paper-vs-plastic.php (accessed February 2008).

Smart Card Alliance. "Sesam Vitale." October 2006. smartcardalliance.org/resources/pdf/Sesam_Vitale.pdf (accessed February 2008).

Staffware.com. "Daisy Brand Uses BPM to Improve Agility," staffware.com/resources/customers/successstory_daisy brand.pdf (accessed January 2007).

Supplychainer.com. "Seven Ways to Immediately Increase Fulfillment Speed." June 22, 2006. supplychainer.com/ 50226711/seven_ways_to_immediately_increase_order_ fulfillment_speed.php (accessed February 2008).

TIBCO. "Daisy Brand Uses TIBCO's Solution to Deliver Fresh Services." *Tibco.com*, 2006. tibco.com/resources/customers/ successstory_daisybrand (accessed February 2008).

UPS. "UPS Supply Chain Solutions." *UPS.com*, 2008. e-logistics.ups.com (accessed February 2008).

Violino, B. "What Can Logistics Do for You?" *Cybermedia*, June 2006. pressroom.ups.com/staticfiles/articles/521.pdf (accessed February 2008).

Vitasek, K., and K. Manrodt. "Perfecting the Perfect Order." *Multichannelmerchant.com*, May 10, 2006. multichannel merchant.com/opsandfulfillment/advisor/perfect_order (accessed December 2006).

CHAPTER 12

Access eCommerce. "Developing Your Internet Business Plan." 2006. access-ecom.info/section.cfm?sid=bp&xid=MN (accessed November 2006).

ACLU. "Libraries, the Internet, and the Law: Adults Must Have Unfiltered Access." November 16, 2006 acluwa. org/detail.cfm?id=556 (no longer available online).

Aptstrategies.com. "Networx Case Study." **aptstrategies.com.au/ case_studies/Networx** (accessed February 2008).

Auckland, J. S. "Davidson Appointed InternetNZ Executive Director." *Computerworld*, May 31, 2005. **computerworld. co.nz/news.nsf/0/C77829204EE51915CC257011006C 7F51?OpenDocument&pub=Computerworld** (accessed February 2008).

Burns, E. "Intellectual Property Threatened by Spyware," *ClickZ Stats*, November 14, 2006. **clickz.com/showPage.html? page=3623943** (accessed March 2007).

Cagni, P. "Think Globally, Act European." *Strategy and Business*, August 30, 2004. **strategy-business.com/enewsarticle/ enews083004?pg=all** (accessed February 2008).

Carr, D. F. "Changing Course amid Turbulence." *Baseline*, September 2006.

CIO Insight. "Top Trends for 2005." December 2004.

Clegg, B., and B. Tan. "E-Business Planning and Analysis Framework," in Khosrow-Pour (2006).

CNN.com. "DARPA Challenge: Build the Ultimate Speech Translation Machine." November 6, 2006. **cnn.com/ 2006/TECH/11/06/darpa.translation.ap/index.html** (no longer available online).

Dell Public. "Building a Business Case for a Technology Investment." August 2005. **whitepapers.techrepublic.com. com/whitepaper.aspx?docid=145883** (accessed February 2008).

Devaraj, S., and R. Kohli. "Information Technology Payoff Paradox and System Use: Is Actual Usage the Missing Link?" *Management Science* 49, no. 3 (2003).

Devaraj, S., and R. Kohli. *The IT Payoff: Measuring Business Value of Information Technology Investment*. Upper Saddle River, NJ: Financial Times Prentice-Hall, 2002.

Dubie, D. "Going Global." *eBusinessIQ*, March 13, 2003. **findarticles.com/p/articles/mi_zd4149/is_200410/ ai_n9476589** (no longer available online).

e-Business World. "Global Imperative . . . and the Pitfalls of Regionalism." January–February 2000.

Egea, J. M. O., and M. Recio. "Menéndez Global Marketing on the Internet," in Khosrow-Pour (2006).

eMarketer. "Small Businesses Expecting E-Sales." December 14, 2004. **emarketer.com/article.aspx?1003177** (no longer available online).

Fortinet.com. "Pierre Lang Jewelers Safeguards Multi-National Enterprise Network," March 30, 2005. **fortinet.com/news/pr/2005/pr033005.html** (accessed February 2008).

Gagnon, D., S. Lee, F. Ramirez, S. Ravikumar, and J. Santiago. "Consumer Power and the Internet." *MIT Sloan School of Management*, June 11, 2002. **mitsloan.mit.edu/50th/ pdf/consumerpowerpaper.pdf** (accessed February 2008).

Ghemawat, P. "Distance Still Matters: The Hard Reality of Global Expansion." *Harvard Business Review* (September 2001).

Green, S. *Profit on the Web*. Auckland, New Zealand: Axon Computertime, 2002.

Harwood, S. "BMW Ban Sparks SEO Clampdown." *Revolution* (London), March 2006.

He, S. "Multilingual Web Sites in Global Electronic Commerce," in Khosrow-Pour (2006).

Helmore, E. "YouTube: The Hustings of the 21st Century?" *The Observer*, March 25, 2007. **politics.guardian.co.uk/media/ story/0,,2042052,00.html** (accessed February 2008).

Hunt, B. "What, Exactly Is Search Engine Spam." *SearchEngineWatch.com*, February 16, 2005. **search enginewatch.com/showPage.html?page=3483601** (accessed February 2008).

InternetNZ. "InternetNZ Strategic Plan: 2004–2007." April 2004. **internetnz.net.nz/reports/plans/archive/2004/ planning040424adoption.html** (accessed February 2008).

InternetNZ. "InternetNZ Strategic Plan: 2006." February 23, 2006. **internetnz.net.nz/reports/plans/archive/2006/ 2006–03–04-strategicplan** (accessed February 2008).

Jelassi, I., and A. Enders. *Strategies for e-Business*. Harlow, England: FT Prentice Hall, 2005.

Johnson, D., and E. Lipton. "Justice Department Says F.B.I. Misused Patriot Act." *New York Times*, March 9, 2007. **nytimes.com/2007/03/09/washington/09cndfbi.html?hp** (no longer available online).

Khosrow-Pour, M. (ed.). *Encyclopedia of E-Commerce, E-Government, and Mobile Commerce*. Hershey, PA: Idea Group Reference, 2006.

Kraemer, K. *Global E-Commerce: Impacts of National Environment and Policy*. Cambridge, MA: Cambridge University Press, 2006.

Lawson-Body, A., and A. Illia. "SME's Perceptions of B2B E-Commerce," in Khosrow-Pour (2006).

Longino, C. "Your Wireless Future." *Business 2.0*, May 2006.

Martin, O. "Configuration Management: A CA IT Service Management Process Map." Computer Associates white paper, June 2006. **wp.bitpipe.com/resource/org_ 1103740304_372/30265_In_Network.pdf?site_cd=bp& asrc=ORG_OSE_GOOGUS** (accessed February 2008).

McKay, J., and P. Marshall. *Strategic Management of eBusiness*. Milton, Australia: John Wiley & Sons, 2004.

Mello, J. P. "Explosive Growth Predicted for Mobile Social Networks." *E-Commerce Times*, December 12, 2006.

Misra, R. "Evolution of the Philosophy of Investments in IT Projects." *Issues in Informing Sciences and Information Technology* 3 (2006).

MSNBC. "Microsoft, Yahoo Test IM Partnership." July 13, 2006. **msnbc.msn.com/id/13833755** (accessed February 2008).

Niven, P. *Balanced Scorecard Diagnostics*. Hoboken, NJ: John Wiley and Sons, 2005.

OECD (Organization for Economic Cooperation and Development). *Enhancing SME Competitiveness: The OECD*. Bologna, Italy, Ministerial Conference. 2001.

Paton, D., and D. Troppito. "Eye on ROI: ROI Review." *DM Review*, March 25, 2004. **dmreview.com/article_sub.cfm? articleId=1000671** (accessed February 2008).

Peppard, J., and J. Ward, "Unlocking Sustained Business Value from IT Investments," *California Management Review*, Fall 2005.

Porter, M. E. *Competitive Strategy: Techniques for Analyzing Industries and Competitors.* New York: The Free Press, 1980.

Porter, M. E. "Strategy and the Internet." *Harvard Business Review* (March 2001).

Puente, M. "Hello to Less Privacy." *USA Today*, February 28, 2007. **usatoday.com/tech/news/2007–02–27-camera-phones-privacy_x.htm** (accessed February 2008).

Rayport, J., and B. J. Jaworski. *Introduction to E-Commerce*, 2d ed. Boston: McGraw-Hill, 2004.

Reuters. "Universal Music Sues MySpace Over Copyrights," *The Financial Express*, January 8, 2007.

Rigby, R. "Splogging Clogging Blogging." *FT.com* (London), October 30, 2006.

Rigby, D. K., and V. Vishwanath. "Localization: The Revolution in Consumer Markets." *Harvard Business Review* (April 2006).

Ross, J. W., and C. M. Beath. "Beyond the Business Case: New Approaches to IT Investment." *MIT Sloan Management Review* (Winter 2002).

SAP AG. "Pierre Lang Europe." 2004. **sap.com/demos/pdfs/CS_Pierre_Lang.pdf** (accessed February 2008).

Sharma, S. K. "E-Commerce in a Digital Economy," in Khosrow-Pour (2006).

Stafford, A. "The Future of the Web." *PC World*, November 2006.

Stone, A. "Breaking Down Language Barriers." *Forbes.com*, October 19, 2005. **forbes.com/enterprisetech/2005/10/19/language-translation-cell-cz_as_1019language.html** (accessed February 2008).

Strader, T. J., and M. J. Shaw. "Characteristics of Electronic Markets." *Decision Support Systems* 21, no. 3 (1997).

Tatnall, A., and S. Burgess. "Innovation Translation and E-Commerce in SMEs," in Khosrow-Pour (2006).

Tillquist, J., and W. Rodgers. "Measuring the Value of IT," *Communications of the ACM* (January 2005).

TNS and TRUSTe. "Consumer Behaviors and Attitudes about Privacy." TNS-TRUSTe Consumer Privacy Index, Q4, 2004.

Veiga, A. "Music Industry Group Targets Students." *FindLaw.com*, February 28, 2007. **ibtimes.com/articles/20070228/downloading-music.htm** (accessed February 2008).

Verizon Wireless News Center. "Wireless Spam Scheme Targeted by Verizon Wireless." November 23, 2005. **news.vzw.com/news/2005/11/pr2005–11–23.html** (accessed February 2008).

Vic.gov.au. "Networx Events." **mmv.vic.gov.au/uploads/downloads/ICT_Projects/eCommerce/NetworxEvents.pdf** (accessed February 2008).

Wang, F., and G. Forgionne. "BSC-Based Framework for E-Business Strategy," in Khosrow-Pour (2006).

Ward, J., and J. Peppard. *Strategic Planning for Information Systems*, 3d ed. Chichester, UK: John Wiley & Sons, 2002.

World Intellectual Property Organization (WIPO). "Splog Alert." *Wilson Quarterly* 30, no. 4 (Autumn 2006). **wipo.int/portal/index.html.en** (no longer available online).

Yunker, J. "Lowering the Currency Exchange Barrier." *Global by Design*, March 3, 2006. **globalbydesign.com/2006/03/03/lowering-the-currency-exchange-barrier** (accessed February 2008).

GLOSSARY

1G The first generation of wireless technology, which was analog based.

2G The second generation of digital wireless technology; accommodates voice and text.

3G The third generation of digital wireless technology; supports rich media such as video.

4G The expected next generation of wireless technology that will provide faster display of multimedia.

802.11a This Wi-Fi standard is faster than 802.11b but has a smaller range.

802.11b The most popular Wi-Fi standard; it is inexpensive and offers sufficient speed for most devices; however, interference can be a problem.

802.11g This fast but expensive Wi-Fi standard is mostly used in businesses.

acceptance testing Determining whether a Web site meets the original business objectives and vision.

access control Mechanism that determines who can legitimately use a network resource.

access log A record kept by a Web server that shows when a user accesses the server; kept in a common log file format, each line of this text file details an individual access.

ad management Methodology and software that enable organizations to perform a variety of activities involved in Web advertising (e.g., tracking viewers, rotating ads).

ad views The number of times users call up a page that has a banner on it during a specific period; known as impressions or page views.

Address Verification System (AVS) Detects fraud by comparing the address entered on a Web page with the address information on file with the cardholder's issuing bank.

admediaries Third-party vendors that conduct promotions, especially large-scale ones.

advanced planning and scheduling (APS) systems Programs that use algorithms to identify optimal solutions to complex planning problems that are bound by constraints.

advergaming The practice of using computer games to advertise a product, an organization, or a viewpoint.

advertising networks Specialized firms that offer customized Web advertising, such as brokering ads and targeting ads to select groups of consumers.

advertorial An advertisement "disguised" to look like editorial content or general information.

affiliate marketing An arrangement whereby a marketing partner (a business, an organization, or even an individual) refers consumers to the selling company's Web site.

Ajax A Web development technique for creating interactive Web applications.

analytic CRM Applying business analytics techniques and business intelligence such as data mining and online analytic processing to CRM applications.

angel investor A wealthy individual who contributes personal funds and possibly expertise at the earliest stage of business development.

application service provider (ASP) An agent or vendor who assembles the functions needed by enterprises and packages them with outsourced development, operation, maintenance, and other services.

application-level proxy A firewall that permits requests for Web pages to move from the public Internet to the private network.

attractors Web site features that attract and interact with visitors in the target stakeholder group.

auction A competitive process in which a seller solicits consecutive bids from buyers (forward auctions) or a buyer solicits bids from sellers (backward auctions). Prices are determined dynamically by the bids.

auction vortal Another name for vertical auction portal.

authentication Process to verify (assure) the real identity of an individual, computer, computer program, or EC Web site.

authorization Process of determining what the authenticated entity is allowed to access and what operations it is allowed to perform.

Automated Clearing House (ACH) Network A nation-wide batch-oriented electronic funds transfer system that provides for the interbank clearing of electronic payments for participating financial institutions.

autoresponders Automated e-mail reply systems (text files returned via e-mail) that provide answers to commonly asked questions.

availability Assurance that access to data, the Web site, or other EC data service is timely, available, reliable, and restricted to authorized users.

avatars Animated computer characters that exhibit humanlike movements and behaviors.

B2B portals Information portals for businesses.

back end The activities that support online order fulfillment, inventory management, purchasing from suppliers, payment processing, packaging, and delivery.

back-office operations The activities that support fulfillment of orders, such as packing, delivery, accounting, and logistics.

balanced scorecard A management tool that assesses organizational progress toward strategic goals by measuring performance in a number of different areas.

banking Trojan A trojan that comes to life when computer owners visit one of a number of online banking or e-commerce sites.

banner On a Web page, a graphic advertising display linked to the advertiser's Web page.

banner exchanges Markets in which companies can trade or exchange placement of banner ads on each other's Web sites.

banner swapping An agreement between two companies to each display the other's banner ad on its Web site.

bartering The exchange of goods or services.

bartering exchange A marketplace in which an intermediary arranges barter transactions.

bastion gateway A special hardware server that utilizes application-level proxy software to limit the types of requests that can be passed to an organization's internal networks from the public Internet.

behavioral targeting The use of information collected on an individual's Internet-browsing behavior to select which advertisements to display to that individual.

biometric systems Authentication systems that identify a person by measurement of a biological characteristic, such as fingerprints, iris (eye) patterns, facial features, or voice.

biometrics An individual's unique physical or behavioral characteristics that can be used to identify an individual precisely (e.g., fingerprints).

blog A personal Web site that is open to the public to read and to interact with; often dedicated to specific topics or issues.

Bluetooth A set of telecommunications standards that enables wireless devices to communicate with each other over short distances.

botnet A huge number (e.g., hundreds of thousands) of hijacked Internet computers that have been set up to forward traffic, including spam and viruses, to other computers on the Internet.

brick-and-mortar (old economy) organizations Old-economy organizations (corporations) that perform their primary business off-line, selling physical products by means of physical agents.

brick-and-mortar retailers Retailers who do business in the non-Internet, physical world in traditional brick-and-mortar stores.

build-to-order (pull system) A manufacturing process that starts with an order (usually customized). Once the order is paid for, the vendor starts to fulfill it.

bullwhip effect Erratic shifts in orders up and down supply chains.

business case A document that justifies the investment of internal, organizational resources in a specific application or project.

business intelligence Activities that not only collect and process data, but also make possible analysis that results in useful—intelligent—solutions to business problems.

business model A method of doing business by which a company can generate revenue to sustain itself.

business network A group of people that have some kind of commercial relationship; for example, the relationships between sellers and buyers, buyers among themselves, buyers and suppliers, and colleagues and other colleagues.

business plan A written document that identifies a company's goals and outlines how the company intends to achieve the goals and at what cost.

business process management (BPM) Method for business restructuring that combines workflow systems and redesign methods; covers three process categories—people-to-people, systems-to-systems, and systems-to-people interactions.

business-to-business (B2B) E-commerce model in which all of the participants are businesses or other organizations.

business-to-business e-commerce (B2B EC) Transactions between businesses conducted electronically over the Internet, extranets, intranets, or private networks; also known as eB2B (electronic B2B) or just B2B.

business-to-business-to-consumer (B2B2C) E-commerce model in which a business provides some product or service to a client business that maintains its own customers.

business-to-consumer (B2C) E-commerce model in which businesses sell to individual shoppers.

business-to-employees (B2E) E-commerce model in which an organization delivers services, information, or products to its individual employees.

button A button is a small banner that is linked to a Web site. It can contain downloadable software.

buy-side e-marketplace A corporate-based acquisition site that uses reverse auctions, negotiations, group purchasing, or any other e-procurement method.

Captcha tool Short for "completely automated public Turing test to tell computers and humans apart," this tool uses a verification test on comment pages to stop scripts from posting automatically.

card verification number (CVN) Detects fraud by comparing the verification number printed on the signature strip on the back of the card with the information on file with the cardholder's issuing bank.

card-not-present (CNP) transaction A credit card transaction in which the merchant does not verify the customer's signature.

certificate authorities (CAs) Third parties that issue digital certificates.

channel conflict Situation in which an online marketing channel upsets the traditional channels due to real or perceived damage from competition.

chatterbots Animation characters that can talk (chat).

Children's Internet Protection Act (CIPA) U.S. law that mandates the use of filtering technologies in schools and libraries that receive certain types of federal funding.

ciphertext A plaintext message after it has been encrypted into a machine-readable form.

civil litigation An adversarial proceeding in which a party (the plaintiff) sues another party (the defendant) to get compensation for a wrong committed by the defendant.

click (click-through or ad click) A count made each time a visitor clicks on an advertising banner to access the advertiser's Web site.

click-and-mortar (click-and-brick) organizations Organizations that conduct some e-commerce activities, usually as an additional marketing channel.

click-and-mortar retailers Brick-and-mortar retailers that offer a transactional Web site from which to conduct business.

click-through rate The percentage of visitors who are exposed to a banner ad and click on it.

click-through ratio The ratio between the number of clicks on a banner ad and the number of times it is seen by viewers; measures the success of a banner in attracting visitors to click on the ad.

clickstream behavior Customer movements on the Internet.

clickstream data Data that occur inside the Web environment; they provide a trail of the user's activities (the user's clickstream behavior) in the Web site.

co-location A Web server owned and maintained by the business given to a Web hosting service that manages the server's connection to the Internet.

collaboration hub The central point of control for an e-market. A single collaborative-hub (c-hub), representing one e-market owner, can host multiple collaboration spaces (c-spaces) in which trading partners use collaboration enablers (c-enablers) to exchange data with the c-hub.

collaborative commerce (c-commerce) The use of digital technologies that enable companies to collaboratively plan, design, develop, manage, and research products, services, and innovative EC applications.

collaborative filtering A market research and personalization method that uses customer data to predict, based on formulas derived from behavioral sciences, what other products or services a customer may enjoy; predictions can be extended to other customers with similar profiles.

collaborative planning, forecasting, and replenishment (CPFR) Project in which suppliers and retailers collaborate in their planning and demand forecasting to optimize flow of materials along the supply chain.

collaborative portals Portals that enable collaboration.

collaborative Web site A site that allows business partners to collaborate.

comment spam Spam sent to all types of messaging media, including blogs, IM, and cellular telephones to promote products or services.

commodity content Information that is widely available and generally free to access on the Web.

company-centric EC E-commerce that focuses on a single company's buying needs (many-to-one, or buy-side) or selling needs (one-to-many, or sell-side).

competitive forces model Model devised by Porter that says that five major forces of competition determine industry structure and how economic value is divided among the industry players in an industry; analysis of these forces helps companies develop their competitive strategy.

competitor analysis grid A strategic planning tool that highlights points of differentiation between competitors and the target firm.

Computing Technology Industry Association (Comp TIA) Nonprofit trade group providing information security research and best practices.

confidentiality Assurance of data privacy and accuracy. Keeping private or sensitive information from being disclosed to unauthorized individuals, entities, or processes.

consortium trading exchange (CTE) An exchange formed and operated by a group of major companies in an industry to provide industry-wide transaction services.

consumer-to-business (C2B) E-commerce model in which individuals use the Internet to sell products or services to organizations or individuals who seek sellers to bid on products or services they need.

consumer-to-consumer (C2C) E-commerce model in which consumers sell directly to other consumers (also known as customer-to-customer commerce).

contact card A smart card containing a small gold plate on the face that when inserted in a smart card reader makes contact and passes data to and from the embedded microchip.

contactless (proximity) card A smart card with an embedded antenna, by means of which data and applications are passed to and from a card reader unit or other device without contact between the card and the card reader.

content The text, images, sound, and video that make up a Web page.

content management The process of adding, revising, and removing content from a Web site to keep content fresh, accurate, compelling, and credible.

conversion rate The percentage of clickers who actually make a purchase.

cookie A data file that is placed on a user's hard drive by a remote Web server, frequently without disclosure or the user's consent, that collects information about the user's activities at a site.

copyright An exclusive right of the author or creator of a book, movie, musical composition or other artistic property to print, copy, sell, license, distribute, transform to another medium, translate, record, perform, or otherwise use.

corporate (enterprise) portal A gateway for entering a corporate Web site, enabling communication, collaboration, and access to company information.

cost-benefit analysis A comparison of the costs of a project against the benefits.

CPM (cost per thousand impressions) The fee an advertiser pays for each 1,000 times a page with a banner ad is shown.

cross-selling Offering similar or complementary products and services to increase sales.

customer interaction center (CIC) A comprehensive service entity in which EC vendors address customer-service issues communicated through various contact channels.

customer relationship management (CRM) A customer service approach that focuses on building long-term and sustainable customer relationships that add value both for the customer and the selling company.

customer-to-customer (C2C) See consumer-to-consumer (C2C).

customization Creation of a product or service according to the buyer's specifications.

cybermediation (electronic intermediation) The use of software (intelligent) agents to facilitate intermediation.

darknets Private online community that is only open to those who belong to it.

data conferencing Virtual meeting in which geographically dispersed groups work on documents together and exchange computer files during videoconferences.

data mart A small data warehouse designed for a strategic business unit (SBU) or department.

data mining The process of searching a large database to discover previously unknown patterns; automates the process of finding predictive information.

data warehouse (DW) A single, server-based data repository that allows centralized analysis, security, and control over data.

denial of service (DoS) attack An attack on a Web site in which an attacker uses specialized software to send a flood of data packets to the target computer with the aim of overloading its resources.

desktop purchasing Direct purchasing from internal marketplaces without the approval of supervisors and without the intervention of a procurement department.

desktop search Search tools that search the contents of a user's or organization's computer files rather than searching the Internet. The emphasis is on finding all the information that is available on the user's PC, including Web browser histories, e-mail archives, and word-processor documents, as well as all internal files and databases.

differentiation Providing a product or service that is unique.

digital economy An economy that is based on digital technologies, including digital communication networks, computers, software, and other related information technologies; also called the Internet economy, the new economy, or the Web economy.

digital enterprise A new business model that uses IT in a fundamental way to accomplish one or more of three basic objectives: reach and engage customers more effectively, boost employee productivity, and improve operating efficiency. It uses converged communication and computing technology in a way that improves business processes.

digital envelope The combination of the encrypted original message and the digital signature, using the recipient's public key.

digital products Goods that can be transformed to digital format and delivered over the Internet.

digital rights management (DRM) An umbrella term for any of several arrangements that allow a vendor of content in electronic form to control the material and restrict its usage.

digital signature *or* **digital certificate** Validates the sender and time stamp of a transaction so it cannot be later claimed that the transaction was unauthorized or invalid.

direct marketing Broadly, marketing that takes place without intermediaries between manufacturers and buyers; in the context of this book, marketing done online between any seller and buyer.

direct materials Materials used in the production of a product (e.g., steel in a car or paper in a book).

disintermediation The removal of organizations or business process layers responsible for certain intermediary steps in a given supply chain.

disruptors Companies that introduce significant changes in their industries.

distance learning Formal education that takes place off campus, usually, but not always, through online resources.

domain name A name-based address that identifies an Internet-connected server. Usually, it refers to the portion of the address to the left of .com and .org, etc.

domain name registrar A business that assists prospective Web site owners with finding and registering the domain name of their choice.

double auction Auctions in which multiple buyers and their bidding prices are matched with multiple sellers and their asking prices, considering the quantities on both sides.

due care Care that a company is reasonably expected to take based on the risks affecting its EC business and online transactions.

dynamic pricing A rapid movement of prices over time and possibly across customers, as a result of supply and demand matching.

dynamic Web content Content that must be kept up-to-date.

e-bartering (electronic bartering) Bartering conducted online, usually in a bartering exchange.

e-book A book in digital form that can be read on a computer screen or on a special device.

e-business A broader definition of EC that includes not just the buying and selling of goods and services, but also servicing customers, collaborating with business partners, and conducting electronic transactions within an organization.

e-check A legally valid electronic version or representation of a paper check.

e-coops Another name for online group purchasing organizations.

e-commerce (EC) risk The likelihood that a negative outcome will occur in the course of developing and operating an electronic commerce strategy.

e-commerce strategy (e-strategy) The formulation and execution of a vision of how a new or existing company intends to do business electronically.

e-CRM Customer relationship management conducted electronically.

e-distributor An e-commerce intermediary that connects manufacturers with business buyers (customers) by aggregating the catalogs of many manufacturers in one place—the intermediary's Web site.

e-government E-commerce model in which a government entity buys or provides goods, services, or information to businesses or individual citizens.

e-grocer A grocer that takes orders online and provides deliveries on a daily or other regular schedule or within a very short period of time.

e-learning The online delivery of information for purposes of education, training, or knowledge management.

e-logistics The logistics of EC systems, typically involving small parcels sent to many customers' homes (in B2C).

e-loyalty Customer loyalty to an e-tailer or loyalty programs delivered online or supported electronically.

e-mall (online mall) An online shopping center where many online stores are located.

e-marketplace An online market, usually B2B, in which buyers and sellers exchange goods or services; the three types of e-marketplaces are private, public, and consortia.

e-micropayments Small online payments, typically under $5.

e-newsletter A collection of short, informative articles sent at regular intervals by e-mail to individuals who have an interest in the newsletter's topic.

e-procurement The use of Web-based technology to support the key procurement processes, including requisitioning, sourcing, contracting, ordering, and payment.

e-sourcing The process and tools that electronically enable any activity in the sourcing process, such as quotation/tender submittance and response, e-auctions, online negotiations, and spending analyses.

e-supply chain A supply chain that is managed electronically, usually with Web technologies.

e-supply chain management (e-SCM) The collaborative use of technology to improve the operations of supply chain activities as well as the management of supply chains.

e-tailers Retailers who sell over the Internet.

e-tailing Online retailing, usually B2C.

e-zines Electronic magazine or newsletter delivered over the Internet via e-mail.

EC architecture A plan for organizing the underlying infrastructure and applications of a site.

EC security program Set of controls over security processes to protect organizational assets. All the policies, procedures, documents, standards, hardware, software, training, and personnel that work together to protect information, the ability to conduct business, and other assets.

EC security strategy A strategy that views EC security as the process of preventing and detecting unauthorized use of the organization's brand, identity, Web site, e-mail, information, or other assets and attempts to defraud the organization, its customers, and employees.

EC suite A type of merchant server software that consists of an integrated collection of a large number of EC tools and components that work together for EC applications development.

edutainment The combination of education and entertainment, often through games.

electronic auction (e-auction) Auctions conducted online.

electronic (online) banking *or* **e-banking** Various banking activities conducted from home or the road using an Internet connection; also known as cyberbanking, virtual banking, online banking, and home banking.

electronic catalog The virtual-world equivalent of a traditional product catalog; contains product descriptions and photos, along with information about various promotions, discounts, payment methods, and methods of delivery.

electronic commerce (EC) The process of buying, selling, transferring, or exchanging products, services, or information via computer networks.

electronic market (e-marketplace) An online marketplace where buyers and sellers meet to exchange goods, services, money, or information.

electronic retailing (e-tailing) Retailing conducted online, over the Internet.

electronic shopping cart An order-processing technology that allows customers to accumulate items they wish to buy while they continue to shop.

electronic voting Voting process that involves many steps ranging from registering, preparing, voting, and counting (voting and counting are all done electronically).

emulation A software emulator allows computer programs to run on a platform (computer architecture and/or operating system) other than the one for which they were originally written.

encryption The process of scrambling (encrypting) a message in such a way that it is difficult, expensive, or time-consuming for an unauthorized person to unscramble (decrypt) it.

encryption algorithm The mathematical formula used to encrypt the plaintext into the ciphertext, and vice versa.

Enhanced Messaging Service (EMS) An extension of SMS that can send simple animation, tiny pictures, sounds, and formatted text.

enterprise application integration (EAI) Class of software that integrates large systems.

enterprise invoice presentment and payment (EIPP) Presenting and paying B2B invoices online.

ethics The branch of philosophy that deals with what is considered to be right and wrong.

exchange A public electronic market with many buyers and sellers.

exchange-to-exchange (E2E) E-commerce model in which electronic exchanges formally connect to one another for the purpose of exchanging information.

exchanges (trading communities or trading exchanges) Many-to-many e-marketplaces, usually owned and run by a third party or a consortium, in which many buyers and many sellers meet electronically to trade with each other.

expert location systems Interactive computerized systems that help employees find and connect with colleagues who have expertise required for specific problems—whether they are across the country or across the room—in order to solve specific, critical business problems in seconds.

Extensible Hypertext Markup Language (xHTML) A general scripting language; compatible with HTML; a standard set by the W3Consortium.

extranet A network that uses a virtual private network to link intranets in different locations over the Internet; an "extended intranet."

fair use The legal use of copyrighted material for noncommercial purposes without paying royalties or getting permission.

FAQ page A Web page that lists questions that are frequently asked by customers and the answers to those questions.

firewall A single point between two or more networks where all traffic must pass (choke point); the device authenticates, controls, and logs all traffic.

forward auction An auction in which a seller entertains bids from buyers. Bidders increase price sequentially.

fraud Any business activity that uses deceitful practices or devices to deprive another of property or other rights.

front end The portion of an e-seller's business processes through which customers interact, including the seller's portal, electronic catalogs, a shopping cart, a search engine, and a payment gateway.

front-office operations The business processes, such as sales and advertising, that are visible to customers.

Geographical information system (GIS) A computer system capable of integrating, storing, editing, analyzing, sharing, and displaying geographically-referenced (spatial) information.

global positioning system (GPS) A worldwide satellite based tracking system that enables users to determine their position anywhere on the earth.

Global System for Mobile Communications (GSM) An open, nonproprietary standard for mobile voice and data communications.

government-to-business (G2B) E-government category that includes interactions between governments and businesses (government selling to businesses and providing them with services and businesses selling products and services to government).

government-to-citizens (G2C) E-government category that includes all the interactions between a government and its citizens.

government-to-employees (G2E) E-government category that includes activities and services between government units and their employees.

government-to-government (G2G) E-government category that includes activities within government units and those between governments.

group decision support system (GDSS) An interactive computer-based system that facilitates the solution of semistructured and unstructured problems by a group of decision makers.

group purchasing The aggregation of orders from several buyers into volume purchases so that better prices can be negotiated.

groupware Software products that use networks to support collaboration among groups of people who share a common task or goal.

hash A mathematical computation that is applied to a message, using a private key, to encrypt the message.

hit A request for data from a Web page or file.

honeynet A network of honeypots.

honeypot Production system (e.g., firewalls, routers, Web servers, database servers) that looks like it does real work, but which acts as a decoy and is watched to study how network intrusions occur.

horizontal marketplaces Markets that concentrate on a service, material, or a product that is used in all types of industries (e.g., office supplies, PCs).

human firewalls Methods that filter or limit people's access to critical business documents.

incubator A company, university, or nonprofit organization that supports businesses in their initial stages of development.

indirect materials Materials used to support production (e.g., office supplies or lightbulbs).

infomediaries Electronic intermediaries that provide and/or control information flow in cyberspace, often aggregating information and selling it to others.

information architecture How the site and its Web pages are organized, labeled, and navigated to support browsing and searching throughout the Web site.

information assurance (IA) The protection of information systems against unauthorized access to or modification of information whether in storage, processing, or transit, and against the denial of service to authorized users, including those measures necessary to detect, document, and counter such threats.

information intelligence Information, data, knowledge, and semantic infrastructure that enable organizations to create more business applications.

information portal A single point of access through a Web browser to business information inside and/or outside an organization.

informational Web site A Web site that does little more than provide information about the business and its products and services.

infringement Use of the work without permission or contracting for payment of a royalty.

insourcing In-house development of applications.

integration testing Testing the combination of application modules acting in concert.

integrity Assurance that stored data has not been modified without authorization; and a message that was sent is the same message that was received and vice-versa.

intellectual property Creations of the mind, such as inventions, literary and artistic works, and symbols, names, images, and designs, used in commerce.

interactive marketing Online marketing, facilitated by the Internet, by which marketers and advertisers can interact directly with customers and consumers can interact with advertisers/vendors.

interactive voice response (IVR) A voice system that enables users to request and receive information and to enter and change data through a telephone to a computerized system.

interactive Web site A Web site that provides opportunities for the customers and the business to communicate and share information.

intermediary A third party that operates between sellers and buyers.

internal procurement marketplace The aggregated catalogs of all approved suppliers combined into a single internal electronic catalog.

Internet ecosystem The business model of the Internet economy.

Internet radio A Web site that provides music, talk, and other entertainment, both live and stored, from a variety of radio stations.

interoperability Connecting people, data, and diverse systems. The term can be defined in a technical way or in a broad way, taking into account social, political, and organizational factors.

interorganizational information systems (IOSs) Communications systems that allow routine transaction processing and information flow between two or more organizations.

interstitial An initial Web page or a portion of it that is used to capture the user's attention for a short time while other content is loading.

intrabusiness EC E-commerce category that includes all internal organizational activities that involve the exchange of goods, services, or information among various units and individuals in an organization.

intranet An internal corporate or government network that uses Internet tools, such as Web browsers, and Internet protocols.

intraorganizational information systems Communication systems that enable e-commerce activities to go on within individual organizations.

intrusion detection systems (IDSs) A special category of software that can monitor activity across a network or on a host computer, watch for suspicious activity, and take automated action based on what it sees.

ISP hosting service A hosting service that provides an independent, stand-alone Web site for small and medium-sized businesses.

key (key value) The secret code used to encrypt and decrypt a message.

key performance indicators (KPI) The quantitative expression of critically important metrics.

keyspace The large number of possible key values (keys) created by the algorithm to use when transforming the message.

keyword banners Banner ads that appear when a predetermined word is queried from a search engine.

knowledge discovery in databases (KDD)/knowledge discovery (KD) The process of extracting useful knowledge from volumes of data.

knowledge management (KM) The process of capturing or creating knowledge, storing it, updating it constantly, interpreting it, and using it whenever necessary.

knowledge portal A single-point-of-access software system intended to provide timely access to information and to support communities of knowledge workers.

latency The time required to complete an operation, such as downloading a Web page.

legal precedent A judicial decision that may be used as a standard in subsequent similar cases.

letter of credit (LC) A written agreement by a bank to pay the seller, on account of the buyer, a sum of money upon presentation of certain documents.

localization The process of converting media products developed in one environment (e.g., country) to a form culturally and linguistically acceptable in countries outside the original target market.

location-based commerce (l-commerce) M-commerce transactions targeted to individuals in specific locations, at specific times.

location-based m-commerce Delivery of m-commerce transactions to individuals in a specific location, at a specific time.

logistics The operations involved in the efficient and effective flow and storage of goods, services, and related information from point of origin to point of consumption.

macro virus (macro worm) A virus or worm that executes when the application object that contains the macro is opened or a particular procedure is executed.

malware A generic term for malicious software.

market segmentation The process of dividing a consumer market into logical groups for conducting marketing research and analyzing personal information.

mashup Combination of two or more Web sites into a single Web site that provides the content of both sites (whole or partial) to deliver a novel product to consumers.

maverick buying Unplanned purchases of items needed quickly, often at non-prenegotiated higher prices.

merchant brokering Deciding from whom (from what merchant) to buy products.

merchant server software Software for selling over the Internet that enables companies to establish selling sites relatively easily and inexpensively.

message digest (MD) A summary of a message, converted into a string of digits, after the hash has been applied.

metadata Data about data, including software programs about data, rules for organizing data, and data summaries.

metrics A specific, measurable standard against which actual performance is compared (quantitative or qualitative).

microbrowser Wireless Web browser designed to operate with small screens and limited bandwidth and memory requirements.

middleware Separate products that serve as the glue between two applications; sometimes called plumbing because it connects two sides of an application and passes data between them.

mirror site An exact duplicate of an original Web site that is physically located on a Web server on another continent or in another country.

mobile commerce (m-commerce, m-business) Any business activity conducted over a wireless telecommunications network or from mobile devices.

mobile CRM The delivery of CRM applications to any user, whenever and wherever needed, by use of the wireless infrastructure and mobile devices.

mobile portal A customer interaction channel that aggregates content and services for mobile devices.

MRO (maintenance, repair, and operation) Indirect materials used in activities that support production.

multichannel business model A business model where a company sells in multiple marketing channels simultaneously (e.g., both physical and online stores).

Multimedia Messaging Service (MMS) The emerging generation of wireless messaging; MMS is able to deliver rich media.

multitiered application architecture EC architecture consisting of four tiers: Web browsers, Web servers, application servers, and database servers.

"name-your-own-price" model Auction model in which a would-be buyer specifies the price (and other terms) he or she is willing to pay to any willing and able seller. It is a C2B model that was pioneered by Priceline.com.

native virtualization Leverages hardware assisted capabilities available in the latest processors to provide near-native performance.

Netizen A citizen surfing the Internet.

nonrepudiation Assurance that an online customer or trading partner cannot falsely deny (repudiate) their purchase or transaction.

nontechnical attack An attack that uses chicanery to trick people into revealing sensitive information or performing actions that compromise the security of a network.

on-demand CRM CRM hosted by an ASP or other vendor on the vendor's premise; in contrast to the traditional practice of buying the software and using it on-premise.

on-demand delivery service Express delivery made fairly quickly after an online order is received.

one-to-one marketing Marketing that treats each customer in a unique way.

online analytical processing (OLAP) End-user analytical activities, such as DSS modeling using spreadsheets and graphics, that are done online.

online intermediary An online third party that brokers a transaction online between a buyer and a seller; may be virtual or click-and-mortar.

online publishing The electronic delivery of newspapers, magazines, books, news, music, videos, and other digitizable information over the Internet.

operational data store A database for use in transaction processing (operational) systems that uses data warehouse concepts to provide clean data.

opt in Agreement that requires computer users to take specific steps to allow the collection of personal information.

opt out Business practice that gives consumers the opportunity to refuse sharing information about themselves.

order fulfillment All the activities needed to provide customers with their ordered goods and services, including related customer services.

organizational knowledge base The repository for an enterprise's accumulated knowledge.

outsourcing A method of transferring the management and/or day-to-day execution of an entire business function to a third-party service provider.

packet Segment of data sent from one computer to another on a network.

packet filters Rules that can accept or reject incoming packets based on source and destination addresses and other identifying information.

packet-filtering routers Firewalls that filter data and requests moving from the public Internet to a private network based on the network addresses of the computer sending or receiving the request.

page A page is an HTML (Hypertext Markup Language) document that may contain text, images, and other online elements, such as Java applets and multimedia files. It can be generated statically or dynamically.

partner relationship management (PRM) Business strategy that focuses on providing comprehensive quality service to business partners.

patent A document that grants the holder exclusive rights to an invention for a fixed number of years.

payment card Electronic card that contains information that can be used for payment purposes.

payment service provider (PSP) A third-party service connecting a merchant's EC systems to the appropriate acquirers; PSPs must be registered with the various card associations they support.

peer-to-peer Technology that enables networked peer computers to share data and processing with each other directly; can be used in C2C, B2B, and B2C e-commerce.

permission advertising (permission marketing) Advertising (marketing) strategy in which customers agree to accept advertising and marketing materials (known as "opt in").

person-to-person lending Lending done between individuals, circumventing the traditional role of banks in this process.

personal area network (PAN) A wireless telecommunications network for device-to-device connections within a very short range.

personal digital assistant (PDA) A stand-alone handheld computer principally used for personal information management.

personalization The ability to tailor a product, service, or Web content to specific user preferences.

personalized content Web content that matches the needs and expectations of the individual visitor.

phishing A crimeware technique to steal the identity of a target company to get the identities of its customers.

plaintext An unencrypted message in human-readable form.

podcast A media file that is distributed over the Internet using syndication feeds for playback on mobile devices and personal computers. As with the term *radio*, it can mean both the content and the method of syndication.

policy of least privilege (POLP) Policy of blocking access to network resources unless access is required to conduct business.

policy-based resource-management tools Automate and standardize all types of IT management best practices, from initial configuration to ongoing fault management and asset tracking.

policy-based service-level management tools Coordinate, monitor, and report on the ways in which multiple infrastructure components come together to deliver a business service.

pop-under ad An ad that appears underneath the current browser window, so when the user closes the active window the ad is still on the screen.

pop-up ad An ad that appears in a separate window before, after, or during Internet surfing or when reading e-mail.

privacy The right to be left alone and free of unreasonable personal intrusions.

private e-marketplaces Markets in which the individual sell-side or buy-side company has complete control over participation in the selling or buying transaction.

private key Encryption code that is known only to its owner.

procurement The process made up of a range of activities by which an organization obtains or gains access to the resources (materials, skills, capabilities, facilities) they require to undertake their core business activities.

procurement management The planning, organizing, and coordinating of all the activities relating to purchasing goods and services needed to accomplish the organization's mission.

product brokering Deciding what product to buy.

product lifecycle management (PLM) Business strategy that enables manufacturers to control and share product related data as part of product design and development efforts.

proxies Special software programs that run on the gateway server and pass repackaged packets from one network to the other.

public (asymmetric) key encryption Method of encryption that uses a pair of matched keys—a public key to encrypt a message and a private key to decrypt it, or vice versa.

public e-marketplace (public exchange) A many-to-many e-marketplace. Trading venues open to all interested parties (sellers and buyers); usually run by third parties. Some are also known as trading exchanges.

public key Encryption code that is publicly available to anyone.

public key infrastructure (PKI) A scheme for securing e-payments using public key encryption and various technical components.

purchasing cards (p-cards) Special-purpose payment cards issued to a company's employees to be used solely for purchasing nonstrategic materials and services up to a preset dollar limit.

radio frequency identification (RFID) A technology that uses electronic tags (chips) instead of bar codes to identify items. RFID readers use radio waves to interact with the tags.

random banners Banner ads that appear at random, not as the result of the user's action.

Really Simple Syndication (RSS) A family of Web-feed formats used to publish frequently updated digital content.

reintermediation The process whereby intermediaries (either new ones or those that had been disintermediated) take on new intermediary roles.

Representational State Transfer (REST) Refers to a collection of architectural principles.

request for proposal (RFP) Notice sent to potential vendors inviting them to submit a proposal describing their product and how it would meet the company's needs.

request for quote (RFQ) The "invitation" to participate in a tendering (bidding) system.

reusability The likelihood a segment of source code can be used again to add new functionalities with slight or no modification.

revenue model Description of how the company or an EC project will earn revenue.

reverse auction (bidding or tendering system) Auction in which the buyer places an item for bid (tender) on a request for quote (RFQ) system, potential suppliers bid on the job, with the price reducing sequentially, and the lowest bid wins; primarily a B2B or G2B mechanism.

reverse logistics The movement of returns from customers to vendors.

ROI calculator Calculator that uses metrics and formulas to compute ROI.

RSA The most common public key encryption algorithm; uses keys ranging in length from 512 bits to 1,024 bits.

RSS An XML format for syndicating and sharing Web content.

RuBee Bidirectional, on-demand, peer-to-peer radiating transceiver protocol under development by the Institute of Electrical and Electronics Engineers.

sales force automation (SFA) Software that automates the tasks performed by salespeople in the field, such as data collection and its transmission.

scalability How big a system can grow in various dimensions to provide more service; measured by total number of users, number of simultaneous users, or transaction volume.

scenario planning A strategic planning methodology that generates plausible alternative futures to help decision makers identify actions that can be taken today to ensure success in the future.

screen-sharing software Software that enables group members, even in different locations, to work on the same document, which is shown on the PC screen of each participant.

search engine A document-retrieval system designed to help find information stored on a computer system, such as on the Web, inside corporate proprietary files, or in a personal computer.

search engine marketing (SEM) Marketing methods used to increase the ranking of a Web site in the search results.

search engine optimization (SEO) The application of strategies intended to position a Web site at the top of Web search engines.

search engine spam Pages created deliberately to trick the search engine into offering inappropriate, redundant, or poor-quality search results.

search engine spamming Collective term referring to deceptive online advertising practices.

Secure Socket Layer (SSL) Protocol that utilizes standard certificates for authentication and data encryption to ensure privacy or confidentiality.

security protocol A communication protocol that encrypts and decrypts a message for online transmission; security protocols generally provide authentication.

self-hosting When a business acquires the hardware, software, staff, and dedicated telecommunications services necessary to set up and manage its own Web site.

sell-side e-marketplace A Web-based marketplace in which one company sells to many business buyers from e-catalogs or auctions, frequently over an extranet.

Semantic Web An evolving extension of the Web in which Web content can be expressed not only in natural language, but also in a form that can be understood, interpreted, and used by intelligent computer software agents, permitting them to find, share, and integrate information more easily.

service-level agreement (SLA) A formal agreement regarding the division of work between a company and a vendor.

service-oriented architecture (SOA) An application architecture in which executable components, such as Web Services, can be invoked and executed by client programs based on business rules.

settlement Transferring money from the buyer's to the merchant's account.

shopping portals Gateways to e-storefronts and e-malls; may be comprehensive or niche oriented.

shopping robots (shopping agents or shopbots) Tools that scout the Web on behalf of consumers who specify search criteria.

Short Message Service (SMS) A service that supports the sending and receiving of short text messages on mobile phones.

signature file A simple text message an e-mail program automatically adds to outgoing messages.

Simple Object Access Protocol (SOAP) Protocol or message framework for exchanging XML data across the Internet.

simulation Attempts to gather a great deal of runtime information as well as reproducing a program's behavior.

site navigation Aids that help visitors find the information they need quickly and easily.

smart card An electronic card containing an embedded microchip that enables predefined operations or the addition, deletion, or manipulation of information on the card.

smart card operating system Special system that handles file management, security, input/output (I/O), and command execution and provides an application programming interface (API) for a smart card.

smart card reader Activates and reads the contents of the chip on a smart card, usually passing the information on to a host system.

smartphone A mobile phone with PC-like capabilities.

SMEs Small-to-medium enterprises.

social bookmarking Web service for sharing Internet bookmarks. The sites are a popular way to store, classify, share, and search links through the practice of folksonomy techniques on the Internet and intranets.

social commerce A subset of e-commerce in which the users and their personal relationships are at the forefront. The main element is the involvement of the user in the marketing of products being sold.

social computing An approach aimed at making the human–computer interface more natural.

social engineering A type of nontechnical attack that uses some ruse to trick users into revealing information or performing an action that compromises a computer or network.

social marketplace An online community that harnesses the power of social networks for the introduction, buying, and selling of products, services, and resources, including people's own creations.

social media Online platforms and tools that people use to share opinions and experiences, including photos, videos, music, insights, and perceptions.

social network analysis (SNA) The mapping and measuring of relationships and flows between people, groups, organizations, animals, computers or other information or knowledge processing entities. The nodes in the network are the people and groups, whereas the links show relationships or flows between the nodes. SNA provides both a visual and a mathematical analysis of relationships.

social network A special structure composed of individuals (or organizations) that is based on how its members are connected through various social familiarities. Web sites connect these people with specified interests by providing free services such as photo presentation, e-mail, blogging, and so on.

software as a service (SaaS) A model of software delivery where the software company provides maintenance, daily technical operation, and support for the software provided to its client. SaaS is a model of software delivery rather than a market segment.

spam site Page that uses techniques that deliberately subvert a search engine's algorithms to artificially inflate the page's rankings.

spamming Using e-mail to send unwanted ads (sometimes floods of ads).

splogs Short for spam blog, are sites that are created solely for marketing purposes.

spot buying The purchase of goods and services as they are needed, usually at prevailing market prices.

spyware Software that gathers user information over an Internet connection without the user's knowledge.

SpywareGuide A public reference site for spyware.

stickiness Characteristic that influences the average length of time a visitor stays in a site.

storebuilder service A hosting service that provides disk space and services to help small and microbusinesses build a Web site quickly and cheaply.

stored-value card A card that has monetary value loaded onto it and that usually is rechargeable.

storefront A single company's Web site where products or services are sold.

strategic (systematic) sourcing Purchases involving long-term contracts that usually are based on private negotiations between sellers and buyers.

strategy A broad-based formula for how a business is going to accomplish its mission, what its goals should be, and what plans and policies will be needed to carry out those goals.

strategy assessment The continuous evaluation of progress toward the organization's strategic goals, resulting in corrective action and, if necessary, strategy reformulation.

strategy formulation The development of strategies to exploit opportunities and manage threats in the business environment in light of corporate strengths and weaknesses.

strategy implementation The development of detailed, short-term plans for carrying out the projects agreed on in strategy formulation.

strategy initiation The initial phase of strategic planning in which the organization examines itself and its environment.

subscriber identification module (SIM) card An extractable storage card used for identification, customer location information, transaction processing, secure communications, etc.

supplier relationship management (SRM) A comprehensive approach to managing an enterprise's interactions with the organizations that supply the goods and services it uses.

supply chain The flow of materials, information, money, and services from raw material suppliers through factories and warehouses to the end customers.

supply chain management (SCM) A complex process that requires the coordination of many activities so that the shipment of goods and services from supplier right through to customer is done efficiently and effectively for all parties concerned.

SWOT analysis A methodology that surveys external opportunities and threats and relates them to internal strengths and weaknesses.

symmetric (private) key system An encryption system that uses the same key to encrypt and decrypt the message.

syndication The sale of the same good (e.g., digital content) to many customers, who then integrate it with other offerings and resell it or give it away free.

teleconferencing The use of electronic communication that allows two or more people at different locations to have a simultaneous conference.

telematics The integration of computers and wireless communications to improve information flow using the principles of telemetry.

telewebs Call centers that combine Web channels with portal-like self-service.

tendering (bidding) system Model in which a buyer requests would-be sellers to submit bids; the lowest bidder wins.

text mining The application of data mining to nonstructured or less-structured text files.

third-party logistics suppliers (3PL) External, rather than in-house, providers of logistics services.

throughput The number of operations completed in a given period of time; indicates the number of users that a system can handle.

time-to-exploitation The elapsed time between when a vulnerability is discovered and the time it is exploited.

total benefits of ownership (TBO) Benefits of ownership that include both tangible and intangible benefits.

total cost of ownership (TCO) A formula for calculating the cost of owning, operating, and controlling an IT system.

trackback An acknowledgment or signal from an originating site to a receiving site.

trademark A symbol used by businesses to identify their goods and services; government registration of the trademark confers exclusive legal right to its use.

transaction log A record of user activities at a company's Web site.

transactional Web site A Web site that sells products and services.

Trojan horse A program that appears to have a useful function but that contains a hidden function that presents a security risk.

Trojan-Phisher-Rebery A new variant of a Trojan program that stole tens of thousands of identities from 125 countries that the victims believed were collected by a legitimate company.

trust The psychological status of willingness to depend on another person or organization.

turnkey approach Ready to use without further assembly or testing; supplied in a state that is ready to turn on and operate.

unique visits A count of the number of visitors entering a site, regardless of how many pages are viewed per visit.

unit testing Testing application software modules one at a time.

Universal Description, Discovery, and Integration (UDDI) An XML framework for businesses to publish and find Web Services online.

up-selling Offering an upgraded version of the product in order to boost sales and profit.

USA PATRIOT Act Uniting and Strengthening America by Providing Appropriate Tools to Intercept and Obstruct Terrorism Act passed in October 2001, in the aftermath of the September 11 terrorist attacks. Its intent is to give law enforcement agencies broader range in their efforts to protect the public.

usability (of Web site) The quality of the user's experience when interacting with the Web site.

usability testing Testing the quality of the user's experience when interacting with a Web site.

user profile The requirements, preferences, behaviors, and demographic traits of a particular customer.

utility (on-demand) computing Unlimited computing power and storage capacity that can be used and reallocated for any application and billed on a pay-per-use basis.

value proposition The benefit that a company's products or services provide to a company and its customers from using EC.

vendor-managed inventory (VMI) The practice of retailers' making suppliers responsible for determining when to order and how much to order.

venture capital (VC) Money invested in a business by an individual, a group of individuals (venture capitalists), or a funding company in exchange for equity in the business.

vertical auction Auction that takes place between sellers and buyers in one industry or for one commodity.

vertical marketplaces Markets that deal with one industry or industry segment (e.g., steel, chemicals).

video teleconference Virtual meeting in which participants in one location can see participants at other locations on a large screen or a desktop computer.

viral blogging Viral marketing done by bloggers.

viral marketing Word-of-mouth marketing by which customers promote a product or service by telling others about it.

viral video Video clip that gains widespread popularity through the process of Internet sharing, typically through e-mail or IM messages, blogs, and other media-sharing Web sites.

virtual (Internet) community A group of people with similar interests who interact with one another using the Internet.

virtual (pure-play) e-tailers Firms that sell directly to consumers over the Internet without maintaining a physical sales channel.

virtual meetings Online meetings whose members are in different locations, even in different countries.

virtual (pure-play) organizations Organizations that conduct their business activities solely online.

virtual private network (VPN) A network that creates tunnels of secured data flows, using cryptography and authorization algorithms, to provide secure transport of private communications over the public Internet.

virtual university An online university from which students take classes from home or other off-site locations, usually via the Internet.

virtual world A user-defined world in which people can interact, play, and do business. The most publicized virtual world is Second Life.

virtualization A technique for hiding the physical characteristics of computing resources from the way in which other systems, applications, or end users interact with those resources.

virus A piece of software code that inserts itself into a host, including the operating systems, in order to propagate; it requires that its host program be run to activate it.

visit A series of requests during one navigation of a Web site; a pause of a certain length of time ends a visit.

voice commerce (v-commerce) An umbrella term for the use of speech recognition to support voice-activated services, including Internet browsing and e-mail retrieval.

voice portal A Web site with an audio interface that can be accessed through a telephone call.

Voice-over-IP (VoIP) Communication systems that transmit voice calls over Internet–Protocol-based networks.

vortals B2B portals that focus on a single industry or industry segment; "vertical portals."

warehouse management system (WMS) A software system that helps in managing warehouses.

Web 2.0 The popular term for advanced Internet technology and applications, including blogs, wikis, RSS, and social bookmarking. One of the most significant differences between Web 2.0 and the traditional World Wide Web is greater collaboration among users, content providers, and enterprises.

Web bugs Tiny graphics files embedded in e-mail messages and in Web sites that transmit information about users and their movements to a Web server.

Web hosting service A dedicated Web site hosting company that offers a wide range of hosting services and functionality to businesses of all sizes.

Web mining The application of data mining techniques to discover meaningful patterns, profiles, and trends from both the content and usage of Web sites.

Web self-service Activities conducted by users on the Web to find answers to their questions (e.g., tracking) or for product configuration.

Web Service A software system identified by a URI (uniform resource indicator), whose public interfaces and bindings are defined and described using XML.

Web Services Description Language (WSDL) An XML document that defines the programmatic interface—operations, methods, and parameters—for Web Services.

Web Services An architecture enabling assembly of distributed applications from software services and tying them together.

Web syndication A form of syndication in which a section of a Web site is made available for other sites to use.

Web-oriented architecture (WOA) A set of Web protocols (e.g., HTTP and plain XML) as the most dynamic, scalable, and interoperable Web Service approach.

Webcasting A free Internet news service that broadcasts personalized news and information, including seminars, in categories selected by the user.

Webinars Seminars on the Web (Web-based seminars).

Weblogging (blogging) Technology for personal publishing on the Internet.

Wi-Fi (wireless fidelity) The common name used to describe the IEEE 802.11 standard used on most WLANs.

wikilog (wikiblog *or* **wiki)** A blog that allows everyone to participate as a peer; anyone can add, delete, or change content.

WiMax A wireless standard (IEEE 802.16) for making broadband network connections over a medium-size area such as a city.

Wireless Application Protocol (WAP) A scripting language used to create content in the WAP environment; based on SML, minus unnecessary content to increase speed.

wireless local area network (WLAN) A telecommunications network that enables users to make short-range wireless connections to the Internet or another network.

Wireless Markup Language (WML) A scripting language used to create content in the WAP environment; based on XML, minus unnecessary content to increase speed.

wireless mobile computing (mobile computing) Computing that connects a mobile device to a network or another computing device, anytime, anywhere.

wireless wide area network (WWAN) A telecommunications network that offers wireless coverage over a large geographical area, typically over a cellular phone network.

workflow The movement of information as it flows through the sequence of steps that make up an organization's work procedures.

workflow management The automation of workflows, so that documents, information, and tasks are passed from one participant to the next in the steps of an organization's business process.

workflow systems Business process automation tools that place system controls in the hands of user departments to automate information processing tasks.

worm A software program that runs independently, consuming the resources of its host in order to maintain itself, that is capable of propagating a complete working version of itself onto another machine.

zero-day incidents Attacks through previously unknown weaknesses in their computer networks.

Index

Note: Page numbers with W indicates Online Files; E indicates Exhibit; A indicates Appendix A; and B indicates Appendix B.

B

C